THORSTEIN VEBLEN

AND HIS AMERICA

THORSTEIN VEBLEN

1920

THORSTEIN VEBLEN AND HIS AMERICA

BY

JOSEPH DORFMAN

[1934]

SEVENTH EDITION

WITH NEW APPENDICES

REPRINTS OF ECONOMIC CLASSICS

AUGUSTUS M. KELLEY · PUBLISHERS

CLIFTON 1972

First Edition 1934

(New York: The Viking Press, 1934)

Reprinted 1935, 1940, 1945 & 1947

Reprinted 1961, 1966 & 1972 by

AUGUSTUS M. KELLEY PUBLISHERS

Reprints of Economic Classics

Clifton New Jersey 07012

By Arrangement with THE VIKING PRESS

I S B N 0 678 00007 7

L C N 64-7662

To

A.J., V.J., W.C.M., R.G.T.,

who at critical moments in the course of this inquiry

forgot the principles of the economic man, and made

possible its completion.

PREFATORY NOTE FOR SEVENTH PRINTING

For this edition some corrections have been made in the text in the light of new information. Also a number of items have been added to Veblen's bibliography.

Joseph Dorfman

Columbia University

January 1966

PREFACE

The realm of scholarship knows of few cases like that of Thorstein Veblen. Thirty-five years have passed since the publication of *The Theory of the Leisure Class*, but its author still remains a figure of mystery and his views an object of controversy. In the hope that an inquiry into Veblen's life history might throw some light on the meaning of his work, this study was undertaken.

I am indebted for information to a host of Veblen's relations, friends, acquaintances, schoolmates, teachers, colleagues. Professors J.M. Clark, Walton Hamilton, R.M. MacIver, and Commissioner Isador Lubin have read various drafts of the manuscript.

Four men from the beginning have watched over the various stages of this inquiry with great care and interest. Virgil Jordan, President of the National Industrial Conference Board, and Professor Rexford Guy Tugwell started the movements making it possible for me to devote my time to the work. To Professor Wesley Clair Mitchell my debts are many and varied. In the decade that has passed since he first encouraged me to carry through this project, the study would have expired on more than one occasion had it not been for his intervention. His apparently casual comments often threw into broad relief what was implied, but not clearly expressed, in the study. Dr. Alvin Johnson, Director of the New School for Social Research, was never formally my teacher, but in comparison with his subtle suggestions and irresponsible conversations, the value of the classroom fades into insignificance.

I am also deeply indebted to Miss Elizabeth Todd, Assistant Editor of the *Encyclopædia of the Social Sciences*, who has worked over the whole manuscript, applying her editorial skill to make sure that the author's meaning, necessarily obscured at times by the close study of the subject, flows clearly and without undue difficulty to the reader. To my wife I owe a great obligation for her typing, patience, and understanding under the strain that dealing with such a figure as Veblen involved.

I owe a great debt to the New School for Social Research, which granted me a fourteen-month fellowship in 1930–31, to write the first and basic draft. In the preparation of this and subsequent drafts I have been dependent for guidance primarily upon Dr. Johnson and Professor Mitchell.

JOSEPH DORFMAN

Columbia University,
September, 1934.

THORSTEIN VEBLEN
AND HIS AMERICA

CHAPTER I

ON July 30, 1857, on a frontier farm in Wisconsin a fourth son was born to the Norwegian immigrants, Thomas Anderson Veblen and Kari Bunde Veblen. He was named for his mother's father, Thorstein Bunde, a man who had been devilled by misfortune in the old country. Thorstein Bunde had been a promising young farmer when litigation forced him to sell his farm, Bunde, in order to meet the fees of the lawyers, a tribe considered by rural Norwegians to be only educated tricksters. Crushed by the loss of his farm he died at the age of thirty-five, and Kari, then five years old, was left an orphan.

Thorstein Veblen's paternal grandfather had also fared badly. In 1818 he had been dispossessed of his farm, Oigare, through the application of one of the rights of primogeniture. According to this right the eldest son, or other senior nearest of kin, had the privilege of recovering possession of a family estate by paying its current owner a price supposedly fixed by legal appraisement proceedings. But Andris Haldorson Oigare was paid in heavily depreciated currency instead of in the old silver money originally agreed upon. He fell from the status of *bonde* or landowner to that of tenant and remained in that position for the greater part of his life. In rural Norway no worse calamity was conceivable. The farm possessed a dignity even more important than its commercial value. The self-sufficient farmstead gave the *bønder* not only sustenance and sometimes wealth, but also that sign of unquestioned social position, the place name, for it was fairly well established by custom that only a *bonde* could add a place name to his ordinary Christian name and patronymic.

From time immemorial the farm was rooted in the minds of rural Norwegians as the substantial reality, and long subjection, first to Denmark and later to Sweden, reinforced this deep-laid agrarian temperament. The urban population was considered a "mixed race, strange exotics planted in an alien soil among alien people whose ways and speech they despised or patronised." [1] These merchants and officeholders, judges, sheriffs, and ministers, were "parasitic," affected with an "aristocratic spirit." The farmers were forced to render military serv-

[1] References are to be found on p. 525 *ff*.

3

ice, but in the army they could not obtain commissions nor could they use their farm names. The office-holding classes forbade the use of such names also to servants and clerks. "The attribute of real aristocracy that resided in this nomenclature," wrote Thorstein Veblen's oldest brother, Andrew, "went against the grain of the class people." The *bønder* became sharply differentiated from what they considered the leisure classes, "not only in customs and language, but also in views and sympathies." They considered themselves the pure Norwegians, "like the very soil itself." [2] For them there was no honourable profession, except possibly the ministry. Even this was viewed with great suspicion, and the rural Norwegians in the nineteenth century supported a lay evangelical movement which was bitterly fought by the hierarchy. Thus the only proper aim of a countryman was the ownership and tilling of a farm.

According to Andrew Veblen the forbears of his family were "altogether of the pure, native strain that had possessed and tilled the land since the settling and clearing of the farms that they held." [3] But Thomas Anderson Veblen was only the son of a tenant on the farm Veblen. His formal education, like that of any poor country youth, had consisted in attending parochial school until he was fourteen, with the goal of passing the confirmation test. The church made little impression on him, but he observed its regulations, and he served his term of military service. Unlike most rural Norwegians he made long trips far away from his native valley, Valders, and had even been to Oslo and to Drammen. He seemed never to become tired, angry, or excited. Slow, deliberate, and without fear, a man of might, poise, and balance, like an "unchiselled grey rock"—this was a man of unusual possibilities. But in a poverty-stricken country where depression was looked upon as normal the future of a carpenter and cabinet-maker held little promise.

Emigration, however, was providing a way whereby ambitious sons of rural Norway could hope to better their condition. Thomas Anderson Veblen's boyhood chum and partner in carpentry, Stephen Olson, left for America in 1846 and became a leader in the Norwegian settlement of Port Washington, near Milwaukee. In 1847, at a severe point of the depression in Norway, two copies of Johan R. Reierson's *Pathfinder for Norwegian Emigrants to the North American States and Texas* appeared in Valders and convinced the community of the new country's possibilities. Among the thousands who left Norway that year were the Veblens. The long journey was seldom a pleasant one for the emigrant. For the Veblens it was especially disheartening. A day before sailing they buried their first born child. When they had got only as far as Hamburg all the passengers were left stranded by their captain, and a month passed before they were able to continue their journey. On board the whaling-vessel whose captain had befriended them Thomas Anderson Veblen contracted a fever, the water supply gave out, and all the children under six aboard died. At Quebec he had to walk supported by his wife and the captain to avoid being detained by the quarantine officers. Practically penniless and physically weakened, the couple reached Milwaukee four and a half months after leaving Drammen. After only one night's rest, Thomas Anderson Veblen walked the twenty-eight miles to Port Washington and immediately commenced work in Stephen Olson's fanning-mill factory. He sent for his wife, and she obtained employment as a maid with a Yankee family. Neither, however, had had sufficient rest to recover from the gruelling journey, and after two weeks they found it impossible to continue working.

Stephen Olson and his brother made it possible for the weakened couple to move to some lands the Olsons had pre-empted. It was arranged that Thomas Anderson Veblen should be given forty acres when the occupancy requirement had been met. As soon as he recovered his strength, he went to work building and finishing houses while his wife took care of the land. But the Veblens, like other immigrants unacquainted with the English language and with the tactics of the speculators, were forced off the claim. A Norwegian visitor, writing home about these claims, said that the "Yankees . . . know how to introduce a certain appearance of law and order into a practice which in the nature of the case is the direct opposite of law and order." [4] Thomas Anderson Veblen, however, worked continually at his trade and kept putting by his earnings until he had enough money to make a first payment on some land. In 1848 his elder brother, Haldor, came from Norway to Wisconsin, and the following year the two of them, partly with borrowed funds, acquired a pre-emption claim for 160 acres of wild forest land in Sheboygan County. They were forced to sell half the grant, however, to meet their loan, which carried an interest rate of approximately fifty percent.

This farm of only eighty acres supported Thomas Anderson Veblen's family of five, his brother, and for a while his mother-in-law's family of four, but it did not satisfy his aspirations. And more important still, their neighbours were not Norwegians. Already they felt keenly the contemptuous attitude of the dominant Yankees. These New Englanders, not unlike the office-holding classes at home, considered the Norwegians in every respect inferior to themselves. The immigrants were called "Norwegian Indians" or "Scandihoofians," and in the Territorial Council of Wisconsin in 1846 it was declared by an immigrant from Massachusetts that the Negroes were "more deserving of a vote and [the] privileges of freemen" than the Norwegians.[5] Only much later was it admitted that "them 'ere Norwegians are almost as white as we are," [6]

The Veblens wanted to be with their own kind. In near-by Manitowoc County, where one section was even named Valders, there was a more Norwegian environment, and Stephen Olson was one of the important figures in the settlement. Thomas Anderson Veblen sold his farm for $800 and with his family and his brother moved by oxen through sixty miles of forest to Cato township in Manitowoc. As a new farm was being wrought out of eighty acres of forest land, Thorstein Veblen was born.

Thomas Anderson Veblen became a leading farmer. He introduced Spanish merinos into that part of the state and sent to New York for the first two-horse-power thresher, in spite of the objections of his wife and in spite of ingrained technological traditions that had prevailed among Norwegians almost as long as farming. By 1860 his lands, now amounting to 160 acres, were worth according to the census the good sum of $3000. The census record of 1860 also reports that he owned 3 horses, 5 milch cows, 2 working oxen, 4 other cattle, 18 sheep, 5 swine. In the preceding year he had grown 100 bushels of oats, 20 pounds of wool, 10 bushels of peas, 60 bushels of potatoes, 700 pounds of butter, 8 tons of hay, 4 bushels of grass seed, and had slaughtered animals worth $50. He was still an excellent craftsman; the house he built in Cato is standing today.

The scheme of things was still that of the self-sufficient farmstead of rural Norway. The homes of the immigrants were usually log cabins, shanties, or dugouts, and often fifteen or twenty persons occupied one little cabin. It was not uncommon that oxen occupied the same room as the family. The pioneer housewives made cheese, churned butter, baked bread, boiled soap, carded wool, spun yarn, wove cloth, sewed clothes. Home-made food, furniture, and garments were customary. The food was of the simple kind upon which generation after generation of mountaineers and seamen had been reared. Coffee and sugar were luxuries. Dress was of the plainest. Thorstein Veblen as a child was not accustomed to an undershirt. Woollen clothing was unknown. Overcoats were made from sections of calfskin. As for overshoes, "it was a common thing to have the neighbours come and ask for a section of the hide that they might make a kind of leather foot covering." [7]

The women, like the men, followed the reapers and bound sheaves. In those Norwegian settlements it could not be said that "propriety requires respectable women to abstain . . . from useful effort and to make . . . a show of leisure." [8] These women were a striking contrast to the typical American woman, of whom the Norwegians said, "all she does is to dress herself, attend church, and take care of her nerves."

The simple agrarian life of the rural Norwegians was part of an un-broken tradition of hundreds of years, whereas the American farmers were foot-loose and shifted easily from country to town, interested pri-marily in the speculative value of land rather than in the farm as a means of livelihood. The near-by towns, such as Clark's Mills, were set-tled by Yankees engaged in exploitation of the country rather than in industry. To these townsmen the rural Norwegians transferred their age-long animosity against the urban classes of Norway. They could see a visible relation between their own productive efforts on the soil and the results in produce, but no such relation between effort and product was apparent in the pecuniary activities of the townsmen. They con-cluded that "the Yankee is simply a financial and political boomer who is too shrewd and unscrupulous to be depended upon." [9]

This situation was ground into the very substance of Thorstein Veb-len's thinking. The Scandinavian immigrants "settled over [the North Middle Region] . . . as tillers of the soil, while the American popu-lation of the East at the same time scattered over the same region in the towns; with the result that the foreign immigrants did the work necessary to the reclamation of this stretch of fertile land, and the native-born in the towns did the business. This business was prevailingly of a prehensile character, being carried on by men well at home in the common law of the land and directed at getting something for nothing at the expense of the foreign immigrants who were unfamiliar with the common law. Being, in the view of their masters, aliens in the land, the foreign immigrants were felt to have no claim to consideration beyond what the laws that they did not know would formally secure to them in case matters were brought to the legal test. The presumption in the mind of honest businessmen at all points was on the side of their own pecuniary advantage, leaving any doubts to be settled by eventual litiga-tion that might be brought by the foreign immigrants—who could with great uniformity be relied on most meticulously to avoid all litigation under a system of law with which they had no acquaintance, before local magistrates (businessmen) whom they had no reason to trust, in a language which they did not understand." [10]

In consequence the cultural isolation of the Norwegians was intensi-fied to an extent never surpassed in any large immigrant group in this country. They seldom met the Yankees except for the necessary busi-ness relations or during political conventions. The "instinct for preserv-ing and guarding their heritage grew strong and articulate." They held fast to the language and literature of their forefathers. Even their thoughts were "rooted in the older civilisation in a vast body of customs and practices and beliefs." Their music, the arrangement of their houses, their needlework and cooking, all their cultural interests, "bore the stamp of the little country across the seas." If a successful farmer wanted a rest, back to Norway he went and flaunted his new-found power in the face of his former oppressors, the office-holding classes, to whom America was a barbarous nation, for "just think, a rail-splitter being president, and a tailor vice-president." The sentiment of the immigrants was well expressed by the opening of an immigrant song: "Farewell, Norway, and God bless thee. Stern and severe wert thou always, but as a mother I honour thee, even though thou skimped my bread." [11] Norwegian politicians fed this growing clannishness, and the pastors, preaching in Norwegian, baptising in Norwegian, intensified the national sentiment. In this process of alienating themselves from the "gentiles," religion was a significant influence. In the early days the austere simplicity of the evangelical churches had prevailed, but with the growth of wealth and national sentiment the ritual and paraphernalia of the powerful Norwegian ecclesiastical organisation were taken over, and the pastors, some of them imported from Norway, increased in power and prestige. The organiser of the first synod, considering no daughter of an immigrant a worthy mate, journeyed to Norway to marry an aristocratic lady. The Lutheranism of the immigrants did not, however, prevent them from preserving some of their ancient pagan ceremonies, such as the sacrifice of the fire two weeks after Christmas. The pagan nature refused to bend too much to authority, and bitter theological warfare resulted.

On all this Thomas Anderson Veblen looked with distaste. As far as possible he avoided any entanglement in community affairs. His countrymen urged him to become treasurer of the local school board so that "the Norwegians could run things" instead of the Irishmen of Catholic faith, abhorred by all good Lutherans. But he was not disposed to allow one group interest to use him against another. His scepticism and simple honesty saw through most of their subterfuges. Some of his neighbours escaped conscription during the Civil War by instituting proceedings to prove that their names in the draft list, which were what English-speaking land officials had made of the foreign names, were not their legal names in Norway. It was suggested to Thomas Anderson Veblen that he might "beat the draft" by this procedure but "he scorned the suggestion as unworthy, because there was no question of who was meant." But his cultural consciousness was so strong that he brought into the family a retired Norwegian official to tutor the older children in Norwegian grammar and literature. As Kari Thorsteinsdatter worked, Andrew, the oldest child, would often read to her from Snorri's

Heimskringla (History of the Norwegian Kings). It was even planned that Andrew should attend the intensely Norwegian Luther College.

The reassertion of the farm name was a significant sign of the cultural consciousness that developed in the Norwegian group. Heretofore the immigrants had not troubled about the farm names, but had allowed their Christian and patronymic names to be used on legal records, such as land entries. In the Wisconsin census records the name of Thorstein Veblen's father was Thomas Anderson. But as the empty-handed immigrants became independent landowners, "their slumbering sense of the historic fitness of things awoke, and so many of them adopted the name of the place they had come from." [12] They began to trace their genealogies through the lands their families had held in Norway and to boast of the length of time, in some cases hundreds of years, that they had been in possession. Thomas Anderson Veblen had already become incensed by the way Yankee district-school teachers were tampering with the children's names to make them conform to English usage. This "name robbery" made it impossible to show to "what people anyone belonged." In 1864 he intended to go into court and have his name made legally Veblen, this to be added to Thomas Anderson.

But circumstances made this action unnecessary. Once more he decided to move. He had become dissatisfied with the rocky and barren farm. In 1864 he and his wife visited his mother-in-law in Rice County, and after seeing the prairie lands of Minnesota, despite the fact that only the previous year Norwegians had been victims of the Sioux outbreak, he could not rest content until he had sold his Cato farm. To the mother with seven children, from an infant in arms to sixteen-year-old Andrew, this meant the breaking up of an established home and accustomed relations and the repetition of many of the harsh experiences of pioneer life. Thomas Anderson Veblen, however, felt that it was best for the children. As he drove with Andrew to the railroad, on the day he made the journey to complete his purchase of land, he talked a good deal about his son's future and his desire that the boy should have the advantage that he had lacked, an "education." At the local bookstore he bought some Latin books for the aspiring classical scholar. But in particular he talked to his son of the name question. Now it could be properly adjusted, and he was determined that the beginning should be right. In purchasing the land he especially insisted that the deed be made out in the name of Thomas Anderson Veblen.

In 1865, when Thorstein Veblen was a child of eight, the entire family moved to Wheeling township in the neighbourhood of what is now Nerstrand. Of the 290 acres 200 were wild prairie land, and the land hunger of the rural Norwegian was finally appeased. Thomas

Veblen had none of the acquisitiveness of the average American pioneer farmer who seized for its speculative value as much of the land as he could hold possession of and thereby made rural life dreary and isolated. While Thorstein Veblen was growing to maturity, his father was content to cultivate his 290 acres.

As in Cato, Thomas Veblen became a leading farmer, although he knew no English. Traditional methods never meant much to him. He was a successful bee keeper and was the first in the section to install drains, to plant an orchard, and to buy a "platform binder" or "harvester." He did all the work of building the dwellings and barns, even hewing the square timber, and he learned something of stone masonry in order to build the basements.

The scheme of life continued to be the same as in the Wisconsin settlements. It was still a self-sufficient economy. Heavy trading in wheat and hogs was unheard of. Women drove the reapers. As late as the seventies the Veblen house remained primitive, according to the account given by a town youth, a "one-story or one-and-a-half-story house like many of the farm houses of that time, with access to the second story or attic by means of a ladder through a trap door." The surrounding towns such as Faribault and Northfield were promoted and inhabited by Yankees of the customary evangelical Calvinist Congregational faith. The leading Northfield banker, whom some might think of "as a cold, calculating man of money . . . wept for joy" at revival meetings when a "rough bum" was converted.[13] Even in physical appearance the towns reminded one of New England.

Meanwhile the little Norways were becoming so nationalistic that a Swedish visitor addressing Norwegians as countrymen or fellow-Scandinavians was greeted with: "You may not say 'countrymen.' . . . We are Norwegian—nothing else." [14] In 1866 the Norwegian synod at Manitowoc resolved that the congregations should establish parochial schools so that the children need not be sent to the public schools. They "could not expect that their Norwegian culture would be transmitted through the public schools, for the culture of the American school is mainly that of New England," with its "dogmatic Calvinistic theology." If any Norwegian intellectual dared to attack this move, as did Hjalmar Boyesen, he soon felt the wrath of the priesthood and found himself outside the pale.

This nationalism in education was not completely achieved in the Veblen settlement, where the sessions of the parochial school, which was called the "Norwegian school," were held between the regular periods of the district or "English school." Circumstances, however, worked toward much the same effect. The teachers in the public schools, partly as a result of the political solidarity in the settlements, were often Norwegians who were themselves equipped with only a rudimentary district-school education. They might insist that English be spoken in school, but the children spoke Norwegian while they played and often even in the classroom. In the Veblen settlement the parochial school led a precarious existence, for the children's labour was needed on the farm, but the public school suffered still more. What little English it could teach was dissipated by the speech at home and in the neighbourhood, which was "a compact mass of Norwegians." Kari Thorsteinsdatter knew English, but she used it so seldom that the children, while in the settlement, never suspected her knowledge. Thus the Norwegian children "spoke the language of their fathers better than they did that of the land of their adoption." "Not until the third generation," said a settler in near-by Goodhue County, "do we find English used in preference to the Norwegian." Second-generation children like Thorstein Veblen did not learn much of the alien tongue while in the settlement and were not touched by the alien culture. "With the best that America might have offered them they had no contact. It was entirely unknown to them." [15] The cultural cleavage had become so great that a second-generation Lutheran asserted that there was a racial distinction between Lutherans and Calvinists as well as between Protestants and Catholics.

The Veblen settlement "was more conservative than the majority of the settlements" and "the people it seems took naturally to authority and followed their leaders," particularly the pastor. Thomas Veblen continued to mind his own affairs. He took no part in the ceaseless theological warfare in the settlements, but he retained membership in the most respectable synod and saw to it that the children observed the customary programme of a Lutheran child: baptism, parochial school, and confirmation. He came to be viewed not only as a leading farmer but as a man of fine intelligence and was respected by his children, the settlement, and even casual acquaintances.

Thomas Veblen was taciturn, but Kari Thorsteinsdatter was a high-spirited individual, "warmly and electrically religious." Like a sturdy, dominant woman of the sagas, she was counsellor, adviser, and often physician and surgeon in the community. Her home was open to newcomers, and her help was often sought by the many relatives who were bruised in the struggle for existence. She knew the solution to her problems without the necessity of reasoning. Thomas Veblen might take days, weeks, often years, in arriving at an answer to a problem, but Kari, with a "brain that was the fastest machine God ever made," solved it "in a fraction of a second." "It was from her," wrote a brother, "that Thorstein got his personality and brains."

Thorstein Veblen, the sixth child of twelve, was his mother's favourite, partly because he was named after her unfortunate father and partly because he was her "oddest" child. He worried her by mischievousness and "queer antics," such as refusing at first to attend school, but this seems only to have increased her affections. He once said his mother thought he was the right kind of son.

Much as Thorstein Veblen admired his father's intellectual qualities and pondered his sceptical comments on the social order and its leisure class, he never ceased feeling that his father was distant and somewhat cold. In the settlement he often wondered whether his father would recognise him if they should meet one another off the farm. Like any other child "in the early stages of his growth," he had need of "friendly human contact" and thus he long remained in that period in which "the child habitually seeks contact with its mother at every turn of its daily life." From her and from the other women he absorbed the folklore of his people.

Other children in the family and the neighbours did not have a very high opinion of Thorstein Veblen. On his first Sunday in Minnesota he was engaged in a fist fight. From then on he fought and bullied the boys, teased the girls, pestered the old people with stinging sarcasm and nicknames of such originality that they stuck through all the years. He not only obtained the easiest tasks but he devised ways whereby the other children did his work. In taking provisions to the workmen at the second farm two miles away, he used the family dog, "Passup," as a transportation vehicle both for himself and the food. But he often neglected even this simple task. It was not uncommon to find him in the attic sleeping or reading back copies of Norwegian newspapers, and the almanacs and "premiums" which came with them, when he should have been working on the farm. But farm tasks were not irksome to him when he could operate machinery, and he drove the harvester when it was first introduced. He had a highly developed sense of economy of effort; one of the men on the farm commented once that he had never seen such a lazy-looking person who performed his job with so few motions.

Despite its general dislike of Veblen the settlement was forced to admit that this "queer" youth was brilliant. At confirmation he proved more than a match for the examiner on the hair-splitting Lutheran church history and doctrine. He was expert in settling the never-ceasing disputes over the meaning of Norse terms which agitated the emigrants from the various rural sections of Norway, with their different dialects. A younger brother remarked: "From my earliest recollection I thought he knew everything. I could ask him any question and he would tell me all about it in great detail. I have found that a good deal he told me was made of whole cloth, but even his lies were good."

Scepticism came early to Veblen. Many a Norwegian youth had been killed fighting for the North during the Civil War, and in the Sioux outbreak of 1862 and 1863 Norwegians had been victims, but Veblen defended the Confederacy and the Indians. He held his tongue, however, about the all-powerful Lutheran church. He cared little for the rite of confirmation but he endured it.

It is impossible to say what would have happened to him if he had continued to live in the agrarian settlement. The only apparent future for him there was as farmer or minister. But Andrew Veblen took a direction which was to have important consequences for his younger brother. Andrew had given up the idea of entering Luther College, where religion was "the core of the whole curriculum." He detested its intense theological bias. In 1871, at the age of twenty-three, he entered the Faribault High School. He was able to stay only a term, but he was determined eventually to enter an American college. His instructors suggested that he investigate Carleton College, in near-by Northfield, which had a preparatory division. He went to Northfield, met the president, and decided to enter the school—one of eighty students. It was not long before he began urging all the children to become students and follow academic pursuits. He became a "rabid crank" on education, much to the irritation of some of his brothers and sisters. But he influenced Thomas Veblen, who wanted his children to be a credit to his ancestors and his nation. The father's deepest ambition was to give the children an education instead of exploiting them as was the customary practice in all pioneering settlements. The neighbours berated him for allowing his children to enter the higher institutions of the native Americans. A farmer's son should have a higher education only for the purpose of entering the ministry, and he should attend only Lutheran schools. The Veblens were accused of putting on airs. But Thomas Veblen had no doubts about what course to follow. In 1874, when he found that the preachers considered Thorstein a suitable candidate for the Lutheran ministry, he decided that the boy should follow the older children to Carlton College Academy. Thorstein was not consulted as to his wishes. He was summoned from the field by one of his father's workmen and placed in the family buggy with his baggage already packed. He first learned that he was to enter Carleton when he actually arrived at the school.

For seventeen years Thorstein Veblen had lived the self-enclosed life of the traditionally agrarian-minded settlement. Now he was entering the life of the alien culture.

CHAPTER II

WHEN Veblen left the settlement, a wave of bitterness against the business interests was sweeping over the entire agrarian West. This hostility continued during his six years at Carleton. In the wake of the psychologically disintegrating effects of the Civil War the money economy was bringing its tragic consequences. The simple scheme of self-sufficient farming was being crushed by a series of revolutionary technological processes which made the period the most remarkable ever seen in wheat growing.

The La Croix purifier, which along with the roller process caused a complete change in flour production, was first set up in 1868 at Faribault. Spring wheat became favoured over winter wheat; the western prairies became a one-crop country; wheat production increased tremendously. Agricultural prices soon began a long period of decline, but mortgage charges had to be met in the original nominal values. The aftermath of the panic of 1873 and the grasshopper plagues wrought havoc with the farmer's living. In the plague-infested areas the summary remedies of mortgage holders often stripped "a helpless family of the last defence against impending starvation." Agricultural machinery agents ruthlessly enforced their inexorable rights of forfeiture. Governor Pillsbury declared a day of prayer and issued a proclamation appealing "for divine mercy for sins" and "for the intervention of the only hand which could stay the pestilence." [1]

The farmers, however, blamed their troubles on the middlemen, from the country-store trader and banker to the railroad company. They complained that they were charged usurious rates of interest, that they were compelled to sell their wheat in a market controlled by the Minneapolis Millers Association, that the "brass kettle" which was used for measuring grades was so manipulated by the members that three different grades could be produced from the same bushel of wheat. The millers were taking advantage of the farmers as they had taken advantage of the inventor, La Croix, an educated Frenchman who was unaccustomed to business ways and who, according to legend, died in 1874 of a broken heart, having been treated "most shabbily by the organised millers" as well as by those who pirated his process. [2]

The railroad companies, which dominated the business situation, were condemned as the greatest sinners. It was the day of promoters, of men who at the "expense of the people" played with railroads under the guidance of

> "The good old rule, the simple plan,
> That they shall take who have the might
> And they shall keep who can."

Western promoters followed Eastern promoters in carrying out the ideals, attributed to Vanderbilt, of charging "all the traffic can bear" and "the public be damned."

In the courts of Minnesota the former receiver of the St. Paul and Pacific Railway, in pursuance of a supposed agreement, was seeking a share of the profits made by James J. Hill and a group of Canadian associates when they reorganised the company into the St. Paul, Minnesota and Manitoba Company. According to the court hearings practically the only funds supplied by the promoters were those needed for printing the securities, the bulk of which went to Hill and his associates.[3]

The Minnesota State Legislature was pressed at every session to pay defaulted railroad securities which had been issued under state auspices as the "Five Million Dollar Loan," even though investigation had convinced the people that these securities were "swindling bonds." Justice Field, speaking for the Supreme Court, declared that "the state is bound by every consideration of honour and good faith to pay them." [4] Local communities went heavily into debt in guaranteeing and purchasing railroad securities; farmers lost their property which had been mortgaged to buy stock in proposed railways for moving their products. In spite of huge grants, estimated in 1873 by the Minnesota railroad commissioner to be sufficient to have built all the railroads of the state, freight rates were high and tending to advance. Even respectable state officials joined with the farmers in denouncing "the continued extortions and discriminations of the railroad companies, controlled by absentee owners." Governor Austin declared that it was "time to take these robber corporations by the scruff of the neck and shake them over hell." [5]

Against these "sinister" interests the farmers had begun a political crusade. The Patrons of Husbandry, or the Grange, first firmly established in Minnesota in 1869, became a power in the politics of the West. In 1873 the quixotic Minnesotan, Ignatius Donnelly, whose forensic abilities were unequalled, was chosen chief lecturer of the Grange. "Wherever amid the fullness of the earth a human stomach goes empty, or a human brain remains darkened in ignorance," he said, "there is wrong and crime and fraud somewhere." The battle of the age was on:

"Could the ordinary man retain his economic independence, or must he become the wage slave of the possessor of great wealth?" After Donnelly's lecture at Faribault "fiery" resolutions were endorsed as "the true ringing declaration of a determined class of men to change the order of railroad government and extortion." At another meeting an Anti-Monopoly Party was started. "We can't look for a remedy in the Republican Party," said Donnelly, for "its brains and its pocketbook are in New England." Most of the farmers were good protectionists, but Donnelly impressed them with the statement that the protective tariff not only allowed Eastern manufacturers to charge unjust prices for the farmer's necessities, but further paralysed him by making it difficult for foreign countries to pay for American wheat.

In 1876 the resumption of full specie payments for greenbacks was set for 1879. The farmers as well as other interests, with debts contracted in a greatly depreciated currency, were up in arms. Donnelly, as temporary chairman of the National Greenback Convention, called for a "party in whose judgment and in whose heart the poorest man who toils in the mines of Pennsylvania or in the mills of New England will outweigh in consequence and importance Jay Gould or Cornelius Vanderbilt." [6] In 1878 Donnelly, nominated for Congress by Greenbackers, Democrats, and a council of workingmen of St. Paul, waged a highly exciting "swindling brass-kettle campaign"; he kept the state in an uproar by contesting the seat for two years on grounds of fraud and bribery.

This state of affairs was a part of Veblen's living experience. Like other farmers Thomas Veblen was burdened with indebtedness and was suffering from the widespread depression. In 1879, according to the census figures, the gross income from the Veblen farms was $1200. A family of growing children added to his cares. The family was deeply interested in the speeches of Donnelly and other spokesmen for the farmers; it was much impressed by the statement of the intellectual leader, Doctor Pentz, that the living of the middleman was a tax paid by themselves. Across the national scene blazed the railroad strike of 1877, which was the greatest labour disturbance on record and almost amounted to a civil war. An American reign of terror lasted for a fortnight, and troops were dispatched and proclamations issued. A new era was dawning in American life.

It was not an easy task for Thomas Veblen to maintain the children at college, but he devised ways of keeping down expenses. He went to town, bought some lumber and a lot adjoining the college campus, and with the assistance of another carpenter built a house within a week. Provisions were brought in from the farm. Sufficient clothing for everyday wear, substantial food, the needed books and tuition, took all the money. Luxuries were unknown to the Veblens.

Such a simple life had been satisfactory in the settlement, but for the college social functions money was required. The Veblens could only resolutely forget the things they could not have. In this community their manners seemed rural, and according to a schoolmate their background in the "Norwegian customs and language" was still apparent. The college faculty and the people of the town might not show any discernible difference in their treatment of the Veblens, but the Veblens themselves felt a distinction. Andrew and Thorstein each won the Atkins prize of $80 for the best college entrance examination, but Andrew, who for a term taught a class in algebra, complained that many of the social honours and privileges which should have been open to him were withheld. Andrew Veblen was somewhat aggressive and determined to show that he was as good an American as any, but Thorstein was highly sensitive. He even preferred to seem unable to answer questions in class rather than betray the fact that he did not have sufficient command of the adopted language to express himself well.

"Carleton College was conceived and organised," wrote Andrew Veblen, "on the Dartmouth-Amherst New England tradition by Yankees, led by the clergy." It was originally established on a precarious footing in 1867 as Northfield College. But Congregational college presidents pleaded that the establishment of college endowments was the noblest monument "any man can rear to his own memory," since it satisfied the "nature which God has given us, to desire the good will and loving esteem of the men of our . . . generation." [7] In the year Andrew Veblen entered the school its aggressive president, the Reverend James W. Strong, persuaded a Congregational merchant from Massachusetts, William Carleton, to give the institution $25,000, and the name was changed.

Carleton College was "thoroughly *Christian,* and distinctly and earnestly evangelical." Such colleges as Carleton were "the training schools of the men who must be depended upon to carry on this home missionary work." [8] Local church service was compulsory, with monitors in attendance. In the settlement it had been customary after the Sunday service to go riding and visiting, but at Carleton such activities were considered deadly sins. "Intemperance, profanity, the use of tobacco in any form," were forbidden, as was also "all Sabbath and evening association between the sexes, except by special permission." [9] One of the trustees declared: "This Christian college is ever our ally, as we seek to combat the superficial scepticism, or coarse but taking infidelity, or vulgar vice. . . . It aims . . . to penetrate the popular mind with the saving truths of religion and science, as in their impressive agreement they shall be set forth by its teachers. In it, therefore, Moses comes before Socrates, David before Homer, Paul before Plato, and Jesus Christ is acknowledged Lord of all."

The faculty, mostly clerical, were devout New England Congregationalists. An instructor was considered capable of teaching any subject as long as "the light of a godly example" was shown in his life and work.[10] One reverend gentleman, whose "consuming aspiration was to attain unto Jesus Christ," taught chemistry, physics, and mineralogy for ten years and then philosophy and biblical literature.[11] "The spirit of God immanent in all His works," was the "fundamental creed" of the professor of astronomy and mathematics, and he opened every class session with a prayer.[12]

Carleton aimed "at the standard of scholarship maintained by the best New England colleges."[13] This meant that the classics, religion, and moral philosophy were stressed. Biology was unknown. There was only a limited amount of textbook botany and zoology. "Natural science" was slighted even more. The college possessed an observatory, but it was conducted as an object of curiosity. "It is . . . a pleasure to say," stated the catalogue, "that visitors from home and abroad, have uniformly been admitted at any time, which is contrary to the practice of other observatories pursuing regular work."[14] The library was stocked with theological works, and a fire in 1879 destroyed most of the books that were not rubbish. English literature was sketchily taught during one quarter of the senior year, and American history was unknown.

In view of the heavy teaching schedules and the intellectual quality of the instructors, the teaching of the classics could hardly have been adequate: There was, in fact, scarcely any appreciation of the classical civilisations. A high standard of scholarship could not be expected, however, in the light of a comment made by the president of the near-by Congregational institution, Illinois College: "We think there can be little danger, that a people so calculating, so intensely money-loving and money-getting as we are, will withdraw more than a reasonable share of their capital from active business for the erection of . . . edifices . . . devoted to education."[15]

The really important courses were those in so-called moral and intellectual philosophy, including the "Evidences of Christianity." Philosophy was an applied science, having relations with morals, politics, and theology, and was usually taught by the president. It stood apart from all the other courses since it contained the principles which fitted the student to command himself and command success. The clerical rulers of the colleges had use only for a philosophy which could be authoritatively taught and on which students could easily recite. It must cast no doubts upon the literal interpretation of the Bible and the allied system of New England morals. The Scottish Common Sense Philosophy, founded by Thomas Reid, eminently suited their purpose. Reid was the representative of Presbyterian Scotland in its quest for a speculative philosophy which would justify as immutable and eternal the prevailing common-sense beliefs against Hume's scepticism. The prevailing doctrine of Locke—that all knowledge is derived from our experience of particular facts, sensations—had been driven by Hume to the conclusion that all so-called fundamental truths, whether of the material universe, religion, or morality, are simply impressions and ideas associated by custom. They are expectations developed in individuals by experience, that is, by habit, and although of great practical usefulness they cannot be rationally established. The existence of fundamental truths assumes the rationality of the causal principle, which Hume denied because it requires the connecting of two concepts—an event and an antecedent cause —between which no necessary connexion of any kind can be detected in the mind. Reid appealed to the common sense of mankind for justification of fundamental truths. They are "principles which the constitution of our nature leads us to believe, and which we are under a necessity to take for granted in the common concerns of life, without being able to give a reason for them." They are "self-evident truths" and "anything manifestly contrary to them is what we call absurd." [16]

During Veblen's college years the thinker of most authority among American philosophers was the last great spokesman of the Common Sense Philosophy, Sir William Hamilton. He held that since sense knowledge is only finite and relative, knowledge is possible only on conditions which compel belief in an Unconditioned Reality which lies beyond. There must be an unconditioned being on whom mankind can depend for preservation, and this being must be unknown since otherwise he would be conditioned. "A learned ignorance" is the consummation of knowledge, and the "last and highest consecration of all true religion, must be an altar—*to the unknown and unknowable God.*" Hence his disciple H.L. Mansel deduced that what is now understandable in revelation must be believed. The dogmas of eternal punishment and atonement, even though they conflict with human ideas of love and justice, must be accepted, for what appear to mere man as love and justice may appear to God as something different.[17] By such means the existing institutional order, which included the dogmatic theology, was also made the divine order. This philosophy prevailed in almost all the American colleges, and the student of Hamilton, President James Mc-Cosh of Princeton, was considered "the American philosopher."

"The criterion of . . . reality is the clear testimony of consciousness," said Laurens Hickok, whose works had been taught to the Carleton professor of philosophy. Any discussion of alien cultures or of the past, if offered at all, should be only a preliminary, to show that unchanging common sense is the unquestioned and necessary beginning of all thinking, and to rule out as not properly belonging to mankind those who do not possess this common sense. Thus Hickok's textbook, *Empirical Psychology*, began with a chapter on "Anthropology" before it proceeded to "Empirical Psychology" proper, and the chapter concluded: "Our short study of anthropological distinctions shows clearly that humanity, though having intrinsic differences, is yet in the common conviction a separate whole, and has a common experience which, while it includes all men, embraces mankind only. This common experience holds all that is peculiar to man, and excludes all that is not in some way common. . . . It thus holds all that it is necessary to be known, in order that we may know what is in man. If then the 'proper study of mankind is man,' the way for man to know himself and his fellows is carefully and thoroughly to study his and their common experience." The common sense "may be attained in various ways; from the languages, laws, manners and customs, proverbial sayings, literature, and history of the race." What happens if one has a common sense that does not coincide with the general consciousness? "If any man allege a consciousness different from that of mankind in general, this can be no matter of any further concern to us," said Hickok, "for if it were true, it would only prove that he was *alterum genus,* and that any facts which were peculiar to him would be of no account in a system which embraces those only of our common humanity." [18]

Since the fundamental principle of common sense is that the original pronouncements of consciousness must be accepted as true, there is an opposition between the individual consciousness and the external world whose reality is attested by consciousness; that is, an antithesis between self and not-self. Therefore the social order, being real, is a part of the natural order of circumstances, and the natural end of man, like that of a businessman, is to take advantage of circumstances. Man is essentially the puppet of circumstances which impress their influence upon him by way of pleasure and pain. Thus the "self-regarding" passions, according to the Reverend Joseph Haven's textbook used at Carleton in the course on Intellectual Philosophy, are the "motive power" to action. The basic desire, if not the all-inclusive one, is the "desire for happiness" or "self-love," which has its "foundation in the constitution of the mind, and which is characteristic of reason and intelligence." The greatest pleasure of man is the pleasure of the ability to exert power, that is, to "control the actions of his fellow man and bend the will of others to his own."

This desire for power may express itself in the form of the "desire for superiority," otherwise known as "the principle of emulation." Today such superiority is attainable principally by the "possession of wealth." "This, as the world goes, is the key that unlocks, the sceptre that controls, all things. . . . No wonder that he who desires power, should desire that which is one of the chief avenues and means to the attainment of power, and that what is valued, at first, rather as an instrument than as an end, should presently come to be regarded and valued for its own sake."

Thus in the textbook on Moral Philosophy the general consciousness reveals "that the desire to possess, to appropriate, lies among the native and implanted principles of the mind." "Man has not only the right to life and liberty, but also to *property*, or the possession and enjoyment of whatever he may, by his own industry or good fortune, or the gift of others, have honestly acquired. . . . It is the labour expended in originally acquiring, or subsequently improving, any object of possession, that constitutes the right of property in the same." Should it be objected that "we possess many things which we call property, on which we have not bestowed labour—many values which we have not ourselves created, as, for example, property inherited or bequeathed, I reply, these values were originally created by labour; they became the property of the original owner in that way; and the right of possession has been conferred by him on the present possessor." Therefore the rich man "has that only which he has acquired by his own toil and economy, or which has rightfully descended to him, from those who in the first instance acquired it in this manner. He has a claim and a right to all that he calls his." [19]

Man has an ethical right to his property "irrespective of all civil legislation." Any denial of this "natural right," whether in real estate or any form of capital, must result "in reducing to a minimum all the motives to production." [20] As Francis Lieber put it, man's "goodness, his greatness, his activity, his energy and industry—everything good and characteristic of him as a man is connected with the idea of individual property . . . the 'nourisher of mankind, incentive of industry, and cement of human society.' " He asks us to imagine for a moment "the idea of property erased from the human mind. "What a state! Nothing but brute force to support each single individual—a pack of hungry wolves." [21] Even the pursuit of knowledge was looked upon from the self-regarding point of view. "We . . . get knowledge" in order to "get wealth." [22]

Property was established by God for the good of man. This was the "final cause" and the axiom of final cause is higher than "the category of efficient or blind causative force"; therefore the efficient causes must be so presented as to portray the "obviously intended beneficent result" of the "pre-established harmony." Disturbances cannot be construed to cast doubt on this basic harmony. Thus, according to McCosh, "a new machine . . . throws a labourer . . . out of work," but such "secondary effects" may be described as "Incidentals" or "Accidents" since "they were not intended." [23]

The philosophy course included a branch in æsthetics, or the "science of beauty." Its texts were written by common-sense philosophers such as Bascom, whose book was used at Carleton, and the material was borrowed from English works such as Archibald Alison on "Taste." The purpose of the course was to refine the feelings, to promote appreciation of aristocratic tastes of leisure. Leisure, the cessation of work, was the great end of the acquisition of wealth. Without "accumulated property," said Lieber, there can be no leisure to engage in "earnest and persevering pursuit of knowledge." [24] A Southern scholar, Jacob Cardozo, thought in the same terms. Writing in 1867 of the pre-war Charleston society of planters and men of commerce, he said that "hospitalities never sit so gracefully as when dispensed by the man of leisure, who embellishes his retreat by the social virtues—and by the liberal culture of literature and arts." When some of the planters, after the reverses of the Civil War, were forced to drive carts and serve as grocery clerks under the supervision of "an ignorant and coarse menial," Cardozo exclaimed: "There is something unnatural in this reverse of position— something revolting to our sense of propriety in this social degradation." [25]

Economics, of course, was taught as an integral part of the common-sense philosophy. The textbooks used were written for the most part by the same theological authors as the textbooks on intellectual and moral philosophy. At Carleton the students used the most popular text in America, that of Bishop Francis Wayland as revised by the Reverend A. L. Chapin, president of the Congregational College at Beloit. Wayland had written the book in 1837, but Chapin in 1878 said that since the "elementary principles have become more or less familiar and apprehended by all . . . scarcely any changes have been made in the opinions presented." The result of his work was merely that the "arrangement and the form of statement have been quite generally *recast*." The "higher principles of Political Economy" are "general maxims" which, from their "obviousness and universality in operation, are in truth general facts, and reasoning founded upon them is eminently practical." All that is needed is "Common Sense and a good knowledge of the English language."

In Chapin's opinion "it is obvious, upon the slightest reflection, that the Creator has subjected the accumulation of the blessings of this life to some determinate laws." For example, "everyone . . . knows that no man can grow rich, without industry or frugality." Economics had not substantially changed since the days of the Reverend John McVickar, who said at Columbia in the thirties: "I go upon facts, and finding from them all that tends to exalt, refine, and give comfort to man, growing up under the patronage of commerce, and united within its bounds, I cannot but reverence the claims of commerce as something *holy.*" Economics was still conceived as *"a business science,"* with man viewed as an "exchanging being." Competition is "a beneficent, permanent law of nature," and self-interest is "the mainspring of human exertion." With these guiding principles, Chapin's typical textbook laid down four fundamental laws of political economy:

1) "God has made man a *creature of desires"* and has established the material universe "with qualities and powers . . . for the *gratification of those desires."* Desire is the stimulus to production and invention. 2) To satisfy desires, to obtain pleasures, man must by "irksome" labour force *"nature to yield her hidden resources."* 3) *The exertion of labour establishes a right of PROPERTY in the fruits of labour,* and the "idea of *exclusive possession* is a necessary consequence." Originally the object belongs to the producer "by an intuitive conception of right, and the act of appropriation is as instinctive as the act of breathing." The right of property may be conceived as "a law of natural justice," as Bowen of Harvard put it, because "the producer would not put forth his force and ingenuity if others deprived him of their fruits." Thus is established 4)*"The Right of EXCHANGE."*

Capital is always the fruit of past labour saved, and takes the form of productive goods. Titles to property indicate capital. Money is a form of fixed capital, a permanent instrument to aid production. Capital is continually consumed for the sake of producing a greater amount, which is measured by profits. An unprofitable investment denotes an unproductive use of capital, that is, a loss of capital.

Since "rent implies *ownership,"* land must be reckoned as capital when appropriated, and thus not questioned. Expropriation of land, even when the owners are paid, is a *"wild scheme of iniquity and folly."* No condemnation was severe enough for Henry George when he asserted, in contradiction to pecuniary common sense, that by the natural right of property no man had a right to more land than he could actually use himself, and that since the value of land was due to society, not to landlords, the "unearned increment" should be expropriated.

Credit, the provision of which is the function of banks, increases *"the sum of wealth available as capital*" and is also indispensable to the most effective development of "*industrial talent*." This is evidenced by the fact that those who have proved most effective in increasing their wealth "have been almost invariably, persons who have begun business with only their own energies and a character to inspire confidence in others." With credit a man of eminent business capacity, which otherwise would go to waste, "is enabled to obtain control of capital, on which his energies may be expended so as to bring in large returns for himself and for who- ever trusts property to his hands."

Money is the medium of the beneficent system of exchange, and through the development of credit and banking the modern system of trade is a "marvellous arrangement" by which goods are really exchanged with one another without the use of an appreciable amount of actual coin. The "metals derive their use as money from their inherent fitness, and the desire of men so to employ them, and not from any agency of government." The remonetization of silver is unjust as "conflicts with the fundamental principles of our science." The act of a government creating greenbacks is "a direct interference with the rights of property and with the fundamental law of exchange, which requires the free con- sent of parties to all transfers, and the maintenance of contracts in full force." It constitutes an abnormal use or a misuse of credit.

By the competitive process of acquisition every man finds the place and reward to which his abilities and talents entitle him. According to this "commercial law" those business men who do not satisfy the public's needs are eliminated, those who satisfy them find success. "Economic, social, and political power gravitate toward the capitalist, and incite him to fresh efforts . . . to carry the nation on its growth." "The tendency to an unequal distribution of wealth" is a fundamental "physical truth" of production. The "enforced equality of property would destroy emula- tion—the constant strain of the faculties, with all classes, in the pursuit of wealth . . . the feverish anxiety to get on."

Usury laws are in "direct conflict with the first principles of sound political economy," for such laws "*violate the right of property*." They contradict "the plainest dictates not only of natural right, but of com- mon honesty."

Since socialism is the "utter negation" of the right of private property, "man is no more adapted to it than the barn fowl is to live in the water." Philanthropy or any other aid of the poor is a violation of the same laws of God and property. All attempts to "relieve the natural penalties of indolence and improvidence" bring about "unexpected and severe evil." The doctrine that the government should provide for the unem- ployed "is the most subversive of all social order." Even the claim of

Ruskin that "all labours of like amounts should receive the same reward," means the suppression of "commercial law," which is "God's
method." If labour and capital are free, as they are in the "order of
nature undisturbed" under "the law of competition," then "the flow of
each . . . toward an equilibrium, is as natural as that of waters of the
ocean under gravitation." In reality the labourer has no complaint against
the competitive system. As Perry put it, employer and employee "come
together of necessity into a relation of mutual dependence, which God
has ordained, and which, though man may temporarily disturb it, he
can never overthrow."

The rate of wages is determined not by the pressure of capitalists but
by the "ratio between the amount of capital and the number of labourers
seeking employment." Thus, according to this wage-fund doctrine, nothing is to be gained by strikes and the "tyranny" of labour unions. Strikes
are a "violation of a most sacred right," the right of a man *to do what
he will with himself, his time, his strength, his skill."* The Reverend
William D. Wilson of Cornell put it more bluntly; in his textbook he
said "it ought to be very emphatically stated and often repeated" that
there may be a tendency for "claiming too much for mere labour and
not sufficiently regarding the rights of capital and the sacredness of the
laws by which it is protected."

Chapin, from a consideration of the prevailing depression, stated that
"it is . . . philosophical and in . . . accord with common sense to say
that wages fall or decline because *industry fails to yield the necessary
profit."* The promoter as distinct from the capitalist is now recognised
as the great industrial engineer and profits as distinct from interest go
to this all-essential "captain of industry" or "entrepreneur," who is assumed to effect "a union between capital and labour" and direct "their
active co-operation."

Some followers of the received tradition were aware of the fact that
the beneficent acquisitive impulse might have unfortunate effects. Bascom declared that the "passions and appetites" which are the basis of the
desire for wealth might lead to the destruction of society. "Vanity, among
the more harmless of these, is yet thoughtless, unsympathetic, intensely
grasping, and delights in that very separation of classes which makes perpetual poverty with its social and moral incidents the inheritance of half
the race. The merely selfish motive, therefore, capable as it is of arousing
the mind, is not able to turn the strength of the higher classes backward
and make it minister to the growth of the weaker and lower; but continually draws the nutriment of all upward, as the wick the oil to the
light, that it may be consumed in the pride and luxuries of the few,
till, the nerve and courage and patience of the nation burned out, it

falls, like Rome of old, with strength all too little to bear the stroke of fate."

This possible outcome, however, would be due to the lack of moral character and intelligence, that is, a self-regarding interest among the "weaker and lower." They are still "barbarians," men of "feeble races" and "savage society," since they do not feel the force of the pursuit of gain. If they felt this "most beneficent law," its unrestricted expression by the productive capitalists would be checked. Therefore, both as a "maxim of political policy" and as "a declaration of rights," the function of government is to let "pecuniary transactions" alone, to furnish "an open field" in which production "may enjoy its own reward."

Chapin noted in a concluding hortatory chapter that "*a mighty power is . . . concentrated in the hands of a few managers,*" a power which could be used against the "interests of the corporation and the public"; that promoters swindled the small purchaser of securities who supplied all the funds, that they bribed legislatures and played fast and loose with the companies for the sake of stock-market speculation. But he had no sympathy for a "blind 'granger movement' of open hostility" against the great corporations. "We hold in highest esteem the benefits conferred on the country by these corporations." The abuses cannot be remedied by legislation, but only by "sound public sentiment . . . which rests on an intelligent regard for the fundamental principles of Political Economy." These principles, demonstrating "the contrivance, the wisdom and beneficence of the Deity," must be used to dispel "popular ignorance and prejudice" which were causing riots and disturbances.[26] As it was put by the Reverend Lyman Atwater, author of the Carleton textbook on logic and lecturer on economics at Princeton, "Civil Government, the family, tenure of property" are "great ordinances of God for the social regulation of man." "True progress" must be based not upon scepticism but on "stability." [27]

No philosophies which in any way threatened common sense were to be tolerated. German metaphysics, particularly that of Kant, was denounced as "disintegrating idealism," a cover for attacking "all the principles of government and social order and for considering a philosophical religion as atheism itself." [28] John Stuart Mill was outside the pale, for he had ruthlessly dissected Hamilton, accusing him of holding up "favourite doctrines as intuitive truths" and of investing intuition, as the voice of God, with "an authority higher than . . . our reason." [29] Spencer and other supporters of the novel doctrine of evolution were accused of a "debasing materialism" and were denounced as propagating a doctrine "too monstrous . . . even to be entertained by competent thinkers." Its spokesmen "are not only at war with all morality and religion, but they are also . . . attacking those institutions of property, the family, and the state, on which the whole fabric of modern civilisation is based." [30] One orthodox Carleton professor was willing to grant that some evolution had taken place in the animal kingdom, but the view that humanity was subject to the same process was not to be tolerated.

The president of Carleton was very much occupied in raising money, and his courses were usually taught by the one man at the school who possessed distinctive intellectual quality. Professor John Bates Clark was officially the librarian and professor of political economy and history, but actually he was professor of "odds and ends," teaching everything from English composition to moral philosophy. As a student at Amherst he had shown unusual independence by refusing to compete for the philosophical prize. The contest required that one adhere with "absolute correctness" to the "text and lecture" of Hickok's system and "defend the philosophy against objections." Clark refused to participate on the ground that he "could think effectively for himself." [31] At Carleton, although he often addressed Congregational gatherings, some of his writings seemed "unspiritual to say the least."

Clark's objections to Hickok were not, however, directed against the fundamental tenets of common sense but only against certain details of Hickok's moral philosophy. The position that Clark held was much the same as that of Haven and Hopkins, two outstanding common-sense philosophers whose textbooks he used at Carleton. He began his writing career by asserting that in the "present state of the public mind financial heresies receive a ready circulation, and, if these false doctrines connect themselves . . . with fundamental errors of Political Economy, it is time that those errors were exposed and their teachers discredited." He proposed to set forth "a new philosophy of wealth" which would avoid the distinction made by liberal English economists between "labour, as productive and unproductive," and which would render "the classification of all labour as productive, both possible and obvious," and make it "easy to place every variety of labourer in exactly the class of wealth-producers where, from the nature of his function, he belongs." Wealth was defined as "relative well-being," pertaining to individual rather than community welfare. A good, in order to be wealth, must of course satisfy a want, that is, possess utility, but its "essential attribute" is appropriability, the attributes "which render ownership possible."

That wealth, property rights, is distributed as equitably as possible under the circumstances is substantiated by anthropological inquiry, such as Hickok's. Political economy, in the light of this anthropological examination, does not treat of man the savage but of man who through ages of unifying processes of social development becomes a part of the social organism "in which each part exists and acts not for itself but for the whole," as in the system of free contract. This social organisation has been achieved by the increase in those higher wants which sum up to a "desire for social consideration." "Civilised man struggles no longer for existence, but for progressive . . . enjoyment," and by a "kindly provision such wants," which "must remain for ever unsatisfied . . . are generally quiescent." The desire for those things "which lie far above the line of necessities and the consumption of which would be classed as unproductive" by the English economists "is the constant motive power in industrial progress." Thus desire for acquisition is the great engine of industrial development and consequently the smooth functioning of society is to be achieved by the distribution of property in "the natural way."

In the natural order of free contract every man obtains the results of his efforts, but in a system of communism, since "acquirement would no longer depend on successful exertion, the springs of ambition would be destroyed and an eager and hungry waiting for a gratuity would be substituted for that natural condition." By equal distribution "the losers in the redistribution would be deprived of what would be the object of an active and intense desire, and would experience great positive unhappiness, which would be intensified to despair by the impossibility of rising again by effort. . . . Absolute communism would be followed by the worst results conceivable, and any approach to it would be attended by a corresponding approximation to them." Therefore, if the citizens knew the principles of political economy, most of them would be "proof against the wild and ruinous doctrines advocated by demagogues in the supposed interest of labour."

Although Clark was opposed to political socialism he favoured a form of socialism which would not contain any violations of the natural ideal order of property. He felt that a "remnant of natural ferocity" existed in business institutions and that the theory of the "modern bargain appears to be that of the medieval judicial combat; let each do his worst, and God will protect the right." But these institutions "contain in themselves the germs of a progress that shall break the limitations of the existing system, and give us the only socialism that can be permanent or beneficial." The predatory order will give way to peace and industry. True socialism is "a general development, directed by the Providence which presides over all history." Little is to be gained by "inventing new schemes of society," but much is to be gained by "reverently studying the course of Providence." Clark declared that he believed in the "teleologic principle," the "optimistic principle, that the world is improving."

In Veblen's senior year Clark elaborated these ideas before the class and before a college forum, in the form of a "philosophy of value" based on "the new philosophy of wealth." In an inchoate manner it presented the logical outcome of the American tradition in economics as refined by Clark's liberalism. Under an ideal system of free contract everyone receives what in reality he produces, or its equivalent. The present system is a close approximation to this condition, and it constantly grows closer by force of the inherent principle of harmony in the evolving social organism. In the light of the pleasure-pain calculus "market value is a measure of utility made by society considered as one great isolated being." The rewards which society thinks the producers are entitled to are established through the functioning of the "laws of property, fixed principles of distribution," which "society is not at liberty to violate." To be sure, "values in use might be augmented" if these naturally established market values could be "arbitrarily changed." But "such a wholesale confiscation would mean the most violent of revolutions, and would lead to a chaotic condition fatal to the welfare of all . . . Yet better systems of social circulation may be before us, in the future, if we can but wait for their development." [32]

Thorstein Veblen did not fit in well at Carleton College, either intellectually or socially. In the words of a trustee the function of such "missionary colleges" was to impress on the West the "ideas and principles" of the East and to combat "the coarse infidelity, the reckless demagogism and old-world socialism so rife in our newer States." [33] But by the test of the common-sense philosophy Veblen was *alterum genus*, and the rising agrarianism, so deplored by the college officials, was the expression of his own people.

He was no better adjusted, however, in the Norwegian community at home. When the Veblen brood at Carleton returned to the farm, they kept aloof from the neighbours. The settlement thought they were snobbish, putting on airs, acting as if they were better than other people. Leading Norwegians, including Pastor Muus and Osmund Osmundsen, the founder of Nerstrand, had established St. Olaf School in Northfield in 1875, but no Veblen child attended it. The clergy still insisted on a rigid maintenance of the traditional scheme of things, and they bitterly fought the public schools. Members of the office-holding classes of Norway were appearing in the settlements, and they too were insisting on the traditional status. The entire community clung to the "old spiritual and cultural values," and the consummation of the process of assimilation "seemed as distant as ever." [34]

Andrew Veblen was somewhat forgiven for his deviations from the right path when he accepted a position at Luther College. Thorstein's unpopularity was aggravated by his "conceit." A member of the family who had always felt a warm affection for him declared that he had become a "conceited jackass." The Norwegian nicknames he had used to torment the neighbours were supplemented now by Greek anathemas, which he flaunted before them and wrote on their fences. An older lad took away his gun one summer and the next vacation period Veblen came back and shot the fellow's dog before his eyes. In another uprising of the hated Sioux, gold prospectors, including some from Rice County, were killed for invading the reservations in Dakota territory, from which the white man was barred. Again Veblen defended the Indians against the general opinion. He was really a lonely youth, most happy when he was laughing with his mother. Most of the time he withdrew within himself and occupied himself with his own ideas.

With his brother Andrew he began a study of Old Norse, in which the sagas of his people were written. He was led to the poetry and prose works of William Morris, based on the Icelandic sagas. The related German epic literature excited him, particularly the Niebelungenlied, and through a near-by settlement of Germans he acquired an excellent command of the language and was able to read the epics in the original. Echoes came to him of the provocative discussions going on in the intellectual world concerning the origin of races and especially the attempt to establish a common origin for the dominant peoples in a race called the Aryan. Acquaintance with Pentz, a German exile from the collapse of the liberal movement, brought him into contact not only with an agrarian spokesman but with a man of high intellectual calibre. Access to Pentz's well-stocked library gave him a first-hand knowledge of the leading German philosophers, particularly Kant. He read Spencer, whom in particular he considered a great contributor to intellectual advance, Mill, Hume, Rousseau, Huxley, Tyndall, and a host of others who tended to free thought and who were kept out of the college courses.

To most of his fellow students at college Veblen seemed "sneering and supercilious," but his good-natured manner and apparent indolence partially disarmed them. "Veblen could say the bitterest things with a smile on his face and a chuckle in his voice." His "dry humour . . . was likely to break out on almost any occasion, especially a solemn one." He liked to corner some very religious student and harangue him, sometimes for hours, on such questions as the advisability of a club for the promotion of suicide. The students considered him a complete cynic. "Whatever is, is wrong," seemed to be his attitude. But even of this they could not be certain. Some of his apparently outrageous remarks disturbed them, but when they questioned him further he would become vague. They accused him of "doing a brilliant thing that won everybody and then in order to be spectacular lying low on the daily task." The attitude of most of the men was described by a classmate: "He was not the kind to whom they could become attached as a friend, or ask for advice or opinions. He was neither sincere nor stable; he lacked character and judgment." But one a little more sympathetic wrote: "As I distinctly remember him in our literary society, he was not selfish or egoistic but felt sure that he had thought the subject through and had the facts in regard to it. His voice and manner were not adapted to addressing large audiences, in fact he wasn't interested in that line of work and seemed to know that his work was thinking and using his pen, talking to a limited number in conference and classroom. He had that keen, cold mentality which held him aloof from friendship with others. He could make mental but not heart associates."

The faculty, too, was not enthusiastic over this youth with a "mind clothed in sardonic humour," as one of them described it. They were a little afraid of him. Clark, who admired his keen psychological insight, was the only one who really liked him. Clark said that as the "college was founded by religious men and for the sake of religious influence Veblen was a misfit," but he considered him the "most acute thinker" among his students. Veblen cared even less for the faculty than they did for him, and spoke "sneeringly and contemptuously" of their abilities and attainments. He heartily disdained the president as "a New Englandish clergyman." He dubbed the rather strict dean of women "mater dolorosa," and the name stuck. Clark he liked very much, but the only teaching of Clark that he remembered was a lecture on suavity, in which Clark spoke of a "suave manner as an aid in giving effect to force of thought." It was an ancient maxim but Veblen had already found it very useful.

The weekly public declamation exercises, or rhetoricals, presided over by the professor of philosophy, provided Veblen with his best opportunity for jarring the faculty and students. While Carleton prayed for the conversion of the heathen, Veblen, reader of Swift, delivered "A Plea for Cannibalism" which threw the faculty and students into an uproar. On another occasion he delivered "An Apology for a Toper." According to the prevailing morals drunkenness would and should bring severe retribution, but Veblen noted how drunkards actually viewed death, not how they should view it, and closed with the statement that "although death is never far away, it has for them few terrors." Clark, who was presiding, asked him if he was apologizing for the toper, but Veblen casually replied that he was simply engaged in a scientific observation. At other times he astonished the gatherings with oratorical outbursts on "The Science of Laughter," "The Face of a Worn-Out Politician," "The Absence of the Gregarious in Student Life," "Companions That Can Be Counted On," "Thrice Is He Armed That Hath His Quarrel Just," "Two Ways of Looking at Facts." "All the time," said a woman schoolmate, "his nasal twang and his subtle smile added an element of—not 'charm'—but of interest to the occasion."

Veblen enjoyed subjecting the textbooks of the philosophy course to public examination. He took up Mark Hopkins's *Evidences of Christianity*, and demonstrated that the "evidences" were cases of poor reasoning. In dealing with *The Philosophical Basis of Theism* by W.T. Harris, the leader of the Hegelians, he attempted to disprove its thesis that partial agnosticism involves complete agnosticism and is therefore untenable. He seemed to be alone in his attitude on religious and moral questions, and found reasons for discussion where most people "would simply affirm, approve, or endorse." Rather than have his attendance at the Sunday service in the local churches checked by monitors, he called himself a Moravian and went to a little German church some distance away to improve his German.

In the more prosaic field of economics he essayed the philosopher's role of prophet and delivered an oration on "The Price of Wheat Five Years Hence," which in the opinion of one auditor was "wretchedly dull" but "logical and learned." In opposition to the rest of the college, including Clark, he took the side of the Greenbackers, and when Henry George's *Progress and Poverty* appeared "he did not hesitate to let it be known that he supported it." He gave little attention to those illtreated subjects, mathematics and sciences. He said he once solved some simple problems in algebra, but he did not know how he accomplished the task. His grade in algebra was 71.

Into the literary societies, ostensibly devoted to the discussion of serious and profound topics, Veblen carried his disturbing tactics. He prepared a paper on the subject of "Noses," which seems to have been a burlesque on Galton's attempt to correlate anatomical facial differences with character. According to a faculty member he submitted an elaborate classification, and attempted to deduce the character of the individual from the shape and other peculiarities of the nose. "It was a fantastic performance presented with the utmost seriousness." At another meeting the official critic called attention to the brevity and poor quality of the papers, declaring that they had little depth and showed little thought in preparation. Veblen appeared at the next meeting with a paper on the philosophy of Mill. For over forty minutes he read it, page after page, very seriously and in a dreary monotone. Without understanding a word the listeners gave it the best attention they could, expecting each moment that he would come to a close. When it was finally finished, the critic was forced to admit that "Mr. Veblen's paper was sufficiently long and sufficiently deep." According to a sympathetic auditor Veblen "fully realized how bored all the listeners were. . . . Yet he read it through and never cracked a smile . . . as though he was standing alone in the room with no one listening. There was nothing oratorical about his speaking or reading."

In the manner of the grand epic style of Morris's Valkyrie poems Veblen wrote a seventy-eight line parody on the traditional New England college sophomore custom of burying Cæsar or Euclid. He headed his poem, "The Following Lines Are Respectfully Dedicated to the Class of '82 by One Who Sympathizes with Them in Their Recent Bereavement." This work included such profanity as "h——," dutifully abbreviated. The poem was privately printed by the students. As a poetic performance it would do credit to the usual college magazine. Veblen also produced in complicated Latin a poem entitled "Carmen," written in praise of the god Bacchus and all his works. A friend said it was done as a "bit of deviltry in the thought that none of the faculty would understand its purport."

Although Veblen was one of the strongest men in the college he walked as if the "effort taxed his muscular system," and when sitting down he "slid his loosely jointed frame to a reclining position." This apparent indolence gave some of the students the impression that he was in school because of his parents' wishes and not of his own free will. But he could show plenty of physical agility if admiration was to be gained by it.

A romance began at Carleton. When Veblen first entered the academy he met Ellen Rolfe, the niece of the president, and "from that first day he cared for no other." She was descended from the Strongs and the Rolfes, old and distinguished families. Another uncle was W.B. Strong, the dynamic personality then making the Atchison, Topeka, and Santa Fe Railroad into a powerful transcontinental organisation. He secured favourable state legislation and aid and engaged in successful warfare with competing companies which reached a climax in the Grand Canyon War, a two-year battle carried on with violence and bloodshed, law suits and injunctions, innumerable writs and counter-writs. Ellen's father, Charles Rolfe, had extensive interests in grain elevators and was a member of the Kansas City Board of Trade. Railroad business thrown his way by W.B. Strong added considerably to his wealth.

Nothing could be stranger than that a daughter of one of the reigning families in the Middle West should be interested in the son of a Norwegian immigrant. It was a Strong who had declared that the Negroes are more intelligent and more civilised than the Norwegians. But Thorstein Veblen, the anthropologist, traced the ancestry of Ellen Rolfe to prove to her that she too was a product of Norway. Her name, he assured her, went back to the first Viking chief, Gange Rolfe, who seized a part of what is now France and formed Normandy. His descendants conquered England and their descendants became the ruling stock of New England.

Ellen Rolfe was a remarkable woman. "Possessed of a sparkling and, at times, slightly caustic wit, brilliant in all her writings as a student, and above the average in scholarship," wrote a classmate, "she was easily the most intellectual member of the class . . . had the brightest, keenest mind . . . and her writings at college clearly foreshadowed a brilliant literary career." [35] She "displayed a subtle power which was nothing short of genius." Like Veblen she was a gifted story-teller, with a leaning towards ghost stories in the style of Poe. The senior class "Prophecy," a subtle parody of the style of "Hiawatha," was her work. In the destiny assigned to her closest friend was a delicate shaft aimed at Clark:

> "Scarcely thrice had rolled the seasons
> When again the voices called her.
> "Who," they cried, "will write a treatise
> Found the science great and noble—
> Teleology—the climax
> Of all science and invention."

She was no better adjusted than Veblen to life at Carleton College. When Ellen was very young, her mother died and her father remarried. Her life at home seems not to have been very satisfactory, and her early maladjustments were not erased at college. The women there were critical of her, just as the men were critical of Veblen. Occasionally she took advantage of the fact that the president was her uncle. Her college mates considered her "dreamy, introspective, disinclined to active physical effort, unable to envisage present duty, lacking in physical fortitude. The painstaking operations of everyday life seemed to interest her less than the smallest details of life far removed. She could more easily draw a vivid picture of the life, perhaps of Pharaoh's daughter or of Nausicaa, than see why she should join in the general activities which all schoolgirls find agreeable and necessary in the care of their individual rooms, clothes, and in a general desire to promote the harmonious and orderly programme of a general dormitory home. This does not mean that anyone took umbrage at Nellie Rolfe's special characteristics. She was placed in a class by herself."

These two misfits spent much of their time together. Even at parties they would "get into a corner and talk—and talk—and in low tones disturb no one," according to a schoolmate, "only we all thought it singularly ill suited to a general student gathering, when we all met and mingled freely and on occasions wherein we believed the rarest social art was to take some responsibility for entertaining the others." Under the influence of Veblen, Ellen read Spencer and quickly "became an agnostic." She, on the other hand, heightened that part of him "which was gentlest and most feminine," and there was much of that. Her great admiration for the idealism of Ruskin had its effect upon him. She said that although Veblen knew no English when he came to Carleton he learned the langauge rapidly and had an agile command of it. He developed "an inclination towards poetry and the best literary prose" and became interested, in fact, in all the arts, except music. Ellen liked his humour and his slow, lazy manner, and she said that he "towered easily above students and faculty in comprehensive outlook and keenness of logic."

Veblen amply demonstrated his superiority during his last year at Carleton. Five years there had made him eager to be free of it, and he asked permission to take both the junior and senior years in one. To the faculty this seemed impossible and at first they refused, but Veblen persisted and reluctantly they granted him the privilege. When his sophomore classmates returned for the junior year they discovered that Veblen had in some way slipped into the senior year and was grouped with the class of 1880 instead of 1881. How it came about they never knew, as "we never knew much about his many movements." The faculty remained hostile but, to the great pleasure of Clark, he carried his purpose with conspicuous success. His highest grade of 94 he scored in "Political Economy" and "Evidences of Christianity." Apparently he could tolerate the "Moral Philosophy," for his grade there was 93, but in "Mental Philosophy" he received his lowest grade of 77. For once the faculty conceded that Clark's opinion of Veblen might be near the truth.

His public oration for graduation was a spectacular performance. Instead of choosing the usual kind of topic, such as "The Duty of a Christian Scholar," Veblen spoke on "Mill's Examination of Hamilton's Philosophy of the Conditioned." The task of expounding one of the greatest English philosophical works did not disturb him. He discussed the mathematical points as if he were a master of the subject, thereby arousing the theological instructor of mathematics, who exclaimed to Andrew Veblen, sitting next to him: "Thorstein is a fraud. He was never any good in my classes." In front of Veblen were his proud parents. "Anyone who looked at the father and mother as they sat in the pew of the

Congregational Church and listened to Thorstein's oration," said a school-mate, "could see that they felt that they were rewarded for all their sacrifice and work in helping him to get his education, and they seemed confident that their hopes for his successful career would be fully realised."

The local newspaper reported that "Veblen, son of Thor, in spite of the heat, hammered away blow upon blow, and with no mean skill, at a subject the bare name of which was almost an overdose for the average reader." All that is known of Veblen's argument is a disarming sentence provided by this same country newspaper: "He held, in a word, that the case of Mill versus Hamilton was clearly one of *non sequitur*." [36] Veblen had chosen the work which was the most annoying to common-sense followers; still one wonders whether this statement could be interpreted to mean that Veblen had found that the difference between Mill's supposedly atheistic philosophy and the common-sense philosophy was as unsubstantial as many were beginning to suspect.

After his graduation in 1880 Veblen, through the efforts of his brother Andrew, secured a position teaching at Monona Academy in Madison, Wisconsin. This institution was under the control of Veblen's synod, and there, for a year, he was thrown back into the life of the Norwegian community. His work was primarily the uncongenial subject of mathematics. The scene was stormy. At the synod's theological seminary, also in Madison, a bitter theological dispute began over predestination and election, Calvinism and strong church authority. During the winter Bjørnson, Norway's national hero and with Ibsen a leader of the rising school of "realism," made a stormy lecture tour through the Middle West, amidst the denunciations of the clergy. In 1879 he had denied the divinity of Christ and, while still professing to be a Christian, he was a pronounced freethinker. All synods and factions were as one in denouncing this apostate and heretic. Bjørnson was accused of denying "all portions of the Bible which treat of governmental authority," and of being "an out and out Darwinist." Lutherans who attended his lectures were threatened with church discipline.[37] But they were attended even by some of the conservative instructors from Monona Academy. The entire Veblen family felt the greatest interest in this reckless Norwegian who was accusing the clergy of acting in opposition to the example of Jesus of Nazareth.

Veblen made the acquaintance of Bjørnson's tour manager, Professor Rasmus Anderson. According to Andrew Veblen, Thorstein helped Anderson with some of his translations from Norwegian literature and substantiated many of the points in old Norse history which were of interest to him. Veblen met also the Reverend John Bascom, president of the University of Wisconsin and author of a textbook in almost every branch of philosophy, including political economy. Veblen found that this New England common-sense philosopher from Williams College was as difficult to understand as had been his textbook on *Æsthetics*, with its involved literary style.

Meanwhile the farmers in the Farmers' Alliance were once more organising for battle with the "sinister interests." Henry Demarest Lloyd published in the *Atlantic Monthly* an immensely popular article against Standard Oil. This company had already undergone several changes in form to meet public outcries and was now being legally made into a trust. Lloyd described it as the "greatest, wisest, and meanest monopoly known to history" and declared that its strength was due in good part to another great monopoly, the railroad companies. The forces of capital, instead of being creatures of the state, had outgrown its control and become its masters. "Our strong men are engaged in a headlong fight for fortune, power, precedence, success. . . . They ride over the people like Juggernaut to gain their ends. The moralists have preached to them since the world began, and have failed. The common people, the nation, must take them in hand. . . . There is nobody richer than Vanderbilt except the body of citizens; no corporation more powerful than the transcontinental railroad except the corporate sovereign at Washington." The power of the people must be used for its industrial life as it was used for its political life "or the people will perish." [38]

Monona closed permanently at the end of the year. Andrew Veblen, who had saved a little money while teaching at Luther College, had decided to study mathematics at Johns Hopkins. He was spurred on by the hope of obtaining a position in some American institution like Carleton after studying at what was extensively advertised as the first real graduate school in the country with a distinguished and able staff and with the best of facilities for graduate study. Thorstein Veblen also was attracted to Hopkins by its publicity. Although he had scarcely any money, the risk was worth taking since he could do very little else. He accompanied his brother to the East, expecting to study philosophy.

CHAPTER III

THE Hopkins scene was not what he had been led to expect by the circulars of information, which he afterwards described as "circulars of misinformation." President Gilman was forced to manage with an income of $90,000 instead of the $200,000 originally contemplated. A part was set aside for a building fund, so that $60,000 was available for instruction. [1] At the opening of the university in 1875 the appearance of Huxley as orator had caused such an uproar that the trustees were very careful in selecting a proper professor of philosophy, and as yet they had appointed none. The eminent English philosopher and psychologist, James Ward, who had been trained as a non-conformist minister, was an unsuccessful applicant because he was not "orthodox enough," [2] and the chair was finally offered to Robert Flint, professor of divinity at Edinburgh and lecturer at the Princeton Theological Seminary, but was declined. [3] For the most part the faculty was very religious, and Gilman was anxious that the members actively identify themselves with some church.

Gilman was "intensely solicitous" of making close contacts between "town and gown." One of his policies was to invite distinguished men of other universities and of foreign countries to give "brief courses of lectures . . . open to the public as well as to students." The regular instructors also were persuaded to give series of brief public courses, and the recording in the official bulletins of the average attendance "according to the doorkeeper's count" was, as one professor put it, "another unique stimulus . . . to hold our audiences." Saturday classes were established for the Baltimore school teachers. Instructors spoke before other institutions, such as the Young Men's Christian Association and the State Normal School. Gilman was pleased by the instruction given on Sunday by "some of our young men" to "the inmates of the penitentiary and in various mission schools." [4]

At Baltimore Veblen found himself in the culture of the South, with its highly developed leisure class. For a while he was a boarder in a family which still clung to its aristocratic traditions. The raw youth was much amused by the family's maintenance of the grand old pre-war style, with servants and meals which cost far more than was received from the boarders. Northerners were still considered outside the pale. The prevalent religion was the familiar Presbyterianism which had developed the common-sense philosophy.

Veblen was lonely and homesick and in his casual conversation with classmates he talked much of his Norwegian settlement. Since he was in serious need of financial assistance almost from the day he arrived, he had no choice but to borrow money. He asked for a remission of tuition, $40.00 a term. He sought one of the ten scholarships paying $250.00.

He took a course in "Sources of Early European History" with Herbert Baxter Adams, a friend and classmate of Clark. Adams was an important influence in the study of history in the United States, but he was not primarily a scholar. He was a man of action, an organiser, interested, in addition to his teaching, in such things as civil-service reform, university extension, and library service. Since Veblen was interested primarily in philosophy, he saw little promise in doing much work with Adams. But he took all three of George S. Morris's courses: "Greek Philosophy," "Ethics," and "Kant's *Critique of Pure Reason*." The centenary of Kant's *Critique of Pure Reason* was being celebrated throughout the world of philosophy.

Heretofore Kant and Hegel had been classed together and denounced as "disintegrating idealists." Hegel was more frowned upon than Kant. In Hegel, according to President Noah Porter of Yale, "facts are scarcely considered at all, but only the metaphysical relations of the psychical powers and processes." [5] The Hegelian analysis seemed to deny that the common-sense truths were rooted in nature as matters of inductive psychology. For Kant, interpreted in terms of the romanticism of Coleridge, there had been not a little sympathy. In Germany Hegelianism was being discarded because of its reactionary tendencies favouring absolutism in politics and religion. Philosophers went back to Kant as the philosopher of enlightenment and interpreted him "in the sober tenor of British empiricism" and the Darwinian theory of evolution.[6] Spokesmen for Darwinism in Germany declared that Kant was the only philosopher worthy of study and that to "him alone" had been "vouchsafed a fore-glimpse of the dawn of true science." [7] This revival of interest in Kant was "something unexampled in the history of philosophy." [8]

But such men as Morris denounced Kant and turned towards Hegel. The protest of William James that Hegelianism was "too fundamentally rotten and charlatanish to last long" had no effect.[9] Hegelianism was beginning to be recognised as offering a better intellectual defence of the common-sense truths of "Puritan morals and religion" than could be found in the common-sense philosophy. Morris's lectures on Kant were a constant polemic against Kant's supposed maintenance of the view that all knowledge is sense knowledge and therefore faith and knowledge are not to be identified. "If all human knowledge were specifically and exclusively sensible," said Morris, "agnosticism would be the last word of philosophy." [10]

Despite his deep interest in philosophy Veblen "thought it best to give more attention to political economy." His teacher was Richard T. Ely, an assistant only a few years older than himself. Ely, an active Congregationalist, had studied under a student of Hamilton at Columbia College. He was trained in the common-sense philosophy, including Wayland's original economics textbook. A stay in Germany, however, where he came in contact with the more optimistic and imperialistic temper of German thought, had served to temper for him the sharpness of the common-sense philosophy. In his first year of teaching he offered one course, "The History of Political Economy," which dealt primarily with German writers. The lectures made Veblen doubt that Ely had read the works he was discussing, and in exploring the library he found a German encyclopædia that contained almost exactly the same material that Ely had been offering. Veblen felt that such lectures might be useful to students who could not easily read this encyclopædia or the work of the writers, but that for him they were unsatisfactory, for "they contained nothing of his own." Ely seems to have cared little for Veblen, believing him to be "a man of fair capacity and inclined to go his own way."

Veblen's disappointment with this course apparently made no difference, however, in his plans to use economics as the basis of his application for a scholarship. Papers on assigned topics were expected from the graduate students in the course, and these papers were often read in what amounted to a seminar in the social sciences, dignified by Adams with the name "The Historical and Political Science Association." Veblen prepared a paper on "J.S. Mill's Theory of the Taxation of Land." Ely firmly believed that rent is an unearned increment, a conviction which represented the English liberal position best presented by Mill. This did not mean that the landlords should be expropriated, but that the land should be purchased by the government. Veblen presented in his paper a summary of Mill's view, but added a comment of his own reflecting the results of land booms in the West. In speaking of the effect of an abolition of future unearned increment by taxation he said: "No immediate redistribution of wealth would take place, but, neglecting all probable undesirable secondary effects of the change on the people, an advantage would accrue from an increased compactness of population, making possible a saving of labour." [11]

In making application to the president for a scholarship Veblen informed him of the paper, "which I have the honour to say has met with the approval of Dr. Ely, and which it is intended shall be read at the next meeting of the Historical and Political Science Association." Apparently he intended to continue this kind of study, for he stated in the application that "at present I am planning and preparing for a paper on the Relation of Rent to the Advance of Population and shall probably have it completed about the end of the present semester."

The letter to the president reveals what the official records do not, that some time after the term began Veblen became interested in the lectures on "Elementary Logic" given by a man who was later to be recognised as a creative intellectual force. This was Charles Peirce, a temporary lecturer. Peirce had already published a series of papers on "The Logic of Science," emphasising that "the whole function of thought is to produce habits of action," that the "guiding principles" of inquiry are "habits of mind," that "thought is an *action*" leading in turn to further thought. He marked a radical departure from the "method of authority" of common sense. He described Mill's classic *Logic* as embodying the "philosophy of ordinary mankind," [12] but declared that most of the examples of scientific induction in the first edition of the *Logic* had since proved to be bad inductions.

Veblen failed to receive a scholarship, although at most there could have been no more than sixty-one candidates who applied. He had no hope of obtaining a foothold at Hopkins. He wanted to be free to pursue his studies as he liked and moreover he was anxious to be away from the supervision of his brother. Under these circumstances the old and "more sedate schools" seemed preferable. He left Hopkins before the term was over and entered Yale, to study philosophy under the president, the Reverend Noah Porter, an outstanding metaphysician and moral philosopher.

Veblen's problem of finding the necessary financial aid was not solved. With a number of other Yale graduate students, he obtained for a while, in return for an hour or two of teaching, what he considered exceptionally poor dinners at the Collegiate and Commercial Institute of New Haven, popularly known as "General Russell's Military Academy." But he lost this free board when some of the students discovered in physical combat that he was not as weak as he appeared. His family was able to help a little. Conditions were far from satisfactory for Thomas Veblen, but he obtained a loan from the bank on his signature and on that of his son Orson, who was in business. As security Thorstein Veblen's life was insured in favour of his father and brother. To various members of the family, however, it seemed that Veblen was merely lazy and irresponsible. Andrew Veblen, with funds running low, did not complete the requirements for a Ph.D. During his second year he accepted an offer to teach at Carleton for the last quarter. Veblen's money was never sufficient and he was

always in debt. Living as cheaply as possible made it necessary to overlook many niceties in dress, and his Norwegian country airs were no asset
in this centre of Yankee culture. His classmates described him as a "foreigner," "a Scandinavian or German from the Middle or North West."

"Yale College," said Porter, its president, "was founded avowedly as
a Christian college. All its . . . arrangements have been inspired and controlled by the definite purpose that the education imparted here should
be emphatically Christian." [13] To Veblen, however, the most impressive
part of its religious service was the scene that regularly followed the
exercises at chapel. At the close of the service the students remained standing while the president passed down the centre aisle. As he passed each
pew, the students in that pew turned towards him and bowed very low.

Since philosophy was still the handmaiden of theology, most of Veblen's classmates in philosophy were divinity students. In this atmosphere
the sardonic attitude he had fallen into at Carleton reasserted itself. He
was more of a sceptic in his twenties, remarked a fellow Norwegian of the
divinity school, "than most men are in their sixties." Veblen declared that
"no patriotic citizen can pass through New Haven without visiting the
Historical Museum on the Green. How can he claim to be up on the
history of his country if he fails to see Benedict Arnold's last pair of
drawers?" The divinity students received substantial financial aid for
their studies, but they seemed to be interested primarily in teaching positions. Veblen asked a group of them: "Do any of you intend to preach the
gospel?" He was asked how he had acquired such an excellent command
of German, and he replied that he had studied the language by looking
intently at the words until finally the meaning came to him. In spite of
all the efforts of his fellow students in and out of class his definite views
could not be determined. He told an associate that he was willing "to
accept God as a metaphysical necessity," but that he was undecided as to
the role of Christ in the scheme of things. Towards the fundamental
doctrine of atonement he took a "decidedly supercilious and cynical
attitude."

Veblen's air of intellectual pre-eminence and Olympian aloofness exasperated many of his associates. Even George Duncan, his friend and
later a professor of philosophy at Yale, said that, although Veblen was
a man of striking intellectual qualities, "he was not an attractive or polished man in character or carriage." A Negro friend, the Reverend
George W. Henderson, described Veblen more sympathetically as a
spectator viewing life from a detached position, "interested in it as an
enticing object of study but [one] for which he had no responsibility." He
had as yet "reached no definite conclusions of his own, but was feeling his
way."

As before, Veblen felt lonely and longed for his home, especially for his mother. He read Ibsen and spread the knowledge of him on the Yale campus. A recent arrival from Norway he greeted as a countryman, much to the surprise of the visitor since "Veblen was born in Wisconsin and I in Norway." Veblen felt drawn to the Norwegian and discussed with him the language, literature, and politics of the mother land.

During Veblen's two and one-half years' residence the Yale atmosphere was tense over the bitter and never-ceasing dispute between Veblen's two most important teachers, Porter and William Graham Sumner. Porter was "a type of the late flowering of the old New England stock," with its "fidelity to the highest known law, and trust in a divine guidance" and its "firm grip on the material world side by side with a searching inquiry into the unseen." He believed in supernatural sanctions and miracles but at the same time "took excellent care of his property . . . was thrifty . . . and commanded the respect of business men in their own field." [14] As a stern defender of the whole traditional culture he exemplified the current theological dominance, with its insistence on the primacy of the classical and moral philosophical training which "has prevailed in New England for two hundred years." [15] Sumner, although a graduate of Yale Divinity School, was opposed to the maintenance of this order of things.

A two-year controversy, concerning the right of Sumner to use Spencer's *Study of Sociology* in his college classes despite the protest of Porter, had just ended in victory for Porter. The book was assailed by Porter for its assumption of "evolution as an axiom" in science, and for its apparent assertion "that a theist . . . cannot accept sociology in any scientific sense of the term." "The offences of Spencer's book against good taste and decency, so far as either require a respect for the convictions which are held sacred by the great mass of Mr. Spencer's fellow countrymen, are almost unparalleled in modern controversial literature." [16]

But on Spencer's American visit in 1882, during which he visited Yale, the treatment accorded him by the leading figures in political, social, business, and intellectual life showed that the tide was turning towards Sumner's attitude. At a farewell dinner at Delmonico's in New York, which was made the occasion for a "fresh setting-forth of the Doctrine of Evolution in its relation to all the higher interests of humanity," a telegram of congratulation was read from President Barnard of Columbia, who in 1866 had written in his annual report to the trustees of "the recent and very plausible and insidious theory of Darwin." Professor O.C. Marsh of Yale, president of the National Academy of Science, responded to the toast: "*Evolution—once an Hypothesis, now the Established Doctrine of the Scientific World.*" Marsh declared that "What the law of gravitation is to astronomy, the law of evolution is now to natural science." It "is no longer a theory but a demonstrated truth, accepted by naturalists throughout the world." Sumner responded to a toast in honour of *"The Science of Sociology."* He credited Spencer with having given the social sciences "a powerful and correct method" and declared that he saw no limits "to the scope of the philosophy of evolution" and that it was destined to "embrace all the interests of man on this earth." Evolution offered a substitute for the worthless "traditional doctrines and explanations of human life." [17]

In March 1884, in an article in *The Princeton Review*, Sumner threw down the gauntlet to the upholders of the traditional curriculum. The existing discipline was a leisure-class discipline, a "caste" discipline. As such it was becoming increasingly useless and so unattractive to the youth of the nation that they no longer cared for a university education as did "the youth of former generations." It "presents the notion that what is useful is vulgar, that useless accomplishments define a closed rank of superior persons, and that entrance into that rank should be made difficult." It was perhaps a useful education when life was on a "military basis." The classics, which "exalt authority," "are the greatest barrier to new ideas and the chief bulwark of modern obscurantism." People trained in them "think that they prove something when they quote somebody who has once said it." The colleges should not ignore facts and doctrines "which are revolutionizing the world of knowledge." Physics, anthropology, archæology, and a host of other sciences offered the stimulus "necessary to draw out youthful energies and to awaken youthful enthusiasm." The recent development of biology and its affiliated sciences provided the key "to a new philosophy destined to supersede the rubbish of the schools." Sociology, although in its infancy, was sure to grow into a great science "as regards utility to the human race."

A month before Veblen obtained his degree in 1884 the faculty approved a committee report making elective a little more than half the junior year and four-fifths of the senior year. Grim old Porter at first refused his consent, but after a turbulent session of three hours he was forced to relent. The distinctively theological features of the university disappeared almost immediately.

Sumner's attitude towards theology did not, however, extend to an attack on the traditional economics associated with it. In his opinion the doctrine of evolution supported a belief in the prevailing competitive order of property as the natural order; in competition nature provided for the survival of the fittest. Evolution was based on property and property was still, as in the older theological tradition, "the condition of civilisation." [18] Thus Sumner and John Bates Clark were not essentially in disagreement. "Recognizing the competitive struggle as the imperfect agent of moral law," said Clark, "a man may participate in it without taint. The bad effects of the contest he does not need to suffer, and to the lower levels, where the golden calf worship is unhindered and blighting, he does not need to descend. . . . He may buy, sell, and get gain, as well as give thanks and worship, with his eyes uplifted to the hills whence cometh his help." [19] Sumner could say the same thing by substituting Spencer's evolutionism for Clark's belief in the unseen hand.

Sumner especially appreciated Spencer's "*laissez faire* attitude and distrust of socialistic tendencies." [20] In 1884 Sumner issued a completely dogmatic and uncompromising presentation of the belief in property in *What Social Classes Owe to One Another*. One reviewer, Lester Frank Ward, wrote that "the whole book is based on the fundamental error that the favours of this world are distributed entirely according to merit. Poverty is only a proof of indolence and vice. Wealth simply shows the industry and virtue of the possessor!" "The labouring class and 'the poor' in general . . . are regarded as sheer intruders and cumberers of the earth." [21]

Certain large industrialists, however, considered Sumner unsound because of his adherence to the formerly orthodox position that free trade is good for business and that protectionism is a violation of natural liberty. Although in general businessmen highly respected him, the protectionists among them carried their animosity to such lengths as to attempt to deprive him of his chair. Sumner believed that protectionism opened the road to socialism and a destruction of private property. In the classroom, in the press, and on the public platform he bitterly denounced the tariff of 1883. He declared that the protective tariff created a "vested interest" and constituted the greatest piece of "jobbery" ever perpetrated on the "forgotten man," who typified the lower middle class. It results "in delivering every man over to be plundered by his neighbour and in teaching him to believe it is a good thing for him and his country because he may take his turn at plundering the rest." [22]

Another controversial problem was raised by the statement in the Treasury report of 1883 that "according to present estimates all bonds payable at the pleasure of the government would be redeemed before June 30, 1887." In less than three years an annual surplus of $85,000,000 or more was expected unless taxes were radically reduced or the remainder of the national debt purchased at great disadvantage. A controversy arose over the question of disposing of the prospective surplus. One group held that it should be distributed among the states, declaring that this plan had been successfully followed in a similar situation in 1837. Sumner maintained, however, that surpluses were a curse and asserted that the surplus revenue of 1837 had not only been squandered by the states but had given rise to the panic of that year. The topic became so important that it was the first of a list of subjects open to all the students for the annual John A. Porter prize of $250 for the "best English essay." Those who chose the topic were to investigate "the history and theory of the distribution, the use made of the funds by the states, and deduce the inferences to be drawn as to the political and economic effects of such a proceeding." [23]

Veblen was in serious need of money to pay his debts. He entered the contest at the last moment and was forced to write his essay hurriedly, but he won the contest over such able men as Edward G. Bourne. The *Northfield News* reported his success and closed with a comment which was not without ironic effect: "The friends of Carleton can well feel delighted at this victory of one of her sons, and it speaks volumes for the college." Sumner thought so highly of Veblen's essay that he suggested that Veblen use it for a doctoral dissertation. But Veblen was still primarily interested in philosophy and, doing most of his work in that field, he was thrown into close contact with Porter, who was also editor-in-chief for the revised editions of Webster's dictionary. William James described Porter about this time as one "possessed of great decision and obstinacy," but he declared that "there is no sort of human being who does not immediately feel himself entirely at home in his company." [24] Porter thought highly of Veblen, not only for his command of German but also for his abilities as a metaphysician and student of morals. They so often took walks together to discuss philosophical questions that students referred to Veblen as "Porter's chum." In the classes the students noticed that Porter regarded Veblen as far above the others intellectually. Veblen alone, it seemed, could respond adequately to Porter's questions. They "dimly sensed that Veblen was able to get the meaning of them." In a class for the discussion of Kant's difficult *Critique of Pure Reason* Veblen and Henderson were the only two students to remain after a few sessions.

Veblen was intent on finding out "why we need not believe in God" and spent two years in the task, writing his dissertation on "Ethical Grounds of a Doctrine of Retribution." In this inquiry Veblen seems thoroughly to have examined Spencer and Kant.

Spencer's *Data of Ethics* was discussed by Veblen in Porter's class in Ethics. Spencer's ethics was considered to be naturalistic as distinct from theological, and in reference to his influence McCosh had said: "What are we to do with our reading youth entering on life who are told in scientific lectures and journals that the old sanctions of morality are all undermined?" [25] Spencer, to be sure, frankly advocated a greater reliance on self-interest than on revelation, but his system was not essentially different from the common-sense utilitarian ethics.

According to Spencer, conduct, no matter how it is viewed, is a necessary adjustment to the circumstances of nature, and man therefore evolves inevitably into the perfect type demanded by the perfect society of free contract. From the physical point of view conduct is a "moving equilibrium." From the biological point of view it is a "balance of functions. . . . The several functions in their kinds, amounts, combinations, are adjusted to the several activities which maintain and constitute complete life; and to be so adjusted is to have reached the goal towards which the evolution of conduct continually tends. Of necessity during the evolution of organic life, pleasures have become the concomitants, the normal amounts of functions, while pains have become the concomitants of excesses and defects of functions." From the psychological point of view "the normal working of the pleasures and pains become incentives and deterrents so adjusted in their strength to their needs that the moral conduct will be the natural conduct." The sense of "proprietary right" becomes clear, as there inevitably arises a "sufficient intellectual power to make inductions from these experiences, followed by a sufficient massing of individual inductions into a public and traditional induction impressed on each generation as it grows up." The fundamental moral intuitions were "originally the result of personal experience of utility," but are now habitual, as a result of the "hereditary experience" or "inherited association."

By some, even among the hedonists, the "hedonistic calculation" was felt to require qualification. Henry Sidgwick contended that the fundamental paradox of hedonism is that the impulse towards pleasure if too predominant defeats its own aim. The greatest pleasure is to be obtained by forgetting about pleasure as the end of action. But Spencer declared that this fundamental paradox is resolved if one recognises that the "pleasures of pursuit are much more those derived from the efficient use of means than those derived from the end itself." By necessary adaptation the pleasure attending on the use of means to achieve an end becomes itself an end. The use of the various means in due order constitutes an obligation. The means must be pursued for their own sake as proximate ends in order to achieve individual and thus social welfare.

For example, "the trader, if asked what is his main end, will say—making money. He readily grants that achievement of this end is desired . . . by him in furtherance of ends beyond it," such as the necessities and comforts of life for himself and his family. "But while admitting that money is but a means to these ends, he urges that the money-getting actions precede in order of time and obligation, the various actions and concomitant pleasures subserved by them; and he testifies to the fact that making money has become itself an end, and success in it a source of satisfaction, apart from these more distant ends." In further carrying out this moral necessity the trader occupies himself more and more with strictly pecuniary employments. "Leaving to subordinates the actual measuring out of goods and receiving of proceeds, he busies himself mainly with his general affairs—inquiries concerning markets, judgments of future prices, calculations, negotiations, correspondence; the anxiety from hour to hour being to do well each one of these things . . . conducive to the making of profits." In this way he is able to discharge his duty to himself, his family, and to others. Strict attention to the pursuit of profits is a moral obligation and contributes to the community welfare. Thus the social equilibrium, the necessary means to the achievement of the maximum pleasure, depends upon the observance of the law of justice, which is fulfilment of contract. This is the "ultimate principle of conduct," the universal basis of co-operation. Here then is conduct from the sociological point of view.

Under the guidance of the increasing personal force of free contract egoism leads to altruism. "As civilisation advances and status passes into contract, there comes daily experience of the relation between the advantages enjoyed and labour given: the industrial system maintaining, through supply and demand, a due adjustment of the one to the other. And this growth of voluntary co-operation—this exchange of services under agreement—has been necessarily accompanied by decrease of aggressions one upon another, and increase of sympathy, leading to exchange of services beyond agreement." All deductions from this principle of justice are of the nature of "absolute truth." State interference with contract is a shielding of the inferior and therefore retards the "reaching of a higher life."

Thus Spencer acknowledged a partial truth in the other ethical theories, particularly the theological and the intuitional. "If for the divine will supposed to be supernaturally revealed, we substitute the naturally revealed end towards which the Power manifested throughout Evolution works; then, since Evolution has been, and is still, working towards the highest life, it follows that conforming to those principles by which the highest life is achieved, is furthering that end." Porter, however, pointed out that the *Ethics* rested upon the argument of divinity against which Spencer was supposedly protesting. "The evolutionists draw more heavily than any school upon an assumed 'far-off divine event to which the whole creation moves.' " Spencer is not really a strict evolutionist for, "if there be such a goal" as Spencer foresees, "the conception of its nature and the belief in its truths cannot be the growth of the tendencies which it governs and controls, and out of which it is evolved. Neither the idea, nor the belief in it, can precede; both must come after the fact." [26]

Even as Veblen was analysing Spencer, theology was beginning to assimilate Spencer's evolutionism. Henry Drummond's *Natural Law in the Spiritual World*, backed by the Scottish aristocracy and published in 1883, had been accepted by Calvinistic Scotland, and the American colleges were extending invitations to Drummond. According to Drummond, "The 'one far-off divine event to which the whole creation moves' is the . . . heart secret of creation. . . . To Science, defining it as a working principle, this mighty process of amelioration is simply *Evolution*. To Christianity, discerning the end through the means, it is *Redemption*. These silent and patient processes, elaborating, eliminating, developing all from the first of time, conducting the evolution from millennium to millennium, with unaltering purpose and unfaltering power, are the early stages in the redemptive work—the unseen approach of that Kingdom whose strange mark is that it 'cometh without observation.' " Drummond made the views of the leading social philosophers, such as Walter Bagehot and Spencer, support this submission to the existing scheme of things. Bagehot's popular *Physics and Politics* was a portrayal of the supposedly progressive, natural disintegration of the "cake of custom" by which savage man is bound until the rational pecuniary animal of modern competitive life is achieved. Drummond asked: "What is the Physical Politic of Mr. Walter Bagehot but the extension of Natural Law to the Political World?" and "What is the Biological Sociology of Mr. Herbert Spencer but the application of Natural Law to the Social World?" Spencer's results "are far from sterile—the application of Biology to Political Economy is already revolutionising the science."

In his *Elements of Moral Science* Porter represented substantially the common-sense philosophy, with its utilitarian ethics and its apotheosis of the rights of property. Porter, Sumner, and Spencer were essentially of the same school, and the continuity of prevailing morals from Carleton to Yale was unbroken. But Veblen specialised in Kant and the post-Kantians.

Kant was of a different mould. His ethics was not hedonistic. As Porter explained it, Kant found "a faculty called the practical reason which presents to the will an authoritative judgment technically called the *categorical imperative*." This moral imperative recognises that man is an end in himself, not a means, but it is not therefore utilitarian, for utilitarianism is not moral. If action is impelled or motivated by any consideration of happiness, even by the satisfaction which is to be derived from right action, it is "thereby corrupted at the root, and ceases altogether to be morally good." [27] In other words, if the self-regarding or hedonistic motive be the guide to behaviour, then the behaviour is "pragmatic." The "categorical imperative," "the *commands* (*law*) of morality" are not to be confused with "the pragmatic sanctions or *rules* of skill, *counsels* of prudence." [28] Naturally Porter assailed the categorical imperative and upheld the pragmatic sanction under the name of the "hypothetical imperative." [29]

Kant, the follower of Rousseau, was inspired with awe by two things: "*the starry heavens above and the moral law within.*" In the language of a commentator, "The sublimity of the starry heavens and the imperative of the moral law are ever-present influences on the life of man; and they require for their apprehension no previous initiation through science and philosophy. The naked eye reveals the former; of the latter all men are immediately aware. In their universal appeal they are of the very substance of human existence. Philosophy may avail to counteract the hindrances which prevent them from exercising their native influence: it cannot be a substitute for the inspiration which they alone can yield." Kant, who was not emotionally religious, "apostrophises Duty in sublime words, as the mainspring of action, even for God!" All of Kant's work was motivated by this attempt to ground morality. "The origin of the Critical Philosophy is in Morality—responsibility for actions." [30]

Kant, like the common-sense philosophers, was started on his inquiry by an attempt to meet Hume's doubts as to the rationality of the causal principle, that is, the rationality of fundamental truths. But on the procedure of the Scottish philosophers Kant made the caustic comment "that a man shows his common sense by using it, not by appealing to it." [31] He attempted instead to investigate the first principles, or *a priori* truths, by reason alone. Kant's *a priori* principles are not primordial first truths but "relational functions . . . activities dynamically creative." They are "not subconscious ideas but non-conscious processes. They are not the submerged content of experience, but its conditioning grounds." Primarily "they are never legitimately applicable as such to the deciphering of ultimate reality. While the principles of common sense are the very guarantees of absolute truth, Kant's *a priori* forms are merely brute conditions of our experience." Kant was the first to state effectively "as the supreme principle in the development of all knowledge . . . the activity of the experient subject itself." Truth to Kant "is only in experience," and "all cognition of things merely from pure understanding or pure reason only is nothing but sheer illusion." Truth is grounded in activity, not in eternity. The "Ideas" of "Soul," "Freedom," "God" are "utterly incapable as well of positive as of negative proof and are therefore relegated to the sphere of practical philosophy." Knowledge and morals are not to be confounded.[32]

The common-sense philosophers were up in arms against Kant. McCosh, who gave some lectures at Yale during Veblen's residence, bitterly denounced this atheistic philosophy with its denial that "truth shines in its own light." To the followers of common sense, truth was "immutable and eternal" and they could have no tolerance for a philosophy which taught that the "constitution of the mind" might conceivably change and "with it the nature of knowledge itself." [33]

In *The Journal of Speculative Philosophy*, the leading philosophical periodical of the day, Veblen published an article on *The Critique of Judgment*, which as yet had not been translated. One of the outstanding Hegelians, Professor George Howison, considered Veblen's article a highly competent piece of work. Veblen held that *The Critique of Judgment* is an attempt to mediate between the outcome of the *Critique of Pure Reason*, "which is the notion of strict determinism, according to natural law, in the world," and the *Critique of Practical Reason*, "which is the notion of freedom in the person," "in order to free activity."

If an agent is to be capable of exercising a "causality on things," the "knowledge furnished by experience is not sufficient. Simple experience . . . cannot forecast the future. Experience can, at the best, give what is or what has been, but cannot say what is to be. It gives data only, and data never go into the future unaided and of their own accord. Data do not tell what the effect of action will be, except as we are able to judge the future by the help of the data given. Judgment must come in, if experience is to be of any use, and morality anything more than a dream. The power of judgment, or of reasoning, must mediate between theoretical knowledge and moral action, and the kind of judgment required is inductive reasoning." In this very solemn journal Veblen characteristically commented that "All this is simple enough. It is so simple and is so obvious that it is difficult to see it until it has been pointed out, and after it has been pointed out it seems to have been unnecessary to speak of it."

Kant, according to Veblen, considered this "power of inductive reasoning" indispensable for morality, but Veblen, showing the influence of Peirce, maintained that it "is no less indispensable in every other part of practical life. Today any attempt, in any science, which does not furnish us an induction, is counted good for nothing." No recourse need be made to the unseen hand. "A knowledge of the teleological end of a given thing, or the purpose of an action or event as considered from the standpoint of the economy of the universe, is not absolutely necessary in order to human life. In truth, a knowledge of ultimate particular ends and purposes is of no use whatever in the affairs of everyday life; and, therefore, the principle of teleology, as being the principle of conscious purpose in the world, is not indispensable in order to such knowledge of things as is required by the exigencies of life. The knowledge we need and use can be got, and got in sufficient completeness for all purposes of utility, without any appeal to, or aid from, the developed principle of finality."

The principle of inductive reasoning is a "principle of search," which as a "guiding principle" becomes the "requirement of adaptation or totality in our knowledge." But this principle does not "give us any new data" nor "tell us anything new about the data we have." It simply "guides us in guessing about the given data, and then leaves it to experience to credit or discredit our guesses." Under this working or regulative principle the "mind has no alternative but to reflect and reflect on the material given it, and make the most it can out of it in the way of a systematic whole; and the requirement of adaptation points out the direction which its search must take. One consequence of this is that the search is never ended, as from the nature of the case, the requirement can never be fulfilled. As soon as a result is obtained by the process of induction, that result becomes, for the purposes of the question in hand, a fact of empirical knowledge, and therefore acquires the character not of a completed whole, but of an isolated and disconnected datum. As fast as one step of induction is completed it becomes a means to another step, which must inevitably follow it." "Yet, singular as it might seem," Veblen said in conclusion, "hardly any part of our knowledge except that got by induction is of any immediate use for practical purposes. For by induction alone can we reduce things to system and connexion, and so bring particular things and events under definite laws of interaction; therefore by induction alone can we get such knowledge as will enable us to forecast the future . . . to tell what will take place under given circumstances and as the result of given actions," and such knowledge "is the only knowledge which can serve as a guide in practical life, whether moral or otherwise."

Both the doctrine of final causes and Spencer's evolutionism, with its insistence upon nature's tendency to evolve into the unmitigated system of free contract, were subjected to vigorous challenge by Darwinian Kantianism. Friedrich Lange, who began the revival of Kant with his classic *History of Materialism*, sharply assailed all those who, in spite of modern science, still clung to "anthropomorphic teleology." "It can now . . . be no longer doubted that nature proceeds in a way which has no similarity with human purposefulness; that her most essential means is such that, measured by the standard of human understanding, it can only be compared with the blindest chance. On this point we need wait for no future proof; the facts speak so plainly and in the most various provinces of nature so unanimously, that no view of things is henceforth admissible which contradicts these facts and their necessary meaning." He denounced the "rationalistic teleology" of political economy, with its insistence on harmony of interests. Based as it is on "dogmatic egoism," political economy has no room for moral motives unless it admits an inconsistency. It attempts "to show that the progress produced by the restless struggle of Egoism always to some extent improves the position of the most depressed strata of the population, and here is forgotten the importance of that comparison with others which plays so great a part among the rich." This emulation or desire to surpass others "is capable of increasing *ad infinitum*, without anything being gained for the well-being of anyone concerned that is not lost to the others. The commercial and industrial statistics of most countries show irrefutably that an enormous development of power and wealth is taking place, while the circumstances of the labouring class show no decided advance, and without the haste and greed of acquisition in the propertied classes being in the slightest degree moderated." Since these egoistic feelings have been "developed into a system of daily life," "they exert their influence even upon those who personally are not without noble impulses." It was a case of what another Darwinian Kantian, Hans Vaihinger, was calling the "Law of the Preponderance of the Means over the End." "It is a universal phenomenon of nature that means which serve a purpose often undergo a more complete development than is necessary for the attainment of their purpose." [34]

Veblen worked not only with Sumner and Porter, but also with the philosopher and psychologist, the Reverend George Trumbull Ladd. In order to combat materialism Ladd had become interested in the relationship between the nervous system and mental phenomena, and he engaged in experimental work in the laboratory. He was determined to protect the soul against the "experimental psychology" of the continent, which was substantially the profane associational psychology. Like other common-sense philosophers, Ladd maintained the supremacy of final causes. Science, say many investigators, has no need of final causes but deals "only with the facts and the working causes out of which spring the facts." Ladd held, however, that "thought and will combining and using efficient causes as means to secure results are everywhere manifested." [35] Veblen never expressed a high opinion of Ladd, but he spoke of him to Andrew Veblen in such a way that it impressed the latter as of importance that Veblen worked under him.

Veblen translated for Ladd a volume of the lectures of Ladd's teacher, Hermann Lotze, who belonged to the Kantian tradition and was considered the outstanding metaphysician of the latter half of the nineteenth century. This volume seems to have been the *Outlines of Metaphysics*. Lotze, who was both a doctor of philosophy and a doctor of medicine, maintained that psychology was a mechanical science of nature and that the uniqueness of organic life was not to be explained by appeal to a mystical vital force, as was done by the romantics and Spencer, but by a "demonstration of the definite and regular manner in which the universal forces of nature work in organisms." This demonstration of the mechanical interconnection of nature will lead to the postulate that ideal principles are the basis of the materialistic conception, that is, the "highest Idea" realizes itself in "mechanism" as the means or "way of behaviour." [36] Lest Lotze be construed as one of "the so-called scientific materialists" and a supporter of pantheism, Ladd informed his readers in the preface of the *Outlines of Metaphysics* that "the disciples of Lotze—should he make any among us—would become uncommonly at their ease concerning the ultimate result upon our fundamental faiths and aspirations, of materialistic science and destructive criticism."

Besides the papers he had written, Veblen had excellent letters of recommendation to help him in securing a position. Clark wrote: "I take great pleasure in certifying that Mr. T.B. Veblen was during his connexion with Carleton College, a student of remarkable diligence, ability, and success; and the work which he accomplished in studies taught by me led me to entertain the hope that he would become not merely a successful teacher, but an earnest and successful investigator, especially in Philosophy and Political Economy." President Porter wrote: "It is with great pleasure that I certify that Mr. Thorstein Veblen, B.A., Carleton College, 1880, Ph.D., Yale College, 1884, has been a student in the Graduate Department in this college for 2½ years and for the most of the time under my immediate instruction. He has prosecuted special studies in Political and Social Science, and in Speculative Philosophy, ethics, psychology, etc. I can give confident testimony to his faithfulness and the critical ability which he has evinced in all his studies. I have in all my experience had few pupils with whom I have had greater satisfaction or who have made more rapid or more satisfactory progress. He is also an excellent scholar in German and other languages. I can confidently recommend him as a very accomplished scholar and a very able man who ought not to fail to occupy a commanding position in some higher seminary of learning."

But even with this impressive array of evidence Veblen was not acceptable at any institution. Whatever prospects he had with Sumner in political science were dissipated by the appointment of Arthur Twining Hadley as a tutor in 1883. College teachers, especially those with philosophical inclinations, were still taken primarily from the ranks of the divinity students. Even Johns Hopkins chose in that year as its permanent professor of psychology and philosophy a holder of a divinity degree, G. Stanley Hall, who declared in his opening lecture that "the new psychology . . . is . . . Christian to its root and centre," and "the Bible is being slowly re-revealed as man's greatest textbook in psychology—dealing with him . . . in all the larger relations to nature and society—which has been so misappreciated simply because it is so deeply divine." [37] No faculty wanted a "Norskie," particularly one suspected of agnostic leanings. Andrew Veblen had been unable to receive a permanent appointment at his old college; Thorstein Veblen had even less of the necessary polish. The worldly wise Porter must have thought that Veblen's career was likely at best to be a stormy one, as he handed him a copy of *La Morale*, by the essentially common-sense philosopher Paul Janet, as a token of his esteem. Veblen went back a defeated man to the settlement from which he had twice departed to ponder further the problem of "responsibility for actions."

As Veblen returned, such radicals as William Godwin Moody were denouncing the great captains as "plutocratic highwaymen." Their seizure of the community's resources had resulted in a tremendous increase in industrial efficiency accomplishing the destruction instead of the welfare of the community. The academic economists were only the satellites of the captains of industry.[38] Professor Laurence Laughlin, on the other hand, told the workingmen that "no one can . . . gain wealth except by sacrifice, exertion, and skill," and every man "has a right to enjoy the products of his exertion to the exclusion of everyone else." Instead of engaging in strikes and boycotts, trade unions should use their reserves for diffusing a better industrial education among their members. He told the community in general that every member of Congress who did not demand the repeal of the Bland Silver Act "to save the business interests of the country ought to be defeated at the next election." In the light of the "almost constant struggle between ignorant legislation and our business prosperity, it becomes us all to know more of our present admirable banking methods." [39]

CHAPTER IV

ELLEN ROLFE said that the only change was that Veblen now spoke with a correct "a." But it was as a failure that he returned to a community where, according to a brother, "they had no use for the man who was satisfied to remain poor." Veblen claimed that he had come home to recover from the effects of a severe case of Eastern malaria which had swept the Atlantic coast in 1883. He attempted not only to convince everybody that he was a sick man, but also to persuade his family that they were all short-lived, tubercular, and physically run down. He was a nuisance to the hard-working children. His dieting necessitated special cooking, and he would take the driving horse and buggy just when they were needed on the farm. He would expound to the family the theory that they could not be successful businessmen because they were not dishonest enough. It was parasitic to buy and sell. Manufacturing and agriculture were "more honest and honourable." Profits were "something stolen or unearned." It did not occur to him, one brother declared, that "profits were largely wages for services rendered." They thought Veblen's theory was a boost for himself as belonging to a superior race of scholars "whose mentality made it unfit for such low dishonest occupations as business."

His brothers were sceptical of his ill health. No one could discover precisely what ailed him and some thought that the best solution would be to force him to shift for himself. "He was lucky enough," said a brother, "to come out of a race and family who made of family loyalty and solidarity a religion. I must admit that I got somewhat disgusted with his loafing. Thorstein was the only loafer in a highly respectable community and he had hard work spending his time. He read and loafed, and the next day, he loafed and read." But, outwardly, Veblen appeared at ease. He retained his sense of humour, and people grew in the habit of laughing in anticipation even before he had spoken a word.

Ellen Rolfe too had not found life easy. After graduation she had attempted high-school teaching with its heavy schedules, but after a few years she suffered a nervous breakdown and went to Colorado to recuperate. She and Veblen became engaged in 1886, but the marriage had to wait. Veblen had no job and his thoroughgoing scepticism at times frightened Ellen.

Veblen did try in his unaggressive manner to secure an income. He did hack writing, and for a while he seems to have written for Eastern newspapers and magazines. He wrote what his brother called "experimental articles," but apparently they remained in their experimental stage. He invented agricultural implements, but he was too late in patenting them. In the winter of 1885–1886 he visited Andrew Veblen at the University of Iowa, where there was a possibility of a position in philosophy, but eventually a Yale divinity student obtained it. It was not unnatural that to Ellen Rolfe he seemed to "lack initiative" and not to "know what he was for."

He read everything he could possibly obtain, including books from the libraries of Lutheran ministers, novels, poetry, hymnbooks, as well as learned treatises. As one pile of books disappeared, he promptly secured another. For days all that one could see of him was the top of his head at the garret window. For intellectual companionship he had his remarkably keen father. He told Ellen Rolfe upon his return from Yale that he had never met his father's intellectual equal. When Veblen was puzzled over some economic problem, he would go out and follow along by his father's plough to talk it over with him. When the day's work was done, Thomas Veblen would leisurely discuss abstruse topics with his son.

Often Veblen camped out in the woods for several days at a time and indulged his interest in botany. One of the few occasions on which he visited Carleton was due to his desire to show the instructor in botany his discovery of some giant puffballs. He became interested in the practical application of physics, but to Andrew Veblen his schemes seemed faulty or incomprehensible. According to John E. Veblen, he had rather impractical theories about running the farm, but "father would listen to him and be influenced to some extent."

Veblen took an active interest in politics. Norwegian political clannishness was still strong, and "fidelity to the Republican party" was "akin to religious duty" in the settlements. Any dissenter was looked upon as a "backslider from the true, established religion." [1] But in 1884 Veblen, as a strong free-trader, supported the Democratic ticket headed by Cleveland, cautioning, however, that Cleveland would bear watching on other issues. He persuaded his father and uncle to change their party allegiance and, controlling thereby three of the four votes cast in the precinct, carried it for Cleveland.

Within the settlements the clergy continued to fight among themselves and against any Norwegian who dared to challenge their control. They still admonished all good Lutherans that "St. Paul more than eighteen hundred years ago said that women ought to be subject to their husbands in all things." [2] They still fought every attempt by the Yankees to get Norwegian children into the public schools, insisting that "first of all, we have our duties to our God and to our souls . . . and then our duties to our race and to our native tongue." [3] A split occurred in the Veblen synod, and the dissenting faction took over St. Olaf school as a college to house its divinity school. Orson Veblen belonged to the rebellious group, but the other members of the family considered the whole matter a joke. During the controversy Veblen said to Ellen Rolfe's sister: "Why believe in God? All it causes is worry." Nevertheless in 1885 he was deeply moved when his favourite brother, Thomas, at the point of death, uttered the words: "I am happy with the Host." The problem of religion was always with him and, according to a sister, formed the central topic of discussion with his father. Even though Veblen thought he had found out "why we need not believe in God," this favourite child of an "electrically religious" mother seems never to have been completely satisfied with his solution.

The condition of the farmers seemed to be getting worse. The panic of 1884 had left its effects and the increasing efficiency of production and transportation helped to bring about an unprecedented decline in the price of wheat. In 1884 it was the lowest since 1869 and had fallen approximately forty percent since 1881. Even a committee of the Minneapolis Board of Trade declared that there was "general dissatisfaction and complaint throughout the great wheat belt . . . and in many of the newer portions, impoverishment, bankruptcy, and general distress." The Northwest Farmers' Alliance rose to prominence, and there began another phase of the agrarian crusade against what the farmers considered the extortionate and discriminatory practices of the banks, milling companies, elevators, and railroads. "How long," exclaimed a writer in *The Pioneer Press* in January 1886, "even with these cheap and wonderfully productive lands, can . . . any agricultural community pay such enormous tribute to corporate organisations in times like these without final exhaustion?"

The greatest "sinners" were still the railroad companies. Costs of almost everything had fallen considerably, but freight charges remained nearly the same as when wheat had brought half again as much. Governor Hubbard in his annual message to the legislature in 1885 stated that "from many points of the state one-half of the value of a bushel of wheat is taken for its transportation to Chicago, while from remote stations the freight and accompanying charges upon certain kinds and grades of grain almost amount to confiscation." One Alliance lecturer declared that "we the people" have given the railroad companies "thousands and thousands of acres of land" but that the companies were causing the ruin of the people. Hill said that he was willing to allow the state to set any rates provided it guaranteed a return of six percent on the actual cost, but the farmers asserted that this interest would be a return on "capital stock never invested at all." [4] A Swedish newspaper declared that "our people" escaped from one slavery "only to become the slaves of one or another railroad company." [5] Even at the St. Paul meeting in 1886 of the National Farmers Congress, composed of the more wealthy and conservative farmers, papers were read, asserting that the farmer was repeatedly duped in politics and demanding stringent railway regulation.

In September 1886 a joint state convention of the Farmers' Alliance and the Knights of Labor was held in St. Paul. Donnelly dictated the multifarious platform advocating measures in behalf of farmers and labourers. So strong was independent voting that for the first time since the Civil War the state sent a Democratic delegation to Congress, and men of supposedly Alliance principles controlled the state legislature. In 1887 the national meetings of both the Knights of Labor and the Alliance were held in Minneapolis. The Alliance made friendly exchanges with the Knights, and suggested that the government should own one or more transcontinental lines as well as control the railway companies.

A court suit was in progress against the great promoters of the Central Pacific, Southern Pacific, and numerous subsidiaries—Senator Stanford, Crocker, Hopkins, and Huntington. The suit was brought by the widow of their ablest assistant, General Coulton, on the ground that they had defrauded her of the general's gains in their promotions. The publication of the early correspondence of the promoters seemed to indicate corruption reaching the highest places of the nation in the course of manœuvres of competing promoters for great prizes.

The government appointed the Pacific Railroad Commission to find why the Union Pacific and Central Pacific were unable to pay the interest on government bonds issued to the promoters for the building of the roads. The manœuvres of the Union Pacific promoters had already been exposed in the spectacular Crédit Mobilier episode and in the subsequent activities of Jay Gould. Testimony regarding the Central Pacific was to the effect that practically no funds had been supplied by the promoters, that tremendous increases in capital structure and other profits through subsidiaries, contracting companies, and similar deals had gone to the promoters. The Southern Pacific was revealed as an imperial power in the West, making and breaking districts and businessmen, with an elaborate organisation for dealing with legislatures and other disturbing forces. The government, however, continued to pay the interest on the bonds. [6]

Senator Aldrich, who believed that social salvation lay in the aristocracy of wealth and who conceived society as an "economic hierarchy" directed by the few great men or captains, strongly opposed an interstate commerce act, which, according to his biographer, sought to lessen the tyranny of the railroads in the West. It was "sacrilege for the Western voters to question the right of the capitalistic East to heap high its hoard regardless of the cost to the country at large." [7]

The outstanding economists found no fault with the great managers. The work of these promoters, according to Simon Newcomb, "lay at the very basis of our civilisation." Newcomb declared through the press: "I think I have made it clear beyond a cavil that it was to your benefit and my benefit that Vanderbilt did not stop making money to become a steamboat hand, but that his grasping love for wealth prompted him to engage in managing steamboats and railways with such success that he accumulated more than a hundred millions." Since the railroad companies lost money, they could not have charged unreasonable rates; they could not have been tyrannical in the light of the "great fact that not one person out of a hundred who reads these papers was ever consciously injured by a railroad corporation or ever received anything but benefits from it." [8] Arthur Twining Hadley of Yale was in favour of controlling the railroad companies to the extent of preventing the ruinous competition between them which did not allow a return on the investment and which could continue for long periods in such large-scale enterprises.

The increasing prevalence of strikes was creating a problem for the followers of the received tradition. In Illinois over a thousand strikes occurred in 1886. The state militia were frequently called out. In Milwaukee they fired into a group of striking Polish workingmen; eight people were killed, and the strike leaders were given stiff jail sentences. The great strike on Jay Gould's Southwestern railroad system resulted in bloodshed, but in the eyes of Taussig of Harvard "the men were endeavouring to secure a share in management beyond that for which they were qualified. The slow and steady movement of society has evolved something like a military organisation. The rank and file are assigned their duties and their places by the captains of industry." [9] Newcomb held that any restriction of the great possessors of property must result in the disappearance of property and thus of civilisation. The workers were admonished that in joining unions they were giving up the "one natural right of humanity which the most heartless tyrant never dared to deny . . . that of every man to make an honest living in his own way, by any reputable pursuit he chooses to follow." The surrender of "individual liberty was not a whit better than an involuntary slavery." "Never was a tyrant, never was a public enemy, seldom was an invading army, engaged in greater cruelty" than that involved in a strike order. Labourers must realise that "our natural progress towards a healthy social state is retarded by the prevalence of false theories which permeate society and control legislation." [10] Any economist who did not have essentially this attitude on the labour question was not a good economist. The conservative Henry Carter Adams was dismissed from Cornell in 1886 because a report of an address on the "Labour Problem" gave to an influential trustee the impression that he was "sapping the foundations of our society." [11]

In far-off New York, George was making a stirring mayoralty campaign. The Catholic hierarchy took a hand and Archbishop Corrigan denounced the Single Tax and allied movements on the ground that they were directed against the right of property. Father McGlynn, a supporter of George, was excommunicated. George's political opponent, Abram S. Hewitt, declared that "the horrors of the French Revolution and the atrocities of the Commune offer conclusive proof of the dreadful consequences of doctrines which can only be enforced by revolution and bloodshed, even when reduced to practice by men of good intentions and blameless private life." [12]

In the stormy summer of 1886 came the Haymarket bombing in Chicago, killing a number of policemen who were attempting to disperse a peaceful labour meeting. Chicago and the nation were thrown into a panic of fear and hatred. Seven anarchists were sentenced to death for the offence and one to life imprisonment, although there was not a shred of evidence to prove their guilt. The *Commercial and Financial Chronicle* demanded that they receive the same treatment as had the policemen. "Their entire following will become convinced of the unsuitableness of America as a campaign-ground for Anarchists." [13] William Dean Howells, William Morris, and a host of liberals protested against what is today considered a judicial murder, but to little avail. The sentences of two of the seven were commuted to life imprisonment and one committed suicide. The only American of the condemned group, Albert R. Parsons, died pleading: "Oh, men of America, let the voice of the people be heard." [14] Around the scaffold crowds sang the "Marseillaise."

The younger group of instructors in the social sciences were organising national societies. In 1884 Herbert Baxter Adams, now an Associate Professor, promoted the organisation of the American Historical Association as a separate body from the American Social Science Association, despite the protest of the latter's president that scientific bodies ought not to be organised for narrow specialisation. Adams's colleague, Ely, formed the American Economic Association from the membership of the American Historical Association. J.B. Clark was made a vice-president.

Clark had just issued a volume of essays, *The Philosophy of Wealth*, which was an expression of Spencerian thought. Each member of the social organism "exists and labours, not for himself but for the whole, and is dependent on the whole for remuneration. The individual . . . produces something, puts it into the circulating system of the organism," and obtains from it what "his being and growth require; he produces for the market and buys from the market. Every producer is serving the world, and the world is serving every consumer." On the basis of this harmony of interests the traditional emulatory propensity is again set forth as the motive for industrial and social progress, the "basis of economic law." The "desire for personal esteem" is a "universal and insatiable" want, for "all men value their standing in the community." It is a "mainspring for the energetic action necessary for the accumulation of wealth"; it "sets for each class a standard of living, and prompts them . . . to maintain it." It tends powerfully to better the condition of the poor, particularly as an important Malthusian influence in checking the number of labourers and thus preventing their increased degradation; "it is a chief incentive to the prodigal expenditures of the very wealthy" and "impels to the accumulation" necessary for large expenditures; "it creates a limitless market" for decorative articles and thus helps to maintain a "stable value for the precious metals, which are the basis of currency"; it "is the basis of fashion" and thus dominates the production of goods into which an "æsthetic element enters"; it "elevates the general conduct of society towards the standard set by its best members. . . . Mercantile honour has its roots in genuine morality; but its visible effects are multiplied by the love of personal esteem." This desire co-operates with virtue where virtue "exists in full measure. The benevolence which founds colleges and hospitals is called out, in part, by their monument-making character. There is much in the name of a public institution." Yet this philanthropy "is not more assisted by this worthy love of esteem than is the virtue which guards men from contamination during the process of acquiring fortunes." The "love of esteem, that universal and not unworthy vanity," creates a "highly expansive market for whatever acts as a badge of social caste" and classes are founded on "differences of social function, and accompanied by real differences in the individual." In an article on "Christianity and Modern Economics" Clark explained that this underlying harmonious arrangement is obscured by the fact that "the things . . . seen are strikes, lockouts, and class antagonism; those . . . not seen are new principles of business life, and the moderating of the cruder forms of self-seeking. The surface phenomena are misleading, and seem to the superficial view, to mean rather the unchaining of demons than the ushering in of God's kingdom in the industrial world."

Ely, secretary of the association, was incensed when a reviewer in *Science* of his *Labor Movement in America*, using the initials N.M.B. (Nicholas Murray Butler), implied that it favoured the "abolition of private property; in other words, the socialistic programme." "While I would not reproach N.M.B. with malevolence," said Ely, "I do bring against him the charge of culpable negligence. . . . N.M.B. is not the only one who exhibits gross carelessness in reviews." "The truth is, I point out many causes for the evils of present society, as intemperance, imperfect ethical development of man . . . unchastity, ignorance of the simplest laws of political economy, extravagance, and in fact 'the wickedness of human nature.' " [15]

The textbook of the new association's first president, General Francis A. Walker, President of the Massachusetts Institute of Technology, succeeded that of Wayland as the most popular in the country. It presented clearly the theory that the captain of industry, as distinct from the capitalist, is the great engine of industrial progress; his income, termed profits, is in the nature of rent paid for his efficiency as master of the industrial process. Labour obtains by "purely natural laws" whatever its efficiency and productivity deserve, and consequently the activities of labour organisations are denounced. By virtue of the requirements of large-scale production, industry tends not towards democracy, but towards the mastership of the captain of industry. But "the American well knows that there is neither hardship nor indignity in working for another man, in his shop, at his task, with his tools, on his terms. . . . He knows that for himself and his children the way is open clear up to the top." Henry George and his single tax are disposed of with the announcement, "I will not insult my readers by discussing a project so steeped in infamy." Usury laws, as well as proposals such as those of the single-taxers, are classified as "invidious treatment of the landlord and capitalist." Designed to confiscate the dues of these groups for the benefit of other classes, their result is a restriction of production. Decencies, those items prescribed by public opinion and composing the standard of living, are the most effective motive for producing wealth or for checking an increase of population beyond the point of the highest per capita production. Walker admitted, however, that "We need a new Adam Smith, or another Hume, to write the economics of consumption in which would be found the real Dynamics of Wealth; to trace to their effects upon production the forces which are set in motion by the uses made of wealth; to show how certain forms of consumption clear the mind, strengthen the hand and elevate the aims of the individual economic agent, while promoting that social order and mutual confidence which are favourable conditions for the complete development and harmonious action of the industrial system; how other forms of consumption debase and debauch man as an economic agent, and introduce disorder and waste into the complicated mechanism of the productive agencies. Here is the opportunity for some great moral philosopher, strictly confining himself to the study of the economic effects of these causes, denying himself all regard to purely ethical, political, or theological considerations, to write what shall be the most important chapter of political economy, now, alas, almost a blank."

Those who refused to join the association—including Laughlin, Sumner, Taussig, Hadley—were known as the "Old School," while the association members called themselves the "New School." Laughlin, like many of the older men, refused to join the association because he thought it socialistically inclined. He declared that principles of economics are "expressions of Christian truth," that social and economic disturbances are due to the foreigners coming from European revolutionary resorts. "Socialistic teaching strikes at the root of individuality and independent character, and lowers the self-respect of men who ought to be taught self-reliance." [16] Walker, too, in his first presidential address, blamed the serious disturbances in the economic system on the "foreign elements." Some of the leading spirits of the association, such as E.J. James, favoured a protective tariff and the restoration of the silver standard as a tonic for depressed business. Laughlin disagreed and asserted that the demonetisation of silver was not responsible for the fall of prices, that prices are determined more by credit, which had made business a refined system of barter, and that the restoration of the silver standard would threaten all business prosperity. Such action would be tampering with a complicated mechanism.

Sumner described society "as an organism . . . as the domain of activities so great that they should appal anyone who dares to interfere with them; of instincts so delicate and self-preservative that it should be only infinite delight to the wisest man to see them come into play, and his sufficient glory to give them a little intelligent assistance." Thus the proper way to deal with the great problem of distribution "is to leave it to free contract under the play of natural laws." [17]

The New School debated with the Old School, but with the New School claiming such orthodox English economists as Alfred Marshall and Stanley Jevons the differences between the two camps were not clear. Ely claimed that the activity of the New School was of "international importance" but included the work of Laughlin and Hadley as within the school. Taussig wrote a letter to *Science* in 1886 complaining that "there is a tendency in the new school to claim for itself perhaps an undue share of credit for the advances in economic thought and economic teaching which have taken place in the last ten or fifteen years." [18]

The most radical thinker recognised in the social sciences, Lester Frank Ward, did not differ substantially from Spencer and the New School. His most important work, *The Dynamic Sociology or Applied Social Science as Based upon Statical Sociology and the Less Complex Sciences*, was devoted to the "philosophy of human progress," or "meliorism." The slowness of progress has been due to the blind working of evolution. What is needed is a diffusion of "a knowledge of the materials and forces of nature," classified and systematised in a hierarchical order of sciences with sociology at the head. If the masses receive this education, "all things else will be added."

His first and fundamental principle is that the "motive of all action is feeling," the satisfaction of desire, the leading characteristics of which are pleasure and pain. The satisfaction of desire results in the performance of those functions demanded by nature's aim—the maintenance and propagation of the race. Between the feelings of the individual and the function of nature, which in principle are antithetical, a "pre-established harmony" results, on pain of race extinction in the course of evolution. Action is merely a connecting link between feeling and function, the consequence of the former, the condition of the latter. Desire therefore is the great agent of civilisation, and fundamentally can lead to no perversion of human interests. Thus the "fundamental law of human nature, and therefore of political economy, is that all men will, under all circumstances, seek their greatest gain."

"The love of money is really the root of nearly all good in civilisation," but its development has been attended with some serious abuses, since "the sole object of human effort was *to acquire*," to achieve success. "The grand rivalry was for the object, not the method. The force of this may be increased, by the antithesis between *getting* and *producing*." But this urge towards acquisition, aided by the "principle of deception," shows superior intellect in circumventing nature and obtaining the means of existence. "The law of force . . . is an essential part of the law of acquisition" and "its method may be denominated *natural justice*." It is the law of "social mechanics": the weaker must yield to the stronger.

Production is a "mode of acquisition," but Ward drew a distinction between production, as such, and the "mere incidents to production," which are business or distributive pursuits. Such operations arouse "no great passion but that of avarice." The mental qualities required in mercantile operations "are of the most ordinary and inferior kind" requiring "no such merit, no such useful quality" as in "the production of the objects sold." It is unusual for a highly skilled artisan to accumulate a competency by attending strictly to his work, but "mere dealers" in his products become millionaires through "shrewd management." At the same time the poor mechanic is taught to look up to the wealthy merchant and banker as superior beings, with the result that production is reduced both in quality and quantity. War is "simply robbery on so large a scale that in the crude conceptions of men it arouses the sentiment of honour," and priestcraft is one of the most successful modes of acquisition and one of the greatest drains upon production. Women are assumed to be the inferiors of men through the "prevalent incapacity to see the plainest facts . . . in any but a conventional light." The inequalities are due not to nature but to the "barbarous conventional code" best expressed in marriage and women's dress, "which is the disgrace of civilisation." But the degradation is fundamentally due to the "rational faculty in man," to his "superior mental power." The real check upon parasitic distributive activities and the subjection of women is education in the laws of social mechanics which by equalising intelligence prevents the illegitimate outcome of superior cunning and force.

Veblen and Ellen Rolfe were married in 1888 on the farm of Ellen's father at Stacyville, Iowa. The Veblen family were not enthusiastic about the match, but they hoped Ellen's money would make it possible for him to continue his scholarly career. Thomas Veblen said: "This is the queerest thing I have ever seen. Two sick people marry and expect some good to come out of it." Her father said, upon hearing of the plans for marriage: "I fear any man who is not a Christian." The clerical President Strong of Carleton felt that, through Veblen, Ellen Rolfe had become an agnostic. Carleton schoolmates and the faculty were dumbfounded. They could not understand why a girl as brilliant as Ellen Rolfe would throw herself away on such a man as Thorstein Veblen. To many the marriage seemed the end of both careers. "Nellie and Thorstein are going to Stacyville to dig potatoes."

The marriage was not altogether an outgrowth of the Carleton romance. Ellen wanted attentions which she thought to find in marriage, and to Veblen it offered a solution for his financial problems. Charles Rolfe had already made provision for his daughters, and it was planned to make Veblen an economist for the Santa Fe, of which William Barstow Strong was president.

Shortly after the marriage, however, the company was involved in financial difficulties. The combination of increased dividends and fixed charges and the dead weight of new track, needless save for the purposes of competition, proved fatal. Strong resigned in September 1889, and the road was taken over by a committee of bankers, but *The Railway Age* praised Strong for not having taken advantage of his opportunity to speculate in the company's securities. His removal had considerable effect upon Charles Rolfe and upon the Veblens.

Life was not too dark, however, for Veblen and his wife. They delighted in rural life, idling or working according to their mood. In remembrance of that time Ellen has said: "We had a cow, a horse and a buggy. . . . There was a river and a boat and the still unspoiled woods where we botanised and held picnics winter and summer." Veblen had ample time to exercise his mechanical aptitude, although he owned little equipment. People preferred to lend him instruments promptly rather than argue with this man of extraordinarily slow speech. He had as a companion his father-in-law's brother, Benjamin Franklin Rolfe, a doctor, participant in the California Gold Rush of '49, writer of no mean ability, mellow philosopher, and keen observer of mechanical processes.

Although Veblen described Stacyville as "rotten," it provided subjects to occupy him and an audience to applaud him. He impressed his listeners at the village centres. Deliberate in his manner and apparently disinclined to put himself forward, he seemed, according to a local teacher, to be telling only a small part of a vast store of knowledge. He always succeeded in routing the leading intellectual light of the community, the village storekeeper, who was "continually attempting to impress people with a supposedly vast and unlimited knowledge, religious, political, and historical." When the local debating teams wanted information on such topics as "The Single Tax Theory" and the "Proper Relation of Labour and Capital," they went to Veblen. He gravely informed their representatives "that he was glad to know that they had taken these questions in charge because the human race had waited long enough for their solution." Ellen Rolfe stood by him staunchly. Her great service to her husband was to give him "the inestimable atmosphere of faith and love, refinement of feeling, assurance of his capacity to do, patience and silence while he went about doing it; making him feel a man, in other words." She gave him direction in this period of indecision and floundering.

Veblen and Ellen returned to the study of Greek and Latin, apparently with an idea of Veblen becoming a philologist, but his Greek was not sufficient. His friend, Rasmus Anderson, brought out a revised translation of Snorri's *Heimskringla;* Veblen, in order to justify his existence to the family and neighbours, undertook to translate the Laxdæla Saga from the Icelandic, though to him such things were what men do "when they grow old." People were impressed, however, when Veblen's wife told them that he was the only one capable of this type of work. There were good reasons for undertaking the task of translation. The Saga was an ethnological document, a competent "record of late-Pagan and early-Christian manners, customs, convictions and ideals among the Germanic peoples at large, but more particularly touching the Scandinavian and the English-speaking peoples at the point of their induction into their feudal and ecclesiastical status in early-Christian times." There would also be commercial advantages for the translation. Morris's poem, "The Lovers of Gudrun," is an adaptation from it, and Morris considered the saga "the grandest tale . . . ever told." It was "the most romantic of all the sagas." [19] Veblen's translation, however, remained unpublished until 1925. No publisher was willing to print it without a guarantee, which Veblen was unable to give even had such a condition been acceptable.

The Veblens read together Edward Bellamy's sensational socialist Utopia, *Looking Backward*. "I believe that this was the turning-point in our lives," Ellen wrote, "because it so affected me." She thought her emphasis on this aspect of her husband's interests may have helped to turn the balance at that "critical period before his life work began."

Unlike most Utopians and reformers, Bellamy believed not in fighting monopolies or the machine process, but in making them the means of achieving the socialist state. In the days of petty trade and handicraft the competitive system may have worked passably well. No distinct cleavage existed between employers and employees since "a little capital or a new idea was enough to start a man in business for himself." Workingmen were constantly becoming employers. But the innumerable small enterprises had surrendered the field to aggregations of capital. "They belonged to a day of small things and were totally incompetent to the demands of an age of steam and telegraphs and the gigantic scale of its enterprises." The "restoration of the old system . . . if it were possible, might indeed bring back a greater equality of conditions, with more dignity and freedom," but to restore the ideal order of small business would necessitate "returning to the day of stage coaches." Although the regime of the great trusts was oppressive, "even its victims, while they cursed it," admitted that because of its efficiency "the wealth of the world had increased at a rate before undreamed of." Early in the twentieth century, according to this Utopian history, "the evolution was completed by the final consolidation of the entire capital of the nation."

It was beyond the comprehension of the inhabitants of Utopia why Bellamy's contemporaries "came to entrust the business of providing for the community to a class whose interest it was to starve it. . . . The wonder with us is, not that the world did not get rich under such a system, but that it did not perish outright from want." The wastes of the "profits system" were enormous. Mistaken undertakings resulted in the failure of four out of five enterprises. "The field of industry was a battlefield" on which "mercy or quarter" was unknown. To rise by the destruction of competitors "was an achievement which never failed to command popular admiration." Each businessman worked "solely for his own maintenance at the expense of the community. . . . If . . . he at the same time increased the aggregate wealth that was merely incidental. It was just as feasible and as common to increase one's private hoard by practices injurious to the general welfare." He would combine with those competitors he could not kill off to make "warfare upon the public . . . by cornering the market. The day dream of the nineteenth-century producer was to gain absolute control of the supply of some necessity of life, so that he might keep the public at the verge of starvation and always command famine prices. . . . This . . . is what was called a system of production. . . . It [seems] a great deal more like a system of preventing production."

At all times there was idle labour and capital, and the Utopian asked: "Could there conceivably be a more conclusive demonstration of the imbecility of the system of private enterprise as a method for enriching a nation than the fact, that in an age of such general poverty and want of everything, capitalists had to throttle one another . . . to invest their capital, and workmen rioted and burned because they could find no work to do?" In the very nature of the system depression was chronic. There were "two years of bad times to one of good." But the followers of the received economics "after endless discussions" appeared to have reached the conclusion that there was no more possibility of preventing or controlling these crises than "if they had been drouths or hurricanes. It only remained to endure them as necessary evils." Instead of maintaining that labour should receive what it produced, Bellamy put forth an argument not usually made by reformers, that every person ought to obtain the same share. A man who can produce twice as much as another with the same effort "instead of being rewarded for doing so, ought to be punished if he does not."

In contrast to the existing system of business enterprise, Bellamy pictured the Utopia of nationalised industry as "the triumph of common sense." No leisure class of property existed, and consequently no competitive emulation, no subjection of women, and no necessity of fashions. There were no deceptions or unnecessary duplications arising in the sale of goods, no separation of pecuniary symbols from the underlying industrial realities, no chronic depression with idle capital and labour. All lived in comparative luxury. No change in human nature was required. "The conditions of life have changed and with them the motives of human action." Men were given honours for the efficient performance of work instead of greater incomes for competitive expenditures. These results were made possible by integrated organisation. "The effectiveness of the working force of a nation, under the myriad-headed leadership of private capital, even if the leaders were not mutual enemies, as compared with that which it attains under the single head, may be likened to the military efficiency of a mob, or a horde of barbarians with a thousand petty chiefs, as compared with that of a disciplined army under one general." With the "perfect interworking" of "every wheel and every hand" all the "processes interlock" so that the different industries could not get "out of step with one another and out of relation with the demand."

Looking Backward helped to revive socialism after the blow it had received from the Haymarket episode. It was the book of the hour, and in a short time a million copies were sold. It may have been a tenth-rate book from the standpoint of consistency of argument, but it caught the prevailing discontent. The newspaper of the Farmers' Alliance offered a copy of *Looking Backward* and a subscription to the paper for $1.25, and the book's teachings were spread far and wide among the farmers through the circulating libraries of the Alliance locals. Men of letters such as Howells organized Bellamy clubs, and a political party, the Nationalist Party, was established to spread Bellamy's doctrines. A labour press association was organised and a magazine published by Bellamy's followers.

Other Utopias began to appear in the wake of *Looking Backward's* popularity, notably Ignatius Donnelly's *Cæsar's Column*, and *News from Nowhere*, by William Morris, the leader of English socialism. These, however, blamed a good part of the world's ills on the machine and offered a handicraft society as the solution. "The refined rusticity of *News from Nowhere*," wrote the official biographer of Morris, "is in studied contrast to the apotheosis of machinery and the glorification of the life of large towns in *Looking Backward*." Morris believed that "individual men cannot shuffle off the business of life on the shoulders of an abstraction called the state, but must deal with it in conscious association with each other." But he felt that the success of Bellamy's book was a "straw to show which way the wind blows." Morris attempted, in fact, to supply an element that Bellamy badly needed. Bellamy had considerable difficulty in discerning "some incentive to labour to replace the fear of starvation which is, at present, our only one." Morris declared that "it cannot be too often repeated that the true incentive to useful and happy labour is, and must be, pleasure in the work itself." [20]

Bellamy's views found scant sympathy from the spokesmen of received economics. Walker delivered before the Providence Economics Club a bitter speech on "Mr. Bellamy and the New Nationalist Party," which was published in the *Atlantic Monthly*. "No epithet short of 'wolfish' will fully satisfy [Bellamy] in application to that state of society in which all of us live, and which most of us cordially support, though always in the hope of steady improvement and progressive amelioration." Bellamy might put the demand for equal distribution "on high ethical grounds" but it "involves the grossest violation to common honesty, as every plain man understands it. . . . One of the dangers of transcendental reasoning about rights and morals [is] that the finest of sentiments are often found in close proximity to the baldest of rascality." Without unequal distribution of wealth "retrogression and relapse" must result. "It is only by the distinction of some that the general character of the mass is to be raised." Walker considered a man "very shallow in his observation of the facts of life, and utterly lacking in the biological sense, who fails to discern in competition the force to which it is mainly due that mankind have risen from stage to stage, in intellectual, moral, and physical power." The ills of society obviously were in no way to be attributed to the money economy, to the businessman's control. "The fact is, that many soft-hearted persons are careless to the point of absolute dishonesty in charging upon the existing social organisation things which are the proper effects of the constitution of nature on the one hand, or of human wilfulness on the other." Injuries might be an "unavoidable incident" of technological improvement. The system of free contract was the ideal order because no man was under pressure to accept the terms.

Bellamy's answer to an attack by Émile de Laveleye carried the argument to a questioning of the natural right of property in any form. "All that man produces today more than did his cave-dwelling ancestor, he produces by virtue of the accumulated achievements, inventions, and improvements of the intervening generations, together with the social and industrial machinery which is their legacy. . . . Nine hundred and ninety-nine parts out of a thousand of every man's produce are the result of his social inheritance and environment. The remaining part would probably be a liberal estimate of what by 'sacred justice' could be allotted him as 'his product, his entire product, and nothing but his product.' . . . The human heritage must, therefore, be construed, and can only be construed as an estate in common, essentially indivisible, to which all human beings are equal heirs. Hitherto the community and equality of rights have been disregarded, the heirs being left to scramble and fight for what they could individually get and keep." [21]

The national scene was growing no less stormy. In Minnesota, Donnelly, as state lecturer, turned his efforts to building up the Farmers' Alliance and was nominated for governor on the Union Labor ticket. At the first constitutional convention in the Dakotas the Alliance men protested against the proposed constitution drawn up by Villard, president of the Northern Pacific, and it was rejected as a "piece of unwarranted outside intermeddling." [22] Charges were made that Kansas was controlled by the Santa Fe, Nebraska by the Union Pacific and Burlington, and Minnesota by the Great Northern.

Speaking before the Chicago Nationalists in 1889, Henry Demarest Lloyd declared: "I can hear the coming notes of a glorious music. The song that was sung for the slave is being taken up for the workingman. We are coming, Father Abraham, nine hundred thousand strong." Through the press, Lloyd broadcasted to the nation "the Strike of Millionaires against Miners" in the coal struggle at Spring Valley, Illinois. He related how "the gentlemen of many millions, sitting under brilliantly illuminated Christmas trees in joyous mansions in Chicago, Erie, St. Paul, New York, by a click of the telegraph, made a present of midwinter disemployment to one-third of 'their' town," and threatened to keep the mines closed if necessary "until the grass grew in the streets." It was a conspiracy to "buy brothers below cost." The increasing practice of using Pinkertons as strikebreakers was bitterly attacked by liberals.[23] "Why is it," exclaimed Palmer, in his campaign for governor of Illinois, "that the state has become an object of such contempt that standing armies are raised in its midst . . . that private men may organise soldiers in the State, hirelings to go with their Winchesters and overawe the people?" [24]

Then in 1890 came what has been called "the most thrilling event ever known in the West." Alliance men deserted the old parties by the thousands. In Minnesota they elected Donnelly and enough other members of the legislature to hold the balance of power. The success of the farmers in Kansas caused a New York editor to say: "We do not want any more states until we can civilise Kansas." [25] Mary Ellen Lease is reputed to have told the farmers that they should "raise less corn and more *Hell*." "The people are at bay, let the bloodhounds of money . . . beware." [26]

Walker, in his presidential address before the American Economic Association in 1890, was disturbed over the fact that "our economists, as a body, should be able to do little in stemming the tide of socialism which has set in so strongly of late." He recalled to his listeners that "our first duty is to see to it that this political and industrial experiment [the competitive order] does not fail." Once more he bitterly denounced the subversive views and influence of Bellamy and the Nationalist Party, and Henry George and the single-taxers. "The bounds of tradition, the barriers of authority have, for the time at least, been swept away. Everything once deemed settled in economic theory is audaciously challenged; the most venerable and well approved of our institutions are rudely assailed; ideas to which, but a few years ago, assent was given so general as to be practically unanimous, are now denounced and scoffed at upon public platforms and in the drawing-rooms of fashion. The ownership of land, individual enterprise in business, even the system of private property are alike threatened." Nevertheless, Walker maintained: "I have little doubt that in due time, when these angry floods subside, the green land will emerge fairer and richer for the inundation, but not greatly altered in aspect or in shape."

Veblen was a keen observer of the changing scene. "To live with him," said his wife, "was to have one of the best instructors of the time." He was reading at this time a curious assortment of books in economics— David Ames Wells, Harriet Martineau, John Stuart Mill, Ferdinand Lassalle, Cliffe Leslie, Spencer.

Wells's *Recent Economic Changes* described "the existence of a most curious and, in many respects unprecedented disturbance and depression of trade, commerce, and industry, which, first manifesting itself in a marked degree in 1873, has prevailed with fluctuations of intensity up to the present time (1889)." Wells, like Hadley, was disturbed by the fact that the nature of large-scale enterprise in competitive society was making it possible for enterprises to continue even when prices were not normal—when they were not sufficient to cover cost of production and a fair profit. "Examples are familiar of joint stock companies that have made no profit and paid no dividends for years, and yet continue active operations." Wells then made the statement which Laughlin considered as the one blemish on Wells's scientific record: "Under such circumstances *industrial over-production*—manifesting itself in excessive competition to effect sales, and a reduction of prices below the cost of production—may become chronic." Wells agreed with Bellamy that the only possible solution was combination. But Wells, who had edited a volume of Frédéric Bastiat's essays and had received the praise of Newcomb, had no doubt about the beneficence of the system of free contract. Although there had been disagreeable accompaniments to the vast industrial changes, he felt that on the whole considerable progress had taken place. In the long run the disturbing features would disappear in accordance with the principles of received economics. "The phenomena of the over-production, or unremunerative supply at current market prices, of certain staple commodities, although for the time being often a matter of diffi-culty and the occasion of serious industrial and commercial disturbances, are also certain, in each specific instance, to sooner or later disappear in virtue of the influence of what may be regarded as economic axioms."

In Harriet Martineau's *Illustrations of Political Economy,* written in the thirties, the orthodox principles were illustrated by the use of ro-mantic tales. "Even the apostles of orthodox political economy, like John Stuart Mill, shivered as they watched Harriet translating each article of the Ricardian creed into terms of human experience with a fidelity that they found embarrassing." Mill was "obliged to agree that the Tales carried the doctrine [of *laissez-faire*] to ridiculous lengths. [27] Sumner declared, however, that his conceptions of economics were all formed by these *Illustrations,* "which I read in my boyhood." [28]

Mill gave the economic axioms their usual expression. "Every re-striction [of competition] is an evil, and every extension of it . . . is always an ultimate good." Political economy deals with man "solely as a being who desires to possess wealth," predicts only the phenomena of the social state resulting from the pursuit of wealth, and "makes entire ab-straction of every other human passion or motive" except those two "per-petually antagonising principles to the desire of wealth; namely, aversion to labour, and desire of the present enjoyment of costly indulgences." [29]

Ferdinand Lassalle, when tried for treason because a speech of his was held to instil the non-propertied with hatred and contempt for the propertied, demanded acquittal on the ground that the Prussian Consti-tution declared that science and all its works are free. In this speech, which was published as "Science and the Workingmen," he declared that he was merely attempting to initiate the workers into the most difficult science, that of philosophy. He was making clear to them "the fact that history is a logical whole which unfolds step by step under the guidance of inexorable laws." He was trying to unite "science and the working-man," a combination which when achieved "will crush all obstacles to cultural advance with an iron hand." Since will and emotion are servants of the intellect and are controlled by it, "every normally constituted workingman must come to hate and distrust" not only the arrangements and institutions of the middle class, but also those profiting by them. The propertied classes are simply "the unconscious, choiceless, and therefore irresponsible products, not the producers of the situation as it stands and as it has developed under the guidance of quite other laws than the direction of personal choice. Even their reluctance to surrender . . . their mastery" is explained by "the laws of human nature, whose character it is to hold fast to whatever is and to account it necessary." The bourgeoisie is only a stage of economic and ethical development in the unfolding evolution of "reason and human liberty," but it is the necessary step for the emergence of the principle of the working class. This principle is the highest manifestation of "the human spirit," the final term of the logical process of history, because it "contains no ground of discrimination, whether in point of fact or in point of law, such as could be erected into a domineering prerogative and applied to reconstruct the institutions of society to that end." We are all workers as long as "we are willing to make ourselves useful to human society in any way." The principle of the working class has asserted itself through "the logical constraint of the course of events, even when such an aim has been absent from the common purposes of the state," even when opposed to the will of those who possessed the power. It is nothing more than a bringing into consciousness and working out on "the ground of free choice" of what has always, though obscurely, constituted the "effective organic nature of things."

Cliffe Leslie, who defended the work of the German historical school among the English, pointed out that the economic theory of this school was essentially the classical view as espoused by Mill and Bagehot, that it was not radical but essentially conservative, and that Wilhelm Roscher, the leader of the school, had asserted that Marx and Lassalle had misapplied the historical method. Properly used this method makes its disciples "distrustful of reforms which do not seem to be evolved by historical sequence and the spontaneous birth of time. . . . No revolutionary or socialist schemes have emanated from its most advanced Liberal rank." [30] Ely was maintaining the same view in this country. In a textbook written for the Chautauqua movement he said that the doctrine of the German historical school was conservative, that "Socialism comes rather from the abstract English political economy." "Socialists claim that developing . . . to their logical outcome the teachings of Ricardo they arrive at socialism, and Ricardo ranks high among scientific socialists. Ricardo illustrates . . . the dangers of the deductive method." [31] Apparently it was unimportant whether one's method was called historical, inductive, or deductive. Spencer, who claimed to validate his conclusions by all these methods, took the same attitude towards socialism as did Ely, Leslie, the German historical school, and the orthodox classical school.

Spencer was completing his synthetic philosophy, which was to show the evolution of society from the system of status to the ideal unmitigated system of free contract. This system is the "beneficent working of the survival of the fittest," or as Sir Henry Maine referred to it, "the beneficent private war which makes one man strive to climb on the shoulders of another." It is the only alternative "to the daily task . . . enforced by the prison or the scourge . . . Every society of men must adopt one system or the other, or it will pass through penury to starvation." Spencer, adopting Maine's position, interpreted the system of status as one of compulsory co-operation and the system of free contract as one of voluntary co-operation. Status characterises the militant type of society, in which the love of applause for subordinating others is the ruling social motive; free contract characterises the industrial type. They are logically exclusive, although in Spencer's evolutionary philosophy the industrial society of free contract evolved out of a necessary militant society of status, and free contract is itself a form of warfare. A society is essentially either servile and predacious, or peaceable and industrious. Its type characterises all its institutions—ceremonial, political, ecclesiastical, professional, and industrial. "The component institutions of each society habitually ex-hibit kindred types of structure." [32] Thus in a militant society women are chattels, and dress, as a ceremonial institution, denotes the force and power of wealth. To Spencer socialism represented a militant type, and he turned his elaborate analysis into an attack on socialism as well as a defence of the system of free contract. Ever-increasing governmental in-terference he denounced as the "coming slavery," and the conflict between free contract and socialism he characterised as "man versus the state."

Veblen continued his study of philosophy in addition to his varied reading in economics. The protest against Hegelianism, associationism, and the common-sense philosophy was increasing, and objections were being raised to the use of the doctrine of evolution to justify the competi-tive order. William James was criticising Spencer and Mill, and calling for an analysis of conduct in terms of the agents' activity rather than in terms of pleasure and pain or common-sense morals. James Ward had put this movement of revolt in high repute by his revolutionary article on "Psychology" in the *Encyclopædia Britannica*. David G. Ritchie was attacking Spencer's and Maine's belief in the "beneficence of the struggle for survival." He asserted that "this talk of beneficence is itself but a sur-vival, not of the fittest, but of the 'theological' belief in a God who wills the happiness of his creatures . . . or of the 'metaphysical' belief in a Na-ture which, if only left to itself, leads to better results than can be se-cured by any interference of man." [33] It involved the doctrines of "natural rights" and "social contract" against which Spencer was sup-posedly protesting. Even T.H. Huxley asked of a correspondent: "Have you considered that State Socialism (for which I have little enough love) may be a product of Natural Selection? The societies of Bees and Ants exhibit socialism *in excelsis*." [34] There was growing in Veblen's mind a project of ruthlessly dissecting the system of modern business enterprise and presenting socialism as the next step.

It was increasingly necessary, however, for him to find employment of some kind. He seems to have done some tutoring at the Cedar Valley Seminary, situated at near-by Osage, and Andrew Veblen made a number of attempts to secure a college position for his unaggressive brother. In 1889 Andrew saw an opening at the University of Iowa, where the professor of political science had just died. Veblen already had letters of recommendation from Presidents Strong of Carleton and Porter of Yale, and from J.B. Clark. He now secured letters from Herbert Baxter Adams, from Sumner, who had been considered for president of Columbia that year, and an additional one from Porter. Adams wrote that Veblen was known to him as an excellent man both in character and attainments, and that his record at Carleton had been highly commended by Clark. Sumner wrote: "Mr. Veblen studied with me as a graduate student two years and gave me good satisfaction. He seemed to me to be a man of very settled and sturdy character and great industry. He wrote a very important thesis which took the prize over some very strong competitors." Porter wrote: "It is with great pleasure that I certify that Mr. T.B. Veblen, B.A. Carleton College, Minnesota, pursued with eminent success a course of study in ethics and metaphysics under my direction, as a candidate for the degree of Doctor of Philosophy, which he received on examination. His capacity and tastes for philosophical studies are uncommon and his opportunities have been improved very diligently. I am confident that he has devoted himself to the study of political science with equal diligence and success."

It seemed almost inevitable that Veblen would secure the place, considering his recommendations, his Ph.D., his published works, and his wife's connexions. But he was unsuccessful. To the president he did not appear forceful enough, and he found it hard to explain his long idleness simply on the ground of ill health. Another factor in his failure seems to have been the opposition of President Strong, who apparently could not forgive the marriage of his niece to an agnostic. Immediately after Veblen had been refused the appointment, Strong demanded the return of his letter of recommendation. The position went to an applicant who lacked Veblen's training in political science but possessed the traditional advantage of a Bachelor of Divinity degree.

Andrew Veblen made attempts on his brother's behalf at other institutions, but nothing came of them. There was a prospect of obtaining the position of superintendent of schools at Warner, South Dakota, where Veblen was sponsored by one Gilbert who controlled the town. Before negotiations were completed, however, Gilbert became involved in financial difficulties and left Warner. Orson Veblen became a trustee of St. Olaf College in 1890, and he and Andrew tried to place Veblen on the faculty. The administration personally liked him, but his religious views prevented his appointment.

Veblen grew extremely moody. Even his botanical interests began to wane and a time came when he could no longer be interested in a "discussion as to whether a honeysuckle or a rosebud should be planted in a certain spot." Andrew Veblen called a conference, and decided that the best solution for his brother was to re-enter academic work, as a student if necessary. The necessity of satisfactorily explaining an inactive period of seven years made it almost impossible for Veblen to obtain a university position. Once he was registered in a well-known university, however, he could prove himself.

Again funds had to be supplied. Ellen had a little money and "that good old man," the father, was once more called on for help. Thomas Veblen was in a better financial position this time than when his son had gone to Yale, though, even as it was, Veblen had very little money with which to begin again.

The choice of a school was a problem. Veblen could never become a teacher of philosophy. Even at this time Johns Hopkins had chosen as professor of philosophy a man with theological training, who had "contrasted the ministry with a professorship to the extreme disadvantage of the latter in point of pleasure and opportunity." Veblen, moreover, noted that "philosophy was too hard." [35] The apparent drift of things intellectual was away from philosophy and to the social sciences, as Sumner had predicted. Cornell, which awarded four fellowships in the social sciences, was the final choice. Veblen set out for the East without his wife.

A decade of frustration was summarised in Veblen's response to a request of the Hopkins authorities for a statement of his activities since leaving Hopkins. "It is some time since I received a postal from you inquiring about my present occupation and my past work since leaving Baltimore. I neglected to answer at the time on account of uncertainty as to what my occupation was to be for the year. I am now lately entered as a graduate student at Cornell. On leaving J.H.U. I went to Yale, where I stayed for 2½ years and received the degree of Ph.D. Since then I have been idle for the greater part of the time because of ill health." A new career was before him, however, and he might have said, like Ibsen: "The time has come for some boundary posts to be moved."

CHAPTER V

VEBLEN registered at Cornell in the beginning of the winter term, 1891. He was reticent about his past, and when he found it necessary to explain his long absence from academic halls he told his story of ill health and recuperation. If it was expedient to mention an occupation, he spoke of his work in Norse literature and history. In the polite words of a fellow countryman, Veblen "dressed plainly and at first glance, there was a suggestion of rusticity about him."

According to the University records, Veblen was "working for an advanced degree." He was formally registered for but two courses, one in American history and one in American constitutional history and law, with the Reverend Moses Coit Tyler. Tyler had been offered a professorship of English literature at Yale. He was known throughout the country for his *Literary History of the American Revolution* and was then writing his *History of American Literature*. He had not stopped preaching, however, and wrote in his diary: "I brood over the possible duty and blessedness of letting my life—what remains—move more completely into the religious work." "I teach American History," he said, "not so much to make historians as to make citizens and good leaders for the State and Nation." [1] He used as textbook the *Constitutional Law of the United States*, by Hermann Eduard von Holst, who believed that the development of American history and constitutional procedure was the unfolding of America's destiny as a great and powerful nation.

Veblen apparently saw better opportunities in economics. The professor in charge of this field was J. Laurence Laughlin, who still refused to become a member of the American Economic Association because he thought it was socialistically inclined, although the members of the Old School were gradually joining. Laughlin was a follower of John Stuart Mill, whose *Principles of Political Economy* he had condensed for a textbook. Laughlin made the work less abstract and omitted what he called the social philosophy—the questioning of traditional *laissez-faire* principles. The neo-classical and Austrian developments in economics were to him simply metaphysical nonsense, since economic principles were matters of common sense.

Laughlin often told the story of his first meeting with Veblen. He was sitting in his study in Ithaca when an anæmic-looking person, wearing a coonskin cap and corduroy trousers, entered and in the mildest possible tone announced: "I am Thorstein Veblen." He told Laughlin of his academic history, his enforced idleness, and his desire to go on with his studies. The fellowships had all been filled, but Laughlin was so impressed with the quality of the man that he went to the president and other powers of the university and secured a special grant.

In May 1891 the People's Party was formed at a great conference of reform groups at Cincinnati. Donnelly, chairman of the committee on resolutions, prevented a threatened disruption of the conference by declaring "we are not here so much to proclaim a creed as to erect a banner under which the marching hosts of reform can rally." Donnelly wrote and delivered the platform's preamble, the most famous document in Populist history. Recapitulating the argument of his Utopia, he envisaged a "vast conspiracy against mankind" and declared that only the intelligent co-operation of the working classes can overthrow the plutocrats. Failure to accomplish this immediately "forebodes terrible social convulsions, the destruction of civilisation, or the establishment of an absolute despotism." At the St. Louis meeting on Washington's birthday, 1892, Donnelly forecast the union of the Democrats and Republicans. The wedding ceremony "would be performed at the altar of plutocracy; Grover Cleveland and Ben Harrison would act as bridesmen; the devil himself give away the bride, and Jay Gould pronounce the benediction." [2] Meanwhile the president of the Union Pacific, writing in the *North American Review*, was insisting that a citizen "commits an impertinence when he questions the right of any corporation to capitalise its properties at any sum whatever. . . . Such transactions are wholly matters of private contract; and . . . regulate themselves." [3]

In economics the traditional positions were still maintained. Alfred Marshall, who was becoming the outstanding economist in the English-speaking world, in his textbook cited with approval Nassau Senior's statement that the desire for distinction is "the most powerful of human passions" since it affects all men at all times. This impulse, said Marshall, is a "chief source of the desire for costly dress." A woman may display wealth by her dress but, since she supposedly has time to take thought concerning it, she must be "well dressed" rather than "expensively dressed." Thus she may be distinguished for her "faculties and abilities" as is the painter of a good picture. The desire for distinction is also the basis for the almost unlimited desire for house room "requisite for the exercise of many of the higher social activities." Furthermore, leisure is now being intelligently used to pursue excellence for its own sake, as in athletic games, which develop ability, rather than in the indulgence of sensuous craving. There was to be remembered, on the other hand, the lessening group of English artisans, without ambition, living in squalid surroundings, and spending their surplus over bare necessities for drink.

The *Christian Register* was circulating a lecture of Clark's on "Natural Law in Political Economy." The law of evolution, as the new phase of natural law, "has won a ready recognition" in the analysis of social organisation, partly because of "the beneficent quality of its operations. . . . That type supplants another which is better for humanity." "Institutions survive because they are adapted to their environment." It was not fully recognised, however, that the "phenomena of the market" —static activities—are also governed by "natural law," by the spontaneous actions of men as distinct from "voluntary action by society in its entirety." Socialism was attempting to supplant natural law by its antithesis, governmental action, on the ground that "poverty is rooted in robbery." Clark disputed this indictment with the theory that society "tends under natural law to give to every man his product."

At this time Spencer and a group of disciples published a *Plea for Liberty: an Argument against Socialism and Socialistic Legislation*. To them socialistic legislation meant even such things as free compulsory education. The author of the concluding essay, "The True Line of Deliverance," asserted that the labourer "has only to let the natural processes go on, to resist all temptation to fight, or to rely upon artificial protection for his labour," and to put "all his spare cash religiously into industrial investments, to become, as he is probably entitled to be, the true owner of this world and all that therein is."

Spencer opened the volume with an essay called "From Freedom to Bondage." Unless immediate action is taken, the militant system of socialism is in the offing. The vicious practices in the competitive order are in good part due "to that lavish expenditure which, as implying success in the commercial struggle, brings honour." This trait is a holdover from the militant life. But the system of free contract has of itself led to the mitigation of evils, and its continued advance must inevitably bring further progress in industrial activity and longevity. The desire for change, which is due to people's restlessness rather than to any rational understanding, means a movement towards compulsory co-operation. "As fast as the *régime* of contract is discarded the *régime* of status is of necessity adopted." "Our existing voluntary co-operation," with its free contracts and its competition, "needs no official oversight." All its numerous activities "are adjusted without any other agency than the pursuit of profit." Socialism will substitute a tyrannical bureaucracy for the "industrial *régime* of willinghood." This cannot ultimately succeed. It is not realised that much misery in the nature of hard labour must still be borne by humanity, for man's savage indolent nature is not yet thoroughly fitted for the requirements of the ideal social state of free contract. The only way to achieve this state is to follow the law of justice; let every man suffer as well as enjoy the consequences of his self-seeking actions. Every social system must have a regulating class. Under the existing system of free contract "the regulators, pursuing their personal interests, take as large a share of the produce as they can get; but, as we are daily shown by Trades Union successes, are restrained in the selfish pursuit of their ends." In socialism, however, the directing class, acting in a self-seeking manner, as do all human beings, would not have the check provided by other self-seeking groups and individuals, and eventually a despotic empire would arise.

Veblen took Spencer's essay as an opportunity for a discussion of "Some Neglected Points in the Theory of Socialism." He said that he was offering a suggestion, in the spirit of a disciple of Spencer, on a point inadequately covered: the economic basis of the current unrest. The legitimacy of the moral or expedient grounds for dissatisfaction was beside the point.

The modern development of industry and industrial organization demands that "natural monopolies" should be controlled by the state, and a constantly increasing number of occupations are developing into the form of natural monopolies. The socialist agitators claim that the existing system is necessarily wasteful and industrially inefficient, and allows one group to live on the community. There is general complaint that the owners of great wealth have unwarranted powers. A feeling of "slighted manhood" prevails.

The existing system is based on the institutions of private property and free competition. It has been contemporaneous with the most rapid increase in average wealth and industrial efficiency ever witnessed. The prevalent dissatisfaction is expressed not by the abjectly poor but by the moderately well off, and the explanation of this fact is to be found in the form that self-esteem has taken in competitive society. From "the standpoint of the average man" the effective desire for esteem is restricted to "economic emulation." This is a striving to be thought better than one's neighbours in industrial-economic ability. Virtuous attributes serve very little purpose as a sign of respectability, and knavery cannot be censured, since in the modern world an individual lives in such a mobile, wide environment that it is difficult to appraise his qualities. Efficiency which is not to a person's economic benefit has little value. It must be pecuniary efficiency. The token of industrial success is the possession of many dollars, and the evidence of possession is an unremitting demonstration of ability to pay. The appearance of success is thus even more desirable than the actual substance. Economic success as a measure of esteem is much stronger in a generation which inherits the belief.

It is necessary to spend as much as one's neighbour, and desirable to be able to spend more. The struggle for decency is the essential element of the standard of living. This insatiable need absorbs the income which remains after physical needs have been provided for, and expenditure for emulation is as difficult to retrench as expenditure for existence. Physical discomfort is endured to provide luxuries which have become necessities, and articles ostensibly for creature comfort are made to serve an antithetical purpose. Articles of apparel owe their value primarily to their effectiveness in protecting the wearer's respectability, not to their protecting of his body. People go ill clad in order to be well dressed, and as a result over half the values of apparel are due to "dress," not to "clothing." The increase in industrial efficiency has been dissipated in economic emulation. Other things being equal, under free competition the greater the advance in industry and the greater the opportunity for personal contact and comparison, the greater will be the straining after economic respectability. No advance in general well-being can lessen or end "this misdirection of effort," since its "aim is not any absolute degree of comfort or excellence."

The struggle of each to possess more than his neighbour is inseparable from the institution of private property. One who possesses less will be jealous of those possessing more. Thus the unrest is immediately caused by the struggle for a higher standard of living, but ultimately by private property under modern conditions. There can be no peace from this "ignoble form of emulation" without the abolition of private property and free competition. Popular sentiment is increasingly adverse to these institutions and thus vaguely favours socialism. There is, however, no inference in Veblen's paper that socialism is the inevitable outcome.

In the second part of the paper Veblen discussed the practicability of complete nationalisation of industry. Modern industry has transformed the "struggle for subsistence into a struggle to keep up appearances by otherwise unnecessary expenditure." Under an organisation allowing no inequality of acquisition or income, economic emulation would become obsolete. The aspect of human nature which appears in this form of emulation should logically find expression in more serviceable activity. It is difficult to imagine it taking "any line of action more futile or less worthy of human effort." Directly and indirectly the struggle for decency is chargeable with "one-half the aggregate labour, and abstinence from labour—for the standard of respectability requires us to shun labour as well as to enjoy the fruits of it." The nationalists might claim, therefore, that even if the new system were not as effective in production the present standard of comfort might still be maintained, and the new regime would be less irksome to common labour. The worker might actually acquire the nobility accorded him in the occasional complacent speculations of the well-to-do. Such a society would have less chance of failure than one where "strenuous labour on the part of nearly all members is barely sufficient to make both ends meet."

Veblen then turns to Spencer's declaration that eliminating free contract means installing the system of status. Natural monopolies, which include an increasing number of industrial activities, do not mark a continuation of the evolution towards a system of free contract, nor towards the system of status, as Maine uses the term. The system of competition has not been discarded and no revolution has been achieved. The industrial systems of all known past cultures may have been organised either on status or contract, but this is untrue of social functions not primarily industrial.

Modern constitutional government "in theory at least" cannot be classified under either category, and "it is the analogy of modern constitutional government through an impersonal law and impersonal institutions, that comes nearest doing justice to the vague notions of our socialist propagandists." "The system of status is a system of subjection to personal authority—of prescription and class distinctions and immunities; the system of constitutional government . . . is a system of subjection to the will of the social organism, as expressed in an impersonal law." Constitutional government is a nationalisation of political functions. Constitutional development takes the direction of the exercise of such powers as the right of eminent domain and taxation. "The later developments made necessary by the exigencies of industry under modern conditions are also moving" along these lines. The socialists wish to identify the industrial community with the political; but the more developed political form will be the ruling one. It is doubtful whether the materials for such a society exist, and their creation is a problem for "constructive social engineering." Even if the change were made, it is highly doubtful that a system of status would be the permanent result, since the people's past development makes such an outcome unlikely. The success of constitutional government among the English-speaking peoples argues, despite its shortcomings, that the question is not whether the perfection of character necessary for a perfect working of the scheme of nationalised industry has been reached, but "whether we have reached such a degree of development as would make an imperfect working of the scheme possible."

A Norwegian friend of Veblen's said that, although supporters of the established order might think the article was propaganda, that was not the opinion of his associates at Cornell. The paper was a metaphysical disquisition. It is said that Veblen obtained his fellowship for the following year on the basis of this article. Before the fellowship awards were announced, Andrew Veblen telegraphed his brother that Ellen was ill and needed him. Veblen could not leave, however, until he was definitely notified that he had won his economics and finance fellowship, paying $400.

After spending the summer at Stacyville, Veblen and his wife returned to Cornell. Apparently no one had known he was married, and his friends were surprised to discover the fact. He was still listed as working for an advanced degree. His wife began graduate work in botany and biology and started a thesis on carnivorous plants, but dropped her work before the year was over.

During the year Veblen published in *The Quarterly Journal of Economics* two notes which gave the impression of considerable dialectical skill in defending Laughlin's common-sense point of view. The first was on "Böhm-Bawerk's Definition of Capital and the Sources of Wages." Eugen von Böhm-Bawerk's *Positive Theory of Capital*, just translated, was being extensively discussed, and Veblen centred his discussion on the wage-fund doctrine.

Böhm-Bawerk rejected this doctrine by distinguishing between what he called "Social Capital" or "Productive Capital," and "Private Capital" or "Acquisitive Capital," which includes in addition to productive capital the means of subsistence of productive labour. Thus "real wages" are not drawn from the community's capital, although from the employer's standpoint they are drawn from his private capital. But Böhm-Bawerk includes in social capital consumption goods still in the hands of dealers and producers, and Veblen gives emphasis to the fact that this incidental point of classification might afford captious critics grounds for arguing that wages thus represent only a general claim on goods still a part of the general capital, and can only be satisfied by drawing on social capital. He felt that the essentially "sterile controversy" over the wage-fund doctrine might be ended by drawing a distinction between "the labourer's share of 'consumable goods,' or 'earnings,' on the one hand, and 'wages,' on the other, analogous to the distinction taken by Wagner —and perfected by Professor Böhm-Bawerk—between capital as a 'purely economic category' and capital 'in a juridico-historical sense.'" Veblen does not point out that Böhm-Bawerk did not regard as fundamental this distinction, originally made by Karl Rodbertus, between capital as productive instrument and as property right. According to Böhm-Bawerk, it led Rodbertus to a faulty theory of interest, namely, that it is an act of robbery achieved by the capitalist through the ownership of the instruments of production. Veblen, nominally following Böhm-Bawerk and Adolf Wagner, who identified the two conceptions, declared that "wages in this stricter definition, and private capital are facts of usage," but social capital and the labourer's income or earnings are intrinsic and fundamental in any theory of industrial society.

Wages is a category of the relationship of employer and employed, of production as carried on by private capital, and the term is not used in the same sense when the discussion shifts to production simply as such, and still less when the point of view is that of distribution and consumption. From the standpoint of the consumption of goods, the labourer is not a labourer, but simply a member of society. The sustenance of men while productively employed is drawn from the product of past industry, and wages are paid out of capital, since wages are a category of private capital. On the other hand, the critics define wages as earnings, and these are drawn from the product of industry, since "earnings are the product, to the labourer, of his labour." Veblen said in conclusion: "All this may seem to be a web of excessively fine-spun technicalities, but in apology it is to be said that it is also directed exclusively to a point of pure theory. And the whole controversy about the source of wages has also been in the region of pure theory, having never directly involved questions of physical fact or of expediency."

The second note, " 'The Overproduction Fallacy,' " is a discussion of the contrast between capital and industrial efficiency. Uriel Crocker, arguing along the lines of received economics, attempted to rehabilitate the general overproduction theory of industrial depression. Relying in part upon Wells's *Recent Economic Changes*, Crocker directed his attack against Mill, who best represented the traditional position of the impossibility of general overproduction. Half of Veblen's note is a dialectic demonstration denying Crocker's argument, since "general overproduction as defined by Mill, 'a supply of commodities in the aggregate, surpassing the demand'—is a contradiction in terms. Aggregate supply *is* aggregate demand, neither more nor less." For Veblen, however, this is simply a preliminary to a presentation of his own theory of depression and general overproduction. "The doctrine of a general over-supply of goods—in the sense in which it has been criticised in economic theory—is palpably absurd," but the "cry of 'overproduction' " that rises in every period of industrial depression has a "very cogent . . . meaning to the men who raise the cry." It stands for an "economic fact" which is significant in any attempt to understand hard times and commercial crises, although its relation to "liquidation" and "depression" has not yet been satisfactorily established. Veblen also used Wells to support his argument, declaring that this economic fact stands for a divergence "between the nominal, accepted valuation and the present value of the property engaged in production, in consequence of which the nominal earnings of capital (and in some cases the real earnings as measured in means of livelihood) are diminished." The basis on which "remunerative prices" and customary profit are computed becomes obsolete. The discrepancy is due primarily to two factors, which reduce the money value of property below its nominal value: a speculative movement and increased efficiency in industry. In either case the result is that the nominal, accepted valuation of the capital exceeds its actual value, indicated by earning capacity. The general aggregate property of the community has been capitalised "above the cost at which it, or its equivalent for purposes of production, could now be replaced." The hard times of the past decade indicated how this result might be reached through a lowering of the cost of production. But the whole matter of overproduction is essentially one of prices, of commercial value. Depression is primarily a readjustment of values, a "psychological fact," and secondly "a matter of the shifting of ownership rather than of a destruction of wealth or a serious reduction of the aggregate productiveness of industry as measured in goods."

Overproduction is a "subjective element." Even though the "dollar is worth enough more to make up for the nominal depreciation," a reduction of one's property in money values is contemplated with regret and submitted to "reluctantly and tardily." Where the nominal owner of the means of production is not the real owner, as in the case of borrowed capital, the decline in the market value of the property means a real loss, although it is only a nominal loss to the man who has his own capital and an unrecognised gain to the creditor. "The cost of production of staple commodities—as compared with the standard of value"—had generally declined during the past ten or twelve years, and there had been a consequent decline of about thirty percent in the nominal earning capacity of property engaged in production. This factor, said Veblen in conclusion, has grave consequences in a community "where so great a proportion of capital is represented by interest-bearing securities." Laughlin felt that Veblen was attacking problems of the greatest importance in the proper manner and that he was destined to be an outstanding economist if he kept to the right path.

Fortunately for Veblen, Laughlin was appointed head professor of economics at the new University of Chicago. Laughlin arranged for Veblen to receive a fellowship at Chicago, paying $520 a year, and Veblen began preparations for a course in socialism.

Before Veblen left Cornell, he had the satisfaction of successfully flaunting his contempt for the theological rulers of the colleges. Orson

Veblen wrote his brother that he wished to get a Norwegian college friend into St. Olaf, but that the administration doubted the man's orthodoxy. Veblen wrote a letter of recommendation, including a statement that the only trouble with the man was that he was too damned orthodox, and he was given the place.

The Populist Party had its first national convention at Omaha in July 1892. Donnelly again delivered the preamble, with a ringing arraignment of the corporate interests, and the delegates staged a tremendous demonstration. One unsympathetic critic wrote: "No intelligent man could . . . listen to the wild and frenzied assaults upon the existing order of things, without a feeling of great alarm at the extent and intensity of the social lunacy there displayed. . . . When that furious and hysterical arraignment of the present times, that incoherent intermingling of Jeremiah and Bellamy, the platform, was adopted, the cheers and yells which rose like a tornado from four thousand throats and raged without cessation for thirty-four minutes, during which women shrieked and wept, men embraced and kissed their neighbours, locked arms, marched back and forth, and leaped upon tables and chairs in the ecstasy of their delirium—this dramatic and historical scene must have told every quiet, thoughtful witness that there was something at the back of all this turmoil more than the failure of crops or the scarcity of ready cash. And over all the city during that summer week brooded the spectres of Nationalism, Socialism, and general discontent." Southern agrarians characterised the nomination of Grover Cleveland "as a prostitution of the principles of Democracy, as a repudiation of the demands of the Farmers' Alliance, which embody the true principles of Democracy, and a surrender of the rights of the people to the financial kings of the country." A Western agrarian leader spoke of Cleveland as a "fossilised reminiscence." [4]

In Minnesota Donnelly was nominated for governor at a meeting addressed by the socialist Robert Schilling of Milwaukee. Donnelly declared that a horde of millionaires expected to become titled aristocrats and, if their progress were not arrested, they would fulfil their wishes. The farmers of Minnesota and the Dakotas, according to Donnelly, were defrauded of a billion dollars by an organised conspiracy of railroad men and grain speculators.[5] The Carnegie Steel Company sent for the hated Pinkertons in an attempt to break a strike at its plants in Homestead, Pennsylvania, and there was a bloody battle when they arrived. The entire state militia was called out, martial law was declared, and the strike leader was held for murder. Alexander Berkman, an anarchist, attempted to kill H.C. Frick, one of the most hated anti-union employers in the country, and a private in the militia was tortured by his officers for publicly expressing sympathy with the act. Davis Rich Dewey declared that the conflict "gave rise to grave forebodings as to the stability of republican institutions." In Congress, in the press, and on the public platform "the Pinkertons, branded as mercenaries and hirelings, were charged with treason and were said to be employed not only to protect the property of employers, but to . . . provoke [the populace] to violence . . . as an excuse for the calling-out of troops." The strikers declared that "the public and the employees aforesaid have equitable rights and interests in the said mill which cannot be modified or diverted by due process of law. . . . The employees have the right to continuous employment in the said mill during efficiency and good behaviour." Laughlin denounced this "inalienable right to continuous employment" and attributed the doctrine to the "one-sided reading" of the strikers, particularly to their exclusive attention to Henry George. Socialism made converts on¹ the apparent evidence "that the individualistic system of competition had broken down." ⁹ The courts ordered the Standard Oil trust dissolved, but a new device, the holding company, made its appearance.

In the midst of this turmoil Veblen made his entrance into Chicago. Heretofore he had been most familiar with country towns; now he was set down in a large industrial centre.

CHAPTER VI

THE new University of Chicago, in recognition of a large endowment, included in its title the words, "Founded by John D. Rockefeller." It "became almost a fashion among Chicago's wealthy and well-disposed to set their names commemoratively among the gargoyles and crocheted gables of scholastic Gothic façades." [1] Within a week after the University opened, the president announced that Charles Tyson Yerkes, whose exploits are chronicled in Theodore Dreiser's *The Titan* and *The Financier*, had agreed at the president's request to build and equip the most complete observatory in the world.

The ambitions of the new university were reflected by its thirty-six-year-old president, William Rainey Harper, who was admiringly described by Walter Hines Page as a type of the captain of industry. Before he accepted the presidency, he had been simultaneously professor of Semitic languages at Yale University, instructor in Hebrew at Yale Divinity School, Woolsey Professor of Biblical Literature at Yale College, president of the American Publication Society of Hebrew, principal of the American Institute of Sacred Literature (through which he conducted a correspondence school for ministers), principal of the Chautauqua College of Liberal Arts, editor of two theological journals, and conductor of four lecture courses at points outside New Haven. He established a system of administration at Chicago which was characterised by *The Nation* as "the dictatorship of the president." It was "one of the greatest errors of American university organisation that so much power is exercised by the president, and so little by the corps of professors. The professors really make the university, and they ought to determine its educational policy." The University Senate, which was "to discuss and *decide*" educational matters, included only "Heads of Departments." This "makes the body ultra-conservative." Even at Columbia, "which has not commonly been regarded as a radical institution, the central organ of the professors, the University Council, consists of delegates from the several faculties"; and in their election "the junior professors and assistant professors have the same voice as their seniors. It is certainly surprising to discover that a more conservative, not to say reactionary, policy has been adopted at Chicago." [2] Harper carried ritualism further than it had been carried in any American university, and established an elaborate system of rankings: deans, head professors, professors, associate professors, assistant professors, instructors, docents, tutors, readers, fellows, as well as lecturers and assistants. The university had five main divisions—the University proper, the University Extension, which included correspondence courses, the University Press, the University Libraries, Laboratories, and Museums, and University Affiliations. A summer school was established. In a short time thirteen magazines were published at the university. Although four other universities issued publications covering economics, Chicago began the publication of *The Journal of Political Economy*. William James had said of such competition in psychology: "I confess, it disgusts me to hear of each of these little separate college tin-trumpets." [3] Harper regarded the department of athletics and physical culture as "one of the great divisions of the university." According to his biographer he brought as head, with the rank of associate professor, "the best-known college athlete of that period," a man very active in Y.M.C.A. circles.

Harper was ambitious in gathering a faculty. The instability of a new enterprise and the "critical attitude" towards what was called "a Standard Oil Institution" did not prove insuperable difficulties in obtaining a staff of eminent men. "Because he wanted the best," wrote his biographer, "he did not hesitate to try for the presidents of colleges and universities" and he got nine of them. He attempted to secure as head of the graduate school that great organiser, Herbert Baxter Adams. At Clark University, where a distinguished science faculty had been gathered, friction had developed, and Harper engaged the majority of the staff without President G. Stanley Hall's knowledge. "I told him," said Hall, "his action was like that of an eagle who robbed the fish-hawk of his prey." When Harper refused to reduce the list, Hall threatened "to make a formal appeal to the public and to Mr. Rockefeller himself to see if this trust magnate (who was . . . at the height of his unpopularity and censure, and who was said to have driven many smaller competing firms out of existence by slow strangling methods of competition) would justify such an assassination of an institution as had . . . been attempted here." [4] Although Harper took almost all the eminent men, he did not take Franz Boas, who was only a docent.

The new university followed the American theological tradition of higher learning. The president considered it as continuing the old Baptist University of Chicago, of which Joseph Haven had once been president. A Universalist minister is reported to have said that the Board of Trustees of the university was composed of fourteen Baptists, one Jew, and six Christians. The university had a divinity school, three theological journals, and three theological clubs, in addition to a Christian Union with a Y.M.C.A., a Y.W.C.A., and a social settlement house. Harper had been an active clergyman, and was recommended for the presidency by an influential Baptist theologian on the ground that "he would do a work in behalf of denominational and Christian education in this country beyond the expectation of those who regard him with the greatest admiration." [5] Out of the original thirty-one full professors in residence, ten were professors of theology and two others had attended theological seminaries. There was also a number of professors like Laughlin, who spoke on the "Spiritual Life" before the Christian Union, and like Thomas Chamberlain, who believed that there "was a divine mind which directed and an earth which executed; the result was good." [6] A department of "Christian Apologetics" was established in the college, and courses were given on "Apologetics" and "Evidences of Christianity." Harper offered the devout George Herbert Palmer of Harvard a salary of three times what he was receiving if he would head Chicago's department of philosophy, but Palmer refused.

"Moral philosophy" nominally was not in the curriculum, but actually it continued to play an important role under the new designation of Social Science or Sociology. Albion Small, who had received an M.A. from Newton Theological Seminary and had been president of Colby College, was made head of the sociology department and dean of the Liberal Arts College. At Colby he had substituted a course in sociology for Noah Porter's course in moral philosophy. The sociology department at Chicago included a division of "Sanitary Science," in which courses were given on "House Sanitation" and "Sanitary Aspects of Water, Food, and Clothing." The most important division was called "Social Philosophy" and was directly conducted by Small. His courses covered almost the entire field of moral philosophy, ranging from "Social Psychology" to the "Organic Functions of the State and Government," in which he was supposed to "determine the premises of political philosophy." "Social Philosophy" was the basis and master science for all the other so-called moral sciences.

The existence of a separate department of economics was not a very serious limitation for Small. He gave a course on the "Psychology, Ethics, and Sociology of Socialism," which was supposedly devoted to "the non-economical content of modern socialistic systems," but the "Sociology of Socialism," if not the other aspects, included economics. Small, an ex-professor of the subject, simply accepted the traditional economics in setting forth the social philosophy of socialism. The "Problems of Social Dynamics" became the capstone of the department. This formula was borrowed from Lester F. Ward, of whom Small considered himself a disciple. Ward's generalised appeal for the control of the social process by society, educated by a proper sociology, provided Small with the sort of opportunistic gospel he needed. He appeared liberal if not radical, when actually he was conservative.

Laughlin stood for the common-sense economics in an undiluted form and was suspicious of sociology because it included "anything from plumbing to philosophy." In the course on "Principles of Political Economy" the textbook was his edition of Mill. This course was but a necessary preliminary for the really important courses on the practical problems facing the business community. The course on "Unsettled Problems in Economic Theory" was occupied with "questions of exchange and distribution," not those of production and consumption. The announcement of the publication of *The Journal of Political Economy* read: "In this day of many complex demands on busy men, it is of the first importance to have at hand a journal . . . which is devoted to the sifting and publication of facts which are vital to the questions every day touching business life in regard to banking, money, railways, transportation, shipping, taxation, socialism, wages, agriculture, and the like."

In the first article of *The Journal* Laughlin declared that economic study must be true to the reality of the common-sense position, although not necessarily true to the facts of the existing situation. Political Economy is not a "body of concrete truth: it does not pretend to be a statement of fact, or a description of actual conditions, or even of future ones. It is a means of analysing the play of economic motives, of measuring their force, of discovering and explaining the relations between concrete truths, and of ascertaining their causes and effects. . . . The reason why we cannot foretell economic results is because in each future case, the facts, although similar to past cases to the casual observer, are in reality different. If we could be certain of all the facts affecting the case, we could prophesy; but in the nature of things we can never be sure of them." [7]

Other head professors in the moral sciences were fundamentally of the same stamp as Small and Laughlin. Von Holst was head professor of history, and the head of the department of political science was Harry Pratt Judson, a devout Baptist and a student of Mark Hopkins. Harper, however, was willing to bear with newer ideas up to a point just short of possible embarrassment in his skating on ice not yet grown thick. The enthusiasm for Edward Carpenter's poem, "Towards Democracy," showed the temper of the university as much as did the respect for traditions.

The original faculty included a number of creative and curious spirits with whom Veblen was acquainted. Albert Michelson was engaged in his great experiments in astrophysics with instruments of his own making.

In the department of physiology Assistant Professor Jacques Loeb was obtaining significant results with the simplest techniques and a strict adherence to what he called a mechanistic interpretation of biological phenomena. The English department included the poet, William Vaughn Moody, as instructor, and Oscar Lovell Triggs, who was making socialist interpretations of literature, as a docent. Assistant Professor Frederick Starr, the eccentric anthropologist, was in the department of sociology. Veblen spoke with "marked respect" of William Caldwell, who was then a tutor in the economics department. Caldwell, primarily a student of philosophy, was sceptical of hedonistic economics as well as of the "experimental psychology," or associational-hedonistic psychology and philosophy. He was at the university less than two years. His reviews in *The Journal of Political Economy* were excellent specimens of subtle thinking, particularly the one on the *Grundriss der Politischen Oekonomie* of Eugen von Philippovitch, a follower of the dominant classical variant. Philippovitch, Caldwell declared, maintains the traditional views "by limiting economic laws to what he calls economic unities or societies, each of which he most carefully defines." The "economic sphere" is "the nineteenth-century idea of some organic economic unity." "One is left to make a synthesis" of his "economic spheres" in order "to find out what economics really is, and what laws govern the industrial organisation of today." His conclusions are consequently of the "hypothetical" sort. Throughout the book "he is strong, because he defines and distinguishes." He admits that the condition of the labourer is "highly unsatisfactory" and that competition has "manifest disadvantages," but here as elsewhere the only remedy he can think of is the "modifying influences of time and public opinion in expressing itself in the state or community." The book "has no predominating interest save a perfectly balanced and lucid treatment of the whole subject of theory," and "many of the definitions are apt to strike one as somewhat formal, and as problems to be solved only by a statement of the conditions of their solution."

At about the time the University of Chicago was opened Peirce attacked the "greed philosophy" of conventional economics, with its strong belief that "all acts of charity and benevolence, private and public . . . degrade the human race." The usual textbooks stated that "intelligence in the service of greed ensures the justest prices, the fairest contracts, the most enlightened conduct of all the dealings between men, and leads to the *summum bonum*, food in plenty and perfect comfort. Food for whom? Why, for the greedy master of intelligence." To say, as did the textbook writers, that "the motives which animate men in the pursuit of wealth" are "in the highest degree beneficial," was the most degrading of blasphemies. In place of the "atrocious villainies of the economists"

Peirce pleaded for man's humanity to man, for sentimentalism, "the natural judgments of the sensible heart." "Soon a flash and a quick peal will shake economists out of their complacency." [8]

While Caldwell was analysing the traditional classifying procedure in economics, George Romanes was pointing out that Darwinism meant causal analysis, not classification. Until Darwin's time scientists had conceived of natural science as consisting "in a mere observation of facts, or tabulation of phenomena." The status of a zoologist or a botanist was determined by the accuracy and extent of his memory instead of any visible "evidence of intellectual powers in the way of constructive thought." These gifts could only legitimately exercise themselves in "taxonomic work." The merit of any brilliant results in observation and experiment lay in the discovery of "facts *per se*," not in the attempts to combine these facts under general principles. But the results achieved when Darwin deliberately disregarded the "traditional canons," have made it "impossible for naturalists . . . not to perceive that their previous bondage to the law of a mere ritual has been for ever superseded by what verily deserves to be regarded as a new dispensation. . . . Natural history is not to [Darwin] an affair of the herbarium or the cabinet. The collectors and the species-framers are, as it were, his diggers of clay and makers of bricks: even the skilled observers and the trained experimentalists are his mechanics." To his predecessors, "the discovery or accumulation of facts was an end, to him it is the means. . . . *The Origin of Species* . . . first revealed to naturalists as a class . . . that not facts . . . or phenomena, but causes or principles, are the ultimate objects of scientific quest." [9]

Veblen was not a member of the original faculty, but only a fellow, registered for courses in economics in the graduate school. He was now thirty-five years old. In the economics department one of his Johns Hopkins classmates, Edward W. Bemis, was an associate professor, and another associate professor was a man younger than Veblen, without even the conventional Ph.D. Another Hopkins classmate, C.W. McClintock, was an assistant professor in another department. Veblen kept aloof from the faculty. Caldwell respected him highly, but was never successful in stirring up a discussion with him. Most of the burden of editing *The Journal of Political Economy* fell upon Veblen's shoulders, but this fact was not officially recognised until some time later. The translation of Gustav Cohn's *Science of Finance* was the first work in a projected series of Economic Studies. Originally it was to be the joint task of the entire staff, but Veblen, with his command of German, did all the work on it. He wrote an article or two for President Harper, and said of this activity: "Harper departed from all his educational ideals. There is evidence of it in a comparison of what he did, with his early addresses. I know, for I wrote the addresses."

A course by Laughlin on American Agriculture was scheduled, but before it was actually given Veblen wrote two articles in the first volume of *The Journal of Political Economy*—"The Price of Wheat Since 1867" and "The Food Supply and the Price of Wheat." The articles seemed to fit the demand for practical work, and Laughlin felt that Veblen should give the course.

In the first article the history of American agriculture was recapitulated. Veblen described the dramatic variations in wheat prices, particularly the great fall in prices that took place during the first half of the preceding decade, and noted the effects produced by the railroad companies, middlemen, and revolutionary changes in technology, and in the traditions of flour production. A student of the Populist movement said the article "concludes that with some exceptions wheat-growing is still generally profitable." This customary reading seems to be due to Veblen's roundabout, strategic literary habits rather than to his actual statements.[10]

If the first article gave the impression that the farmers generally were prospering, the second showed that no fear need be felt of food prices increasing. It was being said at the time that "the date at which the land available for tillage shall have been definitely occupied is near at hand, and that when that day arrives a great and 'sudden' advance in agricultural prices is to be looked for, with its consequences, of great gains for the farmer—for the American farmer perhaps, in an especial degree— and of distress for all peoples who get their supply of food largely from other countries." Veblen contended, however, that in farming as in other occupations "a continual improvement in methods and a steady decline in cost of production, even in the face of a considerably increased demand," may not improbably take place. Thus in view of the farmer's position in the money economy and this technological movement, "even apart from any lowering of the cost of articles of necessary consumption, it is fully within the possibilities of the situation that no permanent advance in farm products need take place at all for a generation or more."

During the last quarter of the year Veblen began teaching his course on socialism. No one could determine whether he was himself a socialist. He used Thomas Kirkup's *History of Socialism* as a textbook and agreed with Kirkup that Rodbertus was not the founder of modern socialism, as spokesmen of classical economics were asserting. Rodbertus's "ideal of the socialist state was a monarchy constructed on the lines of narrowly Prussian tradition." In a review of Kirkup's book Veblen said the author does the socialists a service in calling attention to the fact that "socialists do not propose the abolition of capital." But "much less creditable is the author's acceptance of the socialist interpretation of Ricardo." Kirkup interpreted socialism as the co-operative movement, but Veblen said the view is "forcibly set forth in the concluding pages of the book" that "the whole trend of the modern industrial development is distinctly socialistic, and that socialism (collectivism) is but the logical outcome of the continued growth of democracy under modern conditions." The book "falls short of an exhaustive analysis of the social ills on which the socialist movement feeds, as well as the full scope of the social changes that must be accomplished if the remedy for these ills is to be found in the direction of that movement."

Veblen wrote reviews of anthropological works which dealt with agriculture, and used them as opportunities for comments on the institution of property. In discussing B.H. Baden-Powell's *Land-Systems of British India,* he said that where "as in the case of the Tódas . . . conquest and invasion by alien peoples have not disturbed the ancient order, at least within historic times, the system, and the prevalent concepts with respect to land tenure, which the English found in vogue on acquiring the over-lordship of the country, were of such a simple and primitive character as to baffle the officials by affording no features comparable to the concepts familiar to European habits of thought." Baden-Powell's work was a demolition of the theory of Sir Henry Maine, the historical school, and Spencer, that the original germ of modern industrial and political society was a " 'primitive Aryan village community,' in the sense of a patriarchal-communistic tribal group." Studying the same tribes observed by Maine, Powell found that there was never a stage of "*joint* holding by the tribe collectively." There are two distinct types of village communities. In one there is no claim nor acknowledgment of "joint ownership of the whole estate, or joint liability for burdens imposed by the state." In the other "a strong joint-body . . . has pretensions to be of a higher caste or superior title to the 'tenants' who live on the estate." The first form of the village, of Dravidian not Aryan origin, is one in which the "cultivators—practically owners of their several family holdings—live under a common headman, with certain common officers and artisans who serve them . . . and there is no landlord (class or individual) over the whole." The second or predatory form is thought to have grown out of the first by the "superposition of a landlord," in conquest or in various quasi-peaceable means. "The active factor in producing a joint ownership, vested in a class 'of higher caste' and 'superior title' has been the institution of family property and family inheritance." When the original acquirer of lands dies and "a body of joint heirs succeeds, *we soon find a number of co-sharers*, all equally entitled, claiming the whole estate, and (whether remaining joint or partitioning the fields) forming what is called a 'joint village community.' " A predatory, parasitic class was thus the logical result of the institution of property, which was originally developed, at least ostensibly, to maintain peace and equality.

Chicago at that time was still a new city, with almost unlimited ambitions. The "somewhat forced and pretentious quality of its nascent culture" oppressed sensitive spirits. Hamlin Garland described the city as "only a big country trade centre . . . an ugly, smoky, muddy town built largely of wood" and "its great men were sons of villagers." The contrast between the dwellings on the lake front, where the university was located, and those back of the Yards or in South Chicago, was evidence of the "sharp division of wealth from poverty." Chicago's substantial citizens held that "business is business" and consequently were "annoyed at the very notion of social control." The "city of opportunity," James Hayden Tufts said, had been a "school for forceful leaders," and "the power and the attitude of brooking no resistance . . . gave rise in some cases to a disposition which, if not arrogant, was at any rate little disposed to submit to restraint or dictation. . . . The tendency was rather toward fighting out controversies than toward compromise." [11]

For a short while there was an apparent reign of peace and good will. It was felt by leading citizens that rather than the repressive measures adopted after the Haymarket episode "the only cure for the acts of anarchy was free speech and an open discussion of the ills" of the social order.[12] The Columbian Exposition opened in 1893, and the Fair Grounds and the University of Chicago were side by side. The "White City," the Fair Grounds, rose *pari passu* with the "Gray City," the University. The Divinity School took shape within a few hundred yards of the Ferris Wheel and the Street of Cairo. In the words of Henry B. Fuller, one of the outstanding literary figures of the day, "for the first time cosmopolitanism visited the Western world; for the first time woman publicly came into her own; for the first time, on a grand scale, art was made vitally manifest in the American consciousness." [13] Chicago became for a decade the leading literary centre of the country. A labour meeting, held for the benefit of the delegates to the Labour Conference, adopted the following resolution: "The working men and women of Chicago . . . hereby extend to their brothers and sisters of Great Britain and Ireland, Europe and Australia, greetings of fraternity and fellowship, recognising in the similarity of the problems of unemployed and misemployed men, land, and machinery here and there, that the cause of the emancipation of labour is essentially one and the same the world over; and pledging themselves to unite with all working men in the spirit of international patriotism across all dynastic and tribal barriers to make the world of industry a republic, to make all its inhabitants fellow citizens, and restore to every citizen his alienated though inalienable rights to life, liberty, and happiness here on earth." [14]

To many, however, the gaudy display of the Exposition, the "pseudo-classic" architectural scheme, and the magnificent Krupp exhibit of instruments of destruction, costing $3,000,000, were tokens of an imperialistic nation. The Pullman Palace Car Company, owner and land-lord of the "model" suburb of Pullman, distributed a leaflet declaring "at an early date the beautiful town of Pullman will be a bright and radiant little island in the midst of the great tumultuous sea of Chicago's population; a restful oasis in the wearying brick-and-mortar waste of an enormous city." A social worker asked "Baron" George Pullman "what means the Company took to ally its employees and other residents of the town with its policies," and he tersely replied: "A clause in every lease enables us on short notice to be rid of undesirable tenants." [15] Smouldering class antagonism burst forth again when Governor Altgeld asserted that the whole Haymarket affair had been a judicial murder and pardoned the surviving anarchists. "The press from coast to coast united in heaping vilification upon the head of the executive who thus opened the gates from within to the 'anarchist snakes.' " [16]

There came a panic and a long period of depression. Representative Lane of Illinois declared in the House: "Mr. Speaker, my people do not have to consult Chevalier, John Stuart Mill, Ricardo, or any other writer to understand their conditions." [17] The unemployment problem was worse in Chicago than in any other locality because of the horde of workmen attracted by the Fair. The sleeping forms of the homeless so thickly littered the damp cold corridors and stairways of the old City Hall that one could scarcely pass through without stepping on them. Workmen smashed windows and insulted policemen in order to be jailed, fed, and warmed. The chairman of a city emergency relief committee declared: "Silence, inaction, or apathy in the midst of such distress as exists in Chicago, at present would be a crime. . . . Famine is in our midst." [18] But even the committee ceased its efforts in a short time. Great demonstrations of the unemployed were made on the lake front, and the American Federation of Labor complained that an order "enforced by the chief of police . . . was to club and brutally maltreat all unemployed who gathered" there.[19]

The noted English journalist, William T. Stead, was so moved by the contrast between the ideals of the "White City" and the increasing labour troubles and hideous slums that he issued a city-wide call for a

mass meeting under Trade Union auspices. Side by side on the stage sat
leading businessmen, labour leaders, city officials, representatives of exclusive clubs, preachers, saloon keepers, gamblers, theological professors,
society women, "madames" from houses of ill fame, judges, and anarchists. Stead asked: "If Christ were to come to Chicago today" what
would he think of it? It was a "disgrace to a civilised country" that it
should be necessary for the unemployed to herd with criminals in finding
no place to sleep except the stone floor of a police station. The veteran
socialist leader, Thomas Morgan, created an uproar by exclaiming: "Now
the veil has been torn aside, and you members of the G.A.R., of the
Y.M.C.A. . . . temperance societies . . . and Daughters of America,
have been able to see the skeletons in your closet. Your labouring men
may assemble peacefully on the lake front, begging for work, and with
the strong arm of the law are driven back into their tenement houses,
that the visitors who come to see the White City might not see the misery
of the Garden City which built it. Here and everywhere the puny voice
of those who suffer and have suffered is refused to be heard, is drowned
out in one way or another, by this awful, hopeless social condition." [20]

At an Interstate Anti-Trust Conference held in Chicago, a resolution
was submitted calling for the nationalisation of the railroads and coal
mines. Thirty Populists of the seventy-seven delegates bolted the convention and adopted the resolution.

The American Federation of Labor held its national convention in
Chicago, and the delegates were greeted by the representative of Chicago
labour with the words: "In the name of that homeless wanderer in this
desert of stone and steel, whose hopeless heart lies leaden in his bosom,
whose brain grows faint for want of food—in the name of that unnecessary product of American freedom and prosperity, the American tramp,
I bid you welcome to the Imperial City of the boundless West." [21]
Thomas Morgan submitted to the convention a resolution calling for
government ownership of all the means of production and carrying the
endorsement of the Illinois Federation of Labor. It was barely defeated.
The Populist proposal calling for a government issue of five hundred
million dollars in greenbacks to put the unemployed to work was endorsed, however.

Laughlin reprinted in *The Journal of Political Economy* an address
of J. Shield Nicholson, "The Reaction in Favour of the Classical Political Economy." Orthodox economics cannot be "stifled by socialism."
"Adam Smith did not invent but discovered the system of natural liberty," and any legislative attempts to interfere with the system are "fore-
doomed to failure." That the system of free contract is the order of
nature has become "more apparent than ever through the application of

the comparative and historical methods to jurisprudence; the proposition that the progress of society is from status to contract has almost acquired the force of an axiom."

Ely and his student, John R. Commons, organised an American Institute of Christian Sociology at Chautauqua, composed of "earnest Christian men," who were impressed by the need of "encouraging . . . among the people of America the study of social questions from both the scientific and Christian standpoint." [22] Henry Drummond came to America again to speak on the divine guidance of the evolutionary process, and to help develop among boys the organisations known as "Boys' Brigades." The objects of the Brigades, secured through "military drill and discipline," were "the advancement of Christ's kingdom among boys and the promotion of habits of obedience, reverence, discipline, self-respect, and all that tends toward a true Christian manliness." [23]

Drummond came to the University of Chicago and was impressed by the startling innovation of summer school, "which made the institution wonderful in the way in which classes go on all the year around." He delivered the convocation address, "Some Higher Aspects of Evolution." "Due to the fact that the theory of development became known to the popular mind through the limited form of Darwinism, the whole subject" of evolution "began out of focus, was first seen by the world out of focus, and has remained out of focus to this present day." The teachers of sociology give the proper viewpoint, "and it is to them one would look for the instruction of the country, in the ways and means of betterment, for the illumination of the pulpit, the leavening of the press, the gradual hallowing even of political life, with rational, scientific, and, above all, feasible ideas of progress." [24]

Small, with George Vincent, vice-principal of the Chautauqua system, published an *Introduction to Society* in 1894. Sociology is "the synthesis of the social sciences," "the philosophy of welfare," an "art." It is "the scientific counterpart of characteristic popular convictions." The purpose of sociology is not the "cure of social disease" but the "development of social health." Socialism was attacked because it means "artificial reconstruction." It was suggested instead that sociologists search for "yet unknown facts and relations" for the improvement of an already healthy society. Defectives, dependents, and delinquents are not "properly members of society," but are "unsocial classes," violators of "the laws of nature or of the state." The work of the "Christian Settlement," the university settlement, was praised. Edward Cummings of Harvard, however, sharply criticised the "scholar in philanthropy." "If, perchance," the university settlement "shall publish itself in papers and reports, let the subscription-gathering details of lectures, concerts, and clubs be supplemented now and then by that marshalling of facts, stronger and stranger than fiction, that shall be beyond the peradventure of cavil, holding the mirror up to city life till the 'other half' shall know the wrongs, and right them, if need be, for very shame." [25]

Ernst Grosse's *The Beginnings of Art* was translated from the German under the editorship of Veblen's friend, Professor Starr. The book, written in a sophisticated, sceptical manner, was an attempt to study art in relation to culture through the art of primitive peoples. The factor characterising a culture is the manner in which the social group earns its living. Other cultural phenomena have been formed and developed under the overwhelming pressure of this factor. The Kaffir belief in spirit, for instance, has grown from an independent root, but its form, the "belief in a hierarchal order of ancestral spirits, is . . . the reflection of the hierarchal order of the living, which is . . . a resultant of the prevailing occupation of cattle-raising, with its warlike and centralising tendencies." The "cultural significance of production" is best revealed in the development of types of the family. Where feminine industries, the saving and care of useful plants, develop, the woman as chief supporter and as mistress of the soil is the centre of the family, and the matriarchal form prevails. But the greater part of mankind has advanced along the masculine industries, hunting for animals and cattle-raising. This tends to the form of a centralised military organisation, and thus comes "that extreme form of the patriarchate in which a woman is a slave without rights under a marital lord clothed with despotic power." By predatory pressure and custom the patriarchal system is imposed upon the matriarchal vanquished with the result that all civilised nations today are "more or less sharply marked with the patriarchal family."

The decisive role of production is revealed also in art, particularly in "personal decoration." With the exception of the Eskimos, primitive peoples "are much more richly and carefully decorated than clothed." Body painting is not primitive clothing but decoration. Red, denoting, as the colour of blood, the effect of war and the chase, is "an important part of ornament, especially in masculine decoration." Scarification, denoting family and rank, is highly desirable. Female virtue, indicated by the use of dress, "marks the culmination of the patriarchal form of the family and society" which "punishes every infidelity on her part as a violation of [the husband's] property rights." Primitive decoration owes its effect to "what it represents." Scars, for instance, are an "honourable evidence" of courage and endurance.

No substantial difference exists between civilised and primitive ornament. "Scars, the very rudest form of barbaric ornament, are worn with pride at the central point of the highest modern culture, and are regarded with corresponding admiration. While the sons of our higher rank honour Australian scarification, the lower classes, after the example of Bushmen, delight in tattooing. We have . . . renounced lip-plugs and nose-sticks; but even our cultivated women do not hesitate" to wear the no less barbaric earrings. "Civilised rouging corresponds to certain kinds of primitive painting. . . . The difference between a gold-mounted bead necklace from Venice and a leathern 'tooth' collar from Australia lies not so much in the form but in the material and the workmanship."

In higher stages of civilisation personal decorations have the more extended and important function of serving for class distinctions. Costumes distinctive of ranks and classes do not exist among really primitive peoples because they have no ranks and classes. These societies approach a state of anarchism, and all the members are about equally poor. Primitive styles remain constant, but in the class cultures fashion is the outcome of dress and rank. A certain style is worn at first by only the highest group, and serves as a mark of class. "For this very reason the lower ranks strive all the more earnestly to acquire the elegant dress, and in the course of time the dress of rank becomes the dress of the nation." The higher classes, always anxious "to distinguish themselves from the lower," then "invent or adopt another special form of dress, and the game is begun anew."

Laughlin wrote for *The Chautauquan* an article called "Economic Effects of Changes in Fashion." Whatever difficulties are created by fashion are only temporary, and its changes are beneficent. They are an "influence in steadying the employing of labourers, and maintaining a continuing production," and are inevitable. The total production of the community cannot be affected by changes in fashion.

Veblen, now promoted to reader, continued to develop what might be a workable socialistic economics. In a sympathetic review of Karl Kautsky's *Der Parlamentarismus, die Volksgesetzgebung und die Socialdemokratie,* he said: "A livelier appreciation of the meaning of the dogma that socialism is the 'next stage in social evolution,' that it will be reached if at all by an evolution from existing forms of social organisation, is bringing into fuller consciousness the implication that socialism is the industrial republic, not industrial democracy, and that the means by which it will do its work must be, if anything, a further development and a perfected form of the means employed by the political republic in its sphere." In conclusion he declared: "Perhaps the first reflection which this change, or growth, will suggest to conservative members of society, is that it renders socialism all the more effective an engine for mischief, the more reasonable it becomes on all other heads than its chief characteristic of antagonism to the institution of private ownership."

William E. Bear had said in his *Study of Small Holdings* that a system of small farms and allotments was not only highly desirable for present tenants, but also for landowners. Veblen remarked in his review: "This matter-of-course solicitude for the interests of the landowners is sufficiently naïve, but it is thoroughly characteristic of the British view of the agricultural question." Such an attitude makes it impossible to remedy the situation. "Involuntarily, if not unconsciously, it is implied that a decline of rents is the sole and inevitable remedy for the depression [in agriculture], but it is at the same time similarly implied that a decline of rents is something approaching a moral impossibility."

Emile Levasseur, a follower of the classical school of economics, wrote a book on American agriculture maintaining, said Veblen, that the complaints of American farmers are "not altogether well grounded. The American farmer has the advantage of low rent, or of a low price of land (which is the capitalised expression of a low rent), and this suggests that the remedy ready at hand for the depression in agriculture in France and other European countries" is a lowering of rents to the true value of land as a means of production. Veblen turned the argument to point out the disadvantages of the American farmer. "When the rule is applied to the farming industry of this country, as the facts of the situation today are applying it with constantly increasing rigour, it affects not so much the relation between tenant and landlord as that between debtor and creditor, and what is of equal significance and is submitted to with equal reluctance, it reduces the nominal value, the value in terms of money, at which the 'independent' farmer's property is capitalised." Levasseur's favourable opinion of the future of American agriculture is described by Veblen as "hopeful without being enthusiastic."

CHAPTER VII

THE demand for government issues of greenbacks to put the unemployed to work culminated in 1894 in the march to Washington of armies of unemployed from all parts of the west. The first and main group, known as the "Army of the Commonweal," was organised by Jacob Coxey, who had been converted to the cause at the great Silver Congress in Chicago the previous year. Chicago was the nerve centre of the movement. The slogan of the armies, "the petition in boots," was suggested by Isaac Hourwich, an exile from Russia and a docent in the department of economics at Chicago. He compared the marchers to the movements of the Russian peasants beseeching the Tsar for relief.

Thirteen armies attempted to get to Washington. In Iowa the attorney for the Northwestern Railroad called for the militia, and threatened that if a train were seized he would send a wild engine with the throttle open to meet it, "and the wreck will solve the problem as to whether we are obliged to carry these men without remuneration." Bellamy gave the armies his blessing, and Populists asked if "the bankers and usurer class, who at the present time so completely dominate our government," can appear before congressional committees, why not this "living petition" of the workingmen? The wife of one of the executed Haymarket anarchists told the Chicago Commonwealers that they had "built America" and they "deserved the good things of the earth." It was claimed that the armies were composed of ignorant, revolutionary foreigners, incurable tramps and hoboes. Hourwich made a thorough investigation with a trained assistant, of one of the two Chicago armies, and declared that most of the members were Americans and were willing to work.[1]

"The ostensible purpose of the 'Army of the Commonweal,'" said Veblen, "has been the creation of a livelihood for a great number of people by means of a creation of employment, to be effected by a creation of capital through the creation of fiat money. That is to say, on the face of it, the heart of the 'movement' is an articulate hallucination." But it marks "a new departure in American methods . . . and a new departure in any people's manners of life and of looking at things does not come about altogether gratuitously." The basis "must be something more vital than a feigned sentiment." The movement was a sign that the basic institution of property was being questioned by a great many people.

" 'Capital,' to this new popular sense, is the 'capital' of Karl Marx" not
"that of the old-school economists or of the market place. The concept of
'property' or of ownership is in process of acquiring a flexibility and a
limitation that would have puzzled the good American citizen of a
generation ago. By what amounts to a subconscious acceptance of Hegelian
dialectic it has come about that an increase of a person's wealth, beyond
a certain ill-defined point, should not, according to the new canon of
equity, be permitted to increase his command over the means of production or the processes which those means serve. Beyond an uncertain
point of aggregation, the inviolability of private property, in the new
popular conception, declines. In Hegelian phrase, a change in quantity,
if it is considerable enough, amounts to a change in kind. A man—still
less a corporation—must no longer do what he will with his own, if what
is classed as his own appreciably exceeds the average. It is competent for
his neighbours to appeal for his guidance to the corporate will of the
community, and in default of an expression of the corporate will the
neighbours in question may properly act vicariously for the community."

This change in conception "means the difference between the civil republic of the nineteenth century and the industrial republic of the socialists, with the gradual submergence of private initiative under the rising
claims of industrial solidarity." But "if the industrial republic is to be
floated in on the wave of sentiment which has carried the Army of the
Commonweal, it will not be the anarchist republic of autonomous com-
munes held together in a lax and dubious federation." The nature of the
comprehensive industrial process forbids such a form. The Commonweal
movement is "but an expression of the fact . . . emerging into popular
consciousness, that the entire community is a single industrial organism,
whose integration is advancing day by day, regardless of any traditional
or conventional boundary lines or demarcations, whether between classes
or between localities."

The substance of the movement "has been furnished by the situation"
but its form has been developed by three influences: first, the protectionists with their fiat prosperity and the greenbackers and bimetallists with
their fiat money; second, the Christian socialists, "the gentler-mannered
spokesmen of the pulpit, whose discourse runs upon the duties of the
rich towards the poor, and of rulers towards their subjects—the duty of a
'superior' towards an 'inferior' class; these bear testimony to the strength
and beauty of the patriarchal relation—the Spencerian relation of *status*."
Veblen was here turning Spencerianism against Spencer, who held that
this interest in the defective was an expression of beneficence which was
the outcome of the life of free contract. The third influence came from
the socialists of the chair, believers in the "divine right of the state,"

with their catchword, "look to the state," and their maxim of "political wisdom" that "the state can do no wrong." This belief in "the divine right of the state" was really the old belief in the divine right of the king. The "change of phraseology marks a step in the evolution of language," but "the spirit remains the same as ever," the "spirit of loyalty, petition, and submission to a vicarious providence." This position has been called state socialism, but it is in principle related to socialism as is the absolute monarchy to the republic. But along with the "industrial paternalism" fostered by these three influences "goes a valuable acquisition in the shape of a crude appreciation of the most striking and characteristic fact in modern industrial evolution." "The changed attitude on an economic question . . . is in substance due to a cumulative organic change in the constitution of the industrial community." Characteristically adding a number of clauses denying that such a change was necessarily in the offing or that it made the existing situation better or worse, Veblen concluded: "To use a Spencerian phrase, advancing 'industrial integration' has gone far enough to obtrude itself as a vital fact upon the consciousness of an appreciable fraction of the common people of the country."

The Commonweal movement was a fiasco, but a more significant disturbance followed it. The famous Pullman Strike, or "Debs Rebellion," said Jane Addams, revealed "as did nothing else that distinct cleavage in society, which a general strike at least momentarily affords." The Pullman Company cut wages approximately twenty-five percent within less than a year, but refused to reduce the rents in the company-owned tenements, maintaining that the two businesses were entirely separate investments. The Chicago Council, the Civic Federation, and the mayor asked the company to arbitrate, and William McKinley, then governor of Ohio, sent his brother to intercede with Pullman, but Pullman said that he had nothing to arbitrate. The American Railway Union, to which some of the Pullman employees belonged, ordered a sympathetic boycott and strike, forbidding members to handle Pullman cars and equipment. The company obtained the assistance of the General Managers Association, which determined the labour policy for twenty-four railroads centring in Chicago. Eugene V. Debs said that the "contest is now on between the railway corporations united solidly on the one hand, and the labour forces on the other." By July 6 only six of the roads entering Chicago had unobstructed service.

A sweeping injunction was issued, which made "the very command" of the union leaders "to their striking men . . . an open defiance of the courts." The principal union officials were held under bail for conspiracy under the Sherman Anti-Trust Act, rearrested for violation of the "untenable" injunction, and charged with contempt of court. At the request of the General Managers Association 3600 United States deputy marshals were appointed, and were paid by the railway companies. President Cleveland declared a state of insurrection existing, and sent troops into Chicago. Altgeld said he was ready to send state militia wherever local officials requested them, but protested against the president's violation of state sovereignty. According to Brand Whitlock, a drunken colonel of the Federal troops expressed his wish that he might order a whole regiment to shoot the strike sympathisers, who were wearing white ribbons, "each man to take aim at a dirty white ribbon." "In one hour," exclaimed Lloyd, the Democratic Party "sacrificed the honourable devotion of a century to its great principles and surrendered both the rights of the states and the rights of man to the centralised corporate despotism to which the presidency of the United States was then abdicated." [2]

The Chicago trade unions appealed to the American Federation of Labor to call a general strike. The Executive Board of the Federation hurriedly convened in Chicago, and issued a statement calling Pullman "a public enemy," and protesting against the "array of armed force" of "brutal moneyed aristocracy." "The people are once more reminded of the immense forces held at the call of corporate capital for the subjugation of labour. . . . The Federal Government, backed by United States marshals, injunctions of courts, proclamations by the President, and sustained by the bayonets of soldiers, and all the civil and military machinery of the law, have rallied on the summons of the corporations." [3]

During the strike the convention of the State Federation of Labor met at Springfield. Morgan's nationalisation measure in its original form was again barely defeated, but Lloyd succeeded in having a modified version passed. In Chicago the Populists nominated Lloyd for Congress. The author of the thirteenth amendment, Lyman Trumbull, had become "convinced that the poor who toil for a living . . . were not getting a fair chance," and supported Lloyd's candidacy, thereby creating a national sensation.[4]

On July 13 the American Railway Union agreed to call off the strike if the men were taken back, but the victors were intent on a complete victory, and for years the strike leaders were hunted down and forced out of whatever jobs they could obtain.[5] In August, Altgeld, after visiting the town of Pullman, asked George Pullman to forgo all back rent up to October 1, to help relieve some six thousand starving people. The state, he asserted, had spent $50,000 to protect Pullman's property, but Pullman did not respond, and Altgeld issued a proclamation calling for relief contributions.[6]

In the issue of *The Journal of Political Economy* for September 1894,

Von Holst published a hysterical article on the strike, "Are We Awakened?" He was wrought up over the "subversive tactics" and aims of the strikers and Altgeld. The American Railway Union was an "arrogant intruder." Compulsory arbitration was the "consummation of the rankest socialism." He deprecated the lack in the troops of more ruthless methods, which might have cowed "all organized labour" for "a good number of years." "Bonaparte said: 'Shooting down one thousand at the right time is saving the lives of tens of thousands in the future.' " Altgeld and his group were "wily mischief-makers," and his protests were "impertinent." With such men in power, "popular sovereignty . . . is a dastardly practical joke, played by the people upon themselves, and the sooner they go to Europe a-begging for some well-behaved prince out of employment the better for them."

In the same issue a note on the strike, apparently written by Laughlin, maintained that immigration and the increase of the labour population were the causes of the trouble. "Immigration [is] bringing in lawless hordes who cannot understand our institutions. . . . When labourers are reducing wages against themselves, it is sheer ignorance to put the cause of it on an employer."

At about the same time the Board of Trustees accepted in behalf of the university a portrait of Rockefeller and the president of the board declared: "The man who devotes his intelligence and his energies to building up and managing a great industry or business is a useful and worthy citizen, and the fortune which he acquires is both the badge and the reward of his usefulness." [7]

Ely was now at the University of Wisconsin. Shortly after the strike was crushed, he was accused by an elected official, the state Superintendent of Public Institutions, of justifying and encouraging strikes and boycotts, of giving advice and aid to striking printers in Milwaukee, of entertaining a walking delegate at his home, and of upholding socialism in his works. The university authorities immediately ordered an investigation into Ely's teachings, and the press generally commended this action. *The Chicago Inter-Ocean* said: "Men who feel that it is their mission to teach socialism have no business in our universities." *The Milwaukee Wisconsin* said: "The state cannot maintain a propaganda directed against the political and social principles embodied in the constitution." The newspaper of the opposite political faith declared: "Great harm can be done by a man in Professor Ely's position with a false system of political economy. . . . If he is teaching false doctrines he should be admonished; if he is right he should be vindicated." *The Baltimore Sun*, however, maintained that Ely was no heretic. It quoted with approval from *The Review of Reviews* that "more than any other professor he preaches the truths, which are instinctively believed by the mass of men."

From the platform of the Chautauqua amphitheatre Bishop J.H. Vincent proclaimed throughout the country Ely's lengthy denial of any heresy. "If true, [the charges] unquestionably unfit me to occupy a responsible position as an instructor of youth in a great university." But "I deny" every one of "these base and cruel calumnies." "I have maintained that even could socialism be organised and put in operation it would stop progress and overthrow our civilisation." Said *The Washington News*, "Such a denial was unnecessary for the many persons who know him, and denials as to his socialistic tendencies were unnecessary for those who know him only through his books." [8]

The commission appointed to investigate the "Debs Rebellion" issued a report which put most of the blame upon the employers. The autocratic control of the Pullman Company was sharply criticised, the use of the injunction was questioned, and the General Managers Association was held up as an "illustration of the persistent and shrewdly devised plans of corporations to overreach their limitations and to usurp indirectly powers and rights not contemplated in their charters and not obtainable from the people or their legislators." They do not have the right to form such an organisation "to fix rates for services and wages, nor to force their acceptance, nor to battle with strikers." The development of the association must lead to the question "which shall control, the government or the railroads, and the end would inevitably be government ownership." As long as the companies are allowed to take joint action to fix wages for their mutual benefit, it "would be rank injustice to deny the right of all labour upon railroads to unite for similar purposes." The commissioners recommended that unions be recognised, that labour contracts forbidding union membership be declared illegal, and that some form of compulsory arbitration be established. [9]

Harper's Weekly, voicing business sentiment, declared that the report constituted a "silent revolution," for "the most momentous stage in every revolution is that which takes place silently in the popular mind." "The principles silently assumed by [the commissioners] throughout the report are the negatives of all those on which civilised society has hitherto rested. Economics in their minds is not science but sentiment. . . . The society to which they look is not the Christian and industrial civilisation which embodies all that history has achieved for man, which reverences the moral law, and applies it by guarding vested rights as sacred, but is a vague dream of a socialistic community, in which every man has an undefined claim upon the property and labour of every other. These principles, we firmly believe, need but to be disentangled from the specious disguises of irrelevant fact and plausible thought which fill this report to be rejected by the strong sense of the American people." [10]

Clark devoted his presidential address before the American Economic Association to denouncing "the modern appeal to legal forces" to adjust wages. Society is organised on the "natural or competitive method of adjusting shares in distribution." Compulsory arbitration is socialism. It "would adjust wages in a way that would depart more or less from the standard set by the productivity of labour." Strikes might be more efficient than individual bargaining in bringing about the natural rate of wages, since "the waste is easily smaller," and the "massed idleness . . . is something that can be measured and, in a practical way, dealt with." But those strikes which demand more than labour creates will fail, and as a matter of fact the "pay that could be secured by a strike is often conceded without one." The competitive "form of society that evolution has secured" is a "dynamic one. Competition is a guaranty of a movement that will satisfy the demands of a healthy optimism. . . . By processes that others control, and by wealth that others own, the labourer will get, in the end, the most valuable personal gains. Mastership and plutocracy, in a good sense, yield by natural law a democratic result, for it is by the wealth that these ensure that the productive power of labour must rise." "Whether we shall retain this system or not is not an open question. We shall have to retain it." "The present result may or may not be harmony" but "the ultimate fruit of it is prosperity." [11]

At the same meeting one of the strike commissioners, Carroll D. Wright, pleaded for what Clark called socialism, maintaining that the action of railway companies and other corporate interests denoted a "silent revolution." The railway companies were supporting an expensive lobby at Washington to pass a pooling measure, supposedly in the interest of shippers. Inevitably the demand will arise, said Wright, "that the government shall take charge of the roads—not purchase them— shall take charge of the roads and out of the proceeds of the transportation business guarantee to the existing stockholders of the roads a small but reasonable rate of dividend. Under such a seductive movement the stockholders themselves, conservative men, men in this hall now, will vote for the striking of the blow. All this, as I have said, will be at the demand and in the interest of the railroads and shippers, and not of the labour involved in carrying on the work of transportation, as the demand of today for the enactment of the pooling bill is alleged to be largely in the interest of the shippers and of the public welfare." Wright wondered whether the pooling lobby would demand "the extension of the same principles to labour, and ask for their employees the status of semi-public servants." It would seem "to be inconsistent to demand even partial governmental control on one side and to insist upon *laissez-faire* upon the other. The dictates of the highest patriotism again demand that there should be consistency in these matters."

Most of the economists who took part in the discussion, Arthur Twining Hadley, Elgin R. L. Gould, Edward W. Bemis, Edward Atkinson, Richmond Mayo-Smith, apparently were uncertain of the meaning of Wright's paper. He remarked: "The motive of my paper has not been recognised fully, I see. There was some irony in it. If there is any state socialism going on under national legislation today, the railways and corporations are carrying it out, and they are doing it in the alleged interests of shippers, with great magnanimity on their part." If freight rates are to be fixed by the measure creating "one great trust" in the business of freighting, then the system ought to be completed "by bringing labour into the arrangement as well as the railways and shippers." Since, "as some claim, we are legislating the railroads out of state socialism," by the pooling measure, "let us legislate labour out of state socialism as well." [12]

Radical changes were threatening, but sociologists and economists disputed at the meeting over the proper boundaries of the several social sciences. Small insisted that sociology was the basis of all the social sciences, Franklin H. Giddings of Columbia that sociology was the master social science, but Simon Patten protested against the right of the sociologist to stake off wide and all-inclusive territories without permission from the economists. The controversy apparently became so futile that William Ashley remarked that the "great thoughts which have affected men's minds, and determined our intellectual attitude, have usually come from men like Darwin or Maine, who have cared but little about the classification of the sciences." [13]

Veblen, now a tutor, wrote an article on "The Theory of Women's Dress," which appeared in *The Popular Science Monthly*. Most apparel is worn for both dress and clothing, but for these radically different purposes differentiation in materials is rapidly progressing. "Physical comfort" and "reputable appearance" are "not to be confounded by the meanest understanding." In the development of apparel dress comes first, and continues to be the dominant consideration. "Clothing" is an afterthought. The principle of adornment was the point of departure in the evolution of dress, but in its naïve, æsthetic sense it plays little part in the modern development.

Dress is an economic fact falling within economic theory, since it is an index of the wealth of its owner, that is, the person who has the discretionary control, not the wearer. Over half the values of dress, especially women's dress, are not owned by the wearer, but the owner and wearer must be organic members of the same economic unit. The principles of men's dress and women's dress are substantially the same, but women's dress is the highest manifestation of the principles. In patriarchal society women's dress indicated the wealth of the man; today it indicates the wealth of the household to which she belongs. But the theory of women's dress implies that she is still actually a chattel.

In modern society the basis of social consideration is the visible pecuniary strength of the social unit. Since woman was originally a pecuniary possession, her function is now to exhibit the pecuniary strength of her unit by a "conspicuously unproductive consumption of valuable goods." Today few articles of apparel contain no waste, and "very many . . . in point of economic principle . . . consist of virtually nothing else." Since the object sought is not waste itself, but the display or appearance of waste in order to show ability to pay; consumers are constantly seeking to obtain wasteful goods at a bargain. Producers seek to lower their cost of production, and often such a fall in price results that the goods cease to serve their purpose, and consumption is transferred to other items showing "the wearer's ability to afford wasteful consumption."

Under the motive of "pseudo-economy" it is a canon of good form that the material must not only show lavish expenditure but also give evidence of the wearer's (owner's) capacity for making it go as far as possible in the matter of display. Thus ability to pay may also take the form of a "peculiar manner of life," or manners, breeding, and accomplishments, obviously impossible to acquire and maintain without the leisure given by long-continued possession of considerable wealth. Good form and manners are valuable because, having no direct economic value, their acquired possession indicates pecuniary ability to waste considerable time and effort. They are evidences of one or more lives spent to no useful purpose and are equivalent to considerable unproductive consumption of goods.

Thus the first principle of dress is "conspicuous waste," and has no exception. Dress must not be economical in the sense of effectiveness as clothing. It is evidence of the ability of the wearer's economic group to pay for things useless to anyone concerned.

A corollary, which amounts to a second principle, is novelty, which underlies fashion. Nothing can be worn which is out of date. A new wasteful trinket or garment must constantly supersede an old one. Dress must give evidence of inability to withstand much wear, and in its highest manifestation—ball dress and apparel for similar ceremonial occasions—the maxim is that "no outer garment may be worn more than once." This principle of novelty and the motive of pseudo-economy are responsible for that ever-changing system of sham and deceptive contrivances which figure so largely and openly in the code of dress. The one exception to the principle of novelty is very expensive heirlooms, which can normally be possessed only by a person of "superior (pecuniary) rank." Such heirlooms evidence the practice of waste through more than one generation.

The third principle is ineptitude, which again has no exception. Dress should appear to hamper and injure the wearer. Pecuniary strength is evidenced not only by an "aggressive wasteful expenditure," but by a "conspicuous abstention from useful effort," a conspicuous incapacity of doing anything useful. Woman's function is to exhibit the unit's capacity to endure "this passive form of pecuniary damage. . . . The modern civilised women's dress attempts this demonstration of habitual idleness, and succeeds measurably." This principle is the reason for the mutilations and handicaps endured by modern women, such as constricted waists and cumbrous skirts. Even women who must earn their living must promote the fiction that they live with no gainful occupation, and they encumber themselves with garments especially designed to decrease their industrial efficiency. Dress must make it apparent "that the wearer is permanently unfit for any useful effort, even after the restraint of the apparel is removed." The principle of adornment in the æsthetic sense is of some economic importance, but it is really a handmaid to the principle of novelty. "The fact that voluntarily accepted physical incapacity" evidences possession of wealth, establishes the futility of reforming dress in the direction of physical comfort. As long as the chance of rivalry in wealth remains, no exigency can permanently set aside the principles of dress, which come down to the great requirement of "conspicuous waste." Protests are of only transient effect at best as long as this economic ground remains. For example, a recent and short-lived movement for physical comfort in dress, as a requirement of good form, was usually more concerned with the show of personal comfort than with the substance. Children's dress closely conforms to that of women, and "the child in the hands of civilised woman is an accessory organ of conspicuous consumption, much as any tool in the hands of a labourer is an accessory organ of productive efficiency."

The social sciences were being influenced by the developments in psychology. Lester F. Ward's *The Psychic Factors of Civilisation*, substantially a restatement of his earlier work, was severely criticised by John Dewey for its contradictory psychology of sensation. In analysing the weaknesses of Ward's position Dewey advocated "a psychology which states the mental life in active terms, those of impulse and its development, instead of in passive terms, mere feelings of pleasure and pain." [14] There was a bitter controversy in psychology between the associationists, or experimental psychologists, who believed, as had Mill, that "consciousness is a mere spectator or onlooker, curiously watching the play of material physiological forces, which it is incapable of controlling or modifying in the least degree," and the apperceptionists, who, maintaining the biological or genetic point of view, believed that "the orderly selective and synthetic activity of consciousness is its essential feature, without which the subject tumbles to pieces as an incoherent series of sensations with nothing to give them unity, and to interpret them into a whole." [15] C. Lloyd Morgan supported the apperceptionists, and set up the canon: *"In no case may we interpret an action as the outcome of the exercise of a higher psychical faculty, if it can be interpreted as the outcome of the exercise of one which stands lower in the psychological scale."* [16] Loeb demonstrated that a purely mechanistic theory would account for the actions of lower forms of life, dispensing with explanations based on any form of purposive conscious behaviour. In attempting, however, to explain away consciousness in human beings on the basis of tropisms, he fell back on the Spencerian psychology, maintaining that "consciousness is only a metaphysical term for phenomena which are determined by associative memory." [17] Veblen was sometimes amused at the seeming needlessness of this concept of associative memory, but he had great admiration for the matter-of-fact directness and simplicity of Loeb's experimentation.

Harper at the university was getting more money, building more structures, and bringing preparatory schools and other colleges into the "university coalition." *The Journal of Sociology* was added to the list of publications, and a member of the department declared that the "sociological method is already beginning to revolutionise the mode of thinking in theology, in exegesis, in church history, in ethics, and in pulpit rhetoric." [18] The evangelist, Andrew Fairbairn, wrote from the university: "Chicago . . . is resolved to outdo the world; and Harper will help it." [19]

Franz Boas, then curator of the Field Museum, was illustrating the function of property as the law of "conspicuous waste" in his ethnological study of the Kwakiutl Indians of British Columbia. Their method of acquiring rank and of distributing property is through the potlatch, whose underlying principle is the "interest-bearing investment of property." The recipient of such a distribution cannot refuse the gift, although it is simply a loan which must be later refunded with one hundred percent interest. "Possession of wealth is considered honourable," and each Indian endeavours "to acquire a fortune" in order to "outdo his rival" by means of a potlatch. "Formerly feats of bravery counted as well as distributions of property, but nowadays, as the Indians say, 'rivals fight with property only.' " Corresponding to the modern banknotes of high denomination are the "coppers," curiously shaped copper plates of little value as copper but worth a great deal in terms of blankets, the standard value. The value of the copper "depends upon the amount of property given away in the festival at which the copper is sold." Its value increases with the number of times it is sold, "since every new buyer tries to invest more blankets in it." Its purchase "brings distinction, because it proves that the buyer is able to bring together a vast amount of property." The never-ceasing rivalry finds "its strongest expression in the destruction of property." If a rival "is not able to destroy an equal amount . . . without much delay, his name is 'broken.' " A feast also counts as destruction of property, and the "neglect to speedily return it entails a severe loss of prestige." This apparently ridiculous, wasteful institution "is founded on psychical causes as active in our civilised society as among the barbarous natives of British Columbia." As if in illustration of this the editor of Boas's first reports on these Indians for the British Association for the Advancement of Science declared, apparently on the basis of Boas's data, that the potlatch is "a custom which has been greatly misunderstood by strangers, who have regarded it as a mere parade of wasteful and ostentatious profusion. . . . A thrifty and aspiring burgess, who at one of these gift-feasts had emptied all his chests . . . and had left himself and his family apparently destitute, could comfortably reflect . . . that he had not only greatly increased his reputation, but had . . . invested all his means at high interest, on excellent security, and was now, in fact, one of the wealthiest, as well as most esteemed, members of the community." Where Boas saw a scheme of predation and waste, the editor saw a scheme of productive efficiency. Similarly Boas declared that the "fraternities," or secret societies which control the life of the community, developed "from customs relating to warfare," but the editor, viewing them as composed of "burgesses" or "the middle class," said that they are "by no means ill-contrived for keeping the government of the tribe permanently in the worthiest hands and bringing men of the first merit into the most influential position." The common people are a "rabble" and "therefore a veritable residuum, composed of feeble-minded or worthless individuals, with, of course, in those tribes which practise slave-holding—slaves and their descendants." [20]

The third and final volume of *Das Kapital* appeared in 1894, and a note which bears all the earmarks of having been written by Veblen was published on it in the March 1895 issue of *The Journal of Political Economy*. "Among the surprises of economic literature is the fate that has overtaken Karl Marx's theory of surplus-value" in this volume of *Kapital*. Marx had said that he would explain the mystery in the third volume, and meanwhile "advocates, expositors, and critics of the Marxian

economics have exercised their ingenuity in futile attempts to reconcile
the theory with obvious facts." This "Marxian dogma of surplus-value
has served the present generation of 'scientific' socialists as the fundamental 'scientific' principle and the keynote of their criticism of existing
industrial relations, and its acceptance (on faith) by the body of socialists,
avowed and unavowed, has contributed not a little to the viciousness of
their attack on the existing order of things. And now . . . the 'Third
Book' comes along and explains with great elaboration . . . that the
whole of that jaunty structure is to be understood in a Pickwickian sense.
It appears now that the need which has been felt for some reconciliation
of the theory of surplus-value with the everyday facts of the rate of
profits is due simply to a crude and gratuitous misapplication of the
Marxian doctrine of surplus-value to a question with which it has nothing to do. That theory has none but the most remote and intangible relation to any concrete facts." The fact for which surplus value stands, surplus product, can be stated without reference to economic metaphysics.
"The full extent of the relation between surplus-value and profits is this
. . . that the aggregate profits in any industrial community at any given
time may also be styled 'aggregate surplus-value.' The rate of surplus-
value bears no tangible relation to the rate of profits. The two vary quite
independently of one another. Nor does the aggregate profits in any
concrete case, in any given industry or enterprise, depend on or coincide
in magnitude with the aggregate surplus-value produced in that industry
or enterprise. For all useful purposes the entire surplus-value theory is
virtually avowed to be meaningless lumber." Veblen was simply attempting to free modern socialism, or Marxism, from any foundations in conventional economics, and thereby to avoid the assaults upon it by conventional economists.

In the same issue Veblen reviewed the Reverend Robert Flint's *Socialism*, and reproved him for his misconceptions concerning the subject.
Flint had attempted to dispose of socialism by citing its various inconsistent definitions, but Veblen declared that modern socialism, whatever
its definitions, stands for an economic fact. Flint attacked the definition
of one dictionary writer that socialism has reference to amelioration. Veblen pointed out that originally the term socialism applied to an upper-
class movement of amelioration, such as that of Robert Owen, and that
therefore Marx and Engels called themselves communists. "In the turbulent years of the forties" they "could no more have classed their propaganda as 'socialism' than Mr. Hyndman and Mr. Morris could class their
activity under the head of 'university settlements.' " Karl Marx maintains, said Flint, that "the value of work should be estimated according
to the quantity of socially necessary labour expended, or in equivalent

terms according to the time which must be on the average occupied in the work." He commented that this was absurd, since a man "may spend ten hours' labour in producing what there is so little demand for, that he will get merely the pay of one hour's work for it." Veblen declared that every socialist would deny this construction. The surplus-value doctrine is "infirm enough to inspire surprise at its wide acceptance," but "Marx was too skilful a dialectician (to say nothing more) to base his economic scheme on so undisguised an absurdity" as Flint's attack implies. He charged Flint with confusing the "socialist concept of capital, as a 'historical category,' [the] productive goods which are held as private property and employed by means of hired labour for the production of profit," with an attack on instruments of production. Veblen said Flint's discussion was abreast of the times "in excluding State Socialism and Christian Socialism . . . from the category of modern socialism," and quoted Flint's summary on Christian Socialism: It "will always be found to be either unchristian in so far as it is socialistic, or unsocialistic in so far as it is truly and fully Christian." Veblen concluded that this "volume of refutations . . . will be accepted as conclusive chiefly by those who are already in a frame of mind to accept the conclusions offered. . . . It . . . might have been more useful, and probably would have met with a more sympathetic acceptance at the hands of intelligent people, a generation ago than today."

Members of other departments began to notice Veblen. James Hayden Tufts met him at an oral examination for a higher degree, and later said of the encounter: "When I entered the room the examination had begun, and someone whom I did not know was asking questions. I thought his speech the slowest I had ever heard. . . . I could not make out the drift, and the questions were formulated so slowly (not hesitatingly) but in such slow steady tempo that it was difficult for me to keep the beginning of the question in mind until the end was reached. But after a while I began to see that here was a subtle mind, penetrating to fundamental issues without disclosing its own views, except the one determination to get to the bottom of things, if possible."

Between Laughlin and Veblen there was a similar contrast as, according to Georg Brandes, existed between John Stuart Mill and the great French critic, Sainte-Beuve: "Mill was a man of almost metallic character, rigid, angular, and immovable; the spirit of Sainte-Beuve, on the contrary, was like a lake, broad, tender, elastic and of great circumference yet moving altogether in little ripples of an undefined and varying size. . . . Mill was, as it were, created to be an authority; his tone was that of one accustomed to command, and . . . he seemed, through the very conciseness and confidence with which he substantiated his results, to repulse every contradiction. Sainte-Beuve, on the contrary, never closed a subject entirely and without reservation, he was never quite catholic, nor quite romantic, nor quite imperial, nor quite a naturalist, one thing alone he was absolutely and entirely—Sainte-Beuve; in other words, the critic with feminine sympathy and ever-lurking scepticism. He was of a tiger race, yet was no tiger. He attached himself thoroughly to no one and to nothing, but he rubbed against everything and the inevitable friction produced sparks. Mill's repugnance to him was like the antipathy of the dog for the cat. It was impossible for Sainte-Beuve to write simply; he could not pronounce a verdict without making it dependent on a whole system of subordinate conditions." [21] But Mill despised Sainte-Beuve, and Laughlin respected Veblen and still thought he would have a great future if he would work in the conventional manner.

Veblen had few students. His languid, conversational manner and the apparent irrelevancy of many of his disquisitions were not conducive to popularity. There was nothing polished about his courses, and the customs, conventions, and requirements of the usual classroom procedure were unknown to him. Students could not profitably or easily take notes, and it was his custom to assign papers to occupy the time. His courses on agriculture appeared dull even to the best of his students, and his course on socialism seemed to consist of abstracts of articles on socialism given in an apparently haphazard way. It was still almost impossible to get from him an exact answer on any question. That he was a man of powerful intelligence was conceded, but he was not considered an inspiring teacher, and his reserve prevented strong personal attachments.

But if Veblen's students were few, he seems to have attracted the abler ones. They liked his free spirit and were impressed by his vocabulary, his erudition, and his impersonal discussions. According to one of his students, Sarah McLean Hardy, he seemed to have read everything, but he quoted most, perhaps, from Chaucer, George Borrow, William Morris, and Cervantes. Another student, Henry Waldgrave Stuart, said of Veblen: "It was his feeling always that a man should follow his bent as the surest guarantee of his accomplishing whatever he might, by any chance, have in him the possibility of doing and becoming. He was never more in earnest about anything than about helping a man to discover his true bent by first drawing him out and then bringing to bear upon the view or interest expressed a unique combination of quizzical scepticism and sympathetic interpretation. He had a very genuine and strong interest in any bold and fresh hypothesis backed by conviction and by evidence honestly sought, whatever the field of inquiry or whoever the inquirer might be."

Students in his course on socialism heard "as much about the practices of the Hopi Indians, the Samurai, the Hebrews of the Old Testament, the Andaman Islanders, and the trading pirates of the North Sea as they did about Populism and Karl Marx." [22] Here his noncommittal attitude was described by one student with admiration: "He had the wonderful faculty of discussing without prejudice and with such fairness an extremely controversial subject," such as socialism, "that the students received not the slightest inkling of his own belief or conviction."

Those students genuinely interested in economic inquiry found in Veblen an invaluable guide. Although nominally he taught no course in economic theory he continually raised questions and made suggestions that led students to question the usefulness of conventional economics. He humorously said to one of the Fellows in the department that "psychological and logical analysis in Economics that did not rest upon and reflect an intimate knowledge of business facts could not be true economic theory." Thus speculations like those of the Austrian school are "only the bottle in which economic theory has been," which means that they "bore the same unsatisfactory relation to economic theory that an empty bottle, or the fragrance of an empty bottle, bore to the desirable substance which the fragrance has led one to suppose the bottle contained." He would not agree that just as liquor "must be contained in a bottle if one is to have it at all, so Economic theory must be held in a logical framework of the so-called psychological type if it is to be intelligible or significant."

But although his influence was growing Veblen was still a tutor. John Dewey, who was two years younger and had obtained his Ph.D. in the same year, came to Chicago as head professor of philosophy. Veblen's Hopkins classmate, Elgin R. L. Gould, came as professor of statistics in the department of economics.

To the members of his family his was a ne'er-do-well's status, and at home his domestic troubles were increasing. Ellen Rolfe's attempts to understand his vagaries only annoyed him. Girl students showed an interest in him and, although their attentions were merely amusing to Veblen, they were serious to Ellen. Veblen sometimes "teased" his wife in rather ponderous fashion. In his translation of *The Science of Finance*, for example, he acknowledged assistance from a girl student but ignored the assistance of his wife, who had transcribed the manuscript in longhand as he translated. When he was working on a project, he would read and discuss the matter with her for months, until he was full of his subject, but if she did not retire quickly enough when he wished to be alone he was likely to get angry and say something to offend her.

Veblen never had any desire for children. According to his wife, when it looked for a time as though they might have a child, he fell into a panic and told his wife that she would have to go back to her home and stay in seclusion until it was over. He thought he was not the proper sort of man for a father. He once remarked to a friend that anthropologically the family consists of mother and children, and the father's place in it is of little importance.

CHAPTER VIII

CHARLES YERKES continued his "Napoleonic banditries." "Straphangers pay the dividends." His campaign of financial and political exploitation astonished even the most seasoned representatives of "big business." In 1895 the Crawford bill, allowing the city councils to grant street railway franchises for ninety-nine years instead of twenty years, was safely piloted through the legislature of Illinois with the aid of the leaders of both parties. Altgeld vetoed it, despite the offer of a huge bribe and political preferment. "I love Chicago," said his veto message, "and am not willing to forge a chain which would bind her hand and foot for all time to the wheels of monopoly and leave her no chance of escape." [1]

Chauncey Depew informed the students at the university: "This institution, which owes its existence to the beneficence of Rockefeller, is in itself a monument of the proper use of wealth accumulated by a man of genius. So is Cornell, so is Vanderbilt, and so are the older colleges, as they have received the benefactions of generous, appreciative, and patriotic wealth." [2] Harper said in June 1895: "Any statement to the effect that the university has in any way restricted the liberty of its professors, in the declaration of their opinions, or in the performance of their duties as free citizens, I declare to be absolutely false." Every member should work for better government, but care "should be taken . . . not to mistake popular pleading for scientific thought." When a faculty member makes this confusion, it is time for him to leave, for he has "mistaken the purpose" for which he was appointed and has forgotten that "to serve the university we must employ scientific methods and do scientific work." [3]

Then occurred the celebrated case of Edward W. Bemis, who was unable to secure a reappointment as associate professor of political economy in the extension department. His friends claimed that because of his views on public utilities he had acquired the enmity of "the notorious person whom common fame in Chicago credits with having done more than all other men combined to corrupt the municipal politics of that city, by systematic bribery in the interest of street railway corporations." [4] When the new *American Journal of Sociology* requested subscriptions, it received in reply such comments as "I can look for no lasting good from a work that is conducted by an educational institution founded by the arch-robber of America and which already, by its treatment of Professor Bemis, exhibits a determination to throttle free investigation of sociological or economic subjects wherever there is any danger of running counter to plutocratic interests." [5] The public outcry became so great that Harper reiterated the sanctity of freedom of opinion, and the university issued a circular containing statements by Harper, Small, and Nathaniel Butler, head of the extension department.

The local press supported the university. *The Chicago Journal* asked: "What if one of the reasons of Dr. Harper's action was the refusal of a prominent capitalist to contribute to the university's endowment, as long as it had teachers like Bemis in its faculty? What businessman would retain a subordinate whose obtrusive vapourings were interfering with the financial stability of his establishment? . . . The duty of a professor who accepts the money of a university for his work is to teach the established truth, not to engage in the 'pursuit of truth.' " [6] *The Social Economist*, whose editor, George Gunton, was accused of being subsidised by Standard Oil, declared: "The University of Chicago is a private, not a socialist institution. . . . There is no more reason why those who believe in the present industrial institutions should be surreptitiously made to support teachers of Socialism than there is that Catholics should employ Protestants as priests or Jews instal Christians to preside in their synagogues." [7] Hourwich had left the previous year, and had accepted a position at Columbian University in Washington, but *The Elgin News* said: "Chicago University seems to be singularly unfortunate in its professors of political economy. . . . Dr. Isaac Hourwich is debarred from teaching because he is an avowed socialist, an infidel, a sympathiser with the People's Party. No self-respecting institution should retain for an hour among its lecturers one who holds such dangerous opinions. . . . While the prompt action of President Harper saved the University from serious harm, he should be warned against nominating men to professorships, until their fitness is fully ascertained. It is better to lock the door before the house is burglarised." [8]

Rockefeller gave the university $3,000,000, and a grand celebration was held in honour of the event.[9] Laughlin asserted in a public address that no one could say Rockefeller had "accumulated millions in any way that interfered with the accumulation of others." [10]

The Southern Pacific was attempting to get through Congress a bill providing that the Central Pacific's debt to the government be liquidated in eighty years with a two percent rate of interest. Ambrose Bierce said that Collis Huntington, who was piloting the bill, was "not altogether bad. Though severe, he is merciful. He tempers invective with falsehood. He says ugly things of the enemy, but he has the tenderness to be careful that they are mostly lies." [11] According to the historian, Thomas Beer, of the "mauve decade," there was in the Eastern mind a pleasant confusion between the military engineers, surveyors, and draughtsmen who dragged the Western railroads into being, sweating in the deserts, and the owners and promoters, contemplating the results in an office.

Keir Hardie addressed a Labour Day meeting held under the auspices of the Chicago Trade Union Congress. Debs received an unparalleled ovation upon his release from jail. When the Secretary of the Treasury, who supported Cleveland's gold policy, spoke in Chicago, the *Chicago Record* described him as "coming fresh from the banquet table of Wall Street Goldbugs to tell the idle and the starving workingmen of Chicago" to submit to robbery.[12] Carroll D. Wright told a meeting of Commercial Clubs at St. Louis, according to an account in *The American Journal of Sociology*, that "in the future employers would be held responsible before the law and at the bar of public opinion for strikes; and that it would be held to be the duty of employers during prosperous times to set aside funds for the payment of wages in times of adversity." [13]

Such questioning of business control was directed not against the competitive order of property, but against the power of the holders of the large aggregates of wealth. This fact is illustrated by Lester F. Ward's discussion of "Plutocracy and Paternalism" in *The Forum*. "Society has made wealth a measure of worth. . . . Absence of means is . . . made to stand for absence of merit" and is attributed to defects of character. The only force that works against this attitude is the "wholly dissimilar feeling . . . sympathy," which "is not rational, but illogical." Wealth gives "superiority; and the strongest craving of man's nature is, in one way or another, to be set over his fellows." It is futile to attempt to eradicate the "passion for proprietary acquisition"; almost all will admit that it will "continue to be useful to the end of our present industrial era." The amassing of colossal fortunes is not vicious in itself, since the activity required "stimulates industry and benefits a large number." "The first law of economics is that everyone may be depended upon at all times to seek his greatest gain. It is both natural and right that the individual should be ever seeking to acquire for himself and his; and this rather irrespective of the rest of the world." Natural law once took the form of physical strength; today it is embodied in "business shrewdness." But since this propensity, if allowed to function freely, must eventually destroy society and competition itself, plutocracy, which is "the modern brigandage," must be put down by the strong arm of the state as is physical brigandage. In modern society natural law "instead of developing strength, either physical or mental, through activity incident to emulation . . . tends to parasitic degeneracy through the pampered idleness

of the favoured classes." Government fails to protect the weak and devotes all its energies to protecting the strong, as witness the existence of
monopolies. "Personalities and vituperations are . . . out of place,"
however, since "these things . . . are inherent in the nature of man,
and not . . . peculiar to any class."

Ward was publishing in *The American Journal of Sociology* a series
of papers outlining the relationship between social teleology and his psychology of sensation. He protested against "a certain school of biologists
who are somewhat disposed to sneer at the old-fashioned study of systematic botany and zoology." "To the regular course of the social phenomena as determined by the laws of evolution, we must conceive added
a new force limiting and directing these into special channels and for
special ends." This is the "teleological force, the abstract conception of
which is familiar to all, having formed the basis of theological philosophy," and which he now called "social telesis." The "law of causation"
of science becomes the "law of the sufficient reason" of philosophy.
"Meliorism—the perpetual bettering of man's estate" is "the true doctrine." When the series was published as a book with the title *The Outlines of Sociology*, it was dedicated to Small, "The First to Draw Attention to the Educational Value of My Social Philosophy, the Staunch
Defender of My Method in Sociology."

Veblen's friend, W.I. Thomas of the sociology department, was expressing scepticism of the Spencerian approach to an explanation of culture. Anthropology, he said, "has undergone a change well illustrated by
the difference between the biological botany of today, and the 'herbarium'
botany of the past." Today the primary interest is in "the laws of
growth," the laws of development within a culture, not in classification.
Thomas worked in terms of Loeb's tropisms, but interpreted them in a
manner more akin to Morgan's and Dewey's psychology and philosophy
than to Loeb's metaphysics of sensation. "Differences in temperament in
individuals and races must be regarded as due to the same cause as positive and negative heliotropism or chemotropism in plants and animals,
namely, chemical constitution. The temperament, character, or genius
of a people predetermines within certain limits the spirit of its institutions; it is the direct exponent of the quality of race irritability, and apparently more fundamental, persistent, and inimitable than intellectual
traits. The animal in the protozoan period is played on solely by the
forces of external nature," but in human societies "language and memory
give every member of the group opportunity to play upon the nature of
every other member of the group. . . . Words, ideas, and sentiments
are substituted for light, gravity, and acid." [14]

Thomas gave an interesting group of anthropological courses—Comparative Institutions of Primitive People, Comparative Technology, Animism. The last he described as a discussion of "primitive religious ideas and ceremonials, their relation to other psychic and social activities, and their survival in modern custom and culture." His course on Primitive Art treated of "the origins of the æsthetic sense, and its developmental relation to social consciousness," and included in its scope "mutilation, artificial deformation, tattooing, dress, ornament, painting, poetry, the dance, music, sculpture, architecture, technology, sport, and ceremonial with reference to their æsthetic content." The Somatic and Psychic History of Woman dealt with woman's "somatic, psychic, and æsthetic organisation . . . in relation to her social status—economic, religious, political, legal, technological, and ceremonial." [15]

An anthropological viewpoint which was supposed to revolutionise the social sciences was being spread by Carlos Closson, an instructor in the economics department. He taught the "theory" courses, but was more interested in the subject called anthropo-sociology. The outstanding spokesmen of this subject were Friedrich Ammon and G. de Vacher Lapouge, whose work was presented by Closson in articles in the economic journals, particularly *The Journal of Political Economy*. Lapouge, according to an abstract of Closson's, declared: "Social progress depends primarily upon the quality of population. The quality of population is determined from generation to generation by selective forces, most of which are social rather than natural. . . . The hope for permanent human betterment lies in systematic selection." Two stocks are dominant in Europe, the dolichocephalic, blond *Homo Europæus*, and the brachycephalic, brunet *Homo Alpinus*. All the worthwhile qualities, from the standpoint of an aggressive temperament, are attributed to *Homo Europæus*, a type held to predominate also in the United States. "At its best . . . it is more domineering, enterprising, and self-reliant than other races. . . . Its ambition and courage [are] more impetuous. . . . It understands better how to gain wealth than to save it." "Progress is its most intense need. In religion it is Protestant; in politics it demands mainly freedom for individual activity. It sees far ahead its own interests and those of its nation and race, and aspires to the highest destinies." *Homo Alpinus*, on the other hand, "follows tradition and 'good sense' . . . and is suspicious of progress. In religion he is . . . Catholic, in politics he invokes the protection of the state and tends to attack those who surpass the level of mediocrity. He sees clearly his immediate personal and family interests, but the frontiers of his country are often too broad for his vision. With the cross types, the egoism of the brachycephalic is often emphasised by the energetic individualism of the dolichocephalic and the sentiment of family and race is weakened; there follow extreme cupidity and all the vices of the bourgeois." Military selection works well, but not economic selection, which raises wealth as the standard of efficiency rather than warlike prowess.[16]

Spencer completed his *Synthetic Philosophy* in 1896 with the publication of the third volume of *The Principles of Sociology*. Its last two sections, "Professional Institutions" and "Industrial Institutions," were, like all the rest, supposed to show that the course of evolution is an inevitable process leading from a necessary condition of servility, the militant state, through unperceived "small accumulated changes" to the ordained goal of absolute free contract, which is identified with the industrial state.

The section on "Professional Institutions" dealt with the occupations of physician, surgeon, dancer, musician, orator, poet, actor, dramatist, biographer, historian, man of letters, man of science, philosopher, judge, lawyer, teacher, architect, sculptor, and painter, all directly the outgrowth of the function of the priests as they served, worshipped, and propitiated the powerful living chieftains and the more powerful dead chieftains in the form of gods. Necessarily the "priesthood are distinguished above other classes by knowledge and intellectual capacity," which means "cunning, skill, and acquaintance with the natures of things." Since the priest's power is increased by "those feats . . . which exceed the ability of the people to achieve or understand . . . he is . . . under a constant stimulus to acquire the superior culture and the mental powers needed for those activities which we class as professional." Furthermore, since the priesthood is supported by other classes, it is a leisure class and its members can devote time and energy to that intellectual labour and discipline which are required for professional occupations. The modern scientist is the logical heir of the medicine man or priest. The priest progressed from his duty of "transmitting traditional statements concerning ghosts and gods" to giving instruction in natural things. Thus has been formed the great body of science, knowledge, arts, and the highly developed and integrated industrial processes. State interference would disturb this beneficent, unknowable process.

Industrial institutions meant business institutions to Spencer. The whole of industry today forms an aggregate of mutually dependent parts. Money originated in the militant state through "the wish . . . of subordinating others by outdoing them in decoration," but today it enormously facilitates exchange, without which industrial organisation is impossible. Spencer denounced the British Trade Union Congress for approving by a four to one vote "the wholesale nationalisation of property (which necessarily implies confiscation)." Although there is a possibility of socialism in the near future, and of other rhythmical changes, it is inevitable that the state of absolute free contract will ultimately be reached. Charles Zueblin, a colleague of Veblen, commented that "the Synthetic Philosophy has proceeded, serenely indifferent to the progress of the world." [17]

Patten's *Theory of Social Forces* was a variant of Spencerianism. Using a crude form of the hedonistic-associational psychology, Patten spoke of the development of mankind from a "pain economy" to a "pleasure economy," instead of from the militant system to free contract. Difficulties in the modern order are ascribed to the fact that it is a transitional stage between the old order of pain and the new order of pleasure. The moral man is the self-regarding man, basing his action on "utilitarian calculations." The pleasure economy is destined to be "normal progress" since it is the one in which the natural man, intent solely on pleasure, will be fully adjusted to his environment. There will be no need of the governmental restraints necessary in the pain economy, since in a pleasure economy the "economic bonds" of self-interest are sufficient to "unite individuals into communities, and communities into a social commonwealth." This is substantially Spencer's ideal system of free contract. "The exchange of goods and the growth of credit would develop in individuals and in communities the feeling of honour, the love for truth, and the desire to live up to their contracts." All other virtues, such as "the sacredness of property and the right to undisturbed possession of the means of production," depend upon this development of economic welfare in the individual. Patten criticised the philanthropy of "democratic ideals," which would give the benefits of civilisation to all regardless of the merit or demerit of the individual. These ideals are "static elements," for "they retard the displacement of the less efficient classes and restrict the activity of the more efficient." Reformers forget that "the evils and pains of life" come from the environment, or from the defects of human nature, not from the oppression of men. They are silent about the "pains and obstacles to progress which . . . represent the cost of nature's bounties."

Arthur Twining Hadley's *Economics: An Account of the Relations between Private Property and Public Welfare* became the most popular textbook, supplanting Walker's. The preface proclaimed that it was "an attempt to apply the methods of modern science to the problems of modern business." Hadley felt that the traditional method, which formed the basis of Mill's *Principles of Political Economy*, had been modified by Spencer's principle of natural selection and the modern use of the hedonistic-associational psychology. The details of economic theory expounded in the book remained much the same. Hadley asserted in the opening chapter that titles to property "are more likely to be productive than not, because our industrial arrangements are such that, if men fail to use their capital for things the community needs, they lose money and are eliminated from control of the next period of production." He said that "to the medieval economist the businessman was a licensed robber; to the modern economist he is a public benefactor. . . . So confident are we of the substantial identity of interest between the businessman and the community as a whole, that we give our capitalists the freest chance to direct the productive resources of the community." The labourer is the logical descendant of the ancient slave and the medieval villein. Slavery enforced the habits of due subordination and continuous exertion necessary for production. The institution of property is historically a form of slavery. In ancient days the successful fighters rather than the industrious workers enjoyed the most property. This state, however, marked "the beginning of a higher civilisation." It allowed "domination to take the place of extinction as a habit in peace and a purpose in war," and thereby increased the wealth of the community. It exempted "the children of the fortunate few from the burdens of want which, if equally shared, would drag the whole race down" and prevent progress. The successful acquirer "is led to discourage . . . this method . . . among his immediate neighbours, and to make usage, rather than force, the basis on which society is to recognise rights of possession."

The Austrian theory of value only carries to its logical conclusion the "commercial theory," according to which "the competitive system serves the economic interests of society so well, that the first rule of business morals is to conform thereto." Hadley endeavoured to answer Marx's theory of surplus value on the basis of the Austrian theory, as had Flint. If the producers of objects are paid according to their labour but not according to the social necessity established by the market, "we take away all inducement for the efficient or wise application of labour and capital." If they are paid according to the social necessity, then we have "the commercial theory."

Attacks upon association psychology were increasing. In his celebrated article, "The Reflex Arc Concept," Dewey attempted a formal disposal of the subject on the basis of his action theory. "Instead of a psychical state which is dependent upon a physical excitation, investigation shows in every case an activity which in advance must determine where attention is directed and give the psychical state the very content which is used in identifying it. . . . What we see, hear, feel, taste, and smell depends upon what we are doing, and not the reverse. In our purposively organised life we inevitably come back upon the previous conduct as the determining condition of what we sense at any one moment, and the so-called external stimulus is the occasion for this and not its cause." [18]

Caldwell's lectures as Shaw Fellow at Edinburgh were also arguments for an action standpoint. Philosophy has "the duty of squaring itself not with the atomistic, mechanical, physical naturalism of the eighteenth century, but with the organic, evolutionary, biological, and psychical naturalism of the nineteenth. It may be recognised at the end of this century that the whole genesis-philosophy of Evolution is a piece of unproved and unprovable dogmatism. Evolution refers to process, and not to origin." According to biology, "form—not to mention species—is undergoing constant modification and evolution and adaptation to the endless wants of that mysterious effort after life which characterises all animal beings. . . . Function, structure, type, the organic idea, species itself, can be understood only as the varying expression of evolving life." Consciousness does not mean "a mere intellectual awareness of things. . . . It is far too dynamical a thing for that. Consciousness is always the consciousness of some activity or other." "Thought is only *one* of *many* organic activities," and modern psychology studies "apperception as *always accompanied* by a physical reaction movement which we know from biology to be also a life preservative movement. In thinking we are all conscious of the sense of effort, located somewhere in the head, to adapt our whole organic and mental activity to the perception of the object we are studying in its real connexion as opposed to its many possible connexions. . . . Our whole mental system rejects more or less deliberately or consciously any conception or idea or set of ideas which does not fit in with its established order, which is, as far as possible, the order of ideas most calculated to call forth the action which best furthers our organic development." Action should therefore be the "supreme fact" for philosophy because "action—human, intelligent or motived action—comprises in itself not only mere physical and organic movement but feeling and knowledge." To the disgrace of philosophy, "man's reflective doubts about his actions have often been considered more important than his actions themselves. Action . . . expresses knowledge and something more than knowledge." The development of philosophy should start from the proposition, "I act, therefore I am," as well as from the traditional proposition, "I think, therefore I am." [19]

Veblen persuaded Henry Waldgrave Stuart, who was doing work with Dewey also, to publish in *The Journal of Political Economy* his analysis of hedonism in economics. In the first article, "Hedonistic Interpretation of Subjective Value," Stuart criticised the assumption of Hadley and Patten that "subjective valuation is a process of calculating pleasures and pains, after the manner so elaborately specified by Bentham and his disciple Jevons," and later formulated in economics on the pattern of Weber's law. "Pleasure (or desire for pleasure) is . . . not itself a primary fact of consciousness. . . . Pleasure is the feeling concomitant of certain states or modes of activity. . . . Pleasure in other words results from the attainment of some already existing end of action; it is not itself an end." Man always pursues "actual objective ends." In this article Stuart held that the body of Austrian economics was not fundamentally vitiated by the weaknesses of hedonism, since there was no organic connexion between the two. But in the next two articles, "Subjective and Exchange Value," he came to the conclusion that all the variants of received economics are founded on hedonism, an unknowable pleasure-pain calculus, rather than on the simple basis of the businessman's activity. The seller's valuation is as "real a fact and in itself and for its own purposes as ultimate and natural as any other valuation in the complex economic process," and is not to be obscured by recourse to the inscrutable concept of "normal value," which is in reality market value. "The value of goods is not the use which their possessor may make of them, not what he may do with the goods, but what the goods are able to do to him, and this conception of well-being, whether in this case consciously so or not, is essentially hedonistic. Subjectivity, then, according to the Austrian usage, implies a virtual reference to sensation, and subjective exchange value, *qua* subjective, must accordingly be expressed in terms of future enjoyment." The older classical school represented by Mill and Cairnes also had a hedonistic point of view, since "they have been inclined to regard seller's valuation as in the long run the resultant and accurate representation of the more ultimate or 'original' valuations which labour and abstinence place upon the suffering and irksomeness which they respectively involve, and they have accordingly neglected, and so misrepresented, the psychology of the seller's *own* valuation process." This hedonistic standpoint "prevented an interpretation of capitalist's cost and valuation as self-centred psychological phenomena," an interpretation in terms of the "universal process of the pursuit of Ends and the adaptation of Means thereto." "Pain is incidental to a discrepancy, pleasure to the degree of correspondence, between the end ideally in view and the end which the means at hand are adequate to secure." [20]

"In the writing," said Stuart, "I had [Veblen's] constant encouragement and, in the main, I think, his approval. I distinctly recall that in some remarks on the subject of 'normality' I followed the lead of things I had heard him say. But for his patience and encouragement, the articles would not have been written at all, though he, of course, would not have written in such a manner, himself." Stuart's economic views were not the accepted ones, and it was not long before he turned to the philosophy department.

Veblen's fortunes were slightly improving. In November 1895, while the uproar over the Bemis case was at its height, he wrote Miss Hardy, then teaching at Wellesley: "I don't know yet what the chances of my reappointment for next year may be. It is not altogether improbable that I may be dropped from the budget after the manner of Bemis, when it is made up next month. To make the way plain and smooth, I have struck for higher wages; though I am pretty nearly persuaded that the work I do is worth no more than what I am paid now." He was not dropped, however, but was promoted to instructor. He was then thirty-nine. When Closson left, Veblen was assigned the "theory" courses, which were required for advanced degrees.

Veblen was thinking of writing a book. Apparently he had planned a book on socialism some time before, but had dropped the idea. In his letter to Miss Hardy he said, in reference to the course on socialism: "As we go over the ground again this fall it strikes me again that I should like to write something sometime, and I think I see more clearly what I want to say, too. But I shall certainly do nothing about it for another year. I have little time to spare for loafing, and it will be a long time before I shall get to it, if I ever do. The first volume on the list is *The Theory of the Leisure Class,* and I have taken that up in a small way this month. I am putting in an hour or two a day on it, and have to neglect the class work in order to do that. I have written part of the introductory chapter—which would perhaps make some twelve or fifteen small pages."

In December 1895 he wrote to Miss Hardy: "*The Leisure Class* was of course shelved while the December *Journal* took the floor and went through its customary motions," but the book "is on the boards again. . . . I sit here spinning out the substance of this high theoretical structure. As the writing proceeds, or rather in the attempt to proceed, I find myself embarrassed by an excessive invention of unheard-of economic doctrines more or less remotely pertinent to the main subject in hand; so that, after having written what will perhaps make some fifty or sixty pages when revised, I have not yet come in sight of the doctrine of conspicuous waste, which is of course to constitute the substantial nucleus of this writing." In February 1896 he mentioned to her the "opaque fact" that "in the last three weeks, the *Leisure Class* has been in abeyance, having achieved nothing beyond contributing some half-dozen sheets of handwriting to the waste-basket."

Veblen induced Miss Hardy and most of his abler students to read extensively in anthropological works. He wrote her: "As for the anthropological reading, which I have inveigled you into, I do not know that it will be of much direct use, but it should be of some use in the sense of an acquaintance with mankind. Not that man as viewed by the anthropologist is any more—perhaps he is less—human than man as we see him in everyday life and in commercial life; but the anthropological survey should give a view of man in perspective and more in the generic than is ordinarily attained by the classical economists, and should give added breadth and sobriety to the concept of 'the economic man.' "

Veblen's wife had left him and taken up a claim in Idaho, but he constantly urged her to come back. He casually informed Miss Hardy: "Mrs. Veblen is farming in Idaho. Her health seems slightly improved, but she does not seem well content."

In the summer of 1896 Veblen went to Europe to visit William Morris, whom he considered one of the greatest men of the nineteenth century, but the meeting was a disappointment. Morris had ceased to be an outstanding figure in English socialism, and was occupying himself with attempts to restore the art of printing as it existed before the introduction of efficient machinery.

At that time, however, the International Socialist Congress met in London, and the Fabians laid down their policy of "evolutionary," as against revolutionary socialism. This change in tactics was made prominent by a controversy carried on in the *International Journal of Ethics* between the Fabians and the Hegelian philosopher, Bernard Bosanquet, one of the strongest opponents of collective devices. In the United States a similar change was taking place. Up to 1896 the socialist movement was considered "more or less of an exotic bearing the stamp largely of German socialism," but it was developing now in accordance with Western conditions.[21]

In July the university celebrated its fifth anniversary. Rockefeller visited the school for the first time, and students sang to him: "John D. Rockefeller, wonderful man is he, Gives all his spare change to the U. of C." [22] "Gratitude," said a student spokesman, "is too narrow a word for the deeper, more vital feeling we bear toward him whose work we know is daily remoulding, deepening, sharpening the whole inner meaning and character of our lives." Head Dean Judson declared in behalf of the faculty: "The same largeness of view which characterises modern business is essential for the equipment of modern education. And we greet our founder as one whose sagacity clearly grasped this vital thought —the thought which underlies the University of Chicago." For the trustees it was said: "Mr. Rockefeller is a modest man, and may well ask to be excused from the laudations and congratulations that attend public-spirited and generous acts: but *this greatest and wisest act* so far transcends in importance the average benefaction that we are justified in expressing tonight our appreciation of *its benefits, its spirit, its wisdom, its enduring character,* and the evidence it furnishes that he regards the possession of great wealth as a public trust, as well as a stewardship for which he must give an account to his Maker, to his own conscience, and to the age in which he lives." Harper expressed official gratitude to Rockefeller for his large gifts, inspired by "the love of Christ and of humanity which filled his soul"; to the other donors, including Yerkes and Marshall Field; and to God, "Who prompted the founder's heart to undertake this gigantic work." [23]

On the Fourth of July, addresses were made in "enforcement of the idea that true religion and true patriotism are one." A detachment of the National Guard presented the national colours to the university, and Harper said: "An education which does not carry with it the inculcation of patriotic feeling is a narrow and injurious education. . . . The work of the army and the work of educational institutions are after all closely related. . . . Today the First Regiment of the Illinois National Guard is the teacher, and the University of Chicago is the pupil." [24]

At the convocation Bernard Moses, professor of political economy at the University of California, and then lecturing in the summer school, delivered a patriotic address called "The Conditions and Prospects of Democracy." He attempted to demonstrate that, because of the natural right of property, the "democratic form of society disappears under normal social development." "With no restrictions placed upon the movements of the individual members," in the original state of democratic equality, "the fittest in the several lines of activity acquire positions of advantage, and the less fit fall behind or are crowded to the wall." Every step away from the simplicity and equality of the early democratic agricultural stage towards the complexity of modern urban society is marked by an increasing inequality of material conditions. Government might aid this process, as it has done in the past by "extensive grants of property" and "special exemptions," but this is not essential since "unequal powers in the presence of common opportunities for gaining wealth give . . . unequal possessions." "As a result of free social progress, society, in the course of time, inevitably becomes marked by classes, becomes undemocratic, and this in spite of non-recognition of classes by law." In America there are no "conspicuous obstacles to change," and the country "appears to be drifting towards a state of society less democratic than that of the present." For the weak this means many lives "burned out by an electric current they are unable to bear." This evolution to the inevitable imperial state of subordination should be aided by inculcating a strong religious faith and by an "awakening of the patriotic conscience." [25]

That summer the presidential nomination conventions were held, and the Republicans chose William McKinley. His guiding genius was Mark Hanna, who believed that "some men must rule," and "the great mass of men must work for those who own." To him "life meant war . . . on business associates, on . . . employees, on the State itself." [26]

The Democratic convention was held in Chicago. Fiery attacks were made on Cleveland's financial policies, and the platform demanded free silver. Other sections of the document criticised the Supreme Court for declaring the income tax law unconstitutional, denounced the arbitrary interference of Federal authorities in local affairs as a "crime against free institutions," and objected to "government by injunction as a new and highly dangerous form of oppression by which Federal Judges . . . become at once legislators, judges, and executioners." [27]

Altgeld was the dominant figure in the convention. *Harper's Weekly* wrote of him: "One could not help marking him, at short notice, as the most dangerous influence in the convention—the stamp of agitator who, when the bludgeon had failed of its full work, would be ready with his poisoned knife, and who, in leading a victory-drunken mob, would not hesitate to follow pillage with the torch." [28] His foreign birth prevented his nomination, and the choice went to Bryan after he delivered his famous "Cross of Gold" speech. The Populists, whose program was prepared by Trumbull in Chicago, also chose Bryan. "I feel this year we are squarely aligned," wrote one of the correspondents of Senator Allen, a radical leader. "The honest yeomanry of the land against the pampered owners of wealth." [29]

The Democratic platform was denounced by Republican spokesmen as containing declarations "in favour of free riots," "warfare against the courts," and attacks on "the integrity and independence of the judiciary." [30] Laughlin wrote anonymously a daily column in the Chicago *Times-Herald*, paralleling one in the same journal by W. H. Harvey, whose silverite *Coin's Financial School* was the Bible of the Democratic Party.[31] In the masthead of every issue of *Harper's Weekly* appeared the words: "The Nation's honour must be preserved." Democrats in the East attempted to argue free silver on economic grounds, but the Republicans insisted on making morality the main issue. A writer in *The International Journal of Ethics* commented: "The extreme Republican press endeavoured to take the position that nearly one-half of the American people had gone morally wrong; that the sole issue was one of the Ten Commandments; that the debtor class was trying to cheat the creditor, or, most mildly, the South and West attempting to oppress the North and East." [32]

Altgeld was even more vituperatively attacked than Bryan. Chicago was the real headquarters of the Republican party because of its proximity to the doubtful agrarian states, and Theodore Roosevelt in a speech there said Altgeld was one who would "connive at wholesale murder," who "condones and encourages the most infamous of murders," and who would "substitute for the government of Washington and Lincoln, a red welter of lawlessness and dishonesty as fantastic and vicious as the Paris Commune." [33] Lyman Abbott denounced from the pulpit "the crowned heir and worshipped deity of the anarchists of the North-west." [34] In a box at the head of one of Altgeld's speeches *The Times-Herald* placed Laughlin's comment: "If the governor's figures of the condition of the treasury were correct, the speech is unanswerable, but he has deliberately lied and given false figures." [35]

Under the threats and guidance of Hanna big business openly supported McKinley, "the advance agent of prosperity," and the wealthy deserted the Democratic party as never before. Insurance companies intimated to Western debtors that with McKinley's election five-year extensions on mortgages would be granted. The banks exercised every conceivable form of pressure. Capitalists gave manufacturers large orders, to be executed only if McKinley were elected. On the week-end preceding the election employees were given notice that they could not return if Bryan won.[36] Altgeld declared the Democratic party "was confronted by all the banks, all the trusts, all the syndicates, all the corporations, all the great papers." [37] "The very graveyards," said Paxton Hibben, "were robbed of the names on their tombstones to be enrolled as voters for an honest dollar." [38] Laughlin said later: "If one were to judge from the action of the country in 1896, it must be confessed that in no country in the modern world is there a more cautious and conservative element than the business community of the United States; and that whichever way it turns it generally decides the national election." [39]

After the election there was immense relief. "Long after midnight in a certain Chicago club one of the world's greatest merchants started the old boyhood game, 'Follow the Leader.' He was joined by bank presidents, merchants, Chicago's foremost men; they went over sofas, chairs, tables, upstairs and downstairs, and wound up with dancing in each other's arms." [40] *The New York Tribune* said that the Bryan movement "was brought forth in sin. . . . Good riddance . . . to conspiracy and conspirators, and to the foul menace of repudiation and anarchy against the honour and life of the Republic." [41] Hanna now ruled the land, "a colossus astride of the country." [42]

Yerkes's choice for governor was successful against Altgeld. *Harper's Weekly* exulted: "Exit Altgeld." "He has been . . . the most dangerous enemy to American institutions of all the ruffianly gangs which have broken out of the forecastle of the ship of state and attempted to occupy the quarter-deck and seize the helm." [43] Governor Tanner was inaugurated with a display of military pomp seldom seen before in Springfield.

Economic conditions, however, did not improve, and the murmurs of discontent were by no means silenced. In June 1897 the American Railway Union reorganised into the Social Democracy of America with Debs as its leader. A Co-operative Conference, a movement fostered by John Ruskin, was held in Chicago, and Henry Demarest Lloyd was chosen as the American delegate to the third congress of the International Co-operative Conference at Delft, Holland. Peter Kropotkin spoke at Hull House on his book, *Fields, Factories, and Workshops*.

In the spring of 1897 the reform alderman, John Harlan, made an unforgettable campaign for mayor of Chicago, as an independent against the traction interests controlled by Yerkes. On the stump he called "the roll of eminent citizens who were directors of these corporations, naming them one by one, as though they were on the witness stand. After pretending to swear them in, he proceeded to ask them if they knew that their agents were 'conspiring with public officials to commit grand larceny in burglarising the city of Chicago?' " [44] He lost, but the successful Democratic candidate was pledged to reform.

Yerkes transferred his activities to Springfield, where he expected the legislature to extend his enormously valuable privileges for a period of fifty years. But Bemis was having his revenge. In the Ninth Biennial Report of the Bureau of Labour Statistics, prepared by Schilling and Bemis, it was pointed out that, even according to the fundamental franchise law of 1865, the street car companies would lose their rights to the streets, because the law provided only for horse cars. The report presented a detailed account of Yerkes's manipulations, based on a paper read before the Political Economy Club of the university by a graduate student, Frank Vanderlip. It was "known that the Senate was ready to pass anything the companies asked," but "popular opposition in Chicago to the bills was intense, almost reaching the stage of riot and mob violence." [45] Lloyd prepared for the Executive Committee of the Chicago Federation of Labor an address to the legislature which closed with: "In the name of the happiness, the property, and the liberty of the people of all classes of the present and posterity . . . we protest against the passage of these bills and beg you, our representatives at Springfield, not to lay upon the living and the unborn these two 'dead hands,' of government by syndicates and of monopoly in perpetuity." [46] Citizens marched on Springfield; the legislature was panic-stricken and killed the proposed bill, four to one. Yerkes sarcastically congratulated "the Socialistic element of this city and also the Anarchistic element, which is now working from the top instead of from the bottom as it did eight years ago." A few weeks later a bill empowering city councils to decide on extensions was rushed through by violating the rules of both houses, and was signed by the governor. But the "anarchistic element" rose again when the council was to pass the necessary ordinances. Lloyd said that some of the citizens came with rope and told the aldermen that it was meant for them if the ordinances were passed.[47] The measures were defeated.

About that time the observatory, Yerkes's gift to the university, was completed. Special trains conveyed the trustees, members of the congregation and official guests of the university, from Chicago to Williams Bay, "under the especial guidance of President Harper, whose gracious vigour made him the ideal master of ceremonies." An Amherst professor wrote that "no benefactor of learning has received, or could wish to receive, a warmer or more heartfelt and wholly spontaneous tribute than did Mr. Yerkes at the crowning moment." [48] Yerkes spoke of it as an investment. "I feel that in your attempts to pierce the mysteries of the universe which are spread before you by our great Creator, the enthusiasm of your natures will carry you to success." On behalf of the trustees M.A. Ryerson said to him: "We appreciate highly the liberality with which you have from the beginning encouraged the broadening conception of this great work, and we desire to bear testimony to the breadth of the views which you have always expressed in relation to its aim and its scope." [49]

In a symposium on "Municipal Ownership and Supervision" in *The Independent,* Laughlin took the "opportunity of discussing the points at issue, because, quite without my initiative, some writers have chosen to classify me as an unqualified advocate of *laissez-faire.* I believe there is no ground for this in anything I have written." Concerning public supervision he maintained that "the private company must have large exercise of business discretion on all matters affecting the earning capacity of the property invested." He was not in favour of municipal ownership at present, since public utilities "must be managed on business principles with great ability and sagacity, for a profit." At the Wisconsin Bankers' Convention he denounced any appeal to the state by labour, because such socialistic appeals are confessions of individual weakness.[50]

Laughlin wrote the *Report of the Monetary Commission of the Indianapolis Convention of Boards of Trade, Chambers of Commerce, Commercial Clubs, and Other Similar Bodies of the United States,* which in substance asked Congress to allow the banks to extend their currency issues by securing them on the commercial assets of the bank, instead of being limited, as they were at the time, by government securities. The convention of "representatives of the business men and business interests" passed a resolution testifying to the "very earnest appreciation and gratitude" felt towards Laughlin and the other members of the commission.

Altgeld declared: "The trouble with Professor Laughlin is that the great schemers of the world never take their handy hired men into their confidence. They give each his work and expect him to do it quickly and thoroughly, and under no circumstances to hesitate on account of any question of ethics or morals that may be involved." [51]

Bellamy issued *Equality*, in which he elaborated *Looking Backward*. An inhabitant of Utopia asked: "What hypocrisy could have been so brazen as that pretence"—concerning "the freedom of contract, the voluntary, unconstrained agreement of the labourer with the employer as to the terms of his employment"—"when, as a matter of fact, every contract made between the capitalist who had bread and could keep it and the labourer who must have it or die would have been declared void, if fairly judged . . . as a contract made under duress of hunger, cold, and nakedness, nothing less than the threat of death. If you own the things men must have, you own the men who must have them."

The movement to supplant the older psychology and biology continued. In 1896 C. Lloyd Morgan delivered a lecture at the University of Chicago on "Habit and Custom: A Study in Heredity," which was included in his book, *Habit and Instinct*. Morgan used instinct in a more restricted sense than did James. Instincts are "congenital, adaptive, and co-ordinated activities of relative complexity, and involving the behaviour of the organism as a whole." Man inherits a smaller share "of definite instinctive performance" than any other animal. Instead he "inherits an innate power of acquisition and application, which enables him to cope with an environment of extraordinary complexity, and of a peculiarly specialised nature." In opposition to Spencer and Ward he contended that man does not inherit acquired habits. Mental evolution in human society is due "to the handing on of the results of human achievement by a vast extension of that which we have seen to be a factor in animal life, namely tradition." "Evolution *has been transferred from the organism to his environment,*" created by intellectual evolution itself viewed in a human cultural sense. "The *faculty* of the race [is] at a standstill while the *achievements* of the race are progressing by leaps and bounds."

Caldwell declared that Patten's *Theory of Social Forces*, with its "hypothetical Procrustean framework," was Spencerian. "Our environment is not something that is made for us, once and for all, by an external nature or an unconscious physical necessity, but is essentially something that we ourselves can largely make, or at least modify or idealise." But Patten conceives human force as a very small thing "compared with the force of animate and material nature." He maintains that "physical environment" limits and circumscribes "the possibilities of human development." "The original background of the human race, according to his language, is one of mere force. If it really were such, all the social forces and civic standards, and art and morality would be unequal to the task of socialising it." It must be realised that "we act and we know we act, at one and the same time." "Sociologists will soon get tired of talking as if evolution must be regarded as a process that had happened in time." That is why the *Theory of Social Forces* is essentially "a solution of an imaginary puzzle. It is bent on showing how social forces can be grafted on to essentially unsocial groups of individuals." Patten cited Spencer as his authority, and Caldwell countered that discussions in terms of pleasure and pain were not ethical discussions, and Spencer was not an ethical philosopher. A true student of ethics is concerned with the ends of activity, or the equivalent, not the mere psychology of motives.[52]

Caldwell again presented his action concept before the American Psychological Association meeting of 1897. He attacked E.B. Titchener, who was always insisting that mind is "nothing but sensations and affections," and who did not "allow for the fact (the unique thing in psychology) that psychological happenings and processes are nothing apart from an active, unifying, synthetic self." In the issue of *The International Journal of Ethics* for April 1898, Caldwell elaborated his views in "Philosophy and the Activity-Experience," the *"rapprochement . . .* between philosophy . . . as the 'Theory of Ideas' . . . and the actual practical effort that characterises the life of man, that brings him . . . his experience or wisdom of life." Associationists "claim that there is in the mind of man no evidence of self-engendered effort, of spontaneous activity, of activity essentially different from sensation and affection." "Human beings themselves and history and literature all seem to speak of a life of effort and creative activity and spontaneity as of the very nature of man. . . . The study of evolution," as well as psychology, "has made us aware of the fact that it is 'function,' or adaptation to needs and purposes, that measures reality." We are forced "to think the universe to be what the necessities of our practical nature demand that it shall be." "The data of knowledge and investigation *are* reliable because they tell us the relation that 'things' and the 'world' sustain to the movement of our bodies and the evolution of our life, or the relation that our life sustains to the life or evolution of the universe." If philosophers would think in terms of the activity-experience, "they would gain a consciousness of the relation of the aims and purposes of thought to the aims and purposes of all evolution and effort, to even the industrial and economic activity of man."

Tufts, also using the action concept, analysed Giddings's *Principles of Sociology*. Giddings asserted that psychology is the "science of the association of ideas," and sociology the "science of the association of minds." Sympathy is thus conceived as "merely imitation of emotions," and the increasing sociability of humanity is proved by this imitation process. But Tufts declared that if sympathy is so conceived," it may mean emulation or conflict as well as compassion or sociability. If it is individualistic in its elements, the combination will not be social." "Mr. Spencer," he said, "seems to be the author's chief and almost sole authority in psychology." [53]

The older types of thinking, however, were by no means superseded at Chicago. Small devoted a seminar to a consideration of "The Problems of Social Teleology." At the summer session in 1897 Ward lectured on the "Pain and Pleasure Economy." In *The American Journal of Sociology* for January 1898 he published an elaboration of one of the lectures under the title "Utilitarian Economics," in which he concluded that "under science which makes for *meliorism,* the levelling process will go on, greater and greater numbers will rise above the *Nullpunkt,* and the field of pain economy will shrink as that of the pleasure economy expands." The positive social state is the pleasure economy, and its "end in view" is Bentham's "greatest happiness of the greatest number." Lapouge's article, "The Fundamental Laws of Anthropo-Sociology," translated by Closson, stated that these laws could be reduced to one, "formulated by Closson and designated by him as the Law of Lapouge, *viz., the law of the greater activity of Homo Europæus.*" [54]

CHAPTER IX

D URING this period between the end of 1896 and the beginning of 1898 Veblen's reviews in *The Journal of Political Economy* reflect the development of his thought under the impact of his social and intellectual environment. They are more neutral in tone than previous ones.

Enrico Ferri, in his *Socialisme et Science Positive; Darwin, Spencer et Marx*, attempted to dispose of the criticism that socialism was incompatible with Darwinism. Although Veblen did not commit himself explicitly, his summary of Ferri's statements showed him at least sympathetic towards socialism. The opponents of socialism maintained, according to Veblen's summary of Ferri, that "(a) socialism demands equality of individuals, while the evolutionary process constantly accentuates" the necessary inequality between individuals, "(b) socialism demands the survival, in comfort and fullness of life, of all individuals, whereas Darwinism . . . requires the destruction . . . of the great majority of individuals, (c) the struggle for existence secures a progressive elimination of the unfit and a survival of the superior individuals . . . whereas socialism, by giving all an even chance of life, reduces the aggregate of individuals to a dead level of democratic uniformity, in which the superior merits of the 'fit' count for nothing." Veblen declared that Ferri's answer to these objections was presented in a "rather more convincing form than is usual with the scientific apologists of socialism." Ferri contended, according to Veblen, that (a) the "equality of individuals demanded by the socialist scheme is an equality of opportunities rather than an identity of function or of the details of life; (b) that the struggle for existence, as applied within the field of social evolution, is a struggle between groups and institutions rather than a competition, *à outrance* between the individuals of the group." Therefore, since the struggle is a class struggle, group solidarity is essential for obtaining socially desirable results. Also, the " 'normal' milieu for the competitive development of individuals in society in the direction of availability for the social purpose and a fuller and more truly human life is afforded only by an environment which secures the members of the community a competent and equitable—if not equal—immunity from the sordid cares of a life of pecuniary competition. . . . The closer an approach is made to a condition of pecuniary equality, and solidarity, the better are the chances of a survival of the 'fittest,' in the sense of the most efficient for the purposes of the collective life. (c) It is . . . only by injecting a wholly illegitimate teleological meaning into the term 'fittest' as used by Darwin and the Darwinists that the expression 'survival of the fittest' is made to mean a survival of the socially desirable individuals." It is therefore a "sophism," proceeding "on a teleological preconception—a survival in modern discussion of a concept which belongs among the mental furniture of the metaphysical speculations of the pre-Darwinian times."

Thus Ammon's and Lapouge's theory of "social selection" of type, which they considered a defence of traditional *laissez-faire*, was "turned to socialist account." As if to suggest the irony, Veblen first cited Ferri's words that "it is well known that in the modern civilised world, the action of natural selection is vitiated by . . . military selection . . . matrimonial selection, and especially by economic selection." Veblen then continued: "It is only in the *'milieu normal'* afforded by such an equality of pecuniary competence as the socialist scheme contemplates that the factor of 'choice' has a chance to act and to award the victory to the most normal individuals and types."

Socialism is "atheistic as a matter of course," and the "cults with their entire theistic content will disappear from man's habits of thought as fast as the chief positions of evolutionary science are accepted." It is not denied that "the struggle for existence, and, therefore, the fact of a selective adaptation, is a fact inseparable from the life process, and therefore inseparable from the life of mankind; but while its scope remains unaltered, the forms under which it expresses itself in the life of society change as the development of collective life proceeds"; and Veblen quoted Ferri: "Everything goes to impress upon us with mathematical certainty that when [the] victory [of socialism] is achieved it must in turn give place to further struggles and new ideals among the generations that are to succeed us."

In closing Veblen remarked that "incidentally" the "great Italian criminologist has a word of kindly admonition to say to the students of Sociology and Political Economy." In Ferri's words, "Darwinism and Spencerian evolution" had revolutionised the "physical, biological, and even the psychological sciences," but had "barely rippled the surface of the still waters of that pool of orthodoxy in social science, Political Economy." The explanation is to be found in the fact that "the logical consequences of Darwinism and of scientific evolutionism, when applied to the study of human society, lead inexorably to socialism."

In his review of Richard Calwer's *Einführung in den Sozialismus*, in the March 1897 issue, Veblen called attention to a device which he had already used himself. This socialist textbook, he said, is "not a controversial book. Its purpose is sought to be accomplished by so explaining the meaning and trend of the socialist movement as to leave no legitimate ground for the tendency which it deprecates." The book presents a softened Marxism, in which the " 'materialistic interpretation of history' is no longer obtrusively present in the crude form at every step, although it still remains the fundamental premise." It is a significant departure from the traditional position that the form of modern industry and the rational calculations of the workingmen must of themselves bring about a change of social structure. "But while the evolution of industry, it is claimed, assures the rapid and inevitable socialisation of industry, these mechanical facts and technological events do not immediately or of themselves afford the basis for that growth of institutions which the socialist republic involves. The institutions of the community, whether socialistic or otherwise, rest on psychological ground. The material situation, the state of industry and the arts, may condition the growth of institutions in accordance with the materialistic theory of history, but these material circumstances of environment and of industrial organisation and methods control the growth of institutions and social structure only as they affect the individual's habitual view of things." The psychological factor which is to work out the revolution, "is no longer conceived to be of the nature of a calm resolution, the outcome of dispassionate ratiocination." The psychological motive assumed to bring about the change of social structure is the same as that presented by Veblen in "Some Neglected Points in the Theory of Socialism." "It is bluntly recognised that this motive force is simply sentiment and is closely akin to envy, its basis being chiefly an invidious comparison of the labourer's lot with that of the propertied classes. The decisive fact is the distastefulness of the labourer's social position as compared with his employer. Improvement in material comfort measured in absolute terms counts for very little. You may feed the labourer well, you may clothe him decently, you may provide him with a modest dwelling, in short, you may keep him as a well-to-do man keeps his domestic animals—still the labourer will not be beguiled into overlooking the fact that his place in life is determined by accidents and circumstances which do not permit him to lead the life of a man."

Veblen's views as to the inevitability of socialism through the sheer necessity of the industrial mechanism seem to have undergone a change, but the somewhat rationalistic motivation imputed to the workers remained undisturbed. Veblen's method of emphasising a position which is of interest to himself but not of particular interest to the author is also illustrated in this review. "Socialism is said to hold an entirely neutral position with regard to religion, but this is uttered with an evident conviction that the church and the creeds are alien to socialism and irreconcilable with it in detail." Similarly, socialism is made out to be unpatriotic. Little is said about the family but "it is plainly implied that the traditional form of the family is in an advanced state of obsolescence as far as regards the working classes," although it is conceded that the present marriage relationship is "the form best suited for the well-to-do classes."

Another change is to be noticed in Veblen's thought in his review of Antonio Labriola's *Essais sur la conception matérialiste de l'histoire*, in the issue of June 1897. Labriola's position, said Veblen in summary, was that the "materialistic conception" is the central Marxian position and that "the exigencies of the industrial process determine the features of the society's life process in all other aspects, social, political, and intellectual." All the rest of Marx, including the doctrines of class struggle and of surplus value, is "provisional and tentative," although accepted by Labriola. Using the language of Kant and Peirce in his summary, Veblen declared that the "office of 'the materialistic conception' is that of a guiding principle . . . in the study of social life and social structure." The "economic exigencies" of the industrial process "afford the definitive test of fitness in the adaptation of all human institutions by a process of selective elimination of the economically unfit. They also, through the industrial process through which they work their effect, determine the development of thought and science; the materialistic conception is itself, at the second remove, a product of the industrial process."

Veblen turned from a mere summary of one man's views to a presentation of what he held to be the evolutionary point of view in economics. The dogmas of labour value and class struggle were "giving way before an interpretation of the materialistic conception which does not, in its fundamental position, go much beyond a conception of the evolution of social structure according to which the economic activities, and the habits bred by them, determine the activities and habitual view of things in other directions than the economic one. And in this development the socialists are drawing close to the position of a large and increasing class of economists who are accepting the materialistic conception, or so much of it as is conveniently to be affiliated with Darwinism, whether they accept it under the style and title approved by their socialist mentors or under designations chosen by themselves." These economists he referred to as "of the new evolutionist, or socialist departure." Veblen was now conscious in his thinking of the prevailing action concept, which was replacing the more rationalistic principle of motivation by emulation, characteristic of his earlier work.

In contrast to his sympathetic reviews of Ferri, Calwer, and Labriola, was his depreciation of Werner Sombart's *Sozialismus und soziale Bewegung im 19. Jahrhundert.* Sombart considered himself as the apostle of Marx's method but not of Marx's propaganda. Adhering to a Hegelian romantic approach, he declared that among the lessons to be learned by both parties to the class struggle is that "all social struggle should be determinedly within legal bounds." [1] Veblen declared that "the logical and the only promising line of action for the socialists according to Professor Sombart is to strengthen and accelerate the growth and spread of the modern culture, and carry it to the highest pitch attainable. Oddly enough—though perhaps it seems less odd to an affectionate latter-day citizen of the militant Fatherland—this ideal cultural growth to which socialism should look, it is explicitly held, comprises a large unfolding of warlike activity. Socialism is, on this and related grounds, not apprehended to be, in strict consistency, an international (*a fortiori,* not an anti-national) movement. It is a further curious feature of Professor Sombart's exposition that he finds no logical ground for an atheistic or undevout attitude in the accepted realism of Marx and his followers. This is perhaps as characteristically new German a misapprehension of Marxism as the contrary misapprehension which makes Marxism 'materialistic' in the metaphysical sense is characteristic of the traditional view among English-speaking critics." Sombart's revisionism was not substantially different from Spencer's evolutionism.

In reviewing Max Lorenz's *Die Marxistische Sozialdemokratie,* Veblen pointed out that the author denied that "the substantial core of the Marxian doctrine is the theory of labour-value and surplus-value." Marx's fundamental position was not concerned with a problem of ethics. " 'What comes about comes, according to Marx, not for equity's or morality's sake, but it comes as a causally historical necessary phase of social evolution.' " "While the materialistic interpretation of history points out how social development goes on—by a class struggle that proceeds from maladjustment between economic structure and economic functions—it is nowhere pointed out what is the operative force at work in the process. It denies that human discretion and effort seeking a better adjustment can furnish such a force, since it makes man the creature of circumstances. This defect reduces itself under the author's hand to a misconception of human nature and of man's place in the social development. The materialistic theory conceives of man as exclusively a social being, who counts in the process solely as a medium for the transmission and expression of social laws and changes; whereas he is, in fact, also an individual, acting out his own life as such." Here another change is to be noted in Veblen's thinking, bringing it into consistency with the new psychology and biology without changing his fundamental position concerning the existing order and socialism. "Hereby is indicated not only the weakness of the materialistic theory, but also the means of remedying the defect pointed out. With the amendment so indicated, it becomes not only a theory of the method of social and economic change, but a theory of social process considered as a substantial unfolding of life as well." The fundamental Marxian principle was being interpreted in terms of the action concept, under which socialism would be achieved on the basis of the life of industry led by a worker, instead of through the impact of the motive of emulation. Lorenz, however, prefers "to take up the materialistic argument and carries it out to its logical consequences, with the result of reducing the socialist millennium to absurdity, at least to his own satisfaction."

Veblen's reviews of books on "theory" were written in much the same manner and with the same ends in view as the others. In discussing *Esquisses de littérature politico-économique*, by N. Ch. Bunge, who felt that the historical school's lack of theoretical treatment was a merit, Veblen declared: "What he has learned is what he knew already—that salvation for economic science is to be found in the historico-statistical method alone, and that this method could not be effectively applied until Gustav Schmoller found it and set it in order." Shortly afterwards Veblen reviewed a volume of Schmoller's essays. "Very much of his constructive work" bears out "the criticisms levelled at him on methodological grounds." His work, as well as that of his many disciples, "is of the nature of compilation and description—narrative, often discursive and fragmentary work." Schmoller argues first that "economics is in an inchoate stage" and the proper method therefore is that of "description and collation"—classification, not the causal explanation of phenomena. But the tone of the second essay seems to indicate that "the science is now felt to be rapidly passing this inchoate stage and that the economists may now legitimately turn to constructive theoretical work." Even in his later essays, however, he has much to say as to the "important place of a taxonomic discipline—definitions, concepts, and classification." "It may not be out of place," said Veblen, "to point out, Schmoller gives but scant acknowledgment to the really large and substantial deserts of the classical writers under this head." Veblen considered Schmoller's "most substantial and characteristic move in advance" to be his contention that "observation and description, definition and classification, are preparatory work only. . . . There must remain before our eyes, as the ideal of all knowledge, the explanation of all facts in terms of causation." The "causes at work in the sequence of economic phenomena" are psychical causes, not physical or biological factors. Veblen interpreted this to mean that "the causes in terms of which economic theory must in the last resort formulate its results are psychical facts—facts of human motives and propensities." "The aim of economics, as of any science, adopting any method, must be the determination of uniformities and laws. But the descriptive, empirical generalisation of uniformities, simply, must not be accepted as a determination of the laws of the phenomena under inquiry. Normalisation and taxonomic schedules are not science in the modern acceptance of the word."

What lay behind Veblen's use of psychological and philosophical language and citation becomes less obscure in the light of his review in the June 1898 issue of a book entitled *Aristocracy and Evolution: A Study of the Rights, the Origins and the Social Functions of the Wealthier Classes*, by William H. Mallock. The author had been described by Zueblin as "a prodigal novelist . . . writing automatic defences of individualism." [2] Mallock held that captains of industry belong to the aristocracy, and smaller businessmen to the lower middle class. He was in good repute with the universities and the popular journals. Veblen remarked that after a rough examination of *Aristocracy and Evolution* "one is tempted to dismiss it with the comment that Mr. Mallock has written another of his foolish books." But since the book provides an opportunity for Veblen to discuss the role of the captain of industry, he gave it a rather lengthy review. Mallock "tacitly" identifies the " 'great' man in industry . . . with the captain of industry or the owner of capital." He produces the great share of the product of industry, and it is expedient to allow him exceptional gain for his exceptional product "because on no other terms can he be induced to take care of the economic welfare of the community—and, in the nature of things, the welfare of the community, of the many, lies unreservedly in the hands of the minority of great men." Mallock, declared Veblen, first holds that "productive efficiency is a matter of detailed knowledge of the technical industrial processes of industry," but in his later discussion "the type of productive efficiency" becomes "the counting-house activity of the businessman, who frequently does not, and pretty uniformly need not, have any technical knowledge of the industry that goes on under his hand. His relation to the mechanical processes is always remote, and usually of a permissive kind only. This is especially true of the director of a large business, who is by that fact, if he is successful, a highly efficient great man. He delegates certain men, perhaps at the second or third remove, to assume discretion and set certain workmen and machines in motion, under the guidance of technical knowledge possessed by them, not by him. . . . It is bold irony to call [the captain's efficiency] productive efficiency under the definition of productivity set up by Mr. Mallock. . . . Objection is taken not to the obvious groundlessness of the whole natural-rights structure, but to the scope of the application given the dogmas."

Mallock declares that "the pecuniary incentive is indispensable to modern industry." He agrees with the socialists to the extent of "showing that the pecuniary incentive—the desire of wealth—is in large part a desire for distinction only, not in the last analysis a desire for material, consumable goods. But he denies flatly—what they affirm—that an emulative incentive of another kind might serve the turn if the pecuniary incentive were to fall away." No decisive argument, however, is presented "in support of this denial, which is the central feature of the refutation of socialism." The matter is explained away by an appeal to the uncritical fundamental principle of the associational philosophy and logic—the principle of similarity or uniformity. Through the discussion "there runs the implication that, in order to serve their purpose, at all effectively, the inducements offered the wealth-producer must mechanically resemble the results to be worked out. As on the homeopathic principle like is to be cured by like, so in industry the repugnance to effort spent on material goods must be overcome by a remedial application of material goods. While it seems to be present in the reasoning, it is by no means clear, it should be remarked, that this axiom of similarity has been present in the reasoner's mind."

William Archer, the English literary critic, declared that Chicago "embraces . . . every extreme of splendour and squalor." It "suggests that antique conception of the underworld which placed Elysium and Tartarus not only on the same plane, but, so to speak, round the corner from each other." [3] At the first convention of the Co-operative Commonwealth, in Chicago, a split occurred and the advocates of political action, led by Debs, founded the Social Democratic Party. Another bitter city election was fought in 1898 for reform and municipal ownership, led by a respectable businessman, George Cole, but "the big corporations, the railroads, the great business houses and their friends" took "their business away from him" and he gave up the leadership. [4]

The Spanish-American War began, early foreseen by liberals as a consequence of American investments in Cuba. "From every corner of the land and every variety of pulpit, the humble followers of the Prince of Peace attested their qualifications for slaughter with imagination and enthusiasm." Everywhere liberals denounced the policy of conquest. William Dean Howells declared: "After war will come the piling up of big fortunes again, the craze for wealth will fill all brains, and every good cause will be set back. We shall have an era of blood-bought prosperity and the chains of capitalism will be welded on the nation more firmly than ever." William Graham Sumner immediately after the war, in an address called "The Conquest of the United States by Spain," exclaimed: "My patriotism is of the kind which is outraged by the notion that the United States never was a great nation until in a petty three months' campaign it knocked to pieces a poor, decrepit, bankrupt, old state like Spain. To hold such an opinion as that is to abandon all American standards, to put shame and scorn on all that our ancestors tried to build up here, and to go over to the standards of which Spain is a representative." There was rumour of his expulsion from Yale. William Vaughn Moody's poem, "On a Soldier Fallen in the Philippines," was according to Robert Morss Lovett "a very bold utterance and in a university less tolerant than Chicago would have cost an instructor his position." [5] Harvard began a school of business administration in the belief that an imperial nation needs a trained foreign service; Chicago created a department of Military Science and Tactics, scheduled a course on "Colonial Economics," and planned a college of Commerce and Politics for training students in the direction of business, politics, journalism, and diplomacy.

To the war president, McKinley, the University of Chicago awarded its first LL.D. Small, as vice-president of the University Congregation, said at the presentation: "Your exercise of the presidential prerogative has increased the prestige of the chief magistracy and exalted the standards to which it must henceforth conform. This result is both a splendid national achievement and a glorious national ideal." The Reverend A.K. Parker, in behalf of the trustees, said that the "doctrine of sovereignty of the people leads a precarious existence in the mouths of men who love large-sounding words and have not stopped to consider that it is only a specious form of the ancient blasphemy that might makes right." Altgeld commented that the "President of the United States, standing under the wing of the Standard Oil Company, accepts a proffered honour which is coupled with the declaration that the doctrine of popular sovereignty is a specious form of blasphemy." [6]

In connexion with trusts and other consolidations, the name "promoter" grew suddenly familiar on all the markets, and a new phase of business enterprise, that of the pecuniary magnate, became known. The phrase, "thinking in hundreds of millions," became current. The Chicago Civic Federation held an Interstate Trust Conference to determine how to cope with the menace of large aggregates of wealth. Congress appointed an industrial commission to make an elaborate investigation of economic maladjustments for much the same purpose. H.O. Havemeyer, president of the Sugar Trust, frankly informed the commission that "business is not a philanthropy. . . . I do not care two cents for your ethics. I do not know enough of them to apply them. . . . As a business proposition it is right to get all out of business that you possibly can." [7] The Standard Oil Trust now took the form of the holding company, the Standard Oil Company of New Jersey.

Clark published his *Distribution of Wealth*, which best expressed the ideal logically involved in the dominant economics. In the preface he said: "It is the purpose of this work to show that the distribution of the income of society is controlled by a natural law. . . . At the point of the economic system where titles to property originate—where labour and capital come into possession of the amounts that the state afterwards treats as their own—the social process is true to the principle on which the right of property rests," namely, "the claim of a producer to what he creates." If this were not the case, "there would be at the foundation of the social structure an explosive element which sooner or later would destroy it. For nothing, if not to protect property, does the state exist."

Patten, in his latest book, *Development of English Thought*, reached the conclusion, apparently in accordance with his pleasure-pain calculus, that "classifications of society" based on wealth or social position should be replaced by divisions according to "psychic traits." In a review in *The American Journal of Sociology*, Angell declared: "It must grieve the painstaking critics of hedonism, whose contentions are distinctly relevant as against the view here presented, to hear an enlightened man like Mr. Patten setting down these principles as blandly as though no one had ever questioned them." Veblen, in reviewing the book in Patten's own journal, *The Annals of the American Academy of Political and Social Science*, declared it was based on the conventional economics as formulated in *The Theory of Social Forces*. He dismissed its main argument, based on the traditional preconception of the beneficence of the strong hand, as having no ground in fact and therefore serving no useful purpose. G. Tarde's *Social Laws: an Outline of Sociology* he dismissed for the same reasons and expressed the hope that "the volume may contribute materially to curtail the vogue of M. Tarde's sociological doctrines."

Veblen persuaded Warner Fite, formerly a docent in the department of philosophy at Chicago and later professor of philosophy at Princeton, to discuss Patten's psychological doctrines in *The Journal of Political Economy*. Patten's conception of psychological action, Fite pointed out, is "external stimulus, sensory idea, motor idea, motor reaction. The mental mechanism is thus a static fact . . . the motor energy coming from the environment." But according to the new psychology the "environment is . . . to some degree a function of the organism" and "the adjustment to environment is effected not by the association of sensory ideas with ideas of movement, but by an immediate connexion between the sensory idea proceeding from an external object and the motor reaction itself. . . . Knowledge is not the passive reception of impressions from external sources but a selective activity governed by subjective interests. It is, therefore, impossible to separate the knowing and willing activities since each presupposes the other." He suggested that Patten assimilate James's position that "knowing is always for the sake of doing."

At the 1898 meeting of the American Psychological Association, Caldwell defended J. Mark Baldwin's "genetic" method, which inquires " 'into the psychological development of the human individual in the earlier stages of his growth for light upon his social nature, and also upon the social organisation in which he bears a part.' . . . The reality of the self consists in process and progress rather than stable equilibrium or peculiarity of personal content. 'Man's interests as the intellectual reflection of his habits . . . man's habits as motor phenomena to be explained out of earlier activities . . . and man's wants as a function of the social situation' " will give an insight into the two formulæ used by Baldwin: (a) "that what we do is a function of what we think"; and (b) what "we shall think is a function of what we have done." [8]

Titchener, in replying to Caldwell, branded the Dewey school and Caldwell as standing for "functional psychology," which he declared had not been "worked out either with as much patient enthusiasm or with as much scientific accuracy as has the psychology of mind structure." [9] Caldwell replied with another analysis of the "Postulates of a Structural Psychology." Titchener held that the elementary mental processes are made up of two structural elements, "the sense-element (sensation or idea)," which is constituted of "quality, intensity, duration, clearness, and (in some cases) extent," and the "affection-element, which is constituted of quality, intensity, and duration." But Caldwell asserted that quality, intensity, duration, etc., are not elements; "they are *processes* or phases of *processes*." And processes are "facts of sequence," not "facts of structure." "Indeed, the very fact of process is not a fact of 'structure,' but something more than this." [10]

William James, who had begun the new psychology and philosophy in America, caused another uproar with his public lecture, "Philosophical Conceptions and Practical Results." Claiming to have borrowed the terminology and basis from Peirce's essays on the "Logic of Science," James set forth the philosophy of pragmatism. But it came so close to the traditional common-sense philosophy that Peirce disclaimed the parentage. Caldwell, at the 1899 session of the American Psychological Association, differentiated his "Philosophy and the Activity-Experience" from pragmatism, the philosophy of expediency, with its denial of human objective ends or purposes in conduct. He agreed that science is based on the principle of activity. In science "the idea of *substance*, the idea of different substances in different individual things and the idea of a substance in general, flies before us as we contemplate it or as we investigate its alleged reality, and is actually *disappearing* into the idea of *causality* or the conception (or fact) of measurable energy or modifiable life-process." James, however, "is trying to show us how reasonable it is to regard things as we are compelled to assume them to be; he ought rather to take the ground that the manner in which we are compelled (by genuine practical and *moral* necessity) to assume things to be disposed is the only possible theory of their reality. This perhaps would be the true Pragmatism." [11]

At a conference of the preparatory schools affiliated with the University of Chicago, A.C. Miller made a plea for the encouragement of schools of commerce. "It is no mere figure of speech that has long likened business to warfare and called business heads *captains of industry*." He admitted that in his discussion he had "tacitly accepted the ordinary mercantile view that business is followed for gain, that it is solely a money-getting pursuit," and had attempted "to show what the higher education could do towards developing the business aptitudes." [12] Schools of Commerce, however, could also impart to prospective businessmen a necessary recognition of public interest. The College of Commerce and Administration of the University of Chicago took more definite shape.

In 1899 John R. Commons involuntarily left his position at the University of Syracuse. Professor Herbert S. Foxwell of Cambridge wrote to an American correspondent concerning the tenure of American professors: "Our people cannot understand how you can sit down quietly under this poisoning of the springs of national life. . . . We tolerate at our universities any caprice, any eccentricity . . . rather than . . . tamper with the liberty of professors. They are in fact absolutely independent. . . . In Cambridge we do not recognise any institution as a college unless it has an independent foundation, and all teachers are elected by their colleagues or other experts. No trustees intervene." [13]

At the meeting that year of the American Economics Association, Hadley said in his presidential address that in the reaction against competition and private enterprise, particularly in the public utilities, there was a danger of the people losing confidence in individual initiative. At the same meeting H.C. Emery, in a paper on "The Place of the Speculator in the Theory of Distribution," said that the gain of speculators, such as the traders on the commodity exchanges, could not be determined on the traditional production basis since they are outside the productive process, but since "it is difficult to see how a great world trade in such staples as grain and cotton would be possible without [the speculative market] . . .

speculative gains constitute such claims to the product as are represented in all property rights." In the discussion Thomas Nixon Carver, Franklin H. Giddings, William Z. Ripley, Commons, and Hadley devoted their attention to showing that the speculator was productive, and Emery agreed.[14]

The American Socialist Party was formally organised with Debs as its leader and Chicago as its headquarters. It represented "evolutionary" socialism, following the Social Democratic parties of England and the continent. The Chicago publisher, Charles E. Kerr, began the publication of *The International Socialist Review* and other socialist literature. The new socialism was so inclusive that *The International Socialist Review* included contributions from Christian Socialists, from John R. Commons and Edward Carpenter, and from men who wished to return to a handicraft era. The work of Loeb and the pedagogy of Dewey were considered socialistic.

Veblen was given an excellent opportunity to make use of all these currents of thought. In 1898 it was arranged that in place of the distasteful course on "American Agriculture" he would give one on "Economic Factors in Civilisation," concerned with economic history. The course had been in the catalogue from the first year of the university, when it was scheduled to be given by Caldwell. But Veblen in 1899 gave it for the first time.

CHAPTER X

IN 1898 Veblen had completed the draft of a direct examination of modern capitalism, but he was not satisfied with it and laid it aside. From July 1898 to January 1900 he published in *The Quarterly Journal of Economics* a series of articles indirectly concerned with the same subject, beginning with "Why Is Economics Not an Evolutionary Science?" and ending with three articles on "The Preconceptions of Economic Science." The essays seemingly present a methodological discussion of the obsolete procedure of academic economics, in contrast to the evolutionary method of modern science in physics, chemistry, botany, psychology, anthropology, and ethnology. Veblen discussed the development of economics in relation to other phases of culture and concluded that the antiquated character of economics is due to its retention of discarded anthropological and psychological preconceptions.

Man's view of life is a composite of two incompatible habits of thought. One is that of modern science, whose ultimate axiom is cumulative causation. It adheres rigorously to an impersonal causal sequence. This is the matter-of-fact, dynamic, Darwinian, genetic, evolutionary, materialistic point of view. The other way of thinking is the personal, animistic point of view which belongs to the pre-Darwinian stage of the natural sciences. Its ultimate axiom is an uncritical natural law which inscrutably coerces the course of events, the efficient causes, to achieve the legitimate end, which is the ideal of conduct accepted by the dominant common sense. This preconception of natural law, or legitimate end, has taken various forms—the Creator, the unseen hand, overruling providence, a harmony of interests, propensity or tendency in events, natural rights, natural order, normal order, a meliorative trend in events, a teleological order, final causes, uniformities of nature. The imputation of final causes is met at every turn, in the marketplace as in the pulpit. It is the housewife's belief in lucky days or phases of the moon, the gambler's "haphazard sense of fortuitous necessity." The guidance of the invisible hand operates "through a comprehensive scheme of contrivances established from the beginning." This is the view of classical economics.

The procedure of classical economics is to give a conventional nomenclature to the industrial mechanism and its processes, and to work out its prospective values in accordance with a preconceived pecuniary normality.

A "ceremonially consistent formula" to cover the industrial field is thus manufactured. The "normal case" is used as a control and stabiliser of the economic situation, and features which do not lend themselves to interpretation in terms of the formula are eliminated as disturbing factors. Thus a preconceived normality, established by common sense, is seen as the real order, and to this the actual facts must adjust themselves in order to survive in the inquiry. Phenomena are stated in terms of what "legitimately ought to be according to the God-given end of life rather than in terms of unconstrued observation." The result is a system of logically consistent propositions as to the normal relation of things—"a system of economic taxonomy." It gives "a body of maxims for the conduct of business and a polemical discussion of disputed points of policy."

The historical school of economics is also essentially pre-Darwinian and pre-scientific. It has, when consistent, concerned itself with an enumeration of data and a narrative account of industrial development, thus apparently discarding the taxonomic ideal. But it has not rid itself of the preconception upon which that ideal is based, nor, when consistent, given any genetic, causal analysis of economic phenomena. Even the later and more mature formulations of classical economics are essentially pre-scientific, in spite of their apparent denial of a preconceived harmony of interests, for there is still an insistence upon uniformities of nature, or "colourless normality." Such uniformity can be conceived only as the basis of a dominating principle, and in their case, as with their precursors, the controlling principle is the dominant common sense. What is conceived to be normal is conceived to be right. This identification is the essence of Spencerian philosophy, and the classical economists "are prone to be Spencerians."

"Conjectural history," which plays so large a part in the classical treatment of economic institutions, is a result of this normalistic obsession. The whole narrative is a presentation "of what should have been the course of past development in order to lead up to that ideal economic situation," which satisfies the dominant preconception. The theorist is able "serenely to enjoin" himself from following out an elusive causal sequence by the sacrosanct terminology in which normality is conceived and developed. He can construct without misgivings his theories of such institutions as money or wages or land ownership without troubling himself with the living items concerned, except as a convenience for substantiating and validating the "normalised scheme of symptoms." The distressingly actual and persistent discrepancy between the legitimate and the observed course of things leads theorists to demand that there be no interference with the normal order. This "discrepancy between the actual, causally determined situation and the divinely intended consumma-

tion is the metaphysical ground of all that inculcation of morality and
. . . policy that makes up" so much of Adam Smith's work and that of
"all reformers and moralists who proceed on the assumption of a provi-
dential order." A causal sequence is simply not recognised, for it is substantially inferior to the "normal" order.

Psychologically this concept of normality is based on the hedonistic
conception of human nature. The fundamental principle of hedonistic-
associational psychology, like that of utilitarian philosophy, is that unrestrained human conduct makes for the general welfare. Man "is not the
seat of a process of living, except in the sense that he is subject to a series
of permutations enforced upon him by circumstances external and alien
to him." He is passive, for if he lived his own human life he would interfere with the end demanded by normality. It is accepted that his
prospective pleasures determine what his conduct must be, not that his
aptitudes determine what is pleasurable to him. As a consequence his
reward measures the force he puts forth in production. His returns are
the reward for his personal expenditure in the way of irksome labour or
its equivalent, money expenditures.

Market price and the course of investment measure productive force.
"Hedonistic exchange value is the outcome of a valuation process enforced by the apprehended pleasure-giving capacities of the items
valued." Production means the production of wealth, in the sense of
property rights, and what passes for a theory of production is really
occupied with the phenomena of investment. To the consistent hedonist
this is as it should be, for "the sole motive force concerned in the industrial process is the self-regarding motive of pecuniary gain." Since
"industrial activity is but an intermediate term between the expenditure
or discomfort undergone and the pecuniary gain sought," it is of no concern to the theorist. "Whether the end and outcome is an invidious gain
for the individual (in contrast with or at the cost of his neighbours) or
an enhancement of the facility of human life on the whole," is an
irrelevant question. "In hedonistic theory the substantial end of economic
life is individual gain," and the utilitarian philosophy makes the sum of
the gains of individuals the gain of society, so that an individual in serving his own interests in acquisition serve the interests of society to the extent that he is successful.

Through a more rigorous adherence to the implications of hedonism
later theorists take as their "point of departure the range of market
values and the process of bargaining by which these values are determined." The "average or consistent outcome of such a process of bargaining constitutes normal value." A distinction between higher and
lower pleasures is introduced by the more mature theorists, and this has

the effect of throwing emphasis "on the pecuniary circumstances on which depend the formation and maintenance of non-competing groups," which are of the nature of natural monopolies. It does not lead to emphasis on the actual living industrial circumstances of the community. In the struggle for wealth men endeavour to secure the material means for individual gain "in order to the satisfaction of men's natural wants through their consumption." The hedonistic theory of production and distribution "is complete when the goods or the values have been traced to their disappearance in the hands of their ultimate owners." Thus the "entire range of phenomena comprised under the head of consumption," or the usefulness of wealth, need only be "incidentally considered." "The reflex effect of consumption upon production and distribution" is merely quantitative, pecuniary.

Methods of thinking, however, are ultimately the outcome of the discipline of life. A habit of action constitutes a habit of thought. Fundamentally preconceptions of stability are the outcome of a proces of habituation to a predatory form of life. The dominant note in such a life is personal force or will power. The processes of inanimate nature are to be coerced, as are men and beasts. The scheme of life is one of personal aggression and subservience, partly naïve and partly conventionalised in a scheme of status. "The discrimination enjoined by the canons of status proceeds on an invidious comparison of persons in respect of worth, value, and potency"; that is, value is putative and is assigned not "on the ground of visible efficiency" but merely "on the ground of a dogmatic allegation accepted on the strength of an uncontradicted categorical affirmation." Where "distinctions of status are based on a putative worth transmitted by descent from honourable antecedents," as in the inheritance of wealth and vested rights, "the sequence of transmission, to which appeal is taken as the arbiter of honour, is of a putative and animistic character rather than a visible mechanical continuity." A culture with an institutional framework of "invidious comparisons" implies or involves such an animistic scheme of knowledge. The more unquestionably the "canons of status and ceremonial honour" control the conduct of the community, the greater the facility with which the sequence of cause and effect "is forced to yield before the higher claims of a spiritual sequence or guidance in the course of events."

Those consistently trained to this "unremitting discrimination of honour, worth, and personal force in their daily conduct . . . will not be satisfied with a less definitive ground" when it comes to co-ordinating facts merely "for the purposes of knowledge." If "personal force and invidious comparison" represent the highest criterion and ultimate resort of truth in conduct, then the sense of substantiality and truth in knowledge will be felt only when a "like definitive ground of animistic force and invidious comparison is reached." When this basis is found, the individual rests content with its authentic finality, just as he does in practical life. But "this absolutely right and good final term in conduct has the character of finality only when conduct is construed in a ceremonial sense; that is to say, only when life is conceived as a scheme of conformity to a purpose outside and beyond the process of living." In religion this ceremonial finality is expressed in the concept of taboo. "The habit of appeal to ceremonial finality, formed in the school of status, goes with the individual in his quest of knowledge," as a dependence upon a similar norm of "absolute truth—a similar seeking of a final term outside and beyond the range of knowledge."

The characteristic sciences based on such absolutism are of the nature of alchemy, astrology, metaphysics, medieval theology. Facts are classified according to "a hierarchical gradation of worth or merit, having only a ceremonial relation to the observed phenomena." Unlike the ancient "alchemic symbolism," modern chemistry is not interested in the "honorific bearing of reactions or molecular formulæ. The modern chemist . . . knows nothing of the worth, elegance, or cogency of the relations that may subsist between the particles of matter with which he busies himself, for any other than the genetic purpose." The influence of animism and invidious comparison was transmitted to economic science, however, through the body of knowledge known as natural theology, natural rights, moral philosophy, and natural law.

Although this "animistic formulation of knowledge" is pre-eminent in modern culture, its control has never been altogether undivided. The disciplinary effect of modern industry and of life in an industrial community is inimical to an animistic formulation. The prosy and exacting requirements of the modern mechanical processes induce a matter-of-fact or impersonal point of view. Failure to appreciate the impersonal sweep of these processes brings its penalties ever more surely and swiftly. Men must adapt themselves to their movements. They cannot tolerate personal passions and predilections, and they are no respecter of persons or will power.

This materialistic principle is substantially the fundamental principle of modern science—conservation of energy. Thus the disciplinary effect of the natural sciences reinforces the effect of the industrial processes, of which it is an outcome. The impersonal point of view is indispensable to technological efficiency, and is a selectively necessary consequence of industrial life and the economic interest. Since the stage of culture depends on mechanical efficiency, the greater the prevalence of this point of view the higher the culture. As a result of the selective adaptation of thought to the exigencies of preceding cultural stages, the materialistic method should gain in scope and extent. "The reason for the growing penchant for the commonplace, for the explanation of things in causal terms, lies partly in the growing resort to mechanical processes and mechanical prime movers in industry, partly in the (consequent) continued decline of the aristocracy and priesthood." This attitude has had its greatest effect in banishing the animistic point of view from those branches of knowledge concerned particularly with engineering design and mechanical contrivance. It has had little effect, however, in disturbing the old attitude in the political, social, and spiritual sciences, which deal with intangible realities not visible to the senses.

British economic thinking admits the matter-of-fact point of view more than did the older physiocratic tradition, and this tendency is not unrelated to the fact that English culture, with its respect for impersonal law rather than for a superior absolute, has been less obviously predatory than the French. Also, British wars have been conducted abroad, so that the military class has been segregated, to a great extent, and its predatory ideals and prejudices have not been readily transmitted to civilians. But English culture, too, is by no means free of the animistic point of view. "On all but the higher industrial stages, the coercive discipline of industrial life and the scheme of life that inculcates regard for the mechanical facts of industry, is greatly mitigated by the largely haphazard character of industry." Man continues to be the prime mover, as in handicraft days, and consequently the attention of men looking to the industrial process "comes to run on the personal element in industry." The social, civic, and religious interests of the community usually absorb the greater share of its attention, rather than industrial conduct. "Especially is this true so far as concerns those classes among whom we commonly look for a cultivation of knowledge for knowledge's sake."

Thus the substitution of investment in the place of industry as the central fact in economics, beginning approximately in the middle of the nineteenth century, "is due not to the acceptance of hedonism simply, but . . . to the conjunction of hedonism with an economic situation of which the investment of capital and its management for gain was the most obvious feature." This situation was "what has since been called a capitalistic system." Hedonistic economics is "an interpretation of human nature in terms of the market-place." It did not view the course of events as merely a sequence of unconstrued facts given by the industrial situation, but converted these facts into a pecuniary sequence, in which man's part was to respond swiftly and unquestioningly to the pecuniary situation, and to "adapt his vendible effects to the shifting demand as to realise something in the outcome." A man's gains in this traffic were not held to be losses to those with whom he dealt. They paid only what the items were worth to them, and consequently the pecuniary gain was a net gain to the community. "Those far-reaching organisations of invested wealth which have latterly come to prevail and to coerce the market were not then in the foreground."

The failure of classical economics to distinguish between capital as investment and as industrial appliances is one of the striking "remoter effects of the hedonistic preconception and its working out in terms of pecuniary gain." Invested wealth, as capital, is considered productive. Its increase is the most important factor in the promotion of well-being, and its return measures the degree of serviceability. In discussing industrial improvement it is usually assumed that the state of the arts remains unchanged, but this is to ignore the most important fact in the situation. Since capital funds are mobile, it is presumed that large-scale mechanical processes are easily shifted about. Success in the strategic shifting of security holdings is considered a measure of success in shifting, for industrial efficiency, the industrial appliances controlled by the securities. "By virtue of their hedonistic preconceptions, their habituation to the ways of a pecuniary culture, and their unavowed animistic faith that nature is in the right, the classical economists knew that the consummation to which, in the nature of things, all things tend, is the frictionless and beneficent competitive system." In this perfect money economy "the pecuniary motive . . . guides all the acts of economic man in a guileless . . . unswerving quest of the greatest gain at the least sacrifice." All factors of living are reduced to vendible items, to subservience to the competitive ideal of invested wealth.

Economic laws therefore become expressions of the quantitative—pecuniary—relations existing between the elements of wealth and investment. Such items as credit and population, for example, are treated "as elemental factors acting and reacting" through a variation of values "over the heads of the good people whose welfare they are working out." Classical economics gives a theory of value in which the valuer concerned in the matter, the living community, is eliminated. It is a "theory of life stated in terms of the normal paraphernalia of life," in terms of pecuniary symbols as ultimate realities, not in terms of selectively necessary industrial conduct.

Thus the animistic preconception has controlled speculative thinkers from the time of the scholastic writers, who discussed usury "from the point of view of its relation to the divine suzerainty," down to the classical writers, exemplified by Cairnes and John Stuart Mill, with their laws of natural wages and normal value. The difference is not in kind but in degree. But the fundamental axiom of economic science is, like any other convention, subject to "natural selection and selective adaptation"; when its truth is questioned, its use as a fundamental axiom is over. The process of natural selection, however, has not entirely changed the underlying metaphysics of economics, any more than it has changed the "metaphysics underlying the common law and the schedule of civil rights." Just as in law "the now avowedly useless and meaningless preconceptions of status and caste and precedent are even yet at the most metamorphosed and obsolescent rather than overpassed," so in economics the present generation still clings to the "metaphysics that fixed the point of view of the early classical political economy." This is true even of "those groups of economists who have most incontinently protested against the absurdity of the classical doctrines and methods." Consequently their exposition is "unwieldy, and inconsequent." Economic laws are held to be laws of conservation and selection, enforced by the pecuniary interest, rather than laws of "genesis and proliferation" wrought by economic interest. The pecuniary interest is assumed to be the economic interest, just as the production of property rights is uncritically assumed to be the production of serviceable goods. Thus Alfred Marshall, with his concept of "quasi-rents," resorts to "so essentially taxonomic a category as the received concept of rent" in discussing "such vitally dynamic features of the economic process as the differential effectiveness of different labourers or of different industrial plants, as well as the differential advantages of consumers." "Rent is a pecuniary category, a category of income, which is essentially a final term, not a category of the motor term, work or interest. It is not a . . . feature . . . of the process of industrial life, but a phenomenon of the pecuniary situation which emerges from this process under given conventional circumstances."

Hume, who was not primarily an economist, is the ideal exponent of the impersonal method. His point of view is in sharp contrast with "the Physiocratic discipline," which has been elaborated by the received economics. Hume, that "placid unbeliever," was not "gifted with a facile acceptance of the group inheritance that made the habit of mind of his generation. . . . He was gifted with an alert . . . scepticism touching everything that was well received. It is his office to prove all things, though not necessarily to hold fast that which is good. . . . There is in Hume . . . an insistence on the . . . seamy side of human affairs. He is not content with formulating his knowledge of things in terms of what ought to be or in terms of the objective point in the course of things. He is not even content with adding to the teleological account of the phenomena a chain of empirical, narrative generalisations as to the usual course of things. He insists, in season and out of season, on an exhibition of the efficient causes engaged in any sequence of phenomena; and he is . . . irreverently sceptical . . . as to the need . . . of any formulation of knowledge that outruns the reach of his own matter-of-fact, step-by-step argument from cause to effect. In short, he is too modern to be wholly intelligible to those of his contemporaries who are most neatly abreast of their time. He out-Britishes the British, and in his footsore quest for a perfectly tame explanation of things, he finds little comfort, and indeed scant courtesy, at the hands of his own generation. He is not in sufficiently naïve accord with the range of preconceptions then in vogue."

Veblen did not avowedly discuss the Marxist school in his articles. Its postulates were so divergent from those of "the modernised classical views" as to bar their consideration under the same head. Veblen asked, apparently in parody of the wage-fund doctrine and the accepted variants of interest theory presented by Böhm-Bawerk: "If we are getting restless under the taxonomy of a monocotyledonous wage doctrine and a crypto-gamic theory of interest, with involute, loculicidal, tomentous, and moniliform variants, what is the cytoplasm, centrosome, or karyokinetic process to which we may turn, and in which we may find surcease from the metaphysics of normality and controlling principles?"

To Veblen the fundamental fault of economists was their refusal to realise that the subject matter of their science is economic action, not "a quiescent normal situation," that economics must be studied from the standpoint of the economic interest, not the pecuniary interest, that the economic processes, not their pecuniary corollaries in human action, are the important consideration for the community. "The categories em-ployed for the purpose of knowing this economic conduct with which the scientists occupy themselves are not the categories under which the men at whose hands the action takes place themselves apprehend their own action at the instant of acting." Men thoroughly imbued with the matter-of-fact habit of mind which is demanded by modern mechanical industry have no serious interest in the discussion of the laws and theo-rems of economics treating of the normal course of things. Such discus-sions appear unreal and futile, for "they are not to be apprehended in the terms which these men make use of in handling the facts with which they are perforce habitually occupied."

The "discipline of stability," however, is certain to become increas-ingly inconvenient for the scientist. "With the growth of industrial or-ganisation and efficiency there must by selection and by adaptation super-vene a greater resort to the mechanical or dispassionate method," and the doctrines of the myth-maker will be eliminated. It is only a question of time until the animistic method will be replaced by the matter-of-fact, impersonal method of knowledge, and "the social and political sciences must follow the drift, for they are already caught in it."

CHAPTER XI

VEBLEN delivered before the Graduate Club of the university a series of papers—"The Instinct of Workmanship and the Irksomeness of Labour," "The Beginnings of Ownership," and "The Barbarian Status of Women"—in which he developed his ideas on the nature of the animistic and hedonistic preconceptions of modern business enterprise in terms of primitive culture. They were published in *The American Journal of Sociology*, beginning in September 1898 and ending in January 1899.

In the first paper Veblen declared that, if economics is to be an evolutionary science, it must take the instinct of workmanship as its guiding principle. He began with the hedonistic assumption of classical economics and dominant common sense, that man's ideal is "an unrestrained consumption of goods, without work." Useful effort is considered irksome, and man instinctively revolts against working to supply the means of life. Less distaste is felt for effort which brings gain without giving a product for human use, such as the effort involved in war, politics, or similar employments. Usually there is no avowed aversion to sports or those activities yielding "neither a pecuniary gain nor a useful product." But the repugnance felt for menial service is evidence that the mere uselessness of effort is not sufficient to save it from displeasure.

"The economic man" of the classical economists is an anomaly in the animal world, for no species which has a "consistent aversion to whatever activity maintains" it can survive in the struggle with other species. But the economic man's freedom from the law of natural selection is only apparent, not real. Man's adjustment to the purposes of his species has been fuller than that of his erstwhile competitors, and since he has so far outdistanced them he can now, "without jeopardy to the life of the species, play fast and loose with the spiritual basis of its survival."

Man by selective necessity has, however, an impulse or instinct of workmanship, and this "sense of merit and demerit with respect to the material furtherance or hindrance of life approves the economically effective act and deprecates economic futility." This norm of economic merit is closely related to the ethical norm of conduct and the æsthetic norm of taste. It is not a disposition towards effort, but a wish for achievement. A mature man likes to think he is of some use and he likes to see others engaged in some useful purpose.

The instinct of workmanship and its antithesis—"the conventional antipathy to useful effort"—are found together in "full discord in the common run of men," but, when "a deliberate judgment is passed on conduct or on events," the instinct of workmanship asserts its primacy as the abiding generic trait. "What meets unreserved approval is such conduct as furthers human life on the whole, rather than such as furthers the invidious or predatory interest of one as against another." The conventional aversion to labor, which is the expression of the instinct of sportsmanship, is a habit of thought possible only to a species which has outdistanced all competitors, and it "prevails only by sufferance and within limits" set by the primordial instinct of workmanship. True, the history of mankind as conventionally written is a "narrative of predatory exploits," and a "sportsmanlike inclination to warfare" is found in nearly all modern communities. The prevalent sense of honour, individual or national, is also an expression of the sense of sportsmanship. But throughout human culture the masses have in their everyday life been occupied in turning things to human use. "The proximate aim of all industrial improvement has been the better performance of some workmanlike task." This ideal proceeds from an appreciative interest in the work. Without that there would be only the aimless performance of duties. Material achievement has not been due to compulsion under a predatory regime, for the most striking advances have been accomplished where "the coercive force of a sportsmanlike exploitation has been least."

The selective process through which man has risen to leadership has made him a social, peaceful animal. He is not to be classed with those animals "which survive through overcoming and eating their rivals." Early man was a member of a group which depended for survival on its industrial efficiency and its "singleness of purpose in making use of the material means of life." Self-interest was necessarily thrown into the background. As an "accepted guide of action" it "is possible only as the concomitant of a predatory life." Early man thus had enforced upon him a canon of thought and taste which is "the instinct of workmanship." Even though the tendency towards emulation may have existed, the selective process eliminated "lines of descent unduly gifted with a self-regarding bias," and emulation could not result in "an individual acquisition or accumulation of goods" or a life consistently given to raids and disturbances.

But the instinct of workmanship and the circumstances of social life create a canon of conduct under which men who do not come up to the conventional standard of efficiency suffer a lack of esteem in their own eyes and in those of the community. Under the guidance of the taste for good work men are graded in respect of efficiency "according to a con-

ventional scheme of merit and demerit." There results, instead of a valu-
ing of serviceability, a measuring of capability "on the ground of visible
success." "The award of esteem comes habitually to rest on an invidious
comparison of persons instead of on the immediate bearing of the given
line of conduct upon the approved end of action." The proximate end of
effort becomes the putting forth of evidence of power rather than to
achieve an impersonal end for its own sake, "simply as an item of human
use." Thus under certain circumstances the instinct of workmanship takes
the form of "an emulative demonstration of force."

In the early primitive culture of small peaceable groups the appearance of industrial incapacity is to be avoided and thus there is emulation in
industrial efficiency. The primitive group is not fertile ground, however,
for a "vigorous emulative spirit." Two conditions which are necessary
for its growth are not effectively met in such communities—the "frequent
recurrence of conjunctures," calling for a great and sudden strain, and
the "exposure of the individual to a large, and especially to a shifting,
human environment whose approval is sought." Thus relatively little of
the emulative spirit is found in communities that have retained "the
archaic, peaceable constitution, or that have reverted to it from a higher
culture." In these communities "notions of economic rank and discrimination between persons, whether in point of possessions or in point of comfort," are practically in abeyance. There is only the slightest beginning
of a system of status with its invidious distinctions between classes and
employments.

But with the advance of tools, including weapons, there arises a distinction between "honorific employments" involving exploit, and "humiliating employments" involving the peaceful industrial aptitudes. With
the development of weapons men can devote themselves "exclusively to
the hunting of large game," and so develop this occupation into "a conventional mode of life reserved for a distinct class." With the development of industrial instruments a dense population can be supported, and
the constituted authorities can effectively control this population. Thus
develops that habitual hostile contact between groups which results in
warlike raids. The industrial advance allows the exemption of a portion
of the community from vulgar labour, and supplies the incentive for
prowess in arms. The most serious employment and that in which a spectacular effect may be achieved is conflict with men and beasts. "What is
recognised, without reflection or without misgiving, as serviceable and
effective . . . is fighting capacity. Exploit becomes the conventional
ground of invidious comparison between individuals." The population
becomes habituated to the sight and infliction of suffering and to the
emotions that go with fights and brawls. A man who is careful of his

good name "severely leaves all uneventful drudgery to the women and minors. . . . He puts in his time in the manly arts of war and devotes his talents to devising ways and means of disturbing the peace. That way lies honour." Those employments devoted to "tamely shaping inert material for human use" are debasing and ignoble, and they fall to those defective in predatory capacity, for they involve "no obvious destruction of life and no spectacular coercion of refractory antagonists." In fact, the barbarian, animistic belief in sympathetic magic leads men to avoid, on pain of infection, those occupations having to do with the everyday work of the group. The taboo "against womanly employments and foods and against intercourse with women applies with especial rigour during the season of preparation for any work of manly exploit, such as a great hunt or a warlike raid, or induction into some manly dignity, or society or mystery."

In short, womanly work and living are "ceremonially unclean." It is felt even today that women have no place in occupations such as priestly, diplomatic, or representative civil offices, or in such offices of domestic and body servants as are of a seriously ceremonial character—footmen, butlers, etc. Useful labour is wrong in the apprehension of men "not already beneath reproach," and well-known features of caste and taboo develop from this valuation. With the accumulation of wealth the members of the group divide into a servile class and a leisure class. Labour, as the privilege of the poor, becomes "shameful by force of its evil association with poverty." Physical irksomeness is not itself distasteful if the spiritual incentive be present. The usual recital of a campaigner's experience "carries a sweeping suggestion of privation . . . and loathsome death; the incidents and accessories of war are said to be . . . unwholesome, beyond the power of words." Nevertheless, "warfare is an attractive employment" to those gifted with a suitable habit of mind. "Most sports and many other polite employments that are distressing but creditable are evidence to the same effect." But activity serving the material purpose of the community is spiritually irksome, and is condemned by "polite usage," which is determined by the predatory traditions of the leisure class. For this irksomeness, which is no less real because it is not physical, there "is no remedy . . . short of a subversion of that cultural structure upon which our canons of decency rest." Appeals to taste and conscience have been ineffective. Man is bound by the traditions of decorum, which by prescription and example declare that work is incompatible with the higher warlike activity.

These canons which demand a withdrawal from useful activity rest on the institution of ownership. In the received economic theory it is accepted without question or reflection that "the ground of ownership is . . . the productive labour of the owner." Socialists have used this axiomatic premise to demand that "the labourer should receive the full product of his labour," and classical economists have found it difficult to explain "how 'the capitalist' is the 'producer' of the goods that pass into his possession, and how it is that the labourer gets what he produces." Guided by the preconceptions of a coercive natural order and natural rights, "the classical, pre-evolutionary economists" approach the question of ownership with only an incidental interest in its solution. It seems obvious to them that "the creative effort of an isolated, self-sufficing individual [is] the basis of the ownership vested in him."

But there is no self-sufficing individual, Veblen contended. All production takes place in an industrial community and by its help, for there is no technical knowledge apart from such a community and without technical knowledge production and the possibilities of ownership cannot exist. Since individual productivity and production do not exist, "the natural-rights preconception that ownership rests on the individually productive labour of the owner reduces itself to absurdity, even under the logic of its own assumptions." The natural-rights preconception supported the view that the consumption of such things as weapons and ornaments gives rise to ownership, and "in the eyes of the modern economists," too, such "unrestrained right of use and abuse" over such articles counts as ownership. But in barbarian culture, which colours the later phases of development, especially the "modern civilised communities . . . where the pecuniary point of view prevails," the relation between man and these so-called personal articles is something more vital than formal legal ownership.

The barbarian's animistic preconception covers everything, and he views such things as his name, peculiar tattoo marks, breath—especially when visible—hand- and footprints, favourite weapons, ornaments, and daily clothing as being organically related to him, in the nature of a "quasi-personal fringe." This pervasive personality is implied in sorcery, sacraments, and devout observances, in the adoration of images and symbols, in the almost universal veneration of consecrated places and structures, in astrology, and in divination by means of hair-cuttings and nail-parings. It is best evidenced by sympathetic magic. "If the sorcerer or anyone who works a charm can . . . get at the 'penumbra' of a person's individuality, as embodied in his fringe of quasi-personal facts, he will be able to work good or ill to the person . . . and the magic rites performed to this end will work their effect with greater force and precision in proportion as the object which affords the point of attack is more intimately related to the person upon whom the effect is to be wrought." An article on the margin of the fringe may be eliminated or alienated "either by default through lapse of time or by voluntary severance of the relation." It may pass from one person's sphere into that of another; or, if it is an item lending itself to common use, it may pass into the common stock. "As regards this common stock, no concept of ownership either communal or individual applies in the primitive community." Communal ownership must, by psychological necessity, come after individual ownership, for ownership implies an individual owner, a personal agent, and only by a later refinement in the nature of a legal fiction "is any group of men conceived to exercise a corporate discretion over objects." Corporate ownership is only quasi-ownership, a counterfeit and derivation of individual ownership.

When the idea of ownership gains consistency, the notion may develop that the articles a man owns are pervaded by his personality, but this idea and that of an organic relationship between article and owner do not necessarily coincide. An article of daily use may be in the quasi-personal fringe of a slave or an inferior member of the patriarchal household, but it is owned by the patriarch. The same person may stand in both relations, but the distinction remains. An article may change ownership without passing out of the quasi-personal fringe of the person to whom it belonged, as exemplified in "the mundane ownership of any consecrated place or structure which in the personal sense belongs to the . . . deity to whom it is sacred." So disparate are the two concepts that such items as a person's name, likeness, and footprints are only tardily included under his items of wealth. It is a fortuitous circumstance if they are owned by him, but they hold their place in his quasi-personal fringe. Even in modern civilised communities a vulgar belief includes the footprints and stalls of the domestic animals as a property of the animals, although the latter can scarcely be said to own them.

Thus "ownership is not a simple and instinctive notion . . . included under the notion of productive effort, nor under that of habitual use." Under the servile, feudalistic regime, only the head of the patriarchal household could own property, and the scope of his ownership was greatly limited if he had a feudal superior. "The tenure of property is a tenure by prowess . . . and a tenure by sufferance at the hands of a superior." The chief basis for legitimate ownership is always "the fact of habitual acceptance." The vested interests or prevailing dominating property rights upheld by immemorial usage are "inviolable except in the face of forcible dispossession." Even tenure acquired by seizure quickly becomes sacred through habituation.

In this "barbarian" culture of tenure on the basis of prowess the population is divided into two economic classes: those in the industrial employments, who normally can own nothing; and those in the non-industrial pursuits, such as war, government, sports, and devout observances, "who own such property as they have seized" or as has come to them through usage from forbears who seized and held it. But in the earlier "savage" culture with no such economic distinction "there is no leisure class resting its prerogative on coercion, prowess, and immemorial status; and there is also no ownership." No right of property prevails in communities "where there is no invidious distinction between employments, as exploit . . . and drudgery." Ownership is the differentiating characteristic between the savage and barbarian cultures. It is "the habit of coercion and seizure reduced to system and consistency under the surveillance of usage."

In the "peaceable communistic regime" of savagery ownership could not be tolerated, since "the dissensions arising from any such resort to mutual force and fraud among its members would have been fatal to the group." The group must consume its scanty means of subsistence in common; otherwise it would be defeated by a group which had not given up communal consumption. But although "the idea of individual appropriation of a store of goods is alien to the archaic man's general habits of thought," it arises easily in the warlike barbarian culture with its seizure of captives. The appropriation and accumulation of consumable goods could not have arisen as a direct outgrowth of the primitive horde-communism but it comes in easily and inconspicuously "as a consequence of the ownership of persons."

Captives are usually non-combatant women, whose labour is worth more than their maintenance. Captive women, moreover, are of great utility as trophies of the raid, the woman's character as a trophy is marked by her captor's peculiarly obvious coercive relation to her. He resents any attempt by others to exercise a similar coercive relation towards her and so usurp the laurels of his exploit, "very much as a warrior would under like circumstances resent a usurpation or an abuse of the scalps or skulls which he had taken from the enemy." This customary right of exclusive "use and abuse over an object" not obviously an organic part of his person "constitutes the relation of ownership, as naïvely apprehended." It gives rise to "a conventionally recognised marriage relation" and this ownership-marriage is the original of private property and the patriarchal family. Both these institutions are thus founded on the spirit of emulation. The captive women render personal service to their masters and are employed in the production of goods for them, as are all the peaceful, ignoble members of the group. "When the habit of looking upon and claiming the person identified with my invidious interest, or subservient to me, as 'mine,' has become an accepted and integral part of men's habits of thought," the concept of ownership, with the emulative spirit it embodies, is easily extended to the products of persons owned. The products of the women's labour are seized and valued because they contribute to the comfort and fullness of the master and indicate his superior force by their "conspicuous evidence" that he possesses many and efficient servants. Through the "prescriptive legitimacy" of predatory canons, with selective repression and elimination of those who will not conform, this ownership relation is accepted as the one right and beautiful economic relation between the two classes.

This coercive ownership relation also comes to be considered "the good and beautiful attitude" of men towards women. In order to have "decent standing" a man must attach some woman and thereby enter a "publicly acknowledged marriage relation" sanctioned by capture. But, as the group increases in size, it becomes difficult to obtain wives through capture, and a remedy is sought by a ceremonial capture within the group, which gives "ceremonial legitimacy and decency" to the marriage relation. To the "barbarian," with his animistic preconceptions, this practice of mock seizure is not "fatuous make-believe." He thinks that, if his predatory end is accomplished in the "accredited form and sequence," the same substantial result will be attained as that produced by the process imitated. Thus the male household, as the outgrowth of emulation between members of a group, is a predatory institution, and marriage is essentially "a ritual of . . . servitude," with the same consequences as if it were a real capture. Even after the formula has been softened, it is still the "woman's place to love, honour, and obey." Since the prestige of the patriarch is enhanced as the number of his women increases, polygamy arises. This ideal development is met in the harems of powerful patriarchal despots and chieftains. The patriarchal household, however, has been considerably weakened in western culture. The disintegration of the system of status is most obvious in communities "which have gone furthest in reorganising their economic life on the lines of industrial freedom." The respect for the institution of ownership-marriage has suffered its greatest decline among the industrial classes. Habits of thought developed by modern industrial life are apparently not favourable to it, and "the discipline of modern life—if not supplemented by a prudent inculcation of conservative ideals"—does not make for its rehabilitation.

In the development of culture the predatory male household was probably preceded by the maternal—the household of "the unattached women"—in which the man was disregarded. Where a mixture of the two forms is found, the lower class has the maternal household and the upper the paternal. Such mixtures seem to have been due in good part to the mingling of two distinct stocks, a peaceable and a predatory. The peaceable culture, characterised by common property and the maternal household, is subjected by the more warlike stock with the patriarchal household. But the patriarchal relation does not conform with the most ancient habits of the race. It develops in a system of status, and does not fit any other system. It cannot adapt itself to modern industrial conditions and is visibly breaking down at present. There may be some ground for holding that a reassertion of the generic habits of the race may disintegrate also the correlative institution of private property, "but that is perhaps a question of speculative curiosity rather than of urgent theoretical interest."

CHAPTER XII

VEBLEN was now forty-two years old, and Laughlin was still having difficulties in getting his appointment renewed. He had already served three years as an instructor and now asked for the customary raise of a few hundred dollars in salary. Harper told Veblen that he appreciated his services but would have no objection if he went elsewhere. He did not advertise the university. Veblen replied that he did not intend to do so and wrote out a letter of resignation. He did not really want to leave, however, and Laughlin went to Harper and secured the raise.

In 1899, a month after the appearance of "The Barbarian Status of Women," the last of his three *Journal* articles, Veblen published his first book, *The Theory of the Leisure Class: an Economic Study in the Evolution of Institutions*. He told Stuart that the general ideas of the book had been formed in his boyhood, in large part by his father's remarks, and "Some Neglected Points in the Theory of Socialism" bears testimony that the book had been brewing in his mind before he came to Chicago.

He apparently wrote the last draft while he was living in rooms rented from Starr. "Veblen used to bring it into my room," said Starr, "and read it aloud chapter by chapter." Veblen also read the manuscript aloud to former students and remarked that they would find it polysyllabic. He had to rewrite it completely a number of times before its literary style was acceptable to his publishers. They thought so little of its commercial possibilities that it was necessary, according to Ira Howerth, a colleague, for Veblen to put up a guarantee. From a literary standpoint the book is doubtless worthy of Ph.D. dissertations in English literature. Its extensive use of literary devices, including etymological precision, foggy language, and sharp comparisons and contrasts ever changing in form, has seldom been equalled in a study of an economic and social order. Phenomena which generally appear trivial to the ordinary intelligence are exaggerated to bring out the meaning or consequences of the dominant forces constituting the existing system. Even academic economics becomes a part of Veblen's arsenal.

The book reads as if it were a saga, as if, in accordance with saga traditions, the underlying motif constantly before the listener were the inevitable doom of the industrially advanced, democratic community, through the functioning of the heroic characters who are thrown up as an effective leisure class by conditions supposed to make for peace, and who go also to their destruction.

In the preface Veblen said that "the purpose of this inquiry [is] to discuss the place and value of the leisure class as an economic factor in modern life." More specifically it is concerned with those activities or employments having to do with "ownership—the immediate function of the leisure class proper," that is, the non-industrial propertied class—and with "the subsidiary functions concerned with acquisition and accumulation," or, in terms of three of his chapter headings, "Pecuniary Emulation," "Conspicuous Leisure," and "Conspicuous Consumption." In this organisation of his material Veblen remained true to the letter if not the spirit of the fundamental premises of classical economics, as laid down by John Stuart Mill.

The book falls into two parts of seven chapters each. The first part, an elaboration of the first part of "Some Neglected Points in the Theory of Socialism," is a discussion of the nature of the motive of emulation in pecuniary culture. It closes with "Dress as an Expression of the Pecuniary Culture," which is substantially "The Economic Theory of Women's Dress." The second part of the book is primarily occupied with clarifying the argument of the first. It considers the effect of the survival of the leisure class, or pecuniary culture, under modern industrial conditions. In place of the "composite point of view" of the *Quarterly* essays, the centre of discussion is the economic structure, made up of incompatible pecuniary and industrial institutions. Veblen's spokesman in *The Theory of the Leisure Class* is not the "socialist propagandist" of "Some Neglected Points in the Theory of Socialism" or the "modern scientist" of the *Quarterly* articles, but the "dispassionate common man."

The data, Veblen declared in the preface, "have by preference been drawn from everyday life, by direct observation or through common notoriety, rather than from more recondite sources at a farther remove." The introductory chapter presents the "theoretical premises" of the book. A more explicit statement of its theoretical position is made in the series of papers published in *The American Journal of Sociology*, "but the argument does not rest on these—in part novel—generalisations in such a way that it would altogether lose its possible value as a detail of economic theory in case these novel generalisations should, in the reader's apprehension, fall away through being insufficiently backed by authority or data."

In a modern industrial community the invidious distinction between the leisure class employments of exploit and the unworthy employments has so little obvious significance that it receives slight attention from writers on economics. "When viewed in the light of that modern common sense which has guided economic discussion," the distinction "seems formal and insubstantial." But it persists tenaciously as a commonplace preconception. The prevailing distinction between industrial and non-industrial employments "is a transmuted form of the barbarian distinction between exploit and drudgery."

In the predatory social economy the function of the able-bodied man is to kill and destroy all competitors, to reduce to subservience all alien forces in the environment that assert themselves refractorily against his self-seeking interests. Slaughter and the instruments of slaughter, being honorific, are of high worth and value. An honorific act is a recognised, successful act of aggression. Conversely, industry and industrial employments are dishonourable; therefore productive labour is irksome. The conventional leisure class and the institution of ownership as a conventional equitable claim to extraneous things are results of the same economic forces. In their origin in a predatory culture they are different aspects of the same general facts of prowess. The motive for those chiefly concerned with the accumulation of wealth is pecuniary emulation, never, to any significant degree, the means of subsistence. "The dominant incentive" to ownership "was from the outset the invidious distinction attaching to wealth, and save temporarily and by exception no other motive has usurped the primacy." Selective admission to the leisure class has been proceeding "ever since the fashion of pecuniary emulation set in—which is much the same as saying, ever since the institution of a leisure class was first installed."

Man's sense of purpose and distaste for all futility goes with him "when he emerges from the naïve communal culture where the dominant note of life is the unanalysed and undifferentiated solidarity of the individual and the group with which his life is bound up." Under the regime of individual ownership, "where the self-regarding antithesis between man and man reaches fuller consciousness," the desire for achievement—which is the economic motive underlying the instinct of workmanship—tends to shape itself into a straining to excel others in pecuniary achievement. Distaste for futility reinforces the emulative incentive and makes the struggle for pecuniary reputability more intense "by visiting with a sharper disapproval . . . all evidence of shortcoming in point of pecuniary success." Thus the leisure class culture is an emulative, pecuniary variant of the instinct of workmanship. With this superior leisure class, emulation demands adherence to the ancient prescriptive requirement of conspicuous abstention from productive labour, a canon from which conspicuous consumption of life and goods derives.

Emulation is the most powerful economic motive, with the exception of the instinct of self-preservation, and in the modern industrial community it expresses itself in pecuniary emulation. So far as regards modern society this "is equivalent to saying that it expresses itself in some form of conspicuous waste." Conspicuous waste includes all expenditure incurred on the ground of invidious pecuniary comparison. The word "waste" is not to be taken "in an odious sense, as implying an illegitimate expenditure of human product or of human life. In the view of economic theory the expenditure is no more and no less legitimate than any other expenditure." This expenditure "is here called waste because it does not serve human life or human well-being on the whole, not because it is waste or misdirection of effort or expenditure as viewed from the standpoint of the individual consumer." The latter indulges in it under the guidance of the canon of conspicuous consumption. "To meet with unqualified approval, any economic fact must approve itself under the test of impersonal usefulness," that is, usefulness according to the "generically human" instinct of workmanship. This instinct, rooted in dispassionate common sense, is the final court of appeal. "Relative or competitive advantage of one individual in comparison with another does not satisfy the economic conscience, and therefore competitive expenditure has not the approval of this conscience." The law of conspicuous waste, however, controls the prevailing pecuniary scheme of life. It does not encourage innovation, but is merely regulative. It abjures the methods of life and kinds of goods which are most efficient industrially, because they do not contain the necessary element of superfluous cost on which to rest a complacent invidious comparison. The value of the " 'better' grades" of items is due to this "indirect utility." As a result of this fundamental principle of waste "pecuniary beauty" is confounded with æsthetic beauty, and pecuniary serviceability with brute economic serviceability or the human ends of the community.

The veneration for "the pecuniary or the leisure-class culture" is comparable to the veneration for classicism—a respect for that which is obsolete from the standpoint of modern requirements of compatibility with "the effective evolutionary process." "Conspicuous waste and conspicuous leisure are reputable because they are evidence of pecuniary strength; pecuniary strength is reputable or honorific because, in the last analysis, it argues success and superior force." Thus the conventional scheme of decent living calls for considerable exercise of the earlier barbarian traits. In this scheme conspicuous leisure is of equal importance with conspicuous consumption, both of them based on waste as the means of achieving a good pecuniary name. The choice between them is only a matter of advertising expediency. But conspicuous leisure from useful activities is the older and more comprehensive principle of the leisure-class scheme.

The mature phase in the life history of the leisure class is the "quasi-peaceable" stage, which succeeds the predatory stage. In this phase of the pecuniary culture the constituted authorities and the customs of ownership are more stable. There is a formal observance of peace and order, but life still has too much of coercion and class antagonism to be called peaceable in the full sense of the word. This is the system of status, with its fundamental institution of chattel slavery. The principle of conspicuous leisure is so effective that the community's industry would be limited to the subsistence minimum of the working class were it not for "slave labour, working under a compulsion more rigorous than that of reputability." The leisure-class occupations are still war, government, sports, devout observances, learning. Speculative theorists have argued that these occupations are incidentally and indirectly productive, but the effective answer is that an increase of wealth by productive labour is not the motive of the leisure class in engaging in them. War and government are carried on in good part for the pecuniary gain of those engaged in them, that is, the gain is obtained by the honourable methods of seizure and conversion.

Leisure as an employment is closely allied to exploit, and its criteria are like the trophies of exploit. In its mature development the members of the leisure class customarily assume insignia of honour, which serve "as a conventionally accepted mark of exploit" and indicate its "quantity or degree." The use of trophies develops into a system of rank, title, degrees, and insignia, of which typical examples are medals and heraldic devices. In its highest development, however, the principle of conspicuous leisure expresses itself in immaterial goods, of the character of proficiency in manners and dress and a knowledge of dead languages and occult sciences, which do not directly further human life. That part of the life of leisure not spent in the sight of spectators serves its end of pecuniary reputability "only in so far as it leaves a tangible, visible result that can be put in evidence and can be measured and compared with products of the same class exhibited by competing aspirants" for pecuniary repute.

The taboo on productive labour results also in a spurious leisure class living an abject and precarious life. Its typical members are the decayed gentleman and the lady who has seen better days. Accumulation is not to be obtained by direct seizure, but it is morally impossible for them to stoop to industrial labour. This taboo may even at times prove stronger than the instinct of self-preservation. Great captains and chieftains have preferred to destroy themselves rather than break the prevailing convention against useful labour and make the necessary physical effort to save themselves. On the other hand the appearance of a "cumulative life of leisure" and the effect of "passive habituation" in producing pathological and other idiosyncrasies of person and manner can be acquired by a short-cut process called snobbery. By an arduous training in the pecuniary proprieties a "syncopated evolution of gentle birth and breeding is achieved in the case of a goodly number of families and lines of descent."

The canons of taste, according to which the award of pecuniary reputability is made, are constantly undergoing revision to meet more completely the requirements of the principle of conspicuous leisure. Variations in form and expression, but not in substance, are allowed. The birthright and criterion of the ideal gentleman is irresponsible dominion, and "the base-born commoner delights to stoop and yield" before this attribute of superior worth.

In the predatory, patriarchal culture "women and other slaves are highly valued, both as an evidence of wealth and as a means of accumulating wealth. . . . Together with cattle . . . they are the usual form of investment for profit." But with the development of industry and the accumulation of property in relatively fewer hands women of gentle blood are exempted from industry. Gentle blood is blood ennobled by protracted contact with accumulated wealth or unbroken prerogative. These women are preferred in marriage. Gradually other women are exempted, in the order of their gentility, and a specialised domestic service is formed. Half-caste, impecunious, or marginal gentlemen affiliate themselves by a system of dependence and fealty to the great, and gain from their masters an increment of the means for leading a life of leisure. Uniforms and insignia evidence the source from which these underlings receive their income and distinguish those dependents rendering noble service in predatory pursuits from those rendering humiliating industrial service. The leisure of these servants is vicarious, since it is for the benefit of their master. Maintenance of servants who produce nothing evidences greater wealth, position, and prowess than the possession of slaves who produce goods, for useless servants are proof of the great captain's or chieftain's ability "to sustain large pecuniary damage without impairing his superior opulence." The waste of goods in great competitive entertainments is also especially effective as evidence of pecuniary strength.

The care of the quasi-personal or corporate household in the hands of the housewife performing vicarious leisure must conform to "the great economic law" of "conspicuously wasteful expenditure of time and substance" or effort. If beauty or comfort is accidentally achieved, it must be by methods that are commendable to this controlling principle. Much squalor and discomfort will be endured before the last pretence of pecuniary decency will be put away. The high requirements of pecuniary decency and dominance are ever increasing, since there is no merit in mere spiritless conformity to a standard of dissipation of life and goods "that is lived up to as a matter of course by everyone" in the traffic. This emulation, constantly increasing in scope and narrowing in character, absorbs any "increase in the community's industrial efficiency or output of goods, after the most elementary needs are met." Thus technological advance has not served to lighten the strain of the industrial classes. Because of this element in the pecuniary standard of living, "J.S. Mill was able to say that 'hitherto it is questionable if all the mechanical inventions yet made have lightened the day's toil of any human being.' " A fundamental principle in the quasi-peaceable stage of industry, with its fundamental institution of chattel slavery, is that the "base, industrious class should consume only what may be necessary to their subsistence," and this restriction tends to disappear only formally in the industrial system of private property and wage labour where, in a numerically small though very conspicuous fraction of the community, "the habits of thought peculiar to the barbarian culture have suffered but a relatively slight disintegration."

The leisure class in the nature of things normally receives the luxuries and higher comforts. Intoxicating beverages and costly narcotics are honorific, and thus drunkenness and other pathological consequences of the free use of stimulants, and certain social diseases, tend to become honorific. They are a "mark at the second remove, of the superior status of those who are able to afford the indulgence." Under this pecuniary canon "the thief or swindler who has gained great wealth by his delinquency has a better chance than the small thief of escaping the rigorous penalty of the law; and some good repute accrues to him from his increased wealth and from his spending the irregularly acquired possessions in a seemly manner." In the last analysis "all that considerable body of morals that clusters about the notion of the sacredness of ownership is itself a psychological precipitate of the traditional meritoriousness of wealth."

In Veblen's theory of fashion, dress, too, is conceived as an institution of pecuniary emulation. A sense of beauty is incompatible with the law of conspicuous waste, and although a combination is attempted by make-believe, the effect is only temporary. Forms of dress which will give evidence of pecuniary strength are necessarily of ever-increasing grotesqueness and wastefulness, so that the promptings of the æsthetic sense enforce a change. The new form or detail must, however, also adhere to the principle of conspicuous waste, and there is thus continual change in fashions. The grotesqueness increases and consequently the changes come more rapidly, with ever-increasing disturbance of the community so far as comfort is concerned.

The industrious members of the community, because of their need of the means of livelihood, have the liveliest incentive to reconstruct the received standards and to change their habits of life to make use of technological advance. The leisure class, however, resting on the unequal distribution of wealth and sustenance, is not an organic part of the industrial community, and is not forced, on pain of elimination, to change its habits of life, its theoretical views of the external world. Its function, which conservative spokesmen justify as a matter of policy, is to retard social advance to a conventional scheme of living more in accordance with modern material exigencies.

The human characteristics ordinarily bred by the pecuniary stage proper of predatory culture are essentially unstable and transitory. From the standpoint of the modern requirements of collectivity, they are evidence of an arrested moral development. The traits characterising the man best able to survive in the regime of status are, in their primary expression, "ferocity, self-seeking, clannishness, disingenuousness, a free resort to force and fraud"; that is, "traits highly serviceable for individual expediency in a life looking to invidious success." In the more peaceable stage of predatory culture, in the highly developed pecuniary stage, these "aristocratic virtues" of forcible seizure take a sophisticated form covered by fraud, such as the pecuniary virtues of providence, prudence, chicane, browbeating, falsehood, and administrative ability. But the substitution of chicane for devastation as the best means for accumulating wealth and achieving leisure-class status "takes place only in an uncertain degree."

The peace-disturbing dolichocephalic blonds have a high degree of leisure-class temperament, although men who have scored a "brilliant (Napoleonic) success on the basis of an impartial self-seeking and absence of scruple" have commonly belonged to the brachycephalic brunet type in physique. In distinction to the competitive class, the competitive individual succeeds best if he does not possess the trait of clannishness or loyalty to a chieftain, tenet, or party. Thus, under the prevailing regime of "shrewd trading and unscrupulous management," the individual who "through an exceptional exemption from scruple" can "serenely overreach and injure his fellows" is most successful.

Actually the competitive individual has no place in the modern industrial mechanism, but this anomaly is obscured by the ruling class's maintenance of the traditions of war and rapacity and by the community's fictitious interest in a collective or corporate good fame. "The collective interests of any modern community centre in industrial efficiency," in the vulgar, productive employments which "require honesty, diligence, peacefulness, good will, an absence of self-seeking, and an habitual recognition and apprehension of causal sequence, without admixture of animistic belief, and without a sense of dependence on any preternatural intervention in the course of events." These requirements are met by the generic variant of human nature from that "hypothetical culture" of savagery, where ownership does not exist. His traits are "that instinct of race solidarity which we call conscience, including the sense of truthfulness and equity, and the instinct of workmanship," in its naïve expression "as a non-emulative, non-invidious interest in men and things." These seem to be hereditary characteristics. They have never been entirely eliminated, despite the weakening effects of the modern pecuniary culture "of status and of individual and class antithesis." But this savage nature is a failure according to the standards of a modern enlightened community. The savage traits direct the individual's energy to other ends than pecuniary gain, and, even if he pursues such gain, he adopts the indirect and ineffective methods of industry rather than a "free and unfaltering career of sharp practice." An excess of the peaceable industrial temperament leads to elimination.

Thus a distinction is evident between the pecuniary employments in which lie the economic interests of the leisure class, and the industrial employments in which lie those of the industrial classes. The employments of the leisure class foster the predatory temperament and aptitude and are concerned with those economic functions comprised within "the range of ownership of wealth as conceived in terms of exchange value, and its management and financiering through a permutation of values." These dominating financial operations constitute the function of the modern captain of industry. He is an astute man, but Veblen describes such a man later as of "no economic value to the community," a hindrance to the generic life process. His captaincy is a pecuniary one. His administration of industry is only permissive, and the "mechanically effective details of production and industrial organisation are delegated to subordinates of a less 'practical' turn of mind—men who are possessed of a gift for workmanship, rather than administrative ability" of the predatory sort.

Since leisure-class standards are standards of pecuniary decency, the employments dealing immediately with large-scale ownership and financing are the most reputable. Next come the employments immediately subservient to ownership, such as banking, which suggests large ownership, and law, to which "no taint of usefulness . . . attaches." "The lawyer is exclusively occupied with the details of predatory fraud."

Mercantile employments are high in repute in proportion as they involve a large element of ownership and a low element of usefulness. Thus the retailing of the vulgar necessities of life is on the lowly level of handicraft and factory labour, and "the work of directing mechanical processes is of course on a precarious footing as regards respectability."

Modern pecuniary, or "business" institutions, although fundamentally incompatible with industrial institutions, have developed in response to a more facile pecuniary exploitation of the industrial process. The creation of vested interests, by such means as enactments in regard to bankruptcy, receiverships, limited liability, currency, pools, coalitions of employers or labour, is important to the propertied in proportion as they are propertied, that is, to the extent that they are a leisure class. With the development of corporate enterprise the growing number of the great captain's subordinates and dependents become increasingly exempt from the predatory habits of life given by the pecuniary discipline, since the business becomes reduced to a routine in which there is "less immediate suggestion of overreaching and exploiting a competitor." Thus the pecuniary culture cuts away its own foundation by eliminating the habit of invidious comparison in respect of efficiency or pecuniary gain, and modern competitive business enterprise is revealed as an aimless waste of energy. The captain of industry and "the great leisure-class function of ownership" will become unnecessary as pecuniary institutions develop into "soulless" joint-stock corporations. This consummation, obviously, lies far in the future.

The distinction between the employments of ownership and those of production is not, however, a hard-and-fast distinction between persons, since those engaged in productive employments are also to some extent concerned with matters of pecuniary competition, such as the competitive fixing of wages and salaries and the purchase of goods for consumption. Under the modern competitive regime, survival and success depend proximately on fitness for acquisition, and without something of the predatory traits of cunning and ferocity, even though in a sophisticated form, an individual would be in the position of a hornless steer in a group of horned cattle. If "pecuniary efficiency" were not "incompatible with industrial efficiency, the selective action of all occupations would tend to the unmitigated dominance of the pecuniary temperament," to the dominance of the "economic man," whose "only interest is the self-regarding one and whose only human trait is prudence." Modern industry, however, requires an impersonal, non-invidious interest in the work on hand. This interest in work, without which the elaborate processes of industry would be impossible and would not have been conceived, "differentiates the workman from the criminal . . . and . . . the captain of industry." Since work must be done, there is a qualified selection favouring the spiritual attitude towards work in a certain range of occupations. But the elimination of the economically unfavourable characteristics of the pecuniary culture is an uncertain process.

"The accumulation of wealth at the upper end of the pecuniary scale implies privation at the lower end of the scale." Although private property is in itself of minor importance, being simply a contrivance supposedly for the convenience of men in society, there is a solidarity in the scheme of institutions of the modern propertied class which is a formidable barrier to the simple alteration of any isolated item composing it. By this solidarity, fortified by vested class interests and prescriptive canons of conspicuous waste, industrial exemption and conservatism, pecuniary emulation and pecuniary decency, the leisure class creates a large subservient class, unable to satisfy either its physical needs or the higher needs of decent expenditure and conspicuous hoarding. This relation of dependence and frustration leaves the lower classes without energy for acquiring the habits of thought required by modern industrial efficiency or for appreciating the modern scientific point of view and its implications. Like the leisure class, the indigent class lives by the industrial process rather than in it, and as a result lower-class types take on the qualities primarily belonging to the upper class. Thus the modern pecuniary struggle, by conserving the traits of the leisure class, perpetuates the prevailing maladjustment of institutions. It tends to conserve and rehabilitate the predatory temperament and culture which "the industrial evolution of society in its later stages acts to eliminate."

The ideal pecuniary man—the modern captain of industry—is "like the ideal delinquent in his unscrupulous conversion of goods and persons to his own ends, and a callous disregard of the feelings and wishes of others, and of the remoter effects of his actions." This "modern survival of prowess" is addicted to sport and gambling, to aimless emulation, to a superstitious habit of mind and magical practices, often expressing themselves in a "certain servile devotional fervour and a punctilious attention to devout observances." The leisure-class canon demanding "strict and comprehensive futility" acts slowly and pervasively, by a selective elimination of all useful modes of life, on pain of disrepute. Any activity persistently engaged in "must conform to the generically human canon of efficiency for some objective end," but the instinct of workmanship acts impulsively and is satisfied with a proximate purpose. A member of the leisure class with a slightly reflective habit or a sense of the ulterior trend of his actions will satisfy the generic instinct of usefulness by making himself dominant in sportsmanlike activities.

Sportsmanship—"the predatory and animistic habit of mind"—which is especially characteristic of the hereditary leisure class, is fostered by the pecuniary occupations. Leisure-class status is ultimately determined by fighting capacity, which in its corporate form is called patriotism or the martial spirit. This barbarian way of life is characteristic of boys and the boyish-minded, and the leisure class systematically breeds in the young these habits of adventuresome exploit, exotic ferocity, cunning and status, through "pseudo-military organisations," in charge of "clergymen and other pillars of society." "The pantomime of astuteness is commonly the first step in the assimilation to the professional sporting man which a youth undergoes after matriculation in any reputable school, of the secondary or the higher education." The sportsman resorts continually to make-believe. His destructive apparatus is greater than necessary, and the movements of strategy and manipulation are needlessly exaggerated in order to convince the participants of the seriousness of their games. The result of their activity is to keep "nature" in "a state of chronic desolation," although the love of nature is their ostensible incentive. In athletics and other warlike games a vocabulary of slang is used which makes the struggle seem like actual war.

The leisure class justifies such activities on the ground that they breed the "manly qualities"; that is, although sports are essentially of the nature of invidious exploit, it is presumed that by some remote and obscure effect they develop a temperament "conducive to non-invidious work." But the manly virtues fostered by sports are actually those of "truculence and clannishness." "It has been said . . . that the relation of football to physical culture is much the same as that of the bull-fight to agriculture." The habitual employment of an umpire and "the minute technical regulations governing the limits and details of permissible fraud" show that the game is made up of fraudulent practice, attempts to overreach the opponents, and a "callous disregard of the interest of others, individually or collectively. Resort to fraud, in any guise, and under any legitimation of law or custom is an expression of a narrow self-regarding mind." "The dispassionate common man," however, is beginning to feel that the institution of sport and related institutions from the barbarian past, especially "the entire existing system of the distribution of wealth," lack justification. The unrest regarding sports and related institutions and the increase in apologies for them, are due to the fact that they do not effectively satisfy the generic instinct of workmanship. The emulative predatory impulse, the instinct of sportsmanship, is essentially unstable in comparison with the primordial instinct from which it has developed and differentiated itself. "Tested by this ulterior norm . . . predatory emulation, and therefore the life of sport, falls short."

Another characteristic trait, found alike in the leisure class and in the lower-class delinquent, is the gambling propensity. This belief in luck, or sense of fortuitous necessity, is a belief in the possibility of "propitiating, or of deceiving and cajoling . . . the objects which constitute the apparatus and accessories" of the barbarian games of chance and skill. From this simple animism of the predatory discipline develops a belief in an inscrutable constraining preternatural agency which is endowed with the habits of thought of the predatory barbarian, and which works through the objects with which it is associated, influencing the outcome of any enterprise or contest. This habit of mind counts "as a blunder in the apprehension and valuation of facts" for the purposes of industry and science, although in the peaceable stages of handicraft and agriculture, when a rough equality prevailed, it was not so disturbing. There is a substantial identity between the beliefs in prowess, status, and anthropomorphism. "The predatory, emulative habit of mind here called prowess" is the "barbarian variant of the generically human instinct of workmanship," taking this form "under the guidance of a habit of invidious comparison of persons . . . the relation of status is a formal expression of such an invidious comparison duly gauged and graded according to a sanctioned schedule"; and an anthropomorphic cult is an institution characterised by "the relation of status between the human subject as inferior and the personified preternatural agency as superior."

The practice of devout observances is intimately related to the springs of action underlying the institution of the leisure class. The devout attitude accentuates the divergence between the "self-regarding interest and the interests of the generically human life process," and is characteristic of the classes that live by the industrial process rather than in it. No question is entertained as to the preternatural agent's moral character and purpose in interfering in events. Despite the modern popular conception of God as a father, in accordance with the patriarchal cast of the quasi-peaceable culture, he still remains a warlike chieftain inclined to an overbearing and arbitrary manner of government. The barbarian epithets applied to the divinity "have a high æsthetic and honorific value" to modern worshippers. There is a substantial identity between the consumption in behalf of the divinity and that of a gentleman of leisure—a chieftain or patriarch—in the upper-class society of the barbarian culture. Expensive edifices of an outworn type are set aside for both. The dress of their servants is also archaic. Ceremonial cleanliness insists that the garments of laymen must carry as little suggestion as may be of industrial activity when they enter the sanctuary or audience hall. The normal and deliberately invented sacred or secular holidays and days of fasting are seasons of compulsory abstention from materially useful activity and from consumption conducing to the fullness of life or the comfort of the consumers. The consequent honorific effect, or pecuniary strength, is imputed to the person or striking fact which the holiday celebrates. It is tribute levied upon the community in the form of vicarious leisure.

In the ideal barbarian scheme, the scheme of devout observances, the priestly class not only must abstain from labour believed to contribute to the general material welfare, but is forbidden to seek material gain even when possible without industrial activity. If the priest's own sense of sacerdotal propriety does not prevent transgression, the sense of propriety prevailing in the community will so obtrusively assert itself in his fortunes as to enforce his conformity or his retirement from office. For these highest practitioners of vicarious leisure and vicarious consumption the bounds of permissible indulgence are drawn closer than for laymen. They must avoid the vocabulary of industry, and human matters must be discussed with such "generality and aloofness" as to imply that the master whom the speaker represents is interested in the activities necessary for the community "only so far as to permissively countenance them." Beyond the priestly class, in an ascending hierarchy, ordinarily comes a superhuman vicarious leisure class of angels, saints, etc., with dependent classes performing vicarious leisure for them, as is done by the dependent leisure class under the patriarchal system. The principle of status runs through the entire hierarchical system, both visible and invisible. Some priests diverge from the established schedule and take thought ostensibly or permissively for their own material comfort and that of the community. But they belong to a half-caste priesthood, and their cults are found in relatively young denominations having chiefly a middle-class constituency. They often represent originally a revulsion against the principle of status upon which the institution of the priesthood rests. Such a priest is at first a representative and servant of the organisation or corporation, but with its increase in wealth and its consequent achievement of a leisure-class point of view the priest develops into a member of the special priestly class and spokesman of the divine master.

With due allowance for "exceptions and sporadic departures from the normal," the "classes . . . low in economic efficiency, or in intelligence, or both, are peculiarly devout." Similarly, the woman, particularly the upper-class woman, not standing in direct organic relation to the industrial process, carries over into the realm of the supernatural the logic and the logical processes of her everyday life of status and vicarious leisure, and finds herself at home and content in a range of ideas which to the adult man are "alien and imbecile." Of a like nature are the ideas of the middle class, whose habits of thought are shaped by the pecuniary occupations, with their quasi-predatory character of "arbitrary command and submission and . . . shrewd practice . . . akin to predatory fraud." In the United States the wealthier class of the North is developing a devotional habit similar to that of the hereditary leisure class of the industrially backward South, with its system of status and its habits of sportsmanship, drunkenness, gambling, and duels. "Weddings, funerals, and the like honorific events" among the superior wealthy class are "solemnised with some especial degree of religious circumstance," as in the barbarian culture. The naïve, sensational method of appeal is more used in the sacerdotal structures of the upper leisure class than in those of the lower leisure and middle class. Ritualistic features are accentuated at the cost of the intellectual in devout observance.

The prevailing denominations began with a ritual and a paraphernalia of austere simplicity, but with the growth of their members' wealth they have adopted many of the spectacular elements they once renounced, and the devout habit progressively gains in scope and elaboration among the superior wealthy class. All the apparatus and services in devout observances may be attributed to the great pecuniary law of conspicuous waste of life, effort, and goods. Directly and indirectly this devout consumption lowers the vitality of the community and prevents the necessary institutional adaptation to modern requirements. This effect is obscured by the fact that the sense of human solidarity and sympathy and the "non-reverent sense of æsthetic congruity with the environment" blend with the incompatible motives of the ecclesiastical institution and "contribute materially to its survival in name and form even among people who may be ready to give up the substance of it."

It would seem that the leisure class, free from the direct, grinding strain of the pecuniary struggle to which the lower classes are subject, would give considerable scope to interests which are not invidious. Members of the leisure class, it is true, show an interest in "philanthropic and reformatory effort," such as temperance and similar social reforms and large-scale enterprises for improving the poor. Apparently the "greater number of men who have to do with industry in the way of pecuniarily managing an enterprise take some interest and some pride in seeing that the work is well done and industrially effective and this even apart from the profit which may result from any improvement of this kind." Entrance to the leisure class, however, lies through the pecuniary employments, and only those with a superior predatory endowment are selectively admitted. Without the pecuniary temperament a stock will have its fortune dissipated. Many moves for amelioration are set on foot and many large enterprises are ostensibly devoted to industrial improvement, but all must conform to the ceremonial canons of pecuniary decency, which are reducible to "the principles of waste, futility, and ferocity" so that there is "much coming and going, and a deal of talk, to the end that the talkers may not have occasion to reflect on the effectual economic value of their traffic." Such organisations are undertaken for the good repute and even for the pecuniary gain of the promoters and their supporters. A man may meritoriously take a quantitative interest in the organisation by subscription and be a member of the managing committee, or more meritoriously attempt to elevate the tastes of the poor and to provide opportunities for their spiritual amelioration, but the predatory canons of pecuniary decency pervasively insist that a man in good standing must not show intimate familiarity with industrial life and processes sufficient to make an ameliorative organisation effective for its ostensible material end.

The institutions of the higher learning furnish a good example of what happens to ostensibly non-invidious enterprises under the guidance of pecuniary canons. These institutions of the priestly life have been, at least until recently, conservative, reactionary, and given to devout observances. As in the predatory scheme of status, a hierarchy of ranks—an apostolic succession—prevails, and there is much shamanistic, ceremonial ritual and practice. The modern practitioners of higher education are the logical descendants of the ancient medicine men who, with their sacred apparatus, symbols, and inscrutable realities, attempted spectacular effects to convince the community of their relation with the divinity. The scholastic discipline gives a knowledge of the unknowable, and this occult, inscrutable knowledge is held to be the only true knowledge. In contrast to the lower learning, "the higher learning comprises such knowledge as is primarily of no economic or industrial effect"; it is education for leisure-class membership, not for service to the community. The classics are venerated, for classic means obsolete and therefore reputable. A classical education means industrial exemption, since a considerable amount of effort must be wasted to acquire it. Next to the classics the administrative disciplines, the social sciences, are of highest repute. "These so-called sciences are substantially bodies of maxims of expediency for guidance in the leisure-class office of government as conducted on a proprietary basis." With the substitution of the modern captain of industry for the priest as the immediate director of educational enterprise "administrative ability and skill in advertising the enterprise count for rather more than they once did, as qualifications of the work of teaching. This applies especially in those sciences that have most to do with everyday facts of life, and it is particularly true of schools in the economically single-minded community."

But although the higher learning "is a by-product of the priestly office and the life of leisure," modern science, on the contrary, "is a by-product of the industrial process." Advance in theoretical knowledge does not come from the accepted members of the higher learning—the ideal leisure class. Occasionally contributions from "the modern, economic or industrial, matter-of-fact standpoint" are made by aberrant scions of the leisure class who are sufficiently influenced by the impersonal standpoint to escape the anthropomorphic standpoint of status, but advance comes primarily from members of the industrious class who are not so underfed or overworked that they have no margin of energy left for other occupations than finding daily sustenance. The classes particularly qualified in this way are those whose employment approaches that of the mechanic and engineer, those, in other words, who enter effectively into the industrial life. The discipline to which they are exposed tends to eliminate the animistic, predatory, invidious attitude of interpreting phenomena, and consequently they are inimical to anthropomorphic tendencies and devout observances. They have a proclivity for undevout scepticism, for the materialistic point of view required by industrial activity. These modern scientists are the instruments by which the habits of thought developed by "modern associated life and the mechanical industries are turned to account for theoretical knowledge." Men have come to "systematise the phenomena of this environment, and the facts of their own contact with it, in terms of causal sequence," only to the extent that industrial life enforces the recognition of an impersonal, causal sequence in the practical affairs of life. The modern investigators, savants, scientists, inventors, speculative thinkers, do their most telling work outside the shelter of the schools. The alien body of knowledge produced by this extra-scholastic discipline of the "industrial" employments in the wider sense is finally assimilated by the higher learning when it has long outlived its usefulness. "Men who have occupied themselves" with "new departures which touch the theory of human relations at any point," and have thereby sought "to widen the scope of human knowledge, have found a place in the scheme of the university tardily and by a reluctant tolerance, rather than by a cordial welcome."

The predatory life, however, is beginning to lose its position of dominance, and an attitude of disapproval towards futility in human life is perceptibly returning. In modern industrial communities it is "the average, dispassionate sense of men" that the ideal character is one "which makes for peace, good-will, and economic efficiency, rather than a life of self-seeking, force, fraud, and mastery." Under the impulsion of the instinct of workmanship the vicarious leisure classes, especially women, are beginning to resent their life of tutelage and status and to object to living at second remove from the effective industrial process. But the pecuniary logic still exercises a "selective surveillance over the details of conduct and management in any enterprise," so that appearances of the non-invidious economic interest are only sporadic. In the spirit of the conclusion of "Some Neglected Points in the Theory of Social-ism," and "The Preconceptions of Economic Science," and with particular reference to the "emulative process of accumulation by the quasi-predatory methods of the pecuniary occupations" characterising the modern leisure class, Veblen said that the characteristic attitude of the leisure class "may be summed up in the maxim: 'whatever is, is right'; whereas the law of natural selection, as applied to human institutions, gives the axiom: 'whatever is, is wrong.' "

The first reviewers of *The Theory of the Leisure Class* responded to the book in a spirit not unlike that in which the common-sense philosophers received the doctrine of evolution. D. Collin Wells of Dartmouth declared in *The Yale Review* that such books as this, written by dilettantes, bring sociology into "disrepute among careful and scientific thinkers." The few references bearing on economics are "ill-considered and vicious." It is illegitimate to classify under the one term, "Leisure Class," such unrelated groups as the barbarians and the rich of modern society. The term "status" should not be used to describe the economic relation which "the rich man sustains in a modern community." The book is "crowded with *ex-cathedra* propositions, often of a revolutionary and startling nature," and no authorities are cited. It is unexampled as a "collection of 'things that are not so.' " The "most vicious distinction is that between pecuniary and industrial economic institutions. . . . The climax is capped by an elaborate comparison of the ideal pecuniary man to the ideal delinquent, i.e., criminal; especially in devoutness." Veblen's use of the English language—"futile, archaic, and cumbrous"—satisfies his own canons of conspicuous waste. His style is a "scientific (?) jargon from which no clear meaning can be extracted."

In Veblen's absence the September issue of *The Journal of Political Economy* included as its leading article a thirty-page review written by his former colleague, John Cummings, then at Harvard. The review gave most of its attention to Veblen's analysis of modern business enter-prise. The basic assumption of the book, Cummings declared, seems to be that acquisition of wealth is predatory, an assumption which is clearly expressed in Veblen's fundamental distinction between industrial and pecuniary employments. Both assumption and distinction are "obviously inconsistent with the facts." The captain of industry's income is high because of "the obvious fact" that society needs his services and pays accordingly. The industrial or financial magnate "really earns his $25,-000 a year," as does the ditch-digger his $1.50 a day, because society pays the wages. "Every quality having an economic bearing has its economic value as accurately determined as may be in its economic efficiency." Veblen's terminology suggests the Marxian argument, in which the captain of industry is made out to be a "robber." His denial of ethical judgments in his use of "obviously ethical terms" clearly indicates that he is "a master of sophistical dialectic."

In the next issue of the *Journal* Veblen answered a critic for the first and last time. If he had not been away, he said, he would, as editor, have made suggestions that would have avoided "misdirected criticism." Most of Cummings's objections would have been obviated by a "more facile use of language" in the book. In almost all cases, in fact, Cummings had made his point precisely, but his misuse of the logical principle of the excluded middle had led him to conceive the subject matter of the book in terms of "exclusive alternatives."

Cummings's lengthy discussion of the equity of the existing distribution of property and incomes "assumes the validity of the natural-rights dogma, that property rights rest on production," but this is not a causal relationship. His "advocacy of the claims of the captain of industry to his income . . . proceeds . . . on the bold though ancient metaphor by force of which bargaining is conceived to produce goods."

The fundamental difference between author and critic is the critic's rejection of the distinction between industrial and pecuniary employments. Cummings maintains that both the financier and the day labourer are productive and that the productivity and income-yielding ability of both are due to the intelligence exercised. A distinction is raised in the book, however, in order to indicate the different economic value of the habits of thought and aptitudes fostered by the contrasted employments. It is a difference in kind, not, as Cummings seems to think, in degree. Despite its reality, Cummings fails to appreciate the distinction between aptitudes and employments, since it is not an accepted article of economic theory. Received economics took shape in a world less highly differentiated than the present one. In the earlier phase of modern industry the owner was "at the same time the foreman of the shop and the manager of the 'business,'" and the distinction, although present, did not obtrude itself. But today a person is chiefly confined seriously to one or the other line of employment, although "the disciplinary effect of either is seldom unmitigated in any concrete case."

Veblen then explained more fully his use of the term "industrial." It refers to the material interests of the community, including a social organisation adapted to its exigencies, rather than to mere physical processes; and the term "technicians" means not merely the engineers of a factory, but those intellectual leaders impersonally concerned with these material interests as against those of the modern business man. "The distinction at its clearest marks the difference between workmanship and bargaining." Workmanship characterises the industrial employments, which include the work of directing the processes of industry and contriving its aims and ideals—"such work as that of the artist, the inventor, the designer, the engineer, and the foreman." This range of activity or employments "has to do with adapting the material means of life, and the processes of valuation constantly involved in the work run on the availability of goods and on the material serviceability of the contrivances, materials, persons, or mechanical expedients employed." The worker's interest and sagacity are concerned with "the relation of physical cause and effect." On the other hand, the sagacity, interest, and intelligence involved in the pecuniary employments are directed to contests of shrewdness and personal advantage. The pecuniary activities have to do "with the distribution of wealth—not necessarily with the distribution of goods to consumers." The processes of valuation "run on the exchange values of goods and on the vendibility of the items with which they are concerned, and on the necessities, solvency, cupidity, or gullibility of the persons whose actions may affect the transaction contemplated. These valuations look to the pecuniary serviceability of the persons and expedients employed."

The pecuniary activities, and the pecuniary institutions they develop, "rest on the institution of private property, and affect the industrial process by grace of that institution"; the industrial activities rest chiefly on "the physical conditions of human life," but they too have their pecuniary bearing by virtue of the dominating institution of ownership. "The pecuniary employments are conditioned by human convention, the industrial by the unalterable laws of nature." The objective point of the latter is material use; of the former, pecuniary gain. Modern business, or pecuniary, activities are, "in their immediate bearing, in no degree serviceable to the community, since their aim is a competitive one"; the industrial activities are "commonly serviceable in their immediate effects, except in so far as they are commonly, under the guidance of the pecuniary interest, led into work that is wasteful or disserviceable to the community." Indirectly, as well, the pecuniary employments have considerable effect in shaping industrial life, as when the formation of trusts brings about industrial changes, and "the 'industrial' employments rarely if ever are without a pecuniary bearing."

Cummings, said Veblen, seems to feel that the "consummate diction" of the book "is charged with some malign potency, somewhat after the manner of the evil eye." But if the scientist is to avoid the inscrutable and "paralogistic figures of speech" which "have long afflicted economics" and have given it a reputation of sterility, he "must resort to words and concepts that express the thoughts of the men whose habits of thought constitute the institutions in question."

Fortunately for Veblen, Edward A. Ross was pleased by the book, particularly by its apparent advocacy of the emancipation of women. He recommended it to Charlotte P. Gilman, and showed a copy to his uncle, Lester F. Ward, when the latter lectured at Stanford in the summer of 1899. Ward was so deeply impressed that on his way East he stopped at Chicago to see the author, but Veblen was not to be found. Small asked Ward to review the book for *The American Journal of Sociology.* Ward felt he was "too much a Jacobin," and suggested Ross as a substitute, but was persuaded to undertake it himself. Ross wrote him: "I am looking forward to your review of Veblen's book. How it fluttered the dovecotes in the East! All the reviews I have seen of it so far are shocked and angry. Clearly their household gods have been assailed by this iconoclast." Veblen wrote to Ward: "I need not say that I appreciate the honour of such an attention at your hands. . . . As a matter of course, you will find evidence in the book of my indebtedness to you. The absence of any acknowledgment is due to the fact that I am indebted to so many and various teachers as to preclude detailed acknowledgment."

The review, which Ward said later was from nearly every point of view the best he ever wrote, appeared in the issue for May 1900. He declared that "the book abounds in terse expressions, sharp antitheses, and quaint, but happy phrases. Some of these have been interpreted as irony and satire, but . . . this is the work of the critics themselves. The language is plain and unmistakable, as it should be," and some of it is likely to become classic. "But the style is the farthest removed possible from either advocacy or vituperation and the language, to use the author's own words, is 'morally colourless.' " Critics are unwarranted in asserting that Veblen is attacking existing institutions. Any examination into cultural pedigree always offends. The evolutionary process is necessarily a wasteful one, and Veblen is but showing how the wasteful process proceeds, in co-operation with the conservative force.

The genesis of a great number of occupations, institutions, customs, practices, and beliefs is worked out and their barbaric origin shown. Veblen might have written an equally able book on the instinct of workmanship, but he preferred to restrict himself to the instinct of sportsmanship. He might have shown how the leisure class has aided social progress solely by its leisure, and also how science has grown from the ecclesiastical institutions devoted to vicarious leisure and devout observance, but this is already commonly known, and Veblen tells what is not yet known. He properly confines himself to the economic point of view on the question of wealth, rather than covering a wider area, as economists usually do, to the confusion of everything. "His whole treatise is confined to the 'pecuniary' aspect." Pecuniary value can be shown to be rational only when "we know and can trace its history, and see how, under all the circumstances, it could not have been otherwise." Since the prolonged and laborious exertion required for the production of goods is essentially irksome, it was natural for some to enslave others in order to get consumption goods without producing. Consequently there arises a leisure class enjoying all the good things of life, engaging in sports and warfare, and generally maltreating the lower classes. The antithesis springs up naturally and has persisted to this day. This distinction is characterised by Veblen as "invidious." "This word has been criticised as imputing blameworthy motives. But it is used in a literal sense," meaning "that which has *envy* at its root, for not only does the industrial class envy the leisure class, but every member of the leisure class is perpetually striving to gain the envy of others of that class." It is for this reason that the members of the leisure class build palaces larger than they can comfortably use, and that the captain of industry, while engaged in useful work, has the women of his group keep up the financial appearance of the family by vicarious leisure and consumption. The book throughout is "the application of the fundamental maxim of 'political economy'—the greatest gain for the least effort" but "since effort is itself agreeable, the effort meant is only industrial, productive, useful effort."

Veblen wrote Ward: "I beg to express my very lively appreciation of the honour you have done me in your extended and appreciative review. . . . Your unqualified approval has given me more pleasure than anything that has occurred in connexion with the book, and I can only hope that it will not end with giving me an intolerable conceit."

Veblen felt, however, that Ward had not altogether appreciated his point of view. Miss Hardy, now Mrs. Warren Gregory, had asked Veblen for the review and returned it with some scepticism regarding Ward. Veblen wrote her: "It is not kind of you, and scarcely reverent, to use irony and other allied figures of speech concerning the English of the Patriarch of Sociology, in a case where laudable sentiment gets the better of his diction. What you say is true—as it should be—and what you imply is truer still—as is not surprising—when you speak of the magnanimity and positiveness with which Mr. Ward understands the 'Leisure Class.' I assure you his review has been a great help to me in that respect. It has brought me to a sobering realisation of the very grave importance which my writing, and what I now understand to have been my thinking and my insight, have for the spread of knowledge among men.

"I am unable to share your view that the allegation of 'too much truth' is to be taken as an accusation. I find myself unable to resent it. It is probably to be construed as a superlative, and that being the case I should like to cross out the exclamation point with which you follow it, as well as the one which punctuates the expression 'clear head.' . . .

"It is needless for me to say how sincerely I thank you, not only for your kindness in writing your congratulations, however equivocal, but even more for knowing better than the great men who have been good enough to criticise me."

Veblen's term, "instinct of workmanship," was used by his friend Loeb in the classic *Comparative Physiology and Psychology of the Brain*, which appeared in 1900. "One of the most important instincts," wrote Loeb, "is usually not even recognised as such, namely the instinct of workmanship," and in a footnote he added, "I take this name from Veblen's book on *The Theory of the Leisure Class*."

Before the professional reviews appeared, William Dean Howells devoted the leading article in two successive issues of *Literature* to praise of Veblen's book. Veblen's name, said Howells, "is newer to me than it should be, or than it will hereafter be to any student of our status. To others, like myself, the clear method, the graphic and easy style, and the delightful accuracy of characterisation will be part of the surprise which the book has to offer. In the passionless calm with which the author pursues his investigation, there is apparently no animus for or against a leisure class. It is his affair simply to find out how and why and what it is. If the result is to leave the reader with a feeling which the author never shows, that seems to be solely the effect of the facts." Howells used Veblen's terms beautifully, but read the book as literally as had Ward, as a discussion of the luxurious life of an aristocracy. Howells not only helped to make the book a sensation, but helped to set the fashion of interpreting it as a withering criticism of aristocratic prejudice, as distinct from middle-class prejudice.

Veblen became the god of all the radicals, although he despised them. W.J. Ghent, then something of a Fabian socialist, recalls that in the New York circles of intellectual radicals he always found someone ready with a pat quotation from *The Theory of the Leisure Class*. Its stinging satire was particularly enjoyed. Mrs. Gilman considered it "clear and impressive, and though rather stiff and laboured in part, illuminated by the most brilliant penetrating satire I ever saw," and Tufts considered Veblen the most powerful social satirist since Mandeville. But Charles Edward Russell said he could not see that the book was ironic. It was viewed by many as an example of true artistry in the use of language, and artists' clubs sought unsuccessfully to get Veblen to address them. Dewey said the terminology would survive the book. Such phrases as "conspicuous consumption," "vicarious leisure," "conspicuous waste," were seized upon as fighting terms. Overnight the language on the university campus changed, and it was said that those who read Veblen could be distinguished by their speech. Small suggested that students read the book for its humour. Veblen's schoolmates were surprised at his fame, but Clark noted with satisfaction that Veblen had fulfilled his promise. Spencer even complimented Veblen.

No one was more surprised than Veblen at the book's reception. He was disappointed at the popular view of it as a satire upon the aristocratic classes, although he admitted to Stuart that the book was not altogether free from satire. He came to feel that those who gave the book its popularity were foolish and gullible. A graduate student, Archibald Maynard, told Veblen that he wished to attempt a thesis subject along lines suggested by Veblen's work and that of W.I. Thomas on *Social Origins*, but Veblen advised against it on the ground that such work is not taken seriously. He could speak with knowledge about that, said Veblen, as he had recently tried it and found that people were inclined to "giggle." He cited Karl Bücher's *Rhythmus und Arbeit*, which also made use of a distinction in occupational discipline, as a further proof that unusual work meets with neglect or amused contempt.

In 1900 Veblen was promoted to the rank of assistant professor. After returning from a tour of inspection of the Rockefeller iron mines of Lake Superior, he wrote Mrs. Gregory that "the next book has been named, as you may have noticed, by Mr. Ward, and also by others before him. It is to be called *The Instinct of Workmanship*, a phrase which, perhaps without your knowing it, I owe to you. I have no doubt such a volume on the Instinct will be written before long, but I confess, though I should not like to have it go further, that I don't know what or what kind of things will go into this new book."

CHAPTER XIII

AT the 1900 meeting of the American Economic Association, President Ely gave an address on "Competition: Its Nature, Its Permanency, and Its Beneficence," in which he described the great "economic-juridical institutions of society, such as private property, inheritance of property, and vested interests," as depositories of race-achievement which confine and regulate competition. Struggle in economic life "means rivalry in the service of self, and other selves—rivalry in the upbuilding of the ideal man and the ideal society." "Competition gives us a brave, strong race of men, and the brave and strong are merciful." [1]

At the same meeting Veblen was scheduled to deliver a paper on "Industrial and Pecuniary Employments," but he excused himself on grounds of ill health. This was perhaps fortunate for his would-be auditors, since in print the article is close to fifty pages in length. The title seems to have been due to his discussion with Cummings, but the paper appears to have been written originally as a logical sequel to "The Preconceptions of Economic Science," completing the parallelism between *The Theory of the Leisure Class* and the articles in *The Quarterly*. It shows more clearly that by "market" Veblen means the dominating capital market and the management of industry for profit, and that "capital" refers to the capitalisation of advantages or modern profits, not the incompatible conception of industrial equipment for the material welfare of the community.

Received economics, according to Veblen, is based on the dogmatic, untenable postulate that remuneration measures production. The modern captain of industry is considered a productive agent, who receives in remuneration the equivalent of his productivity, and thus his pecuniary employments or activities are not treated as the controlling factor about which the modern economic process turns, but are assumed to be productive operations effecting the distribution of goods from producer to consumer. Distinctions are drawn between persons, not between activities, so that the modern captain is conceived as a composite of master workman and "business" man. This picture may have been true in the days of Adam Smith, but today the captain is occupied with purely fiscal and financiering activities. Of course, when he steps down from the pecuniary plane and directs "the mechanical handling and functioning of 'production goods,' he becomes for a time a foreman," but in the modern specialisation and maturity of business this vulgar technological activity does not characterise the great dominating and successful captains of finance. Common sense and received economics may declare their services to be extremely valuable and their regime to be the best industrial policy, but these supposedly empirical judgments are based on the tacit "organic concept" of the social-economic function of the captain. They are rule of thumb of common sense, not scientific theory, which is "a formulation of the laws of phenomena in terms of the efficient forces at work in the sequence of phenomena."

The activity of the modern captain is conditioned throughout by the institution of property, which today means the discretionary control of wealth. Thus the captain's activity is neither proximately nor remotely productive industrial activity. It falls into the category typified by the real-estate agent and "the closely related business of promoters and boomers of other than real-estate ventures." He is a man without visible means of support. He may make pecuniary gain by decreasing material efficiency or inhibiting its advance, as well as by letting the processes go their way under the supervision of the technological experts. As a result of the rigorous control of economic life exercised by the market, survival depends on fitness for pecuniary gain, not on material serviceability. Industrial ventures depend for survival on shrewd business management, because such management is necessarily employed by all the competitors in the pecuniary struggle. But this management results in only a relative and superficial success, of little importance to the community in general. If it is increased or decreased, the immediate effect upon industrial efficiency and material serviceability is neutral in comparison with the effect produced by a change in the industrial capacity of those who work. Theoreticians credit the captain with bringing about material economies in production, such as efficient industrial combination, but they overlook the fact that the mechanical possibility of more efficient methods must first be created by the men in industry. The captain's consent is not given until long after the changes have proved industrially feasible, because of the strategic manœuvres and clashing pecuniary interests of the captains. Furthermore, it is overlooked that a given step in industrial integration makes it possible for industry— that is, the working force engaged in industry—to develop new opportunities to be taken advantage of by the captain, and he is thus pushed to make a new concession allowing further industrial efficiency. But when this cumulative sequence is cut off at the start because the captain inhibits or does not allow a development, there is no striking visible result of his inaction and therefore the retardation cannot be calculated.

Consequently there is no warrant in theory for asserting that the work of these highly paid businessmen is of greater substantial use to the community than that of the less well paid. Wages are paid on the basis not of productivity for the community's ends, but of pecuniary serviceability. The natural-rights assumption that the two are equivalent might be true if the aggregate productivity of industry were equivalent to the necessary consumption and if no economic deterioration could take place in the community. As to the first, however, in a modern industrial community "the margin of admissible waste probably always exceeds fifty percent of the output of goods." In many lines the cost of marketing goods equals the cost of making and transporting them. As to the second requirement, which is almost identical with the first, it can be achieved only if the postulate of a meliorative trend is valid. "Instances are not far to seek of communities in which economic deterioration has taken place while the system of distribution both of income and accumulated wealth has remained on a pecuniary basis."

Veblen draws a distinction also between pecuniary and industrial capital, paralleling that between the industrial and pecuniary employments. Here, too, he contrasts the modern captain and the technological expert and processes in their effect on material welfare.

Pecuniary capital is wealth employed in investment or in the management of capital in the business sense of the word. Wealth, material means of industry, physically employed for industrial ends is capital in the industrial sense. The pecuniary employments are concerned with pecuniary capital, and the industrial employments with industrial capital. "Neither immediately in his purely pecuniary traffic, nor indirectly, in the business guidance of industry through his pecuniary traffic . . . can the undertaker's dealings with his pecuniary capital be accounted a productive occupation, nor can the gains of capital be taken to mark or measure the productivity due to the investment." The gain that the captain derives from his capital has nothing to do with serviceability but only with vendibility. Contrary to the doctrines of received economics, the captain seeks not to produce the greatest amount of serviceable goods at the most economic cost, but to produce as cheaply as possible a vendible product, and in the aggregate the cost of production of vendibility is waste. Pecuniary capital is an aggregate of market values, and it varies independently of variations in the magnitude of industrial capital; "it may vary in magnitude with a freedom which gives the whole an air of caprice," its erratic movement becoming "strikingly noticeable in times of panic or of speculative inflation."

The aggregate social (industrial) capital cannot be obtained by adding up individual (pecuniary) capital, because, aside from variations in the market values of given material items, pecuniary capital comprises conventional facts or intangible items, such as good will and effrontery, which are not definitely related to the material means of industry. Ownership is the basis of pecuniary capital, and whatever may be turned to pecuniary gain is comprised in its aggregate. Since ownership is a habit of thought, a convention or institution, matters of convention and opinion figure in the inventory of pecuniary capital. Industrial capital, however, is of a mechanical character subject to the laws of physics and chemistry, not to those of the psychology of acquisition, and "conventional circumstances do not affect it—except as the future production of material means to replace the existing outfit may be guided by convention." Thus items having only a conventional existence are not comprised in its aggregate. The two categories of capital are disparate and incommensurable. Here Veblen's discussion of industrial and pecuniary capital comes very close to his analysis of industrial and pecuniary employments —so close that he seems to admit little difference between capital and employments. "Productivity theories of interest should be as difficult to maintain as productivity theories of the gains of the pecuniary employments, the two resting on the same grounds," that is, ownership. The pecuniary employments, embodied in the modern captain of industry, are the methods of modern capital, the meaning of the institution of modern capital.

This distinction between employments has an important bearing on the question of the survival of modern business enterprise. Marxists who did not know Marx believe that the economic situation affects institutions through class interest, but, without discrediting the claim that class interest counts for something in shaping institutions, the question of growth can be handled better through the disciplinary effects of occupations. The characteristic feature which distinguishes the present economic situation from that out of which it is emerging is the machine process, with its consequent specialised organisation of the working force and plant and its highly developed corporation finance. This cumulative development means that the pecuniary management of industry is falling into the hands of an increasingly smaller class who have no immediate contact with the industrial process and classes. Likewise the industrial classes have only an incidental interest in the business management. Thus the distinction between employments tends to coincide with that between classes. The business occupations are characterised by the business managers, the financiers, and their members work within the lines of the institution of ownership as the conventional norm of truth and validity. But those in the industrial occupations—"the highly trained technological experts and engineers as well as the highly skilled mechanics"—have to take cognisance of "the conditions impersonally imposed by the nature of material things." They are barred from full appreciation of the "cultural graces and amenities" which make up the institution of ownership in modern life. These classes are losing their belief in self-help and the pecuniary incentive of saving.

Socialism is in vogue among the highly trained industrial classes in the industrial towns, but conservatism is the rule in the leisure class and in the relatively indigent, backward, and unintelligent classes and areas, where the differentiation between pecuniary and industrial occupations and realities has not been reached. The agrarian classes in their revolts do not aim to eliminate the institution of ownership, but merely to remedy some of its abuses. Socialistic sentiment among the upper classes means only a "readjustment of ownership under some new and improved method of control—not a contemplation of the traceless disappearance of ownership." But with the higher industrial classes the ownership preconception is becoming "obsolescent through disuse." The industrial mechanism requires thinking in terms of material cause and effect, and thus promotes scepticism of the institution of property—an attitude which Veblen describes as "an effortless iconoclasm." To the disciplinary effect of modern industrial requirements is to be attributed also "the highly irregular, conventionally indefensible attitude of the industrial classes in the current labour and wage disputes, not of an avowedly socialistic character." Similarly the materialistic industrial habits of thought are responsible for the breakdown of domestic life and morality and religion—institutions whose validity depends on the same conventional or metaphysical grounds as those of the institution of ownership.

The socialists were still interested in capturing Veblen, and *The International Socialist Review,* the wife of whose editor, A.M. Simons, was a student of Veblen, declared that, "whether considered as a scientific criticism of current economic thought, a biting satire on classical political economy, or as an exposition of socialist philosophy, this pamphlet must be admitted to be a masterpiece. . . . It takes all the pet phrases of the classical economists of the colleges and uses them to make their teaching ridiculous. How any one of the professors who listened to this talk could go back to their classes and continue their work with sober faces is hard to comprehend." [2]

In reviewing Schmoller's *Grundriss der allgemeinen Volkswirtschaftslehre* in *The Quarterly Journal of Economics,* Veblen's criticisms of the best representative of the historical school were so similar to those that he had made against the main classical tradition as to suggest that Schmoller was merely a means for examining once more the dominant point of view. Veblen declared that the historical school does not adhere to the canons of modern science but merely produces aphoristic wisdom and polemics concerning the beneficence of the present order. Its tacit metaphysics is a belief in the meliorative trend in the course of events. The historical school represents Hegelianism of the right, which was in vogue in those "circles within which lay the gentlemanly life and human contact" of its founders. The Marxians could develop their materialistic conception of history from this same philosophy because they were more fully conscious of the implications of their postulates and less naïve in accepting the prevailing "Romantic commonplaces left by Hegelianism as a residue in popular thought." But the uncritical Hegelians of the right attach no importance to environmental conditions or material exigencies, believing that these conditions must adapt themselves to the personal will of the dominant force. Their work is empirical or historical in the sense that it proceeds on "the Baconian ground of generalisation by simple enumeration." It is concerned with speculations as to the eternal fitness of things, with statements of uniformity or of normality in conformance with the tacit postulate, rather than with statements of the causes at work in the situation.

When Schmoller reaches the existing situation, where "a dispassionate analysis and exposition of the causal complex at work in contemporary institutional changes should begin," he turns from a genetic account, which would study the adaptation of institutions to modern exigencies, to an account of ways and means of maintaining the received cultural form. Thus he strenuously defends the present-day modified patriarchal household, instead of examining the economic exigencies which are forcing a change in this traditional form; nor does he examine the converse question, of similar importance to economic theory, of how the "persistence, even though qualified, of the patriarchal family . . . is modifying economic structure and function at other points or qualifying or accentuating the very exigencies . . . to which the changes wrought in the institution are to be traced." There is no causal analysis of the disintegration of traditional family life among the working population. The discussion of the family and of the relations of the sexes is marked by "unwillingness or inability to penetrate behind the barrier of conventional finality." Schmoller declares that the gravest social effect of machine industry has been the creation of a large class of wage labourers, but he pushes the inquiry no further except to point out an increase in the comfort of the labourers. As soon as a question falls within the sweep of prevailing sentiment, it is settled by "the conventional standards of taste, dignity, morality, and the like."

Schmoller speaks of the technically trained workman of machine industry as superior in character and efficiency to those of all other times

and places; but socialists are considered degenerate. The vital factor of
the radical socialist element is, however, the technically trained population, schooled in the discipline of the machine process. The only other
factor of importance in socialism consists of the students of modern
science. Schmoller declares that a high culture is characterised by high
technical efficiency, and vice versa. Therefore, the socialist constitutes the
high culture, and the proposed elimination of these bearers of technological knowledge would leave a low culture made up of the peasantry,
the slums, the aristocracy, great and small.

Characteristic of Schmoller's treatment is his discussion of modern
business enterprise. He points out that it still retains the commercial
spirit, that its motive force is the "self-seeking quest of dividends." He is
at pains to show, however, that it is guided and hedged by considerations not primarily of a self-seeking kind, so that he can demonstrate the
beneficent working of a harmony of interests and thus show how "a self-
seeking business traffic has come to serve the interests of the community."
He is interested not in the genetic problem, but in how to hold fast and
foster the prevailing form of business enterprise.

Veblen presented his point of view in his own journal through a review article of *Chapters in the History of the Arts and Crafts Movement*, written by his friend and colleague Oscar Lovell Triggs, secretary
of the Industrial Art League. This attempt to rehabilitate the antiquated
handicraft ideal was described by Veblen as a product of romanticism,
"archaism," and "lackadaisical æstheticism." Both on business grounds
and for reasons of economy the scope of the movement is limited "to
those higher levels of consumption" where economy is not important and
"the goods must be sufficiently expensive to preclude their use by the
vulgar." The industrial art method is too costly for modern business
purposes and its products too expensive for general consumption. Business exigencies "demand spurious goods"—that is, goods must cost less
than they appear to—and "modern, that is to say, democratic, culture
. . . requires low cost and a large, thoroughly standardised output of
goods." Any vital reform movement in æsthetic ideals must fall in line
with the exigencies of the machine technology, which is indispensable to
modern culture. "The machine process has come, not so much to stay
merely, but to go forward and root out of the workmen's scheme of
thought whatever elements are alien to its own technological requirements and discipline. It ubiquitously and unremittingly disciplines the
workman into its way of doing and therefore in its way of apprehending
and appreciating things. 'Industrial art' . . . which does not work
through and in the spirit of the machine technology is, at the best, an
exotic," without any chance of life "beyond the hothouse shelter of

decadent æstheticism." The enduring characteristic of an art and industry movement is not an aristocratic ideal, but an "insistence on sensuous beauty of line and colour and on visible serviceability in all the objects which it touches. And these results can be attained in fuller measure through the technological expedients of which the machine process disposes than by any means within the reach of the industry of a past age."

At the university the College of Commerce and Administration was opened and a series of public lectures was given "by friends of the university who have acquired reputation as practical men of affairs." Under the title, "A. Marshall on Economics for Business Men," [3] *The Journal of Political Economy* republished in the June 1902 issue Alfred Marshall's "A Plea for the Creation of a Curriculum in Economics and Associated Branches of Political Science, addressed to the Senate of Cambridge University, April 7, 1902." Veblen complained to a student that, although the university was continually erecting buildings, the library facilities were inadequate and he was not getting a living wage. He felt that President Harper, like Gilman, had learned to a certain extent that " 'honesty is the best policy' even for a college president," but the university publicity was still distasteful to him. The city of Chicago he considered an ugly scramble of money-making.

Beginning in 1899 there was a continued advance in commodity prices, accompanied by a "growth of industrial combinations . . . beyond the imagination of the previous decade," by "sensational speculation in securities and commodities," and by "overshadowing power" acquired by a "handful of immensely wealthy capitalists" through their banks and company affiliations. After a series of strategic manœuvres between the Carnegie and Morgan interests, the billion-dollar United States Steel Corporation was organised. The incorporators made huge sums by a process which Carnegie once described: "They throw cats and dogs together and call them elephants." The Morgan syndicate alone received from the sale of its securities a profit of $62,500,000 beyond its expenses and cash advances. The promotion of the corporation occasioned an outburst of speculation during April 1901 which was "something rarely paralleled in the history of speculative manias." Old and experienced capitalists, as well as younger men, "asserted publicly that the old traditions of finance no longer held," and that a new order of things must be reckoned with. "The 'outside public,' meantime, seemed to lose all restraint." The New York Stock Exchange was forced to declare a one-day holiday to give its members a rest. Newspapers were full of stories of hotel waiters and dressmakers who had won fortunes on the market. But the "poor man" was wiped out in 1901. The stock market was almost wrecked by the battle for control of the Northern Pacific, between Morgan and Hill on the one hand and the Harriman and Standard Oil interests on the other. The parties finally settled the dispute by organising a far-reaching holding company, the Northern Securities Company. Morgan's power and personal authority were such that his will was now law with most of the Wall Street capitalists and institutions. He "frankly and publicly avowed his belief in creating corporations with capital stock so large that existing managements could not be unseated." [4]

Clark asserted that the goal towards which society is tending is not socialism but a continuation of the beneficent competitive system. Workingmen's savings will grow and they will become conservative in their attitude towards property. "The world of the near future . . . will present a condition of vast and ever-growing inequality," but the poor will greatly increase their standards. "The capitalist may become too rich to sleep, while the labourer becomes so relatively rich that he can live in comfort" and peace. The best effect of this evolution will be moral. "When men can regard each other with respect and affection in spite of enormous differences of wealth, there will be some virility in their fraternal feeling." [5]

Meanwhile, after the assassination of McKinley, hatred and the determination to punish anyone who might be charged with anarchistic leanings reached their highest pitch. Men were thrown into jail on the slightest suspicion of being anarchists, and radicals were deported. [6]

President Roosevelt in his message to Congress in December 1901 declared that natural justice assigns great gains to those who produce the most. Great enterprise benefiting mankind can exist only if great prizes are the rewards of success. Tremendous corporate fortunes are due not to "governmental action but to natural causes." Without the captains of industry the immense material development could not have occurred. "The slightest study of business conditions" will satisfy every intelligent person of the necessity of leaving unhampered these "strong and forceful men" devoted to business operations. Unrestricted business action is essential also in order to maintain this country's lead in "the strife for commercial supremacy" among nations. An attack on the business interest inevitably endangers all. Disaster to great business enterprises works its worst effect on the labourers. The capitalist loses his luxuries, but the wage worker his necessities. Now, however, because of the great business leaders, labourers have never before been so well off. [7]

Veblen taught for one term a course called "Economics of Workingmen." According to the *Register:* "The purpose is to treat of efforts made to improve the conditions of workingmen, and the effect of co-operation, profit-sharing, building associations, manual training, trades unions and the like." Veblen had already expressed himself on these subjects in *The Theory of the Leisure Class,* in his discussion of "Social Settlements" work as the propaganda of the leisure-class culture among the lower classes. The course itself, according to student notes, seemed to be concerned with showing that teachers of received economics maintained the wage-fund doctrine and consequently believed that neither labour unions nor combinations of capitalists could so change the price of labour as to violate this economic law, that, in other words, the price of labour measures its efficiency.

The Pennsylvania anthracite coal strike threw a more important question into the limelight. Plants began to shut down for lack of fuel, and in Chicago people ripped up the wooden paving blocks. The entire Pennsylvania state militia was ordered into the mine region, but no coal was obtainable. John Mitchell, president of the miners' union, said that he would accept the decision of any arbitrators appointed by President Roosevelt, but the coal company operators, led by George Baer, read to Roosevelt "a series of typewritten lectures, denouncing the strikers, refusing arbitration . . . and calling upon the President to send federal troops to support the operators." Baer, in writing what he intended to be an ironical response to a private appeal by a clergyman, said that "the rights and interests of the labouring man will be protected and cared for—not by the labour agitators but by the Christian men to whom God in His infinite wisdom has given the control of the property interests of the country, and upon the successful Management of which so much depends." The minister naturally enough did not see the irony and turned the letter over to Henry Demarest Lloyd, who had the reply broadcast through the press. The community at large was not ready to admit that "God was on the side of the Great Industrialists." Darrow nicknamed Baer "George the Last," and the Hearst papers called him "Divine Right" Baer. In Chicago, Turnvereins and religious conferences aided and prayed for the miners, and in New York the Democratic State Convention declared for the nationalisation of the mines. Conservative senators were ready to authorise President Roosevelt to take control of the mines. Finally Roosevelt allowed Secretary of State Root to confer with Morgan on his yacht in New York. Morgan "realised that the country was holding him personally responsible and that the position of his lieutenants 'was untenable and must be given up.' " Three days later he informed Roosevelt that the operators would agree to an arbitration commission appointed by the President. Organised labour demanded a representative on the commission, but the operators "were prepared to sacrifice everything," as Roosevelt said much later, "and see civil war in the country rather than . . . acquiesce." The labour representative was to be E.E. Clark, head of the Brotherhood of Railway Conductors, and Roosevelt discovered that the dilemma could be avoided by calling him an "eminent sociologist."

While the arbitration commission was making a preliminary examination of mining conditions, President Eliot of Harvard in a public speech called the non-union labourer a "good type of American hero." The miners' representatives, including Louis D. Brandeis, Darrow, Lloyd, and Hourwich, arranged that over two hundred human products of mining conditions should appear before the commission. So terrible was the testimony of this "moving spectacle of horrors" that the commission would not hear all of it. Lloyd said to the commission: "These antediluvian captains of industry, who call themselves masters, walk on Market Street or on Wall Street as if it were Mount Ararat, and they were just landed from the Ark. Thanks to their incompetency, the supply of fire in our age of fire has been so disturbed that at least two years will pass before it becomes normal again. Their industrial sagacity has taken their industry and all industry away from its natural foundations on the everlasting hills and put it on the thermometer and the weather-vane, where a south wind means life, a north wind means death."

When the partially successful settlement was reached, 1100 vice-presidents, representing all the labour organisations in Chicago, were on the platform in the auditorium to greet the "three Illinois Conquerors" —John Mitchell, Lloyd, Darrow.[8]

In the meanwhile Ghent's *Our Benevolent Feudalism* was making a stir. Ghent maintained that the concentration of wealth into great trusts, taking the labourer away from the land and making it impossible for the poor man to rise, was resulting in the evolution of society into a feudalistic state, a "morganisation of industry." The state was becoming a hierarchy of classes, with the industrial barons at the top, graded in respect of wealth. The prevalence of the seigneurial attitude was demonstrated by citations from Veblen's "keen satire" in *The Theory of the Leisure Class*, indicating that the aristocracy welcomes the industrial magnate, and that his vast wealth and love of ostentation have set the pace for lavish expenditure. The barons will act together for the sake of their class interests, shrewdly calculating what the traffic will bear and not overstepping this limit. Old-age pensions will be established, and wages and dividends so nicely adjusted as to prevent dissatisfaction. Ghent interpreted the acceptance of arbitration by the coal owners as a sign of the increasing reasonableness of the barons.

In its original form as an article in *The Independent*, Ghent's argument occasioned a response from Clark. The trust magnate, Clark declared, has no baronial power because he is paid his price for a service rendered. That the so-called capitalistic system has continued until now and that its further continuance is regarded with toleration" is proof that it has not the essential quality which the word "feudal" describes, that is, an arbitrary rule destroying freedom or competition. This outcome would be seen in the distance and "its approach will never be permitted." Even though trusts may rob some groups, this is not feudalism since there is no physical subjection. Trusts have reduced the number of competitors, but competition still survives and wages are thus gauged by the productive efficiency of the labourers. "Competition is for ever asserting itself, and if hereafter it were to do no more than it is now doing," even this is sufficient to restrict "the power of great corporations within relatively narrow limits." In the community of the future there will be "great capitals and great labour unions, and the two . . . will . . . make the industrial commonwealth what it should be." [9]

In 1902 a number of magazines began publishing sensational articles dealing with high finance and corrupt politics. Ida Tarbell's ruthless *History of the Standard Oil Company* appeared by instalments in *McClure's*, and in *Everybody's* Thomas Lawson began publishing his sensational experience under the title "Frenzied Finance." *Cosmopolitan* ran a long series of articles on "captains of industry," written by a suave and cynical group. Gifted writers like Lincoln Steffens and Ray Stannard Baker investigated the sinister relations between the big business interests and political life, and between labour unions and business organisations. Veblen was busy on another book. He told Wesley C. Mitchell that its title was going to be *The Captain of Industry: a Romance*.

With the departure of Miller for the University of California in 1902, Veblen taught his course on trusts, "Relation of the State to Industrial Organisation." It was Veblen's custom in this course to have a student take charge of the class and he himself would become a student, asking questions of the temporary teacher. One of them writes: "I recall three very strenuous days during which I took over the outlining of the building up of the capital structure and foundation of the Steel Trust by Carnegie, Frick, and Morgan. He was a merciless questioner when he became a student and caused me no end of discomfiture and created much merriment, mostly at my expense."

Veblen, in reviewing Tarde's *Psychologie économique*, said that Tarde, although he had not assimilated it, had finally arrived at the "central principle of modern psychology, which has been the common property of American and English psychologists of the last generation, ever since Professor James broke away from the earlier empiricism" of Mill.

"The point of departure of modern psychological inquiry is the empirical generalisation that the Idea is Essentially Active," that thinking is an action. If Tarde had been able to make this concept his point of departure instead of his conclusion, "his resulting theories of social conduct would of course not have taken the same form of expression."

Ward published his *Pure Sociology*, which was not substantially different from his other books. Its title was meant to distinguish it from applied sociology, which Ward proposed to discuss in a later volume. "Pure sociology" does not apologise for the facts, does not extol or condemn them; it is not concerned with ethics or with what ought to be. Ward still retained the pleasure-pain calculus, which he called social mechanics, and again he asserted that the love of money is the root of all the good there is in material civilisation. But he presented the defects of the modern system in less obscure language than heretofore, and spoke of "the vested interests" standing behind the politicians, the demagogue, the press, and the law, determining public opinion.

"Fashionable society consists wholly in sham, quackery reigns in the professions and charlatanism in scientific bodies." Strategy in warfare is an act of deception, and so also is diplomacy between nations. Business is of the same character. "Falsehood permeates business, and as you look out a car window, the rocks and trees are placarded all over with lies." Most advertisements, other than mere announcements for public information, are "intentional deceptions." The superlatives "as 'the best,' the strong words as 'superior,' and the word 'only,' almost always occurring in them, are simply falsehoods, and society would be justified in forbidding their use as devices for 'obtaining money under false pretences.' " Declaring that the "philosophy of advertising" is yet to be written, Ward remarked: "Economists know of course that the cost of advertising is added to the price, and it belongs among the facts of 'aggressive competition' which increase instead of diminishing prices." Extensively advertised articles are lower in quality than others in order to cover the cost of advertising without making the price appear competitively too high. "Mr. Veblen," said Ward, "with remarkable penetration applies the term 'predatory' to the leisure class and points out that the methods of the 'pecuniary occupations' even today are at least 'quasi-predatory.' "

The book, according to Ward, was not calculated to please the "vested interests," and the "subsidised press" showed little interest. It was supposed to have been discussed by a group of writers in Small's journal, but Ward wrote friends he felt that Small "is under instructions from the capitalistic censorship that controls the University of Chicago." "I do not of course suppose that Rockefeller or Yerkes descend to petty censorship, but such things are always put in the hands of some clique of small men adapted to manage them, such, for example, as Mrs. Stanford's San Francisco advisers, and the institution is at the mercy of these." [10] Upon receipt of a copy Veblen wrote Ward: "The book needs no commendation from me, but I want to express something of the interest and admiration with which I have read it. It has helped me greatly towards certitude and precision in many ideas that have been present in an undefined manner in my own conceptions, besides giving a comprehensive grasp of social development on lines which no other writer has been bold enough to follow but which must become decisive for the trend of sociological research in the nearest future. The range and volume of materials, as well as the perfect control of them, are fairly beyond the aspirations of lesser men."

In *The Journal of Political Economy* he called it a "great treatise" and declared that only a lifelong specialist could presume to pass upon a book which "presents a system wrought out symmetrically and in detail, with the maturity and poise of half a century's unremitting work and with the fire of unfailing youth." Of the chapters on the characteristics of business he said: "The sections on 'Indirection' offer a bold analysis of the motives and methods of business traffic, of which the dominant note is given by the proposition . . . that 'deception may almost be called the foundation of business.' " Veblen did not point out that this statement appeared in close proximity to a similar point cited from *The Theory of the Leisure Class*. In concluding Veblen declared that, for "economic purposes, Dr. Ward's views on 'The Socialisation of Achievement' . . . converge to the outcome that the trend of cultural growth sets indefeasibly towards collectivism, towards which he finds, on an analysis of the available data, that the most advanced of the industrial peoples have made the most substantial approaches."

In reviewing John Hobson's *Imperialism* Veblen again paid practically no attention to the writer's adherence to the traditional point of view. He praised the book, and, by making citations without comment, gave the impression that Hobson was discussing imperialism as the struggles and activities of the modern captains of industry, with the subject working populations as the enslaved peoples. Imperialism and popular government are incompatible in spirit, policy, and method. The output of industry cannot be entirely disposed of at profitable prices because there is a "very unequal distribution of income," which leaves the masses unable to satisfy their reasonable needs. "Since the income from the larger holdings of invested wealth exceeds the consumptive powers of the holders," there results an automatic accumulation of wealth in the hands of the large possessors, and the increment cannot be invested within the community at rates as profitable as before. Thus opportunity for investment is sought elsewhere under the protection of the flag. The cost of this expansion exceeds by several hundred percent the gains of the business interests. "The ever-recurring contention, apparently indisputable, is that at an exorbitant cost to the nation at large certain business interests derive profit" and that this profit is of no benefit to the community. Contrary to the Darwinian jingoists, such as Karl Pearson and Giddings, the effect of imperialism is to deteriorate the conquering race and, even more, the subject people. In return for the nation's "extravagant feeble-minded trade policy," for its investment in vast armaments and administrative expenses, its politics become demoralised and its people degraded.

In the same issue of *The Journal of Political Economy* appeared a review of Maurice Lair's *L'Impérialisme allemand* which is unsigned but bears all the earmarks of having been written by Veblen. He summarised the argument as if an imperial nation with its policy of commercial and military expansion were a great corporation. "Germany as a commercial world-power, and therefore also as a military world-power," has seen its best days. "The thirty-years' period of prosperity has been of the nature of a speculative inflation, the advantages of which have inured to the large capitalists and have not been balanced by any comparable amelioration" of the masses. The result is political instability, class antagonism, and moral deterioration.

Veblen accorded Sombart's two volume *Der moderne Kapitalismus* more favourable treatment than he had given his *Socialism and Socialist Movements*. He deprecated its cavalier air of conviction and self-sufficiency, its vituperative style, and its excessive detail. But it is a blending of "the historical outlook with Marxist materialism" and, unlike the work of the sterile adherents of the historical school, it "aims at an explanation of the economic situation in causal terms." It is "a genetic account of modern capitalism; that is to say, of modern business enterprise, as an English writer might phrase it." "Characteristic of Mr. Sombart's point of view, and significant of the aim of his inquiry, is a careful distinction with which he sets out between business and industry." Veblen does not point out, however, that Sombart used this distinction principally to show the usefulness of big business.

Veblen felt nevertheless that Sombart did not break as completely from the historical approach as is required by the modern scientific point of view. In examining "the capitalist spirit, the habit of mind involved in diligently seeking gains for gain's sake," Sombart commenced with Germany and Italy instead of taking the British and American situation as the typical, central body of the development, "by comparison with which the ramifications of business enterprise through the rest of the industrial world are best to be appreciated." It is true that in these earlier economies the transition was "effectively made, from the medieval spirit of handicraft and petty trade carried on for a livelihood and governed by corporate regulations designed to safeguard a livelihood, to the modern spirit of capitalistic investment for a profit, governed by some measure of free contract and presuming freedom of competition." But business enterprise died out in those areas when "the era of politics, wars, and church dissensions set in." The "New Legal Basis," to use one of Sombart's chapter headings, is "the system of natural liberty; that is to say . . . the inviolability and equality of property rights, freedom of contract, free competition," and "this institutional foundation of business enterprise is embodied in the English Common Law . . . and is to be found ingrained in the common sense of all English-speaking peoples and prevails nowhere else in anything like the same degree of consistency and tenacity. Institutionally speaking, the British natural-rights development affords the only practicable foundations for a consummate business life, and the other peoples of Western Europe are on this head borrowers and imitators of the British, driven in good part by the exigencies imposed by British competition." Those communities whose institutional situation practically comes nearest the British natural-rights pattern "are the most fortunately placed for purposes of business enterprise."

The material foundation of modern business enterprise—the technology of the machine process—is also of English derivation. "The habit . . . of consecutive and aggressive thinking in terms of the machine process is not confined within the limits of English speech," but its boldest and widest application lies within those limits, and this habit of materialistic thinking is "the spiritual ground of the modern technology." Consequently "business methods and business enterprise . . . have reached their freest swing and their maturest expression among the English-speaking peoples." By taking the essentially outlying German business community as the subject of inquiry, and "the main (English) line . . . only by way of qualification," Sombart obtains a "less clear insight into the working of the mechanism."

Veblen made the same criticism against two Belgian authors, Jules Gernaert and Vicomte de Herbais de Thun, who contended that combinations were in the public interest and that their success depended on their having a proper legal form and a long term of life. Veblen said that for American purposes and probably in many cases for European purposes the conditions might better be phrased: "Any effective coalition will turn out to be legal"; and "An efficient coalition will last as long as it proves itself a business success." The naïveté of the authors is due to the fact that they view their subject matter from the "old-fashioned business situation that prevails in Europe, as contrasted . . . with the maturer business situation of America."

In a review of S. Tschierschky's *Kartell und Trust*, Veblen addressed himself to the author's contention that massive business combinations are a necessary outcome of the current individualistic business method. He declared that Tschierschky's belief in the cartel as the best expedient for continental industry was due to the fact that on the continent businessmen identify themselves with only one concern, a practice which gives these organisations "a quasi-personal character" much greater than that which prevails in the American or even the British. Thus the former have "a degree of initiative and consistent business policy" which the latter frequently lack.

Veblen referred to Mead's work on the United States Steel Corporation, but he cited it in a fashion not altogether expressive of Mead's point of view. "It is, as has been argued in detail by E.S. Mead in the case of the United States Steel Corporation, e.g., to the interest of the individual businessmen concerned to overcapitalise the corporation, in the sense that a large nominal capital will yield larger net gains to the promoters and to the former owners of the underlying companies; although the resulting corporation as such may not gain, or may not gain proportionately." The high capitalisation may "easily lead to a discrepancy between capitalisation and earnings," and thus "to cut-throat competition and eventual overproduction and crisis." Consequently trusts may operate "at the cost of the rest of industrial community, by throwing the pressure of competition on the rest through price variations and the like, and so bringing on a general depression which may in the end spread even to the industries within the trust."

Veblen, in his reviews of books on depressions, reiterated his distinction between industrial and pecuniary conceptions of capital. Theodore Burton's popular *Financial Crises and Periods of Industrial and Commercial Depression* attributed crises to a waste or excessive loss of capital, or to its excessive absorption in enterprises not immediately remunerative. Thus the "shrinkage of the market values of securities and other investments is taken to signify a loss of material means of production." By this pecuniary or "Hibernian logic" Burton contends that the dismantling, destruction, or decrease in efficiency of plants results in large losses, in spite of the fact that it is made necessary by the competition of improved machinery and occurs in countries where there has been the greatest increase in wealth; that is, "a waste of means of production [is] taking the form of an increased aggregate efficiency of the means of production."

Ludwig Pohle, on the other hand, in his *Bevölkerungsbewegung, Kapitalbildung und periodische Wirtschaftskrisen,* traced the periodicity of crises and depressions to "psychological grounds, to the cumulative change of animus in the undertaking class; that is to say, these phenomena are essentially of a speculative nature." But according to Pohle the fundamental factor is a material one, namely, the increase in the working-class population. This increase diverts to consumption savings which might have been capitalised, and as a result there are insufficient funds to "capitalise," or finance, the necessary increase in productive goods. Consequently, with further increase in population, occurs a reduction in employment which is the substantial fact of depression. Veblen argued that on the basis of Pohle's discussion "the funded value of the productive goods in question should be competent, through the introduction of credit relations, to pay for and, therefore, to capitalise, these goods." The workmen could secure a remunerative employment and the necessary increase in consumption goods would be forthcoming. Thus the factors to which Pohle traces depression should on "his own interpretation of the facts, result in brisk times."

In the decennial publications of the University of Chicago, Laughlin and Veblen presented their radically different theories of modern credit. Laughlin once more described credit as the "evolution of a refined system of barter." He considered it self-evident that the function of capital is to bring present goods to the producers whose efforts end in the future. Credit was invented to aid this process, but it is not itself capital, since a transfer of goods is not a production of them. This control of other people's capital by men of affairs is a natural desire "growing out of the evolutionary processes of industry." Credit transactions involve transferable goods and property, and confer the right of destruction in the process of repayment. Thus a lease is not considered a credit transaction, nor is an obligation for the future delivery of personal service.

Credit enables a manufacturer or producer to coin his command over goods or sums due into general purchasing power for further production. This coining of property into a means of payment or a means of deferred payments is performed by banks and similar investment institutions where savings collect. Since these institutions place in the circuit of production a vast amount of property and commodities which would otherwise remain inert, their work is in the category of "the progress of the arts."

The nature of credit is obscured by the fact that credit transactions are in money terms. Only a portion of the community's wealth is, or ought to be, invested in its money machinery, since "money itself is barren." In the ceaseless circuit of goods, in which each exchanges his surplus for other commodities desired, men do not want money itself. Every intelligent manager keeps his money supply at a minimum, since "it earns no interest." Hence the desire to invest it at once. The test of normal credit and sound banking is the repayment of the obligation. An increase of credit is not to be feared, and cannot raise prices, since it is essentially an exchange of goods. But abnormal, illegitimate, speculative credit is the coining of goods and property to an amount greater than the marketable values actually owned by the borrower, and it means that at maturity repayment cannot be made. It raises general prices and provides the situation for commercial crises and a sharp decline in values. In the crash normal credit may change into abnormal credit, but the "panic demonstrates that credit transactions are really based on goods," the fall of prices indicating a return from abnormal to normal credit.[11]

Veblen called his monograph "The Use of Loan Credit in Modern Business," and it shows a close connexion with his previous discussion of the promoter's advantage as opposed to that of the corporation and the community. Once again Veblen is concerned with the dissociation of modern industrial life and modern capital; here his main argument is based on the concept of modern business capital as the capitalisation of prospective earning capacity.

In the beginning Veblen disclaimed any intention of disturbing the established theory of credit, declaring that he wished to examine only the subsidiary problem of credit as an expedient in the quest for profits, in other words, the general consequences of credit extension on the conduct of modern business and the working of the modern industrial system. His inquiry was to be concerned not with deferred payments in the purchase and sale of goods—a type of credit characteristic of small enterprise—but with loan credit, such as debts, notes, securities, call loans, characteristic of modern corporate enterprise and finance.

Contrary to the assumption of economists and men of affairs, said Veblen, credit is necessary not to modern industry but only to modern business competition. It is assumed that credit gives the discretionary control of industry to more competent hands, but the great captain of industry is more competent only in the sense that he may permissively countenance improvements as well as retard them. Credit is rooted in the modern institution of property, and thus, under modern industrial conditions, the so-called abnormal or illegitimate use of credit is inevitable. This "abnormal" credit, exemplified in liquidations and panics, cannot easily be distinguished from normal credit. The former results in an inability to pay maturing loans and interest on securities without cutting into paid-up capital or reducing earnings much below a reasonable rate. Normal credit changes into abnormal credit without any overt action on the part of a borrower, as, for example, when there is a great fall in the value of the collateral for a call loan. The conditions of competition make it necessary for all business managers to take advantage of the pros-

pective profits to be gained from increased credit and the subsequent increase in business operations. But the net effect is that the earnings of
capital plus credit are no greater than was received before on capital
alone. Funds provide the borrower with a differential advantage in bidding against other businessmen for the control and use of material
processes and material, but the competitive demand for credit, while
increasing the volume of business capital, does not in the aggregate increase the volume of industry. Of course a speculative inflation may,
through a rise in prices, lead indirectly to an increased use of industrial
equipment, but this secondary effect of credit extension belongs primarily
in a theory of industry, not in a theory of modern business. In the theory
of business, funds are a pecuniary fact, not an industrial one; they are
important in the control of industry, not in its mechanically productive
work. Loan credit serves to widen the discrepancy between business
capital and industrial equipment. Competitive bidding raises the values
of the material items and thus provides further collateral for further
credit extension to increase business operations, and the process in effect
is repeated *ad infinitum.* Thus the extension of credit is based not on material efficiency but on "the putative stability of the money value"—market
or exchange value, price—"of the capitalised industrial material whose
money value is cumulatively augmented by this extension itself." This
cumulative enhancement of capitalised values does not increase the gross
profits, as counted in terms of material wealth or "permanent values,"
since creditors outside the industrial process must be paid interest on
funds which in the aggregate represent no productive goods and have no
productive effect. This process of inflation turns eventually, however,
into liquidation.

The money value of the collateral is presumed to be its capitalised
value, computed on its supposed earning capacity, but at some point it
becomes apparent that there is a discrepancy between money value and
capitalised value. The nominal value of the earnings "is not increased in
as strong a ratio as that of the business capital," since the demand which
regulates the value of the product "is not altogether a business demand
(for productive goods) but is . . . in the last resort mainly reducible
to a consumptive demand for finished goods." In a footnote Veblen
declared that the market value of the output does not keep pace with the
inflation of capital, because incomes do not increase correspondingly. If
incomes are augmented, the expenses of production are increased and
the inflation of values for consumption goods is destroyed, leaving only
the advance in production goods values as a source of increased earnings.
Liquidation then sets in to enforce a rerating on earning capacity, but if
there were no "competitive investment in industrial material on a large

scale," the liquidation would not occur. In the liquidating period bad debts are written off, and the remaining "gain represented by the credit inflation, goes to the creditors and claimants of funds outside the industrial process proper." Thus the final outcome of a period of liquidation is a redistribution of property, to the advantage of the financiering group.

"But the extension of credit need not take on the cumulative character which it bears during a period of speculative advance, or 'rising prosperity,' unless some effective disturbance of prices and of the market outlook comes in to heighten the incentives that lead businessmen to compete for loans." This disturbance and its opportunities furnish the work of the modern captain of industry and form the background of modern credit. It is this question that Veblen discusses in the second part of his monograph.

In modern business, capital means the capitalisation of presumptive earning capacity, and consequently it involves the use of all feasible credit expedients, and fluctuates with the prevalent presumptions as to the corporation's earning capacity and solvency, and the good faith of its governing board. In the ideal modern corporate organisation, with its elaborate structure of securities, the old-fashioned distinction between capital and credit is illusory. The entire capital, including the whole of the material equipment, is placed on a credit basis. Even the cost of printing the securities is met by the sale of stock. In a well-financed corporation the questions of "stock watering" and over-capitalisation are immaterial. The common stock is nothing but "water"—under the name of "good will," and "over-capitalisation" can mean over-capitalisation only in relation to earning capacity. The adjustment of capitalisation to earning capacity can be made only through the market quotations of the securities, since capitalisation is a question of value and market quotations are the last resort in such questions. Most of the securities offered as collateral for credit extensions, and thus furnishing the means of payment, "are evidences of debt, at the first remove or farther from the physical basis, instruments of credit recording a previous credit extension."

In the beginnings of corporation finance, as in railroad financing for example, the process of expansion by means of debenture credit took some time, but today a corporation starts with a fully organised capital and debt. A coalition furnishes the best means for this credit financing. The avowed motive in the formation of the trusts is increased industrial efficiency, but this motive does not affect the function of modern credit. The real inducements are the presumptive gains of the promoter who is the prime mover; the gains of the stockholders are secondary. The work of these great captains has grave industrial consequences, but it is not of an industrial nature, since it is not concerned with efficiently running the industrial processes. The campaign of business strategy which the modern captain of industry finds necessary "runs, in the main, on credit relations, in the way of financial backing, options, purchases, leases, and the issuance and transfer of stock and debentures." The strategic use of credit differs from old-fashioned investment, because the time element is relatively unimportant and the share of the financiers is calculated not as profits, percent per time unit, but as bonuses, determined mainly by the volume of the turnover. Their share of gain is in effect added to the capitalisation, so that in the language of old-fashioned business the interest due the creditors is incorporated in the capital.

A large proportion of the nominal capital of a trust or holding company is composed of the capitalised good will of the concerns in the merger and to this extent it has no aggregate industrial effect. It is a capitalisation of the differential advantages possessed by the several concerns as rivals in business, and is useful only for competitive business ends. When the rivals are merged, it ceases to be materially useful to the corporation. To this aggregate of essentially imaginary good will is added a good will imputed to the consolidated organisation. The properties of the various parties are equalised by raising the nominal shares of each in the capitalisation. It is only to a fractional and uncertain extent that the values are based on material goods.

Thus the modern captain of industry brings about in a short time an inflation of capital values which might come about gradually in the course of business competition, and achieves without any increase in material equipment an advantageous redistribution of ownership like that which occurs in a period of liquidation. In some respects the trust maker is a substitute for a commercial crisis. The effective value of the new corporation's business capital, as indicated, of course, by the market quotations rather than by its face value, will suffer no permanent shrinkage if its "monopoly advantage (good will) is sufficient to keep its earning capacity up to the rate upon which the capitalisation is based."

In reviewing this monograph *The International Socialist Review* said: "It is always difficult in Professor Veblen's work to determine . . . just how far he is poking fun at the orthodox political economist," but concluded that "the essay is certainly the most keen analysis of modern trust financiering . . . ever published."

Veblen sent a copy to Mrs. Gregory, and in answer to her comments wrote her on June 27, 1903: "Had I known that my pamphlet would disturb you and make you less happy, it should not have been allowed to do mischief. . . . The pamphlet is a chapter out of a prospective book, which has this week gone out to seek a publisher. You may have seen enough to criticise in the pamphlet . . . but the book, I am credibly told, is still more 'beyond,' or, as my friends who have seen it say, beside the point. Its name is the *Theory of Business Enterprise*—a topic on which I am free to theorise with all the abandon that comes of immunity from the facts."

In 1904 the main title of Veblen's course on trusts was changed to "the Organization of Business Enterprise." With the public outcry against the trusts at a fever-pitch, Veblen published in the March issue of *The Journal of Political Economy* an article entitled "An Early Experiment in Trusts." In this essay he returned to the anthropological approach which he had used in much of his previous work, but the discussion of the rise of trusts among the early Vikings is developed in the language of modern capitalistic organisation, with its wage labour and strategy of the stock market.

The culminating achievement of the spirit of adventure and enterprise characteristic of the peace-disturbing dolicho-blond, declared Veblen, is his dominance in business, "and its most finished instrument is the quasi-voluntary coalition of forces known as a Trust." This spirit of enterprise has maintained a "consistent character through all the mutations of name and external circumstances that have passed over it in the course of history. In its earlier, more elemental expression this business spirit was of the nature of "raiding, by land and sea," essentially a corporation in piracy and slave trading. For such traffic there was necessary a "regular market and an assured demand for the output." A relatively large investment had to be sunk, and the period of turnover, the period of production, was necessarily long; the risk was also large. Certain technological requirements had to be met, including the manufacture of weapons. An adequate accumulation of capital goods was necessary, coupled with a spirit of exploit and an available labour supply.

In the course of time the Viking enterprise became transformed from a mere "agreeable and honourable diversion" of well-to-do freehold farmers, and a "lucrative employment for their surplus wealth and labour supply," to the status of a primary occupation, with a "settled business routine and a defined code of professional ethics." The earlier combines were of the nature of loose pools. A combine would be formed for a season between two or more capitalist undertakers, and they employed primarily their own capital, although credit arrangements occasionally occurred. The permanent form of syndicate arose mainly from an increase in the volume of trade and its territorial extension. The technique of trade gradually improved, and there was an increase in the volume of capital invested, with equipment and management reduced to standard form. But overproduction and over-investment were the result, and with them cut-throat competition among the corporations. Violent conflicts destroyed a number of the corporations, and there occurred great losses of capital, the impoverishment of some great families, and demoralisation of the trade.

The coalitions, moreover, encountered the disfavour of the governing authorities. The business has grown so large that the moderately well-off did not possess the intangible assets or good will necessary for the successful promotion of "a new company of freebooters." At best their sons could become only employees and they had few opportunities to rise speedily to executive positions. As the Viking coalitions grew, and as competition became more severe, the blackmail composing the major share of profits grew more excessive and more uncertain and fluctuating. With the disappearance of the small Vikings and the demoralisation accompanying cut-throat competition, the livelihood of the common people, at whose expense the Vikings lived, "grew progressively more precarious, and even their domestic peace and household industry grew insecure." Thus law and order were threatened by popular resentment against the traffic, and politicians were forced to make a show at "trust busting"; but the big stick was usually administered to the smaller corporations, not to those of national importance. These Viking combines were useful for war purposes and brought money into the country, and therefore the politicians made a show of attempting to regulate their activities without disabling them. But the regulation inevitably failed, and severe competition brought such excesses that the politicians were obliged to do something about it.

It became plain that only a combine having an effective monopoly could prosper. The trade in eastern islands had less of a speculative air than that in western islands, and it had that look of stability and conservative management which belongs to an investment business, thus providing the proper ingredients for a combine. As may often happen in such a conjuncture of intolerable competition, "there arose a man of far-seeing sagacity and settled principles, of executive ability and business-like integrity, who saw the needs of the hour and the available remedy, and who saw at the same glance his own opportunity of gain. . . . He was a man of mature experience, with a large investment in the traffic, and with a body of 'good will' that gave him most decisive advantage." He became the first president of the great new corporation, and was given extreme powers for the enforcement of the strict laws concerning the discipline of the personnel and the division of earnings. A charter was granted by the New Jersey of the day, on condition that the company prey outside of its area, and a fortified apparatus was set up. In his long occupancy of the office the promoter exercised his power with great business success. "This neutral, international corporation of piracy rapidly won a great prestige"; that is, its intangible assets, originally composed of the franchise of the good will of the promoter and the underlying companies, "grew rapidly larger." Its policy was essentially that which has since become familiar in other lines of enterprise, except that in those days "the competitive struggle took a less sophisticated form." Syndicates that were sufficiently strong were allowed to submit to the terms of the trust and were brought into the combine; others were forced out or wiped out through bankruptcy. The trust virtually dictated the terms of trade and it became a factor of first importance in international politics. But its attempt to become too thoroughly imperial by subjugating alien communities was unsuccessful, largely because of miscalculation, untoward incidents, and hurried preparations. Its affairs were brought to a spectacular crisis from which it never fully recovered. Other factors in the trust's collapse were its lack of discipline and its arbitrary exactions as it became supreme, but the primary reason was the collapse of the slave trade with the introduction of Christianity, for without a slave market there was no chance of reasonable earnings.

The same month that this article appeared Hobson wrote Veblen asking: "When will your book on Business be out? I am trying to put together an elementary textbook of economics (general) and shall expect to get some definite assistance from your book." Shortly afterwards Veblen published *The Theory of Business Enterprise*, himself paying the cost of the plates and the composition.

CHAPTER XIV

THE *Theory of Business Enterprise* is essentially an expansion of "Industrial and Pecuniary Employments." Authoritative evidence as to the nature of corporation finance was scarcely available when Veblen was writing *The Theory of the Leisure Class*, but now such data were at hand in the nineteen volumes of the Report of the Industrial Commission.

As in *The Theory of the Leisure Class*, each chapter of this book seems to harp on the same theme, but the illusion of an unfolding story is not so well maintained, with the result that the chapters appear disconnected, each complete in itself. Furthermore, the use of numerous mathematical formulæ in lengthy footnotes which repeat the text, a practice needless except perhaps for strategy, and the highly involved and in part repetitious analysis in three chapters in the middle of the book, act as an effective check on full appreciation of the argument. Veblen seems to have used the footnotes to state his main points instead of for reference purposes, but these points are expressed as if they were exceptions to the argument of the text. Another source of confusion arises from the apparent digressions into the "genesis" of such prevailing institutions as capital with no clear indication that genetic explanation means causal explanation. Thus it is difficult to appreciate the fact that Veblen is actually concerned with the modern institution of business and with the non-existent circumstances which the community still believes to prevail, as evidenced in its adherence to the institution; that he is concerned, in other words, with the way in which the acceptance of the institution gives rise to a state of affairs contradicting its presumed foundations. Also, although this, too, is not clearly indicated, the centre of the discussion is great corporate enterprise, not such pre-capitalistic forms of industry as farming, petty trade, handicraft, and small business in general.

The organisation of the book follows so closely that of the earlier book and the *Quarterly* essays that it seems on first impression to be only a restatement of *The Theory of the Leisure Class* in more pecuniary terms. "An Early Experiment in Trusts" and "The Use of Loan Credit in Modern Business" play the same role for *The Theory of Business Enterprise* as do the supposedly anthropological articles for *The Theory of the Leisure Class*, the articles giving in succinct form the theoretical premises of the books. "The Economic Theory of Woman's Dress" and "Dress as an Expression of the Pecuniary Culture" develop the wastefulness of modern dress as an expression of the modern pecuniary culture; "The Use of Loan Credit in Modern Business" develops the nature of modern credit, or capital, as an expression of modern business enterprise. The articles on dress sketch a theory of fashion as the ever-increasing disturbance of comfort through the conflicting dictates of the æsthetic sense and the canon of conspicuous waste; the article on credit sketches a theory of business cycles as the ever-increasing disturbance of material welfare through the conflicting dictates of material needs and processes and the canons of modern capitalisation, as typified by that ideal development of modern business, the trust or holding company. In the first the requirement of conspicuous leisure acts to outlaw material welfare; in the other capitalisation widens the discrepancy between modern capital and industrial efficiency.

The similarity of the concepts, if not the content of these various works, suggests that they were all in Veblen's mind at the same time. Thus he declares that in the mature development of received economics the formulation of its preconceptions has reached such a stage of refinement and intangibility that not only does it have nothing to say concerning the material welfare of the community, but it shows no understanding of the self-seeking interest of the pecuniary individuals. The science is taxonomy for taxonomy's sake.

In the mature development of the predatory culture the instinct of sportsmanship reaches a point not only of almost complete elimination of the naïve instinct of workmanship but of aimless fatigation. For the modern barbarian the institution of property becomes so intangible that it ceases even to serve his comfort. In the ideal development of the institution of the leisure class its members even suffer pains and mortification in obedience to the inscrutable requirements of conspicuous waste. In the maturity of business enterprise the great captains, as well as the community, suffer losses in material values, though not necessarily in funds, in their obedience to the inscrutable pecuniary dictates of the capitalisation process. The result is an elimination of received economics, of the institution of the modern leisure class, and of business enterprise, and the return to a more archaic economics, to the predatory stage proper, and to a feudal regime, unless the discipline of the machine process can effect an evolutionary economics, the reassertion of the naïve instinct of workmanship, and socialism.

So interrelated are the various works that each of them appears to contain the themes of the others. Veblen seems to be playing a number of melodies at the same time, all of which are the outgrowth of the incompatibility between the discipline of the modern industrial process and that of the modern business process, and all of which have their pivotal points in "Some Neglected Points in the Theory of Socialism" and "The Army of the Commonweal." If the term "system" is to be applied to Veblen's work, then *The Theory of Business Enterprise* completes his "system," in the sense that it completes the cycle of thought of the *Quarterly* essays and *The Theory of the Leisure Class*. Thus the argument of the "beginnings of ownership" as deriving from the ownership-marriage relation of female captives outside the tribe and eventually developing into conventionalized seizure of wives from within the corporate unit, is to be completely understood only in the light of the relationship of the financier to the material welfare of the community and then to the corporation, as sketched in this book. Only in the light of all of Veblen's previous work, therefore, can the full implications of *The Theory of Business Enterprise* be understood.

The discussion does not avowedly run in terms of the incompatibility between the impersonal and the animistic point of view, or of that between the savage and the barbarian, or of that between industrial capital and modern business capital, but in terms of the incompatibility between investment for profit and the machine process. These are the characteristic features and dominating forces of the modern economic organisation—"the 'Capitalistic System' or 'Modern Industrial System,' so called."

The scope and method of modern industry are given by the machine. The machine process implies and enforces a sweeping standardisation of processes, goods, services, and consumers. Mankind, in order to get along with the machine process and reap the benefit of its efficiency, must adapt itself to its impersonal, standardised requirements. The machine process denotes a reasoned procedure as against the rule of thumb of the traditional scheme of control, where personal propensity is the dominant feature and where the industrial processes and material procedures must adapt themselves to the needs of the big businessman. Advance in industrial efficiency is due to the comprehensive, concatenated character of the entire process, and the economic welfare of the community is best served by a facile and uninterrupted interplay of its various parts.

But the great gains of the modern captain are made in disturbing the delicate interstitial adjustments between plants and processes. Great profits are achieved not from productive efficiency, but from shifts in the distribution of ownership in vendible capital or securities. The modern captain is interested not in the permanent efficiency of the industrial system or of any plant, but in the control of a segment of the system for the strategic purpose of influencing the security market for the flotation of securities, the manœuvring of a coalition or any other well-known method of manipulation. The result of his manœuvring and strategic activity is a a chronic perturbation of industry, which has become the normal state of affairs. The modern captain does not create opportunities for increasing industrial efficiency, but only watches for opportunities to put his competitors in an uncomfortable position; cut-throat competition, rate wars, duplication, misdirection, wasted effort, and delay of improvements long after they are advisable are the price the community pays. When this game between competing business interests is played to a finish, in a coalition of the competitors under single management, then it may proceed more obviously as a conflict between the monopoly and the community. By virtue of the delicate character of the industrial process as a whole, a small apparent disturbance by the captains has a cumulative effect throughout the system far in excess of the original disturbance and is typified by such phenomena as crises and depressions.

The unquestioned service rendered by the modern captain is the elimination of businessmen as a class, and the cancelling of opportunities for private enterprise. The resulting gains are absorbed by the captains.

The higher reaches of business enterprise have something of the nature of parasitic activities, and whatever goes to maintain the profits of the classes engaged in these unproductive occupations is drawn from the community's productive activity. But the modern business system with its pecuniary aims partially offsets its wastefulness by the added strain it throws upon the productive classes.

The machine process operates on and enforces the impersonal principle of cause and effect, of mechanical or industrial efficiency, but the spiritual basis of business is the institution of ownership. This is derived from anthropomorphic thinking, and belongs in the same category and the same stage of human history as the "principles of (primitive) blood relationship, clan solidarity, paternal descent, Levitical cleanliness, divine guidance, allegiance, nationality." The right of property is an axiomatic premise, a matter of common sense, but from the standpoint of material efficiency the binding relation between property and owner is only putative, no more intrinsic than the relation of the great financier to the industrial processes. The legal relationship to accumulated goods is not a mechanical relationship or one of material efficiency. It is merely a habit of thought which belongs to the eighteenth century. Veblen discusses its derivation in terms that recall "The Beginnings of Ownership." The natural right of ownership is so traced that it seems to be fundamentally of the same character as the notion of the suzerainty of the Creator or of the warlike barbarian. The natural right of ownership is contrary to fact, but it is a matter of ingrained common sense and equity, as given by the pecuniary culture. By the development of this idea the eighteenth century gave the security and ease of credit engagements which have made possible the ideal competitive order of business, the order of unrestricted capital-isation.

The fundamental principle underlying modern pecuniary transactions is the putative invariability of the money unit. It is assumed that the end of modern business traffic is the securing of consumable goods through the medium of money. Thus "the office of the money unit—money transactions, exchange, credit, and all the rest that make up the phe-nomena of business"—is the efficient distribution of consumable goods from producer to consumer. But the pecuniary realities of capitalisation are taken as objective realities, and, although money varies when meas-ured in terms of livelihood and labour, it remains an axiomatic principle that the money unit is stable. Actually great profits and the resulting "savings" which increase capital result from the instability of money. Economists and modern businessmen consider as a matter of common sense that profits are normal. It is presumed that in the natural course of things there must be a stable and orderly increase in money values. Plants and processes are capitalised on their profit-yielding capacity, and investments are made for profits. The ultimate conditioning force in modern business is not the aggregate holdings or the recorded output, but the prospective profits of any move in the strategy of the captain of industry. This great manœuvring and increase of capitalisation are achieved by the use of loan credit, and thus the competitive order becomes a credit economy and takes on its present convulsive character.

Modern business capital bears only a remote relation to industrial capital, since business capital is based on earning capacity. The core in business capitalisation is what is euphemistically called "good will," that is, the profit-yielding advantages of monopoly. These advantages are im-material assets which are serviceable not to the community but to the effective owners. In the received economics they are treated as rents or quasi-rents.

The managers of the enterprise own a very small proportion of the securities of the concern, and this is usually common stock which is of no use to the community or to the nominal owners of the plant, since the plant is more than covered by bonds and similar securities. The earning capacity which affords the basis of business capital is always a matter of conjecture. It is to the interest of the strategists, for purposes of purchase or sale, that there be a discrepancy between the actual and the putative earning capacities of the corporate capital. The managers are interested in the corporation not for the production of goods, but for securing profits for themselves, for increasing the immaterial assets or business capital. Thus the financier can reap profits and increase his business capital by manœuvres which are disserviceable not only to the community but also to the concerns as going business organisations. The interest of those who hold the discretion in industrial affairs is removed by one degree from that of the concerns under their management, and by two degrees from the interests of the community at large.

Furthermore, the securities with which the modern captain plays, and which are the product of his good will, are already reaping incomes from the concerns whose capital or good will they first represented. This secondary use results in magnificent additions to business capital, and gives rise to the great fortunes, but the speculative risk involved in this traffic in vendible capital falls on the community and the corporation, not on the captains. The "good will" of the corporate financier is of a spiritual nature, since it may be present without diminution in every part of the various structures it has created. Its capitalisation in one corporation is used to augment the amount of business capital in the next. When the interest of the financiers so warrants, their good will possesses the additional spiritual trait "that it may imperceptibly and inscrutably withdraw its animating force from any one of its creatures without thereby altering the material circumstances of the corporation which suffers such an intangible shrinkage of its forces." Thus the life of the community is in the hands of the owners of the intangible assets who have only a remote interest in the efficient working of the equipment. "This dissociation of the business control from workmanlike efficiency and from the immediate contact with or ownership of the industrial plant" tends to make the existing system feudalistic.

For the purpose of showing the instability and convulsions of modern business through the workings of business itself, Veblen sketches once more the argument of how the working of credit and capitalisation on the basis of prospective profits results in inflation and inevitable depression. Overproduction or underconsumption is a business, not an industrial fact; that is, the fluctuation and cessation of industrial activity are due not to the material needs of industry but to the fact that industry waits on business capital. New investment, new organisations, reorganised concerns, and new processes perpetuate depressions for fully capitalised concerns. There may be greater production in depression than in times of prosperity, and this productivity makes it difficult for invested wealth to earn its profits. The return in terms of real values may not be less, but big business reluctantly accepts a decline of profits in money values. Thus the efficiency of industry is a never-ceasing threat to capitalised values, calculated as they are on the stability of the money unit. But industry becomes more efficient and more highly integrated, plants are capitalised for prosperity rather than for depression, and the unequal distribution of wealth makes for a continual increase in great savings; under this fully developed regime of business and the machine, depression becomes chronic and normal.

Prosperity is achieved only by some extraneous event in the nature of waste, such as war, land speculation, wasteful consumption. But if industry remains at its present level of industrial efficiency and the unequal distribution of wealth is maintained, waste cannot overtake production and check the tendency towards depression. Combination is inevitable. Trusts, however, face cut-throat competition among themselves, and thus modern competitive business requires a trust comprising the whole field of industry which is dominated by the machine process. The lower orders of businessmen become a "bureaucratic hierarchy," the general body of owners are reduced to the status of pensioners, and the underlying population becomes the raw material of industry, bought at the lowest practical price, which may be even lower than a subsistence wage. In many lines of endeavour this situation is already approximated. But when the last step is taken, there still remains "the competitive friction between the combined business capital and the combined workmen."

The economic or materialistic interpretation of history, applied to the prevailing situation, shows that "modern (civilised) institutions rest in great part on business principles." Under the modern, standardised system the workman's livelihood is dependent on "acceptance of one specific contract," and thus the owners of the industrial processes may bring pecuniary pressure to bear upon the choice of the workmen. But such pecuniary pressure is unknown to the common-sense metaphysics of law and business, conceived as it is in the economic situation of eighteenth-century handicraft. "By force of the concatenation of industrial processes and the dependence of men's comfort or subsistence upon the orderly working of these processes, the exercise of the rights of ownership in the interests of business may traverse . . . the needs of the community at large as, e.g., in the conceivable case of an advisedly instituted coal famine, but since these necessities of comfort or of livelihood cannot be formulated in terms of the natural freedom of contract, they can, in the nature of the case, give rise to no cognisable grievance and find no legal remedy."

The natural freedom of the effective owners of the industrial processes, to let work proceed or not, as the outlook of profits may decide, is a matter of common sense, a matter of the sacred and inalienable character of the " 'natural,' conventional freedom of contract." Limited liability companies might seem a violation of the original postulate of natural liberty, with its implication of personal responsibility, but in the conflict between the main proposition of natural liberty and one of its corollaries, pecuniary liberty, the corollary won because the facts of business ex-

pediency "had outgrown the primary implication of the main proposition." In "the disputes between property rights and naked mankind" it
is natural that property rights—accumulations of funded wealth—take
precedence.

Since modern business is the controlling institution, modern governmental policies are of a "mercantile" character. They consist largely of
maxims prohibiting any "restraint of trade," and are concerned primarily
with fostering business. Patriotism and property are the fundamental
preconceptions of popular metaphysics, and Veblen presents them in
almost identical terms. Pecuniary magnates take the place of princes.
Just as in former times the population believed that what was good for
the prince was good for them, so there is today a "naïve, unquestioning
persuasion abroad among the body of the people to the effect that, in
some occult way, the material interests of the populace coincide with the
pecuniary interests" of the captains of industry. This belief rests "on
an uncritically assumed solidarity of interests, rather than on an insight
into the relation of business enterprise to the material welfare of those
classes who are not primarily businessmen." Although this view is a disserviceable anachronism it "has the deep-rooted strength given by an
extremely protracted discipline of predation and servitude." Equally
strong is the preconception that "the ownership of property is the material
foundation of human well-being, and this natural right of ownership is
sacred." Acquisition of wealth is assumed to be production of wealth, so
that "failure to bargain shrewdly or to accumulate more goods than one
has produced by the work of one's own hands is looked upon with a feeling
of annoyance, as a neglect, not only of opportunity, but of duty." The
result is that the characteristically modern businessmen and the community "by whose means the business gains are secured work together in
good faith towards . . . the accumulation of wealth in the hands of those
men who are skilled in pecuniary matters."

Modern business is closely allied with the current policy of war and
armaments. In fact, Veblen's discussion of international competition is
phrased in such terms that the competition of states appears as the competition of great corporations and financial magnates. The search for profitable
investments, for markets to increase business capital, leads to international competition and force, whether the issue be between princes by
the grace of God or princes by the grace of ownership. The competitive
increase of armaments and war expenditures is profitable business, but,
eventually, it results in industrial exhaustion and business collapse.

Veblen set forth his position most clearly in his second to the last
chapter, "The Cultural Incidence of the Machine Process." The argument runs once more in terms of the distinction between industrial and

pecuniary employments. The fully disciplined workman under the machine regime thinks habitually in terms of mechanical efficiency or impersonal material cause and effect. The machine technology has no use for the "law of sufficient reason" of modern business practice, for the natural right of property or of funded wealth, or for the constraining force of the prevailing pecuniary law and order. The logic of the machine is exemplified in the appreciation of matter-of-fact efficiency by those of the industrial classes who "stand in an engineering or supervisory relation to the processes." Those who serve merely as mechanical auxiliaries of the machine process are not untouched by this working industrial logic, but "it falls upon them blindly and enforces an uncritical acceptance of opaque results rather than a theoretical insight into the causal sequences which make up the machine process." The engineers and the like are required to administer "the laws of causal sequence running through material phenomena," and consequently they must learn to think in the terms in which the process runs. The metaphysical assumptions of such thinking are the same as those of modern science, so that the men occupied with material science are in the class of the industrial experts.

Under modern conditions of specialisation the life of the pecuniary classes and that of the industrial classes differ so entirely that the two classes have no more understanding of one another than have two incompatible cultures possessing radically different ideals and aspirations. The final term of the anthropomorphic pecuniary logic is the purely conventional fact of ownership, which is made to take precedence over the impersonal, non-conventional facts of material exigencies. Training in the pecuniary logic gives efficiency not for mechanical work but for practical management, with "practical" meaning the ability to turn facts to account for the purposes of the accepted pecuniary conventions. It results in conservatism, which means in this case the maintenance of the pecuniary conventions. In other words, the discipline of modern business life has somewhat the "complexion which marks the life of the higher barbarian culture," whereas the "ubiquitous presence of the machine with its spiritual concomitant—workday ideals and scepticism of what is only conventionally valid—is the unequivocal mark of the western culture of today."

The highly skilled industrial experts as well as the factory hands are notoriously improvident and unable to take care of their pecuniary affairs. They have of course an envious appreciation of pecuniary success, but the pecuniary canons enforced by modern capitalisation—conspicuous waste and free expenditure of consumable goods—are against thrift, in a material sense. As a result of the reduction of labour to mobile, interchangeable raw material for the purpose of large organisation, it is practically impossible for a workman to own a home advantageously. A savings account is no substitute for such property as a home which is "tangibly and usefully under the owner's hand and persistently requires maintenance and improvement."

The trade-union spirit is another sign of the weakness of the natural rights preconception among workmen. The necessity for trade-union action is not appreciated by workmen until some time after the introduction of those modern business methods which make it advisable. The trade union is a compromise between what "naturally" ought to be in modern business, and what the situation of the workmen demands. Strikes and agitations may nominally result from the necessities of the labourers, but they involve a disallowance of the sacred rights of capital and of the pecuniary common sense embodied in the prevailing law and order. They are "the means whereby the discipline of the machine industry is enforced and made effective for recasting the habits of thought of the workmen." When the animosity to business principles takes the form of intolerance of all property rights, it is to be classified as revolutionary, and this development, which "overtly asserts the mechanical standardisation of industry as against the common-law standardisation of business," is the logical outcome of trade-union action. Thus socialism is widespread among the advanced industrial peoples. The classes affected by socialistic tendencies have a pronounced sense of "economic solidarity," which "runs on lines of industrial coherence and mechanical constraint, not on lines given by pecuniary conjunctures and conventional principles of economic right and wrong." The entire range of doctrines "covered by the theory of distribution in the received economics is essentially (and characteristically) neglected by the modern socialist speculations."

Socialism is radically different from anarchism, for the latter is based on the prevailing natural rights or romantic postulates. It merely carries these postulates to a more ruthless conclusion, and from the natural-rights point of view it is "substantially sound, though senselessly extreme." Nor has socialism any relation to the modern reform movements interested in reforming the unsound tendencies of machine industry. The line of distinction for potential socialists is to be drawn not between the indigent and the well-to-do, but between the classes employed in the industrial employments and those in the pecuniary employments. Those affected by socialist tendencies are the skilled mechanics of the highly organised urban industries and the men in the material sciences, as opposed to the bankers, the backward rural population, and the general run of the labouring population. The differentiation of occupations resulting from modern industrial methods concentrates the socialistic elements and thus "heightens their sense of class solidarity and acts to accentuate their bias, gives consistency to their ideals, and induces that boldness of conviction and action which is to be had only in a compact body of men." Accordingly, when the machine process and mechanical technology become the tone-giving factor in men's scheme of thought, socialism follows by easy consequence, and the system of status is eliminated.

On the other hand, for the backward classes which belong to the barbaric culture the pecuniary ideals are right and good. The German socialists, in attempting to convert the peasants to socialism, have turned to "measures of compromise, in which the characteristic and revolutionary features of the socialistic programme are softened beyond recognition, if not suppressed." A reduction of the lesser captains to the category of clerks, as a result of the work of the great strategists, does not imply the spread of socialistic views, as socialists claim, because the unpropertied classes employed in business do not become seriously affected by socialist thinking. These dependent classes are the ordinary stockholders, people of small means, and their interest in the institution of property "slackens through the loss of that emulative motive on which pecuniary endeavour proceeds," but they retain faith in its intrinsic rightfulness. Instead of turning to socialism they make excursions into "pragmatic romance, such as Social Settlements, Clean Politics, Single Tax, Arts and Crafts," which touch only symptoms and are therefore a waste of time and effort. Socialism is characteristic of the dolicho-blonds for, according to the work of Closson, Lapouge, and Ammon, the dolicho-blond preponderates in the industrial towns.

The post-Darwinian impersonal conception of causation is essential for the interpretation of modern life. In Darwin's scheme of life God had no place "because . . . He could not be stated and handled in terms of process." Darwin's inquiry "characteristically confines itself to the process of cumulative change. His results, as well as his specific determination of the factors at work in this process of cumulative change have been questioned; perhaps they are open to all the criticisms levelled against them as well as to a few more not yet thought of; but the scope and method given to scientific inquiry by Darwin and the generation whose spokesman he is has substantially not been questioned, except by the diminishing contingent of the faithful who by force of special training or by native gift are not amenable to the discipline of the machine process." This modern conception of causation is making its appearance even in the moral sciences. The older preconceptions have not, of course, been eliminated. Clergymen, naturalistic myth-makers, and the like still personify the process of industrial efficiency, which is the process of cause and effect in economic life, and are thereby enabled to find in it a "well-advised meliorative trend" towards the beneficent process of capitalisation. But the cumulative effect of the machine logic is to make this mythology obsolete.

The concluding chapter of the book, "The Natural Decay of Business Enterprise," is concerned with the thesis that it is only through some factor hostile to the machine process that the pecuniary structure can be maintained, although modern business is dependent upon the machine process for its existence and its gains. Any attempt to rehabilitate the ancient scheme of small business is doomed to failure, either by the requirements of modern business or by those of the modern industrial process, although the working of modern business may eventually reduce the community to a state lower than that of handicraft. Those who hark back to the pre-capitalistic era are simply holding to obsolescent ideals.

Another possible means of preventing the collapse of capitalism is through education, but education itself is of the nature of corporate finance and modern business enterprise. Educators insist upon the practical or useful, and the primary test of usefulness is ability to secure an income. The scholastic accountancy leads to conviction rather than to inquiry, and is therefore a conservative factor. In their competition for students and endowments the schools are much the same as competing corporations. Courtesy and expediency incline them "to cultivate such appearance and opinions as may be expected to find favour with men of wealth." These are businessmen who are "prevailingly of a conservative temper in all cultural matters, and more especially as touches those institutions that bear on business affairs."

The press is part of the educational system, and it too is in the service of modern business. Periodical literature is "scrupulously devout in tone . . . given to laud and dilate upon the traffic of the upper leisure class and to carry on the discussion in the terms and tone imputed to that class." The output issued under the guidance of the advertising office, with its interest in directing the attention of readers "along such lines of investment and expenditure" as may benefit its great advertisers, is "excellent in workmanship" but "deficient in intelligence and substantial originality." Pointlessness and edifying optimism are "the substantial characteristics, which persist through all ephemeral mutations of style, manner, and subject matter." In the interest of its circulation value the press can only laud its advertisers and cannot expose their deceptions.

"National politics" might be presumed to serve as a corrective, but "the quest of profits leads to a predatory national policy." Large fortunes necessitate warlike policies to provide investments, and thus a militant coercive administration develops. The discipline of life given by this system of prowess, status, and despotism might be expected to prove the most salutary check to the machine discipline, but eventually it turns business enterprise into the true predatory culture of feudal status. When European nations were engaged in mutual destruction and turning into the dark ages of depression, as a result of the unfolding pecuniary logic as exemplified in such men as the Fuggers, England was cut off from the most serious effects of this development by its insular position, and thereby took the lead in material development. Now, with the entire world intimately tied up in the network of modern capitalism and industry, it is scarcely likely that such a place for a new start of material advance could be found. Thus mankind is faced either with another regime of status and the dark ages, or with the full development of the industrial republic and machine technology. "Which of the two antagonistic factors may prove the stronger in the long run is something of a blind guess; but the calculable future seems to belong to the one or the other." In either case business enterprise is a transient matter, no more than a biological sport.

The confusion over Veblen's views still prevailed and is again indicated by the reviews. A Dartmouth instructor, Frank Haigh Dixon, writing for *The Yale Review*, said that Veblen's fundamental thesis of industrial and pecuniary employments was presented in a more intelligible form in this book than in *The Theory of the Leisure Class* or in the paper before the American Economic Association, because here "it has been divested of a goodly part of the obscure and impossible terminology in which it has heretofore been clothed." But he thought the distinction was not fundamental and that Veblen had carried it so far that there was a question whether he was sincere. Tufts, however, found the book extremely useful. "I was groping from the outside for some angle at which I could view the ethics of business. Books on economic theory did not help much. Hadley's *Economics* took up ethical questions, but it seemed to find capitalism perfect in theory, even if defective in the case of some of its ramifications. Veblen's treatment, which was an effort to see business as actually conducted, especially in its newer phases, seemed to me to throw light that was much needed on the actual practices and theories of business in this century. It showed the inadequacy of the theories of the eighteenth century for the ethical as well as the economic problems of the twentieth."

The review in *The Journal of Political Economy* was written by a former colleague, Agnes Wergeland, but was far from the character of the *Journal's* review of Veblen's first book. "People will perhaps be repelled" by his "lack of sympathy with and propaganda for anything but the naked and often unlovely truth." This book is vastly less burdened than the other with "unnecessarily studied and anachronistic" terms, but many readers "will lament their absence as withdrawing a peculiar technical flavour from the text. In many respects this volume must be counted a work of larger scope than was its predecessor, but it is fair to say its subject is neither so entertaining, nor its persiflage so spirited and witty."

In *The Political Science Quarterly* Thomas Nixon Carver of Harvard declared that the businessman is not a discretionary agent. "In business enterprise, more than in almost any other field . . . success depends upon adaptation." A man becomes a successful merchant prince because he first took the precaution to find out what people wanted and then supplied it. Such a man does not "dominate the economic world to any degree, and yet all successful business enterprise is fundamentally" of this nature.

Winthrop Daniels, professor of economics at Princeton, said in *The Atlantic Monthly* that its "cosmic irony" gave the book a readable quality, but at the cost of a most unenviable frame of mind. "Professor Veblen has a preternaturally vivid insight into the pathological side of business and society; and he follows remorselessly the poisoned tract which his critical scalpel has discovered." The book prompts "a reflective testing of one's social beliefs and ideals," but its author, apparently mocking humanity in its misery, suggests no cures, and he is blind to the "normal and healthful aspects of industry." As a consequence it is impossible to give the book complete approval, "from either the scientific or the ethical standpoint."

The reviewer for *The Nation* declared: "Such a theory as is here set forth may impress the readers of sensational magazines; but it is a travesty of economics, and an unjust aspersion on our business morality. It may affect the imagination of the half-educated by its ponderous platitudes, its obscure and complicated presentation of simple ideas, even by the barbarisms of the author's style. It may apply to certain notorious phases of modern financial activity; it fails in its assumption that these phases are typical of modern business."

The most reactionary publication, *Gunton's Magazine*, said, however, that "the book is a careful discussion of the theory of business enterprise, and abounds in wholesome suggestions, and is well worth the attention of students of economics and sociology."

The same confusion prevailed among the socialists. A long review in *The International Socialist Review*, written by its editor, declared the book to be "the most searching analysis of capitalism ever published in the English language." The chapter on "The Use of Loan Credit" was mentioned especially, even though it had already been reviewed as a monograph. This chapter is an "ingenious analysis" of how the "modern promoter has been able to 'syncopate an industrial crisis' including all the features from the inflation of credit to the final shearing of the lamb, and doing it all in a single business transaction." Veblen's theory of crises as the outcome of credit operations is, however, "the weakest portion of the entire book." The reviewer took exception to one of Veblen's footnotes, which seemed to imply that the scientific socialism of Marx and Engels, based on the right to the full product of labour, was not modern socialism, which looks to the disappearance of property rights. "We are not exactly sure whether this is intended to be another joke for the purpose of throwing his orthodox readers off the track or not," but the statement is false, for Marx and Engels held to the view of modern socialism. Veblen's final chapter, "The Natural Decay of Business Enterprise," "would in itself make a most excellent socialist propaganda leaflet for use among those who have learned to think in the economic jargon that is taught in the average capitalist university." Veblen's conclusion is all that a socialist could hope for. The socialist "has full faith that the proletariat will see to it that no military regime perpetuates business enterprise or supplants the ruling capitalism." But it is questionable whether Veblen's "sarcastic, cynical style is really one capable of producing results. To a large degree the book is unintelligible to one who has not swallowed the scholastic jargon of conventional economics. We cannot understand, however, how any follower of Laughlin, Sumner, or the standard capitalist economists can read this book and not become, if not a socialist, at least thoroughly convinced of the uselessness of his professionally acquired knowledge."

Another outstanding socialist, William English Walling, who was a former student of Veblen, took a somewhat different attitude towards the book. He made Veblen the centre of his discussion in an article called "An American Socialism," in a subsequent issue of *The International Socialist Review*. Walling declared that Karl Marx is outgrown in Europe and has become a "historical reminiscence" in this country. Veblen, "a professor in the most American of all cities" and "on the payroll of the University founded by John D. Rockefeller," is not a propagandist, but treats his material in a scientific manner. He furnishes the philosophical backbone for the American socialist movement. In contrast to Marx, Veblen holds that the enemy of society is not the capitalist, but the businessman. The capitalistic system will not, according to Veblen, fall of its own weight, since it can easily dispose of its surplus. Working people are socialists not because their interests are different from those of their employers, but because they possess different standards and ideals. To Marx the class struggle is a conflict of interests; to Veblen it is a conflict of minds, of mental characters, of habits of thought. All the

traditional ideals of property, religion, politics, morality, are undermined in the workman's mind by the impinging force of the machine.
Socialism is dependent primarily on economic evolution, not on propaganda. "This American Socialism is not based on any outworn Hegelian
logic, nor on any absolute and therefore unscientific social philosophy."
The modern scientific point of view is characteristic of the American
people, particularily the American manufacturers, for they take a relative
view of life. When the nation turns its attention to politics "with the same
spirit, the same vigour and the same absolute determination to achieve
results with which it has devoted itself to industry and business," the
ruling ideas and working hypothesis will be relative and practical, not
absolute.

In the same journal, however, Robert Rives La Monte, in an article
on "Veblen the Revolutionist," objected to "Comrade Walling's" interpretation of Veblen and his contrast of Veblen and Marx. He said that
Walling's article "is by a writer whose ignorance of Marx is eclipsed only
by his ignorance of Veblen." The antithesis drawn between Marx and
Veblen will unfortunately cause "many revolutionary Marxians to whet
their tomahawks for Veblen," although he is the greatest exponent of
"the psychological effects of economic causes," and "*The Theory of the
Leisure Class* is . . . the most serious contribution to socialist thought
since *The Communist Manifesto*." In "this epoch-marking volume,"
Veblen, "the revolutionary iconoclast," throws around the conventions
and ethics handed down from the past "with all the joyous unconcern of
a bovine male in an emporium for the sale of ceramic products. And how
can a socialist fail to gurgle with glee when he realises that this bomb was
constructed by a Rockefeller employee in the Standard Oil laboratories
at the University of Chicago." But Veblen's "best work is nothing more
than Marxian exegesis."

Perhaps the most striking effect of Veblen's book was that readers began writing to him for advice in making money by the methods of business enterprise portrayed.

VEBLEN AT THE AGE OF FORTY-SEVEN

CHAPTER XV

VEBLEN'S scheme of life was still very simple. "We lived," said his wife, "on $400, $500, $600 a year until 1903 when his salary jumped to $1000." Veblen's courses were given on four days of the week, and during this time he roomed in a flat near the campus. He rose at about nine, had his breakfast at a near-by lunchroom, and went directly to his class at ten. In the afternoon he was sometimes seen around the department library, apparently not very busy, and he did not start his work until after eight in the evening. Maynard said: "I was told he sat at his serious work until 2:00 a.m. His room had only the barest furnishings possible. The only things in the room were a table, lamp, a few plain chairs, a set of plain boxes placed one on top of another, containing books crowded into the shelf-like open side."

The notes taken by students in Veblen's courses during the period between *The Theory of the Leisure Class* and *The Theory of Business Enterprise* are somewhat revealing, even when due notice is taken of the fact that notes represent only what students think they heard, and are selective at best. Copious reading lists and references are given, particularly the more recent studies. His regular courses on "Theory," "Socialism," and "Economic Factors in Civilisation" show striking similarities. Veblen's fundamental antithesis between investment for profit and the machine process, or between the modern pecuniary culture and the industrial republic, seems to have become so deeply ingrained in his thinking that whatever he discussed was presented in such a way as to bring out this distinction. The reader gets the impression of a stage director skilfully manipulating his strange assortment of marionettes in such fashion that they all seem to present the same story.

This is best seen in the notes on his most famous course, "The Economic Factors in Civilisation." More than one student has said that Veblen's books were simply footnotes in this course. Here he discussed the so-called stages of economic development, the American Indian tribes, the great oriental empires and American despotisms, the development of western Europe, currency, religion, art, literature, race theory, the "mark" theory, the family, political organisation, industrial technique, Viking raids, psychology, philosophy, business organisation.

It was necessary, he said, to go beyond western civilisation for "genetic" illustrations because it is of too great complexity for this purpose. Primitive civilisations must be examined, and the American is most convenient, "since material in reference to it is more available and familiar to us." Thus the "hunting" stage of culture was a warlike form of organisation, in which war took the form of raiding and the whole culture rested on portable goods and property. The women "work and weep." Veblen's discussion of the potlatch recalls "The Army of the Commonweal." "Wealth has certain uses to which the community expects the wealth to be devoted. It is a limitation on the idea of property with which one can do as he wills. We have the same current saying that the community is interested in the way a man spends his money."

The dolicho-blonds have developed western civilisation. That "might makes right," in reference to property, was the principle of the ancient dolicho-blond or Aryan. A man might challenge another's ownership of a chattel and, if he obtained it by force, the community would enforce his possession. If the owner refused to do battle for his property, the community justified its seizure by the challenger. The latter "staked" his property against that of the challenged. Indeed the challenger might not himself have much property.

The Viking culture had the characteristics of the piratical activities of Captain Kidd. "These Vikings farmed during the winter and the object of their adventures was to acquire a competence in order to live as 'country gentlemen' on the farm." Swords of the bronze and iron age are evidence of "conspicuous consumption" and thus of a system of status. No fetters and handcuffs are found to give proof of a system of slavery. The Icelandic republic was ostensibly a democracy, but was actually ruled by powerful and wealthy "bosses," each of whom had his partisans. Unless a man stood in with a "boss," he had no chance. Occasionally a new "boss" rose from the common herd, by virtue of his prowess, that is, by force, fraud, arson, murder. The development seems to have been from a loose popular assembly to a system of "bosses," then to a conflict between the "bosses," and finally one "boss" dominated through destruction of the rest, and the popular assembly died out. Much the same was true of Scandinavian culture. Originally the Scandinavians were peaceable on their own land, but their raiding in foreign lands finally resulted in a system of status at home. The mark theory, that western civilisation arose from free village communities of the Aryan, is not valid. Free village communities are not found in the Aryan culture, for it was based on private property. These free communities may have existed outside of the Aryan culture, for example among the peaceable Pueblo Indians.

The chivalrous literature of the Middle Ages is characteristic of a life of status. "You hear of nothing at all except of people who have nothing at all to do and who are continually hunting new ways to do it. You hear of impossibly beautiful women who do not die, or of impossibly heroic men." The piety, honour, and chivalry are of a like impossible kind. The animals mentioned are trained dogs or horses, not domestic animals in service. It is a history of a parasitic class entirely. But the folklore of the industrious classes is the literature of the affairs of working life.

In medieval thinking interest was unjust, since money was impersonal and one cannot gain anything except through persons. The feudal system was one of qualified servitude. Its economic relations were purely personal, between inferior and superior. Christianity, with its hierarchical scheme of fealty and status, showed the same characteristics adapted to religion. In the change to the modern age of handicraft, slavery was formally abolished, but it still existed, for the change from legally coerced labour to hired labour was not, strictly speaking, a change from serfdom to freedom. The fact of labour remained, and it was still labour for the good of others. Man was no longer bound personally, but by pecuniary conditions.

The development of a relatively peaceful state with the free workmen at the centre, such as occurred during the Renaissance, is frequently found in history, but this situation never lasts long. Commercial interests finally conflict, a condition of war results in one way or another, and status is reinstalled.

The system of business organisation is based on a system of profit and is best seen in the growth of loan credit. Business without a system of credit is not worth discussing. The captains of industry come forward with the advent of credit in northern Europe. By buying and selling more than they require for their support they start to make money and rapidly engross the traffic of the towns. By the seventeenth century the business apparatus was as highly developed in western Europe as it was in England and America two or three hundred years later. The Fuggers and other magnates were greater in their time than the financial magnates of today. But their business organisation was destroyed. They went into politics and backed rival princes and emperors, who used their funds in activities which destroyed industry. The result in France was the "ancien régime." When the new industrial era began, after the French Revolution, it started from England.

In the course on socialism Veblen usually began by warning his students that modern socialism means a scheme of society under a democratic organisation, and is not to be confused with state, church, or monarchical socialism. Modern socialists propose to circumscribe the industrial system with restrictions as to freedom of contract. Everyone would receive equal pay, and the right to the means of a living would be a civil right, just as voting is, not a proprietary right. The course was divided into two parts, the first dealing with the history and the second with the tenets of socialism. But Veblen's discussion of origins seems to be at the same time a discussion of modern socialism, and his analysis of its outstanding figures is of such a character as to suggest that their historical reality was of less importance than their function as mouthpieces for Veblen's fundamental distinction between modern business and the institutional requirements of modern economic life.

Marx, said Veblen, was an "unjudaised Jew." Thus he was a freer man, spiritually and intellectually, than a Christian, and had fewer prejudices; also he was thoroughly trained and possessed of the highest intellectual power. He was, in short, one of the most dangerous men in Europe. *The Communist Manifesto* gives the first full expression of the modern socialist attitude. It combines opposition to constituted authority and opposition to the chief institution of the age, that is, property. Adam Smith and his successors wanted freedom "in all respects but one"—property. "They do not say so but looking at their theory I can say it for them." *Das Kapital,* however, is a work that need not be done over again.

Veblen said that the key to Lassalle's work is contained in a query raised in his preface to *Bastiat-Schultze:* "Whether now when property in the direct utilitisation of another man no longer exists, such property in his indirect exploitation should continue." Lassalle's contribution to economic doctrine is his theory of conjuncture or fortuitous gain. Thus an individual's fortune depends not upon himself but on social convention. Wages are not determined by productivity, and a man may acquire wealth while asleep under the convention of ownership. But ownership has no basis except a conventional one, and no claim in equity could be maintained for it. Vested interests count for little, since the owners did not create them. National organisation is also conventional and may be changed or abolished. Lassalle's *System of Acquired Rights* declares that might has been made a right, but that this system of acquired rights must change.

Rodbertus appears in one set of notes as something of a state socialist, in another as a Marxian. In the latter set Veblen imputes to Rodbertus the contention that capital is privately owned wealth utilised for profit. Private property in land and capital means that the wages of the labouring classes constitute an ever-decreasing proportion of the national product, which is itself increasing because of the increasing productivity of social labour. Veblen considered Rodbertus very able in his explanation of crises as resulting from Labour's decreasing share.

Labour unions are not socialistic, but "with every strike the trade unions get nearer and nearer to the idea of municipalisation; they come to have less respect for the employer as a property owner." In America, however, the socialist attitude towards Morgan, Rockefeller, and trusts is almost friendly.

In the second part of the course Marx is the centre of discussion. The most enduring part of Marxism is the doctrine of the class struggle as the method by which an adjustment is effected between economic and other elements in human development. The class struggle does not go back to the beginning of history, as socialists think, and thus the present class struggle concerning property may disappear in the future. But an end to the struggle over ownership would not mean an end to cultural development, for other interests would appear.

"The production of merchantable goods for a price or profit" is Marx's conception of the capitalist system. By capital he means goods or wealth invested with an aim to profits, not merely productive goods, as his critics assume. Because of his "non-recognition of·the big businessman" Marx is not a Darwinian. "The central figure in the industry of the day is the capitalist and we should have a better idea of his function and place, if we explain it in terms in which he expressed himself, that is in terms of profit and loss, instead of in philosophic terms—of the life process—labour." This would require an analysis in terms of cause and effect. Classical economists do not make such an analysis because they proceed on the false theory that men buy and sell in order to consume. The businessman, in so far as he is a businessman, does not aim to get consumable wealth but only to accumulate wealth, as evidenced by the modern corporation.

Marx's doctrine of labour value is the logical outcome of a consistent adherence to the position of conventional economics that labour is the basis of value. Profits—surplus value—can be nothing but exploitation. Veblen declared that the substitution by modern Marxians of surplus product for surplus value makes Marxism into Darwinism. American socialism is based on the two doctrines of surplus value and the natural right of labour to its whole product, especially the latter. The natural-rights doctrine is English liberalism, and when carried to its conclusion by Spencer and Sumner means anarchism. Surplus value is Marxism, and when carried to its conclusion means socialism.

The customary arguments against socialism, such as those of Ely and Schaeffle, are against a paternalistic socialism, not modern socialism. Whether agriculture can be brought under a socialist régime is only a question of standardisation, and this should be possible. In the ancient village communities the broken, non-uniform lands were divided according to certain standards, even though these standards were given from above, by the overlords or stewards.

In discussing whether or not socialism is impending, it should not be asked: "Can human nature be changed to put up with the new order of things?" but: "Will human nature so change as to look with favour upon the proposed system?" The weakness of Marx was that he emphasised inner necessity, self-interest, as factors in the change to socialism, rather than the influence of environment. The defect is being remedied by the modern socialists bringing in the Darwinian principle that the selective principle of survival is adaptation to a changing environment which human activity has itself created, and that unless such adaptation takes place the organism must perish.

The important fact in the environment is the machine process, or "the state of industrial arts"—which means not only industrial skill but the total of machine technology. The business element in the environment has a conservative, anti-socialistic effect, but this is a less important factor in the environment than the machine process. The latter is socialistic, iconoclastic. "We must adapt ourselves to the rule of the machine if we would use it and we have to use it not as we would always wish but as it is determined for us. Society has adapted itself to the machine process. Either you learn to think in its terms or not at all unless you want to go back to the farm and a pretty small farm at that." The machine process is like a character from Ibsen—"an intangible, invisible person against whom it is impossible to fight." Although its discipline falls on everyone, it falls with most effect on skilled artisans who spend their life in closest relation to it. They are not fitted for thinking in terms of the received institution of property, but they understand discussions in terms of cause and effect. Such institutions as property cannot, however, be explained primarily in terms of cause and effect, but only in pecuniary terms, and artisans "ask us to talk about more sensible things." Men engaged in the material sciences are of the same character. The idealist socialism of America does not, however, think in terms of cause and effect, but only in terms of a more just distribution.

The propaganda of socialism is itself a disciplinary effect of the environment, but this does not mean that socialism is a machine product. It existed before the machine, but it has become more dominant with the rise of the machine process. Socialism exists where the machine process does not, as for example in Denmark and France.

Veblen said that his discussion was not concerned with the tenability of socialism; "but the tendency of cultural development," he added, "is toward socialism." The community is coming to look more kindly upon it. Socialism is not necessarily the best thing for the community, but it cannot be stamped out by deporting men like John Turner. "The blood of the martyrs is the seed of the church," and repressive measures must fail unless they reach the basic conditions. This might be done by substituting some other line of habituation, by shifting attention, for example, from terms of cause and effect to terms of imperialism, thus bringing about an industrial feudalism and a loss of effectiveness in industrial organisation. By investing money in such a venture "we would dispose of surplus goods or what might otherwise be available for mechanical appliances. More men would be trained into the régime of fire and sword and trained out of industrial effectiveness." "All this may seem fanciful and is merely speculative, especially at first sight, but there is something in history to bear us out. An example is the era of state making." It ended, to be sure, "in squalor, privation, starvation, and poverty," but by such developments away from the basic requirements of industrial life "the kings and lords would come into their own again."

Veblen's courses on "The Scope and Method of Political Economy" and "The History of Political Economy" had the characteristics of the *Quarterly* essays, but here he had more scope and in his interpretation of the supposedly historical development he proceeded from the time of the Greeks to the period of modern business enterprise. The classical state, he said, was an aristocratic republic, and the Greeks were interested primarily in the proper comportment for a cultured gentleman of leisure. The Greeks were not all gentlemen of leisure, but that was their ideal and it conditioned all their thinking. They did not develop a scientific economics because, living as masters and slaves, they did not develop habits conducive to the impersonal point of view. The Hebrews, however, treated economic matters from the standpoint of practical expediency.

Veblen's discussions of individual economists ran in the terms of his fundamental distinction. Oresme's account of the origin of money as a means of facilitating exchange is entirely erroneous, but Bodin's theory that the increase of commerce raised prices and brought about the growth of banking institutions is remarkably modern. Josiah Child, who favoured the extension of banks and credit instruments, represents the point of view of the modern businessman. The philosophy of mercantilism belongs to the stage of money economy, and the mercantile system is comparable to the modern trust. Adam Smith, with his system of the natural liberty, did not see the complications which arise from the movement towards combinations. The classical school, Ricardo for example, is on the one hand a theory of distribution, on the other, a theory of taxation. It is enveloped in the influence of business methods and machinery and it is for this reason that its members are called "capitalistic economists." Adam Smith holds that capital is used to gain profits, and it does not matter whether it is useful or not so long as it serves this purpose. Mill's work is epoch marking, not epoch making. For him production means production for a market, and thus the distinction between productive and non-productive labour is not the utility of the product but its vendibility. All capital is devoted to production, and therefore productive, but this is scarcely borne out by the value placed on intangible assets. General overproduction is a fallacy according to classical economists, but businessmen insist that there is such a phenomenon. It is possible, Veblen declared, when judged in terms of price, for there is an oversupply when more is produced than will be taken at remunerative prices.

Cairnes is concerned not with industrial activities but with pecuniary data, facts of wealth, such as rates of wages, prices, distribution or exchange. In Ely's political economy, "what the facts are and what they ought to be are never separated." Alfred Marshall attempts to reconcile all schools, including socialism, and the result is an excess of material, a shifting point of view, and therefore eclecticism in the worst sense of the term. The so-called inductive-deductive method of prevailing economics is a "bank account of knowledge. You deduce (draw out) just as much as you might gather in (induce or induct)." J.B. Clark's theory of distribution is an example of the overworking of marginal utility. Accepting the principle that the utility of the last increment of goods measures the utility of the whole, he argues similarly as regards distribution between wages and capital. Thus aggregate wages are computed by multiplying the wage of the marginal labourer by the number of labourers. In this way the pay of the marginal labourer fixes the pay of the rest, and every labourer obtains the full product of his own labour. But it would follow that, as labourers are added, the aggregate productivity of the labourers would decline, and when additions are made to capital the total productivity may decline. This conclusion can hardly be accepted.

The discussion closes on Marx, who according to Veblen attempts to make the views of Ricardo and Smith consistent with their labour theory of value. His theory of value is in terms of human life or human labour, since the active factor in all life is the human agent. Thus the value of the product of labour is the amount of human labour or life that has entered its making. Marx is coming to be more widely appreciated as he becomes better understood.

Of Veblen's own opinions on prevailing questions no one was certain. Students suspected that he was an agnostic, if not an atheist, but they were not sure. According to Maynard he would sometimes speak of a writer as being "pious," but with a definite note of sympathy or approval. A student in the course in trusts would ask what could be done about the situation he described. Veblen's eyes would sparkle, the lines of his face would be drawn into a quizzical smile, and he would answer, in effect: "Mr. —— is not satisfied with the philosopher's statement, 'I want to know.' Mr. —— wants to do something about it." The class would laugh and Veblen would say no more, but often he would tell his students: "We are interested in what is, not what ought to be." Sometimes in his course on socialism his remarks would start excited arguments between members of the class. Veblen would smile, contribute now and then a bit of dry humour, and after a while put an end to the dispute by a pungent remark. Maynard said that he seemed kindly disposed towards Karl Marx, but "did not give us much clue as to his judgment of Marx's arguments." Davenport once became so exasperated with Veblen's apparent evasiveness on socialism, that, while together after class, he told him: "You are outside of class now, and you can say what you think of socialism." But Veblen never gave him a direct answer.

Cummings, who was then a colleague, has said: "I never felt that I knew just what Veblen was thinking about in our casual friendly intercourse. He seemed extremely elusive, rather detached, and disposed to walk by himself." The meeting with President Harper, which had almost led to his leaving the university he described as a matter of amusement. "The experience was told with perfect calmness, punctuated with an occasional titter, and was entirely devoid of any show of feeling." Fite said that no one had ever seen Veblen without his mask of polite irony, although he knew it had been pierced once or twice. "He was capable of sitting for an hour or two, or as many as you please, with another person without saying a word, listening politely to what the other said, but letting the conversation absolutely subside if the other stopped talking." But when Veblen had a proper foil, such as Robert Hoxie, or when he felt in the mood, he could talk for hours on almost any topic. Small complained that Veblen seemed to treat him not as an intellectual equal but as merely a representative of the administration. Small encouraged students to study under Veblen, but whenever he tried to find out Veblen's point of view he was treated as if he were looking for evidence of heresy. When Small criticised Spencer, Veblen declared that Spencer's critics "stand on his shoulders and beat him about the ears." Liberal leaders, such as Darrow and Lloyd, admired Veblen, but when he talked with them they had the impression that he considered them very foolish to occupy themselves with such matters as clean politics, municipal ownership, and other such reforms. Veblen's nephew, Oswald Veblen, who was doing graduate work in mathematics at Chicago and whom Veblen considered the only intellectually capable member of the Veblen family, said that it was two years before their relations became anything near personal. But there was a touch of sentiment in Veblen's nature. On one of his European visits, for example, he had attended a banquet at which the King of Sweden and Norway was present, and he sent the menu card to his mother, who felt deeply moved that her son had met her king.

Veblen's methods of teaching were often eccentric. Once when he was tired of lecturing and wanted the class to engage in discussion, he asked a woman student, who was a church member, what was the value of her church in kegs of beer. But she did not appreciate this method of explaining the theory of value, and became angry. Veblen felt that his students should not take many notes. One meticulous old man, trying to take down Veblen's exact words, asked him to repeat what he had said, but Veblen answered: "I don't think it is worth repeating." Students were free to ask questions, but they had to be careful. Once in a discussion of "conjectural history" a troublesome member of the seminar interrupted Veblen and asked him to explain just what relation existed between conjectural history and real history. Veblen replied: "So far as I am able to see, the relation is about the same as that existing between a real horse and a sawhorse." The student asked no more questions.

Veblen seriously explained to those who asked that his drawl had been inherited from his Scandinavian ancestors among the sharp valleys and on the hillsides of Norway. One student asked him how he could remember so much and with such accuracy, and Veblen replied that he had clearly in mind a general outline of human knowledge and that each new fact automatically took its place in his scheme of things and came into his complete possession. When asked what he thought of an eminent sociologist who contributed extensively to *The Journal of Political Economy*, he replied that "the average number of words on a page is 400 and Professor ——'s articles average 375." Some of his friends were baffled by his scrupulous observance of the formal courtesies and classical language which he apparently ridiculed in *The Theory of the Leisure Class*.

Since Veblen's methods of teaching were scarcely conventional it is not surprising that there were mixed opinions on its value. Undergraduates were discouraged by his heavy assignments in foreign languages, and most of his classes he conducted as graduate seminars, even though they might be listed in the catalogue as undergraduate courses. Aspirants to Phi Beta Kappa were under a disadvantage in his classes, for he refused to give a grade higher than "C." His students considered him very eccentric. One has described him as "an exceedingly queer fish. He never gave us an examination and at the end of the course he would say that with our permission he would register 'C' grade for each of us to conform to the necessary ritual of university life. . . . Very commonly with his cheek in his hand, or in some such position, he talked in a low, placid monotone, in itself a most uninteresting delivery and manner of conducting the class." All his movements, like his speech, were slow and indolent, but now and then a flash of wit lightened up the dreary scene. "I remember once when he had laid it out to us that all moral principles are but shifting social canons, with none commanding universal assent, historically and geographically, I urged in dissent, that surely such a maxim as 'every man is entitled to what he produces' would command such uniform assent.—'Well, possibly,' replied Veblen. 'But if one will change it to run: "Every woman is entitled to what she produces," you will find several parts of Europe that will greet your statement with instant denial.' " He was more reserved than most of the professors, and he never laughed or showed emotion. He was particularly reticent about anything not closely connected with the subjects of study. "We never did really know him or much about him personally. We knew he had a wife and where they lived but that was all."

Some of the graduate students found his apparently philosophical courses too abstract and difficult to follow, and shifted over to other men. There was a belief that Veblen was too lazy to clarify his ideas and that his attitude was "try and find out what I mean if you can." He appeared colourless and unimpressive, with clothing that just escaped shabbiness, a carriage that barely missed being slouchy, and a voice that spoke in a low monotone, without accent on any phrase. He never seemed to raise his eyes from the seminar table, and one at its far end had to strain to catch every word. Looking thin and pale, he seemed to have insufficient strength for the course. He appeared to pay little direct attention to the class, and at times seemed almost asleep. The direction of his discourse was seldom clear; his digressions were numerous, and he liked to ask questions which would give him a chance for an excursion afield. He seemed to care little for consistency. The habit of occupying time by student reports was not altogether satisfactory.

There were some, however, for whom he was stimulating and impressive. One student, the Reverend Howard Woolston, has described Veblen as he knew him in the course on "Economic Factors": "Veblen would come to class looking gaunt and haggard from long nights of study and writing. He dropped a bulky volume of Meitzen's *Siedelung und Agrarwesen* on the desk, and turned the pages with nervous yellow fingers. In a low creaking tone, he began a recital of village economy among the early Germans. Presently he came upon some unjust legal fiction imposed by rising nobles and sanctioned by the clergy. A sardonic smile twisted his lips; blue devils leaped in his eyes. With mordant sarcasm, he dissected the tortuous assumption that the wish of the aristocrats is the will of God. He showed similar implications in modern institutions. He chuckled quietly. Then returning to history, he continued the exposition.

"At times his ironic criticism of church and state disturbed me. One day I met him on the campus. 'Professor Veblen,' I began. 'Do you ever take anything seriously?' He regarded me quizzically and replied: 'Yes, but don't tell anybody.' Perhaps that illustrates his method of prodding docile students into seeking the cause of their restlessness beneath the smooth surface of specious theories.

"Veblen was an impressive teacher and an irritating leader. He encouraged the novice to jump into a bramble bush and scratch out both his eyes. When the smarting youngster came back with tales of grief, the shrewd mentor slyly indicated ways to toughen a tender mind. He often implied if he did not say: 'Read Marx. Uncover the roots of the problem.'

"Veblen's explanations were seldom simple. His major thesis often seemed to be a result of long reflection. His supporting data frequently offered a remarkable evidence of wide erudition. But his argument was not straightforward proof. He devised twists and turns in the discussion, which threw the unwary off their stride, and brought up the rash doctrinaire with a surprising jolt. If a type of thinking can be symbolised by another form of activity, Veblen's course might be compared with the running of a fox—swift get-away, clever doubling, use of heavy cover, sharp holding-in."

As another student put it: "It was not until the conclusion of his lectures that the full import of his argument was realised."

In the courses on "theory," Professor Woods of Dartmouth recalls that Veblen would come into the room with a half-dozen books under his arms "and sit down bashfully behind his desk, and commence mumbling through his whiskers the characteristic economic blasphemies for which he was famous. His inimitable wit played over the field and made what might have been a rather dreary exercise something to chuckle over. Judged by conventional standards he was the world's worst teacher. He seldom knew at the beginning of the hour what he would say or where he would arrive at its end and that pile of books was simply a provision actuarial in its nature, against the too rapid passing of time. I felt that these mumbling lectures were a good deal of a bore to him except for the opportunity they afforded him for flashes of wit and irony, and that he took little interest in the question of whether his students were reading lessons and doing work in the course or not. As a flower garden he was the Sahara desert with occasional gorgeous posies, sticking out of the sand at irregular intervals. When you came on one it was a dandy."

Stephen Leacock says that the students sat around the table and "Veblen lectured into his lap without question or answer or personal contact.

His voice ran from a drawl to a mumble. He had no grace of utterance, but what he said was marvellously good, and spoken without any challenge or false emphasis."

Instead of arguing directly in favour of a view that he might present, Veblen had an unusual faculty of leading the questioner around to a point where he could view the matter himself from a wide perspective. The excursion and the resulting orientation were an intensely interesting and informing experience. This kind of procedure brought him enthusiastic followers. No other scholar, said Sophronisba P. Breckinridge, "unless probably Mr. Dewey, so developed the situation of a master with disciples as was the case with Mr. Veblen."

Maynard's first impression was that Veblen, with his low monotone and his habit of always looking at his desk, was an example of the young overspecialised instructor of limited training. But Harry A. Millis, then a fellow, told him that in a week or two he would "get into the meaning of the work and find it good." The result was as predicted. Veblen's discussions, said Maynard, were "intended to supplement what we could easily get for ourselves by supplying an underground of psychological, anthropological (occasionally) and social philosophical reasons for the people (the economic writers, of course, but also their public) thinking as they did, in their time. Some readings were suggested but not specific assignments except for students' reports." There was no schematised or encyclopædic summaries. "His diction was perfect, of course, and his vocabulary unusually full of the common words and current slang (which he used sparingly) as well as of the erudite and archaic expressions." A very wide range of facts was brought into the discussion. Curious applications were made of them, and often humorous turns given to the talk by apt phrases, but the humour was never brought in for its own sake, nor were the unusual interpretations for meretricious display. He made a thing seem absurd by brief or ingenious characterisation, as for example in his phrase, "rationalised history," but the absurdity was in the thing itself. There were no bitter strictures. "His standpoint," said Maynard, "was the most detached, and his methods the most impersonal and dispassionate I have ever encountered."

A woman student recalls that his keen observations were stated with no more snap and decision than one would use in mentioning that it was a pleasant day. When she dropped out for a semester and on her return, a few days late for the second semester, asked if she might still enter his class, the answer was: "Certainly, we haven't done much and you can make it up easily. How did you like the work you were doing at the Crerar Library, Miss Stern?" "Yet I'd have sworn," she said, "he had never really looked at me in the previous course I took with him and didn't know me from any other red-headed woman on the campus," nevertheless, "he knew why I had taken a semester cut and all about it!"

In spite of the fact that Veblen seemed to most persons extremely shy and retiring, he had a friendly interest in the welfare of his students and often without their knowledge tried to help them professionally. He had great diplomatic skill when he chose to devote himself to the management of others. On one occasion he wished to help one of his students to receive an appointment which was in the power of an influential person not at that moment well disposed towards the candidate. For about a month Veblen carried on a systematic campaign to persuade this person that the candidate deserved the appointment, and after no less than ten or a dozen meetings, by a gradual process of removing prejudice and offering evidence, he effected his purpose. Another factor that cemented bonds of friendship between Veblen and a good number of the graduate students was their walks together in the "Midway" after classes, when they leisurely discussed every kind of subject while dodging bicycles. Cummings, who did not as yet have a high appreciation of Veblen, said: "One thing that impressed me about Veblen was his ability to develop a feeling of personal respect and admiration for him as a teacher and a thinker, one might almost say, personal loyalty, among his students." Cummings said that the younger instructors became Veblenites immediately "and the older ones as fast as they could adjust themselves." In fact, A.C. Miller, then at the University of California, had found Veblen's discussion of the preconceptions of economic science so useful that they constituted the basis of his paper before the St. Louis International Congress of Arts and Sciences.

But Veblen was more at ease travelling in Europe, visiting Icelandic colonies, enjoying the society of artists, scientists, brilliant and beautiful women, than he was in the company of economists. In these lay gatherings his native simplicity and his "drollery mixed with wisdom" were seen at their best. Women were much attracted to Veblen, and he knew how to hold their interest. But in these friendships he seems to have been the pursued rather than the pursuer. His interest in a woman was usually only a passing desire for amusement and diversion, but their interest in him was often so tenacious that for him the affairs became baffling and in some cases even appalling. Veblen seems to have needed the maternal qualities from women; they were his confidantes, men seldom, if ever.

Mrs. Veblen did not appreciate these affairs, and he made the situation more difficult by his habit of leaving in his pockets the letters he received from his women admirers. Every affair seemed to Mrs. Veblen the final crisis which could take away her only possession. Her uncle, the president of Carleton College, thought she took these matters entirely too seriously, but it is true that something of the old streak of cruelty remained in Veblen and he made no effort to allay her suspicions. He did not take her with him on any of his three trips to Europe, or even suggest that she might accompany him. He seemed to be unwilling to take her with him to any social function, although according to a mutual friend she had more social grace than he and won respect in any gathering. Veblen seems to have been annoyed when she attracted attention by her lively and interesting conversation and her remarkably vivid flashes of imagination. He would seldom have anything to do with her own parties, and when she was entertaining her socialist friends he preserved his usual noncommittal attitude towards socialism. She even asked students if they could determine whether or not he was a socialist. Her attempts to read his mind brought only frustration.

When she became particularly angry, she would leave him for a time. Veblen would then become worried and would tell his brothers about the matter, though in a quite impersonal fashion. They said only that he was a Veblen, with the Norwegian traditions of frugality and continual worry. He was very conventional as to his personal comfort and the necessity of regular meals, but she was not a good housekeeper. In fact her stepmother felt that this lack was responsible for most of their difficulties. It brought Veblen to such a state of mind that he began to generalise her ineptitude and to feel that even his own mother was too independent and did not fully appreciate his father or show him due consideration. Veblen seemed to feel that women were intended either to serve men's pleasure or to look after their comfort. But the difficulties of his marital life did not disturb his outward poise, and he told a woman friend that "one gets used to things."

Once when Mrs. Veblen was in Idaho, having left her husband in anger, she went to see an old schoolmate teaching in a near-by college. She was asked to read aloud and, although the friend had expected her to read something from her own work, she chose instead Veblen's *Theory of the Leisure Class*. When her *Goosenbury Pilgrims*, a book for children, had appeared in 1902, he thought it good and told her: "When *The Theory of the Leisure Class* is forgotten, yours will be a masterpiece." At their parting in Chicago he had said that she had made a wonderful companion, and now when she was gone he constantly asked her to return. In spite of their difficulties most of their friends considered them kindred natures, each best fitted for the other.

But the situation finally became so complicated that in 1904, when Veblen returned from a trip to Europe during which he had been seen in the company of one of his admirers, he found it advisable to look for another position. Friends suggested ways of meeting the charges, but Veblen was never able to take the road of prevarication. He was asked to sign a paper declaring that he would have no further relations with the woman involved, but he replied that he was not in the habit of promising not to do what he was not accustomed to doing. Mrs. Veblen said that she went to President·Harper for the purpose of interceding for Veblen. The president appeared uninterested. She went to Laughlin, who said that he wanted very much to keep Veblen and that the situation might be settled if she would return to her husband. But Veblen's days at Chicago were numbered.

In December 1904 he almost received an appointment as editor of a magazine called *Tomorrow,* which Parker H. Sercombe planned to launch. Sercombe who called himself an "expert in right living and correct thinking," was interested, among other things, in promoting a freer sex life and a "school for clear thinking to overthrow leisure-class ideals in education." [1] He sought the support of leading radicals, but without success. During the negotiations Charles Edward Russell met Veblen for the first time, and described him as helpless and good-natured. The magazine appeared for a time, but Veblen had no connexion with it.

Dr. Roland P. Falkner had resigned as chief of the Division of Documents in the Library of Congress in October 1904, and Veblen applied for the position, which included the oversight not only of documents but also of the library's collection of works on economics, politics, and sociology. He informed the librarian that he had carried on research work involving statistics, economic history, and the history of economic science and sociology, that he had the usual university acquaintance with the classics, and a knowledge of German, French, Spanish, Italian, Dutch, and the Scandinavian languages, including Icelandic, that as a teacher he had been chiefly concerned with the history and literature of economics and sociology, including socialism, and had also made investigations in the history of institutions. As references to his character he gave Laughlin, Miller, Clark, W.G.L. Taylor of the University of Nebraska, whose wife had been Veblen's student, and two colleagues of the same rank, William Hill, and Herbert J. Davenport. For personal knowledge of his capacity he referred to Laughlin, Jeremiah W. Jenks of Cornell, Taussig, Bernard Moses, John Franklin Jameson, his colleague, and Ward. Other references were W.C. Ford and J.C.M. Hanson, both of the Library of Congress, and President Benjamin Ide Wheeler of the University of California. He mentioned also Mitchell, Millis, and H. Parker Willis, because as former students "they might . . . be able to give information from a different point of view than the other gentlemen named." He told the librarian that he would send in his application as soon as "I have been able to communicate with my friends to whom I wish to refer, and whose consent I wish to obtain before writing them in as references."

Veblen wrote to Taussig that this move probably seemed unexpected, but he would like to leave the University of Chicago and knew of no available university position for which he considered himself especially fitted. Taussig wrote to the library that, although he did not agree with all of Veblen's views, and was not in a position to judge Veblen's qualifications as an administrator, his material was good and well put, and he had a reputation as a scholar and a thinker of originality.

Veblen wrote to Ward: "I am coming to you for help. As you foretold a few years ago, in a letter which Dr. Triggs was good enough to let me see, the time is coming for me to move out of this University, and you can be of invaluable service to me in helping me to find shelter elsewhere. The kindly interest which you have shown makes me bold to ask a favour. I am applying for the place of Chief of the Division of Documents in the Library of Congress. . . . I need not tell you how greatly I shall appreciate any help which you may be willing to afford me, and I beg you to let my need serve as excuse for my importunities." Ward wrote to the library: "Veblen has shown himself to be one of the ablest men in the country in various lines. I regard his *Theory of the Leisure Class* as one of the most brilliant productions of the country and now his *Theory of Business Enterprise* is out and sustains his high character as a writer and thinker. Other things equal, I believe that a nation can make itself great largely in the proportion that it calls into its service the élite of its people, and I for one would be glad to see the public service and the National Capital adorned by such men as Thorstein Veblen."

Ward wrote a friend: "I heard that Veblen was likely to have to leave the University. They will all have to go ultimately who are above the wretched chauvinism that is required and expected." [2] Also he nominated Veblen for membership in the Institut International de Sociologie, which was limited to one hundred members and two hundred associates and included most of the leaders in the social sciences, such as Marshall, Carl Menger, Böhm-Bawerk, Wagner, Achille Loria, Schmoller.

Clark expressed his conviction that Veblen would be highly successful in the position. "Keen analytical power is his marked characteristic; but he unites with this trait a phenomenal capacity and inclination for work and a natural leaning toward the kinds of work that require exactness of thought and statement and extensive and careful research."

Davenport said: "He is a man who makes strong friendships; while as a teacher he is not especially effective in point of technique and method, he obtains an extraordinary hold both in a personal and scholarly way, upon the more advanced and the better worth while of his students; for graduate work, he is, indeed, the best man of my acquaintance. I speak of this because his quiet manner is likely to be taken for unresponsiveness; the fact is that with any student or investigator who is either in earnest or worth while, Veblen is most helpful and most sympathetic. He is always approachable; his students acquire a great and enduring personal liking for him; and he commands also the confidence and respect, and commonly also the affection of his associates and co-workers. I regard it as a high privilege for any man to be associated with him. . . . I regard Veblen as without a rival in this country in those lines of economic thought lying nearest to Philosophy and Sociology [that is], in the History of Economic Thought, in the History of Economic Institutions, and in the Literature and History of Socialism.

"Finally . . . Veblen is a thoroughly genuine manly, honest, faith-keeping, loyal fellow. As for me, living in Chicago will lose the larger share of its attractiveness if Veblen leaves. But he would go to a line of work for which—piously speaking—he appears to have been providentially designed."

Mitchell wrote: "If ability as a student of social questions is of weight in determining the selection of a man for the post, I do not think there is another man in the country who has qualifications equal to those of Mr. Veblen. Among living economists he seems to me to present the finest combination of originality, sanity, and learning. I know of no one else who has such a sure philosophical grasp of economic problems or who treats them from so scientific a standpoint. Fifty years from now, I think that he will be recognised as the most important figure among economists of this generation.

"As for the more special qualifications of a librarian, Mr. Veblen has a very unusual knowledge of languages and of bibliography. He is distinctly an erudite man, but he is not in the least a pedant; for he possesses in rare degree the power of discriminating between what is important and what is trivial. Further, he has the tact that enables a man 'to get on with' everyone and the qualities that make friendships permanent."

Mitchell persuaded Ernest C. Moore, then president of the State of California Board of Charities and Corrections, to write in Veblen's behalf. Professors Miller, C.C. Plehn, and Hill also commended Veblen to the librarian. A former student who was not on the lists, William H. Allen, then general agent for the New York Association for Improving the Condition of the Poor, submitted a letter upon hearing that Veblen was applying.

The librarian seems to have had a conference with Veblen at Chicago, while attending a meeting of the American Historical Association, and Veblen was told that the incumbent would be expected to give his undivided attention to the work of the division. In submitting his formal application Veblen wrote: "I beg to say that the university administration here expresses a wish to know the success or failure of my application as soon as may be, in order to make any needed readjustment in the departmental staff. . . . Both Mr. Jameson and Mr. Laughlin, who were so kind as to speak for me to you, have spoken encouragingly of my chances for the appointment." Party politics apparently were not neglected. Veblen communicated with Willis, who knew Bascom Slemp, and Willis wrote Veblen: "I have . . . written fully to Mr. Slemp and I think that he will probably do as I have asked."

But he did not receive the appointment. The librarian has said that he considered Veblen a very brilliant man, but he needed more of a routine person. It is evidence of Veblen's inability to take care of his own interests that he submitted the names of Jenks, who thought Veblen was "all bluff," and Wheeler, who was the "conventional embodiment of what by all tradition the head of a great university should be." [3]

In the issue of *The Journal of Political Economy* for June 1905 Veblen once more discussed the prevailing views on credit, somewhat after the fashion of his monograph. He openly assailed Laughlin's "refined system of barter," and asserted that even on the basis of traditional assumptions this concept is not valid. Now, more clearly than before, he held that modern capital is of the nature of so-called abnormal credit, and that the effect of bank credit is only to increase prices; the lenders, financiers, extract their profits from the earning capacity of the community. What is of "immediate interest to modern theory is, of course, the current use of credit in business, and the relation of this business credit to the current price-level, rather than the occasional resort to credit under relatively primitive circumstances." If credit be understood to include such items as securities and call loans, since they involve transfers of property from creditor to debtor, and if it be viewed merely as an expedient of modern business, instead of being tacitly identified with consumable goods and the industrial processes, it would be seen that an increase or decrease of credit leads to an increase or decrease of prices, and vice versa. In other words, "credit and prices are intimately bound up together in a relation of mutual cause and effect."

The significance of credit is best seen in corporation finance. There the credit transaction known as the floating of corporation securities results in a greatly increased market value for the properties involved—an increase sometimes of two hundred percent—and the gain of the promoter comes out of the increase in price and the resulting fluctuation in the price of securities. The immediate effect of an advance of funds can be only an increase in prices. Corporations are organised because they make possible an increase in earning capacity for the benefit of the promoters, that is, an increase in the price of the property involved. The credit transaction is the essential basis for establishing such a monopoly. Like war loans, transactions in corporation finance bring about a decline in the price of fixed investments, thus leading to an increased extension of credit and to profits for the banking class, and in the liquidation which follows there is a redistribution of ownership in favour of the banking class.

When funds are borrowed for investment in permanent goods the immediate effect is a rise in the price of those goods, since credit is a pecuniary, not an industrial fact. But "in the doctrines of the classical economists, who at this point have not been superseded, the phenomena of credit are formulated in terms of their presumed social expediency." The actual motives of the businessmen who seek credit and of those "who carry on the traffic in credit—bankers, brokers, etc.—are disregarded," and in their stead "the presumed beneficial results of the traffic are imputed to these businessmen as the motives of their traffic." Thus "the question of the banker's gain and its relation to credit and prices is commonly not broached in the received doctrines of credit and prices."

In the typical extension of credit on the basis of securities the banker creates credit, thereby adding to the borrowed funds available for purchase and increasing the effective demand for goods, thus increasing prices. The banker secures profit by making advances on "collateral exceeding its own amount," as does the typical financier, who lends more than he has; the profits or discounts are added to his fund, which further enables him to lend more than the whole of it. Through this increase of the values upon which credit is based, the extension of credit takes on a cumulative character, and there is a cumulative increase in prices. "Bank credit acts to raise prices by as much as it increased the nominal purchasing power in the hands of the business community." The bankers' and large businessmen's control of the community has been masked by the cheapened production of goods as a result of technological improvements.

After Veblen's second dissection of the "refined system of barter" Laughlin began to think that Veblen's views were a little too extreme. Spurgeon Bell had taken seminars on credit with both Laughlin and Veblen and had found himself in agreement with Veblen concerning Laughlin's "abnormal credit" theory. When Veblen, along with Davenport, urged Bell's appointment as instructor, Laughlin raised the question as to whether Bell was not a little too rigid in his point of view.

Veblen's review of a translation of *The Code of Hammurabi* is a condensed version of *The Theory of Business Enterprise*. The document is interesting, he said, for "the evidence it affords as to property relations and business traffic among a people living near the beginning of recorded history." The community has a servile, despotic organisation and a blood-thirsty, monotheistic religion. Its guiding principles are those of status, privilege, and differential advantage, and there are harsh safeguards for the privileges of the upper classes. Mutilations, capital punishment, heavy fines, and reprisals are frequent. The most serious offences are those against the servants of the "king" and against the priests and their temples. The prices of everything, including servants, are fixed by the "king." Relations between "merchant" and agent and between landlord and tenant are fixed by statute, but in a violation of contract the merchant and landlord have the advantage. All women are, in effect, in the class of slaves. In this system of subjection and regulation there are "evidences of a traditional freedom of contract."

Beginning with 1906, *The Journal of Political Economy* became a monthly instead of a quarterly, and the active editorship was transferred from Veblen to Cummings. Veblen was still looking for a position. An opening with a civic welfare organisation in New York appeared, and Veblen had a former student investigate the position for him, but the student secured it for himself. Veblen's matrimonial affairs were still full of difficulties. His wife was living alone on a timber claim near Hood River, Oregon. Communications from her friends were few, and she feared that Veblen had turned them against her by telling them she had reported his affairs to the university authorities. "If Mr. Veblen simply guessed and confronted you with it, as though I had 'told,'" she wrote, "remember always that he is subtle and expert, but that I gave no hint." She heard that Veblen had another woman admirer.

Veblen found diversion with artist friends. He was in the vanguard of the artists who began vacationing at Woodstock, New York, and with the painter B.J. Nordfeld he liked to discuss the problems of art. Nordfeld writes: "He seemed to have a passion for an understanding of the problems of painting without having any technical knowledge. I remember that we spent evening after evening trying to get at the fundamental reason for trying this and not trying that." *The Theory of the Leisure Class* was still irritating people, and Veblen gaily showed Nordfeld a letter he had received asking if Veblen would like to have the book translated from the Italian. Medill McCormick became a Veblenite through the influence of his associate, Caleb Perry Patterson, who had been a student of Veblen.

In the academic year 1905–1906 Veblen taught an elementary course in the principles of political economy. It was a bore to Veblen and not much more to his students. One of them has said: "He lounged in his chair, on a raised platform in front of our class of thirty-five or more students and droned in his speech and never rocked from an even keel of steady discourse." He seldom turned his head, but instead moved his eyes from side to side in looking around the room. His personal appearance was not as neat as that of the other professors; and his manner at times suggested a tragic sense of hopelessness. "No doubt, he was so far advanced in his field," said one of his students, "that our immature minds had difficulty in grasping a great many of the by-paths into which he led us." Veblen used a conventional textbook, Seager's *Introduction to Economics*, and asked conventional questions on examination.

Veblen had become such a learned figure that one undergraduate whispered to another as Veblen walked through the library: "There goes Dr. Veblen, who knows twenty-six languages." The graduate students were more and more impressed with him, and the older ones judged the novices on the basis of whether they appreciated his humour. But Veblen was not as approachable as Laughlin and Davenport, and even the best graduate students seemed to feel that he was too indirect in his approach.

In the March 1906 issue of *The American Journal of Sociology* Veblen published the essay he considered his best, "The Place of Science in Modern Civilisation." Stuart has said that the essay was written as a protest against Dewey's pragmatic theory of knowledge but, like all of Veblen's work, it runs in terms of his fundamental distinction between modern business and the material requirements of the community. The paper contrasts pragmatism, conceived as meaning conduct looking to the agents' preferential interest, with modern science, or workmanship, directed to the production of things that may or may not be of advantage to the agent. In the present phase of culture the discrepancy between these "two divergent ranges of inquiry" is wider than ever before.

In "The Instinct of Workmanship," Veblen declared that trait to have been the cause of mankind becoming lord of creation; now he declared that it is modern science, matter-of-fact knowledge, which has given western civilisation its dominion. What distinguishes a civilised people is "an impersonal, dispassionate insight into the material facts with which mankind has to deal," and a civilisation which is dominated by this matter-of-fact attitude in dealing with its means of life must prevail against others. The highest expression of this attitude is modern science, and its highest material expression is the technology of the machine industry.

In its intervals of sober reflection civilised mankind finds that the accumulation of fortunes—which is of similar value to "the making of states and dynasties, the prosecution of feuds, the propagation of creeds and the creation of sects"—is futile in comparison with the accomplishments of modern science. The pursuit and diffusion of knowledge is an end of culture itself, not a means to the higher inscrutable realities, and in the last resort, "enlightened common sense sticks by the opaque truth, and refuses to go behind the returns given by the tangible facts." On any large question the final appeal is to the scientist, and the solution offered in the name of science is decisive until further scientific inquiry sets it aside. This impersonal approach to knowledge arises from the instinct of idle curiosity, which is idle only from the standpoint of the self-seeking pecuniary interest. It is a characteristic trait of savagery, with its story-tellers and myth-makers, who, in formulating their cosmologies, have no interest in interfering with workaday life.

Under the predatory culture, however, this instinct takes the perverted form of pragmatism, and corresponds to the perversion of the generically human instinct of workmanship into sportsmanship under the competitive culture, or to the confusing of business and industry in the mature credit economy. Pragmatism is characteristic of the higher barbarian culture, where the institutions are "conventionalised relations of force and fraud," and where questions of life and death are "questions of expedient conduct as carried on under the current relations of mastery and subservience." The system of knowledge falls into the like terms of personal force, personal claims, prejudices, graded dignity, and servitude, though the higher generalisations may formally retain the complexion given by the peaceable life of savagery. In this higher barbarian culture the canons guiding idle curiosity are not those of homely life, but are cast by the scholastics in terms of a "feudalistic hierarchy of agents and elements," and the causal relation between phenomena "is conceived animistically after the manner of sympathetic magic." The deity or deities are conceived as arbitrary rulers of the facts. The natural laws of scholasticism are "corollaries under the arbitrary rules of status imposed on the natural universe by an all-powerful Providence with a view to the maintenance of his own prestige." The flourishing sciences are those in which the symbolic force of names is "looked to for an explanation of what takes place." But in the modern era industry is the tone-giving factor in culture, and cosmologies take on the character given by the life of workmanship.

Veblen now used the term animism in such a manner as almost to describe what he had formerly established as its opposite. With the exception of mathematics no scheme of thought can avoid all trace of animism, since animism represents essentially a life history and phenomena are interpreted animistically so they may be organised into a dramatic sequence. Those, like Pearson, who deny the essentially metaphysical preconception of causation, and those, like the association psychologists, who insist on a colourless mathematical formulation of scientific theories, fall back upon animism in an uncritical form—that of the modern businessman—as soon as they go to work. In this use of the animism concept Veblen was emphasising the fact that inquiry must always be open, that established points of view are always on the defensive, and that systems of thought and activity are intimately related to human aspirations, ideals, and ends. Such systems, whether that of impersonal socialism or that of modern business enterprise, are for human beings and are limited by the simple human nature of hypothetical savagery.

Veblen declared that modern science is not itself practical, that is, it is not directed towards practical ends. But the output of modern science can be turned to practical account, for both modern science and modern technology are matter of fact, the former being an outgrowth of the latter. Modern science runs in the terms employed by the mechanical engineer. The employment of scientific knowledge for useful ends is technology, in the broad sense of the term which includes not only the machine industry proper and such branches of practice as engineering, agriculture, medicine, and sanitation, but also "economic reforms."

Pragmatism, however, inhibits and misdirects scientific inquiry. In the direction of systematic formulation the highest achievements of pragmatism consist of "didactic exhortations to thrift, prudence, equanimity, and shrewd management." Pragmatism is a body of shrewd rules of conduct, designed in great part "to take advantage of human infirmity." It is the dominant characteristic of the barbarian life of "competitive expediency for the individual or the group, great or small, in an avowed struggle for the means of life," and is thus the ideal of the businessman as well as the politician with barbarian traditions. The training of "business tactics" is like that of theology, law, diplomacy, military affairs, and authoritative political tactics, in that it is subversive of the sceptical scientific spirit. The so-called sciences associated with the pragmatic discipline, such as the social sciences, "are a taxonomy of credenda." The effect of unmitigated pragmatism is seen in the human flotsam left by the great civilisations of antiquity, such as those of Egypt, India, and Peru. During the dark or barbarian ages, any non-pragmatic movement was found among the lower classes, who lived below the reach of the active class struggle, but the folklore of this homely life is highly treasured. Even the "meanest and most romantic modern intelligence" uses the language of the industrious classes, because "the gallantries, the genteel inanities, and devout imbecilities of medieval high life would be insufferable," even to him.

The scientific formulations of mankind are still phrased, however, in "romantic and Hegelian" instead of "realistic and Darwinian" terms. The causal relation between vulgar work and product is not made a basis for comprehensive analysis but is vaguely taken for granted. Under the guidance of the shortsighted the formalism of modern science has been considered scholarship, which is not formalism but "a systematic familiarity with past culture achievements." Under the same guidance and confusion, the study of literature and the appreciation of literary taste and form are turned into philology. But, in the last analysis, as long as the machine process is the dominant disciplinary factor, modern science is the one self-sufficient and ultimate end of endeavour, although, "even in the apprehension of those who most rejoice in the advances of science," "the ideal of human life is neither the finikin sceptic in the laboratory nor the animated slide-rule." The race has developed through most of its history with little of "this searching knowledge of facts," and the normal man, considering his inheritance, has good cause to be restive under the dominion of "passionless matter-of-fact."

The Journal of Philosophy, Psychology and Scientific Method apparently saw such wide implications and importance in this article that it was given a long review by Stuart.

Ward sent Veblen a copy of his *Applied Sociology*, which accepted the traditional common-sense pragmatic approach to problems of conduct and knowledge. Ward felt that there is no such thing as the pursuit of knowledge for its own sake. The purpose of science is ethical, and modern science, including traditional economics, is the agent of advance. Veblen wrote Ward: "I have lately (last spring) ventured on a discussion of the place and nature of science, as a sociological phenomenon, in which, I foresee, that I shall find myself somewhat at variance with you."

In April 1906 Veblen took advantage of another opportunity to urge the incompatibility between pragmatism and modern science. He secured a two weeks' leave of absence to deliver a series of lectures before the Harvard department of economics, where he was paid out of a fund originally established in the sixties by Boston gentlemen who wished to bring lectures to Harvard to combat the "heresies" of the regular Harvard professor of economics.[4] Three of Veblen's lectures were on "Followers of Karl Marx" and were given in Carver's class in "Methods of Social Reform." A fourth lecture called "The Distribution of Socialist Sentiment" was given in the seminar in economics. In each lecture Veblen gave long lists of references, and his style was relatively simple, as in his course on socialism. Subsequently the lectures were published in two essays in *The Quarterly Journal of Economics* under the title "The Socialist Economics of Karl Marx and his Followers," but in published form the literary style is as highly polished and elusive as that of the *Quarterly* essays.

These essays reflect the development that had taken place in Veblen since "Some Neglected Points in the Theory of Socialism." He was still the sophisticated alien with agrarian roots, sceptical of the intangible money power, and appreciative of an industrial republic. But in his earlier work, influenced by Bellamy and the agrarian crusades, he considered the republic to be imminent; now he felt it was an open question. Then, having lived on farms and in country towns, he had little taste of what industrial civilisation meant; now he had felt its impact, and there were some doubts in his mind. These essays are the outcome of fifteen years' teaching of socialism and thinking in its terms under the unfolding of the money economy.

"The Theories of Karl Marx" is the subtitle of the first essay. "Marx," said Veblen, "was neither ignorant, imbecile, nor disingenuous, and his work must be construed from such a point of view and in terms of such elements as will enable his results to stand substantially sound and convincing." But as in the case of his discussion of the ostensibly right-wing Hegelian, Schmoller, so now in his discussion of the left-wing Hegelian, Marx, Veblen interprets his subject in various, almost contradictory, ways so as to state his own point of view. The philosophy of self-interest, hedonism, and natural rights, which characterises classical economics, is permeated by the philosophy of inner necessity which characterises Hegelianism or romanticism, and Veblen declares that Marx's seemingly "fallacious" conclusions are drawn from the postulates and preconceptions of classical economics and the historical school. Marx is merely more ruthlessly consistent in working out their content than are his natural-rights antagonists in the liberal classical school. The Marxian concept of class consciousness is the outcome of a belief in the progress of humanity, the unfolding of human destiny, through the calculation of the main chance. The final term and end of the struggle is socialism. But this analysis is not Darwinian; that is, it is not a dispassionate statement of the facts. The class struggle is perhaps a highly efficient factor in the social process, but it is in itself no guarantee that mankind will not retrogress as readily as it will advance. It can hardly be said that the social process tends to the final equilibrium of a classless economic structure.

Marx is interested primarily in the current phase of the process—the capitalistic system, which is the "system of modern business traffic." Capitalism means production of goods for the market by hired labour under the direction of employers who own (or control) the means of production and are engaged in industry for the sake of profit. " 'Capital' is wealth (primarily funds) so employed." In the past the products of industry were used as aids to further production, but under capitalism all industry hinges on "the price of marketable goods." Thus the theory of value is the point of departure for the analysis.

Veblen not only grants that Marx offered no adequate proof of his labour theory of value, but declares that to Marx it was self-evident that "value = labour-cost," and that he therefore did not attempt to prove it. The traditional economists translate the unfolding life of the human spirit into terms of the material life of man in society, and deduce that the ultimate reality is the balance between pleasure and pain. But from the same premise Marx deduces labour power as the "metaphysical substance of life." Goods, as facts of production, are identical in their true value, but under the capitalistic system of self-interest and competitive profit-making "distribution is not in any sensible degree based on the equities of production, and the exchange values of goods . . . can therefore express their real value only with a very rough, and in the main fortuitous approximation." Under a socialistic regime, where the labourer would receive the full product of his labour, or where the whole system of ownership and consequently of distribution would lapse, "values would reach a true expression, if any." The difference, which goes to the capitalist, is surplus value. The existence of the capitalistic system can be explained by surplus value and exchange value. In the received economics there is no conception of surplus value, since it is assumed that a labourer will stop producing if he does not receive the equivalent of his pains. The degree of irksomeness is considered a measure of both the labour expended and the value produced, so that what the labourer receives measures his production. Labour does not produce in excess of its wages, and thus the enhanced productivity of industry is to be explained by the "irksomeness of the capitalist's abstinence," and consequent necessity for profits. This constitutes the classical theory of production. But according to Marx there is a discrepancy between the value of the labour expended—the market value of labour—and the value created by the expenditure of labour power, and thus surplus-value arises. Wages are the price of the labour power, and therefore the surplus cannot go to the labourer; by force of the wage contrast it goes to the capitalist in the form of profits, which are the source of the accumulation of capital. Since wages are measured by the value of labour power—its serviceability to the employer —and not by the greater value of the product, labourers cannot buy the whole product of their labour, and capitalists are "unable to sell the whole product of industry continuously at its full value," that is, its value in terms of the capitalised structure of industry. Thus "difficulties of the gravest nature in the capitalistic system" arise, such as so-called over-production.

This fundamental law of "accumulation of capital out of unpaid labour," and its corollary, the doctrine of the reserve army of the unemployed, form the basis of Marx's system and of his exposition of the causes which must lead to the collapse of the capitalist system. The capitalist does not spend all his profits, but adds the remainder to capital. Thus the larger the surplus value through the wage contract, the more rapid the increase in capital, that is, the "greater the increase of capital relatively to the labour force employed, the larger the surplus product available for accumulation." The process of accumulation is a cumulative one, but it is based always on "an unearned increment drawn from the unpaid surplus produce of labour." With an appreciable increase of capital, labour-saving devices are used to a greater extent, constant capital is increased, and the "wage fund" used for the payment of labour—variable capital—is relatively reduced. Proportionately less labour is needed and consequently a reserve army of unemployed arises. Thus from capitalist control and increasing technological efficiency results a cumulative increase of capital and unemployment. Since the purchasing power of labourers, as represented by their wages, is the largest part of the demand for consumable goods, and since in the nature of things this purchasing power is progressively less adequate for the purchase of goods produced, as represented by the price of the products produced, it follows that the market is progressively more subject to glut from overproduction and hence to commercial crises and depression. The capitalistic system breaks down, and socialism arises. Crises and depression put the labourer in a frame of mind to bring about this consummation.

The achievement of the goal is aided by the fact that the reserve army, ever increasing with the increase of capital, is used by the capitalists to depress wages. Every period of depression hastens and accentuates the depression of wages, so that wages are reduced even below the bare subsistence level—"that which is necessary to keep up the supply of labour at its current rate of efficiency." When capitalistic production occupies practically the entire field of industry and has "depressed the condition of its labourers sufficiently to make them an effective majority of the community, with nothing to lose . . . they will move, by legal or extra-legal means" to absorb the state and eliminate private ownership of the instruments of production. All of this derives from the fact that "private ownership of capital goods enables the capitalist to appropriate and accumulate the surplus product of labour."

Marx's argument, says Veblen, is apparently most vulnerable in its implied doctrine of population. The concept of the reserve army of the unemployed involves the assumption that population increases independently of the means of life, and hostile critics—the classical economists—have attacked this point of view. Marx might have reached the conclusion that population can be arrested, but he was barred from that by his theory of evolution as development. According to Marx's premises the capitalistic system would mean the death of humanity if population did not continue to increase. Veblen added, however: "But Marx is a Hegelian."

In the second essay, subtitled "The Later Marxism," Veblen declared that it is to the experience of the English liberal utilitarian school that Marx "owes (probably) the somewhat pronounced individualistic preconceptions on which the doctrines of the Full Product of Labour and the Exploitation of Labour are based." The older Marxism is Hegelian and pre-Darwinian, based on the personal point of view. The facts of the economic order are "construed to take such a course as could be established by an appeal to reason between intelligent and fair-minded people." But mankind has obviously not acted in this logical manner. Continuity in the given facts is not to be imputed in personal terms but only in terms of cause and effect. They represent a scheme of "blindly cumulative causation," in which the outcome is not foreordained as good. When the economic interpretation of history is translated into the concepts of Darwinism, the question is whether or not the industrial classes will respond to the economic exigencies upon which their survival depends. From the point of view of their mutual interest it is logical, reasonable, and convincing that the underlying population should join hands and proceed in a class struggle against the propertied classes, "until it should have put an end to that diversity of economic interest on which the class struggle rests." But man's reasoning is controlled more by sentiment than by logical and intellectual processes, so that the upper-class interest and the training of the industrial classes in subservience to their employers may "bring them again to realise the equity and excellence of the established system of subjection and unequal distribution of wealth." Thus it is an open question whether the working classes will go forward along the lines of socialist ideals and enforce a new order in which there will be no economic discrepancies, no international animosity, no dynastic politics. Heretofore, in the game of dynastic politics, which alone their sportsmanlike rulers consider worth while, they have enthusiastically allowed themselves to be ground under foot.

The accredited socialists with strong aspirations but "with relatively few and ill-defined theoretical preconceptions" have surrendered, under the guidance of "opportunist politicians," their belief in the efficacy and inevitability of the class struggle. The doctrine of progressive proletarian distress has also been given up by the "idealists." "As a matter of reasoned procedure, on the ground of enlightened material interest alone, it should be a tenable position that increasing misery, increasing in degree and in volume, should be the outcome of the present system of ownership, and should result in a well-advised and well-consolidated working-class movement that would replace the present scheme with one more advantageous to the majority." "The experience of history," however, "teaches that abject misery carries with it deterioration and abject subjection."

Veblen followed a similarly indirect procedure in discussing the Marxian theory of value. "In any evolutionary system of economics the central question touching the efficiency and fitness of any given system of production is necessarily the question as to the excess of serviceability in the product over the cost of production." It is in this excess of serviceability over cost that the chance of survival lies for any system of production, "in so far as the question of survival is a question of production." If surplus product, however, be substituted for surplus value, "the doctrines and practical consequences which Marx derived from the theory of surplus value would remain substantially well founded." The question is then phrased not in terms of a natural right to the full product of labour, but in terms of "what scheme of distribution will help or hinder the survival of a given people or a given civilisation." A competent theory of value "dealing with the excess of serviceability over cost," would leave a doubt as to "the advisability of the present as against the socialistic regime," but economic theory has yet to handle value theory in such a modern manner. On this question the recognised socialists are as innocent as others, unless "the current neglect of value theory by the socialists be taken as a negative symptom of advance, indicating that they at least recognise the futility of the received problems and solutions, even if they are not ready to make a positive move."

Veblen concluded with a discussion of the opportunistic departures from the Marxian doctrines. Trade unions were bitterly opposed by the original Marxian socialism, whose spokesmen were as hostile "as the loyal adherents of the classical political economy." Trade unionism is an attempt by labourers to deal with capitalism on a business basis, but "the great point of all socialist aspiration and endeavour is the abolition of all business and bargaining." Socialists now argue, however, that an improvement in the working class is the first requisite for the advance of the socialist cause, and unionism is therefore considered an instrument for the achievement of socialism. In other words socialism is to be attained through an acceptance of capitalism. It is contended "that the socialist revolution must be carried through not by an anæmic working class under the pressure of abject privation, but by a body of full-blooded workingmen gradually gaining strength from the improved conditions of life."

Similarly there has been a softening of doctrine in connexion with the farmers. According to the older Marxian doctrine, under the development of modern business and industrial methods the class interest of the agrarian population, which is in effect reduced to the state of the proletariat, should throw the farmers into the socialist movement, along with the workers. But this conclusion is not true, according to Darwinian principles of cause and effect. The revisionists seek to enlist the sympathies of the agrarians by holding that socialism would not disturb their property rights. Although the farmer operates on the principle of ownership, he is in fact not a capitalist. Under the "current regime of markets and credit relations, the small agricultural producer, it is held, gets less than the product of his own labour, since the capitalistic business enterprises with which he has to deal are always able to take advantage of him." Thus he is caught in "the web of vexatious exactions of his creditors and the ruinous business traffic." The aim of opportunistic, revisionist socialism is to enlist the sympathies of this "obstinately conservative element for the revolutionary cause" by leaving it alone.

The growth of patriotism is another effect and characteristic of revisionism. Marxian socialism is, of course, opposed to "warlike establishments and warlike policy" and is "characteristically inclined to peaceable measures," but the up-to-date liberals and socialists stand for "national aggrandisement first and for international comity second." They are first of all patriots and secondly socialists, "which comes to saying that they are . . . working for the maintenance of the existing order, with modifications." They are not revolutionists but reformers, whose ideas are those of English liberalism instead of Marxian socialism. The educated socialist seems to be tending towards the ideal of "imperialistic liberalism" or "imperialistic democracy." Habituation to warlike ideals, said Veblen, is leading to the sterilisation of "revolutionary socialism."

Veblen said that Taussig would have liked to have him made a member of the Harvard faculty, but other members objected. A new position soon appeared through Jacques Loeb at Stanford. Its head, D. S. Jordan was engaged in a contest with the trustees, who were attempting to make the university more of a vocational school. Veblen, a prominent figure, would strengthen his side. Jordan said to Maynard that Veblen was "the most subtle man in the business. What he cannot reverse and make appear the opposite of what it purports to be isn't worth reversing." President Jordan knew of Veblen's matrimonial difficulties, but he expected that Veblen would observe the customs when given the best opportunities, including a good salary. Veblen was to teach as little as he wished and devote his time to writing. Also he could have a tutor to help him build up the library along his lines. President Jordan offered Veblen an appointment to an associate professorship for the academic year 1906–1907, and he was to commence work in the latter part of August.

Veblen's father died in August, and less than six months later his mother passed away. Having been more interested in the welfare of his children than in accumulating a fortune, Thomas Veblen left only a modest estate of $8000, and in the division the cost of Veblen's education was taken out of his share.

Ellen Veblen had never told her husband where she was. One day when she had almost completed the necessary residence for her timber claim, she looked out of her door, her dog having barked with alarm. She saw Veblen strolling towards her. Remarking that she had a fine stand of timber on her claim, he asked her how much longer she would have to hold it down, and how she would like to go with him to Palo Alto when she had finished her residence. He stayed with her until she could leave and they departed together for Palo Alto.

CHAPTER XVI

VEBLEN stayed at Stanford a little more than three years. His cottage was located in a grove of pine and cedar trees, in an isolated spot on the Stanford campus, and for a short time, said his wife, they were as happy as they had been at Stacyville. But in a few months Veblen's matrimonial affairs were again entangled. He seems to have complained that his wife spent too much for clothes; she declared that she was ill provided for; Veblen said she had money of her own. One of his Chicago admirers wrote Veblen that she wanted to be the mother of a great man's children, not thereby making the situation any less difficult. It was not long before Mrs. Veblen left him again, but one rainy day she looked up from her work once more to see him standing in the doorway of the lonely cottage. He was holding up a long black stocking which she had lost from the laundry she had carried home, and he asked: "Does this garment belong to you, Madame?" He stayed with her there until she was ready to return to their home in Palo Alto.

This continual cycle of separation and reconciliation might appear almost comic if it were not that it was caused by such tragic maladjustment. The Veblens, both of them untamed and unconforming, had much in common and much to give each other. Certainly her gifts were of a sort that were useful to him, and might have continued to be. Like Veblen, she had many idiosyncrasies, but like Veblen she had many loyal friends who forgave them. She could be extremely generous, not only with money but also with her personality. Henry Cowell, the composer, was one of her protégés. She gave him his first music lesson, and once, to help him financially, she dropped some money where she knew he would pass.

But eventually there came the final break. Veblen was forced to turn over half of his salary to his wife. She built herself a shack near his house, and they often passed one another, but were scarcely on speaking terms. Apparently, however, they knew of each other's movements. On one occasion Mrs. Veblen, while in Los Angeles, heard that Mrs. Millis was ill. She wrote a desperate letter begging that someone inform her of the condition of her friend, and received in answer an unsigned telegram informing her that Mrs. Millis was better. The telegram could not be traced to any of the friends of Mrs. Veblen or Mrs. Millis, and the former felt certain that it was sent by Veblen. He remarked once that the "president doesn't approve of my domestic arrangements. Nor do I."

Veblen appeared to be happy, however. His surroundings were congenial, and he fondly likened the California hills to the "lands that never were outside of William Morris's romances." [1] Veblen had forty chickens and two cows on his place, and often rode horseback. There was plenty of opportunity for his mechanical ingenuity. He had taught himself to work flints and turn out arrow-heads and the like, and he could make repairs swiftly and ingeniously. He secured what the earthquake had left of the chickencoop belonging to the Stanford family; hauled it by wagon to an isolated spot on the top of a mountain range between Santa Clara Valley and the sea, and built a cabin. It stands on a redwood stump, with a pair of large second-growth redwoods flanking the doorway. On one side is a forest of redwoods, on the other an uninterrupted view over range after range of hills to the sea. He was proud of having driven what he considered a shrewd bargain for the wreckage with the Stanford administrator.

Veblen solved his household cares by bringing in an entire family, sometimes two, to manage his home. In this way Robert Duffus and his brother William met part of their college expenses. Veblen could be quite generous with his resources. The father of the Duffus boys, who was ill, stayed with him for a time, and a tubercular student, whom Millis had told him of, was allowed to pitch a tent on the property and Veblen helped to nurse him. He showed infinite patience and interest in little children, and was able to tell stories that entranced them. When Mrs. Veblen's sister and her daughter visited the house, the child was so delighted with Veblen that on the day of departure she waited patiently for two hours before his bedroom door until he appeared, and when he left them in the Pullman she awakened the entire car with her cries for him. To a child's question as to what "T.B." in his name stood for, he answered: "Teddy Bear."

Veblen became interested in the Arnotts, a working-class family of old-time socialists. Their house, two miles from Veblen's, was a headquarters for travelling radicals and socialist agitators. On one occasion Veblen walked there to meet three workers, one a stone carver who had come to do work on the carving at Stanford, the second a bricklayer who had travelled all over Europe, South Africa, and America, and the third a painter who had lost the sight of both eyes and earned a precarious living by writing and speaking on the socialist movement with his wife acting as reader. Veblen talked to them until two o'clock in the morning, and commented that the evening had been a revelation, that he had never met three more intelligent men.

Upton Sinclair, who admired Veblen's work and later embodied in his *Love's Pilgrimage* part of what was considered Veblen's discussion of the degraded position of women, declared on meeting him that "he was one of the most silent men I ever met. I do not think I ever met a man who would sit in a company and listen so long without ever speaking." Once Veblen was present at a lecture by Jack London on socialism, and some of his students also attended, at his request. London read from his forthcoming socialist novel *The Iron Heel*, and at the conclusion of the lecture Veblen was called upon to make some remarks. He modestly rose and bowed, and said he had none to make. The students had looked forward to a verbal combat between London and Veblen, and were keenly disappointed. After a similar occurrence at a banquet of the Ruskin Club in Oakland, which he reluctantly attended, Veblen said to Mrs. Arnott: "They asked me to speak, but I knew better. I would have driven them out of the house."

E.W. Scripps tried to interest Veblen in the investigation of the corrupt San Francisco "labour government," which was said to be backed by the "sinister corporate interests." Guido Marx, professor of machine design at Stanford and president of the Palo Alto League of Justice, was the intermediary. According to Marx, Veblen "replied rather distantly that he was not interested, that it was a move of the middle class directed against the workers. I was flabbergasted and asked him . . . to explain that to me. Still distantly he remarked that he hadn't time. I was too much interested to be otherwise than amused at the snub, so later on, one evening at the faculty club, I captured him and said: 'Now we had plenty of time. . . .' He escaped in his most characteristic fashion by smiling wickedly and saying: 'Well, you know, I really don't think I quite understand it myself.' I accepted the second refusal as final."

Veblen's place at the university was similar to what it had been at Chicago. President Jordan in the annual report referred to Veblen as a well-known author in economics, and Allyn Young, as executive officer of the department, said in his report to the president for 1906–1907: "It is hoped that the new courses offered by Professor Veblen will especially contribute 'to the end of offering' some opportunities for advanced study and research to those students who are interested in the study of economics for its own sake." [2] But Young was made a full professor in 1907, and Henry Waldgrave Stuart received the same rank in the department of philosophy in 1909, while Veblen remained an associate professor. He was not an administrator, nor was he, in terms of registration, a successful teacher. His classes were large for the first few days, but before long only a handful remained. In "The Economic Factors in Civilisation" the highest registered attendance was twelve, and in his last year it was only three.

His course on the "History of Political Economy" varied from three to eleven, and in a five-hour "Thesis" course which he gave in his last year the only member was William R. Camp, a graduate student devoted to Veblen. His average schedule of six hours was lighter than the customary one.

At Chicago Veblen had been accustomed to handling graduate students but here practically all his students were undergraduates and he cared very little for them. According to Ira Cross, a former student, assistant, and follower, Veblen avoided a heavy teaching load by asking the prospective student if he could read French and German, and whether or not he were conversant with psychology, philosophy, and other such fields. Here too Phi Beta Kappa candidates were not enthusiastic about Veblen's methods, since he paid practically no attention to marks. On one occasion he encountered a Phi Beta Kappa student who could not harness his horse, and Veblen mentioned it in class with some amusement. One student contended that "maybe that wasn't his line," but Veblen answered: "He was just a fine Phi Beta Kappa."

Student opinion was generally against Veblen. For one thing, his personal appearance was not in his favour. One student said: "The first time I saw him, ambling along the Quad, with a slouch hat pulled down over his brow, with coat and trousers 'hanging'; with untrimmed hair and moustache creating a general unkempt appearance, I thought he was a tramp." But he could be conventional when he cared to be. Once, at a dinner party given by a student, he even appeared in a dress suit. Also, the students generally considered him a poor lecturer, and felt his lack of interest in undergraduates. He still spoke in a low, monotonous voice, and put most of them to sleep. A student in "Socialism" recalled the course "as about the driest subject I ever attempted to study." In fact, the taking of naps became so notorious one year that Veblen resorted to the traditional device of unexpectedly setting an examination. Another student said that most of the time Veblen was "over my head and beyond the range of both vicarious experience and academic reading." Still another considered him a kindly, unassuming old man, and felt himself to be "in the presence of somebody who did not belong to our world at all but who was away up somewhere in the vague realm of the abstract, and the true. I always felt as if I were listening to one who literally knew everything, and who was benevolently trying to improve our little world, but I understood precious little of what he actually said."

Some of Veblen's old Chicago students were becoming somewhat sceptical of his work. Stuart felt that Veblen's strict reliance on such concepts as "idle curiosity," "opaque cause and effect," reflected the one-sided development of a man too much influenced by Spencerian evolutionary notions. Millis told Camp that he did not consider Veblen understandable. Spurgeon Bell, whom Veblen had sought as a tutor to assist him, at Stanford, declared: "I found out rather early that a younger man with a less profound background than Veblen had, could get nowhere scientifically by following Veblen's practice of bold generalisation unsupported by conclusive proof. We frequently believed and accepted the conclusions of Veblen because the man himself with the profound scholarship and established background inspired our confidence. What he said often appealed to one as being true when given the setting he alone could give it."

Most of Veblen's fellow-professors seemed scarcely to have heard of him. His books were not light reading and he did not mix easily with his associates, usually remaining silent in their company. A few real friendships developed, however, notably with Guido Marx and Henry W. Rolfe, professor of Greek. Marx was actively interested in bringing about a more adequate and equitable salary scale and a more dignified and influential position for university professors. At the suggestion of a mutual friend he attempted, without success, to have Veblen look at a series of charts on the subject, in the hope that he would write an accompanying text. When he published the material with his own text, however, and sent Veblen a copy, Veblen spoke highly of the work, and "from then on," said Marx, "I felt as if he 'accepted' me as worth being bothered with."

Henry Rolfe was so attracted to Veblen that he regularly attended the course in "Economic Factors." Of this class Rolfe has said: "We scattered round a long table; Veblen sat at the head, tolerant, amused, humorous, witty, subtly ironical, sarcastic never (sarcasm being the weapon of incompetence), pausing willingly for questions or attempted rebuttal, drawing on vast stores of knowledge (bookish, technological, and what not), wielding a wide vocabulary with the precision that one admires in his writings. Almost every factor of civilisation appeared as economic and he disclosed the pattern of man's life and the threads that made it from arboreal days to this century. He had an amazingly full and accurate knowledge of the life of man in all time and all climes—knowledge drawn from sources historical (including documentary), literary, archæological (he had handled masses of archæological materials in European museums, including great reserve stores of paleolithic and neolithic implements, and had visited sites), anthropological, etc. He was a scholar in ten thousand. But he was modest and never paraded his knowledge. His books are footnotes to that great outpouring." In conversation "he preferred to abide 'in the quiet and still air of delightful studies.' . . . Very little that was controversial, very little that was personal, came from him. He was too dignified for such discourse. Only in his seminar did he let himself go a bit. There he would not infrequently speak cuttingly, very, of remote persons or times, with a chance piercing at the present, but always mirth-provokingly. He seemed to me like a Heine who was always kindly, never sardonic, yet just, and a bit grim."

Veblen was continually experimenting with minor and outlandish tongues. He managed his large number of languages without an accent, and had the ability to insert foreign phrases into English discourse, and to slip from the English to the continental system of vowels and back again, without any lingual embarrassment. Reading was his greatest indulgence, but, thorough as it was, it was for the purpose of securing bullets, just as his reviews were only excuses for setting forth his own position. For books as possessions he cared little; as he moved from place to place he usually left most of them behind. Their use exhausted, they became useless baggage. In many respects he felt the same towards people.

In 1909 Camp proposed that Rolfe, Veblen, and himself should study Homeric society together. "Camp selected passages," said Rolfe, "came to me, listened to the suggestions that I made concerning them from the point of view of their literal meaning, went to Veblen and got his interpretations and comments, and brought them to me for further discussion. . . . Ridgeways's theory of an intrusive civilisation was their especial object of study." Camp and Veblen were strongly of the opinion that "the Homeric poems mirror a period when Minoan institutions had been broken up and new ones (of today's type) were beginning to form, as the Achæan raiders from the north settled down in the rich land." The excavations going on in Crete were of deep interest to the group. Veblen considered the diggers better at finding than at interpreting, for they seemed to him to lack the "perspective of the field."

At the 1907 meeting of the American Sociological Association, Hoxie attempted to use Veblen's distinction between industrial and pecuniary employments by drawing a distinction between the industrial and pecuniary psychology, and thereby showing the inevitability of class conflict. He thought he had Veblen's approval. But Hoxie held that these differences in discipline cannot be obviated, since they seem to be a necessary aspect of the developing life process in society. "Without these differences no division of labour, no specialisation, no development of efficiency and individuality could exist. To obviate them we should have to accept the simplicity, stagnation, and atrophy of the small communistic community.".[3]

In 1908 William McDougall's *Introduction to Social Psychology*, with its "instinct" psychology, created a furore in the social sciences. McDougall asserted that the traditional political economy was useless and that economic science needed a more adequate psychology to replace its tainted hedonism. "As an example of the happy effect of the recent introduction of less crude psychology into economics discussions" he cited *The Standard of Life* by Mrs. Bernard Bosanquet, who was a Hegelian of the right and one of the most uncompromising opponents of socialism. The point of view was that of the "moral philosophy" of Clark, of the principle of self-realisation of the historical school, and of the Christian sociologists, approaches which Veblen had identified as essentially one with the hedonistic point of view.

Loeb was still insisting that he had no metaphysical principles, that all scientific laws must be reduced to mathematical form and equations. Veblen often chided him with the accusation that his materialism was a metaphysical principle.

In Veblen's course at Stanford on "Economic Factors in Civilisation" the anthropological attitude was much in evidence, but for the year 1907 an interesting variation took place in the opening lectures. Veblen began with a discussion of *The Communist Manifesto* and of the "Marxian Materialistic Interpretation of History," interpreted as meaning the survival value of a culture. Any culture, Veblen declared, must adjust itself to economic exigencies on pain of destruction. Some, like western culture, with its technological efficiency, which allows a wide margin between highest and minimum efficiency required, can afford to waste much in the competitive struggle between the members of the dominant economic class. But it is possible to cross the deadline and perish, as Spain did. "Mankind is older than the class struggle"; according to the socialists, said Veblen, the "class struggle began in cannibalism."

In all other years Veblen began this course in his more indirect fashion. All types of activity from religion to literature were discussed, and students wondered at the slight attention he gave to the modern scheme of things, to modern capitalism. He frequently used in the classroom those excellent strategic devices—"in the light of modern science," and "but with that we are not concerned." When a student asked ingenuous questions Veblen would simply answer: "I don't know, I'm not bothered that way."

Cultures are to be contrasted, Veblen held, by their differences in kind rather than by their stages. The traits of the warlike, pastoral culture and of the peaceable, agricultural, persist among all tribes all over the world in at least a general way. In contradiction to the assumption that in the competitive system livelihood can be reduced only temporarily below the minimum required for efficiency, Veblen spoke of the depauperate forms, that is, forms which have been stunted for generations. A depauperate stock is not necessarily one that cannot survive, but it is likely to be best able to survive under the conditions that produced it.

The course in "History of Economic Thought" followed the framework of previous years, but it was perhaps less obscure than at Chicago. Even so modern a treatise on money as Laughlin's gives the same explanation as Oresme: the prince is the vicar of God and money is instituted for the good of the community. Turgot represented the best endeavours of the politician of his time to avert a catastrophe. He might have saved the situation and worked out practicable reforms if it had not been for the opposition of the interests. The vested interests, secure in their "graft," went too far and collapsed, just as a parasite fails when its host fails. Turgot almost gave an explanation of modern capitalisation, but he had no adequate terminology.

In Adam Smith's day capitalists did not habitually do business on borrowed money; hence there was no distinction between interest and profits. The current rate of profits is what a capitalist will accept, and is accordingly dependent upon a moral standard. Malthus's doctrine of population is based on the assumption of a pastoral life; he thereby takes account of institutional factors. The theory of markets is the great contribution of the classical school. It recognises the fact that the difficulty of capitalism is that of not producing more than can be sold, so that the market will not be overstocked. But in its theory of production and distribution the labour supply is taken for granted. The discretionary power of the capitalist is inevitable, and his operations determine how much will go to capital and how much to wages. Thus wages are a fixed fund, and an increasing share of funds goes to machinery and a decreasing share to wages. Clark, Hobson, and Sombart assume the validity of Mill's theory of production as investment; they accept, in other words, his belief that the industrial system is carried on for profit, and that consumption is adjusted to the financial market.

Today the sole test of productivity is vendibility. In the modern corporation the discretionary agent is in a material sense far removed from the products. Manipulation in copper stocks has only an intangible relation to the mines, but it may have more effect than physical fact. The prevailing assumption is that assets are productive goods and that there are no intangible assets, yet Ivory Soap's greatest asset is the intangible slogan, "It Floats," in spite of the fact that it produces nothing. The accepted theory fits the situation of a hundred years ago, when the manager's gain came out of the success of the enterprise under his hands. Today the practice of borrowing on the future is the source of great profits. Skilful capitalisation leads to automatic "saving," but it is concerned with securities, not goods. When the Steel Trust was organised, Carnegie became three times as wealthy as he was six months before, but in this period he did not, in the traditional sense, save $116,000,000. Hill says that there has been no gain to his three railroads since the start, but he is worth $200,000,000. His ostensible position is that of the paid head of the railroad, but the railroads have "saved" nothing and he has made a fortune.

Veblen's writings at Stanford are directed more obviously towards an analysis of modern corporation finance, although his work still shows much of his old roundabout style. In reviewing Albert Schatz's *L'Individualisme économique et social,* he wrote: "An interesting outcome of this study is the emphasis thrown on the continuity of economic science and of liberal policy throughout the period since the predominance of mercantilism. Seen in the light of their philosophical preconceptions the various schools appear to be variants and phases of a common scheme, gradually unfolding and maturing by the help of controversies that prove in the outcome to have been nothing more serious than factional disputes about matters of detail. Substantial discrepancies are absent from the general scheme of modern economic science. They occur only between the successful main line of individualistic thought and the transient reassertion of older ideals. But hitherto individualism has held the field, even though its forces have latterly been scattered and disorganised in a greater degree than once was the case." Veblen finally dismissed Schatz as a follower of the historical school. Reviewing Reeve's *The Cost of Competition,* he declared that the author was a physiocrat, but as usual he made full use of the work for his own purposes. Reeve describes value as "the potentiality of a thing for the support of human life and growth," a concept contrary to the usage of conventional economics. "By the Cost of Competition" the author "means the same as would be signified by the Cost of Business Enterprise," that is, primarily a waste of goods and work, and secondly "the evil consequences of business in the way of hardship and moral, æsthetic, and intellectual corruption." The appreciation of such facts stands in sheer contrast with the views of business traffic current among the older generation of economists, who show little interest in "the stupendous sweep of events in the modern market-place" as achievements of modern "capitalism."

For the younger generation the point of departure is the distinction "between industry and business." "Industry, productive activity, is the source of all wealth," but business, in so far as it is competitive, merely dissipates wealth. By comparing the statistics of income of the competitive or business classes, and those of the productive classes, the substantially accurate conclusion is reached that in 1900 the dissipation due to competitive business was seventy percent of the total annual product, as against fifty percent in 1850. Under a "free and consistent business regime the share of competitive business as contrasted with productive industry, must grow at such a rate as to take up any amount by which the total product exceeds the minimum necessary to induce the productive classes to go on with the work." It might be objected that the greatest part of the larger incomes is added to capital, so that the community gains more than it loses in yielding the income to businessmen. But even if it were conceded that increased productivity results, this increased investment gives businessmen a valid claim to a correspondingly greater share of the output, with the result that the community is about as well off as it would have been "if the businessmen had dissipated their share of the total income." In fact the eventual result is a heightening of the spectacular effect of dissipation.

Veblen declared that the greatest shortcoming of Reeve's work was its lack of an adequate account of the elaborately wasteful consumption of wealth, a process which is inseparable from the regime of competitive business. Wealth is acquired competitively in order to be wasted competitively. Appreciation of this motive of modern business would have "strengthened Mr. Reeve's position, both as regards the wastefulness of the current regime, and as regards his optimistic appreciation of a conceivable non-competitive future."

In his more important articles Veblen discussed these principles of modern pecuniary action in greater detail. These articles suggest that Veblen had now grown tired of his distinction between industrial and pecuniary employments, between the comprehensive machine process and investment for profit. He had exhausted its possibilities, and its reiteration resulted only in confusion or in the assertion that he was concealing a truism behind a play of rhetoric. Most of the articles now drew a distinction between technology, or "the state of the industrial arts," which is described as a group heritage, and intangible assets, which represent the misuse of technological knowledge in behalf of modern capital. This analysis marks something of a return to the argument of "The Beginnings of Ownership," and reinforces the distinction between industrial capital and pecuniary capital. But Veblen's discussion of the "state of the industrial arts" makes it clearer that in his usage "industry" refers to a state or scheme of living which is in contrast to a predatory scheme. It makes more intelligible his usual anthropological approach, as involved, for example, in his comparison of modern business to invading barbarians, or in his comparison of an industrial republic to hypothetical savagery. Also it provides the foundation for the concept of the "engineer" as the responsible person who, in contrast to the financier, stands at the centre of modern technology, thereby satisfying Veblen's aristocratic bent and his lack of faith that the poor man as such can take the necessary steps to achieve a workable scheme of institutions.

For *The Quarterly Journal of Economics* Veblen wrote a long review of Clark's *The Essentials of Economic Theory as Applied to Modern Problems of Industry and Public Policy*. Veblen's personal feeling towards his teacher is shown in his remark that Clark has "in a singular degree the gift of engaging the affections as well as the attention of students in his field." But Veblen was interested here in Clark's work "as a competent and consistent system of current theory," and for this analysis he adopted the unusual procedure of referring primarily to the *Distribution of Wealth* instead of to the book supposedly under review. Indeed, Clark and his *Essentials of Economic Theory* become so subordinate in Veblen's discussion that, if this article were read as a review, Veblen's comments would appear contradictory, inconsistent, and frivolous. Veblen was so absorbed in examining modern business enterprise that it is scarcely to be expected that any important review he wrote at that time would serve any other purpose than this.

Thus Veblen referred to Clark as "a spokesman for the competitive system, considered as an element in the Order of Nature." Clark's conjectural anthropology explains away modern capital by reference to a situation where capital does not exist. It is overlooked that the important fact in the material welfare of the community is the technology of the economic situation, which is a group heritage, the accumulated experience of mankind. In primitive life, with its scheme of petty trade and handicraft, "capital-goods" are of little consequence; but with the advance of the industrial arts the capital necessary to put the commonplace knowledge into effect "is greater than the common man can hope to acquire in a lifetime." This advance in the industrial arts has enabled the owners of production goods to corner the accumulated experience of the race, the intangible assets of the community. These are the substantial core of all capital and in comparison with them the goods which are formally owned are an adventitious and transient factor.

Received economic theory consists in the definition and classification of economic life, in terms of the definitive, hypothetically perfect, beneficent, competitive system of complete capitalisation to which the prevailing system closely approximates. The only changes or variations recognised are quantitative, pecuniary ones, so that the ideal dynamic system is the hypothetical static system of perfect capitalisation or monopoly, where the actual living forces of modern industry are repressed. Because of hedonistic preconceptions and pragmatic ideals, capital is viewed as a congeries of physical goods, not as "the central claimant in the current scheme of distribution," as it is revealed to be by prevailing corporate practice. Intangible assets, as the term is actively understood in modern business, particularly by the great financial magnates, are not known to the traditional economists. Thus the shifting of capital funds is conceived to be the shifting of industrial factors for increased efficiency, instead of a shifting of ownership; increasing technological efficiency, resulting in a lowering of pecuniary values, is viewed as a destruction of capital as industrial equipment.

Actually, however, the capitalist's gain arises from his "monopolisation of a given portion of the intangible assets of the community at large," from his differential advantages in having legally seized the material contrivances by which the technological achievements of the community are put into effect. If capital is thus interpreted as a historical category, the road is open for curbing the trust-makers' discretionary management of capital, as is apparently advocated by Clark and anti-trust sentiment in general. But also the field is "left equally free of moral obstructions to the extreme proposals of the socialists."

In received economic thought there is no question as to the equity or expediency of the existing conventions concerning rights of ownership and initiative. The valuation of the financial market is assumed to be the standard of society and thus the measurement of productive efficiency. The argument reduces itself to the dictum, "The value of a thing Is just as much as it will bring." Accepting the hedonistic postulates without their corollaries Veblen deduced some striking conclusions. The competitive price, which includes competitive wages and interest, reflects the valuations which the marginal unfortunates among both labourers and consumers are willing to concede under stress of competition. According to Clark's doctrine of effective utility, however, the maximum net productivity is set at the point "at which a perfectly shrewd business management of a perfect monopoly would limit the supply; and the point of maximum (hedonistic) remuneration (wages and interest) is the point which such a management would fix in dealing with a wholly free, perfectly competitive supply of labour and capital." Thus Veblen discussed Clark's doctrine of "effective utility" as if it were the doctrine of maximum capitalisation.

In this essay Veblen came closer than ever before to presenting the hedonistic calculus as the principle of modern financial enterprise. The hedonistic calculus expresses itself in the principle of "all the traffic can bear," the principle that a large value may be had by raising the return per unit to just that point beyond which the demand will be curtailed. This is done not only by reducing the output of goods, but by reducing wages and by leaving labour only partially employed. As applied by Veblen to the problem of monopolies, Clark's law of "natural distribution" is only a product of reformist thinking. Clark and the reformers might consider monopolistic gains to be "robbery" and "plunder," but according to hedonistic theory these gains—to which must be added such losses to the community as the cost of monopolistic management and deprivations due to a restriction of the principle of increasing returns—are the " 'natural' remuneration of the monopolist for his 'productive service' to the community in enhancing its enjoyment per unit of consumable goods to such a point as to swell its net aggregate enjoyment to a maximum."

The characteristic features of the modern capitalistic business situation are the negotiability of securities, and the holding company, which allows "sufficiently few men to control a section of the community sufficiently large to make an effective monopoly." The vendible securities (common stock) which are the basis of monopolistic control should, according to received economics, be "simply the formal evidence of the ownership of certain productive goods and the like." Actually, however, these securities are used in such a way as to pre-empt control of the industrial equipment; in other words, owners of securities, standing "in certain, immaterial, technical relations to certain other securities, are enabled arbitrarily to control the use of the industrial equipment covered by the latter." The intangible assets represented by these securities are the most important feature in modern capital. They have a "total effective utility," that is, a market value. These assets are the outgrowth of freedom of contract under the conditions imposed by the machine technology, but the reformers attempt to suppress this category of intangible assets without considering the suppression of either the machine technology or freedom of contract. Attempts to suppress the trust have been futile, for the only result has been the emergence of the holding company, and this experience should provide an object lesson. The problem of monopoly might be more competently understood if there were an appreciation of the meaning of modern business capital. Even on the conventional assumption of hedonism, that man's only gift is that of "appraisement and calculation" for his own advantage, the futility of the modern system is evident. Under its operation man's pleasures and profits are not actual but speculative, and in anticipation of them man's pains or costs are adjusted, so that in the nature of things the net result of modern competitive enterprise is hedonistically a deficit for the community.

In conventional economic thought the natural order of competition is believed to guide the course of economic affairs, that is, the only institutions to be considered are those of pecuniary capital. In proposed measures of reform, which are the short-sighted proposals of "pre-Darwinian hedonism," there is no conception of the uncertainties and cumulative changes involved in the development of modern machine technology. "No doubt presents itself but that the community's code of right and equity in economic matters will remain unchanged under changing conditions of economic life." But the institution of capital is secure only as long as it is currently believed to be just and equitable.

Shortly after this review appeared, Clark met Veblen and said that the article had called attention to at least a few corrections he ought to make. When Clark had left, Veblen turned to a student and declared that Clark was a gentleman. Davenport thought that Veblen had superbly exposed the weaknesses of Clark's position, but if Davenport had looked a little more closely he might have suspected that his own type of pecuniary economics was not free from Veblen's scrutiny.

Veblen's review of Irving Fisher's *Nature of Capital and Income* developed further his conception of the nature of modern capital. Veblen began with his customary recital of methodological criticisms. Fisher's analysis of capital follows from an uncritical acceptance of the modern competitive system as beneficient. Capital is that which yields "psychic income" and modern business income is conceived as of this kind. It is held to include persons, even though modern business posits a distinction between the capitalist and his capital. The inclusion of persons avoids the substantial fact of modern business, intangible assets, by holding that these assets are an unfortunate misnomer for roundabout claims to concrete (tangible) items of wealth. Actually modern capital comprises the value of the differential advantages of one business as against another, thus adding a fictitious volume to the total property rights of the community. These, like other assets, are capitalised and made the basis of credit extensions, "serving to increase the aggregate claims of creditors beyond what the hypothecable material wealth of the debtors would satisfy. Hence, in a period of liquidation, when the differential advantages of the various concerns greatly contract, the legitimate claims of the creditors come greatly to exceed the paying capacity of debtors, and the collapse of the credit system follows." The failure of prevailing economic thought to recognise intangible assets is responsible for the lack of an intelligent account of credit and crises. Fisher, like Clark, assumes that "capital wealth," or productive goods, is substantially the same as "capital value," or pecuniary capital. Fisher's analysis is of capital value, but the capitalisation of values is held to be the value of tangible objects, productive goods. Wasteful, disserviceable, or futile acts are supposed to have no place in the normal scheme of life, and the "current competitive capitalistic business scheme" of differential advantages and gains is normal when rightly seen in the light of the traditional hedonistic preconceptions.

A year afterwards Veblen reviewed Fisher's *The Rate of Interest, Its Nature, Determination and Relation to Economic Phenomena*, which, he said, was based on "so good and authentic a utilitarian theorist as John

Rae." According to Fisher's adaptation of the received doctrine, interest is paid for a service, and arises from a preference for present income, psychic income, over future income. This is not a theory of production or of industry, but a theory of distribution or business in terms of non-pecuniary factors. Interest is, however, said Veblen, a phenomenon of credit transactions alone, and rests on the mature development of the institution of property, or the credit economy. Thus it is a pecuniary fact, "having no validity (except by force of an ambiguity) outside of the pecuniary relations of the business community." Interest is therefore to be explained in terms of modern business, and not converted into terms of livelihood of the community or into terms of the sensations of consumption.

Because of the traditional hedonistic preconception, appreciation and depreciation in the standard of payments, which are essentially a variation in price, are looked upon by Fisher as a variation in the commodity rate of interest. But the economist asserts that "businessmen habitually do not (adequately) appreciate variations in the commodity-value of money"; that is, "with rising prices they simply do business at a high money profit and pay a high rate of interest without suspecting that all this has any connexion with the 'commodity interest' of Mr. Fisher." These so-called exceptional or anomalous facts are the unavoidable rule as long as business is done in terms of money, and indicate "that money value has an institutional force in the counsels of businessmen"; consequently modern capital is not identical with the facts of livelihood.

Fisher said in reply that Veblen's criticisms were "almost all generalities on methodology and concepts and for the most part they disregard the special conclusions which differentiate my books from others on his *index expurgatorius*." He declared that his own criticisms of method were like those of Veblen, and that Veblen had misinterpreted his attitude towards *laissez-faire* economics. "My views on this subject are largely based on John Rae's stimulating book, and are not unlike those of Professor Veblen," as stated in the *Theory of the Leisure Class*.[4]

Veblen presented a direct statement of his mature views on modern capital in two essays "On the Nature of Capital" in *The Quarterly Journal of Economics*. In these articles he carried his concept of intangible assets so far that he seems to have reformulated Marxian doctrines in the light of modern corporate practice. In Marx the productive agent in economic life is labour, in Veblen it is the accumulated experience and initiative of the race, techniques created by man for human use. Veblen, like Marx, holds that capital goods cost nothing but labour, and that all gains to capital, aside from those going to the working community, are surplus gains, but Veblen maintained that capital goods are instruments of production only by virtue of the technological knowledge possessed by the industrial community. In Marx surplus value arises from the control of the instruments of production by the capitalists, and causes the accumulation of capital with the consequences of increasing misery, the casting out of the bourgeoisie into the ranks of the proletariat, the increasing reserve army of unemployed, depressions and crises of ever-increasing intensity, until the capitalist system collapses. According to Veblen, the pecuniary magnates, possessors of the intangible assets, have cornered the technological knowledge of the community through control by modern credit of the instruments of production, and have thereby increased capital, viewed as a pecuniary magnitude. The pecuniary magnitudes of capital are increasingly dissociated from the material welfare of the community, depression becomes normal, and the ordinary business-men are placed in the same relation to the great captain as the workmen are to the ordinary businessmen. Veblen places more emphasis on the age-long experience of mankind than on the comprehensive standardised machine process of his earlier work. According to Veblen the idleness of plants enforced by modern investment has an unfavourable effect on technology which is far more serious than the actual amount of idleness produced or the elimination of human beings, since the restriction in population reduces the common fund of knowledge, which is only to a fractional extent known by any one person, and thus reduces the efficiency of the community.

The subtitle of Veblen's first essay is "The Productivity of Capital Goods." The ancient institutions of ownership, slavery, and landed wealth, he declared, have much the same effect. The effect of the latter two, which are characteristic of mature ownership, was to make the community's industrial efficiency serve the needs of the slave-owners and the land-owners. In modern capitalism the predominant feature is the owner-ship of industrial capital and the consequent strategic advantage for en-grossing the community's livelihood. This institution of capitalism is so much a matter of prevailing common sense that "we find ourselves hesi-tating between denying its existence, and affirming it to be a fact of nature antecedent to all human institutions."

The single-tax argument should logically be pushed to the conclusion that "all land values and land productivity, including the 'original and indestructible powers of the soil,' are a function of the state of the in-dustrial arts." The preferred status of the landlord, as a claimant of the net product, consists in his legal right, whether, how far, and in what way men shall put this technological scheme into effect in those aspects of it which involve his piece of land. This concept of the unearned incre-ment can be applied to capital goods in general. The productivity of the instrument or that of the maker is a function of the immaterial equipment, which is the outcome of the community's age-long experience.

The characteristic trait of capitalism, from the technological point of view, is the fact that the pursuit of industry requires a larger unit of equipment than one individual can achieve by his own labour, and larger than one person can make use of. The required equipment is held exclusively by the capitalist employer. In the last analysis gains and the consequent accumulations of capital arise from "bargaining between those who own (or control) industrial wealth and those whose work turns this wealth to account in productive industry." The capitalist employer characteristically possesses business knowledge, but this knowledge is useless for industry. On the other hand, the efficiency of the control exercised by the engineer or "whatever term may be used to designate the technological expert who controls and correlates the productive processes—this workmanlike efficiency determines how far the given material equipment is effectually to be rated as 'capital goods.' " This technological knowledge is turned not to the advantage of its bearers, but to the profit of the capitalist employers, minus the wage which the working population is able to demand. From the point of view of the employer wages can be reduced to their most economical basis by consolidating all material assets under one business control. It is an open question whether the working community would be better off in this state or in the current approximation to it, where competitive bidding stills exists. The only factor that prevents a neater adjustment to the minimum of subsistence—which would represent the *de facto* monopolisation of the immaterial equipment by the owners of the material wealth—is the opportunity which still exists for a small fraction of the community, such as those occupied with housekeeping routine, to " 'pick up a living,' more or less precarious," without recourse to large-scale industry.

The second essay, subtitled "Investment, Intangible Assets, and the Pecuniary Magnate," described the process by which the finished business state is being achieved. Under modern investment the pecuniary, differential, advantage of capitalist managers takes precedence over the economic advantage of the community. In modern business the avoidance of pecuniary losses and of pecuniary wastes and the achievement of pecuniary savings take the form of intentional idleness of plant and a waste of the community's goods and efforts. These strategic advantages and obstructive tactics are fully capitalised in intangible assets. The comprehensive principle of modern investment is the charging of "all the traffic can bear," or raising prices and thus increasing the net gain of business by limiting the supply of goods and, in effect, impoverishing human life. The recurrence of hard times is evidence of the effective inhibition of industry resulting from the ownership of capital under the modern price system, "the rule of pecuniary standards and management. The capitalisation of inefficiency, through the control of invested funds, is exemplified in advertising, armaments, saloons, gambling houses, and houses of prostitution, which "simply take their stand on the (institutionally sacred) 'accomplished fact' of invested wealth."

Modern capital is based on intangible assets. These are capitalisations of differential advantages, as against other persons and in the last analysis as against the community at large. Such advantages constitute modern pecuniary gain, but they cost the community more than is received by their beneficiaries, the captains of finance. Capitalisation of the rental value of land might be roughly taken as the measure of its current serviceability as an item of material equipment, but promoters and real-estate agents, in assuring prospective buyers of an increased value, will increase the selling price of this "tangible" asset. Thus capitalised rental capacity is in the nature of an intangible asset, a preferential or monopolistic claim to income without productive service from the effective owners. The effective ownership of means of production in sufficient amount to control the market, whether for purchase (as of material or labour) or for sale (as of marketable goods or services), gives rise to the intangible assets which are the cornerstone of modern profits. In the final sales transaction, however, the merchantable goods are valued by the consumer not as assets signifying an instrument of profit, but as means of livelihood. Depressions are the result of this discrepancy in valuation. Eventually these consumer transactions act as a check on the capitalisation of values.

The analysis of intangible assets was only a preliminary to Veblen's discussion of the pecuniary magnate. In modern business the most important sources of income are not capitalisable, but they yield a legitimate business income. In the prevailing common sense, reflecting the "technologically obsolete" pre-capitalistic stage, this income is presumed to be legitimate wages of superintendence, entrepreneur's profit. In fact after the theorist has satisfied himself that such income-streams are traceable to a personal source, it has even been attempted, as by Fisher for example, to rate the recipients themselves as "capital." Actually the great gains of the pecuniary magnates are due to their managerial ability in financial operations, to the strategic position of their wealth, as in underwriting and the like. These men are not notable for any productive sagacity and initiative, as the manœuvres of the United States Steel Corporation with Carnegie, and the pettifogging tactics of Standard Oil so well indicate. But the assets used in these operations of high finance are already earning a return. In contrast to the old-fashioned industrial business, dependent on the causal sequence of the industrial process, there is in this modern financing no definite time relation between the underlying assets and the gains they produce. In the long run these great gains are drawn from the products of industrial efficiency, and there is a time relation between them only in the sense that a day of reckoning, in the form of a crisis and depression, must eventually be faced. Proximately, however, these great gains are achieved at the expense of other businessmen through an increase of nominal capital "based on a (transient) advantage inuring to the particular concern whose capitalisation is augmented." Since there is no corresponding increase in the community's material wealth, the increased capitalisation amounts to a redistribution of wealth, a subtraction from the community at large. Thus these gains are a "tax on commonplace business enterprise, in much the same manner and with much the like effect as the gains of commonplace business (ordinary profits and interest) are a tax on industry."

The capitalistic efficiency of the capitalist employer lies in his ability, through suitable bargaining, to force the industrial community to surrender to him as much of its product as is in excess of its requirements for a livelihood. His fortunes are dependent on the market, the conjunctures of purchases and sales, and his aim is to secure some intangible asset, some monopoly value. The pecuniary magnate, however, is superior to the market. By the mobility of his investments, he can, as profits decide, make or mar its conjunctures of advantageous purchase and sale of goods. His capital can be characterised as capital at large, as distinct from capital invested in a given industrial enterprise. The capitalist employer becomes an instrumentality of extraction and transmission of revenue from the community to the pecuniary magnate, who, in the ideal case, would leave him only enough to induce him to continue in business. It should logically result that the pecuniary magnate's "relation to business at large will be capitalised in some form of intangible assets after the manner in which the monopoly advantage of an ordinary 'trust' is now capitalised." But this development would have only "a speculative interest . . . for the working classes, who own nothing to speak of and whose only dependence is their technological efficiency, which has ceased to be their own" since it "is already virtually engrossed by the capitalist employer's ownership."

Veblen's views on the nature of capital gave the organising principles for his paper, "The Evolution of the Scientific Point of View," delivered at the University of California Kosmos Club, of which Mitchell was secretary. In this essay, as elsewhere, Veblen seems to use the concept of evolution in the sense of necessary growth or adaptation to the modern material exigencies. The unavowed postulate of the modern scientist is consecutive change, and thus every goal of research is necessarily only a point of departure, every term transitional. This concept of change is "an unproven and unprovable postulate," a metaphysical preconception, just as the ideal of the general material welfare is a preconception. In a footnote which is itself a minor essay Veblen ostensibly attacked those who, like Loeb, deny the concept of causation and contend that there is only an idle concomitance of variations, a mathematical formulation suggesting the logic of sensation-empiricism. The footnote is more fundamentally concerned, however, with the role of causation in modern economic life, and with the creative part that can be played in the modern economic system by the scientist or the master technician, if he but recognised his role. "The shrewd insight and bold initiative" of the great scientist must be tested by experiments. The great advance in science has been made by assuming the metaphysical postulate that action can take place only by contact, not at a distance, just as in modern industry the advance is by the growth of the technological experience through the contact of the working community with the material processes. "It is only the 'occult' . . . 'Sciences,'" such as those of modern business, "that can dispense with this metaphysical postulate and take recourse to 'absent treatment.'" Thus, since science cannot avoid a certain amount of "animism" in its organising principles, there must be some form of personal control. The question is whether this control is to be that of the technician, with his postulate of consecutive change, or that of the pecuniary magnates, with their postulate of supernatural justification for their arts of exploitation.

Returning to his main argument, Veblen declared that in the last analysis science and the scientific point of view are by-products of cultural growth, and cultural growth is the adaptation of men's habits of thought to the material exigencies of the community. Primitive systems of knowledge are construed along thoroughgoing animistic lines, but there prevails also a divergent, obscurer, matter-of-fact body of knowledge which is concerned with the material means of life. The evolution of the scientific attitude has involved a shifting from the first to the second of these incompatible points of view.

The higher learning of the barbarian culture has more room for "profoundly picturesque speculation" than for matter-of-fact generalisations. Its "excursions are not so immediately and harshly checked by material facts"; that is, it is not "guided, undisguised and directly, by the habitual material (industrial) occupations. The fabric of institutions intervenes between the material exigencies of life and the speculative scheme of things," and thus the latter is formed in the image of the prevailing cultural scheme of status, coercion, and differential authority. The discipline of such institutions as slavery, ownership, or royalty is not the same for the master as for the serf. If the scheme of institutions is in the hands of one class engrossed in maintaining the prevailing law and order, and the workmanlike activities are in the hands of a class to whom the maintenance of law and order "is at the best a wearisome tribulation," a considerable discrepancy arises between the two systems of knowledge. The workaday generalisations fall into deeper obscurity, mirroring the depth of indignity to which workmanlike efficiency falls under such a barbarian scheme, and they only remotely check the current speculative scheme. Reality and fact become widely dissociated from each other. But if the institutional fabric, the community's scheme of life, changes so that the habitual interest of the people is centred on the immediate material relations of men to brute actualities, then the discrepancy is not so great between the speculative realm and workaday generalisation of fact, and the spirit of modern science has a chance to rise.

Matter-of-fact theories are beneath the dignity of the ancient sciences, with their intangible realities of status. But the modern machine technology has created new scientific preconceptions. "These machine-made preconceptions of modern science, being habits of thoughts induced by the machine technology in industry and in daily life, have . . . most consistently affected the material sciences." They threaten the disappearance of the ancient preconceptions of differential reality, creative causation, invidious merit. In such disciplines as economics, however, which lie far afield from the technological domain, it is an open question whether the metaphysics of the machine technology will supersede the prevailing metaphysics of the code of honour.

The influence on economic thought of this metaphysics of the code of honour was elaborated by Veblen in an article on "The Limitations of Marginal Utility," published in *The Journal of Political Economy*. In the comparable essays, "Why Is Economics Not an Evolutionary Science?" and "The Preconceptions of Economic Science," his inquiry was phrased in terms of the difference between the animistic and the evolutionary, matter-of-fact points of view; now, a decade later, it is phrased in terms of a contrast between efficient and sufficient reason. His inquiry was now, in Hegelian language, whether the fact that the prevailing financial system of control exists is sufficient reason or justifiable ground for its existence, as is presumed by conventional economic thought.

Marginal utility economics becomes for Veblen the comprehensive term for prevailing economic thought, just as differential gain became his comprehensive term for characteristic modern business enterprise. The practitioners of marginal utility economics are not concerned, as are modern scientists, with the growth of the industrial arts in the sense of their adaptation and needs; in other words, marginal utility economics has nothing to say about the growth of modern business enterprise. The institutional facts of modern capitalism and modern industry are "taken for granted, denied, or explained away." The preconceptions of economic science themselves represent "a certain institutional situation, the substantial feature of which is the natural right of ownership," and the hedonistic calculus is a wise adaptation to the demands of the main chance. But these postulates give the point of view of sufficient reason rather than efficient cause. Veblen presents the contrast as if it were one between the activities of the pecuniary magnate and the requirements of material circumstances. In their consequences the two are incompatible. "The relation of sufficient reason runs by way of the interested discrimination, the forethought of an agent who takes thought of the future and guides his present activity by regard for this future." It "runs only from the (apprehended) future into the present, and it is solely of a subjective, personal . . . character and force; while the relation of cause and effect runs in the contrary direction, and it is solely an objective, impersonal, materialistic character and force."

The principles of marginal utility, however, "commend themselves to all serious and uncritical persons at the first glance. They are principles of action which underlie the current business-like scheme of economic life, and as such, as practical grounds of conduct, they are not to be called into question without questioning the existing law and order. . . . Men order their lives by these principles and practically entertain no question of their stability and finality. That is what is meant by calling them institutions," or methods of action arrived at by habituation and convention and agreed upon. But modern science, instead of assuming their stability, makes a causal, that is, a genetic inquiry into their relation to the other phases of culture, namely the material exigencies of life. The basis of "hedonistic discrimination" is property, ownership, "conceived to be given in its finished (nineteenth-century) scope and force." But Veblen creates a certain confusion by using "hedonism" now in a sense almost contradictory to his previous formal use of the term. Modern business traffic, in which pecuniary gain is not to be identified with the sensations of consumption or with material serviceability, he now describes as unhedonistic. Hedonist economists refuse to realise that extraneous pecuniary aims control the exigencies of life for the community.

Productive efficiency and distributive gain are measured in terms of pecuniary serviceability; that is, the institution of price accountancy, the institution of property or money values, "dominates the current common sense in its appreciation and rating" of the "non-pecuniary ramifications of modern culture," although it is an extraneous standard of excellence. Hedonist economists may admit upon reflection that preoccupation with extraneous commercial interests has "commercialised" the rest of modern life, namely material exigencies, but the commercialisation of commerce is not conceded. "Business transactions, and computations in pecuniary terms, such as loans, discounts, and capitalisation, are without hesitation converted into terms of hedonistic utility, conversely."

The run of the facts of modern business shows that increases in capitalisation, that is, credit extensions tending to inflate credit, raise prices, and overstock markets, occur without a visible basis in the material items of the state of the industrial arts or in the sensations of consumption, to which hedonistic theory reduces all phenomena. The pecuniary magnate seeks not consumable goods or the sensations of consumption, but accumulations of wealth in excess of the limits of practicable consumption. He does not intend to convert this wealth by a final transaction into consumable goods or sensations of consumption. But the hedonists explain away these characteristic pecuniary phenomena, out of which "the conjunctures of business life arise and run their course of felicity and devastation," as due to aberrations and faulty logic on the part of the modern businessman. Thus the entire money economy, with all its machinery of credit, disappears into a refined system of barter culminating in a maximum of pleasurable sensations of consumption.

Veblen's last article at Stanford, "Christian Morals and the Competitive System," is almost suggestive of *The Communist Manifesto* and its ringing close. The instinct of workmanship is here translated into an ethical norm of conduct, of brotherly love or mutual aid. The setting is ostensibly the period of devastation and subjection by imperial Rome, but the article reads more like a description of the period of depression after the panic of 1907. Veblen compares the morals of Christianity and those of competition, emphasising again the incompatibility between material welfare and investment for profit. The two kinds of morals are incompatible codes of conduct, institutional by-products of two different cultural situations, and the question is which one will decay.

The fundamental principles of Christian morals, said Veblen, are first, brotherly love and mutual service, and second, non-resistance or humility. The first is basic, an inherited trait. It antedates Christianity and is characteristic of the peaceable savage culture. "When the pressure of conventionality is removed or relieved," the savage heritage "springs eternal." It is doubtless because this principle of conduct is inherited that it has persisted "even in later times, when the external conditions have not visibly favoured or called for its exercise." The second principle, non-resistance or humility, is not altogether compatible with the life of a free man, and is not so firmly rooted among free peoples. It is the less humane principle, and arises from the discipline of coercion under imperial masters. The subject peoples, having been ground down by their masters, and having no rights which the latter were forced to respect, acquired the conviction that non-resistance to the exactions of their masters, "was the chief of virtues if not the whole duty of man." Neither this trait nor that of mutual service is characteristic of the master classes.

The lower classes, as a result of their experience of "Roman devastation and punishment-at-large," lost whatever class distinctions and privileges they had enjoyed and found themselves in a uniform state of subjection, "in which one class or individual had little to gain at the cost of another, and in which . . . each and all obviously needed the succour of all the rest." The conventional distinctions inherited from the past were fictitious and meaningless in the current situation. "The pride of caste and all the principles of differential dignity and honour fell away, and left mankind naked and unashamed and free to follow the promptings of hereditary savage human nature." This principle of mutual service "is for ever reasserting itself in economic matters, in the impulsive approval of whatever conduct is serviceable to the common good and in the disapproval of disserviceable conduct even within the limits of legality and natural right. It seems, indeed, to be nothing else than a somewhat specialised manifestation of the instinct of workmanship and as such it has the indefeasible vitality that belongs to the hereditary traits of human nature." It is not, however, to be confused with the principle of thrifty charity or pecuniary fair play, which closely resembles the modern business principle of "all the traffic can bear."

From Christian morals in the Roman period Veblen turns to modern business morals, interpreted as an outgrowth of the handicraft era. Under the conditions of handicraft and petty trade, the right of ownership made for equality rather than inequality. The handicraft situation emphasised the workman's creative relation to his product, as well as his responsibility for it and for its serviceability to the common welfare. Honesty was the best policy. The principles of ownership were in close touch with the "ancient human instinct of workmanship which approves mutual aid and serviceability to the common good." But under the machine technology and corporation organisation, with delegated management, credit, and distant markets, there is no longer such a "close and visible touch between the workman and his product, as would persuade men that the product belongs to him by force of an extension of his personality." There is no visible relation between serviceability and modern acquisitive business. The pecuniary principles have lost the sanction afforded by the human propensity for serviceability to the common good. Except, therefore, "for a possible reversion to a cultural situation strongly characterised by ideals of emulation and status, the ancient racial bias embodied in the

Christian principle of brotherhood should logically continue to gain ground at the expense of the pecuniary morals of competitive business."

Veblen had begun work on what he had originally scheduled as his second book, *The Instinct of Workmanship*, but once more his personal affairs led him into difficulties. One of his feminine friends had come to Palo Alto, and, when his friends suggested that her presence might cause trouble, Veblen only replied: "What is one to do if the woman moves in on you?" In December 1909 he was forced to resign. A young woman who had come from the University of Nebraska in 1909 to study under Veblen has said that the greatest disappointment in her student career occurred in January 1910, when Veblen did not reappear to continue his courses. Young met the class on "History of Economic Thought" and said he would teach that course but could not undertake "Economic Factors." "That course," he said, "is taught in no other place and by no other man —it is Dr. Veblen's own course." Veblen might have defended himself, but he refused. His friends on the faculty did not, he felt, stand by him as strongly as they should have. He wrote Katherine Bement Davis, a former student, to believe in him regardless of what she heard.

Veblen applied for a position at various schools. To James Mavor, who was in charge of economics at Toronto, he wrote that he was anxious to secure an appointment there because he wished to compare university conditions in Canada, where there was a strong Scottish influence, with those in the United States. This interest suggests that Veblen had begun revision of his rejected 1904 manuscript on the higher learning. Mavor consulted someone who warned him against Veblen, and as a result the application was not successful. Veblen was a difficult undertaking for any department. His severance from Stanford was of such a kind that it was difficult for other institutions to offer him a position. The only possibility seemed to lie in his securing a research grant from some foundation for a few years. Such organisations as the Carnegie Institution and the Archæological Institute of America often backed anthropological expeditions, and the Pumpelly expedition to Turkestan had achieved some spectacular results. His friends turned to these organisations.

Veblen began writing an ostensibly anthropological paper on "The Mutation Theory, the Blond Race, and the Aryan Culture," which was later published as two separate articles, "The Mutation Theory and the Blond Race" and "The Blond Race and the Aryan Culture." Here the contrast is between Darwinian doctrines and the Mendelian mutation theory. The main postulate of the Mendelian theory is the stability of type, and without such an assumption any ethnological inquiry must degenerate into mere fantasy. But ethnologists have also accepted the incompatible Darwinian doctrine "that racial types vary incontinently

after a progressive fashion, arising through insensible cumulative variations and passing into new specific forms by the same method, under the
Darwinian rule of the selective survival of slight and unstable (non-
typical) variations." On the assumption of stability of type it follows that
these racial types have arisen not by the cumulative acquirement of unstable, non-specific traits, but by mutation or some analogous method, and
this view must find its way into anthropology and "questions of cultural
origins and relationship." "Hence an inquiry into the advent and early
fortunes of the blond stock in Europe will fall, by convenience, under
two distinct but closely related captions: The Origin of the Blond Type,
and The Derivation of the Aryan Culture."

Veblen's fundamental distinction between modern business and the
requirements of the machine process so pervades his thinking that it is
apparent here too in the structure and organisation of his inquiry. Even
the discussions of climate, topography, and language, comparing the
blond race and the Aryan culture, run in the familiar terms of the antithetical institutions of modern economic life. It is as if Aryan speech were
the speech of modern business enterprise; as if Aryan culture were modern
pecuniary culture; as if the triple relationship between the Mediterranean
stock, the Alpine or Aryan which subdued it, and the dolicho-blond, were
comparable to the relationship between the eras of small business, big
business, and the industrial republic; as if the process of Aryanisation
symbolised the growing dominance of business civilisation; and as if
the contrast between Darwinism and mutationism were a contrast between liberalism and revolutionary socialism.

The stable, generic type that underlies modern mankind is now represented as the dolicho-blond. It arises as a mutation from the Mediterranean type, which is a composite of producer and marauder. The Aryan
is a predatory, commercial race intruded upon the blond from outside
Europe. In the diffusion of the pastoral (patriarchal and predatory) institutions of this Homo Alpinus "the language and in a less degree the
domestic and civil usages and ideals bred by the habits of the pastoral
life might of course come to be dissociated from their material or
technological basis and so might be adopted by remoter peoples who
never acquired any large measure of the material culture of the pastoral
nomads whose manner of life had once given rise to these immaterial
features of Aryan civilisation." This is a supposition of "conjectural history," but it is supported by certain considerations. "Insubordination,
which is the substance of free institutions, is incompatible with the prosperous large-scale pastoral culture of the predatory Aryan. The social
structure is an organisation of graded servitude, in which no one but the
overlord is his own master, and almost unavoidably the tribal organisation

of the group becomes eventually a despotic monarchy. The classic Greek and Roman republics seem to have been of this nature, but not the pagan Scandinavian culture. Certain writers have imputed a fighting, class organisation to the Scandinavian culture, by plainly "construing Germanic facts in Roman terms, very much as the Spanish writers of a later day construed Mexican . . . facts in medieval-feudalistic terms." In the migrations the wandering Scandinavian hosts achieved a clan organisation through exposure to warlike discipline, but their "loose-jointed proliferous European paganism" still persists, even after a long period of Aryanisation.

The theory of the European origin of the dolicho-blond is faced by the apparently insurmountable fact that the languages of early Europe are almost universally Aryan, but this can be explained by the trade activities of the Aryan. The language of the people who carry on trade is the language which becomes dominant. Dealing with "many men of varied speech, and carrying their varied stock of trade goods," they will impose their own names for the articles bartered, thereby contributing much to the jargon vocabulary. The intrusive words, which are the names of intrusive facts, "will in so far find their way unhindered into current speech" and displace the indigenous language. The idioms of Aryan speech were in their beginnings "little else than crude vocabularies covering the commonest objects and most tangible relations. . . . By time-long use and wont the uncouth strings of vocables whereby the beginners of these languages sought to express themselves have been worked down through a stupendously elaborate fabric of prefixes, infixes, and suffixes, etc., etc., to the tactically and phonetically unexceptionable inflected languages of the Aryan family as they stood at their classical best." The European jargons are not as close to the ideal pattern as are the best Asiatic, which lie "nearer the centre of diffusion of the proto-Aryan speech and technology." Thus Veblen denied the existence of an Indo-European language stock and implied the Sanskrit might have been a trade language, like the modern Chinook pidgin, built up out of odds and ends of existing languages. This theory, he later confessed, put him at no little variance with the philologists.

After finishing this work Veblen stayed for a time on some property in Idaho. His work was interrupted by an attack of pneumonia, but when he recovered he prepared a memorandum "As to a Proposed Inquiry into Baltic and Cretan Antiquities" and a statement of expenses for such an inquiry, hoping to receive a Carnegie grant to carry it through. "The problem on which my interest in prehistoric matters finally converges is that of the derivation and early growth of those free or popular institutions which have marked off European civilisation at its best from the great civilisations of Asia and Africa." He seems to have considered that the central areas for such free institutions were Crete and the Aegean Mediterranean, and also—since there were trade relations with the north —the Scandinavian shores. "A study of other primitive cultures, remote and not visibly related to this early European civilisation, shows a close correlation between the material (industrial and pecuniary) life of any given people and their civic, domestic, and religious scheme of life; the myths and the religious cult reflect the character of these other—especially the economic and domestic—institutions in a pecularly naïve and truthful manner." Evidence of the technological bent which is peculiarly characteristic of western civilisation runs very far back in the North Sea-Baltic culture, and later explorations in Crete and its cultural dependencies suggest that the prehistoric Aegean culture possessed a similar aptitude for technological efficiency. The problem that interested Veblen was what constitutes "the nature and force of the correlation, if any, between this peculiar development of technological efficiency and the early growth and character of that scheme of free institutions which today is as characteristic a trait of western civilisation as is its pre-eminence in point of technological efficiency." It was desirable, he said, that such an inquiry be pursued co-operatively, since it is a most common trait of scientists, "particularly when occupied with matter that is in any degree novel and growing, that they know and are willing to impart many things that are not primarily involved in the direct line of their own inquiry and many things, too, to which they may not be ready to commit themselves in print."

Veblen estimated that the expedition would take three years and that the expenses would be between $16,000 and $20,000. As to his own remuneration, he wrote: "Since my retirement from university work leaves me without an income, some provision of that character would necessarily be involved in my taking up this inquiry. I am accustomed to a salary of $3,000, but in this matter, I shall, of course, be glad to defer entirely to the discretion of the Executive Committee."

Veblen sent the article and statement of the project to President Jordan, who forwarded them, with a letter of his own, to the Carnegie Institution at Washington. He wrote that Veblen was "one of the highest living authorities in certain specialised lines, one being the economic theory, and the other the theory of the origin and development (especially economic development) of primitive man. He wishes to devote his life to the latter type of study, and if possible without the burden of teaching. He resigned his professorship here on January 1, 1910. . . . The details of his giving up teaching can be explained, if necessary. Dr. Veblen is an unworldly sort of man, who is bound up in his scientific studies. He has a mind that, in certain lines of subtlety and keenness of apprehension, has no superior in this country."

There was no lack of letters of recommendation. Allyn Young referred to Veblen's special competence in economic theory and added: "On the basis of a somewhat varied academic experience I feel no hesitation in saying that Veblen is the most gifted man whom I have known. His scholarship is extraordinary, both in range and thoroughness. Moreover, he carries it lightly—he has none of the marks or methods of the pedant. . . . Professor Taussig of Harvard recently wrote me that he regarded Veblen as one of the very few men who have given distinction to American work in the field of economics. . . . I regret in many ways that Veblen expects to abandon the teacher's profession, even temporarily. He has never been very successful in dealing with large numbers of under-graduates, and has never been a good 'drillmaster.' But on the students of adequate preparation and range of interests who have come under his influence he has had an extraordinary influence, and the same is true with reference to those of his colleagues who have had the fortune to know him at all intimately. . . ."

Taussig wrote: "I am able to say . . . without hesitation that Profes-sor Veblen is a brilliant and many-sided scholar. His work has covered not only Economics, but has crossed the border line into Sociology. It has been original and stimulating. A brother economist, in whose judgment I have much confidence, once remarked to me in conversation that Veblen came as near to being a genius as any economist we have; and I am in-clined to think that the remark was just. Any man whose views run out-side the beaten track is accused of being radical, and of lacking sound judgment. Such accusations have been brought against Veblen. I am free to say that on some topics I myself am of the opinion that Veblen has not shown sound judgment. But I believe his work has been of very high order indeed, and amply deserves the encouragement of such a body as the Carnegie Institution."

Davenport, who was then head of the department of economics at the University of Missouri, expressed as usual his high admiration and added that "the University of Missouri has for some time been pressing for Professor Veblen's promise to give next year his course here upon the economic factors of civilisation." Starr and Laughlin also wrote in Veb-len's behalf. Mitchell secured a recommendation from David Barrows, and Rolfe secured one from Jameson, who was now director of the de-partment of historical research in the Carnegie Institution.

At the same time a similar move was made to enlist the interest of the Archæological Institute of America. Camp secured the aid of the Stanford professor of Latin, H.R. Fairclough, a former president of the institute,

and of Warren Gregory, a leading San Francisco attorney. But nothing
came of either plan. Archæologists who were consulted were not impressed. At first the Carnegie officials showed some interest, and Veblen
was immensely pleased over the possibilities of the trip, but later they
announced that, although they thought well of the project, no funds
were available for its execution. Veblen felt that President Jordan had
not supported him as he might have.

But Davenport came to his rescue. Davenport had nothing of the cosmopolitan learning of Veblen, and in almost every fundamental respect
he was a radically different type of person, but Veblen had been his
teacher and was, he felt, a great intellectual force. Despite the danger,
risks, and conventional inhibitions, Davenport remained true to his intellectual conscience and persuaded President A. Ross Hill to bring Veblen to the University of Missouri. Veblen considered Davenport the
"salt of the earth."

Late in 1910 Veblen departed for Columbia, Missouri, to begin teaching in February 1911. He gave Camp his varied assortment of books, including Marx's *Capital*, the nineteen volumes of the Industrial Commission Report, a set of Spencer, and volumes of the ethnological reports
of the Smithsonian Institution, around which so much of his work had
revolved. It was the close of one cycle of his life, the beginning of another
one more mature. The era of articles for the professional journals was
over, and the unfolding of the credit economy was demanding a less
roundabout analysis.

CHAPTER XVII

THE great outcry against "big business" was reaching the close of another phase. In 1911 the House of Representatives appointed a committee to investigate the United States Steel Corporation. The Bureau of Corporations made a report on this "greatest industrial concern in the United States . . . the most conspicuous example of the modern corporate organisation of great business," maintaining that the formation of this holding company arose from attempts to prevent a threatened steel war and to achieve great profits through the flotation of securities. Over half its original capitalisation of $1,400,000,000 was "water," that is, based on intangible merger factors. Its iron ore reserves were valued by the bureau at $100,000,000 whereas the corporation valued them at $700,000,000. The bureau report stated that the ore reserves, which were the dominant factors in the steel industry, were "made to stand for the excess of capitalisation over value of tangible assets." Of the stock, over $150,000,000 "was issued either directly or indirectly (through exchange) for mere promotion or underwriting concerns." From 1901 to 1910 the average rate of profits on the tangible value of the investment was twelve percent, and this would be considerably increased if allowance were made for the fixed rate of approximately five percent interest on bonds. The corporation's lease of Hill's enormous ore properties, "with an unprecedentedly high rate of royalty and other onerous conditions, is a striking instance of the policy of the corporation to maintain a high degree of control of ore." [1]

The majority report of the investigating committee, after lengthy hearings, declared that the "daring financiers" used the "steel industry as basis for the fabrication of 'bonds,' not billets," by a "monotonous repetition of the old process of the inflation and exchange of securities." They practically paid themselves out of the securities, "which were so lavishly issued," in actual disregard of "the rights of the stockholders or the welfare of the industry." The interests in control derived a "greater profit from their operations in the stock market than the manufacture of steel." "Gary dinners" and similar arrangements helped to prevent price competition.

Unionisation was opposed, according to the executive records of the corporation, and a study of the United States Commissioner of Labour showed that of the 153,000 employees in the blast furnaces, steel works, and rolling mills, 50,000 customarily worked seven days a week, and twenty percent of them worked eighty-four hours or more a week, which meant a twelve-hour day, including Sunday. Labour conditions in the company's plants were far below "the American standard of living among labourers in our country. Some of the details are revolting, both as to sanitary and moral conditions." The wages paid, assuming constant employment and the ordinary family as the basis, "are barely enough to provide subsistence."

The corporation made heavy contributions to political parties, particularly for the purpose of maintaining the protective tariff against competing items. The report criticised most severely the "inside management," and the record is full of "the pernicious effect sometimes upon the Steel Corporation itself, and more often upon the public generally, of this interlocking of directorates." Specific instances of abuses directly traceable to the community of interest between a few powerful individuals in control of a great number of corporations were the "enormous sums" paid in the purchase of various properties, rebates on purchases to Standard Oil Company, "the purchase of supplies by the International Harvester Company and the American Tin Company at greatly reduced rates, the complicated web of agreements in restraint of competition, low costs in sliding-scale contracts," the huge sums paid Frick and others for certain properties, and the "inordinate sums" paid to the promoters and underwriters. The power wielded by the directors was to be measured not only by the size of the corporation itself, but by the ramifications of the far-reaching interests of its directors and by its control, amounting in effect to monopoly powers, in banking, transportation, and manufacturing. "The holding company is not an evolution, it is an abuse of corporate power." "The enormous earnings of the Steel Corporation are not due to a degree of integration or efficiency not possessed by its competitors, but to the ownership of ore reserves out of all proportion to its output or requirements and to the control and operation of common carriers, and to concessions in the nature of rebates, obtained from other railroads through inequitable divisions of rates and inordinate terminal allowances."

Carnegie and Gary suggested federal government control, but the majority report declared for full publicity of the operation of the Steel Corporation and similar organisations, for enforcement of the law against the use of "cunning devices" to secure unfair advantages over competitors, and for the prevention of an industrial concern's owning an interstate carrier.[2] The Standard Oil Company of New Jersey, the master holding company, was dissolved by the Supreme Court in 1911, but the court laid down the rule of reason in judging combinations. The effect of the dissolution was more formal than substantial, since the chief stockholders received proportionate shares in the underlying concerns, and continued their concentrated control.[3]

The election of Wilson seemed to mean a change, although in his "devout faith in the beneficence of competition," according to Witt Bowden, a writer of American industrial history, "there was something suggestive of the metaphysical preconceptions of the classical economists, which Veblen delighted to talk about in words of learned length if not of thundering sound."[4] The New Freedom drew a distinction between "big business" which was justified, and the trust, and thus followed in the traditions and legal distinctions of Presidents Roosevelt and Taft.

In 1911 Loeb, in defending "the mechanistic conception of life," paid tribute to the forces that Veblen contrasted with "big business": "We are active, because we are compelled to be so by processes in our central nervous system; and as long as human beings are not economic slaves, the instinct of successful work or workmanship determines the direction of their action. The mother loves and cares for her children . . . because the instinct of taking care of the young is inherited just as distinctly as the morphological characters of the female body. We seek and enjoy the fellowship of human beings because hereditary conditions compel us to do so. We struggle for justice and truth since we are instinctively compelled to see our fellow-beings happy. Economic, social, and political conditions, or ignorance and superstition, may warp and inhibit the inherited instincts and thus create a civilisation with a faulty or low development of ethics. Individual mutants may arise in which one or the other desirable instinct is lost, just as individual mutants without pigment may arise in animals; and the offspring of such mutants may, if numerous enough, lower the ethical status of a community. Not only is the mechanistic conception of life compatible with ethics, it seems the only conception of life which can lead to an understanding of the source of ethics."[5]

Veblen's Chicago students began paying back their intellectual debts. Hoxie had now realised that Veblen's distinction between industrial and pecuniary employments was a guiding principle, not an explanation, and that Veblen's apparently methodological criticisms of academic economics were something more vital than the mere charge that received economics is unconscious apologetics for things as they are. Thus he turned to a more effective examination of labour, in terms of the spirit of workmen's organisations, of workmen's ideals and aspirations under the pervasiveness of business principles. Mitchell was diverted to the study of business cycles, partly by Veblen's paper on "Industrial and Pecuniary Employments," and in 1913 published the outcome of his studies, based on the principle that pecuniary discretion or profits is an end in itself in modern economic life. The money economy was beginning to be examined as such, instead of as a refined system of barter.

Veblen continually asked Ellen Rolfe to secure a divorce so that his position would be less precarious, but she always felt he would come back to her. In January 1911 she wrote to a friend: "He now once more wishes me to get a divorce. The situation is still so complicated that I don't know which way to turn." She owned a number of houses and her Oregon timber claim was worth $4000, but she complained that she was very poor and had received nothing from Veblen for years. Within a year of this letter she relented, however. "After months of parleying back and forth," she wrote, "I was finally divorced in fifteen minutes and before three men only, on charges of non-support!!! . . . What a horrible rupture divorce is! Incredible! . . . Mr. Veblen through his part of the bargain is to furnish me with $25.00 a month, probably will not do it." President Hill wrote President Jordan about Veblen, and Jordan replied that he saw no reason why Veblen should not be retained since he was now divorced and could straighten out his matrimonial difficulties.

In 1914 Veblen married Anne Fessenden Bradley, a divorcee, whom he had known in Chicago and California. A former student who was devoted to Veblen felt very certain that the latter did not wish to marry, and tried to help him to avoid it, but after he had with difficulty arranged what seemed a satisfactory solution Veblen informed him that he was old enough to take care of his personal affairs himself and that he intended to be married immediately. The Veblen family felt that "only trouble has come from marriage outside of our people."

Mrs. Veblen took excellent care of Veblen, did all his typing, washed all the laundry, made clothes for her children. Some acquaintances marvelled that this "amorous little wife and mother should mate with such a dry quizzical man." One student, who recalled her as a quiet little mouse, said: "I remember distinctly that several times we laughed about the fact that he had married a woman who was apparently not high brow, and we simply passed it off with the comment that in matrimony there was no accounting for tastes." She was intent on having a child by Veblen, but there was no heir. Mrs. Veblen was a radical, according to a neighbour, but of a type precisely opposite to that of Veblen, "impatient, explosive, and very doctrinaire. She was immensely attracted by the thought of the movement and sense of progress involved in violent destruction, the clearing out of the way of what she hated, so that rebuilding could take place on a clear site." She would argue the merits of socialism with other faculty wives. Veblen would become bored with these discussions, and would remark that the disputants could find enough books in the library to prove either side of the argument.

Mrs. Veblen brought up her two daughters in accordance with what she read literally in *The Theory of the Leisure Class*. The children wore long dresses while the fashion was short ones. A neighbour has said: "I wonder if he could not see how mistakenly their mother brought them up. She was very indignant once because someone said to her, I think of your girls as little quiet mice. Nevertheless it was a fair comment and while it was an unintended, it was certainly a result of her training. She had no mercy on them as children who ought to be allowed to live in and enjoy the world as it is, and be taught to criticise it later when they have more developed minds. Doctrinaire persons are often unconsciously cruel and I felt that Mrs. Veblen was so, in certain respects, to her children. Her personal affection was great, but she simply could not understand and would certainly not have admitted children's need for being allowed to enjoy uncritically when they are young." Veblen was blamed because it was felt that some of Mrs. Veblen's tactics were due to her feeling that the great man must have absolute quiet. The children were enrolled in the university demonstration school, but they were likely not to arrive until eleven o'clock or even until the afternoon. The director spoke to the children, but it had no effect, and finally he sent Veblen a note saying that he could not have the school discipline demoralised. No notice was taken of the note. The director sent a letter saying that unless the girls came on time they would have to be withdrawn. Veblen answered that he felt the children must have all possible rest and sleep and that he was unwilling to waken them in the mornings.

Ellen Rolfe, in a letter to a friend telling of some business deals, said: "Have never received a cent of help since divorce, though was awarded alimony. Such is men's gratitude." She knew Veblen had married and she declared: "I do not give him one thought."

For a time before his marriage Veblen lived with the Davenports. He occupied a tent in the basement and the entrance was through a window. One year he stayed with the Stewarts, and there he had a carpentry shop, where he built furniture and other things. His pen was one of his own construction. Davenport tells of Veblen doing such things as taking the clock apart to see how it worked. After his marriage Veblen set up his own establishment. He made nearly all the furniture himself, out of dry-goods boxes which he covered with burlap. The "chairs" were hard and they lacked backs, but they were not unsuited to a hardy product of pioneer conditions. The only expensive thing in the house was Veblen's cigarettes, which cost $3.50 a hundred, but these were supplied him by Max Handman, a student and colleague. Veblen refused to have a telephone in the house. He once wrote that the telephone not only has the drawbacks of the typewriter, which "has appreciably more than doubled the volume of correspondence necessary to carry on a given volume of business and quadrupled the necessary cost of such correspondence," but in addition the telephone "involves a very appreciable nervous strain and its ubiquitous presence conduces to an unremitting nervous tension and unrest wherever it goes." [6]

Veblen was convinced that the time of women in the home is too much taken up with household duties. He had a theory that if the work were properly organised it would not take more than an hour a day, thus leaving ample time for the housewife to have a career if she chose. In his house the ceremony of making beds was considered a useless expenditure of energy, and the covers were merely turned down over the foot so that they could be easily drawn up at night. Dishes were washed only when the total supply was exhausted. They were stacked in a tub, and when all of them had been used the hose was turned on, and after the water had been drained off they were allowed to dry by themselves. Veblen also advocated the making of clothes out of paper.

Veblen's ill health was now more aggravated. He was very susceptible to colds, and they were of such severity that he had to stay in bed. His wife believed that his delicate health was the result of an overdose of calomel which he had taken sometime in his early thirties.

Columbia was the first country town where Veblen had stayed for any length of time, and it was abhorrent to him. The local Chamber of Commerce offered a prize for a slogan for the town, and Veblen told Walter Stewart, a student and colleague, that it ought to be described as a woodpecker hole of town, to which he later added, "in a rotten stump called Missouri." In discussing the nature of modern capital in his course on "History of Economic Theory" Veblen compared the early German mercantile and feudal states to Columbia, and the guilds to the commercial club. The only difference between them, he said, was that the guilds did not have a printing press.

During his entire stay of seven years at the University of Missouri Veblen's rank was that of lecturer, and his appointment had to be renewed annually. Every year Mrs. Veblen was greatly worried when the time came for the renewal of his appointment. As against his Stanford salary of $3000 he received here $1920 in 1913 and $2400 in 1917.[7]

The university atmosphere was not to Veblen's liking. When he ate in the faculty dining-room, he usually left the table promptly after he had finished. He considered President Hill the best college president he knew, but declared that the best of men after ten years as president become highly undesirable characters. Once in class he referred to President Jordan as a pseudo-scientist but, when a student criticised Jordan after he became Chancellor, Veblen remarked that the university had not yet improved upon him.

Veblen's faculty position for the greater and latter part of his stay was in the School of Commerce, of which Davenport was dean. The catalogue read: "Its aim is to equip students with a thorough knowledge of the general principles of business, to prepare them for the investigation and mastery of the practical organisation and administration of any business, not to train them for particular lines of business." Its curriculum "is especially intended for those students who are looking forward to (1) a career in some one or other line of business, or (2) teaching in the field of economics or commerce, or (3) secretarial or governmental or public commission work." [7] The curriculum included Veblen's courses on "Corporation Finance," "Trusts and Combinations," "Economic Factors in Civilisation," and "History of Economics."

Class attendance was a very important matter at Missouri, and a student absent more than a certain number of times automatically suffered a reduction in his grade. The supervision of examinations was also supposed to be strict. But Veblen's laxness concerning grades and attendance was notorious. According to a student, Montgomery Wright, he told his class at the opening session: "The fact that you are here as mature and serious scholars is proof to me that you are deeply interested in this course and that you will not miss a lecture unless absence is unavoidable. The university authorities, however, feel that a roll should be called. I should be the last man to go against constituted authority." He then called the roll of students, each of whom was listed on a separate card. When two or three failed to respond he looked up in extreme surprise and placed their cards at the farthest corner of his table. The others were placed with exaggerated care in front of him. "Now the roll is called," he announced. "In this course we shall first turn our attention . . ." and as he continued he picked up the two piles of cards and shuffled them, as if absent-mindedly. Once towards the end of a semester he passed cards to each member of the class and requested that the students enter the number of times they were absent so that he might produce a class roll for the authorities.

At the end of a course he allowed the students to hand in suggestions for examination questions and selected a few at random. He never returned the completed papers; students doubted that he ever read them. On one occasion, after his last lecture for the term, Veblen asked an undergraduate if he were coming the following Tuesday. The student, surprised, answered that he was, that Tuesday was the day of examination.

Handing him the examination questions, Veblen said that if the student would write on the blackboard his answers to the questions it would save him the trouble of coming himself. In most of the courses he never gave an examination, and all the students were given an average grade. Just before examination Veblen would tell his classes: "You know that an examination is scheduled for this class tomorrow. I will be in the classroom at the time scheduled. If any student or students show up for the examination, it will probably be so severe that you could not make a passing grade. If no students show up, all members of the class will be given an 'M,'" the average grade. Usually, even when examinations were given, all the grades were the same.

Veblen's apparent lack of interest in the apparatus of university life was sometimes trying to his students. When Walter J. Shepard was at Missouri, he had a very able but shy student named Vogel, who was also taking a course with Veblen. Shepard asked Vogel how he was getting along with Veblen, and Vogel replied that he was enjoying the course, "but Professor Veblen has confused me with another student by the name of Wolfe and always calls me Wolfe and calls Wolfe Vogel. I am afraid that at the end of the term I shall get Wolfe's grade and Wolfe will get mine." Several times Vogel called Veblen's attention to the confusion but at the end of the term, when Shepard asked him about his grade, he announced: "Well, it was just as I expected; I got Wolfe's grade which was very low, and he got mine." When Vogel applied for a scholarship, the committee noticed that his only low grade was in a course given by Veblen, and asked Veblen about it. The latter answered that they should pay no attention to it. "My grades are like lightning," he drawled. "They are liable to strike anywhere."

Wright, although he had taken sufficient hours of work, needed a higher than average grade in order to graduate, because of the regulations which limited the maximum hours to be taken in any one term for credit. He went to Veblen, who wrote a note to the dean of Arts and Science stating that "I reported Mr. Wright's grade for the second semester in my Economic Factors as 'medium.' I now report an error. It should have been 'superior.'" The dean was annoyed, recalculated the student's grade, and announced, not without a certain satisfaction: "Mr. Wright, you still lack a fraction of a point!" Wright returned to Veblen, who wrote a second note stating that the grade should have been "excellent." Within ten minutes of his first visit to the dean Wright was triumphantly laying the second note on his desk. The dean said: "I can't understand how Dr. Veblen could be so careless," laying his emphasis on the last word. Veblen seems to have told Davenport about this, and at commencement, when Davenport and Veblen passed together, as the ranking members of the School of Commerce, with the students standing at attention, Veblen rolled his eyes sidewise and grinned at Wright; Davenport, towering in dignity in his cap and gown, turned and winked.

One woman wanted to enter Veblen's class in "Economic Factors" because she had heard that he did not want women. She told him her reason when seeking permission. Veblen chuckled and asked her if she belonged to a sorority. She answered that she did not belong to social organizations but was a member of two honorary sororities, and asked him how membership in a sorority concerned his course in economics. "I don't say that I will fail any member of a sorority or fraternity," Veblen replied, "but no member of such an organization has ever yet passed one of my courses." Once when a student asked about bringing her sister to visit the class for the term Veblen answered that it was against the rules but his eyesight was bad.

To be admitted to Veblen's class in "Economic Factors" a student was required to have completed considerable work in history, political science, sociology, economics, and other sciences, to have done better than average work in most of his preparatory courses, and to be recommended to Veblen by the head of a department. The statement of his course on "The History of Economic Thought" contained a note stating that students should correlate it with courses in philosophy, political science, and sociology. Readings suggested were usually found to be two-volume works. Thus Veblen continued the practices he had followed at Chicago and Stanford, and his classes were small.

Some of the students felt that it was Veblen's intolerance of grade seekers that brought about the comedy of the door plate. According to custom a card was placed in the door at the beginning of the term to announce the time of conference periods. Veblen's card one year was worded: "Thorstein Veblen, 10 to 11, Mondays, Wednesdays, and Fridays." It was reported that Veblen was seen making the first change: "10 to 10:30, Mondays, Wednesdays and Fridays." Other changes by his students followed quickly—"10 to 10:10 Mondays, Wednesdays, and Fridays" . . . and at last "10 to 10:05 Mondays." Wright happened to see Veblen glance at the last card and smile, but in the months that followed he never troubled to have a new card slipped into the little glass frame on his door.

Veblen continued to avoid direct participation in political and social affairs. One year Shepard, who at the time did not know Veblen well, ran as an Independent candidate for the Missouri City Council, as representative from the ward which contained the university community. The strong Democratic machine undertook to defeat him, and every possible vote was needed to elect him. One of Veblen's colleagues in the economic department finally persuaded Veblen to vote, arranging to call for him at his home at four o'clock in the afternoon and accompany him to the polls. But at the appointed time Veblen could not be found. He had escaped into the woods and did not return until after the polls were closed.

When Veblen came to Missouri, he was an outstanding figure, almost legendary, and was lionised by a number of the faculty. Charles Elwood, professor of sociology, remarked in class that Missouri University had one of the greatest scholars in the United States, and that if he could write a book of the lasting value and rank of Veblen's *Theory of the Leisure Class* he would consider his scientific endeavours well spent, even if he were to accomplish nothing more. Albert T.E. Olmstead said that Veblen was the biggest man on the campus. A group of lawyers, physicians, and members of the faculty were in the habit of meeting in one another's homes to discuss the relations between the sciences. Veblen was asked to join this group, which came to be called "The Sacred Sixteen" by other faculty members. He stipulated that he would join on condition that he speak only when he felt like it. He would go to meetings and never say a word. Even when Olmstead thought that a certain paper should interest him particularly, Veblen would make no comment. If Veblen did not rise, however, when a meeting was supposedly over, the members knew that he was preparing to talk, and they waited and heard a brilliant analysis or devastating criticism.

Veblen was a puzzle to the faculty here as elsewhere, and to a number of them he seemed to be wearing a mask. Stewart said that Veblen's demeanour gave no inkling that his previous experiences had embittered him. Some of the liberal members felt that Veblen was only an observer, always humorous, never very sympathetic, and usually critical. Olmstead said he gave the impression of a man who would not have been happy anywhere. In the words of Max Meyer, professor of psychology: "He tended to keep his light under a bushel. The time probably was not quite ripe for his teaching. I believe that few students of the university realised that they had a chance to meet in the classroom a teacher who had the genius of looking under the dazzling surface of things and seeing the realities of social life. It is a pity that Veblen never said a word in a faculty meeting and rarely said a few words at the meetings of our social science fraternity, Alpha Pi Zeta, although he attended the latter meetings regularly. But he did open his mouth at these meetings when virtually no one else saw the truth of a new viewpoint presented by someone, and then he defended the new idea."

The relations between Veblen and Davenport were very close, in spite of the fact that intellectually they had little in common. The Davenports showed a kind of brooding protectiveness towards him, and Veblen's stay at Missouri was relatively free from the unpleasant episodes that had marred his careers at Chicago and Stanford. Davenport was a dynamic, argumentative personality, always insisting on immediate answers, and he was a firm adherent of traditional academic economics. Veblen, on the other hand, was slow and deliberate, always sceptical and aware of complexities and implications. On a number of occasions Davenport was seen walking with Veblen to the very door of Veblen's lecture room, eagerly arguing some point at which Veblen was making slow but effective thrusts. Loyal as he was to Veblen, Davenport used to admit in his advanced classes that "Veblen says this and I don't know what he means by it."

Davenport disturbed one student who took him too seriously by remarking: "You students of Veblen don't believe there is any such thing as theory, do you?" It has been said that students would go to Davenport's classes and receive the absolute truth, then to Veblen's classes where it was all explained away, and would finally complain to Davenport that they had been spoiled as theorists. Davenport in solemn glee told Veblen that on the Judgment Day he would have to account to his Maker for having spoiled so many promising theorists. Veblen retorted: "I have written only two books: *The Theory of the Leisure Class* and *The Theory of Business Enterprise*," in each title emphasising the word "theory." Orthodox instructors in the department used to inform students inquiring about Veblen's course in "Economic Factors" that it contained no economics. Though some of Veblen's promising students gave up economics and went into other social sciences, Davenport constantly urged the students in his elementary courses to study with Veblen, insisting that his own work was in some way preliminary to that of Veblen. Davenport said to Shepard that there might be wiser men dead, but there was no wiser man living than Thorstein Veblen, "intellectual magician that he was."

Veblen used Davenport's textbook to illustrate the confusion concerning the nature of capital, declaring that Davenport conceived of capital in two ways, first as productive goods, and second as anything which brings an income. But Veblen commented to John H. Urie, a student who lived with him in 1916–1917, that his outstanding "pupils" were, in order, Mitchell, Davenport, and Hoxie. For his own outstanding teachers he had a strong sense of personal loyalty. He used to dissect Sumner in class, but Sumner seems to have been the only man for whom he expressed, in conversation, a deep and unqualified admiration. He spoke of President Noah Porter's views as obsolete, but at the same time said that he was a great thinker.

One year a professor of rural economics, who had been a treasurer of one of the United States colonial possessions, took Veblen's advanced

course in "Economic Theory," and he and Veblen showed a rather reserved respect for one another's judgment. A student said of Veblen in
this course: "I suspect in our classes he kept up some of the barriers of
his innermost thinking and talked more or less on accepted principles,
and I noticed that he was always wary of what the Professor might
think." Veblen's advanced classes were popular with students from the
Bible College, who tilted with him frequently over the implications of
some of his theories. A number of faculty members also took Veblen's
courses. One of them, Grover C. Hosford of the law faculty, recalls a
street conversation with Veblen in 1911, in which Veblen predicted that
before many years had passed a political economic revolution would
occur in Russia, in which the execution and bloodshed would far exceed
that of the French Revolution. Also at that time he was not at all hopeful
of the continuance of peace, but looked for a European war to start at
any moment.

Two former Stanford students, Camp and Leon Ardzrooni, came to
Missouri to continue their graduate work under Veblen. Bell once more
took the "Economic Factors." It did not make any difference how many
times one took the course, for it was always different. The history department fell into the habit of sending their best students to Veblen's
"Economic Factors," which was considered by some of the historians
as the best history course on the campus.

During the early years Davenport used to invite frequently for supper
four or five of the students who attended his own and Veblen's courses,
and Veblen usually joined them. One of the members of this group,
Dr. Leslie B. Hohman, later of the medical faculty of Johns Hopkins,
writes that, "although we were a rather impudent bunch of youngsters,
I rather think he enjoyed us. When he did not appear, we would frequently go down the basement and rout him out and bring him upstairs
to talk to us. The five of us had a silly secret society to which we initiated
Mr. Veblen but we could never persuade him to wear a pin. I remember
one of the occasions in which we grabbed him and announced that we
wanted to discuss religion. In his humorous and quiet fashion he informed
us that he knew nothing about religion but would be delighted to discuss
theology with us."

There were a number of socialist students in the university at the time,
and they hoped to claim Veblen. But enlightened opinion held that he
certainly was not a Marxian, even though it was beyond question that he
was not orthodox according to the classical tradition in economics. Nevertheless Veblen told Urie that he did not see why his works were not used
more by the socialists as they were "very good argument" for them.

Many readers of Veblen have been irritated by his device of taking some popular word, pouring into it a meaning apparently of his own, and adding it to his vocabulary in his own peculiar sense. He used such words in conversation as well as in his writing. However, the dictionary and etymology were always on Veblen's side.

A shaggy head of hair and a frizzly beard were the most obvious traits of Veblen's general appearance. Students recall him as being slow, sleepy, and very unkempt. His clothes looked like "cast-offs," and if his coat and vest matched it was an unusual achievement; his collar was always several sizes too large. In the small pocket of his vest he carried a watch on a piece of black ribbon, which was pinned to the front of his vest with a large safety pin. His seminar in economic theory he met at home, shod in moccasins. A casual acquaintance, said Shepard, would never have thought that Veblen gave a single thought to his dress and personal appearance, but "Davenport told me that he had a meticulous concern with regard to his wardrobe and that he was particularly discriminating as to his underwear and had a large wardrobe of the finest kind of garments." One student has said that his Vandyke beard, his eyeglasses on a ribbon when spectacles were the usual thing in the faculty, and his excellent quality beaver hat, which was unusual in that part of the country, showed his fastidious tendencies in dress. But when he sat down before his class and comfortably drew up his trouser legs, his sturdy woollen hose was revealed to be held up by equally sturdy safety pins. If the weather were cold and the lecture room seemed chilly, Veblen would sit down wearing his heavy overcoat, a huge woollen muffler wrapped around his neck, a fur cap with its flaps securely tied under his ears, heavy woollen gloves, and, looking around the class, would remark quietly: "If any of you wish to keep on your wraps it will be all right with me." Then he would begin his lecture, apparently oblivious of his wrappings.

One student has said that he looked in wretched health. He was thin to the point of emaciation. His skin was wrinkled and drawn like that of a person both old and ill, and had a gray pallor that was deathly; his dark muffler only enhanced the corpse-like appearance of his face. He talked, walked, and moved his arms and hands in a slow and measured manner that seemed to indicate an utter lack of physical vigour. He would sit at his desk with his eyes closed, occasionally peering out from behind his bushy whiskers to ask a question. It was his habit, said one of his students, "to carefully place his watch on the table in front of him, to seat himself, and with slightly lowered head and low voice, develop his subject . . . seemingly almost forgetting at times the presence of the class."

"I remember," writes C.F. Clayton of the Federal Department of

Agriculture, "the first time I attended one of Veblen's classes. I think it was the course which he gave in Economic Factors of Civilisation. The class was composed of twelve or fifteen persons, all seniors or graduate students. We sat in the conventional arrangement of chairs in front of the instructor's desk. Veblen drifted into the classroom, walked over and seated himself in a kind of huddle behind the instructor's table, drew a watch of ponderous size from his pocket and placed the watch carefully on the table before him. At this action there was a flutter of suppressed amusement from the class, to which Veblen responded with a half-whimsical smile. He then cleared his throat, which was the last distinctly audible sound during the remainder of the class hour. Veblen's lips were perceptibly moving. Evidently he was saying something, but what that something was, it was impossible to tell. He spoke in a sort of monotonous, droning voice, so that it was impossible to distinguish a word at a distance of a few feet from his desk. This procedure was repeated at the second meeting of the class, after which we held a council of war with the following result. When Veblen appeared for his next class, he found the entire class grouped in a semi-circle around his table. A student seated on one end of the half-circle had his knees parked against one end of the table. A student on the other end of the circle had his knees parked against the opposite end of the table, while the student directly in front of Veblen had his knees jammed against the centre of the table opposite to where Veblen sat. The effect of all this was to bring the whole class into a radius of the speaker's voice, which would permit conversation on a level adapted to the most secret, confidential, or intimate discourse. On entering, Veblen met this revised arrangement in the seating of his class with his usual half-whimsical smile, but said nothing. He merely seated himself, parked his watch on the table, and began with his slow, monotonous talk about the Eskimo or some other topic which appeared to be far removed from the life of the present and the problems of western civilisation. I may add that those of us who sat with Veblen and learned to know his thought, ultimately learned that what so often appeared irrelevant to the problem in hand, represented in reality the probing of a remarkable intellect into the roots of our modern civilisation."

A number of students were attracted by the fame of the author of *The Theory of the Leisure Class,* but the half-audible voice and the monotone soon discouraged them. One said that his physical appearance suggested that "we were in for another dry course which stood between us and the coveted diploma." His technique of teaching differed sharply from that of the dynamic Davenport, who emphasised his points by vivid illustrations. Those who took economics as a chore to fulfil the requirements of the curriculum often found Veblen vague, a failure as a lecturer. One student has said he felt that Veblen taught only because it was necessary to earn his living. The lectures seemed disorganised and without system; he seemed to be thinking out his thoughts as he went along, instead of delivering a fully prepared address. He might digress for three days on some subject brought to his mind by a question from a member of the class. Undergraduates usually took him for a "freak" and considered his courses "easy."

A graduate student has said: "What a fund of information he possessed, how widely and how deeply he had read and it seems that his fertile mind added to what he read rather than forgot any of it." Myron Watkins, expressing the attitude of the abler students, described him as Kant and the *Encyclopædia Britannica* put together. Veblen used to explain his vast erudition on the ground that he had a "court plaster" memory, when he found a fact that might be useful he stored it away until needed. Students marvelled at his learning in physics, chemistry, and the technology of production. One class period he spent almost completely in tracing the history of heels on women's shoes, describing the various types of heels and how they had come into use. Legends grew up concerning his erudition. It was said that on walks in the woods with professors of biology he would disagree with them as to the classification of some insect or animal, and reference to the authorities would always prove him right. Similar stories were afloat concerning his knowledge of botany. He was referred to as a "systematic botanist," one of the three at the university. In the fields of psychology and sociology most of his students preferred his ideas and points of view to those of their own department heads, and would take delight in quoting him to their other professors.

Wright says that his method in discussion was to listen patiently with a cryptic smile, then quietly make some remark that blasted the argument. One of his students recalls that one day a member of the class in "Economic Factors" suggested individual achievements as one of the factors contributing in a major way to civilisation. This was dismissed by Veblen with the comment, "Well, you will find, Mr. ——, that all through history, when there was need for a sermon to be preached, there appeared a preacher to preach it." His quickness in answering questions was in sharp contrast to his indolent movements. Dean Howard Taylor of the Oklahoma College for Women recalls Veblen's keen sense of humour as he lectured on the inner workings of the United States Steel Corporation, in the course on "Trusts and Combinations." He had intimate knowledge of the personal weaknesses and prejudices of the men involved, and enlivened his very serious discussions with many funny stories of the great and the near great.

Veblen was never discourteous nor did he ever become excited in an argument. Once in class a student interrupted him with the question, "But, Doctor Veblen, is that a scientific fact?" Veblen beamed on him benignly and patiently and answered slowly: "I don't know of any other kind." Once after a five-minute dissertation by an undergraduate Veblen announced dryly: "I think you are right, Mr. ——. I arrived at that opinion about three weeks ago and have been trying to tell the class about it ever since."

Although he always appeared to be conducting his lectures and discussions in the most serious and earnest fashion, one would suddenly become aware that without changing his voice he had interpolated some sly joke. Sometimes he used a phrase of current slang, and this delving into the commonplace produced a startling effect, coming from one who looked so "otherwordly." There was no little shock in hearing this erudite person quoting the popular song of that day, "I don't know where I'm going but I'm on my way." Once after discussing the Southwest Indian festivals and ceremonials in the most deliberate and dignified manner, he turned suddenly to the religious import of these functions and declared they were "religious in the same way and to about the same extent that a Sunday School picnic is." Veblen said that early man's relation to his domesticated animals was the same as that of a fraternity man to his bulldog—what Giddings calls "the consciousness of kind." He would smile, his eyes sparkling, his teeth exposed—the nearest he ever came to "breaking into a laugh"—whenever a student gave any indication that he had detected the hollowness of one of Veblen's notorious circumlocutions.

One of his students, Elizabeth Nardin, has well expressed what might be considered the enlightened opinion of his students. In the course on "Economic Factors," she said, the effect "was quite a bit as if a beginner were out in a plane piloted by a great geographer circling over vast continental contours and spacious shore lines, a geographer who made quiet unemphatic comments but never gave his passengers a neat little map of what they were to discover.

"A guest whom I once took with me said: 'Why, it was creepy. It might have been a dead man's voice slowly speaking on, and if the light had gone out behind those dropped eyelids, would it have made any difference?' But we who listened day after day found the unusual manner nicely fitted to convey the detached and slightly sardonic intellect that was moving over the face of things. His detached, free-ranging intellect attracted, and yet it seemed a mutilated personality. The scholarliness of his mind was amazing and delightful. He held in memory detail that would have overwhelmed most minds and become an end in itself, and never lost the magnificent charting of large design. He lectured without notes; he rarely consulted a memorandum in giving assignments to read, though these ranged over geography, anthropology, ethnology, biology. The quiet voice might in one minute make the most adroit use of a bit of current slang or popular doggerel to point out an opinion and the next might be quoting stanza after stanza of a medieval Latin hymn.

"What did one unready person make out of the course? Well, no doubt only a misty fragment of what was there. Not a Marxian economic determinism as to the shaping of civilisation by economic factors. The richness, the concreteness of Mr. Veblen's mind saved him, it seemed to me, from falling into the pit of such narrow abstractness of theory. And yet in the main one found the margin of freedom from economic shaping not too large. No, not too large for the comfort of one whose interests were centred really on that margin!

"The whole effect was towards criticism, scepticism of watchwords, fine sentiment, prides, prejudices, no passion of hope or preference, no scornful explosives or condemnations, just a remorseless massing of facts that drove home the plasticity of the human mind under economic facts, however free it fancied itself.

"I think we Middle Westerners recognised in him a real citizen of the world, and we liked the wit and urbanity we found in him personally."

Mrs. Winifred Sabine, wife of Professor George H. Sabine, has said of his classes in economic theory: "One needed to get close to Dr. Veblen to 'get' . . . the small and delicate shadings of meaning he was eloquently, but not forcibly conveying." Questions were offered by the students "with a background of immense respect." Veblen "would take a very poor or incomplete idea, sympathetically develop it, give it a new bearing or two, and hand it back, one might feel, scarcely the same idea . . . and encouraging one to go on with it from that point. Or if an idea had to be discarded, it was done with so much urbanity and so fine a play of understanding for the state of mind that offered it, that the result was equally valuable in encouraging the student." In the classroom, as in his books, "he had the same wickedly innocent tone of objectivity when he wished to hold something up to ridicule and the same air of complete detachment from any emotional connotations a subject might possess." Difficult as his historical evolutionary approach in economics was, "we all strove greatly to understand, but without entire success. I came finally to wish strongly that Dr. Veblen could have found time . . . for writing . . . a history of economic thought. A related difficulty . . . was that the evolutionary approach to doctrines of the present was equally implied and was even more difficult for students. No training outside the class prepared for it."

His articles on economics, said Mrs. Sabine, were no easier for the students "than they have been for generations of loyal followers who have tried to erect on their foundation a system. I came at last to feel that there was a second great task Dr. Veblen needed to undertake for students and economists, and it was to carry his point of view into a more systematic and constructive stage than he ever had found time to do. It was not merely the compact statement that seemed lacking to help us although that might have helped. It seemed probable that with his interest primarily in social institutions, he had not given time to working his ideas far enough to see just what they would come to. One was left in a critical stage. Everyone in the class stretched to the utmost his intelligence to grasp what seemed both from its manner and content to be cryptic, baffling, yet enormously significant. But the task was too great. I don't think anyone ever knew at the end what Dr. Veblen's own constructive economic theory would be.

"He seemed to delight in intellectual difficulties and new problems. His face would always beam just a little when he made once more a remark which was a stock expression with him, on those occasions when analysis led you into further problems in place of elucidations. 'Where one problem bloomed before,' he would announce happily, 'two are now blooming.'

"Finally it seemed to me that the irony, the understatement, the objective unconcerned tone might almost be thought of as devices for concealing feelings too deep to desire easy expression. When a question arose which naturally involves feelings (a criticism probably of going concerns), it was interesting to observe the slight and yet unmistakable evidence of feeling which could be hidden behind the imperturbable manner never given up in the large. No one could fail to be impressed by Dr. Veblen's eyes. So extraordinarily clear and expressive. The faintest of alterations in the lids, in the expression of the mouth, and in particular, a slow flush rising through the thin skin betrayed a disturbance that never was allowed to break through into direct and more explosive expression."

Mrs. Sabine had the impression reinforced in watching Veblen and Mrs. Veblen together. Her modes of expression "were necessarily and rigidly excluded from Dr. Veblen's vocabulary. It may be taken for certain that he would not have been in intellectual agreement with all of it. Yet I used to sense in him sometimes when Mrs. Veblen . . . would let off a bit of steam, quiet and barely perceptible evidences of satisfaction and sympathy. In a word, I had the feeling that the tight-fitting lid he kept on his own reactions permitted him, perhaps helped him, to get a certain pleasure from hearing someone else 'explode a little.' "

Veblen described himself to Urie as a mutant, declaring that in the

Veblen family this mutant strain showed markedly in mathematics. Veblen said he could extract the eighth root of a number without computation on paper, simply writing down the answer, and his nephew, Oswald Veblen, was able to go into fields where even expert mathematicians could not follow. A sport on the desirable side of the "ordinary," said Veblen, was a "genius"; on the undesirable side an "idiot"; and he declared that he was of the latter class. Both classes, however, were sports. One day when Urie asked him about his religious leanings, Veblen said he was a follower of the Lutheran church. Urie asked why, and he replied: "Because there is no Lutheran church nearer than fifty miles." But he continued with a very serious discussion of the "materialistic sciences," their "spiritual" assumptions and untenable conclusions. So long, he said, as even the findings of science were in such illogical shape, he preferred to believe that there was some kind of omnipotent Providence.

In "Economic Factors" Veblen declared that France is the centre of civilisation today and that her role in the advance of culture is greater than that of other peoples. To him French culture had neither the ponderousness of the German nor the aggressiveness of the English and American; it would not have condemned his way of life in such arbitrary fashion as did the latter. His subtlety and elusiveness would have been appreciated for what they were worth, and not been made the main subject of criticism. There may have been something of Veblen's feeling of his own alienation in his discussion of the Swedes in Russia. "They seem to have been quite a few thousand people speaking a foreign language and considering themselves to be aliens to the Slavic people with the status of aliens much as a German miner today may feel that he is an alien in this land, not because he likes to but on the whole because he belongs to another culture. He may know a great deal about American institutions but yet feel that he is not of them."

In his course in "Economic Factors" Veblen declared that before the coming of the white man the American Indians were generally agriculturists, not hunters. The white man wanted furs and precious metals, and to secure his goods in trade the Indians turned to the hunt and away from the raising of crops. There was a radical improvement in the technology of the hunt, and thus an obsolescence of agricultural techniques. The consequence was a continual movement westward, exhaustion of the supply of furs, wars with other tribes, and elimination. The Indians suffered from contact with the whites, from their diseases, their alcohol, and their guns.

Representative art is characteristic of hunting life. For magical reasons hunters need a true representation of animals, but the human figure is seldom used. Later, impelled by the motive of economy, the representation becomes more symbolic. After constant repetition a figure will be made with fewer strokes and only those features will be used which are held to be essential by prevailing superstition. With the displacement of a hunting culture by one of agriculture and a more settled life, there is less need of magically true representation.

In a peaceable sedentary culture the maternal type of organisation seems to prevail. The family is an institution of motherhood, the children belonging primarily to the woman, and the household is shaped by human needs. The woman is physically and perhaps spiritually better fitted for steady work than the man; with more persistence and equanimity she provides the daily living. With the growth of wealth, however, that is, with a shift to the higher barbarian culture of hunting activities, the men become masters and the women are property, to be bought and sold. The village is ruled by chiefs from families that are strong, both in numbers and in wealth. Property descends in the male line, in close entail or in primogeniture, so that it may not be scattered. The patriarchal household reaches its fullest development in the pastoral culture.

During the absence of the Israelites in Egypt, the people of Palestine grew rich and strong, their land flowing with milk and honey. The agricultural state was very advanced. When on the return from Egypt God told the Israelites that the land was theirs, these agricultural people were able to resist. The predatory hosts of the Israelites retreated into the wilderness for a while, and finally they were successful in conquering the land. Speaking a different language and possessing a different god, the invaders kept their tribal organisation and formed the ruling class. The tribes were united under a loose federation, but they were distinct from one another and quarrelled continually. This is known as the period of the Judges. The judges proved inefficient against the development of predatory life, and a reorganisation took place, in the form of a union under one king, in order to meet outside enemies. A despotic organisation, practically without a constitution, emerged.

The growth of the priesthood is closely correlated with the growth of property rights. The priesthood derives an income from its possession of property, and it also profits from the taboo on certain objects which are sacred to priestly use. As the institution of property becomes more settled and wealth accumulates, the priestly office comes to have peculiar value, and the priest is industrially exempt because of his magic. Large sacrifices are made, most of which go as food to the priesthood, and it receives also the revenues from tributary towns. When both the spiritual and secular rule are combined in one, the economic advantage is especially great. The king of such a community is in a position to claim everything, and the example of Israel, as finally developed under Solomon, is only typical of other known instances. Economically speaking either the spiritual or the secular power is able to take care of the surplus; it is not that they are greedy, but their claims are of such character that they may be extended, and where circumstances are favourable they will claim whatever is available. Other things being equal, the wealthier the community and the greater its loyalty towards its gods, the more splendid, and therefore costly, will be the property of the church and the priesthood. Nothing is too good for the house of God in wealthy, more advanced cultures; and goods are measured in terms of market price.

As the civil organisation becomes more monarchical, the gods do likewise. Until the individual has sworn fealty to God, he is a sinner—"Those who are not for me are against me." Men, in order to be of God, must be converted, but those who have had only an agricultural training seem quite unable to compass the view that they are sinners. This is the greatest difficulty facing missionaries.

The antecedents of the prevailing American culture were described by Veblen as deriving from northern Europe. The race of that area is the blond who has developed the superior technology. The blond community is an adventurous, protesting, experimenting one. The traits of political freedom, Protestantism, and technological mastery are found together. One who thinks not in terms of the fear of God, but rather in terms of mechanical forces, is likely to be a better technologist than one who thinks in terms of Providence, interference and priestly authority. "I do not mean that it was a mistake for our devout forbears of the scholastic age to paint the devil black. . . . But it seems that the greatest detriment has come to the church from the blond with red hair rather than from the dark brunette."

Veblen described the Minoan culture as consisting of a number of depressions, ending finally in a collapse. The culture was not altogether peaceable, as shown by the prevalence of the bull in its religion, and the axe. Its latter period shows a good deal of wealth and many weapons. The succeeding culture was based on trade, and revenue was obtained by force of arms. The great cities were situated on trade routes, and the best of these routes must have passed through Troy, for otherwise the Trojan war would not have occurred, since it was a fight for customs. The warriors of the time, however, exhausted the traffic upon which they lived, and civilisation sank again into a state of collapse. The presence of 100,000 Greeks before Troy for seven years was bad for trade and for those who lived on the trade. The Homeric poems were written at least two hundred years after the event, and in the meantime, conditions had changed so greatly "that what was a matter of course with the poets was a matter of novelty with the heroes."

Some savages, declared Veblen, spend all their leisure time hunting and killing one another. Their chief interest is collecting the heads of others. These savages have their fraternities, and though they do not wear Greek letter pins as insignia they carry skulls around to show their prowess. Today men compete in laying up dollars. Honour comes in having bank accounts of several figures. This would mean nothing to the savage, for, if one knows no difference in having big bank accounts and small ones, the whole matter of laying up dollars is senseless.

In the "History of Economic Thought" Veblen declared that Adam Smith and John Bates Clark were both evolutionists, but their evolution stopped with their time. In the mercantilistic scheme the gain of the prince, who was "the discretionary manager of the community," was held to be the gain of the community; and today the gains of his heirs, the "individual traders," are considered the gains of the community. The animus between areas in the days of mercantilism was of the sort that "now exists in local commercial clubs."

Veblen illustrated the logic of modern mercantilism by the example of Prussia under Frederick the Great. "The advantage of Prussia is the disadvantage of others. The disadvantage of others is the advantage of Prussia. The greater the net return, the better off the individual who gets it." Thus "the more Prussia gains the better off it will be; hence the greater the surplus of receipts over expenditures, the better off Prussia will be." With the passing of time, however, "the tendency has been to shift the emphasis of the purpose of mercantilistic policy. For example in England and the United States, perhaps, the mercantilism seems to flourish for the benefit of the businessmen. In Germany, however, imperialism for the crown still remains." On the basis of a similar logic concerning capital, "men of affairs continually harp against reduction of earnings of industry today and that the return on the capital of various industries should not be cut down. At the same time they know this capital is only the capitalisation of the earning capacity in question."

Sir William Petty, said Veblen, felt that the costs of the French court had trenched on capital, but to him and his group, speaking the "common sense" of their day, "some court was necessary, and the idea of eliminating the court and landed class was so far out of their horizon that it never appeared to them worth while considering." The same is true today in regard to the diplomatic service. "Nobody knows what they are good for but we know that we must have it, and we never even think of doing away with it. Today they are taken for granted. In the future, they may be questioned." In the same way the right of property may be questioned in the future; the holders of property are like "many people in England [who] . . . claim descent from those who stole the land from the Irish, with the aid of Cromwell. They claim respect for holding on ever since those days of licensed piratage and they do not want their licences revoked."

Of the Malthusian theory Veblen said: "The world hitherto has everywhere been underpopulated and hence there has been no chance for the Malthusian law to operate. The premises of the theory are not sound. They have never thus far applied to the given world situation. Hitherto the population has never pressed on the means of subsistence, except in the cases where the artificial factors such as the distribution are poor. Under the modern state of the industrial arts, what makes the Malthusian theory plausible is the subdivision of the world into nations and the class strata of rich and poor."

In Veblen's discussion of Marx there is another possible suggestion of his own isolation. Jews, he said, are usually unorthodox in economics, in institutions, in religion. The Jew, as an alien, is born into a community with traditions different from those of the gentile community. He sees that his own traditions will not do, but he sees just as plainly that the gentile's traditions are no better; hence he becomes a sceptic and an atheist. Thus Marxism is not historical economics. The latter arose within the academic circles, where gentile traditions ruled, but socialism arose outside the university. Veblen declared that Clark and Fisher, in fact, the leading economists of the present, are in effect members of the historical school.

The Theory of the Leisure Class was still popular, but Veblen referred to it as "this chestnut." Cummings expressed his astonishment that its language was becoming that of the man in the street. Macmillan's thought so well of its possibilities that a special cheaper edition was issued in 1912, and for the new edition Veblen changed the subtitle from *An Economic Study in the Evolution of Institutions* to *An Economic Study of Institutions*. Had Veblen used the shorter phrase originally he would doubtless have prevented much confusion and as much of the criticism as was based on the belief that he was concerned with the genealogical pedigree of institutions rather than with the present-day functioning of business enterprise, of modern capital.

There was a possibility of revising *The Theory of Business Enterprise*. Professor Bell, then a colleague of Veblen, writes: "I frequently argued with him to the effect that he had not taken due account of the limitations of the extension of bank credit in his explanation of the limits in the expansion of stock values. . . . He was convinced . . . that the book should be expanded so as to include a theory of bank credit in its relation to reactions in business. . . . He suggested to me that I undertake the writing up of such material with a view to its inclusion in his

Theory of Business Enterprise in an enlarged and revised edition." But nothing came of it.

Writing was difficult for Veblen. One afternoon, when a student asked him what he had been doing, he drawled: "Well, I tried writing, but my sentences were so crooked, they wouldn't lie down on the page, so I went out to help the goats in clearing up the thicket." He confessed to Urie: "Never tell it on me, but I never use an outline." Much of his difficulty in writing came from his demand for precision in the use of words. He was so meticulous in this respect that he declared there are no synonyms in the English language.

Veblen was occupied with completing *The Instinct of Workmanship*. His colleague, Maurice Parmelee of the sociology department, declared that in Veblen's first year at Missouri, "Veblen was writing his *Instinct of Workmanship* and I was writing my *Science of Human Behaviour*. Naturally we were constantly discussing the biological and psychological questions involved. He was for using the term 'instinct' in a wide and rather vague sense while I insisted upon limiting it to its strict biological meaning." *The Instinct of Workmanship and the State of the Industrial Arts* finally appeared in 1914. It is essentially a summary of his famous course on "The Economic Factors in Civilisation." Once, when asked why he did not publish his lectures, he is said to have replied that one could beat about the bush in a lecture, but it was difficult to secure sufficient accuracy to warrant publication. Veblen felt that such a book should have been written by a sociologist, by William I. Thomas, for example. This is the only book of Veblen's that contains a dedication—to "B.K.N."—and this in itself is somewhat revealing of his method and style. The initials, he told Stewart, compose the first names of his wife and his two stepdaughters. There is, perhaps, a suggestion of "B.K.N." when the names Becky and Anne are pronounced quickly together.

After he had ceased writing Veblen declared that *The Instinct of Workmanship* was his only important book. It closes a cycle which began with "The Instinct of Workmanship and the Irksomeness of Labour," and it is fundamentally an elaboration of this essay. Under machine technology, he declared, the result of the modern institution of capital is to make the public at large feel aggrieved at the outcome in price that it must pay for the activities of the capitalist employers. The labouring classes resort to unionism and so work "what mischief they can to their employers and to the public at large, always blamelessly within the rules of the game as laid down of old on the pecuniary principles of business discretion." "The 'money power' comes in . . . with ever-increasing force and incisiveness, to muddle the whole situation mysteriously and irretrievably by looking after their own pecuniary interests in a fashion even more soberly legitimate and authentic if possible, than the workmen's management of their own affairs." In the last chapter he reiterates his judgment that "always and everywhere invention is the mother of necessity." The invention of the credit economy is the substantial basis of its necessity in uncritical common sense. "The prevalence of salesmanship, that is to say of business enterprise . . . is perhaps the most serious obstacle which the pecuniary culture opposes to the advance of workmanship. It . . . contaminates the sense of workmanship in its initial move, and sets both the proclivity to efficient work and the penchant for serviceability at cross purposes with the common good." Workmanship is confused with salesmanship.

Thus the fundamental argument of the book is not unlike that of any of Veblen's important works. In fact all his work seems to merge together in this book, and it combines in its sweep all the basic concepts and devices for presentation he had used before. The instincts of workmanship, of idle curiosity, and of parental bent have so much in common that even Veblen finds its difficult to distinguish between them, and often he seems to consider a distinction unnecessary. They all seem to signify the survival and advance of the "generically human" being, and thus of humanity, as opposed to the beast of prey, and they suggest the fundamental realities of Kant—"*the starry heavens above and moral law within.*" The instincts are "characteristically human predispositions," with objective, impersonal ends instead of personal proximate pecuniary ends. To Veblen the instinct of workmanship is essentially a logical term, and it "may as well be taken to signify a concurrence of several instinctive aptitudes, each of which might or might not prove simple or irreducible when subjected to psychological or physiological analysis." In the language of Kant it is a regulative principle, not a constitutive one. The parental bent is conceived as an interest in the welfare of the race, an abhorrence of waste of life and goods. Idle curiosity is so intimately related to the instinct of workmanship that "the long-term consequences of the common run of curiosity, helped out by such sporadic individuals in whom the idle curiosity runs at a higher tension, count up finally because cumulatively, into the most substantial cultural achievement of the race—its systematised knowledge and quasi-knowledge of things."

Veblen's conception of these "instincts" is best revealed in a note taken in the course on "Economic Factors" in 1911, when he was working seriously on the book. The human animal, he declared, is, like other animals, at the mercy of his instincts. There is no profit in inquiring into the purpose, as they are themselves the purpose. The individual has certain bents, instincts, which decide what he will aim towards. But human activity, as distinguished from that of animals, is impersonal, imma-

terial. Only proximate activities are personal. Thus men have a solicitude
for the incoming generation, but this "paternal bent" is separate from
the urge for children and is not to be confused with the sexual impulse.
Men would like the next generation to do better; they prefer future
goods to present goods; they prefer the welfare of the filial generation
to their own. It is not for one to say why this preference—this fear of
race suicide—exists in human nature, but all men are able to understand
the thesis that we should not squander the resources needed by the incoming generation. This is an abhorrence of waste, an urge towards the
conservation of life. Thus economy, efficiency, an effective direction of
forces in consumption and production, are approved. War is wasteful of
life and resources, which is felt to be wrong. It ministers to the sporting
instinct, but man wants also to accomplish something. Sport develops because of the teleological necessity of action, but what is wanted is serviceability to the race, the satisfaction of accomplishing something in the
approved method of workmanship. There are few men who have not
wished they had done better, and even Darwin regretted that he had
not been of greater service to mankind. This instinct is allied with the
parental bent in its solicitude for the future. Men seek knowledge for
other than pragmatic reasons; the search for knowledge, the instinct
of curiosity, is directed towards other than money ends. In times of great
strain this instinct of idle curiosity is not predominant, but when the conditions of life run more smoothly men become curious.

But by habituation man may modify his instincts; the instincts may
be contaminated by one another, or may be held in abeyance under a given
scheme of institutions. Thus, although men do not like waste, it is equally
true that they waste their resources, that other things are desired which
run counter to the wish for conservation. Thus, too, although the instincts
of workmanship and of beauty may blend and fortify one another, the
instinct of workmanship may also become an end in itself rather than the
means. Towards the close of an era of art, for example, when the inspiration of the movement has passed, technique flourishes and becomes
overloaded with detail, and the only purpose is to produce an elaborately
perfect, finished piece of work.

Veblen thus described the instinct of workmanship as the source of material welfare, as the controlling principle of mankind. It is the substitute
for Lassalle's "idea" of the workingman as the guiding principle of
history. But the sense of workmanship has been contaminated by the
competitive principles of business, so that "men are conceived to serve
the common good somewhat in proportion as they are able to induce the
community to pay more for their services than they are worth." According to the prevailing pecuniary common sense, based on a handicraft

situation in which capital goods were inconsequential, property rights and free contract make for the common good, for an expression of workmanship. But by force of habituation property—invested wealth—has become in fact an end in itself and now has "barred out any move that might be designed to reinstate the workman in his effective freedom to work" as he chooses or "to dispose of his person and product" as he sees fit. It also effectively bars the facile workings of the material processes necessary for the welfare and survival of the community. Veblen speaks of this transition, from the savage plane of free workmanship to the barbarian plane of pecuniary control, as one of the most significant mutations in man's history.

Thus the fabric of institutions, or the logic of the ways and means of the money economy, has so intervened between the functioning of the instinctive human impulses and their realisation in the achievement of effective serviceability for the community, that it is an open question whether the "native common sense," the naïve instinct of workmanship, will reassert itself and radically revise the scheme of institutions before it is too late and the prevailing precarious situation takes its course to a collapse. If the estimates of efficiency engineers are to be believed, the waste of life and products is not less than fifty percent under the prevailing institutional scheme with its principle of natural rights which vest unlimited discretion in the owners of property. "History records more frequent and more spectacular instances of the triumph of imbecile institutions over life and culture than of peoples who have by force of instinctive insight saved themselves alive out of a desperately precarious institutional situation, such, for instance, as now faces the peoples of Christendom." "Even in those members of the community who are most directly and rigorously exposed to its discipline the machine process has hitherto wrought no such definite bias, no such positive habitual attitude of workmanlike initiative towards the conventions of industrial management," as distinct from technological procedure, "as to result in a constructive deviation from the received principles."

It is not at all necessary for a highly developed industrial technological scheme to be managed by pecuniary experts, as is evidenced by the culture of the peaceable Pueblos and Eskimos, where property rights are vague. But with the growth of culture, the rise of property rights and of machine technology, and the consequent importance of the ownership of capital goods, the priestly classes have grown so powerful that, although in the more primitive scheme they lived on a precarious margin, it is now the community that lives on that margin for the sake of the welfare of these priestly classes.

From one point of view *The Instinct of Workmanship* can be considered to close the cycle of articles ostensibly on methodology which began with "Why Is Economics Not an Evolutionary Science?" The book discusses the correlation that "runs through modern intellectual life between technological use and wont . . . and the preconceptions of scientific theory." The preconception of the meliorative trend is discussed as the preconception of prowess in the predatory culture, and the contrast between the matter-of-fact and the animistic preconceptions is discussed as the contrast between the logic of handling external facts from the standpoint of their serviceability for the material ends of the community and the logic of handling them from the standpoint of due respect to their imputed natures. The conventional belief in property rights, funded wealth, as contributing to the needs of the community is of this latter kind, but the economists continue to yield allegiance to this and to other old-fashioned conceptions that are embodied in the law and supposedly govern industrial enterprise. The perverted instinct of workmanship, the fundamental " 'business proposition' . . . of how to get the most in price for the least return in weight and tale," is one of differential gain —a differential as "between the businessman and the unbusinesslike generality of persons with whom directly or indirectly he deals as customers, employees, and the like." Thus the theory of exchange value is the central and controlling doctrine for the orthodox economist, and "with easy conviction" he traces this value "back to an individualistic ground in the doctrines of differential utility—'marginal utility.' " But since the technological scheme is a community product, it would seem that the controversy as to the productivity of the recipients of incomes should shift ground from the "nature of things," the natural right of invested wealth, to "the exigencies of ingrained preconceptions, principles, and expediencies as seen in the light of current technological requirements."

The reviews seldom went farther than to acknowledge Veblen's ability. The attitude of those who were not former students is well represented in a review by Alvin Johnson in *The Political Science Quarterly:* "You cannot read the book without conceiving an admiration for the sheer intellectual power of the author. Your admiration extends even to his style, baffling and shifty as it is. You gasp at his facility in handling polysyllabic and recondite words, as at the feats of a sword-swallower. And you pray that his style may not spread as an infection among the social philosophers to come."

In his *Inventors and Money-Makers*, which appeared shortly after Veblen's book and dealt with the same subject matter, Taussig referred to *The Instinct of Workmanship* as a "brilliant and original book, like everything that comes from his pen," but was sceptical of the instinct and the deductions Veblen drew. Taussig declared it to be obvious that "if the confidence imposed in persons having fiduciary obligations, such as directors and managers . . . had been always and everywhere abused, the whole system of delegated management would long ago have broken down." He concluded that "under the subtle influence of a pervasive sentiment of interdependence and of spontaneous approbation for public-spirited action, greater regard for the general good may be expected even in ordinary pecuniary operations."

In class Veblen spoke of Norway in such glowing terms that students sometimes accused him of being a Norwegian chauvinist. In 1914 he made a trip there. As a man of distinction he was given a free pass for the first-class coaches of the Norwegian railways. Once he donned overalls and, as he expected, was threatened with removal. He showed his pass and the officious attitude turned immediately to obsequiousness. He was in Europe when the war came. When he returned to the university, he said that Germany did not attempt to avoid the war, and therefore it was a fight to the finish for the English-speaking peoples. Had Germany really desired peace, the trouble on the Russian front could have been avoided by the use of a little "gumption." If Germany had turned her back on France, leaving the French frontier unprotected, her attitude, said Veblen, would have been respected by France and England.

In the year 1914–1915, instead of beginning with neolithic and paleolithic man, in the course on "Economic Factors," Veblen took up Bernhardi's *Germany and the Next War*. He outlined how the United States would be involved, explained why Germany's policy could not succeed, ridiculed the Nordic theory espoused by the German writer. Students who had taken the course in previous years were surprised, and concluded that Veblen had a new book in process. After three or four lectures, however, he went back 50,000 years to neolithic man. But it was true that he was busy on a new book. *Imperial Germany and the Industrial Revolution* was to mark a significant change in Veblen's procedure.

CHAPTER XVIII

THE *Theory of Business Enterprise* had predicted war as one of the alternatives facing mankind, as one which would lead to a regime of feudal status and the collapse of occidental culture. In *Imperial Germany and the Industrial Revolution* the war became the occasion for determining which alternative would win —the industrial republic or a despotism which would be feudal in fact, whatever its form. Veblen's other books had taken years to write, but on this one he spent only a few months, as the date of the preface indicates. The book betrays haste, but his very haste prevented him from building up the strategic devices by which he customarily masked his meaning. What the book lacks in urbanity it makes up in effectiveness.

It was probably Veblen's haste that led him to place at the end of the book, in five lengthy notes in the nature of essays, material that belonged in the main text. But a striking effect is achieved by this procedure. The notes refer to passages in the text, separated at times by a hundred pages, but when they are read together they form almost a book of their own, somewhat resembling *The Theory of Business Enterprise*. The first is on the dolicho-blond, who has the characteristic qualities for survival in occidental civilisation; the next two refer to the development in Iceland from a small-scale scheme of life to an aristocratic republic, and its collapse; the fourth is a discussion of the country town as a reflection of modern business principles; and the last discusses war and its effect upon the redistribution of wealth.

In *Imperial Germany* there are only an occasional footnote and a few pages in the conclusion to indicate that a war was in progress. Veblen stated in the preface that the work was projected before the war occurred, "though the complexion of subsequent events has also doubtless had its effect on the particular direction of the argument at more than one point." England plays as much a role in the study as does Germany, and by England Veblen refers to English-speaking peoples in general. The inquiry, he said, was not primarily concerned with the war, but with a "comparison and correlation between the German case on the one hand and the English-speaking peoples on the other hand, considered as two distinct and somewhat divergent lines of the cultural development in modern times," and the comparison is based on "the economic, chiefly the industrial circumstances that have shaped the outcome in either case." Little of the material is new, and the "anthropological" material on the "old order" of Baltic culture is practically identical with that presented in the course in "Economic Factors" which Veblen gave during his first year at Missouri.

Veblen's customary contrast between the generic presumptively savage culture, where ownership does not exist, and the unstable advanced barbarian pecuniary culture now takes the form of a contrast between the generic neolithic culture, with its "anarchistic savage," and the modern dynastic state, with its fighting prince carved in the image of the pecuniary magnate. The early culture of the Germanic peoples and their pre-German forbears, which include the English-speaking peoples, "is made use of as a term of contrast against which to exhibit the characteristic traits of the modern era, and as showing the cultural point of departure of these peoples, towards which any drift of reversion in their case will necessarily set." Industrially "the current German situation is a derivative of the English and an outcome of the past development of the industrial arts as worked out in Great Britain." "The English-speaking peoples are democratic, indeed anarchistically democratic, in principle," said Veblen, "but by reason of common-sense expediency fortified by a pervading respect of persons—what is sometimes disrespectfully called flunkeyism—the effective degree of freedom enjoyed by the individual, as restrained by law and custom, is only moderately greater than that which falls to the lot of the German subject whose point of departure in the regulation of conduct would appear to be this same flunkeyism, dignified with a metaphysical nimbus and mitigated by common-sense expediency." In notes taken in the course in "Economic Factors" the year the book was written the similarity between the English and German conditions is elaborated somewhat further. In small Denmark the poorest class is not as badly off as the poorest class in either England or Germany. There are no large industries in Denmark and no class comparable to the employees of mines and collieries in England and Germany, who live in abject misery. Norway is poorer in soil, resources, and population than Denmark but it is generally accepted that the common man is better off even in Norway than in England or Germany. The richer the country, the poorer the people.

As in *The Instinct of Workmanship*, Veblen speaks in *Imperial Germany* of the basic difference between heredity and habit, between the enduring, characteristically human predispositions and the transitory unstable dominant scheme of human institutions; and he speaks here of the modern composite, hybrid population as he used to speak of the composite point of view. But while in most of his other writing much space had to be covered before he discussed the relationship between modern business enterprise and technological efficiency, in *Imperial Germany* this relationship is stressed almost at the beginning, although it is introduced first in a footnote. The United States Steel Corporation, he says in the footnote, was organised so that the technologically obsolete equipment of underlying companies, which for business reasons could not be summarily scrapped, might be shifted gradually to a modern basis; that is, the "monopolistic position of the new corporation" enabled it to make the community at large pay for the temporary lower efficiency which resulted from the refusal to make a radical shift to the requirements of the new technological situation. Its control later of southern coal, iron, and lime was for the same purpose. In other words, modern business control under the changed industrial system has the same effect upon the general welfare as if it were consciously directed towards retarding material efficiency. Business enterprise takes over the control of industry, and the pecuniary gain of the businessman in whom the discretionary power rests becomes the test of industrial efficiency.

In the course in "Economic Factors" that Veblen gave the same year, he converted this principle into terms of dynastic statecraft. The transformation of Prussia from a group of warring principalities to a large-scale dynastic state was accomplished by Frederick the Great and diplomatists masterful in lies. Prussia was in a position to take the lead in the growing movement, necessitated by the new state of the industrial arts, for a larger-scale organisation. To qualify for modern competition the state must be a large-scale organisation. The "merger" or combination process was already going on among the smaller states, and inevitably the stronger ones absorbed the weaker. Prussia, aided by her lack of restraint in diplomatic ethics, secured the lead and kept it, although the smaller states were growing. Moreover, what representative institutions existed were only nominal, and in no way impeded the crown's policy.

The modern German statesmen have in no way changed the policy. The pressure for home industry is apparent, for example, in the production of steel. By tariffs and other encouragements the Germans have forced the development of ore beds, nine-tenths of which it would have been uneconomical to touch in America. This procedure, however, provides them, at such times as the present, with the equipment and process necessary for utilising such ore as they have available at home. The same is true of copper. But in spite of all protection, and all efforts to employ substitutes, an increasing percentage of the supply during the last forty years has been secured from Sweden and Spain.

In *Imperial Germany* Veblen declared that in modern economic life the principles of "conspicuous waste," or the great investors' considerations, take care of the margin between production and productive consumption, so that at least fifty percent of the current product is wasted. But the waste and unemployment entailed in the modern institution of property follow from principles which are conceived to make for the general welfare, the principles of natural liberty.

Here Veblen turns back to what he calls the "pagan anarchy," or "quasi-anarchistic scheme of social control, resting on insubordination." Under this scheme civil power was vested in the popular assembly, made up of all the free men, and the executive power was slight. The whole scheme rested on neighbourly surveillance, or the principle of live and let live. Under the simple technological scheme of mixed farming which prevailed then, the scheme worked passably. With the advance of the industrial arts, however, the possessor of the required means is able to extend his enterprise beyond the bonds within which neighbourhood surveillance is effective. The uncritical sense of group solidarity is so strong in such a community that gains to its members only add to the standing of him who makes them, "as all pecuniary gains do in a culture that makes much of property." This sentimental sophistry results in the community unreflectively furthering such enterprises "at a palpable cost to itself and with the certainty of getting no gain from the venture." The effective presence and uncritical efficiency of this propensity is best seen in international trade, "where the trade is carried on for the gain of the businessmen immediately concerned and where the benefit presumed to accrue to the community at large from such gains for the home-bred businessmen will bear no scrutiny."

In the small-scale kingdom of the "Old Order" the interest of the citizens lay in defeating the ambitions of the crown to extend its patrimony, but instead, in violation of sound logic, they went to considerable lengths to further such projects of dynastic aggrandisement. The king played one neighbourhood against another, with the result that obedience to the crown took the place of the "pagan" traits of insubordination and initiative. Local kings extended their domains and displaced those that fell short in the struggle for empire. Restless young men formed bands of adventurers and followed a similar procedure, or ran to waste in the turmoil. In the end the old order of quasi-anarchistic autonomy gave place to irresponsible authority and subjection. The rule of live and let live eventuated by its own working into the rule that the king is to live as he sees fit and "the common man is to live as the king of his grace will let him."

This process is further elaborated in the two supplementary notes on the old order at the end of the book. The classical writers on the Germanic tribes are best exemplified by Tacitus, whose work is a *Tendenzschrift*, a rationalised account reflecting the views then prevalent among

Latin scholars concerning primitive social conditions, and "drawn with an eye to the discipline and edification of his Roman audience." His account is taken from tribes that have notoriously wandered long and far from their ancestral homes, engaged in profitable seizure, and made themselves, at least provisionally, a master class over a population already settled on the land. These accounts describe a more or less mature state of predatory culture. A better source is the saga literature, which was contemporaneous with the breakdown of the pagan anarchy and its dissolution into a dynastic dependency. Snorri's work is that of "an artist gifted with a Shakesperian sense for the ludicrous." Whatever the gods may have been in their legendary shapes before he touched them, they are figures of no great stature as deities after they leave his hands.

The Viking trade was made possible by the great improvements in the technology of boat-building and navigation, but since no substantial equivalent was gained from the traffic a surplus population and productivity must have existed in order to make the considerable investment required. The Viking traffic was in slave labour, superfluities, trinkets, precious metals, but with due regard to these imports, which were of slight value, and to the mutual raiding that took place, the equipment, supplies, and personnel that went into the Viking traffic were a total loss. The result was the insecurity of person and industry, an increase in the number of slaves, an increase in their hardships, and a decline in their price.

Social classes in the age of the Vikings are sketched by Veblen in terms very like those he had used in describing the hierarchical organisation of modern business enterprise. At the bottom were the slaves, who were the chattels of their masters and differed from them neither in speech nor in physical characteristics. Above them was the larger class of half-free tenant cottiers, or the dependent working classes. Above these in turn, and constituting the main body of the population, was the freehold farm population. Then came the earls and the king, whose place in the social organisation is not clear. In these petty kingdoms the king was primarily a gentleman farmer, and in Veblen's description he appears as a composite of industrial technician and businessman, merely the chairman of the assembly and having little power except in war. This ancient small scale of things still lives in popular folklore, although it has disappeared from popular experience. "The folk tales carry the suggestion, to be taken for what it may be worth, that this small-scale, half-anarchistic, neighbourhood plan of society is . . . the one plan in effect, to which they will drift by natural bent and in which they instinctively see the land of the heart's desire and the empire of content for their kind."

But in these principalities the tenure of property and the incidents of ownership were precise and of fundamental consequence beyond any

other, like their modern counterparts. There is some evidence of the use
of machinery and of production for a market. With the growth of the industrial arts the neighbourhood scheme broke down, and the consequent
dynastic triumph "cannot be well characterised as anything but imbecile
and nasty." In small communities the instinct of workmanship might stir
the neighbours into activity to put down an "obnoxious superfluity of
naughtiness," but in general the institutional framework gives rise to conditions which, under the new technology, break the hold of the neighbourhood scheme. The accumulation of wealth gives a differential advantage
to its owner, so that with the same free hand as his neighbours, and with
the added reach given by his means, he is in a position to engross the
community's natural resources and technological knowledge. Thus the
private accumulation of wealth "works, from its beginnings, at cross-
purposes with the principle of live and let live," until the democratic
regime dissolves into rapine and destruction, as exemplified by the Icelandic republic at "the close of a protracted season of internal raids, lawlessness, civil war, and assassination carried out in the endeavours of these
magnates each to live as good him seemed." On the other hand, the institution of property, the institution of ownership with full discretion in
the use of property, is an intrinsic effect of the rule of live and let live.
"All this, of course, implies no criticism or derogation of the institution
of private property at large, either as to its defensibility on moral grounds
or as to its expediency on economic grounds. . . . It is only in its consequences that it comes in conflict" with the rule of live and let live in the
course of institutional growth.

Again the notes taken in Veblen's course in "Economic Factors" in 1911
are useful in understanding his analysis of the old order and its relation
to modern business enterprise. A few burial places which survive from
the Baltic Stone Age attest the possession of property at that time as well
as poverty. Judging from the grave mounds people lived in a great many
relatively small villages. The roads are along the lines of these mounds
and indicate the use of wheeled vehicles. By the middle of the Bronze
Age the workmen became so proficient that they were making chains, and
towards the close of the Bronze Age the wealth of the country seems to
have increased. Apparently gold was plentiful at that time, but with the
transition to the Iron Age gold disappeared and silver took its place, although silver was never abundant. There are indications of great disturbances and of marked changes in culture. Weapons became more
abundant and representative art developed. "It is believed that these
representations of animals have a magical meaning; something like the
designs on our coins." At the close of paganism in Norway, the constitution of society was formally of a free nature, but aristocratic. There was

a certain degree of preference before the law, but freeholders ruled, and the legal fiction of absolute equality was never denied, in spite of the growing tendency to prerogative in fact. The privileges of the freeholders were closely connected with property. If a freeholder lost his property, he might cease to be a freeholder and lose his citizenship. He might even lose his freedom and become a slave either voluntarily or by outlawry. Originally the king was usually the largest farmer, the chairman of the assembly. He formally had no executive powers. In theory the king is always present although he inherits little. But gradually he achieves executive powers and engrosses the revenues. The system is based on property and descent, with inheritance of both property and status. The culture is one of mixed farming and of piracy, although there are some merchants who are not pirates.

The Icelandic community illustrates the situation. A meeting of the whole country would be held annually. The main business of this general assembly was litigation, and it had a supreme court of nine judges. But an extra-legal system of bosses and of combinations of bosses developed, and, although the forms of free equality remained, they failed in practice. In 1235 there were two permanent factions; in their fights the courts were of little importance and their awards were given little consideration. The republic came to a close in this civil warfare, without the interference of any higher power and without the growth of a kingly power.

Baltic culture was organised on a small scale at that time, and its institutions were not suited to the management of a community on a larger scale with larger interests. Originally the wealthy were proud of being good workmen, but in the end they appear as a distinct leisure class of fighters. The habit of independence comes from the small-scale culture, where each neighbourhood governs itself, but this situation was changed by the invasions. The invaders probably killed off some of the original cultivators, but most of them they allowed to live on condition they furnish their owners a livelihood. Thus the barbarians settled not on the land but on the people. This scheme has been tried almost everywhere. It failed in America only because the people would not submit to slavery. It develops a society in which the freemen govern themselves and also their subject workmen, and the outcome is a system of feudal status, in which a free citizen has one or more villages assigned to him. The classical theoreticians who espoused the mark theory saw only the ruling class of freemen, not the insignificent subject classes, and deduced a democratic village. As a result of this incursion into Europe of men bred to freedom and self-government the underlying population was reduced, at least for a while, to a condition of servile subjection to warlike enterprise.

The notes on the Mediterranean culture, taken in the course in "Economic Factors," tell the same story. The greatest era of fighting was in the Iron Age, the era of Mycenæan culture. This was the era between the Homeric and the classical periods, and the fighting continued in the latter, through the collapse of Rome. Cattle and the pastoral culture came with the Bronze Age. The European learned the domestication of cattle and developed it farther, since in taking it over he avoided the load of magic and superstition. The Alpines, with their superior technology and aristocratic organisation, were at first successful against the Europeans, but after the Europeans absorbed some of the Alpine culture they were able to thrash the brunettes.

In *Imperial Germany* the chapter on "The Dynastic State" shows the petty principalities developed into petty dynastic communities, not unlike the competitive business organisations that engaged in warfare before the great trust and holding-company era. The formation of imperial Germany as a dynastic state is a medieval anachronism. The dynastic state is necessarily of a "competitive, or rapacious, character, and free to use any expedient that comes to hand." It took over the mechanically more efficient devices of the new age because it would thereby enjoy a differential advantage over conservative neighbours, and would in the end supplant them in statecraft and seize their substance. The old order of self-sufficient principalities had no chance of survival when the state of the industrial arts made national organisations possible. The dynastic state was reorganised and its administrative machinery differentiated to make possible a more detailed and exacting control of the source of revenue. By a policy of warlike aggression and by a system of bureaucratic surveillance and unremitting interference in the private lives of the subjects the necessary servility of the population has been obtained. Successful warfare, the disciplinary effect of preparation for war, indoctrination with warlike arrogance and ambitions, have sustained the submissive allegiance of the underlying communities.

The discipline of personal allegiance to the dynastic state or sovereign is in sharp contrast with the discipline of the machine industry, which constantly enforces the futility of personal force and prerogative in the face of the impersonal requirements of the mechanical process. Liberals, however, held their "intellectual convictions on such 'academic' tenure—that is to say, so uniformly without reinforcement from their own experience of mechanical fact—that with the best intentions they never succeeded in infecting the people at large with their own ideals of a new order, or in disturbing the incumbents of office in their tenure and usufruct of the old order." In the disturbances of 1848, for example, "the enlightened conceptions and impulses of the literate minority here joined hands with the irritation of the illiterate due to intolerable conditions of physical discomfort, with a transient appearance of success, and with the net result that in the end both parties to the misunderstanding were convicted of contumacy."

The situation of imperial Germany is that of an organisation whose industrial technology is modern but whose scheme of controlling institutions belongs to a past predatory era, just as the modern economic organisation is comprised of the incompatible principles of business and the machine technology. German technology has been borrowed from England, but the scheme of free institutions which is the concomitant of that technology has not been borrowed.

The English culture is distinguished from the German by its preoccupation with "material realities," or the mechanistic conception, as distinguished from the romantic preconception of status and differential dignity. The drift in the direction of the mechanistic conception has proceeded with such a degree of consistency that "the mechanistic conception has the appearance of a goal towards which the discipline of modern life has tended." The habit of thinking in workmanlike terms of efficient causes is "one of the most ancient and incorrigible metaphysical habits of the race," and under the relative peace that England has enjoyed the result has been a relative predominance of insubordination and free institutions. Its handicraft technology passed over insensibly into its machine technology. In fact, "except for the fear of giving annoyance, one might find survivals of the gild-regulation concept of natural laws in the work of scientists still living, particularly perhaps in those sciences that lie farthest afield from the technological domain and so come least in touch with the logic of mechanical engineering." In England as elsewhere, however, the right of property has the sanction of law and custom, so that in the transition to machine technology pecuniary enterprise has not assumed the nature of petty trade subservient to handicraft, but has become master of the industrial system, owner of the industrial equipment, and beneficiary of the community's technological efficiency. The English capitalistic system has influenced economic life in two directions: first, in its effect on industry, or production, under the principle of competition; and second, in its effect on the consumption of the product, under the principle of conspicuous waste, also called the standard of living.*

The consequences of the modern businessman's control are strikes, lockouts, idleness, trade union rules, and similar disturbances of the industrial process, that is, an "exploitation of the human raw material of industry that has at times taken quite an untoward scope and direction," in the way of overwork, underpay, and bad working conditions. Thus

* In his lectures Veblen said that the standard of living is the same as the cost of living, and he expressed a preference for the term "standard of livability."

modern capital has resulted in an "appreciable population of 'depauperate' workmen, sufficiently damaged in their physique to transmit their debilities to their offspring and leave them doubtfully fit for any efficient use, 'unto the third and fourth generation.' " The privileged wealthy classes, sheltered from the need of adjustment to modern requirements, might also be characterised as depauperate. These two, the indigent and the leisure class, are found together since they are the outcome of the same conditions—"the era of business and industry, peace and prosperity, brought on by the technological advance in modern times." Competitive salesmanship and the other strategic expedients of competition are the essence of modern business enterprise. The more mature the development of business enterprise, the greater the share of product wasted on salesmanship.

Modern industrial technology has rendered obsolete the prevailing industrial equipment and methods, which include more than physical relations, but "it is by no means an easy matter to find a remedy . . . that will approve itself as a sound business proposition to a community of conservative businessmen who have a pecuniary interest in the continued working of the received system, and who will (commonly) not be endowed with much insight into technological matters anyway." So long as the obsolescence gives rise to no marked differential advantage of one magnate as against another it follows logically that no remedy will be sought, particularly since the adjustments required today are not simply matters of detail, but are in the nature of an economic reorganisation. Under the competitive pecuniary interests of the businessmen in control, there is "a fatal reluctance or inability to overcome this all-pervading depreciation by obsolescence." This is the penalty for taking the lead in industrial development under business principles. "The shortcomings of this British industrial situation are visible chiefly by contrast with what the British might be doing if it were not for the restraining dead hand of their past achievement, and by further contrast, latterly, with what the new-come German people are doing by use of the English technological lore." The English are now paying the penalty for having taken the lead in capitalisation. The situation of Germany makes it plain that it is immaterial equipment which is of prime importance, not the accumulation of productive goods. "These 'production goods' cost nothing but labour"; the immaterial equipment of technological proficiency, the state of the industrial arts, considered as a system of habits of thought, "cost age-long experience." But the "economists have not been in the habit of making much of it, since it is in the main not capable of being stated in terms of price, and so does not appear in the statistical schedules of accumulated wealth." Funded wealth invested in industrial business is industrially of slight importance, since business capital means in the aggregate merely "a pseudo-aggregate of differential claims on the usufruct of the industrial equipment, material and immaterial." As a result of the extensive use of credit and corporate organisation the aggregate of capitalised wealth greatly exceeds the aggregate market value of the material items.

The discipline of the machine industry is inimical to the stability of personal government, of "subordination to the discretionary call of a personal superior." Instead it induces a due appreciation "of the sweep of mechanical processes, impersonal and in that sense equitable." But when the business control of industry takes extensive effect personal discretion again becomes dominant. "The authority of ownership, enforced by pecuniary pressure, takes on a coercive character that grows more comprehensive and unavoidable as the scale of industry and investment grows larger. Under latterday large-scale conditions, this authority of ownership has the harsh aloofness of irresponsible tyranny, but it has none of the genial traits that may relieve even a very ruthless despotism. The subordination which it enforces is of a sullen, unenthusiastic character tending more and more to a grudging disloyalty, as the scheme of business control grows more comprehensive and settles into more rigid lines." The result is an antithesis, emulation and disparagement between classes which is like the relation between hostile cultures or between culturally distinct communities, and "the outcome is a state of aliency between the two, which may on slight provocation rise to the pitch of manslaughter."

Under the rising standard of living, or increase in conspicuous waste, of the advanced pecuniary culture, the function of the perfect gentleman is to waste as much as he can engross of the community's resources and product. Under the canon of pecuniary efficiency "the conspicuously wasteful consumption of the gentleman must not incidentally or by leakage conduce in any degree to the physical well-being, or to the pecuniary gain, of anyone else. . . . The staple product of the pecuniary culture in England in the way of gentlemen (and gentlewomen) is as good as human infirmity will permit." The population's preoccupation with sportsmanlike activities, with such a *"tour de force* of inanity" as big-game hunting for example, results in a wasting of the products and energies of the industrial system and the perversion of the sources "from which the efficiency of the industrial system is to come."

The success of the German people was achieved in spite of the imperial state, not because of it. Because of their more recent entrance into what constitutes western civilisation, the Germans were able to take over the technology of Great Britain without the faults of its comprehensive business control. "The borrowers are in a position of advantage intellectually, in that the new expedient comes into their hands more nearly in the shape of a theoretical principle applicable under given physical conditions; rather than in the shape of a concrete expedient applicable within the limits of traditional use, personal, magical, conventional," or of "pecuniary use and want." "It is, in other words, taken over in a measure without the fault of its qualities." The premises and logic of this machine technology "are patent to the meanest understanding at the first contact." They may often be overlaid with an alien, "practically impermeable crust of habits of thought," but the substantial basis "is unavoidably and indispensably familiar to the common man in all his commonplace dealings with the commonest inanimate objects that surround him. Its point of departure and its scope and method are summed up in the phrase, 'matter of fact.' "

"The epoch-making intellectual achievement of the English technologists and their like, who prepared the Industrial Revolution and have afterward worked out its consequences in technology and the material sciences, is not so much that they gained a new manner of insight into the nature and working of material things, as that they were, by force of circumstances, enabled to forget much of what was known before their time." The most important of these circumstances appears to have been the decay of personal government consequent on the decay of dynastic enterprise. "By atrophy of the habitual bent for imputing anthropomorphic qualities and characters to the things they saw, they were enabled to interpret these things in terms of matter-of-fact." "This does not mean that everyone, or any community is ready forthwith to evolve the working technology of the machine industry out of his inner consciousness, provided only that no one interferes with his cogitations. Even given the premises and the logical insight, there is a large field of empirical, matter-of-fact knowledge to be covered under the working-out of these premises; and this can be had only at the cost of . . . experience and experimentation, for the details of this knowledge are of the opaque nature of all empirical, particularly physical, information and are to be had only by the narrow channel of sense perception."

In contrasting German material development with that of the English-speaking peoples Veblen refers to his eight-page supplementary footnote on the country town, which illustrates the backwardness of American business. American business has had unexampled material resources and workingmen, but under the unlimited opportunities for profitable business, the industrial outcome has been inferior to that in Germany. Taxation in America has fallen not on the businessman in control but on the farm population and other classes not engaged in business. Nowhere have businessmen so controlled the laws and administration, nowhere have they had such opportunities, and nowhere have they fallen short of their opportunities by so wide a margin. The mature American businessman is of the same character as the American politician. He is a product of the country town, "considered as an institution and an engine of cultural discipline." The immigrant rural population of the Middle West and its productive activity were mercilessly taken advantage of by the Yankee leisure class of substantial citizens which constituted the institution of the country town. "This politico-pecuniary enterprise in municipal pre-requisites is a case of joint action rather than of collective action," since "each and several of the participants, overt and covert, takes part as a strategist or diplomatic agent for his own pecuniary interest." The characteristic enterprise of the country town businessmen is real-estate speculation, a businesslike endeavour to get something for nothing through engrossing the technological efficiency and practising what are actually acts of prevarication in promoting this speculation. Those who pecuniarily succeed must be conservative, prehensile, and endowed with the capacities of cupidity, prudence, and chicane. Their enterprise and efficiency is in pecuniary strategy, pecuniary intrigue, also called finance, not in industrial innovation. "Adventures in new, untried, unstandardised industrial projects and expedients are alien and anathema to the prudent, conservative business community." The mechanical inventions which have given America its industrial importance have not been made by the businessmen or with their support. The modern pecuniary test of survival rejects candidates who are endowed with technological insight or with an aggressive curiosity in matters of industrial management. The incredible amount of waste in equipment, resources, and manpower is due to the businessmen's lack of even "the degree of technological insight necessary to appreciate the pecuniary loss involved in their own astute mismanagement." But the waste is increased severalfold when account is taken of the unemployment or the stoppage of workmen and plant which result from the pecuniary strategy of these conservative businessmen.

The operations of large-scale American business finance by business financiers who hold the industrial fortunes of the country in their hands are eminently of this country-town character. Their controlling incentives are those of the security market, not those of the output of goods. Final discretion rests not on the engineering staff or manager of the work, but on the financial house whose ostensible relation to the industrial concern is only that of an underwriter. The trust movement was a device of the great financiers to manœuvre concerns into difficulties so as to obtain bonuses and similar gains through recapitalisation, and these concerns have continued in a state of dependence upon the irresponsible financial houses. The relationship is so commonplace as to call for no censure. The greatest financier and discretionary controller of industrial enterprise maintains that the directors of a corporation are not responsible for the condition of work in the concern since they are merely financial agents. Another great financier holds that, in justice to the full discretion of these directors, their establishments must be left without control by public authorities.

The German captains of industry of the new era did not, however, graduate from the training school of a country town, with its rule of "prehension, division, and silence." They made good under the selective test for fitness in the aggressive conduct of industrial enterprise, not in the closed circuit of financial strategy. They could install the best of equipment since they were not constrained by the invisible hand of capitalisation. They were not captains of finance but captains of industry, and chose their staff on the basis of industrial insight and capacity, not on the basis of street-corner politics and "astuteness in ambushing the community's loose change." While the American community was being brought under the control of the financial strategist, the German was being brought under the rule of the technological expert. The salaries of captains of industry and their staff were not high, since they were accustomed to a frugal way of living. The German workmen had not reached a pitch where industrial activity and interests were conventionally irksome.

But the fundamental principle of the price system, with its continual bargaining, is the principle of conspicuous waste, and thus in any community where industry is controlled by the price system there eventually arises some sportsmanlike endeavour, which is expensive and unprofitable from the standpoint of the material interests of the community, but which gives an appearance of activity, so that the sense of workmanship is not entirely frustrated. In Germany, too, the great rule of corporate finance, which conserves and increases the funded wealth at the cost of stopping the community's material wealth, has resulted in a relative decline of home consumption and an increasing demand for foreign markets for investment and similar purposes. Fixed charges cumulatively increase and cut into the industrial advantage. The early differential advantages have been duly capitalised under the regime of credit and the capitalist system, so that with the phenomena of obsolescence comes a discrepancy between accepted capitalisation and effective earning capacity. By a curious twist of logic the imperial statesmen have felt that this inevitable and cumulative drawback could be remedied by the acquisition of colonies. The consequent rising standards of conspicuous waste bring on labour troubles, which threaten the "living profits" to be paid on capitalisation. But these "living profits," based on what the traffic will bear, are the fundamental element in the pecuniary standard of living, and are given up only reluctantly and tardily. Ultimately the decent waste of time and substance, or increased charges and costs, threaten the disappearance of the disposable surplus between industrial output and current consumption.

A settlement by war was inevitable, but Germany's best opportunity was a half-dozen years ago, when it ceased to gain in industry and commerce relatively to the situation at large. Its increase in warlike capacity has not kept pace with that of its competitors. "The resulting massive aggregate of increase in warlike capacity among the nations with whom imperial Germany has had to make up its account has been such as would, during the last few years, throw the net balance of the differential gain slightly against the Empire's score."

The economic system of a dynastic state is operated on the principle of fighting capacity. Railways are laid out from the standpoint of strategy, and the lordly classes obtain pecuniary concessions. Any popular sentiment against the imperialistic aggression of the strategists is repressed by "drastic exercise of the police power, and a free recourse to juridical excesses," by censorship of the press and of education, by pensions, insurance for disabilities, etc. Universal military service is the most effective corrective of socialistic propaganda and similar movements of insubordination. Without the training this warlike service gives in personal authority the socialist movement would hardly have fallen into its present state of "innocuous desuetude." The whole scheme rests fundamentally on martial law, and the single-minded aim of dynastic aggrandisement is obstructed by no consideration of equity or humanity. "A dynastic state cannot be set afloat in the milk of human kindness"; from its great warlike enterprise the common man has nothing to gain but frustration and hardship. But "so seen in its historical setting and in the light of the circumstances that have shaped it and that will continue to determine its further life history—that is to say, considered genetically—this variant of the western civilisation is evidently an exceptionally unstable, transitory, and in a sense unripe phase."

It cannot be otherwise, for it combines archaic metaphysics and the modern industrial arts, an institutional scheme handed down from medievalism and a technology resting on matter-of-fact. It is true that the English commonwealth, which is something in the nature of a joint-stock company, is not the embodiment of free institutions that is imagined. Discrepancies of wealth were not provided for in that ancient hereditary bent towards free institutions which made "the petty anarchistic groups of the Baltic culture a practicable engine of social control" and which is reasserting itself now in democratic discontent. In fact, in the light of the de facto consequences of property rights, it is doubtful whether a free, indigent workman in the modern industrial community is in a better situation than a workman on a servile tenure under feudalism. But at least it is now believed that the common man has paramount dominion, and that class distinctions are against human dignity. The cultural drift is towards free and popular institutions. As the machine technology renders obsolete the imputation of occult powers and qualities in the conception of objective reality, the similar imputation of occult grounds for privilege, authority, and subservience will become obsolescent in the institutional scheme. "Free institutions and insubordination" are the concomitants of the mechanistic industrial system, "inseparable from it in the long run because it is made of the same substance as this technological system." But the "long run" has not yet been achieved in the German case.

So Veblen sketches the natural decay of the dynastic state. In his analysis the dynastic state seems unlikely to endure in competition with free institutions and the modern state of the industrial arts, unless there is a reversion, a general destruction of civilisation. The modern large-scale dynastic state violates the technological foundation upon which it rests. "The Imperial system of dominion, statecraft, and warlike enterprise necessarily rests on the modern mechanistic science and technology, for its economic foundations and its material equipment as well as for its administrative machinery and the strategy necessary to its carrying on. In this, of course, it is in the same case with other modern states. Nothing short of the fullest usufruct of this technology will serve the material needs of the modern warlike State; yet the discipline incident to a sufficiently unreserved addiction to this mechanistic technology will unavoidably disintegrate the institutional foundation of such a system of personal dominion as goes to make up and carry on a dynastic state." But whether the imperial state wins or loses, the struggle stands for "a substantial, though presumably temporary, impairment and arrest of western civilisation at large."

Veblen seems to find some advantages to the community, however, "in times of stress, as in a season following warlike devastation," just as he found some advantages to the community in a depression. Such times of stress show clearly the waste and maladministration of modern business enterprise, for then industry and industrial life show themselves able to continue in spite of the devastation of the governing authorities. In *The Theory of Business Enterprise* depressions are shown to entail the liquidation of security values, the competition of new industry with lower fixed charges, the suspension of a large proportion of conspicuous waste, so that a greater amount of goods is produced than in high prosperity. In *Imperial Germany* the argument is somewhat similar. If seasons of great warlike raids are not too protracted, industrial values recover, because the state of the industrial arts is not damaged. The loss in equipment and special personnel is easily made up. In such a season of stress the demand for the superfluities required by pecuniary decency is seriously demoralised, and the taboo against productive achievement falls somewhat in abeyance. Thus the net production of the community rises nearly to the level of its gross productive capacity, or at least comes much nearer to that level than in the piping times of peace. Under the settled conditions of peace and commonplace prosperity over fifty percent of the conventionally necessary consumption is in items whose use is "only conventionally necessary," such as capital values, and can be easily dispensed with to the advantage of the material welfare of the community.

Veblen's final digression in a supplementary note is concerned with war finance. The aggregate of war taxes, plus liens and similar obligations, indicates roughly the aggregate wealth consumed in prosecuting the enterprise, not including the incidental waste due to devastation. These war loans, presently funded, are greater than they appear, because they are of a perpetual character. The demand for war loans in effect advances the rate of interest and lowers the capitalisation of outstanding securities with a fixed income. Property is in reality capitalised at a higher rate of interest. As an effect of the war loans the financiering houses "trade on a thinner equity," and the available industrial equipment in effect is bid up. A voluminous credit extension results, and, since in the season of hostilities the traffic in war loans unavoidably goes on, neither the rate of discount nor the price of such goods as are wanted is likely to return to the antebellum level so long as these conditions remain. The net result after a period of hostilities is that the businessmen in the war industries have gained, other industries have lost, and industrial property has been recapitalised on a thinner equity and at an increased rate of dividend. To the old irrevocable capitalisation is now added the government securities covering war loans, the interest on which constitutes a fixed charge on the community wealth and income, a deduction of the community's earning capacity. This deduction may conceivably rise to one hundred percent of the net income, and may even pass that point. A season of war prosperity is followed by a liquidation, in order to bring the capitalisation into correlation with earning capacity and to determine the ownership of the net earnings.

In the main text of the book Veblen declares that in the season of hostilities the volume of obligations added on the basis of the industrial property is almost the same as the amount of war obligations. But neither the aggregate property in hand nor the industrial efficiency of the competitive nations is increased at a comparable rate; there is more likely a decrease in these items. Since no wealth or productive capacity is created, the result of the new claim on industrial enterprise is, in effect, to transfer to the holders of the new securities an undivided interest in the com-

munity's wealth, amounting approximately to the face value of the securities issued. It would be hazardous to estimate by how great a margin
the newly credited claims, amounting practically to an aggregate seizure
of the productive capacity, fall short of the total wealth in hand.

A serious effect of the great competitive warlike enterprise is the loss
of industrial morale, the lowering of industrial efficiency, because of
irregularities rising from the discipline of military service and from exposure to the vicissitudes of an occupation which in reality amounts to
arson and murder. Perhaps one deduction should be made, however, in
favour of warlike enterprise. The officers, drawn from the wealthier
classes, are gentlemen, from the economic point of view, and have appreciably less than no industrial value to the community since they are typically
unproductive consumers. Therefore the mortality of officers, the discretionary agents in the warlike enterprise, should be credited to the net gain
of the community, and the economic relief is something more than a per-
capita rating. Those who believe that the effect of the great modern
competitive enterprise is to drain off and destroy the best people—those
best for warlike enterprise—should have no fear. If the condition of warlike activity remains, the breeding of depauperate stocks from the
delinquent, defective, and dependent will produce the same kind of manhood.

In an article on "The Opportunity of Japan" in the July 1915 issue of
The Journal of Race Development, one month after the publication of
Imperial Germany and the Industrial Revolution, Veblen made an analysis of Japan that was almost identical with his analysis of the imperial
German state. "In effect, the people at large are the government's chattels, to be bred, fed, trained, and consumed as the shrewd economy of
dynastic politics may best require." The underlying population is exploited for the glory of the intangible imperial state and for the gain of
the governing authorities. In Japan, as in Germany, the anachronistic
medieval scheme of institutions was not displaced by the reception of
western technology, but the latter was taken over without the magical
practices and conventions that hindered its further development in its
place of origin. The Japanese have not yet worked out that scheme of free
institutions based on insubordination which is a basic element in western
technology, but have allowed the material gains to be appropriated by
the imperial establishment for dissipation in warlike endeavours. The
feudal institutional foundations of Japan are being threatened, however,
by the new mechanistic technology, since its "matter-of-fact conceptions . . . induce the working-out of a corresponding fabric of matters
of imputation-principles of conduct, articles of faith, social conventions,
ethical values." The feudal regime of Japan must give way either to

business enterprise or to a scheme of institutions adapted to modern material exigencies.

The system of business enterprise is closely involved in the principle of the dynastic state, and it entails so much waste that it must eventually exhaust the surplus which was hitherto available for the use of the feudal establishment. Pecuniary management results in "what might be called the 'sabotage' of capitalism—the competitive working at cross-purposes of rival business concerns and control of industrial processes by considerations of net gain to the managers rather than of material serviceability." Equipment is rarely, if ever, worked to its capacity, and "products, whether goods or services, are turned out with a view, in respect of kind, time, place, and sophistication, to their profitable sale rather than to their serviceable consumption." Because of this unavoidable "capitalistic 'sabotage' the industries in the maturer commercial countries fall short of their theoretical normal efficiency by something more than fifty percent." With competitive gain comes "competitive spending as its legitimate counterfoil," and this leads to a "ubiquitous system of 'conspicuous waste.'" Closely allied to these pecuniary developments is "the well-worn principle of modern politics that 'public office is a means of private gain,'" and a comprehensive system of "graft" develops. It was this comprehensive principle of graft which allowed "the great organisation of Russian officials to be defeated by the Japanese," but the system must develop in Japan, too, in due course of maturity. Through the competitive wage system and other channels of commercial indoctrination, such as sabotage, this "same principle of competitive consumption comes to permeate the industrial population and presently induces a higher standard of living or more accurately of expenditure"; thus the surplus is still further diminished. The dynastic statesmen do not realise that these conditions bring about a decline in the rapid rate of material gain which material efficiency has already produced. If the Japanese are to utilise these new-found gains for dynastic aggrandisement in Asia, they must strike within the effective lifetime of the generation now coming to maturity. "The imperial government must throw all its available force, without reservation, into one headlong rush; since in the nature of the case no second opportunity of the kind is to be looked for."

The striking similarity of the underlying argument in *Imperial Germany* and "The Opportunity of Japan" is more than a coincidence. Veblen had begun *Imperial Germany* before the war, and the declaration of war threw a different light on what he had written. He told Urie that he had made some alterations in his material and relabelled it "The Opportunity of Japan." He could, in fact, have made similar alterations in "the opportunity of Japan" and made it apply to the opportunity of modern finance in the United States. These substitutions were made possible by the fact that the emergence of modern Germany, modern Japan, and the modern United States occurred at about the same time—Germany in 1870, Japan in 1863, and the United States in 1861.

The reviewers of *Imperial Germany* took the book rather literally and viewed it as an examination of the imbecility and eventual downfall of Germany. It was admired by both conservatives and liberals, more properly reformers, although conservatives were more outspoken as to Veblen's "characteristically cumbrous style" as the reviewer in *The Journal of Political Economy* called it. The reformers gave high praise to Veblen and his attitude on Germany, but they were puzzled, as socialists and liberals had been puzzled by Veblen in the past. Walter Weyl of *The New Republic* wrote: "In the end we lay down Professor Veblen's book with a certain sense of frustration. The theory he advances is large and original, but the very detachment of the author baffles us, and the ironic and elusive treatment of a subject matter which lends itself to a more direct handling, gives us a feeling that Veblen has said only a few things that were in his mind."

Graham Wallas, in *The Quarterly Journal of Economics*, called the book a sociological treatise and Veblen a genius. "If someone would write a 'Secret of Veblen,' summing up (with an index!) the four books which have so far appeared, Professor Veblen's position in the universities of the world would be assured." Wallas expressed the hope that Veblen would write a new book, "in which he shall drop the irony and reticence which is such an admirable means of self-protection for a sensitive teacher who thinks for himself."

Doubtless the interest in the war was responsible for the fact that Veblen's analysis of modern business enterprise was generally ignored. But to Veblen this seems to have been the most important element of the book, judging from the trend of his course in "Economic Factors" during the year he was writing *Imperial Germany*. The second semester his course deviated from the usual "anthropological inquiry." Ostensibly the course followed the book, with perhaps more emphasis on the contrast between the German and American situation. The supplementary note on the country town became of considerable importance, and the strident note beginning to appear in Veblen's books is more obvious in the lectures.

Modern large-scale industry was introduced in America at about the same time as in Germany, and accordingly the two nations may justifiably be compared. But the contrast between Germany and America is greater than that between Germany and any other country that has stood for much in modern industry. Germany is far inferior to the United States in resources and manpower, and it has serious disadvantages in its heavy public expenses, but it has outstripped the United States in efficiency and left it far behind.

The American businessman "brags" of enterprise, but actually he is extremely conservative. In the development of the United States the typical businessman was a small dealer in real estate, or a holder of real estate as a side issue. The essence of this business is to get something for nothing, and almost without exception the landowner has found himself suddenly possessed of a fortune. The situation was in favour of real estate and undeveloped resources, and there was no need of industrial speculation or industrial pioneering. The German businessman, however, was necessarily speculative in industry. The land in Germany was not so available, and it could be used in business undertakings only as a complementary factor to much greater wealth of other kinds. Since there was no Michigan white pine to be stripped, the businessmen had to develop a process, some special technology. They were men of liberal education, scholarly enough to work along with the experts, but in America the businessmen have neglected or even fought the technological expert. They have tried to avoid experimentation, but when the effectiveness of new processes is demonstrated they reap the profits. Great industry has been developed not by the enterprise of the businessman, but in spite of him. It is true that there is much gambling in business, but high capitalisation is provided for that purpose, and the industrial organisation goes on its way without encouragement and in a different sphere. The American businessman aims to keep out of industry, to make money without impairing his health. He lacks the German's education, which would enable him to look into the future and see the product before it is demonstrated, and thus he waits until the experimentation stage is over and then "fleeces the lamb." Usually he does not understand even an algebraic formula, and he has an aversion to anything he does not understand.

This relationship between business and industry in America is due to the American educational system. In the pre-industrial era, that is, before the Civil War, the American community had only a rudimentary training, and education was eminently practical. This was considered necessary because of the seemingly small margin above the means of subsistence, but the margin was not as close as was believed. When the early industrial era developed, the educational system offered the student no subjects likely to make him capable of dealing with large projects, of grasping the theoretical formulations which are essential in modern industry. Education was based on the requirements for efficiency in a handicraft system, but in Germany the common school system was made responsive to new industrial conditions. The extreme practicality of American education was solely for the purpose of pecuniary efficiency. There was no self-sufficient foundation for education because the people had no further horizon than pecuniary ideals. In Germany ideals of efficiency rose largely from early traditions established by scholarly businessmen who had other than pecuniary standards of excellence. Short-time calculation was discouraged. Even in America there are limits beyond which the standard of pecuniary success becomes odious, but on the whole the men who have stripped the country of its resources, and stripped the people of their money, are regarded with the utmost popular approval. The people applaud them for founding libraries, foundations, and universities (Cornell, Stanford, Chicago).

The American businessman is not content with merely getting a living. He is interested in the immediate gain which he himself is able to extract from the process, and he discounts heavily any long-term motives. In America business enterprise seldom looks more than eight or ten years ahead, usually less, whereas in Germany twenty years' foresight and calculation is not uncommon. Gary, Indiana, was obsolete before it was finished, as the result of business management with no knowledge of and no foresight for industrial details. Germany has not been so burdened with this kind of obsolescence, and she has been able to accomplish in fifty years what required three hundred years in England.

Capital, an accumulated fund, is essential to carrying on modern industry, but Germany did not need so much capital as America and could get it more cheaply and with less difficulty. There the methods of credit arrangements were more minutely looked into, and business speculation was not so widespread or so rooted in formulated tradition. In America better collateral was required, for American business enterprise was more speculative. It rested on real estate, which is an insecure investment. Even transportation adventures were entered into for the sake of a real-estate boom. In the United States there was scarcely a corporation of any size that did not have some kind of franchise or privilege which it depended on for unearned gain. Enterprises involving any considerable flotation of securities were presumed crooked till proved straight. Industry was always watching for opportunities for manipulation, gambling, and speculation. The consequent high pecuniary risk to lenders and investors was a cause of the high interest rates, although it is not usually recognised as such by orthodox economists. This situation gave Germany an advantage in the world market, for investment is made on a basis of expense and not cost as the orthodox economist knows it. Since the natural resources of Germany were neither of as good quality nor as plentiful as those of the United States, Germany was forced to develop the machine technology more assiduously. The machine discipline was acquired more thoroughly. It was not so easy for German businessmen to get something for nothing, and industry was therefore conducted more on the basis of legitimate gain.

The United States is essentially a mature colony, a branch of the British colonial system and of British culture. In England the situation from Elizabeth's time to the present has been one of steady and, on the whole, uninterrupted advance in productivity per capita. This, however, has not meant any significant improvement in the material well-being of the working class, as the early classical economists candidly admitted. They spoke of the iron law of wages, the subsistence minimum, and the Malthusian law of population. There has been sufficient time for the appropriation of the surplus to develop into an elaborate system of unproductive consumption. England is best habituated to this unproductive consumption and unearned gain. Germany can never become so efficient as England in disposing of surplus wealth which does not go to the worker. The methods must become conventionalised; they are then considered noble. In the United States there were no conventionalised means of disposing of surplus gain.

Compulsory military training in Germany reached its greatest effectiveness in about 1880–1885. Since then the military officialdom has been a visibly growing burden, insubordination has declined, and loyalty to the dynastic state has increased. The net efficiency of the German economic system continued to rise until about 1906, but since then the net product has probably remained constant, that is, the rate of the deductions has caught up with the rate of increase of gross product. Veblen declares that Germany was not gaining at a higher rate than the Allies either in spiritual or in material equipment after 1912, and that if German imperialistic statecraft had been wise and uninfluenced by sentiment a war would have been started in that year.

An element of basic importance which is clearer in the notes than in the book is the role of the technical expert. In mechanical industry the expert is one who knows the complete theory of production, who has discretion and insight into industrial processes, not one who has a manual dexterity and is equipped with apprenticeship training. The expert studies the detailed working of the process. Patent-office diagrams and designs cannot merely be transferred into terms of three dimensions instead of two, they must pass through the hands of the experts, and be adapted to theory, before they can be operated as mechanical bodies.

In handicraft industry the labourer was an embodiment, an impersonation, of the industrial process, and hence in handicraft industry the personnel was all-important. Skill and manual dexterity were the keynote to the system and these could be acquired only by long training and the development of traditions. In borrowing the handicraft system from the continent England had either to import workmen or to send workmen to Europe to spy upon the technology she was borrowing and learn it by training. She was aided in her acquisition by the continental wars and by the banishment of many of the best workmen from those continental countries. But Germany's borrowing from England was easier and more simple. It involved only the adoption of machines and a process worked out by experts and directed by experts. The workman is now only auxiliary to the process. The expert is the central fact; it is he who is informed on the theoretical meaning of the process.

Ultimately and basically the discipline of technology works at cross-purposes with that of the dynastic state or business enterprise. As the expert technician gains increasing sway, as is essential in the nature of his work and in the growth of material sciences, the greater are the troubles of the captains of finance, for the captain becomes increasingly an obstacle to advance and the technician becomes increasingly the responsible agent. The work of the expert makes it necessary for the captain to increase his depredation of material welfare, in order to maintain and increase capital values. Nevertheless the expert's substitution of formulæ and comprehensive theoretical principles for personal supervision and skill, suggests the answer to the gravest objection to socialism. The technical expert becomes not merely the substitute for the modern captain of finance, but the instrument for achieving the downfall of capitalism.

He again prepared to publish *The Higher Learning in America: a Memorandum on the Conduct of Universities by Business Men*. Like *Imperial Germany* it was written in less than a year. In fact, Veblen told a former student that it now took him about ten weeks to write a book, and that he used no notes. Before the book was finished in March 1916, Handman asked Veblen what the subtitle was to be, and Veblen replied: "A Study in Total Depravity." Ardzrooni said that the first draft was the most vitriolic writing he had ever seen. He told Veblen that the book would give people the impression he was mad. Veblen accepted criticisms without any comment, and made amendments. Originally it was planned to publish the book in the University Studies, but President Hill advised both the editor and Veblen against publishing it in the series. President Hill said that the book was one of the cleverest pieces of writing Veblen had done, even though his point of view seemed somewhat extreme, but "there were so many paragraphs that reflected on educational leaders of the universities that I considered it might seem discourteous for the University of Missouri to become officially responsible for its publication and distribution." He told Veblen that the time was not ripe for such a book, and Veblen accepted his advice. Veblen told Urie that he would not have the book published until after his death.

Veblen's influence was growing with a small group. Francis Hackett, who had become probably the outstanding literary critic in the country through his work on *The Chicago Evening Post*, was now literary editor of *The New Republic*. He lost no opportunity to praise Veblen, and also interested other literary editors in him. In reviewing Edgar Lee Masters's *Songs and Satires* in *The New Republic* in 1916, Hackett said that the confusion concerning Masters was due to "his arrival on the stage at a period of economic and moral transition. For the right clues to this transitional period there is no observer so fertile, so brilliant, so inexorably honest as the author of *The Theory of Business Enterprise*." Hackett quoted extensively from "The Cultural Incidence of the Machine Process" and concluded with the statement that Masters represents that modern population which Veblen calls "iconoclastic and materialistic." In reviewing Harry T. Baker's *The Contemporary Short Story, a Practical Manual*, under the title "The Fiction Factory," Hackett made Veblen the centre of his discussion and suggested that Veblen's analysis of magazine and newspaper work under the guidance of business principles showed a better understanding of the situation. This year the Institut International de Sociologie made Veblen a vice-president.

In 1915 it was understood by the seniors in the School of Commerce that Stewart and Davenport had been offered better positions in other schools but were staying on that year in order to have the benefit of their association with Veblen. Stewart told a colleague that the University of Chicago made him an offer because it wanted someone who could present Veblen's methods of research and inquiry. Unfortunately for Veblen, Davenport found conditions not altogether satisfactory at Missouri and left in 1916 for Cornell. Stewart departed for Amherst at the same time.

When Hoxie died in 1916, Alvin Johnson wrote in *The New Republic* that "every man who has come under the direct influence of Veblen has been marked by it." Although there is doubtless an explanation for Veblen, he "seems to be something new in the cosmos to anyone who knows him only through his writings." Veblen was deeply moved by the death of Hoxie, and when he was asked about his influence on Hoxie he replied that it was about the same as Hoxie's influence on him.

By the end of 1916 Veblen clearly realised that the United States, under the guidance of President Wilson's policy of "Peace with Honour," must shortly join the Entente cause. He declared that England's tactics in violating American neutrality were in effect similar to those of Germany, but England had shown more skill in execution. The Germans, he said, lacked an appreciation of the psychology of the English-speaking peoples, and he cited the different attitude of the Germans and the English in dealing with American shipping. The affronts of the English were as numerous and, with the exception of the sinking of the *Lusitania,* as offensive, but the English, having stopped American shipping, were very profuse in their apologies, while the Germans made no effort to disguise their "high-handed" violation of American rights. Veblen had a furtive admiration for the skill of the English, and he never ceased to be curious as to the explanation of England's successful strategy in maintaining world headship.

According to Urie, Veblen was very anxious that America should enter the war, and sometimes lost patience with President Wilson for his slowness in taking what he considered an inevitable step. Veblen received newspapers from the Scandinavian countries and gleaned considerable information that seeped through from Germany, and he was therefore in a better position than most Americans to appreciate the situation of the Germans.

Socialists and liberals of the left had an impression that Veblen was strongly against the United States entering the war. Max Eastman's sister arranged an anti-militarist meeting at the Park Avenue home in New York of Amos Pinchot and Veblen was supposed to lead the discussion. He came to the Eastman home for dinner before the meeting. Eastman who, "had admired him extravagantly all his life," says that "he refused to talk at all about any political or intellectual question, both throughout dinner and at the meeting. . . . He came to life only in a frivolous, or at least 'lowbrow' conversation with a very beautiful girl whom we had the sense to put beside him at the table." But she, unlike the beautiful women of Chicago, considered Veblen a "chimpanzee."

Shortly after Wilson was re-elected Veblen began writing, at the rate of 1000 words a day, *An Inquiry into the Nature of Peace and the Terms of Its Perpetuation.*

CHAPTER XIX

I N the early part of *The Nature of Peace* the date for the current
scene is given as December 1916; in the middle part it is January
1917; and the preface gives February 1917. With the exception
of *The Theory of the Leisure Class* none of Veblen's books contains an index, but *The Nature of Peace* contains a detailed table of con-
tents. This, however, was not prepared by Veblen but by Urie. According to Isador Lubin, who was Veblen's assistant at Missouri, Veblen
paid the publishers $700 to publish the book.

The preface contains some of Veblen's most earnest writing. "It is now
some 122 years since Kant wrote the Essay, *Zum ewigen Frieden* . . .
Many things have happened which the great critical philosopher, and no
less critical spectator of human events, would have seen with interest.
To Kant the quest of an enduring peace presented itself as an intrinsic
human duty. . . . Through all his analysis of its premises and of the
terms on which it may be realised there runs a tenacious persuasion that,
in the end, the regime of peace at large will be installed. . . . The title
of the following inquiry—On the nature of peace and the terms of its
perpetuation—is a descriptive translation of the caption under which he
wrote. . . . The aim and compass of any disinterested inquiry in these
premises is still the same as it was in Kant's time; such, indeed, as he in
great part made it, viz., a systematic knowledge of things as they are. Nor
is the light of Kant's leading to be dispensed with as touches the ways
and means of systematic knowledge, wherever the human realities are in
question. . . . The quest of perpetual peace at large is no less a paramount and intrinsic human duty today than it was."

Kant held that critical philosophy has its origin in morality, in responsibility for actions, and this belief is implied in all of Veblen's work.
In the middle of the book he raises the problem in his customary roundabout fashion. The question is the visiting of penalties upon the German
people for their outrages, and Veblen attacks the problem of whether
the dependent working classes are to be considered guilty for the transgressions of the great pecuniary captains. "The chief relation of this
common run, this underlying population of German subjects, to the inception and pursuit of this Imperial warlike enterprise, is comprised in
the fact that they are an underlying population of subjects, held in
usufruct by the Imperial establishment and employed at will. . . . The

warlike enterprise of the Imperial dynasty has already brought . . . a good measure of punishment on this underlying population, whose chief fault and chief misfortune lies in an habitual servile abnegation of those traits of initiative and discretion in man that constitute him an agent susceptible of responsibility or retribution. . . . It would be all the more of a pathetic mockery"—an inversion of all the equities in the case—"to visit the transgressions of their masters on these victims of circumstance and dynastic mendacity. . . . To serve as a deterrent, the penalty must strike the point where vests the discretion; but servile use and wont is still too well intact in these premises to let any penalty touch the guilty core of a profligate dynasty." Since this ethical canon applies to the entire leisure class, and since in Veblen's analysis imperial Germany is merely a type form of the essential characteristics of ostensibly democratic nations, it is not surprising that in Veblen's description captains of finance are shown as sinister figures, moral delinquents.

Although warlike enterprise inculcates in the community a heightened warlike animus, the conduct of modern warfare, which is a technological affair, decreases the common man's respect for the abilities of his superiors, the gentleman officers, for the gentlemen of the leisure class are as unable to command in modern warfare as in industry. The common man is of the underlying population, the ninety percent which owns only ten percent of the wealth. The privileged class is the ten percent which owns ninety percent of the wealth and engrosses the community's technological efficiency.

The preconceptions that Veblen examines in this book are those of patriotism and dynastic loyalty. The analysis is primarily of the motives behind the patriotic ardour for destruction, as expressed in the national spirit, but they are described as not far different from the motives behind modern capital, as expressed in the spirit of pecuniary gain. The categories of "dynastic ambition and business enterprise" have "the common trait that neither the one nor the other comprises anything that is of the slightest material benefit to the community at large."

The sole function of the modern state, with its principle of sovereignty, or inalienable right of aggression, is warlike enterprise. It is only in spite of the state that an enduring peace can be achieved. Veblen disposes of the students of political science on substantially the same grounds as he disposed of the received economists. "Quite properly and profitably that branch of scholarship is occupied with the authentic pedigree of [government] institutions, and with the documentary instruments in the case," with "a formally competent analysis of the recorded legal powers. . . . The *de facto* bearing of the institutional scheme on the material welfare or the cultural fortunes of the given community" is "substantially extraneous to the structure of political theory." If questions of this kind are to be considered, "the specialists in the field cannot fairly be expected to contribute anything beyond an occasional *obiter dictum*. There can be no discourteous presumption, therefore, in accepting the general theorems of current political theory without prejudice, and looking past the received theoretical formulations for a view of the substantial ground on which the governmental establishments have grown into shape, and the circumstances, material and spiritual, that surround their continued working and effect."

It is an axiomatic premise of political science that modern governments possess the same irresponsible coercive discretionary right that belonged to the feudal chieftain. But, as is illustrated by the Icelandic republic, these powers of coercion over the individual derive from an acquired bias, not from an underlying trait of human nature; they are a matter of habit, not of heredity. The Icelandic republic of insubordinate citizens collapsed under the systematic abuse produced by the accumulation of wealth, with the aid of legal fictions and constitutional formalities. Under the present state of the industrial arts such a republic is impossible, if the sacred rights of ownership are to be maintained. The rise of ostensible democracies can be conceived at best "as a transient weakening of nationalism by neglect, rather than anything like the growth of a new and more humane ideal of national intercourse."

It is for the benefit of the controlling investment interests that the governmental establishments engage in their warlike policies and in the incredibly stupid but inevitable competitive race in armaments which must lead to warlike enterprise. Such enterprise costs the community more than the gains it brings the business interests, but the common man bears enthusiastically this burden for the benefit of his wealthier neighbours, because in some occult manner he believes he profits by it. The "honour," or "spiritual capital," traded in by the governmental authorities carries no connotation of honesty, veracity, equity, liberality, or unselfishness, but is entirely worthless from the point of view of the material interests of the community. It is of a magical character, but the community will lay down its life to defend it, given the proper stimulus under the guidance of the interested business classes. Veblen compares those spirits animated by patriotism to the enterprising spirits of the Spanish Main and, in the present day, to the "even greater number of no less single-minded spirits, bent on their own 'life, liberty, and pursuit of happiness,' according to their light, in the money-markets of the modern world." In the spirit of his definition of modern capital Veblen says that "patriotism may be defined as a sense of partisan solidarity in respect of prestige." The patriotic spirit is one of emulation and invidious comparison, of sportsmanship rather than workmanship, and like these "is bent on invidious success," which basically and normally involves "as its major purpose the defeat and humiliation of some competitor," that is, "a differential gain as against a rival." The spirit of patriotism will not tolerate any public interests which traverse this all-pervasive preconception of waste and damage, whether the individual "be engaged on a rapacious quest of gain, as a businessman within the law or as a criminal without its benefit." The population at large—except for the "appreciable contingent of morally defective citizens" that are the leaders in such invidiously competitive enterprise—demands a conformance with the underlying generic human principles. But this moral sense is easily satisfied with a modicum of equity, and by cumulative excitation the support for the patriotic policy of aggrandisement can be achieved. The patriotic spirit, however, works at cross-purposes with modern life, with the civilised cultural and technological system. "In its economic, biological, and cultural incidence, patriotism appears to be an untoward trait of human nature."

Today property rights have displaced community of usufruct, and from the point of view of material interests the people are divided into two contrasted classes: those of great wealth, who own, command, have authority and are masters; and those of poverty, who work, are servants, and obey. With this development of property, and of similar prescriptive claims of privilege and prerogative, joint enterprise becomes beneficial to only one class. Under these conditions such enterprise works by methods of inhibition which lower the aggregate efficiency, in order to secure a differential gain. The interest of the governing classes in the common welfare is of the same kind as the interest of a parasite in the well-being of his host. The notability of the vicars of the national honour rests on nothing more substantial than a slightly subnormal intelligence, and their claims to serviceability for the common good, which are easily conceded and acted upon by the underlying population, are conceivable only in the "light of glory shed by the blazing torch of patriotism." In the aggregate the services rendered by the constituted authorities of the competitive governing establishments are only a remedy for evils of their own creation.

The two great administrative instruments available for imperialistic statesmen are the protective tariff and commercial subvention, which Veblen handles as if they were substantially identical. These devices, like "commercial turnover," are a patent imbecility, but the increase they bring in pecuniary activities is rated by the common man as an increase of his "psychic income," because he has an uncritical preconception of group solidarity instead of any clear perception of the facts of the case.

Veblen's description of the rise of the German dynastic state suggests the muckrakers' accounts of the rise of large fortunes. "When the Fatherland first comes under [the] light [of history] it presents a dark and bloody ground of tumultuous contention and intrigue, where princes and princelings, captains of war and of rapine as well as captains of superstition, spend the substance of an ignominiously sordid and servile populace in an endless round of mutual raiding, treachery, assassinations, and supersession." The common people who supported this structure of sordid mastery can have survived only by oversight. The embellished history of the time is devoted to the life of the master class, a life which they, their chroniclers, and the servile population considered admirable. This history "doubtless plays up the notable exploits and fortunes of its conspicuous personages, somewhat to the neglect of the obscure vicissitudes of life and fortune among that human raw material by use of which the admirable feats of the master class were achieved, and about the use of which the dreary traffic of greed and crime went on among the masters." Later this turmoil fell into lines of settled and conventionalised exploitation. Throughout his discussion it is clear that Veblen considers imperial Germany and imperial Japan merely type forms, the consummate development of patriotic enterprise, and that he considers it to be highly questionable whether the so-called democratic nations, with their mature property rights, have lost much of their barbarian heritage.

In Veblen's description even the "German Intellectuals" appear in the same class as the received economists and seem to embody the highest ideals of modern business. These intellectuals have borrowed the abstract theorems on cultural aims and national preconceptions, since "they are, in the spirit, citizens of the cosmopolitan republic of knowledge and intelligence," but these theorems of civic life of maturer nations have been apprehended and developed "in terms and by the logic of the dynastic system of control known to them by workaday experience—the only empirical terms at hand." Thus in the hands of the "German Intellectuals" the formidable development and elaboration of the modern civilised principles of liberty and freedom have "uniformly run out into Pickwickian convolutions, greatly suggestive of a lost soul seeking a place to rest."

In the achievement of peace the fundamental alternatives are either a submission to the imperial state or an elimination of these dynastic regimes. The first might be compared with submission to an all-powerful trust. It would mean non-resistance and submission to an omnipotent combination, and its outstanding feature would be the devastation wrought by the masters. The situation of the Chinese may be taken as a type form. Gains in civilisation, industry, and arts have always been made by the subject Chinese, with their alien masters contributing nothing but imbecility and corruption. But the Chinese, in spite of this handicap of misrule, waste, and decay "have held their place and made headway in those things to which men look with affection and esteem when they come to take stock of what things are worth while." " 'This fable teaches' that a diligent attention to the growing of crops and children is the sure and appointed way to the maintenance of a people and its culture even under the most adverse conditions, and that eventual death and shameful destruction inexorably wait on any 'ruling race.' Hitherto the rule has not failed" because it "is grounded in the heritable traits of human nature, from which there is no escape."

It might be contended that the rule of one great dynastic regime would result in such savings as the elimination of competitive armaments, and that the centralisation of authority might reduce "overhead" charges to a minimum. But the comprehensive principle of "Conspicuous Waste," the cost of which is borne by the subject people, would become more pervasive, and the provocation to the creation of this "good will" would not be diminished, for such a want is always indefinitely expansible.

The nature of this principle of monopolistic management becomes clearer as Veblen discusses more directly the pecuniary nature of the modern ostensible democracies. The citizens of these advanced nations are not masterless, for under the impersonal rule of pecuniary magnitudes a greater pecuniary force will always stand in a relation of mastery towards a lesser one. Under the "current regime of law and order, according to the equitable principles of Natural Rights, the man without means has no pecuniary rights which his well-to-do pecuniary master is bound to respect." It is felt to be right and good that the pecuniary majority, the ten percent composed of the pecuniary masters, should hold unabated rule over the material means of life in all matters of public policy concerning the general material welfare. This is evidenced in the scrupulous regard with which such a body of public servants as the Interstate Commerce Commission will safeguard the claims of the railroad companies to a "reasonable rate of earnings on the capitalised value of the presumed earning-capacity of their property." Under the surveillance of "big business" the community at large or the common man who makes up such a community "comes into the case only as raw material of business traffic—as consumer or as labourer. . . . He is, of course, free, under modern principles of the democratic order, to deal or not to deal with this business community, whether as labourer or as consumer, or as small-scale producer engaged in purveying materials or services on terms defined by the community of business interests engaged on so large a scale as to count in their determination. . . . De facto he is only free to take [the terms offered]—with inconsequential exceptions—the alternative being obsolescence by disuse, not to choose a harsher name for a distasteful eventuality."

Only a concern which has sufficient resources to make it a formidable member of the system is endowed with discretion. It makes very little difference for the common man whether the concerns act in collusion or severally. There would have been before now an adjustment to the principle of all the traffic can bear, exerting the utmost pressure on the common man, were it not for the insignificant backward trades and the lack of perfect mutual understanding and confidence among the discretionary businessmen. "The system is after all a competitive one, in the sense that each of the discretionary directors of business is working for his own pecuniary gain, whether in co-operation with his fellows or not."

Responsibility of ownership is inoperative in the characteristically modern industries. A concern will consume its manpower not at the rate that would be most economical to the community at large, because of the high cost of the replacement of workers, but at the rate which will yield the largest net pecuniary gain to the employer, because the cost of production of the worker is borne by the community. Thus under so-called scientific management the working community is pushed at high pressure and its members ruthlessly discarded, just as corporations are exploited by the captains of finance. Under control by discretionary business of large-scale industry, business strategy, discretion, and sagacity are reduced in effect to a judicious use of sabotage. Idle plant, duplication, waste, retardation, incompetence are the consequences of the free competitive enterprise of captains of finance. The businessman's remedy is the consolidation of competing concerns, and monopoly control. But to the common man the proposed remedy is even more vicious than the malady, for such a monopoly may fairly be depended upon to use its advantage unsparingly under the business principle of charging what the traffic will bear.

As a result of capitalistic sabotage production is less than fifty percent of capacity and hard times are normal. But the highly productive state of the industrial arts, although systematically and advisedly retarded or arrested by the thorough control of the instruments of production by investment considerations, "is at the same time the particular pride of civilised men and the most tangible achievement of the civilised world." The war is making it clear that business control is intolerably incompetent in a season of desperate need, when the nation requires the full use of its productive forces, equipment, and manpower, regardless of the pecuniary claims of individuals.

It is not the material means of life, nor the life conditioned on these means, that is conceived to be the ultimate ideal, but some higher intangible reality, such as fighting for the sake of the sovereign's renown. "Even the slightest and most nebulous reflection would make it manifest that in point of net material utility the sovereign's decease is an idle matter as compared with the loss of an able-bodied workman." A sovereign, like a businessman, "may always be replaced with some prospect of public advantage." The national integrity, however, is too strong a preconception to be seen in the dry light of the material interests of the community. It is not yet clear among the English-speaking peoples whether the industrial classes or the commercial classes will secure the hegemony. The dynastic state and modern mechanistic industrial life characterise two contrasting cultural eras, habits of mind, schemes of knowledge, with incommensurable systems of logic and appreciation.

The basis of enduring peace is the neutralisation of the rights of citizenship, including the preferential claims of investment and trade. "A neutralisation of citizenship has of course been afloat in a somewhat loose way, in the projects of socialistic and other 'undesirable' agitators," but nothing much has been achieved. Privilege and royalty would be eliminated, and a pacific league of neutral peoples established. The German aristocrat, the British gentleman, and the ideal American businessman are much alike in effect, "under the skin." They are "kept classes." For the British and American gentlemanly investors the usufruct of the community's productive efforts rests on a vested interest of a pecuniary sort, sanctioned by the sacred rights of property, with a routine of "subreption, trover, and conversion" as a result, "very much as the analogous German dynastic and aristocratic usufruct rests on personal prerogative, sanctioned by the sacred rights of authentic prescription, without afterthought."

But the war is teaching the underbred common man the futility of gentlemen and investment, and of "business enterprise designed to eventuate in investment." The superstition that industry is limited by lack of funds is being dissolved. When the national establishments become insolvent, they seem to get along much better without the accustomed roundabout method of accountancy and allowance of profits. Under these urgent material exigencies, investment, euphemistically called savings, has "the appearance of a gratuitous drag and drain on the process of industry." On the return to "normal" conditions the common man, who gathers nothing but privation and anxiety from the owner's discretionary sabotage, "may conceivably stand to lose his preconception that the vested rights of ownership are the cornerstone of his life, liberty, and pursuit of happiness." In America, land of "abounding faith . . . in business enterprise as a universal solvent," "the unreserved venality and greed" of businessmen has resulted "in furtherance of profitable abuses, of such a crass and flagrant character that if once the popular apprehension is touched by matter-of-fact reflection on the actualities of this businesslike policy the whole structure should reasonably be expected to crumble."

Under the neutral league, colonies, as conventionally understood, would have no place. "In the imperial colonial policy colonies are conceived to stand to their Imperial guardian or master in a relation between that of a stepchild and that of an indentured servant; to be dealt with summarily and at discretion and to be made use of without scruple." The people of the dynastic states might have to be put in tutelage, because of their ingrained habits of servility. Their masters, who are the responsible discretionary agents and therefore the guilty factors, are to be put away not as defeated antagonists but as public nuisances.

The bill of particulars for Germany is typical of the desirable procedure for all dynastic states: (1) Definitive elimination of the Imperial establishment and of the subsidiary order of privileged classes; (2) Removal or destruction of all warlike equipment; (3) Cancellation of the public debt of the Empire and its members; (4) Confiscation of such industrial equipment and resources as have contributed to the carrying on of the war; (5) Assumption by the neutral league—which would include America and the people of the defeated nations—of all debts incurred by the Entente belligerents or by neutrals for the prosecution of or by reason of the war, and the distribution of this obligation impartially among the members of the league. Civilians in invaded territories would be indemnified for injuries by the confiscation of "all estates in the defeated countries exceeding a certain very modest maximum, calculated on the average of property owned, say, by the poorer three-fourths of the population—the kept classes being properly accounted accessory to the Empire's culpable enterprise." Veblen's disposition of this typical case goes even further, for "the neutrals of the league must all be shorn over the same comb," and undemocratic institutional survivals must be eliminated. There is a suggestion that even the differentials and privileges of labour unions are to be eliminated.

Should gentlemanly government still be maintained after the close of hostilities, the pecuniary burdens placed on the defeated peoples will be shifted to the underlying population, without seriously touching the responsible parties. This will only feed the patriotic animosity, as in the case of contests between corporate financiers, "and offer a new incentive to a policy of watchful waiting for a chance of retaliation."

In the last analysis "the theory, i.e., the logical necessities of . . . a pacific league of neutral nations is simple enough, in its elements." War is to be avoided by putting away the means and motives of warlike enterprise and warlike provocation. This means the elimination of the price system, so that industry and livelihood are no longer managed by the rule of investment for the private gain of the captains of finance. The price system, the managing of industry or investment for a profit, permits no violation of the principle that all transactions must show a profit in terms of price, in terms of capital values. The only purpose of national interests is to keep the people in a state of mutual envy and distrust.

The preconceptions of "national solidarity and international enmity" are of a feudal character, but they are an integral part of the unwritten constitution underlying modern nations, even those that have departed most widely from the manner of life to which their peoples owe these ancient preconceptions. Hitherto the discrepancy between workaday experience and the received institutional preconceptions has been overborne by the unremitting inculcation of the patriotic virtues by those interested classes who speak habitually for the received order of things—"the beneficiary or kept classes," "nobles, gentlemen, or businessmen." The business interests, particularly the American business interests, look to short-term gains to be derived from the country's necessities. "The order of things which is known on its political and civil side as the feudal system, together with that era of the dynastic States which succeeds the feudal age technically so called, was, on its industrial or technological side, a system of trained manpower organised on a plan of subordination of man to man. On the whole, the scheme and logic of that life, whether in its political (warlike) or its industrial doings, whether in war or peace, runs on terms of personal . . . relations. Politics and war were a field for personal valour, force, and cunning, in practical effect a field for personal force and fraud. Industry was a field in which the routine of life and its outcome turned on 'the skill, dexterity, and judgment of the individual workman,' in the words of Adam Smith."

Warlike enterprise is still a matter of skill, cunning, dexterity, personal force, and fraud, even though the logic of war has come to be of the same mechanistic nature as modern technology. And the standard economic theories form a defensive hedge about the competitive system, seeing it as a necessary condition of their own validity; they assume the rights of property and contract as axiomatic premises and ultimate terms of analysis, the beneficence of which is unquestioned. These theories may have fitted the handicraft situation, but when applied to the later situation, which has outgrown the conditions of handicraft, they are nugatory or meretricious. Under corporation finance and modern industry the good old plan is archaic, and the common man is feeling the pinch of it.

The large owners of invested wealth have ordinarily contributed nothing to the technological knowledge which enables them, through their control of the material equipment, to draw their gains. This technological knowledge is a free and exclusive gift by the community at large to the owners of industrial plant. The large owners as a class are characterised by the successful businessman—"astute, prehensile, unscrupulous." They have a well-advised interest in retarding or defeating improvements, and in bringing about privation and starvation, for thereby they maintain or increase capital values. But the common man is beginning to doubt the expediency of the management of industry on the basis of private property and "by persons who can show no equitable personal claim even to the most modest livelihood, and whose habitual method of control is sabotage—refusing to let production go on except it affords them an unearned income." The modern captains of industry are in effect "captains of sabotage," and modern capital is little else than a "capitalisation of chartered sabotage," although for them such sabotage is legitimate and the term is "morally colourless." "It is only when measures of this nature are resorted to by employees, to gain some end of their own, that such conduct becomes (technically) reprehensible." "The large gains of the large corporate coalitions are commonly ascribed by their promoters and by sympathetic theoreticians of the ancient line, to economies of production made practicable by a larger scale of production. . . . What is . . . visibly true on looking into the workings of these coalitions in detail is that they are enabled to maintain prices at a profitable, indeed at a strikingly profitable, level by such a control of the output as would be called sabotage if it were put in practice by interested workmen with a view to maintain wages. The effects of this sagacious sabotage become visible in the large earnings of these investments and the large gains which, now and again, accrue to their managers. Large fortunes commonly are of this derivation."

In a peace that would abolish formal international dissension the division of classes would take the form of a division between "those who stand on their ancient rights of exploitation and mastery, and those who are unwilling longer to submit," "between those who live by investment and those who live by work." Those substantial citizens who speak for peace imagine a return to the old scheme managed by pecuniary equilibration with peace and security merely added on the surface. Under such a peace "the hold which business enterprise of the large scale now has on the affairs and fortunes of the community at large is bound to grow firmer and to be used more unreservedly for private advantage. The increased technological efficiency will necessarily be neutralised to a greater extent than heretofore through the freer scope of the large coalition of invested wealth." Under the greater security, with the maintenance of the existing system of property rights, "larger coalitions than before are due to come into bearing with more facile recourse to the rule of all the traffic can bear."

When widely separate passages in the book are brought together, it becomes clearer how Veblen's conception of the imperial state and a negotiated peace is influenced by his philosophy of the modern industrial mechanism, modern competitive business, and trade union practice. Germany, he declared, is still a dynastic state, for its national establishment is in effect a self-appointed and irresponsible autocracy which holds the nation in usufruct. Because of its very nature such an establishment, bent on dominion for its own sake, cannot keep the peace. A peace which allows imperial states to remain intact is merely an armistice, a temporary truce for warlike enterprise. To the discretionary authorities of these warlike combinations force is the only arbiter, and solemn engagements are to be broken at any opportune moment.

"The old-fashioned—that is to say nineteenth-century—plan of competitive defensive armament and a balance of powers has been tried and found wanting. . . . The era of defensive armaments and diplomatic equilibration, as a substitute for peace, has been definitively closed by the modern state of the industrial arts." In another passage Veblen presents much the same argument: "The ideal of the nineteenth-century statesmen was to keep the peace by the balance of power; an unstable equilibrium of rivalries, in which it was recognised that eternal vigilance was the price of peace by equilibration. Since then, by force of the object lessons of twentieth-century wars, it has become evident that eternal vigilance will no longer keep the peace by equilibration, and the balance of power has become obsolete" in the face of the new and inevitable policy of the defensive offensive. The logic of dynastic control has only one end, undisputed dominion for its own sake; a negotiated peace puts events into shape for submission of the peoples to the imperial powers.

Under the negotiated peace, which would be like the Roman peace or the peace during the Victorian era, the logical result would be an accelerated rate of accumulation of the country's wealth "in the hands of a relatively very small class of wealthy owners"—the "class of gentlefolk or legally constituted wasters." Under them would come the class of menial servants, the bailiffs or stewards of vested wealth for the leisure class in the proper sense. There would be a relatively inconsiderable semi-dependent middle class of well-to-do, "with the mass of the population even more nearly destitute than they are today." The resulting regime of feudal status seems not unlike the mature regime of the pecuniary magnate and modern capital. The middle class or dependent businessmen have illusions of independence, and throw their voice and interests on the side of their pecuniary magnates, safeguarding private property and the fabric of prices and credit through which the income stream flows to the pecuniary magnate. The logical result, under the heightened efficiency of large-scale investment, is that the middle class with independent means obtains a more meagre livelihood, particularly since its livelihood includes a considerable amount of conspicuous waste, the fundamental element of pecuniary traffic.

The situation of the farmer is typical of the middle class. It may be possible for him to earn a living wage if he has independent means enough. He calls himself an "independent farmer," and believes that in some occult way he is independent of the market, which is controlled by the paramount investment interests in the background. Recently farmers have attempted to influence the market, but they have not reckoned with the great investment interests. The farmer's interests are those of a working class, but "he clings to a belated stand on the side of those who draw a profit from his work."

Pedigree is a pecuniary attribute, "a product of funded wealth, more or less ancient." "The canons of taste and the standards of valuation worked out and inculcated by leisure-class life have . . . run, with unbroken consistency, to pecuniary waste and personal futility. In its economic bearing, and particularly in its immediate bearing on the material well-being of the community at large, the leadership of the leisure class can scarcely be called by a less derogatory epithet than 'untoward.'"

A mature system of investment for profit results in the suppression of cultural talent among the industrious classes. "The working of that free initiative that makes the advance of civilisation, and also the greater part of its conservation," is allowed only in the erratic member of the kept classes, and there it must work against the side draught of the conventional pecuniary usage, which discountenances any useful activity. The entire leisure class makes up at but only ten percent of the population and in actual effect the retardation or repression of civilisation by this means should reasonably be expected to count up to something appreciably more than nine-tenths of the gains that might presumably be achieved. All useful activity is teamwork, and where only a dwindling element has this cultural interest, its best endeavours will be nugatory. Thus the domination of the impersonal price system has in many American towns overruled all inclination to "cultural sanity" and put it definitely in abeyance. The barrenness of the American university is also evidence of the dominion of investment for profit.

But circumstances are enforcing a change. Technological improvements take place and new processes and equipment are now and then introduced in the process of seeking differential gain. Besides, the mechanistic technology requires intelligent workmen. Under the unremitting discipline of the machine process such a supernatural phenomenon as the basic institution of property must necessarily be divested of the superstitions that surround it. There is a strong and stubborn material interest bound up with this fundamental article of the pecuniary faith, and the class in whom this material interest rests is, in effect, invested with the coercive powers of the law. If any move be made to disallow the obsolescent rights of ownership and investment, all the coercive apparatus of law and order will be brought into action. But as soon as the workman realises that these prerogatives which do not run in the mechanistic logic work to his material detriment, as soon as he has lost the will to believe in these supernatural realities, it is to be expected that he will take a stand as uncompromising as that of the Englishmen against the irresponsible rule of the Stuarts. These kings were also within their prescriptive rights, but the outcome was not thereby affected. When each of two antagonists is convinced of the justice of his cause, the logical recourse, in the absence of an umpire, is the wager of battle. In such a conjunction history teaches that "the outworn institution . . . faces disestablishment."

In the present situation, therefore, the alternatives are that either the price system with modern business enterprise will disappear, or the pacific nations will conserve their pecuniary scheme of law and order, at the cost of returning to a war footing and of preserving the rights of ownership by force of arms. An enduring, unwarlike state of peace can be achieved only by an attempt to abate and eventually abrogate "the rights of ownership, and of the price system in which these rights take effect." If the modern pecuniary scheme of "competitive gain and competitive spending" is to be maintained, promoters of peace should make only such "a peaceable settlement as would result in a sufficiently unstable equilibrium of mutual jealousies; such as might expeditiously be upset whenever discontent with pecuniary affairs should come to threaten this established scheme of pecuniary prerogatives."

Shortly after completing the book Veblen, in a review in *The Dial* of *England; Its Political Organisation and Development and the War Against Germany* by the German historian Eduard Meyer, wrote: "In the apprehension of any outsider, of course, there is not much to choose, as touches the common good, between the warlike aggrandisement of an imperial dynasty, and the unearned increase of pecuniary benefit that accrues to a ruling class of gentlemen-investors. The nearest approach to serving the common good that is made by either of these contrasted national establishments and national policies is a make-believe backed with just so much of concession to the public needs as will serve to keep popular discontent from rising to the point of revolt; the material differ-ence being that the committee of gentlemen-investors who rule the commonwealth under parliamentary auspices are habitually constrained to concede something more, being more readily accountable to their underlying community."

Reviewers of liberal tendencies interpreted *The Nature of Peace* as a warning that the German and Japanese militaristic regimes must be eliminated, and that government aid and protection should not be ex-tended to foreign investments and trade in order that enduring peace be achieved. Some of them were impressed with Veblen's peace terms, and re-printed them in full. The more conservative organs were a little disturbed by the last chapter, with the relatively unguarded title "Peace and the Price System." *The North American Review* said that "it is only when one reaches the final phase of Mr. Veblen's argument that one clearly perceives that the whole work is, in effect, a bitter criticism of the existing social order. Yet at lowest, Mr. Veblen's analysis is clarifying and his warnings are well aimed." *The Springfield Republican* declared that "it may be urged against his latest book, that it is little more than an elaborate statement of orthodox socialism, and so perhaps it is." Some of the so-cialists were more confident. According to *The Call:* "The reasoning is the dialectic method applied by Marx and other great socialist writers, and in this method Veblen is a past master."

George Mead, Veblen's former colleague in the philosophy depart-ment at Chicago, said in *The Journal of Political Economy* that Veblen uses rigid categories and that "his formulas are too simple and abstract to do justice either to social movements or to the psychology of the in-dividual." He lays too much stress on the gravitation of wealth in the hands of a small class, to be spent in "pecuniary waste and personal futil-ity." The content of the British Labour Party programme, which is not a movement to abolish private property, gets no recognition from Veblen.

Floyd Dell, in *The Masses*, after describing Veblen as "the most bril-liant and . . . profound thinker" on modern society, "the author of that masterpiece of analytical satire, *The Theory of the Leisure Class*," said that the book "should result in his being either appointed to the Presi-dent's War Council, or put in jail for treason." Reading it is a "perilous adventure." "Professor Veblen may be compared to that mildest-mannered pirate that ever made a lady walk the plank. In this book he bears, indeed, a certain ironic resemblance to that eminent Russian trouble-maker who was intimate to the councils of both the secret police and the revolutionaries; and who cheerfully assisted his friends on each side in sending his friends on the other side to hell or Siberia as the case might be. In the realm of the intellect these duplicitous operations, resulting in a dreadful slaughter of familiar beliefs on both sides of the fence, are not ethically reprehensible. They are merely inconvenient to the reader, who is accustomed to be told at the outset whether he ought to believe it as he goes along. The peril of reading Veblen is that, whether your beliefs are pacifist or militarist, they will have been damaged severely at his hands before you realise your danger."

A fortunate occurrence for Veblen was Hackett's review in *The New Republic*. "So little is he known," wrote Hackett, "that a pretentious man the other day met my mention of *The Nature of Peace* by saying: 'Ah, of course, a new translation.' . . . Mr. Veblen is an American writer but the kind of American writer whose merit is rather more clearly recognised abroad than at home, an American who ought to have been a foreigner to be appreciated in America. . . . He is a mountain—stubborn, forbidding, purgatorial"—and "the area he unrolls is strategically chosen and significantly inclusive." His work is tortuous reading and one cannot skim through it. The greatest justification of the pain he exacts "is the final sense conveyed by him that he has had a singular contribution to make, and has made it with complete regard to the formidable requirements of responsible unconventional utterance." *The Nature of Peace* is the "most momentous work in English on the encompassment of lasting peace." In *The Theory of Business Enterprise* Veblen showed that the war and America's participation in it were inevitable. "The same rigour of intellectual standard that gave him a command of the situation at that time is discernible in this present volume, and gives him dominance now. Such severity of mind as Mr. Veblen exhibits is not likely to win him many readers, despite its Brahms-like quality, but the recommendation of Mr. Veblen is not merely the recommendation of a great philosopher of industrialism. It is not his relentless logic alone that elevates him. It is the democratic bias which *The Nature of Peace* indicates."

Hackett's review came at a psychological moment and played a role similar to that of Howell's review of *The Theory of the Leisure Class*. Instead of remaining a satirist Veblen became now an international figure, an authority on the problem of enduring peace. Letters began coming to him from all parts of the world. "Now," he said, "they are beginning to pay some attention to me." The Carnegie Endowment for International Peace purchased five hundred copies of the book, for distribution mainly to international relations clubs in colleges, universities, and normal schools. But Robert La Monte, who had officially left the socialist party, now with citations from *Imperial Germany*, urged socialists to purchase Liberty Bonds, join the troops, and suppress the activities of pacifists.[1]

On the basis of his books alone, Veblen's position regarding the war might seem rather difficult to determine, but the entrance of the United

States on the Entente side seems to have pleased him. When Japan also joined the Allies, Veblen wrote *The New Republic* that the Japanese statesmen, "these shrewdest, most callous, and most watchful of all adepts in unashamed statecraft," had given up all hope that their natural predatory ally, imperial Germany, would remain substantially intact after the war, and they therefore joined the victorious side. Veblen drew a distinction between winning the war and supporting what he had called in *The Theory of the Leisure Class* organisations devoted to devout observances.

Shepard has said: "I shall never forget the conversation I had with him soon after the United States entered the Great War. The entire country was, of course, wrought up to a high emotional pitch and the feeling against slackers was intense. A campaign was organised in Columbia to raise a certain quota of money for the Y.M.C.A., and I was delegated to solicit contributions from my neighbours. It was the intense feeling of the community that everyone should contribute at least something. I called on Veblen and presented the case and his response was an immediate and positive refusal. I was naturally somewhat angered and undertook to argue the matter and to bring the usual type of pressure that was used in coercing compliance with the general social demand. But I got nowhere. Veblen was quite impervious to any sort of social pressure. His answer was simple and direct. He had no use for the Y.M.C.A. He considered it a bourgeois and capitalist agency to defend the existing order. This conversation . . . revealed to me more of a socialistic attitude on Veblen's part than is to be found in any of his books. I do not mean to suggest that Veblen was a socialist. He was one of those people who are incapable of being pigeonholed or classified or placed in any category, but on this occasion he did talk the language of Karl Marx."

Veblen welcomed the Russian Revolution, which he had predicted not only before the war but again in *The Nature of Peace*. But when the Kerensky regime was overthrown by the Bolshevists, he was disheartened, particularly after the signing of the treaty of Brest-Litovsk, for he feared that as a consequence Germany might win the war.

Veblen's course in "Economic Factors" after the American entrance reflected his animosity against the Germans and their allies. In speaking of the fact that domestic animals did not originate in Europe he said: "The only animal domesticated in Europe is the cockroach. It was 'made in Germany.'" In a discussion of the barbarian raids he referred to the German pretension to a pure culture going back thousands of years. "I hate to disturb the boundaries of the Fatherland, but 3000 years ago it was not German at all. They came as invaders, taking the loose articles they found. As others came along, some settled down. So the whole traffic goes on. The history, the prehistory and early history of the Fatherland is of that sort." The Turks, he said, have always been in the minority. All ruling classes must be in a minority, for they produce nothing, and if they are in a majority, there will be nothing for them to consume. In Turkey the producing majority has not been allowed to have enough to live, and as a result they will soon be unable to produce enough for the leading class which rules. This has happened many times in southeast Europe, with the consequence of innumerable successions of ruling classes which have sooner or later died out. When the drain on the producing majority is more than the traffic will bear, the result is that both producers and consumers perish.

At the 1917 meeting of the American Economic Association, Carleton Parker delivered a paper on "Motives in Economic Life," in which he showed a literal acceptance of Veblen's instinct of workmanship and of the instinct of display, vanity, ostentation. He even included an "instinct" of acquisition, collecting, ownership, which was distinct from the instinct of vanity and, like other instincts, had to be satisfied and not thwarted. Mitchell objected that Parker made no allowance for the fundamentally important institutional factor.

There seemed to be a possibility that Veblen might go to Clark University, which he felt was closest to his conception of a true university. Veblen thought that a group in economics might be gathered together, composed of such men as Stewart, Mitchell, and Walton Hamilton, to make researches into current economic activity. An exchange of letters took place between President G. Stanley Hall and Veblen, but the matter fell through, ostensibly because of the limited financial resources of the university. President Hill and Davenport began negotiations with the Cornell authorities for dividing Veblen's services so that he could teach graduate students at Missouri one semester and at Cornell the other. In October 1917, while these negotiations were pending, Veblen took a trip to Washington, D.C. He wanted to be at the centre of things, and he hoped that he could be made use of on the paramount question of the plans for peace. He saw the Secretary of War, Newton D. Baker, and Supreme Court Justice Louis D. Brandeis, but no one in high position was deeply interested in the author of *The Nature of Peace*. He was discouraged and ready to return to Missouri, but friends sent a telegram to Mitchell in New York to come to Washington and see what could be done. Mitchell was busy at the time and telegraphed Veblen to come to New York. For a while it looked as if Veblen might be given an opportunity to develop his proposals.

In the fall of 1917 President Wilson requested Colonel Edward M. House to collect a group of men who could bring together all the available definite material in the form of facts and opinions, concerning the terms of a possible peace settlement. On the basis of these data House was to prepare a memorandum to guide the president in his peace manœuvres. House instituted the Inquiry which bears his name. President Sidney E. Mezes of the College of the City of New York was named director, and Walter Lippmann, then of *The New Republic*, was made secretary. Headquarters were established in New York and "specialists with practical experience were invited to join the staff." [2] Veblen prepared some memoranda for the Inquiry. One, "Suggestions Touching the Working Program of an Inquiry into the Prospective Terms of Peace," was a brief paper in the form of an outline, and discussed the use of the inquiry in establishing a pacific league of nations in the interest of enduring peace.

First Veblen raised the question as to whether peace was to take the form of the customary "diplomatic compromise," which would only eventuate in another war, or of a "neutral league of Peoples," which would take notice of such things as "trade discriminations, and the commercial engrossing of natural resources," only "to disallow them." Secondly, he discussed the need of "open diplomacy" in the matter of publicity in conducting the inquiry, so that public sentiment could be thoroughly canvassed and guided. Thirdly, the inquiry must eventually take sides between "favouring the vested interests at some risk to the maintenance of peace at home and abroad, or favouring a workable realignment of the country's available resources designed to keep the peace even at the cost of some appreciable derangements to these vested interests." Fourthly, if it be assumed that the settlement will result in a "League of the pacific Peoples," then the United States should show its idealism by taking the lead in establishing a league of neutral peoples, to be built at present around the chief Entente belligerents, and to serve as a "core of the eventual Pacific League." Veblen suggested that the inquiry, as an "organ of the administration," should turn its efforts to determining the "lowest terms and the most neutral claims on which such a working coalition can be made sufficiently compact for this purpose and can be held together as a going concern."

A notation on a copy states that it was submitted in December through Walter Lippmann, and "its date indicates," says Mr. Lippmann, "that we received it at about the time when we were preparing the memoranda for the fourteen points" speech on January 8, 1918.

In Veblen's second memorandum, "An Outline of a Policy for the Control of the 'Economic Penetration' of Backward Countries and of Foreign Investments," his discussion was primarily of the "Pacific League," although he admitted incidentally that this discussion did not directly concern the point at issue. It is assumed as a major premise, he said, that keeping the peace is the paramount consideration, and that the keeping of the peace would be the abiding purpose of the projected league of pacific peoples. It is thus implied that the people would divest themselves of all commercial discrimination and national ambition. The League would prove nugatory unless a large and consequential proportion of civilised mankind can be brought into it. The world, according to President Wilson, is to be made safe for democracy, and "Democracy may be described as that frame of mind by virtue of which a people chooses to be collectively fortunate rather than nationally formidable." The ancient principle of a balance of power to keep the peace must be given up, and one of the duties of the league is to eliminate formidable nations. It is being appreciated by the chief belligerents of the Entente that no profits of commercial enterprise or national aggrandisement are worth the hazard of a return to the *status quo ante*.

The core of the league and its prime movers would be the English- and French-speaking nations, and also the Chinese. Other nations who could answer to democratic specifications would also be included on equal standing. The organisation would be something like the American structure, with these peoples corresponding to the "states," in which the overruling sovereignty rests; the nationalities under German, Austrian, Bulgarian, or Turkish rule would correspond to the "territories"; and the pronouncedly backward peoples, now under the nations which will presumably exercise the discretion in laying down the policy of the pacific league, would correspond to the "outlying possessions."

Although cultural integrity or solidarity would be unimpaired, all national lines and national establishments would be obliterated, with a consequent disallowance of national discretion in commercial matters. There would be instead a neutral scheme of administrative divisions. All extraterritorial jurisdiction and enforcement of pecuniary claims, both between the several peoples of the league and between them and the peoples not in the league would be disallowed; that is, all pecuniary claims and obligations would be neutralised. The league would conserve the natural resources of the "backward" countries "with a view to the least practicable infraction or exhaustion of the resources that so are taken over in trust," and this supervision applies "to 'economic penetration' of undeveloped countries more at large, apart from the special case of those outlying virgin resources of the savage world." It has been uncritically assumed that the fastest and most comprehensive development of all hitherto idle resources is best for the inhabitants of the countries possessing those resources and for the citizens of the enterprising nation. But it can be seen from the past history of colonisation that such penetration and conversion to use may be too swift for the continued well-being of the native population. The pacific league, in order to hold fast to what is good in democracy, the policy of peace and good will, must not allow an exploitation of helpless wards and dependent neighbours. "Considered simply as a matter of moral profit and loss, dishonesty is not the best policy."

Industrial penetration is to be retarded on the grounds of "equity and of self-preservation from moral dry rot." Contrary to prevalent conceptions, most of these outlying resources are not needed. The available natural resources are sufficient for the calculable future, but the strategy of competitive investment prevents the use of resources otherwise available. The clamour for "development" comes from promoters and financiers, who are the only beneficiaries. Their objective is commonly a competitive advantage as against rival concerns, a monopolisation of materials with a view to the control of the market. "In those countries where this pursuit of private gain at the cost of the country's resources has been allowed freely to run its enthusiastic career, as, e.g., in America . . . the gravest mischief has been a pervasive deterioration of industrial enterprise into a collusive chicanery and a speculative traffic in unearned gains." Thus natural resources are not to be alienated to private enterprise; the furthest concession should be granting them on lease, for short terms and under such provisions as would reduce to the lowest terms the inducements offered to private enterprise. The permanent improvements and plant necessary to the working of these resources would be held in common usufruct by the common authority.

Foreign investments are made in order to secure a higher rate of profit. A part of the available resources are drawn out of the country, and thus the rate of profits in the country is raised or kept up, since production is reduced. Activity may result in industry so long as prices are advancing, but this is not always the case. The net result is a loss to the community but possibly a gain to the interested business concerns. The gains are in cash or its equivalent, and the well-to-do investors who receive the gain will spend it chiefly on superfluities. This diverts production away from goods for satisfying the ordinary needs of the community, and thus acts to keep up or advance the cost of these necessary consumable goods, thereby increasing or keeping up the cost of living. The nations which are outside the league are outside because they adhere to the old-fashioned principles of statecraft and to archaic illusions of commercial chicanery. It is assumed that the greater proportion of industrial resources and peoples are within the jurisdiction of the league, so that the force of the league might serve as a deterrent. The industrial relations of members with nations remaining outside would help to make the latter observe the requirements of enduring peace, and might eventually bring them in. They are "small and commercially dependent as compared with the League." If these nations, however, passed the limit of tolerance, relations with them would be curtailed by such measures as export duties on goods destined for them, and in urgent cases an embargo on traffic with them would be imposed.

The general policy of the league would be to extend the free-trade policy to include foreign investments and commercial traffic. The difficulties of this policy are difficulties of adoption, not of its successful administration. As a collective policy for collective peoples, directed towards the control of economic penetration and investment, it is very simple in principle, "amounting to nothing much more than a collusive disallowance of privileges and preferences, with safeguarding of the weak and destitute and without respect of persons."

"Under such a policy private enterprise is not to be supported or countenanced in making use of backward peoples or their resources; foreign investors will take their chances where they find them, without capitalising the support of their home government; justiciable questions will be decided under the law of the place where they arise, without prejudice by the litigants' domicile."

On the surface Veblen's conclusion seems far distant from his conclusion in *The Nature of Peace*, where the solution rests in the elimination of property rights and pecuniary magnates. But the whole discussion of foreign investment lays bare the incompatibility of modern capital and the modern industrial process, and emphasises the advisability of freeing the industrial process from the alien jurisdiction of pecuniary magnates. Veblen's Pacific League suggests once more a working industrial republic. Veblen's meaning becomes less obscure in the light of an address "On the General Principles of a Policy of Reconstruction," which he delivered in New York on January 18, before the National Institute of Social Sciences.

Since the Great War was engendered by the scheme of life of the *status quo ante*, declared Veblen, the re-establishment of this scheme may confidently be expected to lead to the same disastrous issue. All thoughtful persons are agreed that the peace must be kept. Disputes which rise to the dignity of warfare always turn on National Ambition or Business Enterprise, and usually on both together. America, despite its formal statements, entered the war for the ends of enduring peace and security. The question is between national business enterprise and free trade. The best assurance of peace lies through a pooling of the issues of business traffic, and thus the disestablishing of the national state as a handmaid of private commercial enterprise. If America took the lead in such a policy, other pacific nations might reasonably be expected to follow.

In the American commonwealth there is such a cleavage of interests as may reasonably be taken to augur a stormy reckoning ahead. As a going, living concern it is in a precarious condition, and the present is thereby the appointed time to survey the situation and make any necessary changes in the domestic policy, even at the cost of deranging vested rights and vested interests. The vested rights both of organised labour and of the employer, as seen from the standpoint of the material interest of the community, amount to the right to exercise unlimited sabotage to gain a private end, regardless of the community's need that work go on at full capacity and without interruption. There are few lines of industry or trade where vested interests do not work at cross-purposes among themselves or at cross-purposes with the common good, and the exercise of these vested rights amounts "to cheating the community of the full benefit of the modern state of the industrial arts." The inefficiency of railway enterprise, as seen from the point of view of material efficiency, has under the war situation forced the Administration to act. The same charge of costly incompetency is to be levelled against shipping and against the privately owned production and distribution of coal, and the handling and distribution of food products; "the oil, steel, copper, and timber supply are only less obviously getting into the same general category of public utilities legitimately mishandled for private gain."

The working at cross-purposes rises to disturbing proportions when and insofar as the industrial process concerned takes on such a character of routine automatic articulation, or mechanical correlation, that it can be controlled at a distance by means of accountancy, at the disposal of a modern business office. The result of the activities of big business and financial control is ill will between employees and employers and mischievous waste, expense, and disservice imposed on the concern's customers. Antagonism and inefficiency arise out of the disjunction of ownership and discretion from the personal direction of the work. This is most obvious where the discretionary control vested in ownership is exercised by an employer who has only a pecuniary contact with the industrial process, with the employees, or with the persons whose needs are supposed to be served. Under such a situation this superior control might better be exercised by one who has no pecuniary interest in the enterprise, and can therefore operate it at its fullest usefulness, eliciting the least amount of ill will on the part of the employees.

Veblen presented a "workable scope and method of reconstructing the existing scheme of law and order on such lines as will insure popular content." "(1) Disallowance of anything like free discretionary control or management on grounds of ownership alone, whether at first hand or delegated, whenever the responsible owner of the concern does not at the same time also personally oversee and physically direct the work in which his property is engaged, and in so far as he is not habitually engaged in the work in fellowship with his employees; (2) to take over and administer as a public utility any going concern that is in control of industrial or commercial work which has reached such a state of routine, mechanical systematisation, or automatic articulation that it is possible for it to be habitually managed from an office by methods of accountancy." Any plan of reconstruction must violate either the equities of the vested interests or the equities of the common good.

In all this there is no "socialistic iconoclasm . . . either covert or overt." It is merely a matter of material expediency. Already it is more than doubtful if the community at large will continue to be content to leave its large material interests, its larger industrial concerns, at the mercy of business methods. Business management has shown itself to work such waste and confusion as cannot be tolerated at a critical time. "The system of vested rights and interests is up for revision, reconstruction, realignment, with a view to the material good and the continued tranquillity of the community at large. . . . In this bearing, the meaning of 'reconstruction' is that America is to be made safe for the common man—in his own apprehension as well as in substantial fact. Current events in Russia, for instance, attest that it is a grave mistake to let a growing disparity between vested rights and the current conditions of life overpass the limit of tolerance."

Veblen no longer speaks of the material exigencies enforcing a change through habituation, but the conclusion he reaches is substantially the same as that implied in the earliest of his work. In *The Theory of the Leisure Class* Veblen had declared that under the leisure class institution of ownership the captain of industry can be dispensed with as fast as pecuniary transactions are reduced to routine, although this consummation lay far in the future; now he was proposing to eliminate the leisure-class gentleman and the prevailing leisure-class scheme, and to substitute the technological expert for the captain of finance.

Veblen also began writing for the literary journals. Helen Marot, who owned some stock in *The Dial*, became interested in Veblen's views and persuaded him to prepare some articles for that magazine. In one of these, "The Passing of National Frontiers," he declared that national frontiers, although they presumably had some usefulness in the old handicraft scheme, when they acted as a preparedness measure for the handicraft workers, interfere with the modern state of the industrial arts, and "serve substantially no other purpose than obstruction, retardation, and a lessened efficiency." But of course such restrictive measures are good for business. Business gets its gains from industry but in competition with rivals, and thus it becomes the aim of business concerns to hinder the productive efficiency of those industrial units that are controlled by their rivals. From this situation develops what has been called "capitalistic sabotage." The New Order that is coming in must recognise the fact that the nation as an industrial unit is out of date. The question of retaining the national establishment and its frontiers, of combating repression and waste of life and efficiency, "becomes in effect a detail of that prospective contest between the vested interests and the common man out of which the New Order is to emerge, in case the outcome of the struggle turns in favour of the common man."

Despite Veblen's prominence and his work he was not given a permanent part in the House Inquiry, and Allyn Young was put in charge of economic questions. Veblen felt that the heads of the inquiry did not appreciate the economic realities involved in achieving an enduring peace. He was, however, given an opportunity to serve the government in a minor position.

One of Veblen's friends, Alice Boughton, was assistant to Raymond Pearl, who was in charge of the statistical division of the Food Administration. During the fall of 1917 she suggested to Pearl that, since Congress would sooner or later begin to inquire into the procedure of price-fixing, it might be advisable to prepare for this contingency by having an economist of standing on the staff. Pearl and some of the subordinate heads in the statistical division who were fixing prices were biologists, not economists. She suggested that Veblen be offered the place, and gave Pearl some of Veblen's books to read. Veblen's biological approach appealed to Pearl, and he secured Veblen as a special investigator. Allyn Young, who felt too that Veblen's views might be of value in that connexion, had also something to do with the appointment. President Hill gave Veblen a leave of absence, and in February 1918 he joined the Food Administration.

While Veblen was in Washington he lived at first at the home of A.P. Winston, who had been one of his students at Chicago. He was friendly with a group of engineers, including Joseph Pogue, and according to Pogue he suggested to them that engineers collectively have a potential power which they have never exercised. Veblen submitted to the navy a scheme for catching submarines. The plan, which was based on his discovery that a wire in water will wrap itself around anything which strikes it, involved a set of wires to descend from a stout vessel and sweep through waters where submarines might be found. Veblen said that the admiral to whom he explained the plan was solid wood above his collar button.

Veblen was dissatisfied with the way his books were being handled by the publishers. *The Nature of Peace* was practically unavailable and Hackett took him to B. W. Huebsch, who arranged in February to take over the plates of the books held by Macmillan, who had published all but *The Theory of Business Enterprise.* Then Hackett secured $250 from Judge Learned Hand, Elsie Clews Parsons and others to advertise *The Nature of Peace.*

In the same month *The Nature of Peace* began giving Veblen a good deal of unfavourable notoriety. In an early chapter, "Peace without Honour," Veblen sketched in his strategic manner the advantages of unconditional surrender and submission to the imperial dynastic regime. Professor William H. Hobbs of the department of geology of the University of Michigan wrote to *The Detroit Free Press* that "one is fairly stupefied in contemplating the moral depths to which the flabby conscience of this pacifist has permitted him to descend." The newspaper published the letter with headlines reading, "Submit to foe, urges teacher. Permit Kaiser to rule world to save gold and blood, writes pacifist. Yet professor is retained as instructor of youth in state university." Hobbes also wrote a letter to *The New York Times,* for he was disturbed over the fact that the book was used at Columbia University. "This alone gives sufficient ground for an attack upon the book in print." Henry A. Wise Wood, chairman of the Conference Committee on War Preparedness, sent the Hobbs letter to *The New York Tribune* with additional comments. He said that "Professor Veblen's thoughts, logic, and arguments are of the sort that started the Huns on their present mission to conquer the world," and that the book was the "most damnable piece of pro-German propaganda that the Federal Authorities have overlooked." Complaints were made to the Department of Justice.

In Kansas City, President Hill publicly defended Veblen against a public attack by a visitor from the East. *The New Republic* thought the professor of geology should be given "the booby prize," and that Mr. Wood gave no evidence "that he has ever opened the book he is attacking." When Mr. Wood cited specific passages to *The New Republic,* the editors retorted that he did not appreciate the irony. *The Dial* commented that although "war offers small opportunity for laughter" the work of the self-appointed censors takes the character of "opéra bouffe." *The Tribune* retracted the letter and said that the incident had caused them to lose "faith in intuition." An army lieutenant wrote to *The New Republic:* "Mr. Henry A. Wise Wood and Company should have a vote of thanks from all radicals and also from those whose heads and eyes are still reasonably unclouded. Denunciations of Veblen's *Nature of Peace* have gained to the book at least one reader who would not have read it. They have converted me—to Veblen." One story which is probably not historically true but illustrates the confusion over Veblen is that, after the complaints to the Department of Justice, the book was read by an agent of the department who, although he could not understand Veblen's vocabulary, found the programme for the punishing of Germany so far ahead of anything that had been proposed by the Entente that he concluded that Veblen was a superpatriot, and refused to pay any attention to the complaints. The assistant attorney generals in charge of such work in the Department of Justice were admirers of Veblen, and one of them, in answering the complaint of the American Defense Society, added that incidentally Professor Veblen was in Washington in government service with the Food Administration. Lubin wrote George Creel, head of the Committee on Public Information, about using the book for propaganda. Creel replied that the material was valuable, but he did not think it advisable to use it at the moment.

Imperial Germany was also attacked. The executive head of one patriotic organisation heard with great chagrin from his scouts that Veblen was in the government service. But the attacks on the book continued. It soon became evident that two arms of the government service had radically different opinions about *Imperial Germany*. The Postmaster of the City of New York wrote the publisher that in accordance "with advice from the Solicitor for the Post Office Department you are hereby notified that the book entitled *Imperial Germany and the Industrial Revolution* . . . is non-mailable under the Espionage Act." Within the same week, a New York newspaper asked the publisher for permission to reprint certain chapters, because the Committee on Public Information thought the book was good propaganda. The publisher discovered from the newspaper that the official propaganda bureau of the American government had written: "We call your attention to certain penetrating chapters and passages in Veblen's *Imperial Germany and the Industrial Revolution*, especially with reference to how this feudal group has made terms with the industrial revolution which everywhere else has made for democracy, but which they in Germany have so dominated as to make it fit into their political and social scheme."

As William Hard said: "The Committee on Information thought that the book was damaging to Germany. The Post Office thought it was damaging to America." [3] B.W. Huebsch went to Washington and was introduced to an assistant attorney general by Felix Frankfurter, an admirer of Veblen. The assistant attorney general was sympathetic, but Huebsch found that no influence, not even official, availed against the war machine, of which the Post Office Department was one of the most effective instruments. Veblen talked about the matter in a jocular fashion, but he was glad to have influential friends take up the matter with the Department of Justice. Their efforts, however, were not successful. The question had serious implications for Veblen, because the recent report of the Committee on Academic Freedom and Academic Tenure, of the American Association of University Professors, had, in the words of *The Nation,* proclaimed "the right and duty of the 'academic authorities' to dismiss the officer who, without violating the law, is in *their judgment* acting in a manner contrary to that required by the national interest." [4]

President Hill felt that it was these public attacks on Veblen's books that led the Cornell authorities to veto the plan of dividing Veblen's services. But an alternative plan seems also to have been discussed. According to a minute of the Executive Committee of the Board of Trustees of Cornell, dated March 9, 1918, "arrangements have been made for securing Thorstein B. Veblen as Professor of Economic Institutions for the year 1918–1919 at a salary of $3500, of which $2500 is to be contributed to the University; and the appointment was approved and the details as to the contribution and possible further service referred to a committee consisting of the President and the Chairman." But on April 13, 1918, there is a minute stating that "the President reported that negotiations looking toward the securing of Professor Veblen for a temporary appointment next year had been discontinued." Some students of Veblen felt that the negotiations failed because too much anxiety was shown in dealing with the Cornell authorities.

Veblen stayed in the government service less than five months. Although he started his work with a feeling that he might do some good, a friend writes: "I think from the first month of his contact he realised that nothing would come of it." Some of the work was statistical and in that Veblen was almost helpless.

While he was working in the Food Administration, Veblen prepared a memorandum entitled "A Schedule of Prices for the Staple Foodstuffs (with Accompanying Tables and Charts)," which was the outgrowth of a study made by his assistant, Lubin, concerning the effects of government price-fixing upon the production of the small grains not affected by price stabilisation. It was a plan of price control in the interest of the production of the staple foodstuffs required by the Allies. Since the underlying purpose of any such regulation was the more effective prosecution of the war, the plan called, among other things, for guaranteeing to the farmer, for his "main staple foodstuffs," a suitable minimum return per acre of crops planted, and "perhaps a similar insurance per head of livestock in hand at the opening of the season." The producers would thus be relieved of the risk of losses "due to crop failures, or to unforeseen losses of livestock due to drought, hard weather, or disease." Under the existing emergency conditions "the production of foodstuffs is quite unmistakably a joint enterprise for the prosecution of the war," and "as far as practicable the risk of loss should be borne by the nation as a whole—on the well-known principle of mutual insurance."

An opportunity arose for Veblen to do some field work. General Enoch Crowder had just made his first call for a large quota of men, and complaints were coming in to the Food Administration from farmers all over the country stating that if their sons were going to be taken away from them they would be unable to harvest crops. Veblen and Lubin were sent out to investigate the possibilities of getting a labour supply. On reaching Minneapolis, however, Veblen became ill with a severe cold, and instead of continuing the trip he went to his home in Columbia, Missouri, to recuperate, and Lubin continued the work.

In one report *ad interim* to Pearl, Veblen called attention to a "particular political muddle" in the North Dakota area, and to "the mischief which it is causing just now" and the consequent "necessity of prompt and independent action on the part of the Food Administration if it is to save the grain crops" in that region. The Minneapolis office of the Farm Loan Corporation, which was a branch of the Treasury Department, refused for formal reasons to lend to the farmers who needed funds for the purchase of seed. Veblen declared that the "Farm Loan people, in collusion with the A.F. of L. representatives of the Department of Labor and equally political representatives of the Department of Agriculture, are collusively playing politics to queer the Non-Partisan League (which is in control of North Dakota) at all costs. The fortunes of the War and the chances of famine are a secondary consideration in the County, State, and National party politics of these northwestern states." In any attempt to relieve the situation "I gravely suspect the Railway Administration will lend itself to political manœuvres for defeating the Non-Partisan League." Nothing could be done for spring wheat and corn, but barley might be saved if pecuniary principles, such as the limitation of industry by capital could be laid aside. "To get the seed into the farmers' hands the Food Administration will have to disregard formalities and go over the heads of the Farm Loan people as well as of the representatives of the Agricultural Department. It appears to be not a question of placing Farm Loans and of the purchase of the seed by the farmers, so much as it is a question of distributing the seed and getting it planted, and then patching up the monetary questions involved afterward." For the sake of a labour supply Veblen suggested that all Federal indictments and prosecutions against the I.W.W. be "immediately quashed," and measures taken to prevent county and state authorities from similar activities, which he considered "also a political complication" and "closely bound up with the campaign of the old-line politicians against the Non-Partisan League."

Veblen reworked Lubin's first draft of the report, and on his return to Washington he submitted a detailed report buttressed by a number of exhibits. One exhibit contained affidavits concerning the beatings and other mistreatment administered to the I.W.W. by government officials, and by groups of citizens and members of Commercial Clubs. There was a list of men "who appear to have been indicted by oversight or in undue haste," and this document was "held by the informant to show an inexpedient animus." Some of the men indicted had long before been expelled from the I.W.W.; some were in foreign countries; others were dead, or had long been inactive in the organisation, or were not even members. One was accused by the organisation of being a labour spy. The close of the exhibit bears the following notation: "Is it any wonder that the I.W.W. feels that it is being persecuted by the government? How is such an error in judgment to be repaired?"

Veblen recognised that he was engaged in "special pleadings," but "it is intended as special pleadings for the grain crops of the northern prairie states." It was expedient "to discountenance and disallow any measures that will bear the appearance of persecution or partisan manœuvre," and to remove any hindrances to the most efficient use of the I.W.W. or any other available contingent of farm labour. Even if "they may not be in the right," their efforts are sorely needed and "they can be used to good effect only by way of generous treatment and fair dealing."

Veblen proposed that instead of prosecuting such organisations the Administration enter into "direct and official relations" with them. He made a suggestion, backed by affidavits from men in the forestry service and by a letter from an I.W.W. official, that a "scheme of regimentation be put into effect by which the workmen will be enrolled, under officers of their own choice, as members of a collective labour force to be distributed and employed at the discretion of agents of the Administration with suitable powers—always with the proviso that these agents be vested with advisory rather than coercive powers and be enabled to offer inducements sufficient to give effect to such advice as they may offer; that facilities be constantly afforded for men to enroll in these regiments of workmen, without other qualifications than a willingness to work and to submit to majority rule within their own regiment." Thereby the necessary mobility of labour, and the highest efficiency, might be achieved. Since the migratory workmen distrusted the Department of Agriculture and its agents, and also the Department of Labor with its A.F. of L. point of view, the arrangements "should be left in the hands of the Department of War and the Food Administration, preferably in the hands of a joint bureau representing both and consulting with both, but in the last resort answerable to the Secretary of War."

Veblen even discussed the matter with the Department of Justice.

Alfred Bettman, then an assistant attorney general, has said that one morning he was called into the office of John Lord O'Brian, who had charge of the enforcement of the Espionage Act, and was introduced to a gentleman whose name, however, he did not understand. From what the stranger said it was obvious that he had been sent by the Food Administration to the agricultural regions of the Northwest, evidently to report on the conditions holding back agricultural production. He had found that the "migratory labour," on which such production was to some extent dependent, was being antagonised by the campaign of the War Department Intelligence Service against the I.W.W. This was pictured as an example of two separate departments of the same government following inconsistent and contradictory policies. He was describing this situation for the purpose of persuading O'Brian to take some action which would cause better co-ordination and remove this I.W.W. persecution, for the benefit of agricultural productiveness.

"My first impression of the physical appearance of the stranger," said Bettman, "was not particularly favourable, by which I mean that it did not give the expectation that I would hear anything particularly interesting or important. As he spoke, I became alertly conscious of the fact that, whoever he was, here was a man of keenest wit and intelligence, clear and picturesque vocabulary, somebody exceptional, and I became eager to know who he was and managed to find out by a side glance at the visiting card which he had placed on Mr. O'Brian's desk, and lo and behold, he was none other than Thorstein Veblen! Of course, I immediately became doubly alert and interested, and think I said to Mr. O'Brian after the interview, that there was the keenest-minded person, who had come into the department while I was there."

When a hundred and one I.W.W. leaders were brought to court in Chicago, on charges of conspiring to obstruct the selective draft and hindering the government's war work, Veblen, along with such men as Robert Bruere, John Dewey, Carleton Hayes, James Harvey Robinson, signed a public appeal for funds to secure the best legal defence and a fair trial. Veblen felt that the long terms of imprisonment meted out by Judge K.M. Landis were evidence of hysteria, bordering on insanity.

In connexion with the same problem of obtaining a farm labour supply, Veblen prepared another memorandum on "Farm Labour and the Country Towns," which was substantiated by statistical data brought together by Lubin at Veblen's suggestion. After Veblen left the government service, he elaborated it and published it in a series of four articles under the title "Farm Labour for the Period of the War" in the single-tax publication, *The Public*. The editors said that Veblen had explained "the leisure class in a book that threw more light and cleared up more muddled thinking than any in a generation." The original memorandum is only slightly different from the published article, although in the former the style is more restrained. The published article calls more attention to the effective control exercised by the packers and millers over the farming population, and the consequent distrust felt by the farmers. In this article he refers to the vested interests of certain corporations of labour, by which he seems to suggest the A.F. of L., but this matter is omitted in the original memorandum.

The prosecution of the Great War, declared Veblen, depends most critically on the season's grain production in the prairie states. But the vested interests of certain organisations, both of labour and of capital, hinder an effective farm labour supply. The reason why the war has not been ended, with a victory for democracy, is that the American people have not been able to decide that they would disturb the vested interests and make unreserved use of all resources, including manpower. As a working force, as a going concern engaged in the prosecution of the War for Democracy, the American people are made up of the American farmers and workmen. The destiny of the democratic nations rests upon teamwork between these two free constitutents of the American population. The vested interests are certain fractions of the community who have a customary claim to a preferred share of the community product, and this vested right will be surrendered only when its retention involves palpable risk of its total loss. Any neutralisation of these rights depends upon what the farmers and workmen demand in the way of effectively prosecuting the war.

Because of its specialised character, requiring something of an apprentice period, the farm-labour supply cannot be immediately created out of urban people. The country towns, however, are made up to a great degree of persons drawn from rural occupations and therefore suitable for farmwork. Veblen now describes the town living off the country, much as in his other works he described modern business living off the working community. The "farmers" can almost be taken as a symbol for the entire industrial population. The country town is an organisation of middlemen, or businessmen, who make a profit in buying and selling. They sell the farmers' products at an advance in the central markets, and from the central markets sell products at an advance to the farmer. The living of the country town comes from the difference, which is in the nature of an unfair advantage.

The excessive number of retail concerns results in a waste of seventy-five percent of all men and resources employed. A great proportion of the country-town retail trade is appreciably more than useless, from the point of view of the net productive efficiency of the community which is supposedly served by this traffic. "The spectacle of ten well-fed bankers at the county seat" is "a striking evidence of the community's ability to pay." But "the prestige-value of a superfluity of well-fed bankers must not be allowed to cloud the issue of national efficiency." " 'Business as usual' means 'Uncertainty and retardation as usual,' " and in war times this production of waste, inefficiency, and fashionable discomfort is a matter of public concern, even though in time of peace citizens of any well-conducted democracy "are presumed to owe no active duty to the country in which they live."

With due allowance for the proportion of useful work performed by some concerns, two-ninths of the number of concerns and workmen employed would be sufficient to do all the useful work performed by the country town. The fraction would probably be even less, since much of the retail trade serves the population of the town itself, just as much of the trade in capital serves the corporate financiers. At least seven-ninths of the country-town population is supernumerary for all material purposes. It might be contended that by this elimination of waste and duplication the "benefits of competition would be lost." But the established retailers habitually act in collusion in matters of price and competition, under the guidance of the Commercial Club and with the aid of the town government which represent the "larger vested interests." In peace times, when only the creature comforts of the farming community are at stake, such a situation might be tolerable, but war-time expediency requires that the American people—farmers and workmen—"quit being squeamish about the vested right of the country-town merchants and speculators to get a 'reasonable return,' " which amounts only to surreptitious gain "on capital sunk in waste and duplication." The statesmen of the old order, the Commercial Clubs, the spokesmen of business as usual, suggest that moral suasion be brought to play on the sensibilities of those substantial citizens responsible for the impasse. But experience teaches that the best effects of moral suasion "are likely to be slight and transient where it runs counter to a settled legal right." Thus Veblen proposes a "sane and economical" plan of marketing and distribution which comes close to Bellamy's Utopia. The government would not bring administrative pressure against local concerns "beyond that equitable pressure of competition that is implied in the buying and selling of goods at cost." But such pressure should logically result in the greater number of these concerns quitting business, their personnel returning to the farm.

The plan contemplated a combination of the methods and working forces of the parcel post, chain stores, and mail-order houses. The Federal Administration should "install a system of farm marketing and of retail distribution of staple merchandise at cost, to be organised as one undivided administrative undertaking under the parcel-post division of the United States Post Office, and designed to serve all those places and persons whom the Parcel Post can effectually be made to reach." The mail-order house equipment and personnel would be taken over, present restrictions on the parcel post lifted, and transport facilities and freight handling placed indiscriminately at its disposal. The result would be considerable saving of the "overhead charges" of wasteful business, when concerns are consolidated in a trust or pool. Such concerns as express companies and other common carriers would be seriously affected, but present exigencies must be allowed "to take precedence of any vested interest in wasteful practice and special privileges."

The mail-order houses, despite superfluous business practices and the undying hatred of commercial clubs, have been so successful that the leading concerns are capitalised at something more than ten times the value of their material assets. Under the new plan the procedure for filling orders for goods would be the same as under the mail-order house system, except that the local post office would act as agent of the central office of distribution and the letter carrier would take orders, accept payments, etc. The money transactions would be handled in the fashion of periodical clearings. The post office would do all the banking business, in relation, if need be, with the Federal Reserve, and would become a station for the purchase and receipt of farm produce. Relatively little remittance of funds would be needed, because of the offsetting of credits and debits in the clearings. Most of the banking is now commercial, inflated on the same scale as the commercial business it serves, but under the plan more than one-half of it would be eliminated, and the remainder so simplified that it would be difficult to recognise as banking.

The experience of mail-order houses and the logic of the plan make it necessary to reach back among the jobbers, mills, factories, and packing houses. The great industrial enterprises supplying the farmers' needs cannot be allowed to "be managed by their owners for a profit, even under the most stringent standardisation and inspection." No system of inspection and legal remedy can keep up with the ingenuity of the interested parties. "Legal remedy by litigation after the fact is the merest foolishness in these premises." Veblen's proposal was "a plan for taking care of the farm products all the way over the circuit from the farm; when the goods leave the farmers' hands at the local market as raw materials; through the process of working them over into staple goods for consumption; and back again through the processes of distribution until they reach the farmers' hands as wrought goods ready for use." All the working parts needed for putting the plan into effect are at hand, and can be "co-ordinated into a balanced system directed from a single centre, instead of being left, as now, out of touch and frequently working at cross-purposes."

The ideal role of the entrepreneur and of money, as taught in the standard economic textbooks, would be performed by the central bureau, whose work would be in the nature of traffic management. The "market 'bureaux' . . . would transact very little that could properly be called 'business,'" since no bargaining and no salesmanship would be involved. Prices "would be offered quite impersonally, on a basis of standards and tests, as computed in a system of cost accounting." The change is fundamentally not in the mechanics of the traffic, but in the underlying principles. Under the present system the packers, for example, make the price at which the raw materials are bought and the finished goods are sold, but the principle is that of all the traffic can bear, which means the largest net profits to those who set the price. Under the new plan, however, the Administration, "through its local traffic agents connected with the parcel-post distributing system, would make its offer of prices on a cost basis, as adapted by skilled accountants to the special circumstances of each locality; and the producers would 'take it or leave it,' knowing all the while that the price so made is made without a view to profits and that no man has any motive of gain in determining it." The Administration will so arrange its schedule of prices as to induce the farming community to produce the largest practicable output of those staples needed for carrying on the war. For the satisfying of customers' everyday minor needs, and also as a further check on competitive duplication of equipment, the parcel-post system would necessarily comprise a system of local branches, in the nature of general merchandise stores and operated on the plan of chain stores.

The net result of the new plan, Veblen calculated, would be a reduction of the country-town population by nine-tenths, and a consequent increase in the available labour supply. This change is "of course, to be counted as a passing interruption of that regime of wasteful duplication, unearned incomes, and collusive division of profits that now goes to make up the everyday life and habitual interests of the town's population." The original memorandum was submitted to leaders of finance and industry, and Bernard Baruch, Chairman of the War Industries Board, gave it some consideration, but the plan did not interest the administration. Henry A. Wallace, whom Veblen visited while on the road trip, was impressed with Veblen and his quiet and unassuming manner, and Veblen expressed a high regard for Wallace's opinions and felt that he knew more about the realities of agriculture than did the officials at Washington. According to Wallace, Veblen felt that his colleagues' real interests were not in increasing the food supply but in conserving the profits of certain dealers in the manufacture of food.

While still in the government service Veblen wrote another article for *The Public*, entitled "Menial Servants during the Period of the War," in which he offered another suggestion for relieving the labour shortage. Even in the present emergency of war, he said, popular interest and administrative policy are bent on the maintenance of the status quo—the status of competitive gain and competitive spending—instead of on an elimination of "the nugatory interests and usages of peace." The chief use of domestic servants, menial servants, is not the physical well-being of the employer, but the intangible prestige value, or psychic income, which they represent. These intangible values and invidious distinctions are like sand in the bearings of the industrial and military mechanism by which the war is to be won. Nevertheless the better classes, while professing patriotic devotion to the country's efforts, continue to draw on the labour force for menial servants with whom to keep themselves in countenance as licensed wasters with ability to pay. In view of the great opposition to a direct conscription of the labour supply for productive use, Veblen suggested the taxation of such intangible values.

"It should be practicable to lay a steeply progressive tax on those same persons who still go on employing a staff of unproductive domestics to uphold their own personal prestige in the face of the nation's sorest need. There will, for example, be two able-bodied man servants, coachman and footman, in waiting at the curb while their patriotic and spendthrift mistress within the gate sits in self-appointed council on the state of the Republic at large with a quorum of ladies as scrupulously ignorant as herself in all those things that have any slightest significance for the work in hand. Indeed, merit is still to be acquired in that way." A household of five, including two children under the age of five, would have one tax-free servant. An additional servant would entail a tax of one hundred percent of his wages and living expenses; the tax on a second additional servant would be two hundred percent; on a third, three hundred percent; and so on. But as Veblen continues, he includes in the list of menial servants all labour engaged in the production, sale, or consumption of superfluities. The resources thus made available could be used for the material needs of the community. Butlers and footmen "are, typically, an eminently able-bodied sort, who will readily qualify as stevedores and freight handlers as soon as the day's work has somewhat hardened their muscles and reduced their bulk." This labour force devoted to superfluities is shown to occupy a place in the productive scheme not dissimilar to that of financial executives in service to capital, and in Veblen's conclusion there is even a Marxian suggestion of the effect of casting businessmen into the working classes. The effective law-making body, he said, would be reluctant to install a measure to "equalise the condition of life as between the servant-keeping class from which the law-givers are drawn and the common man to whose class the released domestics would bring an increment of numbers and discontent."

The editorial announcement of this article exemplifies the old and never-ending controversy over Veblen: "It is a sign of the times that we are left wondering for a moment whether to regard his article as a brilliant bit of playful irony or as the proposing of a war-measure which can be expected to receive serious consideration at the hands of the Federal Government." But the editors believed that "Professor Veblen was never more in earnest, as a careful reading . . . will show." A later editorial comment said: "Apropos of Dr. Veblen's recent articles, proposing heavy taxation of employers of servants, readers of *The Public* must have been particularly interested in the recommendations of the Treasury Department, recently submitted to the Ways and Means Committee of the House, for a tax identical in method and intent, although differing somewhat in rates, with that urged by Dr. Veblen."

Pearl submitted to Herbert Hoover Veblen's memorandum on the I.W.W. Pearl, who had grown to respect Veblen and to agree with much of his thinking, considered the report good. It was discussed at a meeting of the War Boards, but, as one colleague wrote, "it caused some consternation," in view of the aspersions it cast upon various government bodies, and its attitude on the I.W.W. Veblen and Lubin were not told what happened to the memorandum, but when requests for information or memoranda ceased to come to them from any of the offices of the Food Administration, they took the hint and resigned. Veblen was somewhat chagrined and discouraged with his experience in the government service. In his opinion the discretionary authorities considered the war already won, and were therefore interested mainly in retaining the *status quo*. He felt that the packing interests were in control of the Food Administration, and that it was they who were responsible for his leaving. He asserted that Hoover went to Europe to take charge of food activities there so that he would not be put in the position of taking orders from the packers and putting the data secured by the Food Administration at the disposal of these interests.

Before formally ending his services with the Food Administration Veblen wrote a memorandum which he submitted to leading educators and published in *The Dial* under the title of "The War and Higher Learning." The ostensible reason for the memorandum, according to Lubin, was that Veblen was disturbed over the possibility that the hatreds developed by the war and the loss of income experienced by foreign universities might cause a void in the contribution of scientists to the world's knowledge. Interested businessmen, he said, act as if the nation's industrial system may best be served by hindering the nation's industry from taking advantage of that freedom of intercourse in the use of resources and technology which the modern industrial system presupposes as an indispensable condition to its best work, and thus they have enforced such measures of restriction and retardation as the protective tariff. The functioning of the higher learning is similarly restricted by such measures as restrictive tariffs on apparatus and the disbarment of aliens from teaching. But a civilised nation has nothing to lose and everything to gain from unguarded co-operation in the necessarily joint pursuit of knowledge, just as it needs co-operation in technology. In the pursuit of knowledge the loss of one is acknowledged to be the loss of all, and any substantial loss or defeat is recognised as the most shameful setback that could be suffered. Thus the condition of the higher learning in the aftermath of war is a problem of greatest consequence. In the higher learning, as in technology, the war is resulting in a tremendous depletion of forces, breakdown of necessary co-ordinations, decay of the spirit, and impoverishment in material means. These effects, which will not end with the formal close of the war, are best exemplified by the "moral dilapidation" and incapacity for sound work shown by the German scholars. By denunciation, debauchery, and diversion to alien interests they not only hinder the scientific work of the present but also prevent the rise of a new generation of scientists.

The Americans, however, have been less exposed to the disorganising experience of the war, and they have the necessary material means for the conservation and reconstruction of the world's joint enterprise in science and scholarship. Any degree of reflection will show that the American community is in no danger of material impoverishment in the further course of the war. It would seem obligatory, therefore, that the American schools provide sanctuary and allow free and impartial use of their resources to students and teachers, regardless of nationality, who give any evidence of fitness. Heretofore the higher schools have been rival concerns, doing a wasteful competitive business in student registration, scholastic real estate, and funded endowment. In times of peace, prosperity, and universal price rating such waste may be endured, but in time of war it is intolerable, and this competition for trade in erudition should be eliminated by co-ordination. The schools should be brought out from the underbrush of rivalry and intrigue, should pool their scholastic issues and thereby give rise to something like a central office. It would "serve as a common point of support and co-ordination," as a "focus, exchange, and centre of diffusion for scholarly pursuits and mutual understanding," and would be "an unattached academic house of refuge . . . for any guests," both domestic and foreign, "strays, and wayfaring men of the republic of learning." The institutions of the higher learning, by placing their resources and good offices at the service of the world at large, would thus in reality serve their ostensible purpose, which has hitherto been served to a considerable extent in name only.

Charles Beard of Columbia University told his class on the American Constitution that the most original work on the economic basis of government structure was being done by a man named Thorstein Veblen in a small college called Missouri. Wesley Mitchell told R.C. Journey, a student and colleague of Veblen's at Missouri, that Veblen was the most profound scholar in the social sciences, with Marx in second place. In class Mitchell said: "Veblen is a man . . . who has been more misunderstood than any other American economist of his day, and misunderstood primarily because of his highly original temperament as well as because of his highly original frame of mind." To look upon prevailing ideas of right and wrong as of the same nature as certain superstitions "is, to people who have not had any experience in that kind of inquiry, often a very disagreeable experience." Thus many readers of Veblen have been badly shocked and put in such a state that "they either could not go on reading at all or could not go on reading in a frame of mind which allowed them to understand what is being said. I think that, more than anything else, accounts for the fact that this extremely penetrating theorist has, until recent years—at least the last two or three—had comparatively little recognition, outside a very small circle of people, who largely for personal reasons, have understood what he is doing, better than the great majority." Practically all of Veblen's graduate students "have felt his extraordinary powers and have been inclined to attach a great deal of importance to the problems he has seen more clearly than his contemporaries, and also to solutions, at least to some of the solutions which he has provided. But it is not until a man has had a considerable education of a rather unorthodox sort that he begins to see the real significance, either of the problems or of the solutions that are offered, and it has only been recently that there has been any considerable number of people interested in economics who have gotten a sufficient glimmering of these problems and their importance to give Veblen anything more than a sort of esoteric recognition." Intelligent students should try to view him with calmness, "not getting unduly excited over the writer's mannerisms, or unduly frightened by the conclusions to which he seems to be conducting us."

Stewart and Walton Hamilton were instrumental in securing Veblen for a series of lectures at Amherst in May 1918. These lectures were provided by the William Brewster Memorial Foundation, and the catalogue said of them: "Four or more lectures are given each year on the Modern Point of View. The purpose of the donors is 'to assist the College in throwing light in a genuinely scientific spirit on the relation of present-day research, discovery, and thought to individual and social attitude and policy.' " [5] Veblen's lectures at this old New England college, the intellectual home of Hickok and Clark, were on "Economics of the War and the Modern Point of View." According to Hamilton, "Veblen stuck his tongue in his cheek and declared that the modern point of view in economic thought was a product of the eighteenth century."

Jett Lauck, a former Chicago student who was executive secretary of the War Labor Board, offered Veblen a job with the board at a salary of $4800 a year. Veblen's title was to be Examiner, but Lauck expected Veblen to be of great service in giving the board the benefit of his prophetic insight into what policies should be followed and particularly what was to be done in the light of the expectation that the cessation of the war would not mean the ending of the board's functions. Veblen at first felt that in a body whose chairmen were Frank Walsh and ex-President Taft he would not be congenial. However, Lauck told him he would find a great number of radicals on the staff, and Veblen agreed to join the board. But he dropped the matter when he saw a possibility of joining *The Dial* staff, although he could not expect the salary that Lauck offered him.

In June Veblen prepared *The Higher Learning in America* for publication again, after adding "War and Higher Learning" to the introductory chapter, with slight alterations. It was the first book that Veblen did not have to subsidize.

CHAPTER XX

IN this book, too, as in all his others, Veblen's analysis is concerned with the dominance of modern capital. The higher learning is carried on under the guidance of the personal end of pecuniary gain. The never-ending competitive accumulation of wealth for the sake of competitive expenditure of life and substance, so that there may be further competitive accumulation of wealth, becomes in the institutions of higher learning a competitive seeking of endowments and an increase of students from among the reputable, so that life and substance may be expended for a further accumulation of funds and immature students. There, too, capital is the objective, and the consequence is a steady elimination and repression of the one end conceded by sober, civilised mankind as the only undisputed end, just as in the economic organisation, modern corporation finance leads to the repression and elimination of the material welfare. The factors that are ostensibly only the means of life have become the ends of life, to the destruction of civilised humankind. "It will avail little to speculate on remedial correction for this state of academic affairs so long as the institutional ground of the perversion remains intact," so long as the institutional ground is "the current system of private ownership."

Even in denying to technological schools a place in the university, Veblen seems to be emphasising not only the fact that the lines of free inquiry and criticism must be kept open, but also the incompatibility between the business schools and modern business principles, and the impersonal ends of mankind. For the modern captain of industry and the boards of directors discussed in other works Veblen substitutes now the captain of erudition and the governing boards, composed to highly successful businessmen. The role assigned elsewhere to national patriotism or to good will is given now to university prestige. Education, like business, is rated in terms of earning capacity, and the ideal of efficiency is the pattern of shrewd management whereby a large business concern makes money.

"There is . . . a work of reconstruction to be taken care of in the realm of learning," said Veblen in his supplementary introduction, "no less than in the working scheme of economic and civil institutions." Here, too, "if it is to be done without undue confusion and blundering, it is due to be set afoot before the final emergency is at hand." But since "competition is well ingrained in the habitual outlook of the American schools," such a foundation as the Carnegie Institution "might serve as a practicable nucleus" for the "proposed joint enterprise," provided some of its restrictions could be removed. This freely endowed joint enterprise would serve as "an international clearing house," and "students of all nationalities, including Americans with the rest, may pursue their chosen work . . . as guests of the American people in the character of a democracy of culture." The resources are available, because "the experience of the war, and the measures taken and to be taken, are leading to a heightened industrial productiveness and a concomitant elimination of waste." The universities may turn to what is supposed to be their aim, and "forgo their habitual preoccupation with petty intrigue and bombastic publicity," for the sake of competitive prestige, "until the return of idler days."

Any system of knowledge runs back to two impulsive native traits of human nature: Idle Curiosity and the Instinct of Workmanship. Knowledge is idle in the sense that it is sought impersonally as an end in itself, not for the personal end of pecuniary gain. Such knowledge will be turned to account in various ways by the instinct of workmanship, which gives the basic canons of truth and validity. The important factor in systematising knowledge is the current technological scheme, but workmanship today is made to conform with the system of ownership and pecuniary value, which is alien to the current state of the industrial arts. Modern technology is a matter-of-fact, impersonal pursuit of knowledge, and the inquiries of modern men, in so far as they are modern, are tested by canons of mechanistic effectiveness. But the American community appears to be divided "between patriotism in the service of the captains of war, and commerce in the service of the captains of finance."

The university is the only institution upon which the quest for knowledge unquestionably devolves, and the conservation and advancement of learning are recognised as its only duty. The quest of learning involves, first, scientific and scholarly inquiry, and, second, the instruction of students for the sake of carrying on the quest. A university is a body of mature scholars and scientists, and all else but the quest for knowledge is incidental. The student is presumed to have scholarly and scientific aspirations, and he has a legitimate claim to an opportunity for such personal contact and guidance as will give him familiarity with the ways and means of the higher learning, for the university is not a penal settlement. The controversy between those who speak for the modern university and those who advocate that culturally obsolete institution which includes lower and professional schools—such as schools of commerce and finance for the training of successful businessmen—is a controversy between "those who look to make use of the means in hand for new ends and meet new exigencies," and those who "wish to hold fast that which once was good" in a barbarian scheme. There is no place in the university for an undergraduate department, for the latter is only a place for preliminary training, and today it is chiefly concerned with affording a rounded discipline to those whose goal is the practical pecuniary life of "fashion and frailty." The effect of joining the undergraduate school with the graduate is to impose upon the latter the alien and incompatible standardised routine and formalities of the former.

There is a substantial bond of community between the proper work of the university and such technical schools as engineering, since the mechanistic technology is the working logic and basis for both. But just as the industrial expert is contaminated by pecuniary ideals, the academic technologists, under the current regime, are trained in the use of pecuniary strategy and adroitness. They are necessarily and habitually impatient of any scientific or scholarly work which does not lend itself to some practical pecuniary use, and they join with the lawyers, another product of the professional schools, and with the businessmen at large, in repudiating whatever does not look directly to a utilitarian pecuniary outcome. Thus they shift the university forces from disinterested science and scholarship to the practical, expedient end of profit and loss. By intimate association with these utilitarians the scientists and scholars also take over the characteristic pecuniary bias, with its disastrous effects on modern knowledge. The professional and undergraduate divisions resent any interference in their conduct of affairs by the scholars and scientists, much as the captains of finance resent any interference in their pecuniary activities.

It has been contended that, since historically the university was a collection of professional schools serving practical ends, it should have the same purpose today. But this is no different from a contention that modern industry should return to handicraft technology. "The historical argument does not enjoin a return to the beginning of things, but rather an intelligent appreciation of what things are coming to." The medieval and early modern university was a barbarian institution reflecting the unmitigated pragmatic, utilitarian, worldly wise culture then prevailing. Only by a sophisticated subsumption of their activities under some line of interest and inquiry ostensibly serving the glory of the predatory gods or chieftains, were university men able to carry on disinterested scholarship. But the modern community "will not enduringly tolerate the sordid effects of pursuing an educational policy that looks mainly to the main chance, and unreservedly makes the means of life its chief end." Universities which make an experimental reversion to vocationalism, to the worship of Mammon, and violate "the long-term drift of the modern idealistic bias," "unavoidably return presently to something of the non-professional type on penalty of falling into hopeless discredit." If they turn unreservedly to the practical, that is, to the "pecuniarily gainful," the result is the same liquidation and depression that comes ultimately to business corporations and civilisations which unmitigatingly pursue pecuniary principles.

This estimate of the place the university occupies in modern civilisation, and more particularly of the manner in which it is to fill its place, is an "ideal logically involved in the scheme of modern civilisation, and logically coming out of the historical development of western civilisation hitherto, and visible to anyone who will dispassionately stand aside and look to the drift of latterday events insofar as they bear on this matter of the higher learning, its advancement and conservation." But today the unremitting habituation to the current competitive system of acquisition and expenditure exercises the same devastating effect on the higher learning as was exercised formerly by dynastic and theological principles. The contest is now between the claims of science and scholarship on the one hand, and those of business principles, business enterprise, and pecuniary gain on the other.

The discretionary control of the universities rests in governing boards made up of businessmen and of politicians who are like businessmen. They are of no material use in any connexion, and their sole effectiveness is in interfering in matters that lie outside their competence and interest. The reason for the retention of these aimless survivals is the prevalent uncritical respect for such organisations and methods of control as have been found "advantageous for the pursuit of private gain by businessmen banded together in the exploitation of joint-stock companies with limited liability."

In footnotes Veblen discusses the relation of the governing board to the university corporation in much the same terms as he customarily used in describing the relation of a captain of finance to dependent corporations and the community. The discretionary control of large funds may be pecuniarily profitable to the members of the governing board, and office on such a board may thus be sought for business reasons as well as for the similar reason of its prestige. It has been claimed, said Veblen, that the businessmen governors of a certain university managed its $30,000,-000 endowment for their own pecuniary advantage. The investment yielded three percent when first-class investments usually yielded six to eight percent. Out of this income, forty-five percent was required for the current use of the establishment. What happened to the remainder is not altogether clear, but it is presumed to have been kept for eventual buildings. Half of the forty-five percent was put in a sinking fund for future contingencies. Less than one percent of the total investment was available, and out of this came also a sinking fund for the eventual use of the library, which at the time was seriously handicapped by lack of funds for current needs. Thus the academic establishment was "managed on a basis of penurious economy—to the present inefficiency and the lasting damage of the university."

The modern American is "the most admirably thorough-paced business community extant." American business enterprise is managed in "a spirit of quietism, caution, compromise, collusion, and chicane." The inventors and technicians are bold and resourceful, but they are not represented in the management of business and usually they die poor. The wealth and serviceable results of "these enterprising and temerarious Americans" go to those who "are endowed with a 'safe and sane' spirit of 'watchful waiting,' " which is characterised by the saying that "the silent hog eats the swill."

It is only by getting something for nothing that a man achieves such success in business affairs that he will command sufficient awe to sit upon governing boards. America has been a land of free and abounding resources; that is, in terms of economic theory, "it is the land of the unearned increment." Those who were endowed with the retentive grasp, and had "the patience or astuteness to place themselves in the way of this multifarious flow of the unearned increment" created by technologists, inventors, and the bearers of technological knowledge, were given wide opportunities. "Putting aside the illusions of public spirit and diligent serviceability, sedulously cultivated by the apologists of business, it will readily be seen that the great mass of reputably large fortunes in this country are of such an origin." In a footnote Veblen declared, much more directly than was his custom: "The typical American businessman watches the industrial process from ambush, with a view to the seizure of any item of value that may be left at loose ends. Business strategy is a strategy of 'watchful waiting' at the centre of a web; very alert and adroit, but remarkably incompetent in the way of anything that can properly be called 'industrial enterprise.' "

The endeavour of modern business enterprise and that of the higher learning are as widely out of touch as possible. The guiding principles of the large business enterprise are those of strategic manœuvres, in a game of competitive guessing and pecuniary coercion, a game which depends for its movement and effect on personal discrepancies of judgment, or the fluctuating margin of human miscalculation. But "science has to do with the opaquely veracious sequence of cause and effect," dealing with the facts of this sequence without the ulterior purpose of business expediency. The "astute and invidious character of cunning," indispensable to the conduct of business affairs, works at cross-purposes with the dispassionate animus of scientific inquiry, shaped by the discipline of the mechanical industries.

It is contended by "the spokesmen of content" that the larger businessmen of the governing boards do not interfere with scholarly affairs and that the scholarly interests are actually in the hands of scholars headed by the president. Such a view overlooks the control exercised through the budget and the great appreciation of tangible pecuniary values and vendible property by the directors. The board may decide to spend most of the funds available in "improving and decorating its real estate," and consequently the staff will be so underpaid that its working capacity is reduced, funds will be set aside for future use, or current needs cut down. The intangible, non-pecuniary uses for which a university is established "are *prima facie* imbecile and . . . distasteful to men whose habitual occupation is with the acquisition of property."

From the point of view of the interests of the higher learning and the means of the institutions, no reason exists for competition between universities, but the precedents of competitive business have made competition a necessity. Competitive publicity, and its maidservant conventional observance, or respectability and dissipation, have like advertising services no scientific motive and serve no useful purpose. They only divert the resources and energies of the university and staff to the greater glory and service of the discretionary heads, who have the boyish and make-believe kind of mind typical of business experience.

Any executive unable to satisfy the pecuniary test of successful business is eliminated, just as in modern business enterprise. The executive's notable traits of character are an accentuation "of the more commonplace frailties of commonplace men." The executives fall into the class of the "professional politician of the familiar and more vacant sort." The function of an executive head of a business concern is to get the better of rival concerns and to engross the trade, and consequently "financiering tact" is the prime prerequisite. The captain of erudition must also be a "strong man," with the successful businessman's traits of irresponsible and arbitrary dominion. He must have the autocratic and arbitrary power of hiring and dismissing so that his staff will work with him loyally in achieving those pecuniary realities which are gratifying to the governing boards. The staff is not to question the executive's policy, for they are merely his employees, hired to turn out "certain scheduled vendible results." A hierarchy of ranks is established, as in commercial business. The academic tradition is a drag on the thoroughgoing businesslike organisation that the captain of erudition aims to achieve. The formalities of the tradition are observed, but the substance is evaded by use of an adroit group of servile lieutenants who, like their chief, are expert parliamentarians, proficient public speakers and administrators, having a "ready versatility of convictions and a staunch loyalty to their bread." These men are given advanced academic rank, and "so will take a high (putative) rank as scholars and scientists."

Veblen coined the term "philandropist" to describe the executive, and added that the captains of erudition are visibly affected by "those characteristic pathological marks that come of what is conventionally called 'high living.'" The executive must have a "conspicuously profound conviction that all things are working out for good, except for such untoward details as do not visibly conduce to the vested advantage of the well-to-do businessmen." The need of the president's office is a matter of invention, and the office serves no useful purpose today. The ways and means of controlling the faculty by the president's office have become so settled that they belong under the "category of legal fiction rather than that of effectual prevarication." The "misdirected cowardice" of the pecuniary-minded captains of erudition, however, not only cripples the higher learning but also discredits "the executive and his tactics in the esteem of that workaday public that does not habitually give tongue over the cups at five o'clock." The executive is caught between the necessity of satisfying scholarly ends and of satisfying pecuniary principles of visible magnitude, bureaucratic control, and vocational education. "It should seem beyond reason to expect that a decade of exposure to the exigencies of this high office will leave the incumbent still amenable to the dictates of commonplace tolerance and common honesty." When a scholar becomes a directive head he is in effect "lost to the republic of learning" and, like a technical expert who takes financial office, passes to the ranks of business enterprise. Even discretionary heads who start with scholarly pretensions must succumb to the pecuniary exigencies, on penalty of elimination. Indeed, executives of this kind are more of an evil than those not so blessed. The academic staff will work with better effect "the less effectually its members are interfered with and suborned by an enterprising captain of erudition."

The higher learning cannot tolerate autocratic rule, hierarchical gradations, or anything of the spirit and characteristic apparatus of competitive enterprise. It is business ideals which put in the forefront of university activities the undergraduate division, with its extra-scholastic traffic and its dissipation, exemplified in sports and in the life of a gentleman of leisure. The scholastic interest of these students may be said to centre in unearned credits, just as the businessman's interest centres in unearned income.

For the purpose of controlling the great volume of perfunctory labour required of the undergraduate instructor, his work is reduced to standard, interchangeable units—"academic bullion." "One line, somewhat narrowly bounded as a speciality, measures the capacity of the common run of talented scientists and scholars for first-class work. . . . The alternative which not unusually goes into effect is amateurish pedantry, with the charlatan ever in the near background." Members of the various departments, instead of co-operating, mutually distrust and hinder one another. The conferences of executives are ostensibly for the purpose of reducing inter-academic rivalry, but actually they are means of discussing other affairs of joint interest to the guild of executives, such as the "inter-academic, or inter-executive, blacklist." Following sane competitive practice, the executive pushes into an increasing number of extra-scholastic fields, with a limited amount of resources, so that the sweatshop system or piece-rate plan of wages goes into effect. It is "bad business" to offer a better grade of goods than the market demands, particularly to customers who do not know the difference. The result is such great waste, inefficiency, and stultification as should humble the pride of scholars and cause rejoicing among the captains of erudition.

Knowledge cannot be bought at a price, any more than can material efficiency, but the canons of conspicuous waste inherent in the pecuniary culture require that the college be operated as a gentlemen's school. The result is that successful athletic coaches are given the highest scholastic ranks and salaries, although in point of scholastic attainment it would be a stretch of charity to say that such a "professor" is of "quite a neutral composition." The material equipment of the university is handled by the directors and executive so that it may create "good will," that is, prestige and publicity, just as in corporation finance it is attempted to obtain something for nothing by the arts of salesmanship or the illusion of serviceability. The plant is laid out not with regard to modern architecture and the requirements of the academic staff, but for the purposes of decorative real estate, which merely curtails the efficiency of the staff. The result is a meaningless juxtaposition of details, which "prove nothing in detail and contradict one another in assemblage." This "may suggest reflections on the fitness of housing the quest of truth in an edifice of false pretences." But successful men of affairs "find these wasteful, ornate, and meretricious edifices a competent expression of their cultural hopes and ambitions."

Services are required of the academic staff which are extraneous and incompatible with the higher learning, services which, however, have a business value and are calculated to enhance the prestige and the pecuniary gain of the institution at large, the pecuniary advantage of a given clique, or the profit or renown of the director head. In political organisations payment for such services is called graft. The domination of business values is shown in the choice and promotion in the faculty of men of wealth and wealthy contacts. They can strengthen relations with the opulent patrons of learning, and can serve to show the pecuniary reputability of the institution as a worthy recipient of funds. The transactions in funds have no reference to creature comforts, but begin and end within the circle of pecuniary respectability. It is morally incumbent on the staff to engage in such conspicuously expensive amenities as will show the collective good repute. In this game of emulation the pace-maker man of wealth is invaluable, for he serves to raise the standard of living, which is paid for in part out of the salaries of the faculty.

To elicit the donation of funds there are spectacular ceremonial functions and pageants. These are aimless survivals of the archaic belief in magical efficacy, and are also found in the larger business enterprises, such as those concerned with the competitive sale of securities and with the mature development of retail trade, as seen in their formal openings and "shrewdly conceived harangues" before select groups "setting forth the alleged history, adventures, and merits, past and future, of the particular branch of the trade and the particular house." The academic requirements of pomp and circumstance have such results as the necessity of avoiding children. Extra-scholastic matters, such as domestic infelicities, will have an untoward effect on the university member's fortunes, whereas activities which give a reputable notoriety, such as addresses before an audience of devout and well-to-do women, are of more weight than scholarly activities. Academic men, it is true, take easily to the ceremonial yoke of ritual dissipation, just as technicians fall in with the routine of business sabotage, but the fact remains that "without the initiative and countenance of the executive head these boyish movements of sentimental spectacularity on the part of the personnel would come to little, by comparison with what actually takes place."

If the prevailing business principles of quasi-scholarly proficiency and propagandist intrigue were free to work out their logical consequence in the universities, the result would be the elimination of the pursuit of knowledge. But the consummate sweatshop scheme has not been achieved because the purpose of the university is still ostensibly scholarship, and if this were completely eliminated the business administration would be left without anything to administer. Even businesslike university members have usually started with scholarly aspirations, and they still harbour a feeling that scholarship is higher than official preferment, so long as it does not touch their own preferment. They may view "the naïve children of impulse" with amused compassion, but on the whole kindly and sympathetically, if not with envy. The arbitrary rulers must also pay some attention to scholarly achievement; their competitive manœuvres must, in a sense, be carried out surreptitiously, disguised as a non-competitive campaign for the increase of knowledge without fear or favour. Moreover, distinguished scientists have to be tolerated to a considerable degree, since they have great publicity value, and they may influence the course of events towards the scientific bent. But such influence comes primarily from the material sciences.

In the so-called moral and social sciences a "clamorous conformity . . . to the conventional prepossessions of respectability, or an edifying and incisive rehearsal of commonplaces, will commonly pass . . . for scholarly and scientific work." If a member's scholarly activities lead to the possible estrangement of the affections of potential donors, or involve anything like overt disloyalty to the executive head, an appeal to the base sentiments, by such measures as defaming a man's domestic life, his religion, or political status, is resorted to. Under modern business principles, statements of fact are controlled by the pecuniary end to be accomplished, rather than by antecedent circumstances of scholarly accomplishment. "Such statements are necessarily of a teleological order." As in other competitive business, the facts have in this connexion only a strategic value.

Men are chosen on the basis of their reputation among the unlearned wealthy, the superannuated captains of industry who control the material welfare of the community, and in the range of the moral sciences the estimate of the unlearned is necessarily in the wrong. These sciences are concerned with inquiries into the prevailing law and order. "No faithful inquiry into these matters can avoid an air of scepticism as to the stability . . . of the received articles of institutional furniture. An inquiry into the nature and causes, the working and the outcome, of this institutional apparatus will disturb the habitual convictions and preconceptions upon which they rest." But a scientist in the realm of institutions can secure the businessmen's approval of his scientific capacity "only by accepting and confirming current convictions regarding those elements of the accepted scheme of life with which his science is occupied." An inquiry which violates the prevailing opinion merely stamps the inquiry as "spurious and dangerously wrong-headed." A sceptical or noncommittal attitude towards the convictions of the well-to-do will be tolerated "only as regards the decorative furnishings, not as regards the substance of the views arrived at. Some slight play of hazardous phrases about the fringe of the institutional fabric may be tolerated by the popular taste, as an element of spice, and as indicating a generous and unbiased mind; but in such cases the conclusive test of scientific competency and leadership in the popular apprehension is a serene and magniloquent return to the orthodox commonplaces, after all such playful excursions. In fact, substantially nothing but homiletics and wool-gathering will pass popular muster as science in this connexion."

The reluctance of these quasi-scholars to encounter present-day facts hand-to-hand or to trace out the causes of current conditions is not due merely to their fear of traversing the opinion of the pecuniarily superior upon whom they are dependent, for they are free to conduct their inquiries as they see fit. But they have been chosen because their intellectual horizon is bounded by the same limit that binds the governing boards and the president, and thus they express and fortify the preconception of the conservative middle class. Mediocrity is requisite for leadership. The putative social scientists reach conclusions innocuous to the prevailing system of ownership and the distribution of wealth, for their interest is in what ought to be done "to conserve those usages and conventions that have by habit been imbedded in the received scheme of use and wont." Their leadership serves to stabilise the opinion of the elderly businessmen, and their inquiries rest on the archaic canon of expediency and prescriptive authority in contrast to the iconoclastic ground of cause and effect and genetic sequence. "Such a quasi-science necessarily takes the current situation for granted as a permanent state of things; to be corrected and brought back into its normal routine in case of aberration, and to be safeguarded with apologetic defence at points where it is not working to the satisfaction of all parties." Thus the discipline of the social sciences is "conducive to a safe and sane, if not an enthusiastic, acceptance of things as they are, without undue curiosity as to why they are such."

To the pragmatist, value is synonymous with pecuniary gain, and good citizenship means proficiency in competitive business. Expediency and practical considerations have come to mean considerations of pecuniary gain, and are useful only for pecuniary purposes. But to ask what is the profit of learning is not far different from asking what is the use of a baby "as a means of speculative gain." In his more thoughtful moments even the most businesslike pragmatist will avow that the pursuit of knowledge, like the material welfare of mankind, is an end in itself, but in his pecuniary traffic his working experience is at cross-purposes with his ideal, and "the barbarian animus, habitual to the quest of gain, reverts," and the deliberation turns on the usefulness of knowledge, in the business system of competitive gain and spending.

The incursion of pecuniary canons of taste and ideals into academic policy is seen at its broadest and baldest in the schools of commerce and finance, whatever their designation. Such schools are the appointed keeper of the higher business animus. Unlike the technological schools, they need take no cognisance of the achievement of science, and the proficiency they inculcate has no serviceability for the community. It is possible to organise a school of finance "on lines of scientific inquiry, with the purpose of dealing with business enterprise in its various ramifications as subject matter of theoretical investigation," but neither the avowed aim nor the actual work of these schools is of such a character, except by inadvertence. The training given by the American school of "commerce" is detrimental to the community's material interests, because the principles which dominate them are the business community's principles of financiering and salesmanship. Such training results in "an enhancement of the candidates' proficiency in all the futile ways and means of salesmanship and 'conspiracy in restraint of trade,' together with a heightened incapacity and ignorance bearing on such work as is of material use." It is only by a euphemistic metaphor that businessmen are conceived to be producers of goods. Their gains are only differential, achieved at the expense of the community or other businessmen. Increased business efficiency entails a net loss on the community at large, for it leads to the businessmen acquiring a greater share of the product and leaving the community poorer by that much. A college of commerce serves an "emulative purpose only—individual gain regardless of, or at the cost of, the community at large." As far as the collective cultural purpose of a university is concerned, it is in the same category as a department of athletics, and the support and conduct of such schools at the expense of the university's ostensible purposes of disinterested learning "is to be construed as a breach of trust." The furtherance of the work of schools of commerce is in the nature of malpractice.

Law schools are also an expression of the higher pecuniary culture. Both in the training they give and in their unscientific character they are like the schools of finance and belong to the medieval era. They are, in effect, devoted to the training of practitioners in duplicity and to the inculcating of the strategy of successful practice, which is not unlike military strategy. The less numerous they are and the lower their proficiency the better off is the community, through the avoidance of litigation and cost of training. Schools of law and commerce and finance are, in effect, supported by the public against whose interests they are directed. Hitherto, however, the colleges of commerce have amounted to no more than secondary schools for bank-clerks and travelling salesmen, with a subsidiary department of economics.

The recent establishment of foundations might appear to be a solution for the academic defeat, but it is no real solution, for these institutions serve only the end of research and take no cognisance of the indispensable correlate function of teaching. Should they turn to teaching, "the dry rot of business principles and competitive gentility" would consume their tissues, too, as it has that of the universities. Without the give and take between teachers and students it is only in exceptional if not erratic cases that it is possible to avoid "the blunting of that intellectual initiative that makes the creative scientist." The foundations breed no new scientists, and consequently, when the academic sources fail them, as they must with the increasingly efficient application of business principles in the universities, they will have no other alternative than the same sands of "intellectual quietism."

All that is required in the interests of the higher learning is the abolition of the academic executive and the governing board. "Anything short of this heroic remedy is bound to fail, because the evils sought to be remedied are inherent in these organs, and intrinsic to their functioning." Objections to decentralisation are based on the "unreasoning faith" in the "pecuniary efficiency of large capital, authoritative control, and devious methods in modern business enterprise." With the methods and organisation of the trust as the ideal, there is a steady process of annexation and innovation, such as summer schools, extension, correspondence, and sewing schools. The dissolution of the trust would do away with the intangible element of prestige and magnitude, and also with the necessity for the office of the present-day academic executive. The decentralised units would require little control and administration. They would operate on the form of a democracy instead of an autocracy, and there would be that necessary personal communion and contact between student and teacher. The graduate school, having been freed of the drag of the undergraduate school and the vocational school, "should come into action as a shelter where the surviving remnants of scholars and scientists might pursue their several lines of adventure, in teaching and inquiry" free from the disturbance of the academic executive and governing board "who clamour for the greater glory" of funded wealth.

The socialists viewed the book as another example of Veblen's irony and praised it. *The New York Call* reviewer said that "there is no higher learning in America because there is only one Veblen." The liberals expressed the opinion that this was the profoundest and most important study yet made of the subject, but they read it literally and made criticisms which doubtless Veblen knew of before he wrote the book. Harold Laski, in reviewing it in *The New Republic*, declared that Veblen was unquestionably right in his criticisms of schools of journalism and commerce, but unquestionably wrong in his criticisms of the normal graduate school and law school. The great danger of Veblen's plan was that it would lead to professors establishing a closed society. In a review article in *The Dial*, entitled "The Hire Learning," Beard called attention to the same danger, and said that, if control did not rest with the financier, it would rest with a board of aldermen. In such a choice the "busily and heavily preoccupied benevolent despot" is preferable. Likewise, if an industrial democracy should eliminate or cut in half the income yield of the investments of such a university as Veblen proposed, "could that democracy expect a cold and passionless judgment from the professor of political economy?"

Brander Matthews of the department of English at Columbia wrote a review of the book for *The New York Times* in which he spent most of his space in criticising Veblen's grammar and rhetoric. "So frequent and so flagrant are Mr. Veblen's violations of accepted usage that I was moved to look him up in *Who's Who*, and I was astonished to learn . . . that he is not only a college graduate but that he is even a doctor of philosophy. It is evident enough that Mr. Veblen does not write cleanly because he does not think clearly." Veblen not only arrogantly assumes the right to look down upon the rest of mankind, but he discloses "absolute ignorance of the institution he has taken for his topic," and the book "is unusual in its bad manners and perhaps, I should say, in its bad morals. There is a discourtesy very close to dishonesty in slandering by insinuation. The man who comes straight at us with a bowie knife in his hand may be dangerous, but he is not despicable, like the creature who comes up stealthily with a stiletto to deal a stab in the back." In *The New Republic*, Francis Hackett under the pseudonym "Salann" declared that it was unfortunate that *The Times* had not chosen someone among the solid old-line professors to attack the book instead of a "popgun" like Brander Matthews. "Professor Matthews' discourtesy, it is clear, is of a different order. But isn't there something in the product of Professor Veblen's long and bitter experience as a teacher besides these horrible limitations? Can he be disposed of by this simple method of shrill abuse? Thorstein Veblen stands above this kind of attack, but it is too typical of the degenerate condition of criticism in academic America. For years Veblen has been one of the most salient social critics in America, yet instead of living in an atmosphere of healthy recognition he has been a pilgrim in the wilderness trailed by a bunch of over-heated admirers. His style is beyond doubt one result of his experience. It is a cactus style. But healthy recognition would have done a great deal to change that. When one thinks of the prompt recognition that is granted to the shrewdly compliant professor, and the cold dubiety that greet a subversive critic like Veblen, the sickening atmosphere of professorial cowardice is unmistakable. To this patent fact Professor Matthews pays no attention. He is content to complain that Veblen is ungrammatical and obscure. More correct and more suave Veblen could surely be, yet suavity is not everything. There is, after all, the impeccable suavity of the pimp."

everything. There is, after all, the impeccable suavity of the pimp."

Although *The Higher Learning in America* contains some of the clearest expressions of Veblen's conception of modern business enterprise and modern capital, the book dropped quickly into obscurity, largely, perhaps, because the war and post-war problems were the paramount interests of the day.

In the meanwhile, Helen Marot thought that *The Dial* should begin emphasising the importance of organising economic activity in times of peace with the unified machinery that the war had brought into action. Horace Kallen suggested that Veblen's services be obtained. Miss Marot found that both Dewey and Veblen were ready to lend their support to a reconstruction policy based on the realities of productive capacity. A board was to be formed and Veblen was to settle in New York.

CHAPTER XXI

IN the issue of *The Dial* for June 6, 1918, the announcement was made that with its removal to New York the magazine "has determined to extend the editorial policy to include, in addition to the present literary features, discussion of internationalism and a programme of reconstruction in industry and education." The editors were to be John Dewey, Thorstein Veblen, Helen Marot, and George Donlin. The associate editors were to be Clarence Britten, Harold Stearns, Randolph Bourne, and Scofield Thayer. Veblen was to contribute "articles dealing with economic and industrial reconstruction," and the magazine was referred to as the "Veblenian *Dial*." The journal which Ralph Waldo Emerson had founded had now as a star contributor a man whose entire work was directed towards undermining the Emersonian pragmatic philosophy.

In the fall of 1918 Veblen and his family arrived in New York and presented themselves to Leon Ardzrooni, who was teaching at Columbia University. From that time Ardzrooni became Veblen's *fidus Achates*. He settled the arrangements with *The Dial* for Veblen's services, and it was agreed that Veblen would receive $2500 for one year and would write when and how much he chose. Veblen, although present at the meeting, did not say a word, but after it was ended he turned to Ardzrooni and said he did not think he was really worth twenty-five cents.

Not long after Veblen's arrival in New York, his wife began having delusions that he was being persecuted. She suffered a nervous breakdown and had to be removed to a sanitarium. The stepchildren were sent to the Stewarts at Amherst. Ardzrooni handled these matters, and Veblen became more helpless than before. Late in 1918 it was necessary for Ardzrooni to return to his raisin vineyard in California, but someone had to take care of Veblen. He telegraphed Lubin to come to New York. Lubin was then working in Washington under Mitchell on the War Industries Board, and Mitchell told Lubin that he could take his work to New York and look after Veblen.

The interest of *The Dial* editors in advanced social philosophy did not diminish their belief in the ordinary canons of literary style and journalism. They asked Veblen to limit his articles to 1000 words, but Veblen said that it took him that much space to get started. His characteristic literary style exasperated the editors. Miss Marot says that Veblen "gave meticulous care to every article he wrote and charged me with the pleasant task of seeing that no punctuation mark was ever omitted or changed after it had left his hands. I always enjoyed the tussles which ensued in the office with the literary editors who considered these articles of Veblen impossible journalism. But only once did they ever have the opportunity to delete and change the text. It was a first and last time. Veblen would not stand for it." This incident seems to have been the one later described by Lewis Mumford, then also on *The Dial*. "Veblen had characterised Samuel Gompers as the sexton beetle of the American labour movement. In preparing the MSS. for the printer, one of the editors had automatically changed this over to sexton beadle, in order to make sense. Veblen was furious: his white ashen face was more ashen than ever with anger— such anger as seemed especially terrible in the mild and reticent person that Veblen always was. He wanted to know if the unknown dunder- head who had mutilated his copy did not realise that a sexton beetle was an insect that spent its life in storing up and covering over dead things? Besides, there was an overtone in the allusion: Gompers looked more like a beetle." [1]

"As the office predicted," writes Miss Marot, "the public would not stand for Veblen to the extent of supporting a magazine weighted with such portentous material. The point of difference was clear—should *The Dial* continue or should Veblen be published while we had the chance. The continuation of *The Dial* was to me unimportant in comparison to the publication of his articles, charged as they were for those few who read them with creative and revolutionary import."

The editorial page of the October 19, 1918, issue of the magazine announced that Veblen, along with Dewey and Miss Marot, were "In Charge of the Reconstruction Programme." Later the title of the editorial page was changed to "The Old Order and the New," a name which Veblen is supposed to have suggested. With the October 19 issue Veblen began a series of papers on "The Modern Point of View and the New Order." They ran until January 25, 1919, and in March were published in book form, under the title, *The Vested Interests and the State of the Industrial Arts*. Thus there is apparent in Veblen's usage a rough parallel between the "modern point of view" and the "vested interests," and between the "new order" and the "state of the industrial arts." In the preface Veblen said that "in point of scope and logical content this dis- cussion resumes the argument of a course of lectures before students in Amherst College in May 1918." Hamilton says that some of the chapters were elaborated by the introduction of new material, but the remaining parts were scarcely changed for publication either in *The Dial* or in the book. The book, however, is rather more than a mere résumé of the argument presented at Amherst.

Before the series was half finished, the war ended, and negotiations for peace and a league of nations were begun. These changes and events furnished new terms of contrast for Veblen. He changed his mind about Bolshevism, and began now to use this, as he had machine technology, as a term of contrast to the prevailing control by corporate magnates and corporate capital.

The entire series of articles, which was actually an inquiry into "the nature and uses of the vested interests," was concerned, like his other works, with modern capital and with the modern leisure-class gentleman in the guise of the pecuniary magnate. But Veblen's method of stating the consequences of modern business enterprise as if they were conscious motives of the pecuniary magnates, led him at times to be somewhat careless in his use of language, and the book lacks the precision of *The Theory of the Leisure Class*. It betrays a new tone in keeping with a literary journal rather than with a professional periodical, and indicates that Veblen was attempting to break away from the involved apparatus which had become the master of his style and thought instead of his creature.

"The more matter-of-fact the frame of mind of the common man" the narrower appears to be the margin of tolerance for the prevailing institutions of law and order, for the prevailing imponderables or make-believe. A scheme of institutions centring on property rights may have worked passably well in the eighteenth century, but Adam Smith never foresaw the modern use of credit and corporation finance for the collective control of the labour market and the goods market, usages which are the outgrowth of the principle of property under machine technology, and which are hard to distinguish from that unfair combination between masters for the exploitation of their workmen which was denounced by him. For those habituated to the modern point of view it is difficult to appreciate the "larcenous use of the national establishment" in protecting investments and abetting the characteristically modern business practices. This is actually in the nature of a protective tariff for the benefit of the vested interests at the expense of the community.

A mutation in the state of the industrial arts has taken place, and today the place of the personal employer-owner "is filled by a list of corporation securities and a staff of corporation officials and employees who exercise a limited discretion." In other words ownership has become impersonal, taking the shape of an absentee ownership by anonymous corporate capital, and in the ordinary management of corporate capital the greater proportion of the owners have no voice. Ownership of capital is today in effect a claim on the earning capacity of the corporation, and constitutes a liability of industry, an anonymous pensioner living on its product. Of course the "reasonably skilful economist—any certified accountant of economic theory"—still believes that capital is a physical magnitude used in the production of goods. The efficiency of industry is conditioned by the state of the industrial arts, which is a joint product of the working community, but the "investors, owners, kept classes, or whatever designation is preferred" characteristically possess little if any of this technological knowledge. This joint stock is the "substance of the community's civilisation on the industrial side," and "constitutes the substantial core of that civilisation." It is not as intelligent persons, but only as large owners of material ways and means, as vested interests, that those who possess the discretionary control of industry are able to secure that part of the product not taken by costs, which include subsistence and replacement of equipment.

Unrestricted property rights, which are presumed by the obsolete metaphysics to give the common man equality of opportunity, actually, under the new circumstances of industry, promise "to be nothing better than a means of assured defeat and vexation for the common man." Under the modern corporate practice of investment and credit over one-half of the net product of the country's industry goes to those persons in whom the existing state of law and custom vests a plenary power to hinder production. These are the possessors of the intangible assets, which "represent a 'conscientious withdrawal of efficiency,' " and upon which modern business enterprise rests. The community loses more, however, than these vested interests gain, since production must be hindered in order to achieve the gain. Today (October 1918), under the bitter shame of need and surveillance by government authorities, the production may approach fifty percent of normal capacity. That it does not exceed fifty percent, even under the present emergency, is due to the fact that the jealous public officers are capable businessmen with a frame of mind native to the counting house. "They still find it reasonable to avoid any derangement of those vested interests that live on this margin of intangible assets that represents capitalised withdrawal of efficiency." Industry is too productive for the reasonable profits of the beneficiaries or kept classes, and reasonable profits are all the traffic can bear. In describing the effect of modern capital on the industrial community Veblen uses the same quotation from John Stuart Mill that he had used in *The Theory of the Leisure Class* to describe the effect on the working community of the increasing pecuniary standard of living: "Hitherto it is questionable if all the mechanical inventions yet made have lightened the day's toil of any human being."

In view of the delicate and comprehensive character of the modern industrial process it would seem reasonable that "its control would be entrusted to men experienced in the ways and means of technology, men who are in the habit of thinking about these matters in such terms as are intelligible to the engineers," but by historical necessity, by virtue of the eighteenth-century point of view in a twentieth-century scheme of industry, the control vests in the captain of finance, "the master of the financial intrigue." Meanwhile the system grows unmanageable by business methods, that is, with every successive move this discretionary control of the vested interests "grows wider, more arbitrary, and more incompatible with the common good." Business enterprise in the narrower sense, in the sense of corporation finance, is occupied with obstruction, friction, and retardation of the industrial process, since it consists in holding out for a better price, or in withholding necessary information. In discussing these competitive manœuvres of corporate financiers Veblen declared, "it has been rumoured that one of the usual incentives which drew the patriotic one-dollar-a-year men from their usual occupations . . . was the chance of controlling information by means of which to 'put it over' their business rivals."

Businessmen claim that they are resourceful at every readjustment, and full of initiative and enterprise, but they also assert that the "ordinary and normal processes of private initiative will not, however, provide immediate employment for all of the men of our returning armies." This amounts to saying that the largest net return in terms of price cannot be had by full capacity, even though the community may be suffering privation and want. The result of business management in America has been, on the whole, a fairly high level of prosperity. This has been due, first, to the great natural resources and, second, to the growth and spread of population. The legalised seizure and rapid exhaustion of the resources has been profitable to business, but it has impoverished the underlying community. The growth of population has furnished businessmen with an expanding market for goods and a copious supply of labour. "Hence the American businessmen have been in the fortunate position of not having to curtail the output of industry harshly and persistently at all points," but always there has been a very appreciable amount of unemployment, idle plant, and waste of resources. The free income resulting from the strategic interference with the material welfare is an intangible asset, a vested interest, and is duly capitalised and held legitimate under the prevailing law and order. To such effect have commonly been the findings of courts and boards of inquiry, of Public Utility Commissions, and of such bodies as the Interstate Commerce Commission, the Federal Trade Commission, the public price-fixing and production-restricting bodies, and also, in certain decisions and recommendations, the War Labor Board.

The result is that in a successful corporation the fair value, the market value, of its vendible securities always considerably exceeds the total value of the underlying industrial equipment and resources. A corporation which has no vested interest is one on the edge of bankruptcy.

In such typical concerns as the United States Steel Corporation and similar organisations in the oil industry, the material equipment is the least valuable of the assets. The intangible assets of capitalised free income, of monopoly privilege, amount to several times the total value of the material assets which underlie them, and such gains in capitalisation, the normal gains of corporate magnates, are of no interest to the community except as an overhead charge on its production and production capacity. The coalition of ownership involved in a modern corporation such as a holding company is in effect a conspiracy in restraint of trade, and so frequently does this restriction enhance prices and increase unemployment that there is a popular belief that such "is the logical aim and outcome of any successful manœuvre of the kind." The new and large business concern is in a position to make its own terms with the workingman, and its principle here as elsewhere is all the traffic can bear, charging what will yield the largest net profit in terms of price.

The question arises as to why these powerful concerns do not exercise their autocratic power to drive the industrial system at full capacity and expropriate the additional gain over the present restricted capacity. The answer is that the vested interests are bound by the limitation of the price system. They seek net profits in terms of price, not in terms of goods. The vested rights are carried as overhead charges to be met in terms of price, that is pecuniary gain, and this does not allow an increase of net production regardless of price. "The free income . . . goes to support the well-to-do investors, who are for this reason called the kept classes," and their keep "consists in an indefinitely extensible consumption of superfluities."

The chapter that follows this discussion of "The Vested Interests" is entitled "The Divine Right of Nations," and this juxtaposition suggests that the vested interests and the divine right of nations are manifestations of the same spirit. Indeed Veblen declares that there is an evident resemblance and kinship between the vested interests of business and the sovereign rights of nations.

The war was the outgrowth of the modern point of view embodied in free contract. Now there is a move to restrict the inalienable right of self-help on the part of nations, and the demagogues are alarmed at the danger threatening the national sovereignty, just as the vested interests are alarmed at the danger to the sacred rights of property. But no statesman has been audacious enough to lay profane hands on the divine, irresponsible right of nations to seek their own advantage at the cost of the rest "by such means as the rule of reason shall decide to be permissible." The problem is merely one of provisionally disallowing "all insufferable superfluity of naughtiness," just as within the nation statesmen have set about tentatively protecting "the free income of the less vested interests against the unseasonable rapacity of the greater ones." All the while the underlying community is left as a free field for the vested interests, big and small. Under modern technology, as the war has shown, a great power in exercising its inalienable rights of self-determination will suppress any smaller power that gets in the way. The ancient system of remedial adjustment after the event, of balance of powers and court litigation, may have the support of ripe statesmen and of over-ripe captains of finance, but it is futile under the dominion of the comprehensive, delicate machine system. It is safety first or none, and the onward movement of the machine system is making obsolete the scheme of things represented by captains of finance, vested interests, and remedial diplomats.

Under modern technology, since the ownership of property in sufficiently large blocks will control the country's industrial system for the private income of the kept classes, the natural right of property operates in the same way as the divine inscrutable right of nations, or the irresponsible right of the strong monarch, so far as the common man in the ostensibly democratic countries is concerned. In the democratic commonwealth, however, "the common man has to be managed rather than driven —except for minor groups of common men who live on the lower-common levels, and except for recurrent periods of legislative hysteria and judiciary blind-staggers." Chicanery takes the place of corporal punishment. "Imperial England is . . . a milder-mannered stepmother than Imperial Germany." The common man in America knows, of course, that the profits of business go only to the businessmen, the vested interests, but he still has the hallucination that any unearned income going to the vested interests whose central office is in New Jersey is inscrutably paid to him, and that the gain of the vested interests domiciled in Canada are a net loss to him.

Anyone not bound by the superstitions of the price system knows that such measures as the protective tariff are an obstruction of industry insofar as they are effective, and that, like other forms of business sabotage, they cost the community more than the vested interests gain. It has been argued by protectionists, with some reason, that the more reasonable tariffs have been more damaging to industry than the most imbecile. This is true, because industry waits on profits, and business prosperity is the only manner of prosperity known or provided for among civilised nations. A protective tariff is only an alternative method of business sabotage, of making business profitable by restricting production. As long as investment controls industry, the community welfare is bound up with the prosperity of business, and modern business cannot allow full productive capacity on pain of inability to meet fixed charges and collapse of the entire business structure, as in periods of so-called overproduction. Waste is essential for business prosperity, and the nation, like the discretionary businessman, has a divine right to use its irresponsible discretion to cripple the effective use of the common stock of knowledge. But the cost of these gains to the vested interests is paid for in the goods and blood of the common man, who swells with pride at the increase of the pecuniary magnitudes of the captains.

In the problem of self-determination for small nations and oppressed nationalities the elder statesmen will not allow these adventurous pilgrims of hope to go about their own business in their own way, any more than the courts will allow the I.W.W. to go their own way. These new establishments must be organised on the good old plan of competitive units, with protection to vested interest and property, on the Balkan plan of embryo imperialism. In *The Nature of Peace* Veblen had described the typical Balkan state as the land of the double-cross. In subject lands the common man, hard ridden by vested interests, thinks that if the people become a nation their life may be easier. But the common man in Rumania or imperial Japan is doubtless worse off in point of hard usage than he is in Ireland, subject to England. Nevertheless, in subject lands, in the absence of the apparatus of "managerial sabotage," of national establishments working at cross-purposes, "substantially the same results would have to be got at by the less seemly means of a furtive conspiracy in restraint of trade among the vested interests." But there is an increasingly evident cleavage of interest between industry and business, or between production and ownership, or between tangible performance and free income, and thus a matter-of-fact project of reconstruction "will be likely materially to revise outstanding credit obligations, including corporation securities," or perhaps even bluntly to disallow these claims to free income upon which modern enterprise rests through managerial sabotage. This shift in ground from vested interest to tangible performance might be deplored by captains of finance, but the destruction of wealth would directly touch only the value of the securities, not the material objects covered by the securities. Such a cancellation of ownership would cancel the fixed overhead charges resting on industrial enterprise, and thus further production by that much.

In the last chapter, "The Vested Interests and the Common Man," Veblen declared that today, under corporation finance and machine technology, the population is divided into two classes, the common man and those who own wealth in large holdings and thereby control the condi-

tions of life for the common man. It is a division between the vested interests and the working community. Those who do not own wealth
enough to count belong in the category of the common man. It is his lot
not to be vested with a prescriptive right to get something for nothing
through controlling the traffic at one point or another, and this will increasingly be his lot as long as the modern point of view rules industry.
The "distinguishing mark of the common man is that he is helpless within
the rules of the game as it is played in the twentieth century under the
enlightened principles of the eighteenth century." But he allies himself
with his superiors, the kept classes of large invested wealth. The officers
of the A.F. of L. are in the category of kept classes, and the rank and
file, although they are not visibly endowed with a free income, feel that
under the existing system they gain a little more by not throwing in their
lot with the undistinguished common man. In other words, they have a
vested interest in a narrow margin of preference over the lot of the common man; but it is obtained by the businesslike method of sabotage and
restriction of output. Their conditions of life, man for man, are not distinguishable from the common lot, and the spirit of vested interest which
animates them is an aimless survival.

Likewise the farmer, who is typical also of the small businessman, still
thinks he is independent, but his property, by the impersonal working of
the price system, is in the discretion of those massive vested interests that
move obscurely in the background, buying cheap and selling dear. Actually
the farmer has ceased to be a self-directing agent, and "the conditions of
life should throw the American farmer in with the common man who has
substantially nothing to lose, beyond what the vested interests of business
can always take over at their own discretion and in their own good time."
The reason the farmer has been led to ally himself with the vested interests is that he also is the owner of speculative real estate, and expects
to get something for nothing in the unearned increase of land value. But
he overlooks the fact that the future increase of land value is already dis-
counted in the price of land. As all those know who are informed, holdings
in the typical American farming region are overcapitalised; that is, their
current market value is greater than the capitalised value of the income
to be derived from their current use as farmlands. In fact the farmer,
judged as a "going concern," is an example of negative intangible assets.
He is caught in the new order, but does not belong to that order of modern
business enterprise characterised by the pecuniary magnates, "in which
earning capacity habitually outruns the capitalised value of the underlying
physical property."

The mechanistic logic of the mechanical industries and of material
science leads to a rating of men and things in terms of tangible perform-

ance instead of legal usage, and to a disallowance of the rights and thus
the incomes of ownership, whether in the form of tangible or of intangible assets. But the cleavage thus being achieved by the new order
of industry and businessmen has not yet fallen into clear lines. The common man does not know himself as such, since he has not emancip ted
himself from the American tradition. The farmer, workman, consumer,
the common man, still makes believe that he has vested interests at stake
in maintaining the modern point of view in behalf of the massive interests
moving obscurely in the background. These massive interests have law
and order on their side, but the common man cannot effectively take
his part without getting on the wrong side of law and order.

Under the stabilised principles of the eighteenth century the investor
is a producer, but according to the mechanistic calculus "brought into
bearing by the mechanical industry, and material science," this rating is
"palpable nonsense." "The peculiar moral and intellectual bent" which
marks the I.W.W. "as undesirable citizens" to be repressed runs closer
"to that of the common man than the corresponding bent of the law-
abiding beneficiaries under the existing system." The dread word, Syndi-
calism, is "quite properly unintelligible to the kept classes and the adepts
of corporation finance," but the notion of it is easily assimilated by these
others in whom the discipline of the new order has begun to displace the
archaic preconception. The agrarian syndicalists, in the shape of the non-
Partisan League, are, for the vested interests, passing the limits of tolerance. "It is not that these and their like are ready with 'a satisfactory
constructive programme' such as the people of the uplift require to be
shown before they will believe that things are due to change." But they
represent a development that is very familiar in history, the situation that
arises when established principles do not fit material requirements. To
these untidy creatures of the new order common honesty appears to
mean vaguely something more exacting than pecuniary freedom of contract. "And why should it not?"

After the series was finished, but before the book was published, Veblen restated the argument in an article in *The Dial* under the title "Bolshevism Is a Menace—to Whom?" Bolshevism, which has become for
Veblen another name for the industrial republic, aims to carry democracy
and majority rule into the domain of industry, and is a menace to property
and business, to the vested interests in contrast to the common man. Consequently the elder statesmen, being faithful to their bread, are taking
measures to safeguard the common man against infection. "The Bolshevist scheme of ideas comes easy to the common man," since it simply
requires him to unlearn older preconceptions that no longer have the support of the material exigencies necessary for his survival. The training

of a mechanically organised community works at cross-purposes with the prescriptive rights of ownership, and makes it easy to deny the validity of these rights as soon as there is sufficient provocation. Business traffic gives support to the right of ownership, but business traffic is not the tone-giving factor in the life of the common man. Out of this ever-increasing division of material interests arises an unreserved recourse to force, and the consequence of the righteous opposition, intrigue, and obstruction of the vested interests of property has been strife, disorder, privation, and bloodshed, with an evil prospect ahead.

Despite the accounts of the Associated Press, which is described as an instrument for the maintenance of big business, the Soviet regime seems to have done very well. Cut off from supplies abroad, the Russians have been able to maintain themselves and their transportation system successfully against their enemies. This, like the war experience of America, demonstrates the fact that a disallowance of private gain makes for heightened efficiency, in spite of the blunders and confusion incident to taking over industry. Those who seem to be suffering famine in Russia are the superfluous businessmen, who are undesirable citizens to the Bolshevist, but are most desirable in the American scheme, as exemplified by the country town, in which nine-tenths of the population is useless, but whose reasonable profits are safeguarded. Even if food were plentiful, the Bolshevist might deprive the vested interests of food, on a cool calculation of military necessity, since these undesirable citizens, kept classes who consume without producing, can be counted on to intrigue against the administration and obstruct its operation wherever opportunity offers. By a "roundabout process of production," by sophistication in pecuniary solidarity, the common man may believe that Bolshevism is a menace to him, and thus he pays in lost labour, anxiety, privation, and blood for the maintenance of the Russian investments of the bankers and vested interests in general. From the matter-of-fact point of view, "The Bolshevik is the common man who has faced the question: What do I stand to lose? and has come away with the answer: Nothing."

In reviewing *The Vested Interests and the State of the Industrial Arts* for *The Dial*, Veblen's friend Robert L. Duffus said: "In a less dangerous field of inquiry work comparable with that of Thorstein Veblen would win recognition as the beginning of an important new school. It is only because most of us are too deeply a part of our own institutions to be able to consider them scientifically" that Veblen's books have not won him "a formal place in the front rank of contemporary thinkers and prophets. The so-called difficulty of Veblen's style has nothing to do with the scant recognition that the Brahmins have accorded him. He is as easy to read as any man with as much to say." *The New York*

Call said: "There is none like [Veblen], and in this book he maintains his prestige as intellectual iconoclast untarnished." The effectiveness of his method is questionable, however. "If Eugene Debs had spoken at Canton with that philosophic aloofness and subtle sarcasm which Thorstein Veblen employs so gracefully," the government agents could not possibly have understood him and he would not be in prison, "but at the same time, his audience would have been composed of no more than two or three dozen intellectual liberals and radicals." *The New York Times* reviewer said that the book would be appreciated by those who like to think that an elimination of the vested interests would be the one great boon. "It is well written from that point of view, which is held by so many that it is time to make a stand against the defiance of experience."

Veblen's former students and sympathisers were not pleased. A former Missouri student who held a high government post wrote Veblen that *The Dial* articles were giving people the misleading idea that he was radical. In general this group felt that Veblen was not at his best in such essays and that the agitator and phrase maker was taking precedence over the thinker. Their attitude was clearly expressed by Hamilton in a review in *The New Republic* entitled "Veblenian Common Sense": "Those who regard Veblen as an acute critic of modern industrial society, but who, like Veblen himself, are no Veblenians, will get more of psychic income than of intellectual ammunition from the volume." Veblen should return to the work he did when he was a "certified economist." Readers of this popularly written book will take over its phrases, but in a good many cases they are quite imponderable when analysed. Apropos of the misunderstanding to which Veblen's books were subject Hamilton remarked that "the opinion of a German committee on responsibility for the war that Veblen's pen persuaded the capitalists of the Allied nations to attack Germany rests upon inadequate documentary evidence."

Veblen's prestige in the world of letters had considerably increased. Randolph Bourne in a *Dial* review of Meredith Nicholson's *Valley of Democracy*, which berated the farmers for their restlessness and sedition, called attention to Veblen's discussion of the country town in *Imperial Germany*. "Town, in the traditional American scheme of things, is shown charging Country all the traffic will bear." Reading *Valley of Democracy* in conjunction with Veblen's discussion "is to experience one of the most piquant intellectual adventures granted to the current mind." Maxwell Anderson in a letter to *The Dial* said: "I once asked a friend if he had read *The Theory of the Leisure Class*. 'Why, no,' he retorted, 'why should I? All my friends have read it. It permeates the atmosphere in which I live.'" A professor of biology at Amherst, "Tip" Tyler, who was an old-fashioned, genially sceptical New England scholar and a great reader of Veblen, partly because of Stewart's influence, used to insist in conversation with other faculty members that the requirement of Latin and Greek be dropped, and Veblen substituted. "It will give the same disciplinary values, especially in translation into English, and the student is likely to get something very much worth while for his terrible bother." Virgil Jordan has said that "it might not be very inaccurate to call Veblen, the Freud of economics," for his work "was the first to point out the influence of certain psychological forces in the maladjustments of industry and in the economic attitudes of certain classes, and to glimpse the influence of what might be called an economic libido." [2]

In 1919 Mencken wrote an essay on Veblen in the magazine *Smart Set*, which was later republished in his first *Prejudices*. Until 1917, said Mencken, Professor Dewey was the great thinker in the eyes of the respectable literary weeklies, a role he had fallen into after the death of William James. "Then, overnight, the upspringing of the intellectual soviets, the headlong assault upon all the old axioms of pedagogical speculation, the nihilistic dethronement of Prof. Dewey—and rah, rah, rah for Professor Dr. Thorstein Veblen!"

"In a few months—almost it seemed a few days—he was all over *The Nation, The Dial, The New Republic* and the rest of them, and his books and pamphlets began to pour from the presses, and the newspapers reported his every wink and whisper," and "everyone of intellectual pretensions read his works. Veblenism was shining in full brilliance. There were Veblenists, Veblen clubs, Veblen remedies for all the sorrows of the world. There were even, in Chicago, Veblen Girls—perhaps Gibson Girls grown middle-aged and despairing." But Veblen's domination is declining now, largely because a reader of Veblen "has to struggle with what is not only intolerably bad writing, but also loose, flabby, cocksure, and preposterous thinking." As an example of such thinking Mencken cited Veblen's assertion in *The Theory of the Leisure Class* that cows are not kept on one's lawn because "to the average popular apprehension a herd of cattle so pointedly suggests thrift and usefulness that their presence . . . would be intolerably cheap." "Has the genial professor, pondering his great problems," asked Mencken, "ever taken a walk in the country? And has he, in the course of that walk, ever crossed a pasture inhabited by a cow? And has he, making that crossing, ever passed astern of the cow herself? And has he, thus passing astern, ever stepped carelessly, and—" After the essay appeared, Veblen remarked to Lubin: "Now I am an agricultural economist."

A number of people were alienated from Veblen because of his apparent inability to carry on a conversation. Distinguished economists from abroad, such as R.H. Tawney, came to see him; industrial experts would visit him at his invitation, but he would have nothing to say. The visitors thought he was adopting the pose of a god, but after his guests departed Veblen always bitterly regretted his inability to find anything to say. His protective mechanism of silence had become his master. Often, however, he asked questions in order to avoid being questioned. Once Davenport asked if a certain professor had Jewish blood, and Veblen answered that the man was one-fourth Jewish. "How do you know?" asked Davenport. "Well," replied Veblen, "I had lunch with him, the other day, and if I had not asked questions, he would have."

Some of Veblen's friends considered his helplessness not entirely excusable. He and his stepchildren stayed much of the time at the Stewart home in Amherst, and his whims were not easy to live with. The stepchildren had to take especial care not to disturb him, and they were required to rise very early in order to get Veblen's fresh cream from the milkman.

When Veblen was still with the Food Administration, he had lunched one day with the editor of a leading Jewish magazine which was strongly Zionist. The important part played by Jews in the growth of knowledge was discussed and the question as to whether their influence would proceed at an accelerated rate in a land which they could call their own and which would be free from the bans and taboos that prevail against Jewish intellectuals in the gentile world. Veblen offered to write on the problem, and understood that he was to receive $250. He finished the article on July 4, 1918, but instead of describing the pre-eminence of the Jews in the intellectual world as the result of national genius, or race, or the Jewish cultural heritage, he described it as a result of the fact that in the alien gentile world the Jewish intellectuals have been made to realise the make-believe character of both Jewish and gentile cultural foundations, and have thereby been enabled to appreciate the facts as they are. Thus their peculiar intellectual position is due to their character as renegade Jews, and in their own homeland they might make good Talmudic scholars but would not contribute to modern science. The magazine sent Veblen a check for $100. He was annoyed, returned the check, and sent "The Intellectual Pre-eminence of Jews in Modern Europe," to *The Political Science Quarterly*, where it appeared in March 1919. The subtitle of the original article—"Its Nature and Causes"—was now omitted.

Veblen's description of the intellectual Jew carries a strong suggestion of the renegade who had broken out of the Norwegian community into the New England scheme. The argument has a strictly academic air of philosophy, but, when its metaphysical terms are translated into equivalent terms of institutions or action, the spirit of a rebel is revealed, and also something of bitterness. The analysis is the same that Veblen had used before in explaining Marx's role as a great creative intellectual force. Jewish and gentile cultures are described in terms that Veblen had made familiar; in this essay it is the renegade Jew that takes the role elsewhere played by the modern scientist, the engineer, the socialist propagandist, the hypothetical savage.

In the intellectual life of western civilisation, in institutional change and growth, in science and scholarship, Jews have an importance out of proportion to their numbers, "particularly among the vanguard, the pioneers, the uneasy guild of pathfinders and iconoclasts." But only when the Jew escapes from his archaic culture and becomes a naturalised though hyphenated citizen in the gentile world, does he become a creative leader in the world's intellectual enterprise. Any inquiry in modern science that will bring enduring results rests upon a sceptical mind; that is, emancipation from the dead hand of conventional finality is requisite in that pioneering and engineering work of guidance, design, and theoretical correlation without which "the most painstaking collection and canvass of information is irrelevant, incompetent, and impertinent." The intellectually gifted Jew, like other men in a similar position, secures immunity from intellectual quietism "at the cost of losing his secure place in the scheme of conventions into which he has been born, and . . . of finding no similarly secure place in the scheme of gentile conventions into which he is thrown. . . . He becomes a disturber of the intellectual peace, but only at the cost of becoming an intellectual wayfaring man, a wanderer in the intellectual No Man's Land, seeking another place to rest, farther along the road, somewhere over the horizon. They are neither a complaisant nor a contented lot, these aliens of the uneasy feet."

The Jew's traditional intrinsically thearchic culture, with its beautiful efficacy of ritualistic magic, bears the mark B.C., and runs on a logic of personal and spiritual traits, qualities, and relations, "a class of imponderables, which are no longer of the substance of those things that are inquired into by men to whom the ever-increasingly mechanistic orientation of the modern time becomes habitual." When the gifted young Jew, still flexible in his mental habits, is set loose in the mechanistic scheme of life, his archaic scheme falls to pieces, just as the prevailing pecuniary order seems insubstantial to a modern scientist or technician. But this disintegration does not lead to an acceptance of those preconceptions which make the safe and sane gentile conservative and complacent, which blur his intellectual vision and leave him intellectually senile. The sceptic does not uncritically accept the "intellectual prepossessions that are always standing over among the substantial citizens of the republic of learning." Thus the Jew "is in a peculiar degree exposed to the unmediated facts of the current situation; and . . . takes his orientation from the run of the facts as he finds them, rather than from the traditional interpretation of analogous facts in the past." By virtue of this enforced scepticism towards the prevailing dominant institutions, "he is in line to become a guide and leader of men in that intellectual enterprise out of which comes the increase and diffusion of knowledge among men, provided always that he is by native gift endowed with that net modicum of intelligence which takes effect in the play of the idle curiosity" on the received institutions.

Although such a Jew intellectually becomes an alien to his own community, spiritually he will likely remain a Jew, "for the heart-strings of affection and consuetude are tied early, and they are not readily retied in after life." Regardless of the intellectual assets he brings, the attitude of the safe and sane gentiles towards him is not one that is likely to lead to his personal incorporation into their community. "The most amiable share in the gentile community's life that is likely to fall to his lot is that of being interned."

But this method of approach was not one adapted to the current scene or to Veblen's work on *The Dial* or to the forces that were driving him on to a clear expression of what he had called the evolutionary point of view. Popular interest was centred in the peace, the League of Nations, and Bolshevism, and it was to these matters that Veblen turned his attention. He became particularly interested in Bolshevism, anxiously read the newspapers as to its success, and began learning Russian. During the summer of 1919 he followed with interest the military movements against Denikin and Kolchak, which Geroid Robinson recorded from day to day on a map in the *Dial* office. Veblen frequently attended editorial conferences, and he was interested in the *Dial* workers' soviet which was formed that summer, but he never participated in the discussion, except perhaps to ask an occasional question.

Late in 1919 a meeting took place between Veblen and Lenin's recently announced representative in the United States, Ludwig C.A.K. Martens, who was an engineer and who had been, during the later period of the war, the representative in the United States of the Demidorff Steel Works of Russia. He was described by the gentleman who introduced him to Veblen as "a large gentleman, almost painfully shy." He announced himself just as the Great Red Scare was rising to its height, and thereafter his days and nights were a nightmare of legislative and administrative investigations and third-degree quizzes by policemen, secret service agents, and official and amateur patriots.

"Veblen expressed . . . a desire to meet Martens and ask him some questions. In due course I asked Veblen and Martens to lunch. Both men were shy. I sat between them. After shaking hands they said nothing. I sat endlessly making conversation, trying to stumble on a topic that would serve as an open sesame for their talk. The meal was almost over—it had seemed eternal—when I happened to press the right button in my groping talk, my monologue. Veblen turned suddenly from gazing off into space, and began to ask questions. It was like a skilled surgeon wielding a scalpel. He turned Martens inside out; he turned the whole soviet experiment inside out. He got, in the course of possibly an hour or so, all that there was to know. Martens was put at ease at once. He responded beautifully. It was an impressive example of one keen, orderly mind excavating another." Both Veblen and Martens totally ignored their host.

On the question of the peace negotiations Veblen felt that President Wilson had been given an extremely rare opportunity of shaping the course of events to an enduring peace at home and abroad, but that, although the whole world was at Wilson's feet when he went to the Peace Conference, he had not risen to the occasion. But Veblen appreciated the president's integrity, his sacrifice of his health and fortunes for the sake of an ideal. In Veblen's apparent criticisms of the president and his policies it is difficult to be sure that he is not in reality directing his attack against the prevailing system of arrangements which the president allowed to stand.

In April 1919, Veblen began writing a number of unsigned editorials in *The Dial*. Their titles appear only in the index, the editorials appearing in the magazine without headings. The first, "Bolshevism Is a Menace to the Vested Interests," is familiar material. Bolshevism is a menace to the vested interests of privilege and property, and consequently a problem to the elder statesmen. The measures taken and planned against the Russians by the great powers cannot be successful; the blockade can scarcely do more than starve the remnants of the Russian vested interests. In the main Russia is self-supporting. It has the defects of its qualities, but it has also the qualities of its defects; it is incapable of serious aggression but it is also incapable of conclusive defeat by force. Soviet Russia offers an attractive market for American equipment and goods. If the blockade is maintained for some time, the smuggling trade will appreciably increase, to the substantial profit of the Scandinavians and other expert smugglers and blockade runners. The great powers, whose national integrity has been provisionally stabilised by American participation in the war, are placing an embargo on the goods for which Soviet Russia, the only country which puts no obstacles in the way of import trade, is making a cash offer. It is an interesting question "how long will those American vested interests which secure an income from foreign trade," patiently forgo assured profits from open trade with Soviet Russia "in order to afford certain European vested interests" a dubious chance to continue securing "something for nothing in the way of class privilege and unearned income."

In his editorial on "Sabotage" Veblen shifted to a topic more closely related to his view of corporation practice. Sabotage is one of the late and formidable terms, loan words, of the English language. "Graft," "good will," "intangible assets," and "vested interests" are uncouth terms, but they are indispensable in describing "facts which are very much in evidence and which are not otherwise provided for." Graft is at least as old as the Egyptian dynasties; sabotage is quite inseparable from the price system, and is perhaps the first-born of those evils that are said to be rooted in the love of money. Doubtless graft and sabotage have been running along together through human history from its beginning. "We should all find it very difficult to get our bearings in any period of history or any state of society which might by any chance not be shot through with both." But the terms were not so necessary before the last quarter of the nineteenth century, doubtless because of the fact that sabotage and graft, despite their massive and far-reaching character, "did not . . . stand out in bold relief on the face of things." But since the price system and all its ways have reached that mature development which is familiar to this generation, both terms have become indispensable in current speech.

In another editorial Veblen cited as an example of sabotage the congressional filibuster, the action of the constituted authorities in turning back industry to private gain, and in refusing to take measures eliminating private gain. Congress, he said, adjourned without passing measures to pay for the railroad administration bureaux. The employment bureaux, which it required so much trouble to build up, have been reduced from seven hundred to about fifty or sixty, the training school has been eliminated, and the work of the bureaux left to be taken care of by the smaller political units.

In the issue for May 3 Veblen's editorial was "Immanuel Kant on Perpetual Peace." "Immanuel Kant once wrote a sketch a century and a quarter ago on Perpetual Peace. He prefaced it with a jest . . . to say that the running title under which he wrote—*Zum ewigen Frieden,* that is to say, The House of Peace Everlasting—was borrowed from the signboard of a certain roadside tavern adjoining a certain ancient churchyard. Compounded of bar-room and graveyard, this wise man's jest will to many readers doubtless have seemed as pointless as it is tasteless. But that will be true only of those readers of Kant who have not the inestimable fortune to live through these days of returning peace and to witness the maudlin deliberation of that conclave of elder statesmen who are now arranging to make the world safe for the vested rights of international dissension. The point of Kant's jest is plain now. Today his readers are in a position to marvel that even that wise old man should have been so wise as all that. It is quite uncanny."

Two editorials, one appearing in the issue for May 17 and one in that for May 31, cannot be unequivocally attributed to Veblen. The first stated, "One may turn from the outdoor turmoil in Europe, and even in the United States, as from a bad dream to the report of the Commission on Industrial Labour Legislation of the Peace Conference and be assured that the hour of peace has struck and 'all is well' in industry." High aspirations are stated which might even be supported by the Chamber of Commerce, but mystery surrounds their enforcement. "The ways of enforcement, it is understood, are fraught with technicalities which must perforce take precedence as they are concerned with the realities of routine rather than the abstractions of human rights." In the contemplated scheme, involving trade wars against nations who do not observe the business ethics, the wage standard of the regular unions "are to be protected as the prices of commodities are now protected by the United States tariff, and special labour interests like special business interests will be cared for." Stand-pat business and stand-pat unionism join hands. "Such a contemplated scheme, naïvely supported by reformers in a spirit of universal uplift, has as much relation to a progressive civilisation as a tariff imposed for the support of infant industries, but no more." The familiar statement of Samuel Gompers, re-echoed in the declaration of the High Contracting Parties, is that human labour shall not be an article of commerce, but this is precisely the position of labour in the wage system which Gompers and the High Commissioners support. The statement can be cleared of cant only if it carries with it a plan "which will do away with a *market* where labour is bargained for collectively according to trade-union practice, or where individually sold and purchased. But such a proposal would re-echo the outdoor movement of the workers of Europe, and that we know is not the purpose of the Peace Congress."

The other editorial applied to the treaty the theory of the "offensive-defensive." "By and large the terms of the Great Peace were drawn to secure two objects; one offensive—the destruction of Germany; one defensive—the preservation of the present economic and political system." The capitalist system made the peace, and the terms are so heavy that German capitalism will be crushed out of existence, and the subject classes of Germany will be united in a hatred born of nationalistic rebellion and the class war, aimed at the "foreign" kept classes, whose only function, so far as Germany is concerned, is the absorption of profits. If the governing and owning classes of Germany are retained, they become merely agents of commutation for the higher parties. For the first time the class that owns and the class that works appear in the undecorated roles of the taxer and taxed. "Whether or not this reductio ad absurdum of the old order will have an appreciable effect upon the taxed classes in the Allied countries remains to be seen. Already it seems safe to predict that Allied and German labour will find friendship in adversity." These matters have escaped the critics of the treaty, who feel that the Allies may be killing the German goose that is to lay the golden eggs of indemnity. The deeper fact implied, is that "the real goose is an international bird; as long as labour and brain power in Germany and elsewhere are organised for production incident to the preservation of life, the goose lives. It is the system for collecting the eggs that is everywhere in danger."

In the same issue Veblen wrote an article entitled "Peace," which is on the face of it perhaps his most seriously written article. It was in this article that the grievous substitution of beadle for beetle was made. The Peace Covenant, Veblen declared, was created in the image of nineteenth-century imperialism or Mid-Victorian liberalism, and is consequently irrelevant in the twentieth century. It is America's covenant, made and provided for by the paramount advice and consent of America's president. It provides for no abatement of the devastating nationalist intrigue that so seriously deranges the industrial mechanism, for no elimination of the increasingly obstructive control of production by the vested interests of commerce and finance. This capitalist sabotage is fast approaching the limit of popular tolerance, but the answer to the common man's cry for enduring peace, for industrial prosperity and content, is the provision of armed forces sufficient to curb any uneasy drift of sentiment among the underlying populace with the due advice and consent of the dictatorship established by the elder statesmen.

A settlement should logically be in the hands of those who know the needs of the industrial system and are not biased by commercial incentives, that is, it should be entrusted to production engineers. "These men, technical specialists, over-workmen, skilled foremen of the system" and their like, "know something of the material conditions of life that surround the common man," and they should logically be allowed "to frame such a settlement as will bind the civilised peoples together in an amicable footing as a going concern, engaged in a joint enterprise." Without these specialists the working of the industrial system, whether in peace or war, is impossible. The cost, the work, of the war, both at home and abroad, fell on the soldiers and workmen; the vested interests and spokesmen of commercialised nationalism risked nothing and lost nothing. But in the soviet of elder statesmen, which has conferred the dictatorship on the political deputies of the vested interests, no soldiers and no workmen's deputies are included. Neither their wishes nor their welfare has been consulted in drafting the covenant; that is, the interests of the industrial system have been ignored. Slight attention need be paid to the statement that the "American workmen may be alleged to have been represented at this court of elder statesmen, informally, unofficially, and irresponsibly, by the sexton beetle of the A.F. of L."

Veblen's editorial of June 14 shifts back directly to the domestic scene. *Panem et Circenses* was the formula on which the politicians of imperial Rome relied to keep the underlying population from being restless. The politicians, spokesmen of the vested interests, were forced to allow the underlying population a ration of bread, at some cost to the vested interests, in order to count on their support. This is the closest they came to the modern democratic institution of the breadline. "To those democratic statesmen who now bear up the banners of the vested interests— also called the standards of Law and Order"—this conduct is viewed as prodigal and a sign of weakness. But the politicians of Rome did not have the use of Liberty Loans and machine-guns, and apparently the underlying population was less reasonable and patient as regards promises and procrastinations. Today mechanical appliances for upholding law and order have been greatly perfected, and by suitable fiscal methods "the underlying population which is to be 'kept in hand' can be induced to pay for these mechanical appliances" for controlling them. Thus the democratic statesmen are able to let the breadline take the place of bread, and save the net output of the republic's industry more nearly intact for the use of the kept classes.

This businesslike age is also more economical in its *circenses*. The Roman *circenses* cut rather wastefully into the ordinary earnings of those vested interests for whom the Roman imperium was administered, whereas the movies of the twentieth century are a business enterprise in their own right, a source of earnings and thus a vested interest. In ordinary peace and war they are adequate for that dissipation of attention which is politically so salutary. But in times of stress, as now, when large chances of profit and loss for the vested interests are in the balance, something more enticing must be done. Thus the rant and swagger of subsidised heroes, and the pomp and circumstance incident to a victory loan, have good use in stabilising the doubtfully manageable popular sentiment. Similar devices are the "heroic spectacles" of a " 'victory fleet,' together with parades, arches, and banners—miles of banners, and square miles of heroic printed matter"; and an "overseas flight; particularly if it is abundantly staged and somewhat more than abundantly advertised." The common man's afterthought must not be allowed to "run along the ground of material fact, where it might do mischief," but must be kept in the upper air of fancy. Such shows are expensive, but the cost need not be watched too closely since it is borne not by the vested interests but by the common man, who is for ever in danger of getting into mischief by "reflecting unduly on what the statesmen have been using him for." It is no more than reasonable that he should pay the cost for being saved from obnoxious afterthought. "*Panem et circenses:* The Bread Line and the Movies." In the issue for July 12 Veblen discussed the president's betrayal of democratic aspirations. The president proclaimed a policy of "open covenants openly arrived at," but the elder statesmen have guarded their meetings with jealous secrecy in order to "give out no information which might be useful to the enemy," useful, that is, to the underlying population of the great powers. Democratic ideals have gone into abeyance because the elder statesmen realise that their avowed ideal of democratic rule is hopelessly out of date, and that an ever-widening cleavage of interest has arisen within each nation between the vested interests and the underlying populations. The latter are in effect falling into the position of subject peoples, in the nature of alien enemies. Recent and prospective American legislation bears a striking resemblance to the notorious British Rowlatt acts for India. Both the Indians and the Americans are to be kept in hand for the good of the vested interests. The underlying population wants peace and industry; the elder statesmen are by their nature committed to the maintenance of law and order for the vested interests, the *status quo*, at the cost of the underlying population, despite the smoke screen of secrecy and prevarication thrown up by the "seven censors and the Associated Prevarication Bureaux."

The high-hearted crusade to make the world safe for democracy by open covenants openly arrived at has come to a tragic end because Bolshevism is a menace to the vested interests of privilege and property. For the utter defeat of democratic ideals the paramount responsibility is to be attributed to America's spokesman. No important move could have been made in this negotiation without his advice and consent. Without America's backing, the high contracting parties are practically bankrupt; no two of them could reasonably trust one another out of sight. Thus the achievement and the commitments of this conclave of elder statesmen are in effect the achievement and the commitments of America's spokesman.

The editorial which immediately followed, entitled "A World Safe for the Vested Interests," continues the argument. America's spokesman began with a high resolve to make the world safe for the Mid-Victorian commercialised democracy, that is, a democracy for the safeguarding of the vested interests of property. But the Bolshevism of Soviet Russia is a menace to this goal. It is easily to be seen that their own material interest would incline the underlying populations in other nations to fall in with the soviet policy just as soon as "they come to realise they have nothing to lose." To meet this menace the older statesmen have necessarily entered into working arrangements with all the irresponsible shameless forms of reaction and reactionary enterprise. "Needs must when the devil drives, and Bolshevism is largely believed to be of that breed."

There is no certain evidence that the next editorial is Veblen's work, but it conforms with his argument. The outstanding feature of the government's international policy is the effort to stabilise capitalism at the expense of social reconstruction. "The great body of citizens is probably reactionary only out of apathy, but the groups which are effectively organised—the politicians, the labour unionists, and the financiers—have formed a Triple Alliance in the interest of active reaction." In the light of the world situation, however, the increase in production called for by the financiers cannot be accomplished except by a thoroughgoing reconstruction of the industrial process; that is, it requires the active participation of the worker in the management, and the transferring of authority "from the pecuniary strategists of the antiquated financial regime to the new subordinate controllers of material and personnel." Capitalism apparently can survive only on condition of being "transformed out of all recognition. Therefore the hope of reconstruction lies not in the liberalism of America" but in the needs of an impoverished and prostrate mankind.

About this time the investigations of radical opinion, carried on by the notorious Lusk Committee of the New York State Legislature, were being denounced by liberals. Offices of radical organisations had been raided, supposed evidence of sedition issued to the press, and over a thousand arrests made. *The Dial* charged that the A.F. of L. was one of the agencies behind the raid. Protests were made by the organisations, by liberal newspapers, and by such citizens as Samuel Untermyer that the organisations were not allowed to present their side of the case. The Rand School inserted an advertisement in *The Dial* appealing to the people of the United States for the simplest right of self-defence.[3] The Lusk Committee included Veblen among its dangerous radicals. Veblen's offence consisted not only in being an editor of *The Dial*, but in having aided the I.W.W. and the Civil Liberties Union in preparing the latter's pamphlet on "The Truth about the I.W.W." Actually his only contribution was a paragraph quoted from one of his works. In this, as in other similar quotations, the authorship was clearly indicated, and also the fact that it was an extract.[4]

Veblen paid his respects to these alarmist organisations in two editorials entitled "The Red Terror—at Last It Has Come to America," and "The Red Terror and the Vested Interests." The Red Terror is "running wild among the guardians of Business as Usual; official, semi-official, and quasi-official; courts, camps, and churches; legislative, judiciary, and executive." The ordinary citizen is immune and apathetic, but "the Guardians of the Vested Interests are panic-stricken, all and several, certified and subsidiary and surreptitious. The commercialised newspapers all see Red. So do the official and quasi-official conspiracies, such as the Lusk Commission, the Union League Club, the Security League, and the Civic Federation, as well as the Publicity Police, the Workday Politicians, the Clerics of the Philistine Confession, and the Wild Asses of the Devil generally." Anyone not visibly identified with the vested interests is under suspicion and in effect assumed to be guilty. "Acute paranoia persecutoria" is coming to be rated "the chief of the civic virtues." Actually, however, the "confederated paranoiacs" have already "assembled much curious evidence of undue sanity" and "seditiously excessive sanity" among the vulgar. Veblen cited from the committee's own exhibits letters, sent in by alarmists, which demonstrated imbecility and incredible foolishness by their display of evidence which told the opposite story. "These particular exhibits may perhaps lay bare the Red state of mind of the Guardians in a more picturesque fashion than the common run of these uncanny keepsakes of the demented which they have been assembling in the course of these raids." But the Red alarmists are "busily accumulating more of the same kind, by fair means and foul."

As an "outcome of the dispassionate sweep of forces which no man can withstand or deflect," it seems that the vested interests are "riding for a fall." Only the Guardians of the kept classes are unable to see the matter in that light, because it is their whole duty "to endeavour by all means, fair or foul, to deflect the sweep of events over which they have no control. Such a change of base as is now coming in sight is in the nature of a moral impossibility for the keepers of the Old Order." The Guardians as a result of the war and post-war experience are beginning to realise that the vested interests run at cross-purposes with the material welfare of the underlying population. It is universally known that "the Vested Interests of business are driven by business considerations to waste, mismanage, and obstruct the country's productive industry, unavoidably and unremittingly, and to divert an ever-increasing share of the country's income to their own profit"; and the Guardians are unable to continue keeping this information secret. But they believe that, should the community at large appreciate these facts, a popular revolt would follow, sweeping out of existence the vested interests of privilege and property. In this they overlook the massive institutional fabric of uncritical habituation that in effect makes the population submissive to the interests of the kept classes. The Guardians are presumably right in believing that the situation in business and industry should logically lead to a revolutionary overturn, but grounds of sentiment rather than logic have to be taken into account in such a case. "Popular sentiment, as well as the strategic disposal of forces, is still securely to be counted on to uphold the established order of vested rights and Business as Usual. The Guardians have allowed the known facts of the case to unseat their common sense. Hence the pitiful spectacle of official hysteria and the bedlamite conspiracies in restraint of sobriety."

Veblen was still convinced that something might be done to prevent a repetition of the events of pre-war days, and in the summer of 1919 it seemed as if he would have an opportunity to realise his ambitions of guiding a group of able students in an investigation of the economic order. A group of persons connected with the Federal Council of Churches had conceived the idea of collecting a staff to make a thorough analysis of economic conditions, and the Inter-Church World movement had a large amount of money available for the project. In July 1919, during a week-end at Amherst, where Veblen was staying with a group including Stewart, Lubin, Hamilton, and Leo Wolman, a representative of the Federal Council of Churches discussed the plan with Stewart and Veblen, but nothing came of it because the interests behind the Inter-Church World movement thought the idea too radical. F. Ernest Johnson, executive secretary of the Council's Department of Research and Education, had a conference with Veblen and Helen Marot. Veblen was chiefly interested in the credit system and seems to have wished to make the use of loan credit the point of departure. He estimated that the study would cost $25,000, but the money, according to Mr. Johnson, was not available. The Council turned instead to an investigation of the great steel strike. Veblen was greatly interested in the investigation, and he questioned David Saposs, one of the investigators, with great thoroughness.

President Wilson arranged for an industrial conference in October to discuss the prevailing economic situation. An editorial in *The Dial* referred to the fact that the president reproaches the community for not wishing peace as much as he does. On the other hand, he appoints Judge Gary and Mr. Rockefeller to represent the public at the conference. "Some lesser lights, mostly from the banking fraternity, and two renegade Socialists complete the list." It is such people, apparently, that the president has in mind "when he tells us that he voices the sentiments of the American people—about peace. . . . We note that the ablest labour leaders have not been snatched away from their personal interests and impressed into the service of the general public; and we recommend for careful consideration the sacrifice the President has required of the largest employers of labour in the United States."

Veblen's last editorial, "The Twilight Peace of the Armistice," appeared on November 15, 1919. Its occasion was the first anniversary of the armistice. The eleventh of November, he declared, is dedicated to the "white boutonnière of peace," but the peace that prevails is one of martial law, not of good will and tranquillity. The peace was concluded in order to engage in a fight; it shows a steadily rising tide of warlike expenditure, hostilities, bankruptcies, and is made of intrigue, fire, famine, and pestilence. The year since the armistice "will show a larger expenditure for military operations and a larger total of warlike atrocities than any recorded twelve months prior to the Great War." This is a negotiated peace, in the nature of a compromise in order to prevent the collapse of the German military establishment. But the entire imperial organisation, including the military establishment, remains virtually intact under a perfunctory mask of democratic forms. The hasty compromise was due to a realisation that the Entente's vested interests of property and class must join hands with those of the Central Powers, if they were to cope successfully with the common enemy—the increasingly uneasy underlying population on both sides. If the German military organisation had been rendered prostrate and discredited, as it would have been in another three months, the country would have turned Bolshevist. But the guardians of the vested interests, the elder statesmen, needed the bulwark of a practicable German Empire to serve as a bar against the spread of Bolshevism out of Soviet Russia. Their purpose is to defeat Bolshevism by fire, sword, and famine, in and out of Soviet Russia. The policy of the Entente, in war and peace, is wholly comprised in the proposition that Bolshevism is a menace to absentee ownership. But it is an open question how closely the elder statesmen "are likely to realise their sanguine hope of subduing Soviet Russia by use of a subservient German military establishment."

In December *The Survey*, in an article entitled "The Way Out; a Symposium of the Industrial Situation Now before the President's Conference and the Country," gave the results of a canvass of "employers," "labour leaders," and "industrial experts" for constructive suggestions as to means of alleviating the wave of industrial conflict and unrest. *The Survey* felt that there was a great demand for creative statesmanship in the field of industrial relations, and Veblen was asked for his opinion as an "industrial expert." He replied: "To my great regret I have no answer to the question on which you have been kind enough to ask my opinion for publication in *The Survey*. In fact I find myself more interested in what is likely to happen than in what should be done about it."

CHAPTER XXII

A SERIES of essays in *The Dial*, beginning in April 1919 and ending in November, paralleled Veblen's editorials and extended their argument. Along with "Peace" and "Bolshevism Is a Menace—to Whom?" they were intended, according to an announcement in *The Dial*, to compose "a series on Contemporary Problems in Reconstruction, a concrete application of [Veblen's] theory outlined in The Modern Point of View and the New Order." Later the essays were brought out in book form under the title of *The Engineers and the Price System*. Only the last three essays in the book appeared originally as a unit—"On the Dangers of a Revolutionary Overturn," "On the Circumstances Which Make for a Change," and "A Memorandum on a Practicable Soviet of Technicians"—representing the three sections of the article on "Bolshevism and the Vested Interests in America." The first three, however, also form a unit—"On the Nature and Uses of Sabotage," "The Industrial System and the Captains of Industry," and "The Captains of Finance and the Engineers." The order of the essays is not, however, of great importance, for, like the individual chapters of his other books, they all tell the same story. In this book, as in the others, the second half offers a less obscure presentation of the argument of the first.

Investment banking is now the centre of discussion, and the investment banker is seen as the dominant figure in economic life. The vested interests are the financial powers, and the old-time corporation financier has ceased to be a captain of industry and become a lieutenant of finance, "the captaincy having been taken over by the syndicated investment bankers and administered as a standardised routine of accountancy, having to do with the flotation of corporation securities and with their fluctuating values, and having also something to do with regulating the rate and volume of output in those industrial enterprises which so have passed under the hand of the investment bankers." In Veblen's fundamental contrast the material welfare is represented now by the engineers. "The two pillars of the house of corporate business enterprise of the larger sort are the industrial experts and the larger financial concerns that control the necessary funds."

The first chapter, "On the Nature and Uses of Sabotage," reads like a popular version of his more academic discussion of the nature and uses of capital. When this essay appeared in *The Dial*, the demand for it was so large that it was republished as a booklet. The common welfare in any community organised on the modern price system, declared Veblen, cannot be maintained without recourse to capitalistic sabotage, to obstruction and retardation of industrial efficiency in order to maintain reasonable profits—all the traffic can bear—and so guard against a business depression. Considerations of sabotage are now extremely important to businessmen and officials, in their attempts to tide over a threatening depression and a consequent period of hardship for the classes dependent on free income from investment. The habitual recourse to ordinary, legitimate sabotage of manpower and resources is not usually discussed by the spokesmen of business. They dwell instead "on those exceptional, sporadic, and spectacular episodes in business where businessmen have now and again successfully gone out of the safe and sane highway of conservative business enterprise that is hedged about with a conscientious withdrawal of efficiency, and have endeavoured to regulate the output by increasing the productive capacity of the industrial system at one point or another." The populations of the civilised countries are in great need of the means of subsistence and are suffering ever-increasing privation and want, but plants continue to shut down because of "insufficient income to the vested interests which control the staple industries and so regulate the output of product."

An appreciable decrease in the net earnings of a large well-managed concern in the staple industries will bring it to bankruptcy under the routinised requirements of the price system as it takes effect in corporation finance. The overhead charges which represent free income, that is, the costs of inefficiency, or pecuniary salvation, have precedence over physical salvation, but it is an open question whether this businesslike sabotage can bring the community through this grave crisis without a disastrous shrinkage of capitalisation and a consequent liquidation. A more comprehensive, more co-ordinated organisation is needed to help the business community enforce the necessary restrictive measures, and the national authorities have the duty of providing such an organisation. The protective tariff, the conscientious mismanagement of the railways under federal control so as to discredit government operation, the sabotage through press and post office of information which might give the underlying classes an appreciation of the grave state of affairs, are of this nature. Veblen seems also to suggest that the Federal Reserve system can be characterised in this way.

The next essays are more directly concerned with the role of the engineer as opposed to that of the financier. Although the state of the industrial arts is a joint stock of knowledge derived from past experience, and is held and passed on as an indivisible possession of the community at large, it is not recognised as a factor in production by received economics, which assumes that productivity is measured by profits since the state of the industrial arts is no man's individual property. The modern businessman has been taken account of in the received economics because he has become increasingly important as the recipient of an increasing share of the community's income, and thus he is held to be an important industrial factor. The typical entrepreneur is the corporate financier, the investment banker, in big business rather than small. The corporation, as exemplified in the holding company, is characterised by combination and restriction, its emergence coinciding with the need of restricting production for the sake of profit percent. The end of free-swung competitive production at the close of the century is evidence of the fact that industry has passed into the hands of the corporation financier. Financial management has been reduced to a routine of acquisition and running sabotage, so that the corporation financier is taking on the character of a bureau chief. Industry is in the hands of the syndicated investment bankers, and administered as a standardised routine of accountancy. But the investment banker, by virtue of his addiction to strictly financial manœuvres, to a safe and sane policy of watchful waiting to absorb any gain created by engrossing the community's technological efficiency, is out of touch with technological needs, and cannot even appreciate the pecuniary losses he himself may suffer, not to mention the greater loss suffered by the community.

Veblen declared that the "financial interest here spoken of as the investment banker is commonly something in the way of a more or less articulate syndicate of financial houses, and it is to be added that the same financial concerns are also commonly, if not invariably, engaged or interested in commercial banking of the usual kind." With the maturing of private property and the machine technology this quasi-syndicate of banking interests that make use of the country's credit for corporation finance is able more efficiently to sabotage the material welfare of the community. The substantial credits and debits, the large-scale credit transactions, are in effect pooled within the syndicate, and the multiplication of securities and extension of credit, with resulting inflation of values, can take place to a greater extent, but need not bring any risk of liquidation. No effective derangement of the credit situation can take effect except by the free choice of the quasi-syndicate of investment banking houses, that is, they will allow a derangement only to the extent that such a move is profitable.

In this characteristically indirect fashion Veblen places the responsibility for depression upon the investment bankers, with their creation of a make-believe stable structure of credit and finance, in the free pursuit of profits and capital. Credit, which is now merely a method of accounting and make-believe, "is also one of the time-worn institutions that are due to suffer obsolescence by improvement." The process of pooling and syndication has been greatly helped by the establishment of the Federal Reserve system and other similar devices which provide unified control to the large financial interests of the country's credit system. The ideal of a definitive stabilisation of business is now closely reached, but, since this maturing of corporation finance reduces financial traffic to a riskless routine, it may also result in the obsolescence of corporation finance and eventually perhaps of the investment banker, who has already displaced the old-time promoter and the captain of industry of popular tradition.

The comprehensive mechanism of the modern industrial system, upon the due working of which the material welfare of the community depends, "is of an impersonal nature, after the fashion of the material sciences," on which it is constantly drawing. It requires the use of trained and instructed workmen and technologists born, bred, trained, and instructed at the cost of the people at large; that is, the special knowledge of the technologists, as well as that of the workmen, is a community heritage and product, for it is drawn from the community's joint stock of accumulated experience. Highest efficiency requires that a free hand be given to the technologists, for they alone are competent to manage the industrial system. But the captains of finance work deliberately to derange the system for the sake of special gain, with the result that there is increasing unemployment, retardation, and maladministration. Their "trained ignorance" of industrial matters, coupled with their pursuit of the main chance, work effectually to the creation of a state of chaos. "Politics and investment are still allowed to decide matters of industrial policy which should plainly be left to the discretion of the general staff of production engineers driven by no commercial bias."

Industrial integration and consequently financial integration have proceeded farthest in the underlying key industries which shape the main conditions of life, such industries as meat packing, transport and communication, textiles, the production and industrial use of electricity, water power, coal, oil, iron, steel. The date does not seem far distant "when the interlocking processes of the industrial system shall have become so closely interdependent and so delicately balanced that even the ordinary modicum of sabotage involved in the conduct of business as usual will bring the whole to a fatal collapse." Recently the technologists, with the experience of four years of war, have begun to be uneasily class conscious. They are increasingly recognising the tremendous waste and mismanagement achieved by "absentee owners, now represented, in ef-

fect, by the syndicated investment bankers," and are beginning to realise that they are the indispensable general staff of the mechanical industries upon whose unhindered teamwork depend the due working of
the industrial system and therefore also the material welfare of the
civilised peoples. In thus perceiving the all-pervading mismanagement
of industry they come to a realisation of "their own shame and damage
to the common good." The older generation of engineers, however, has
had its habitual outlook shaped by its apprenticeship to the corporation
financiers and investment banks, and therefore it still looks upon the
industrial system "as a contrivance for the roundabout process of making money." Engineers have heretofore been acting in effect as keepers
and providers of free income for the kept classes, but the new generation
now coming on is "not similarly true to that tradition of commercial
engineering that makes the technological man an awe-struck lieutenant
of the captain of finance." These younger men view men and things from
the standpoint of tangible performance, in the way of productive industry, and accordingly they are coming to appreciate that "the whole fabric
of credit and corporation finance is a tissue of make-believe. . . . Corporation finance and all its work and gestures"—the time-worn fabric
of ownership, finance, sabotage, credit, and unearned income—are simply
a nuisance in the working scheme of the engineers, and this activity could
be barred out without deranging the system, "if only that men made up
their mind to that effect." It is difficult, of course, to determine just when
the engineers will make the move.

As it is, the system is at the mercy of endless and inconclusive negotiations between the vested interests of federated workmen and those of
syndicated owners. As long as ownership of industrial resources and equipment is allowed, such negotiations can effect only insignificant concessive
mitigations of the owner right of interference with production. These
bouts of bargaining are games of chance and skill, "played between two
contending vested interests for private gain," and the industrial system
as a going concern, the material welfare of the community and of the
workmen, "enters only as a victim of interested interference."

Neither numerically nor in their habitual outlook are the engineers
such a "heterogeneous body and unwieldy, as the federated workmen,
whose numbers and scattering interest have left all their endeavours
substantially nugatory." The engineers could easily arrange a compact
organisation, and a common purpose for their efforts is supplied by the
all-pervading industrial confusion, obstruction, waste, and retardation
which business as usual continually throws in their face. Also, they are
the leaders of the industrial personnel, which is now becoming restless
and inclined to follow its leaders in any adventure that holds a promise

of advancing the common good. These industrial workers have more than an even share of the sense of workmanship, in its naïve unsophisticated form of appreciation of tangible performance, and they are also endowed with the common heritage of respect for the rule of live and let live. To them the disallowance of the make-believe customary right of ownership would not be a shocking innovation. "A general strike of the technological specialists in industry need involve no more than a minute fraction of one percent of the population; yet it would swiftly bring a collapse of the old order and sweep the time-worn fabric of finance and absentee sabotage into the discard for good and all." It would be only an incident in the day's work to "the engineers and to the rough-handed legions of the rank and file." Such a move depends on the council of technological workers and soldiers' deputies; "the industrial dictatorship of the captain of finance is now held on sufferance of the engineers and is liable at any time to be discontinued at their discretion, as a matter of convenience."

The last three essays are those that were begun in *The Dial* in September. They were written at the height of the Red hysteria, and are conspicuous for their recklessness and their savage use of inverted meaning. Students of the situation, said Veblen, predict a revolutionary overturn in two years; others, not so intimately acquainted with the facts, suggest a longer period. Veblen constantly reiterates that the guardians have nothing to fear, but with a repetition that becomes almost annoying he adds, "just yet." The hysteria of the American Guardians of the Vested Interests is putting them in the position of deliberately bringing about a revolutionary uprising. They should take a lesson from the gentlemanly British government, which has "grown wise in all the ways and means of blamelessly defeating the unblest majority," through a policy of gentlemanly compromise, collusion, and conciliation. A movement to dispossess the vested interests can be permanently successful only if it is undertaken by an organisation competent from the start to take over the country's industry as a whole and administer it on a more efficient plan than that now pursued by the vested interests. No such organisation is yet in sight. As for the A.F. of L., "at the best its purpose and ordinary business is to gain a little something for its own members at a more than proportionate cost to the rest of the community."

It is organisations like the I.W.W., not the A.F. of L., that shatter the nerves of constituted authorities. Bolshevism is the danger that the vested interests are facing, and "the Elder Statesmen are . . . in a position to know, without much inquiry, that there is no single spot or corner in civilised Europe or America where the underlying population would have anything to lose by such an overturn of the established order as would cancel the vested rights of privilege and property, whose guardian they are." In other words, "it has been argued and it seems not unreasonable to believe that the established order of business enterprise . . . is due presently to go under in a muddle of shame and confusion, because it is no longer a practicable system of industrial management under the conditions created by the later state of the industrial arts." Since the industrial system necessarily becomes more integrated, with a more comprehensive control of the labour supply, "any businesslike control is bound to grow still more incompetent, irrelevant, and impertinent." To the extent that the state of affairs becomes understood by the underlying population, "its logical outcome is a growing distrust of the businessmen and all their works and words."

Salesmanship is "the whole and the substance of business enterprise," and "the spokesmen of this enterprise in conspicuous waste are 'pointing with pride' " to the ever-increasing amounts devoted to such enterprise of mendacity and prevarication. Success in salesmanship is the characteristic trait of the captain of finance. In the form of increased sales cost, salesmanship is the remedy for the evils of underproduction, and it constantly increases as the condition of the community grows worse. It is "the chief factor in that ever-increasing cost of living, which is in its turn the chief ground of prosperity among the business community and the chief source of perennial hardship and discontent among the underlying population." An elimination of salesmanship and all its voluminous apparatus and traffic would cut down the capitalised income of the business community by something like one-half.

The deliberate sabotage and restriction required by the system of absentee ownership and capitalised income is a visibly sufficient reason for a revolutionary overturn. An "unbusinesslike administration—as, e.g., the Soviet—will be relieved of the businesslike manager's blackest bugbear, a 'reasonably profitable level of prices,' " and production could be increased several hundred percent. Because of the increasing integration of industry, the captains of industry are enabled, in fact they are driven, to plan their strategy of material defeat and derangement with ever-increasing reach, to the ever-increasing hardship of the community, until the point of tolerance is passed. Industrially speaking, the captains of industry are bound to go wrong, despite the most benevolent and pacific intentions.

It is argued that monopoly, in such forms as syndicates, pools, interlocking directorates, employers' unions, is now covering the field, instead of competition, thus leaving the underlying population more unreservedly at the disposal of the coalition of interests. "The underlying corporations of the holding companies, e.g., are no longer competitors among themselves on the ancient footing," but they are as much as ever bent on strategic dislocation and mutual defeat. Fundamentally there is competition between the great captains who buy cheap and sell dear, and the community from and to whom they buy cheap and sell dear. Whether the commodities they traffic be in securities, labour power, or goods, the result is the same—a dislocation of industry and idle manpower. There is also competition between the pecuniary magnates, even when they temporarily join together, for each one looks out for his opportunity to take advantage of the rest. The temporary syndicates are like temporary alliances, and they are, "in effect, in the nature of conspiracies between businessmen each seeking his own advantage at the cost of any whom it may concern." There is no ulterior solidarity of interests among the participants in such a joint enterprise, just as there is none between two dynastic states who may temporarily join together. Business is still a competitive pursuit of private gain.

When and as far as vested rights give way, the material welfare of the community passes to the technician. "There is no third party qualified," and, if a soviet should arise in America, it would necessarily be a soviet of technicians. As long as no such change takes place, a continuing regime of shame and privation and disturbances is confidently to be expected. But the technicians have the A.F. of L. businesslike attitude and unreflectingly act in severalty and in obedience to the dictates of the captain of finance. They have without much reflection lent themselves and their technical powers freely to the obstructive tactics of the pecuniary strategist, thus in effect betraying the community's joint stock of knowledge. Without the technicians the captains of industry would not exist, since there would be no income, but the captains are not indispensable to the technicians. Indeed they are merely obstructions, and the technicians, by their strategic control, could easily eliminate the pecuniary magnate and absentee ownership. "But there is assuredly no present promise of the technicians turning their insight and common sense to such a use."

In the last chapter, however, "A Memorandum on a Practicable Soviet of Technicians," Veblen sketches what they should do if they used their common sense in this way. The duties and powers of the new order of technicians will "converge on those points in the administration of industry where the old order has most signally fallen short; that is to say, on the due allocation of resources and a consequent full and reasonably proportioned employment of the available equipment and manpower; on the avoidance of waste and duplication of work; and on an equitable and sufficient supply of goods and services to consumers."

Included among the technicians are consulting economists or "Production Economists." By force of commercial pressure and traditions, the economists have "habitually gone in for a theoretical inquiry into the ways and means of salesmanship, financial traffic, and the distribution of income and property, rather than a study of the industrial system considered as a ways and means of producing goods and services." But among the younger generation there are some who have learned that business is not industry, and that investment is not production. The economists would give the necessary insight into the play of economic forces at large and into the wider relations of the economic mechanism. In modern industrial statesmanship they would play a role analogous to that which "legal counsel now plays in the manœuvres of diplomatists and statesmen." Men who have had business experience, particularly in the larger organisations, would be barred from positions of responsibility, discretion, and trust, since they are accustomed to the misleading valuations and accountancy of salesmanship and earnings.

If such a group of engineers and economists made a move towards this new order, preparatory work would have to be done in two directions: first, an inquiry must be made into existing conditions and means; and, second, practicable organisation tables must be set up, covering in some detail the country's industry, energy, resources, materials, and manpower. "And bound up with this work of preparation, and conditioning it, provision must also be made for the growth of such a spirit of teamwork as will be ready to undertake and undergo this critical adventure." The group of technicians, including economists, would also have to engage in a campaign of publicity in order to acquaint the public with the inherent defects of the businesslike regime and with the purposes of the new order. It must bear constantly in mind the fact that the state of the industrial arts is a joint product; that is, a common understanding and solidarity of sentiment must be worked out between the technicians and the general working force in the underlying population. The latter would be represented by deputies and commissioners in the general administration.

In its elements the revolutionary project is simple and obvious, but its working out will require much painstaking preparation. "In principle, all that is necessarily involved is a disallowance of absentee ownership; that is to say, the disestablishment of an institution which has, in the course of time and change, proved to be noxious to the common good. The rest will follow quite simply from the cancelment of this outworn and footless vested right." The initial move would be a cancellation of all corporation securities. Since the underlying industries, controlled by absentee ownership, are the industries which control the main conditions of life, the taking over of these industries from the dead hand of the

captain of finance will result in the disallowance of small business enterprises without any formal elimination. They could be taken over by a
conscientious withdrawal of efficiency, which would be in effect a general
strike. The engineers could do this in a few weeks, but unless they have
the aggressive support of the trained working force in the primary industries they will accomplish nothing more than "a transient period of hardship and dissension."

As yet the production engineers have not drawn together but are still
content to take orders from the deputies of absentee owners; the working
forces of the great industries are out of sympathy with the technical men,
and are bound in rival organisations; the underlying population is still
uninformed of the state of affairs leading to disaster. All these groups
still believe uncritically that absentee ownership is the salvation of civilisation.

Stewart, Mitchell, and Ardzrooni selected the best of Veblen's earlier
essays and had them published under the title, *The Place of Science in
Modern Civilisation and Other Essays*. Stewart and Mitchell considered
the title essay to be Veblen's best, and, when Stewart suggested it as the
most satisfactory title, Veblen merely agreed without question. In addition to this essay the volume includes "The Evolution of the Scientific
Point of View," "Why Is Economics Not an Evolutionary Science?"
"The Preconceptions of Economic Science," "The Limitations of Mar-
ginal Utility," "Professor Clark's Economics," "Schmoller's Economics,"
"Industrial and Pecuniary Employments," "The Economics of Karl
Marx," "Some Neglected Points in the Theory of Socialism," "An
Early Experiment in Trusts," "On the Nature of Capital," "The Muta-
tion Theory and the Blond Race," and "The Blond Race and the Aryan
Culture."

The reviews of this collection reflected the usual difference of opinion
over Veblen. The socialists consigned him now to the despised class of
liberals. The reviewer in *The Call* declared that, if Veblen intended his
original style to keep him clear of too close an identification with radicals, he had succeeded admirably. "He would be rash, indeed, who suggested that the word 'Veblen' conveys the same meaning to all minds.
. . . Mencken cries 'Pish! Posh!' while humble Columbia instructors
spend their salary increases in adding his books to their libraries. . . .
Each reader will find in it what he is looking for." The college senior
will point aghast at Veblen's highly involved and ponderous sentences,
but the faithful liberals will be impressed with his wide erudition. Congratulations may well be extended to those who succeed in unravelling
the maze. "The absence of rhetorical brilliance will prove his sober penetration. . . . Nowhere in them is there any indication of that subtle

wit, the telling thrust, the finely pointed characterisation that rewarded the hours of toil through his other writings." If the caution shown here was due to the fact that Veblen's public was college professors, his subsequent flight "from university circles to New York City is deserving of sympathy." The articles will not be of particular interest to revolutionaries, not even to "parlour Bolsheviki." The essays on socialism imply the scantiness of information available in Veblen's day, "the inhibition enforced by a scholastic environment," and a state of public opinion which viewed the slightest departure from orthodox economics and established procedure as subversion of public morality. "While our author's standing as a humanist is enhanced by the essays, his reputation as an economist will not be." The specialists in political economy may find his other articles of interest, but for the general reader there is nothing in them that is not better presented in his books. Taking Veblen's work in general, "it is the university instructor, the philosophical liberal," who is drawn to him, the class which turns away from orthodox thinking but which cannot, because of either prudence or previous conditioning accept the only adequate system. Veblen "takes the materialistic interpretation of history and socialistic economics, subdues them, envelops them in a metaphysical terminology, arranges them in a striking design, and finally offers them for public consumption. Nothing could appeal more to our closet intelligentsia," for they can now accept socialism "without the stigma attached to the term, and yet offer it as the expression of their own muddled liberalism."

The "philosophical liberals," however, had their own quarrel with Veblen. Hamilton's review of the book declared that "the danger of ignoring [Veblen] because he is far in advance of the scrimmage line is gone. The present danger is that his work will be appraised in terms that are indefinite and cosmic. There is already a tendency to make him responsible for all that is new in economics; and in history and psychology as well. . . . And the movement has reached the laity. In this season's most 'significant' novel the heroine who fights the smugness of the small town with affectation reads Veblen." The glib phrases of his books have "convinced many of their readers that they have understood Veblen." But *The Place of Science in Modern Civilisation*, which "presupposes a specific acquaintance with economic theory" and is addressed to the professional economist, "enables the cosmic judgments of Veblen's place in economics to be reduced to finite terms."

The orthodox economists, those who felt themselves to be the only true professional economists, did not assign Veblen a very high place. Frank Knight of the University of Chicago said in his review in *The Journal of Political Economy* that Veblen was "not a close or clear thinker" and that he could hardly be followed as a "constructive leader" in economics. "The most serious defect of the Veblenian philosophy comes out in the contrast between pecuniary and industrial employments." Even Veblen's secretary, Babette Deutsch, said of the book in *The Dial* that there are passages throughout that "rouse impatience because of the author's very carelessness of pragmatism."

Veblen's career as an editor came to an end after one year, when *The Dial* turned into a literary magazine. It had been dependent on subsidies in one way or another, and these finally ended. But in the New School for Social Research, established in the fall of 1919, Veblen had already found another temporary resting place, which at first, as so many others had done, gave promise of offering him the opportunities he had been seeking.

The first announcement of the New School for Social Research declared: "The people of America as well as those of Europe now face a tide in the affairs of men such as will scarcely pass without a searching readjustment of the established order of things. In view of the difficult situation in which humanity finds itself a group of men versed in the various branches of knowledge relating to mankind have drawn together for counsel, for the correlation of their investigations and the establishment of a centre of instruction and discussion where serious-minded and mature students may gather to carry on their studies in a spirit of scientific inquiry.

"It is, in short, the purpose of the New School to seek an unbiased understanding of the existing order, its genesis, growth, and present working, as well as of those exigent circumstances which are making for its revision."

In further agreement with Veblen's ideals, although not altogether, it was stated that the standard of all the work in the school would be " 'post-graduate' in character although an academic degree is not required for admission." There was to be no irrelevant ceremonial apparatus or hierarchy of ranks. The students "will be presumed to be pursuing each his special study for its own sake according to his particular aims and interests, and there will therefore be no prescribed 'course of study' or fixed curriculum." There was some provision for fellowships. A distinguished faculty was assembled, including Veblen and also Charles A. Beard, James Harvey Robinson, and Wesley C. Mitchell, all of whom resigned from Columbia University. They were referred to as the "Big Four." John Dewey, who retained his Columbia professorship, agreed to lecture at the school. Others in the first faculty were Graham Wallas, Leon Ardzrooni, Alexander Goldenweiser, Horace Kallen, Leo Wolman, Harold J. Laski, Harry Elmer Barnes, Elsie Clews Parsons, Dean

Roscoe Pound, Robert Bruere, Ordway Tead, Moissaye Olgin. Veblen
was scheduled for his famous "Economic Factors in Civilisation." For
the benefit of selected students he gave a course, limited to ten, entitled
"Special Studies of Economic Factors of Civilisation," and another course
was devoted to individual conferences. Veblen's salary was $6000 a year.
In the first two years $4500 of it was contributed by a former Chicago
student who had been greatly influenced by Veblen. Veblen, like a
frugal Norwegian, saved most of it and turned it over in large part to
Ardzrooni for investment in the latter's raisin vineyards in California.

The New School was a fine, simple building in old Chelsea, with its
windows facing a pleasant garden. For a while Veblen and Ardzrooni
shared an apartment in a near-by building owned by the school, but early
in 1920 Ardzrooni went to Dr. Alice Boughton and said that Mitchell
and Robinson had sent him to inquire if she had place for Veblen, for
they felt that he was not getting proper food or care. Dr. Boughton and
Miss Mildred Bennett were living in a house of their own, and they
gladly consented to have Veblen with them. They both admired him
greatly and felt that someone should take care of him because he was a
"national asset." Veblen came the following Sunday and stayed on without ever mentioning the matter. He became interested in detective stories,
although he never admitted it, and whenever Dr. Boughton missed one
of hers she could be sure of finding it hidden under Veblen's mattress. He
was immaculate in his habits, and never left his room until it was entirely
in order.

Veblen was continually encouraging his former students to write for
publication, and if they had manuscripts completed he would accompany
them to his publishers. When the authors pointed out the great probability of the failure of the volume, Veblen said that he had never dreamed
that *The Theory of the Leisure Class* would become so popular.

Dewey, who was more than ever turning to political programmes and
measures of reconstruction, said: "I always found Veblen's own articles
very stimulating and some of his distinctions, like that between the
technological side of industry and its 'business' aspect, have been quite
fundamental in my thinking ever since I became acquainted with them."
Veblen, now grown more mellow, said after hearing an attack on Dewey
and James by a leader of behaviouristic psychology: "He will never
know as much as Dewey and James forgot."

Harold Laski, in a letter of his impressions of Veblen during his first
years at the New School, has said: "I first met Professor Veblen shortly
after the opening of the New School for Social Research. He was very
shy, and, in the first weeks of our acquaintance, it was difficult to get
on intimate terms with him. But, once the initial barriers had been over-

come, he was an entrancing companion. He delivered himself, in a half-oracular, half-ironical way, of extraordinarily pungent judgments upon men and things. I remember particularly his admiration for Marx . . . his praise of F.J. Turner and Charles Beard. . . . He used to insist that we had entered upon an epoch of revolution and he doubted whether any American of his time would see again the kind of social peace characteristic of America in his youth. . . . He impressed me greatly both by his sudden flashes of insight—a streak of lightning which revealed unexpected vistas—and the amazing range both of his general knowledge and his memory for almost esoteric facts. It would have been easy to describe much of his talk as cynical; but one saw quite early that this was in fact merely a protective colouring beneath which he concealed deep emotions he did not like to bring to the surface. I was moved by his patience, his willingness to consider difficulties, his tenacity in discussion, and his anxiety, in matters he regarded as important, to discover common ground. When I first knew him, he was beginning to get the recognition he deserved; and it was profoundly moving to watch his shy delight in realising that his long struggle was at last beginning to bear fruit. . . . I do not remember discussing anything with him without receiving illumination; and his kindness to a much younger teacher remains one of the abiding memories of my years in America."

But there were many who still found themselves quickly blocked in attempting to pierce his mask. Once when asked if he really believed a certain fantastic race theory that he was seriously expounding, he replied that it was good for those who found it good. When a colleague said to him that, if Veblen was a Marxian, all the other Marxians were wrong, he retorted that every man was entitled to the credit for his own originality. There was scarcely a faculty member, however, who did not recognise that his was a great creative intelligence. Veblen never called any of his friends by their first names.

In spite of the fact that Veblen was rather a diffident person, there was something of the showman in his nature. Alvin Johnson has said that Veblen's Norwegian accent was very noticeable when some distinguished visitor was in his class whom he wished to impress. Veblen was not unwilling to attend gatherings when he was the centre of attention, but he never allowed a Mæcenas relation to develop. He refused to make any effort to attract students or to make contacts with those who were influential or wealthy, even though he must have realised that he was relatively unknown to the trustees and that in the light of his large salary and small classes they might consider him an expensive luxury. On the other hand, he could be diplomatic enough when the interests of others were concerned. When Davenport was suggested in 1920 as president of the Economic Association, he refused to be considered, because the association had never made Laughlin president. But Veblen encouraged the sponsors, and, when Davenport was actually offered the nomination, which was equivalent to election, Veblen was with him and made him accept.

The other members of the "Big Four" drew and held large audiences, mostly from Columbia University, but Veblen and Dewey were not so fortunate. Students would pack their classes on the first day, but would gradually dwindle to a handful. Veblen actively discouraged students by suggesting that they take other courses, and his monotonous voice was a further deterrent. When a class of seventy was gathered together for him in order to pay his salary, Veblen seems to have taken pains to speak in a lower voice than usual. But he was tired of teaching, and as affairs grew more complicated he felt tired and ill. Since the school gave no degrees, other universities refused to grant credit for work done there, and thus the best type of student was rare. In some respects the students were less satisfactory than undergraduates. Veblen's absence from classes increased, presumably because of ill health, but, whenever his health was examined, nothing wrong could be found.

Veblen was a different person at his summer camp on Washington Island, which was an Icelandic settlement. There he was able to indulge his interest in botany and he even did some sculpturing, in the company of a niece's husband. He planned fictitious holidays and birthdays for his guests and neighbours and arranged amusements and hunts. He could outrun any of his guests, including even the younger ones. Veblen called on his Icelandic neighbours regularly with great formality. He bought all his supplies from them and, seeing them as an instance of the common man in opposition to the vested interests, he paid higher prices than were asked. But even here Veblen's laughter and humour seemed to some of his friends to be a little forced. After the vacation, when he returned to New York, the task of teaching, small as it was, proved too much, and he resorted to the same defence mechanism that he had used after returning from Yale.

As before, however, there were some students who found him interesting and who delighted in his flashes of humour. McAlister Coleman has said that Veblen's lectures on politics in the machine age were a "witheringly ironic, sometimes consciously concealed attack upon the salients of the stuffed shirts. . . . John McConaughy [another radical] once said: 'That man can kick them without once showing his foot.'" It was with the greatest difficulty, and only now and then, that "any of us" could "catch a sly, shrewd, deflationary word or so," but "all of us agreed . . . that we would rather have one of Veblen's swift summations of a situation, muffled and inaudible as some of it might be, than a tankful of the customary academic gas."

When the New School began to function in the fall of 1919, Veblen was writing the series of articles leading to a memorandum for a soviet of technicians. He had become obsessed with the important role of the technician, and felt that the New School provided the opportunity and headquarters for the group he planned. On October 19, 1919, he wrote Guido Marx, in California: "Now, it is an intimate part of the ambitions of the New School to come into touch with the technical men who have to do with the country's industry and know something about the state of things and the needs of industry. In fact, some of us are beginning to see that 'social research' means, in good part, industrial research of a very objective and even mechanical character, if it is to mean anything substantial. At the same time the younger generation among the technicians appear to be getting uneasy on their own account, with very much the same notion, and are loosely drawing together and entering on an inquiry into the industrial conditions and speculating on a way out of the current muddle. All of which leads up to this. Can you offer a course of lectures at the New School, on any topic which this state of things may suggest to you, during the second semester of this school year? . . . These lectures at the New School are not all the reason for my breaking in on you, and as far as concerns my own interest they are not the chief reason for wishing to see you here. Several of us who take an interest in the run of affairs want the help of your judgment and information, particularly as this winter promises to bring on something of an organised inquiry and publicity bearing on the industrial situation, both from the side of the economists and from that of the engineers. In effect, there is something for you to do and New York is the likeliest place for you to do it." Later, because of "a slight indisposition of Dr. Veblen's," Ardzrooni took up the correspondence with Marx. On December 10, Marx, who was relinquishing a half-year's salary at Stanford, telegraphed that he preferred to come without compensation. On December 11, Ardzrooni wrote to Marx: "The situation is this: I have been hobnobbing with some of the members of the A.S.M.E. [American Society of Mechanical Engineers] and find that they are very much upset about the present industrial muddle throughout the country. Some of them, with the connivance of certain prominent newspapermen, had nearly perfected plans to get together and discuss matters under the guidance of H.L. Gantt. They are all convinced that there is something wrong somewhere, but they are still groping and need proper leadership. As you have probably heard, Gantt died quite recently, and, in speaking about the plans of these engineers, I told them we had in you the proper leader and, in case it was possible for you to come to New York, you would meet with them once a week, or oftener, and talk things over."

On December 18, Marx sent a description of the course as "The engineer considered in his relation to the natural resources and to the organisation and direction of the industrial enterprises which utilise them." Ardzrooni wrote Marx what he felt to be a faithful paraphrase of this statement for the purposes of the catalogue. There the course appeared under the title, "Conferences on the Social Function of the Engineer," and was described as follows: "The production and distribution of goods is now fundamentally an engineering as well as a social problem. The engineer's function is to insure the full use and unimpeded operation of the material resources and industrial equipment of the nation with a view to secure a larger volume of production and a more adequate distribution of the output. The course of lectures and conferences with technical men is intended to be a study of these questions with a view to reach some common understanding of these industrial and social conditions."

Marx says that when he reached New York "no mature members of the A.S.M.E. appeared in the picture." Howard Scott was "one of two men brought around for me to interview. I was not favourably impressed with him. I could not believe he was a trained technician, his use of technical terms being highly inaccurate and his thought processes, to my mind, lacking in logical structure and being basically unrealistic. His chief idea at that time was an industrial survey which would have required the complete staff and facilities of a census bureau. In brief, I chose to have as little to do with Scott as possible and advised Veblen and Ardzrooni to that effect. . . . Veblen never gave me to understand that he doubted my judgment of Scott." Marx arranged a dinner and conference to bring the faculty of the school in contact with leading technicians, "in line with what I thought would best fulfil Veblen's plan." Among the technicians present at the conference were Colonel Fred J. Miller, president of the A.S.M.E., Calvin Rice, secretary of the A.S.M.E., Morris L. Cooke, director of Public Works of Philadelphia, E.J. Mehren, editor of McGraw Hill publications, and the architect Frederick Ackerman. Among the faculty members who attended were Veblen, Robinson, Mitchell, Barnes, and Ardzrooni.

According to Marx there was substantial agreement as to the part the technician plays in the scheme of things and his responsibility to society to lead in the direction of order. But an editor of engineering publications summed up the majority sentiment "when he said that as an editor, 'if he pulled any harder on the tow rope, he would merely break the rope.' Remember, these were the days of Mitchell Palmer and his acute 'red scare.' Anything that touched the established 'order' of things was 'red.' "

Morris L. Cooke met Veblen a few times at an Armenian restaurant, where Veblen taught him to eat Armenian food. According to Cooke, Veblen was on one occasion somewhat amused when some communists at the table quite glibly discussed the problem of feeding New York City during the impending uprising, but he was unwilling to say anything that would dampen the enthusiasm of youth. He was quite pleased, however, according to Mitchell, when someone told him he was laying the foundation of modern socialism. Veblen became deeply interested in the work that Cooke was doing, and often discussed with him the larger function of the engineer in the organisation of society. He took a great deal of interest in the Giant Power Survey and in the fact that it was being carried out by engineers rather than by politicians. But Cooke said, as had so many others: "I must say that all my contacts with him were rather tenuous because he struck me as a man who was almost too frail for any kind of contacts. He was a bully good counsellor, but only as to theory. There was too little physique there to help on action."

It had been agreed that Marx was to be given $250 for his expenses in coming from Stanford, but because of the smallness of the group the New School lost financially on the venture, although not as much as Marx had sacrificed. He had so enjoyed his association with the faculty and his group of students, however, that he sought some way to show his appreciation. His niece was Blanca Will, the sculptress, and, when she expressed a wish to make a portrait bust of Veblen, it seemed to Marx an excellent solution for his problem. He arranged to give her the $250 he was to receive from the school, and with Ardzrooni's help he persuaded Veblen to consent to the necessary sittings. According to Miss Will, "when Veblen was asked to pose, I think he did not like the idea especially but was very kind and gentle about it, saying only something whimsical to the effect that he might as well sit there as any place since he wasn't any good for anything else anyway." The bust was first put in the lounge of the school, where the faculty frequently foregathered, but Veblen was sensitive about so constantly encountering himself, and it was removed to the library.

In the summer of 1920 Veblen made a visit to California. Through the carelessness of real-estate agents his mountain cabin had been included in a sale of surrounding property, but Camp's sister, who handled Veblen's property interests, had made an arrangement with the owner of the surrounding property whereby Veblen's title was recognised and a small rent paid. The signs, however, had not yet been rectified, and Veblen had not been told of the mistake. Veblen, Ardzrooni, Camp's sister, and three or four others drove up to the cabin in an automobile. Veblen thought the neighbouring landowner had seized his property. He took a hatchet and methodically broke the windows, going at the matter with a dull intensity that was like madness, the intensity of a physically lazy person roused into sudden activity by anger. If there were to be any disputes about the ownership, he intended to make the place thoroughly uninhabitable for all concerned. Ardzrooni, under the spur of Veblen's excitement, helped him on the job, and Camp's sister was too terrified at the sight of Veblen's anger to attempt any explanation of the situation. Most of the group were acutely embarrassed. In time they got themselves back into the car, and in a brave effort to return to normal behaviour someone asked: "And what is going to be the title of your next book, Dr. Veblen?" "*Absentee Ownership*," he answered, and said nothing more on the way home. The irony of the remark was not fully appreciated until three years later when the title of *Absentee Ownership* was actually announced. Veblen had a sign put on the property stating that it was the private property of Thorstein Veblen, and after his return to the New School he commenced writing the book.

Lubin, then at the University of Michigan, delivered a paper before the Michigan Academy of Science, in 1920, on "The Economic Costs of Retail Distribution," based on the material that Veblen had had gathered by the Food Administration. Data, largely statistical, were gathered for 1200 towns, and Veblen's earlier discussion of the untoward nature of the country town and of retail distribution is shown to have been more an understatement than an exaggeration. Waste and duplication were rampant. The data as to retail grocery prices showed that food prices were not cheaper in those towns where duplication was most extensive; "indeed, many instances may be cited where the opposite was true." In spite of the low profits and the high percentage of bankruptcy in the retail field as compared with the manufacturing field—11,923 failures in the former and 3691 in the latter in 1917, a year of unparalleled profits and prosperity—the number of retail establishments shows no decrease. "Emulation, the desire to supplant one's competitor through the lowering of prices or through better service, seems to have disappeared," and the "consumer for whose benefit the institution of competition is apparently maintained continues to pay for the maintenance of the institution with no gain to himself."

Veblen's attitude towards international politics and finance was reflected in a note by Stewart on "Financing Revolutions in Mexico," in *The Journal of Political Economy.* "When in the course of human events it becomes expedient for a people to dissolve the economic bands which have connected them with their past, a decent respect to the opinions of the investing classes requires that they should recognise all outstanding obligations. These classes, having been legally endowed with certain inalienable rights, among which are their claims to the virgin resources beneath the surface of their lands, are entitled to the protection of the law both at home and abroad. To secure these rights governments are instituted among men." As to the treatment of foreign investments, "here . . . as elsewhere in matters of finance, the final appeal is to the investment bankers. . . . The investment bankers act with the decisiveness and finality of those who control the source of supply." Thus an International Bankers Committee on Mexico has been organised, with J.P. Morgan as chairman, and when Mexico asks for funds in the great financial markets she will be politely referred to the committee. "Before passing on the application, the then existing Mexican government will be expected to validate outstanding obligations in addition to making new pledges. . . . Investors of all countries unite for the financial conquest of Mexico."

Cooke asked Veblen to write an article dealing with the general topic of labour management and production for the September 1920 issue of the *Annals* of the American Academy of Political and Social Science, of which Cooke, Samuel Gompers, and Colonel Miller were the editors. Veblen passed the assignment on to Ardzrooni, whose article was called "The Philosophy of the Restriction of Output."

Veblen wrote on much the same topic in *The Political Science Quarterly,* in the guise of a review of John Maynard Keynes's *The Economic Consequences of the Peace*. Veblen wrote his review a year after the book appeared, but said that did not make any substantial difference. This piece has much in common with the earlier essays dealing with the received economists. Keynes's attitudes, declared Veblen, is that of the dominant common sense, of "men accustomed to take political documents at their face value." The treaty is not a conclusive settlement, as Keynes imagines, but a point of departure for further negotiations, for further warlike enterprise. The bargaining out of which the treaty resulted was conducted with the characteristic "vulpine secrecy" of the elder statesmen. Keynes's discussion of the treaty is a commentary on its language rather than on the consequences which were designed to follow from it or the uses to which it is lending itself. The treaty and the league have not brought world peace, but have only provided a screen for the elder statesmen's never-ceasing policies of imperial aggrandisement and chicane. The most binding provision of the treaty and the league is the unrecorded one, by which the governments of the great powers are bound together for the suppression of Soviet Russia. Except for this, the elder statesmen are still engrossed with mutual jealousies and cross-purposes.

Keynes's criticisms of President Wilson are unwarranted. Absentee ownership is menaced by Bolshevism, but the elder statesmen are by native temperament and by the duties of their office committed to this paramount institution and abiding purpose of the political traffic of the imperialistic nations, including America. When President Wilson drew up the fourteen points, based on the humane spirit of Mid-Victorian liberalism, without realisation that the Mid-Victorian liberalism had grown into the Democracy of Property Rights, of commercialised imperialism, the Bolshevist demonstration had not yet become a menace. But when the question resolved itself into a choice between the humane principles of Mid-Victorian liberalism and absentee ownership, it was inevitable that absentee ownership came first, and that the fourteen points were scrapped. The guardians of the democracy of investors, of commercial imperialism, are driven to root out Bolshevism at any cost, regardless of international law or the law of human rights.

This need to safeguard the democracy of absentee owners is seen in the "notable leniency, amounting to something like collusive remissness," in the question of the German indemnity. The stipulations have proved to be merely provisional and tentative, something in the nature of diplomatic bluff, to gain time, divert attention, and keep the claimants in a reasonably patient frame of mind, "during the period of rehabilitation" needed to re-establish the reactionary German regime "as a bulwark against Bolshevism." The indemnity stipulations have already been substantially modified, and "there is no present reason to believe that any of them will be lived up to in any integral fashion." They are apparently in the nature of a base of negotiations and are due to come up for indefinite further adjustment as expediency may dictate. The expediencies are determined by the necessity of defeating Bolshevism in Russia and elsewhere, and by the necessity of the "continued secure tenure of absentee ownership in Germany." Germany must not be so effectively crippled as to leave the "imperial establishment materially weakened in its campaign against Bolshevism abroad or radicalism at home." The indemnity must not exceed what can be thrown on the underlying propertyless working population, "who are to be kept in hand," that is, it must not be so large as effectively to endanger "the free income of the propertied and privileged classes, who alone can be depended on to safeguard the democratic interests of absentee ownership." Therefore the provisions of the treaty avoid any confiscation of property. An adequate indemnity could be collected, however, without materially deranging the country's industry and without hardship to the underlying population, if the German war debt, imperial, state, and municipal, were entirely repudiated and if the freed resources were diverted to the benefit of those who suffered from German aggression; in other words, if absentee ownership were disregarded by "a comprehensive confiscation of German wealth, so far as that wealth is covered by securities and is therefore held by absentee owners," the parties guilty of the war.

But the statesmen of the victorious powers, in order to safeguard the prevailing democracy of investors, have taken sides with the war-guilty absentee owners, against the underlying population. The indemnification of war victims has been enforced with a particular bias in favour of the German imperial *status quo ante*. The provisions touching disarmament and the discontinuance of warlike industries and organisation "have been administered in a well-conceived spirit of *opéra bouffe*."

In November 1920 a new edition of *The Vested Interests and the State of the Industrial Arts* was issued, with the title changed to *The Vested Interests and the Common Man*. The change is indicative of the vital meaning that Veblen attached to "the state of the industrial arts."

Veblen and Ardzrooni were giving a course at the New School on "The Productive Use of Resources," and Captain Otto Beyer was continuing Marx's work. According to Beyer his purpose was to enlarge upon some of Veblen's contributions concerning the relation of the engineers to modern economic society. Howard Scott, Stuart Chase, and others participated, and listened also to Veblen. About the same time Scott and his friends set afoot an organisation called the Technical Alliance. Scott proposed that the organisation of technicians should perform "the function of a mutual service between technical members, and the function of a training service for those organisations which wish to subscribe to it," and that its programme "must not be one of sympathy towards any ideal." Friends disagreed. One wrote to Scott that the Technical Alliance must have a specific point of view, saying it was his opinion "that through a release of the technical resources of the country, living in it would become more worth while for everybody, that the businessman cannot on account of the business system release these technical resources, that the labour movement may release them, provided the technicians and the labour movement can be brought into some working alliance. . . . You can organise paid technicians or a staff 'to give progressive bodies the plans and data of the present mechanism of industry' but you can't . . . organise a group of volunteer technicians to assist this staff unless they understand what it is all about." If the technician does not have such an ideal, or point of view, "he is going to ask 'what do I get out of it?'" The idea of mutual service would not interest any technician "unless it implied some sort of an employment service which would assist him in getting a more remunerative job."

The printed prospectus of the Technical Alliance omitted the question of the ideal, and presented what was in effect a garbled account of Veblen's memorandum for a soviet of technicians. An elaborate organisation, to engage in applied engineering and pure research, was set forth, and, significantly, the concept of technician was interpreted with the comprehensive meaning given it by Veblen. Scott set himself down as chief engineer. The temporary organising committee listed in the prospectus was composed of two physicians, Allen Carpenter and John C. Vaughan; two architects, Frederick L. Ackerman and Robert H. Kohn; three electrical engineers, Bassett Jones, L.K. Comstock, and the great Steinmetz; a housing expert, Charles H. Whitaker; a statistician, Leland Olds; an accountant, Stuart Chase; a forester, Benton Mackaye; a physicist, Richard C. Tolman; a chemist, Carl C. Alsberg; and two "educators," Alice Barrows and Veblen. Ardzrooni, in the copy of the prospectus which he sent to Marx, wrote under the list of names: "I have learned that most of the men whose names . . . appear here were never consulted nor informed of any meeting, e.g., Veblen. Veblen gave them a calling down for using his name without asking him about it." But Veblen was apparently deeply interested, although he felt that the established engineers did not appreciate the situation, and he was somewhat incensed at their attitude of letting nature take its course and expecting things to work out their way in the long run. Ardzrooni seems to have been rather active in the work of the Technical Alliance, although he felt that Scott was too vague. The Alliance did some service for Jett Lauck, and for the I.W.W. it did some work on a lumber investigation, and it made reports on coal, milk distribution, and luxuries.

In February 1921, Veblen's *Engineers and the Price System* was issued. *The Dial* commented that "certain phrases, like 'the underlying population' and 'Vested Interests,' occur too often and too complacently even for the purposes of irony. One feels that the thinker has been swallowed by the propagandist." A woman who had known Veblen when he was writing *The Theory of the Leisure Class* said that *The Engineers and the Price System* had none of the sting of the earlier book. "It is mellow and balanced. . . . Dr. Veblen in his later years seems to have been a very different man from the drolly gay and cynical man I knew." The radicals also were not impressed. Max Eastman said in *The Liberator* that "Veblen could not point out the weak spots in the [social and economic structure] with a more dry and masterly accuracy, if he were consulting engineer to His Satanic Majesty who contrived it." But "Veblen's 'Soviet of Technicians' may be set down as a soviet of abstractions— interesting as an intellectual experience, but irrelevant to the problem of defining and organising a dynamic force sufficient to alter the essential course of history."

In May *The Freeman,* which was published by Huebsch and supported by a single-taxer, although it was directed towards views far more
radical than the single tax, published Veblen's article "Between Bolshevism and War." The principle of action of Bolshevism is the disallowance of absentee ownership, and such a disallowance amounts to a
revolt against the constituted authorities by the underlying population.
This revolutionary movement may signify a peaceable substitution of
the new order for the old, or a resort to violence. Bolshevism, in point
of method, or ways and means, is committed to the soviet—a form of
government of, by, and for the underlying population—and thus it implies the elimination of the prevailing parliamentary form, in which the
government is of the underlying population, by and for the substantial
citizens, or absentee owners. The soviet is closely analogous to the town
meeting, as known in New England history.

"The certified socialists are among the staunchest enemies of Bolshevism." They support a belief in the eventual obsolescence of all ownership "by force of a natural law which governs the sequence of human
affairs." They "had hoped to preserve the established political organisation intact, and eventually take it over for their own use." But "socialism
is a dead horse," and socialists are realising that Bolshevism is rendering
the orthodox preconception obsolete.

Under the prevailing law and order, absentee ownership comes first,
and other interests are tolerated only so long as they are subservient to
the main interest. As soon as the underlying population appreciates its
de facto disinheritance, the drift of sentiment to the Red Flag will be
appreciable. The practicable corrective is warlike preparation and warlike
enterprise, which induce patriotic animosity and servility in the underlying population. In the material respect warlike expenditure is a net
loss, but ninety percent of federal expenditures is for this purpose. The
factor that still stands in the way "of a free-swung Bolshevist temper
and a consequent bull-headed Bolshevist adventure in these civilised nations is the belated conservatism of the passing generation," which is in
effect a spiritual holdover out of an obsolete past, in which "absentee
ownership had not yet taken over the nation's industrial system." The
experience of the recent past plainly shows that the established businesslike system of ownership and control cannot provide a decent livelihood
for the country's population; it is patently unfit to take care of the country's industry and the material fortune of the underlying population.
For the last two and one-half years the captains of industry and statesmen have laboured to turn the unexampled industrial resources of the
country to some account under the rule of absentee ownership and business as usual, but the result of their concerted effort is an "uneasy state

of industrial 'twilight sleep,' hedged about with nightmares of famine, pestilence, and Red riots"; and under the continued management of absentee ownership and business enterprise, this "incredibly shameful" state of affairs has been growing worse.

But in spite of its plight the world had failed to achieve the prophecy which Veblen made in *The Theory of Business Enterprise*. A depression had arrived and his radical colleagues were convinced that a revolution was about to occur, but the depression began to clear and there was no panic and no revolution. Veblen seems to have taken the red hysteria almost as seriously as had the authorities; he said, in fact, that the politicians had led him astray. He told Babette Deutsch that he did not expect a revolution to occur in his lifetime, but he was embittered none the less. Former students of orthodox convictions, such as H. Parker Willis, who had been secretary of the Federal Reserve Board, felt that Veblen had completely changed, that he did not care for his old intellectual associates, and that the personal contacts between them and Veblen were not as close as before.

But the Technical Alliance had a brief existence. Financial support was lacking; some of the clients complained that services arranged for had not been performed; and there were complaints that the chief engineer was too arbitrary. On March 25, 1921, an executive committee, which included Ardzrooni, Scott, Ackerman, Comstock, Bassett Jones, Sullivan W. Jones, and Whitaker, was set up, to have full powers and reorganise the Alliance. On May 16 the members of the committee, with the exception of Scott, reported that they had requested Scott, then in possession of the books and property of the Alliance, to "turn over all cash to the Committee's Treasurer; make an inventory of all property and report it to the committee; turn over all books and accounts to an auditing committee composed of Messrs. Ardzrooni and Whitaker. Mr. Scott himself present at the meeting agreed to do these things at once. The undersigned have since learned that he declines to comply with the request and, lacking power in the matter, and without inclination to proceed further, the undersigned consider themselves as discharged."

The New School underwent a radical change in 1922. Of the "Big Four" Beard, Mitchell, and Robinson resigned. Financial support practically disappeared, and in order to maintain itself the school broadened its activities. Veblen's position was a precarious one, but he had nowhere to go. Attempts to find him a post in the city universities proved unsuccessful. Davenport tried again to bring him into Cornell but, aside from other difficulties, Veblen could not stand the Ithaca climate. At one time there was a possibility of his joining the faculty of a leading Scandinavian university, but every time terms were agreed upon, the changes in exchange rates required new terms, and in the end the plan fell through. Veblen attempted to persuade Alvin Johnson, the new director of the school, to raise $40,000 to help develop his ideas on the role of the engineer, but not even a small fraction of that sum could be raised, since those who had money either did not know of Veblen or did not care for his ideas, and those who were interested in him were generally without means. Veblen felt deserted. He was still interested in his old report to the government on "Farm Labour and the Country Towns," and felt that the government should have originally published the report, and particularly its elaborate statistical data. He seems to have had an expectation that it might still do so.

Early in 1922 Wallace W. Atwood, president of Clark University and Mrs. Veblen's brother-in-law, was thinking of adding Veblen to the faculty of Clark, according to Harry Elmer Barnes, who was then teaching there. In March the Liberal Club of the college brought the socialist Scott Nearing to address them on "The Control of Public Opinion in the United States." The president's consent was obtained, but the meeting hall had to be changed because President Atwood, whose specialty was geography, had arranged to have a noted geographer from Washington speak in the originally assigned hall. Only a handful attended the geographer's lecture, but the Nearing meeting was packed and a good number of the faculty were in attendance. President Atwood, after the end of the geographer's lecture, happened to pass the Nearing meeting place, where the lights were still on, for Nearing had not yet finished. President Atwood came in, dissolved the meeting, and instructed the janitor to put out the lights. This action excited the entire student body, and a protest was signed by the head of every undergraduate student organisation of Clark University. The local press took the president's side, garbled the Nearing address, and referred to the student body as "children who should be spanked" or "sincere young people of an impressionable age." The dispute developed into a question of academic freedom, and the president maintained the traditional common-sense position. At a student assembly, where President Atwood attempted to clarify his position, he declared that, in carrying out his responsibility of deciding what speakers the students might have, "I shall be guided by the very best motives for your good and the desire that the university may retain the respect and confidence of the American people." When "all professional experts in the social sciences recognise their responsibility to the community, and give adequate assurance that scientific methods are followed in their practice of their profession, the problem of academic freedom in these fields will disappear." According to the students' account, "about fifty percent of the students felt like rising at that point to inform the President concerning the high standing of this institution in the very fields he had been mentioning, but they controlled themselves."

The significant feature of the matter is that Nearing used Veblen's works as authorities throughout his address. Thus he is reported as saying: "In our own society, as Professor Veblen has indicated in his *Theory of the Leisure Class*, the governing group is that which possesses the majority of the property of the country, and it attempts to create a public opinion justifying this possession, and its uses and advantages." Or again: "The higher education, as Professor Veblen has shown in his *Higher Learning in America*, has also come to reflect the philosophy of the present-day businessmen." The president of the Liberal Club, whose "testimony . . . is supported by that of other witnesses," told the investigating committee of the American Association of University Professors that, when President Atwood appeared at the meeting, "Nearing . . . was speaking on the control of education by the 'vested interests' and their ability to control the development of thought, quoting freely from works by Thorstein Veblen, a relative of the president." [1] According to one story it was while Nearing was quoting from Veblen that the lights were ordered out. While the episode was still in the public eye, President Atwood asked Veblen to give a series of lectures, but Veblen declined on his customary ground of ill health.

In *The Freeman* for June 1922 appeared what was perhaps Veblen's most scathing article on the established order, entitled "Dementia Præcox." Here he returned to the argument of his last editorial in *The Dial*, and expressed his opinion of the effect to be expected from the loss of the great steel strike, of the Bolshevik scare, and of the policy of the Federal Reserve system in attempting to prevent a complete liquidation in the depression of 1920–1921. The article is prophetic of the great inflation and resulting depression of 1929. America's entrance in the World War, he declared, resulted in Europe "balancing along the margin of bankruptcy, famine, and pestilence, while America has gone into moral and industrial eclipse." In the absence of American intervention the old order of kept classes in Germany, resting on privilege and property, would have been effectively liquidated, and an industrial democracy might have arisen instead of "the camouflage of a *pro forma* liquidation in 1918–1919 and the resulting pseudo-republic of the Ebert Government. Noske could not have functioned and the Junkers would not have been war-heroes." If Imperial Germany and Imperial Russia had dropped out as effective war powers, the French government, which is typical of the continental countries, "would have had no practicable war-scare at hand with which to frighten the French people into a policy of increased armament," and France would have returned to a peace footing. "Coercion and submission would have ceased to characterise its internal affairs, the existing Government of French profiteers would have lost control; and expenditures would have been covered in part by taxes on income and capital, instead of the present deficit-financiering and constantly increasing debt." The continuing of hostilities during the winter of 1918–1919 would have resulted in exhausting resources and inflating indebtedness to such a point as to ensure a drastic and speedy liquidation of commercial and fiscal affairs, "with a recapitalisation of assets at a reasonable figure," which would have permitted "trade and industry to make a new start within a reasonable time." American interference ended the war before the exhaustion of resources and liabilities in Europe had reached the breaking point, and thereby it allowed the vested interests to keep their footing on a nominal capitalisation in excess of the earning capacity of their assets, in order to maintain prices and restrict output. The result has been unemployment, privation, disorder, and an inconclusive peace looking towards future hostilities.

Of course it is possible that such a conclusion would have followed if America had not intervened, but the American people would have escaped much of "the increased armament, a good share of the profiteering incident to the war and the peace, and all the income tax would have been avoided." American statesmen might have continued to be the bankers' henchmen in Nicaragua, manhandle the Haitians, put the white man's burden on the blacks of Liberia, and back Polish interests and the Siberian adventure against the horrid Bolsheviks, all for the vested interests, but there might not have been such activity as that of the Lusk Commission, the American Legion of veterans organised for a draft on public funds, the enforcement of law and order on the unfortunate, the prosecution of pacifists and conscientious objectors for "excessive sanity." The Americans might have come through "in a reasonable state of buncombe and intolerance without breaking down into the systematised illusions of dementia præcox."

The past three or four years of dissension, disorder, privation, debauch, and disease have cost in wasted time, substance, and lives twice as much as the cost of continuing hostilities five months more for a definite conclusion. The logical faculty, the advance of matter-of-fact and material science, have been prostrated and have given way to the barbarian beliefs in magical efficacy, superstition, and devout observances for the sake of inordinate gain. "The profiteers do business as usual and the federal authorities are busied with a schedule of increased protective duties designed to enhance the profits of their business." Pacifists, I.W.W.'s, communists, are statutory criminals who continue to be subject to cruel and unusual punishments unparalleled in American history.

The course of events has shown that they were contending for the wiser course, but although they are *de facto* in the right they are *de jure* in the wrong. The prevailing distemper, enforced by the heightened businesslike ideals, is characteristic of the adolescent, the devout, and boyishminded. It is evidence of puerile mentality, of arrested mental and spiritual development, and the persons so affected might be called "morons." In practical effect it is these characteristics that form the basis of selection for governing offices. "A degree of puerile exuberance coupled with a certain truculent temper and boyish cunning is likely to command something of popular admiration and affection, which is likely to have a certain selective effect in the democratic choice of officials. . . . A run of persecutory credulity of the nature of dementia præcox should logically run swiftly and with a wide sweep in the case of such a community endowed with such an official machinery, and its effects should be profound and lasting."

Veblen's last book, *Absentee Ownership and Business Enterprise in Recent Times; the Case of America,* was nearing completion.

CHAPTER XXIII

VEBLEN was very tired. Everything seemed to have gone wrong. The writing of *Absentee Ownership* was difficult for him, and he resorted more often than before to Roget's *Thesaurus*. He showed the manuscript to a friend as he wrote, and asked that repetitions be pointed out, but most of Veblen's friends felt that he could never be repetitious. In some ways the book is inferior to his other works, particularly *The Theory of the Leisure Class* and *Imperial Germany*. It has neither the subtlety of the former nor the magnificent sweep of the latter. On the other hand it is not as vitriolic as *The Higher Learning*, nor does it lend itself to the accusation of being propaganda, as does *The Engineers and the Price System*. It has much of the blandness of *The Instinct of Workmanship*, but the starkly terrible character of the underlying argument is more obvious than in *The Theory of Business Enterprise*. In this sense it is the most mature of his work.

All of his other works suggest the imbecility of modern business enterprise and an expectation that the underlying population will take matters in hand, but the tone of *Absentee Ownership* suggests more the imbecility of the underlying population for continuing to put up with the current state of affairs, and an expectation that business enterprise will tend to become more feudalistic in character until modern civilisation collapses. This attitude of despair was perhaps a factor in Veblen's bringing into fuller expression in this book the substantial objective of all his analysis: the nature and control of the "money power" of investment banking and corporate capital and modern credit, as against the efficient working and survival of the community. The contrast here is between capitalised overhead charges and the underlying population.

The controlling institution of absentee ownership has much in common with the institution of the leisure class. In fact, *Absentee Ownership* gives a more profound meaning to *The Theory of the Leisure Class*, and the latter, on the other hand, reveals more fully the implications of *Absentee Ownership*. For example, Veblen's declaration in *Absentee Ownership* that the executive power and judicial control over the material life of the community are held by "the high magistrates of solvency"—the "One Big Union of Financial Interests"—by virtue of their sovereign power of large credit, is to be fully understood only in the light of his discussion of the institution of the leisure class. But in the later book it is seen more clearly that Veblen is concerned not with personalities but with working arrangements, with institutions, and that, when he phrases his argument in terms of personalities and conscious motives, it is only to bring out the consequences involved in this arrangement. Thus in speaking of monopoly and monopolistic action, he refers rather to the effect of the dominant institution of capital than to conscious design of the great captain. He makes more frequent use than before of such phrases as "in effect" or "practical consequences."

In this book Veblen brings into play every type of analysis that he had used before, from that of the country town to that of dynastic politics, from metaphysical principles to theological canons, but whatever device he uses, its function is to throw light on the nature of large-scale credit. In *Imperial Germany* Veblen had made use of a series of supplementary notes to present his discussion of capital in a more pointed manner than in the main inquiry. Also in *Absentee Ownership,* under the general heading of "The Case of America," he presents in the middle of the book five essays to illustrate more concisely the nature of modern credit. Thus the essay on "The Self-Made Man" seems to have reference to the captain of finance; the one on "The Country Town" to the industrial corporation; "The Independent Farmer" to the working community and general owners; "The New Gold" to credit; and the last, "The Timber Lands and the Oil Fields" to the outcome of modern credit.

The aim of the book, declared Veblen, "is an objective, theoretical analysis and formulation of the main drift, as determined by the material circumstances of the case, including the industrial arts, and by the dominant institution of absentee ownership, including the use of credit." Absentee ownership rests upon modern credit. The first part of the book is occupied with a series of essays ostensibly presenting the economic circumstances that have led up to the present impasse, but it tells much the same story as the second part, which is a more direct discussion of modern credit as the basis of absentee ownership.

"In a long run, of course," said Veblen, "the pressure of changing material circumstances will have to shape the lines of human conduct, on pain of extinction. . . . But it does not follow that the pressure of material necessity, visibly enforced by the death penalty, will ensure such a change in the legal and moral punctilios as will save the nation from the death penalty." Of this the present condition of civilised nations is evidence. Whether the people come through this period of "enforced change alive and fit to live, appears to be a matter of chance in which human insight plays a minor part and human foresight no part at all."

The customary adjustments which are made in order to meet the situation, such as the expansion of credit, the use of the injunction on industry and labour, are in the nature of forced movements, animal conduct, tropisms, rather than national reasoned adjustments to the material welfare of mankind. The outcome is the sovereignty of great financial interests.

Thus Veblen comes once more to a discussion of dynastic states, "dynastic corporations." "To the end that these adventures in damage, debauch, and discomfort might be carried to a fitting conclusion, as they commonly have been, the several dynastic corporations claimed, and enforced, an undivided usufruct of their underlying populations and all their ways and works." This natural right "became a perpetual and inalienable asset" of the princely corporation and by force of severe habituation the underlying population came to believe that what was good for their predatory masters was good for the community. In the nature of things these competitive princely corporations were always working at cross-purposes, and in this game of competitive force and fraud for differential gains, there was no place for scruples of any kind.

The democratic commonwealth of absentee ownership has taken over the theologic-metaphysical exaction of the unquestioned subservience of the underlying population to and for the warlike ends of the absentee owners, that is, the divine right of obstruction or chicane, just "as a modern oil corporation will take over all the powers and liabilities of any individual promoters whom it has bought out." But the national welfare, by force of the "hip-shotten logic" exemplified by the protective tariff and embodied in the modern right of ownership, is conceived to be dependent on an increase in pecuniary magnitudes. The more mature, vicious developments of the policy of commercial sabotage are indicative of the dominance of absentee ownership; that is, "any gains to be derived from such restraint of trade always accrue to one and another of the vested interests of the absentee owners, at the cost of the underlying population." The right of absentee ownership in the democratic commonwealth becomes, in essence, the policy of speaking softly and carrying a big stick.

With the elimination of this footless nonsense of absentee ownership, and thus of "patriotic inflation" or increasing capitalisation, the commonwealth would become "an unsanctified workday arrangement for the common use of industrial ways and means." The democratic commonwealth would become what they profess to be—"neighbourly fellowships of ungraded, masterless men, given over to 'life, liberty, and the pursuit of happiness.' " Under the paramount consideration of large capitalisation and a substantial rate of earnings, the prevailing administration is in effect a "Soviet of Business Men's Delegates," a "Big-Business Administration," at the cost of the underlying population. "Born in iniquity and conceived in sin," the spirit of nationalism which animates modern business has bent human institutions designed to serve the common good to the "security and free income of the absentee owner." Such has been the unguarded drift of habituation to the institution of ownership, under modern circumstances.

Veblen's description of the feudalistic regime is phrased in terms of the pecuniary regime of the investment banker. As the feudalistic regime matured, became more efficient, and settled down to its work, it grew progressively more irksome to the underlying population, "as would naturally happen in the case of any system of absentee rights and powers, and as has happened more than once since," for such a balanced scheme of submission and personal control is based on organised and standardised hardship. The feudalistic regime, like its modern counterpart, offered no net material advantage to the common man, but only "material hardship overlaid with spiritual pomp and circumstance." It had no place for the masterless man. He was an institutional misfit, a social, industrial, civil, and political encumbrance. His situation was very much the same as the present situation of an I.W.W., "who is endowed with no absentee ownership and who disclaims that standardised allegiance to the national establishment" of pecuniary reality. "And, then, as now, the whole duty of loyal citizens in dealing with these homebred aliens," who threaten the scheme of absentee ownership, "was that which is embodied in the watchword of the Legion—'Treat 'em rough!'"

The effective owners of the controlling natural resources—land, forests, water power, mineral deposits, franchises, etc.—do not own them by virtue of having produced or earned them. Their ownership is based not on the workmanlike ground that they are making use of useful things in productive work, but on the feudalistic principle of seizure by force and collusion. Under the circumstances of modern technology the principles of natural laws and rights, which may have worked well in Adam Smith's day, play now the role of a "dead hand," the role of obstruction and devastation. The great creative factor in industry is the state of the industrial arts, "which is a joint stock of technological knowledge and practice worked out, accumulated, and carried forward by the industrial population which lives and moves within the sweep of this industrial system." But the ownership of the essentially ephemeral material assets created by the living structure of technology confers a legal right of sabotage, a right to enforce unemployment and, to that extent, render useless the technological knowledge. This is the natural right of investment, and is accomplished by the modern use of credit. "Ab-

sentee ownership vests the owner with the power of sabotage at a distance, by help of the constituted authorities whose duty it is to enforce
the legal right of citizens." It is this right of sabotage that makes ownership worth while, that gives pecuniary gain to the effective owners, and
the necessity of sabotage is enforced by the canon of investment for a
profit, the canon of maintaining and increasing capitalisation.

The "Era of Free Competition" was the era of personal business enterprise, carried on under the immunities of impersonal investment, and
it results in the modern captain of industry. The chief virtue of the
pursuit of enhanced income from investments was the steadfast cupidity
displayed, the steadfast spirit of the business enterprise of getting a safe
margin of something for nothing. By settled right the absentee owners
obtained the new wealth created by the advancing state of the industrial
arts. "The kept classes made a notable growth in numbers and in the
conspicuous consumption of superfluities, while the underlying population steadily fell into arrears, underfed and underbred in an ever more
pronounced fashion as this era of free competition ran its course and
brought the community nearer to Senior's 'Natural State of Man' "—
that "state of commercial felicity for which by a happy destiny mankind
have been brought out upon the surface of this planet and placed under
the governance of certain natural laws" of capital leading to this eventual
consummation in absentee ownership. The old-fashioned free competition in price between producers has given way, by virtue of the control
exercised by modern credit in the key industries, to the characteristic
devices of salesmanlike prevarication, thát is, businesslike curtailment,
and to competition in publicity in the manipulation of securities, resulting in a scarcity of livelihood for the community. Such devices of sabotage
were resorted to because of the greater expedition and larger pecuniary
gains percent on the investment to be had from a more exhaustive use
of credit. The principle of the characteristically modern corporation—
the holding company—is what the traffic will bear, which means a proper
balance of unemployment, but faith in the creative efficiency of capital
funds and capitalised savings is one of the axioms of the business community.

Capitalisation is a transaction in funds, credit, not in the production of
physical goods, and in effect it gives the corporation financier an increase
of funds for the purpose of increasing capitalisation and the purchasing
power of the concerns for which he acts. For the community it amounts
to an inflation of prices, an increased valuation of material assets to the
extent of the capitalisation. This increased capitalisation has a cumulative character, so that "the endless use of credit has enabled the wealth
in hand to multiply far and away out of proportion to the increased pro-

duction of goods due to the advance of the industrial arts." At times, of course, the inflation of credit has broken down, but the more unified control of the credit resources by "collusion of the greater credit institutions, has virtually done away with these unadvised fluctuations of prosperity and depression; although even yet a general liquidation may be, and a general depression already has been brought on by a credit-inflation of such unexampled sweep as to exceed the capacity of that apparatus of control that has been made and provided for the stabilisation of this business." Under the control of the captain of finance, and under the continued increase of capitalisation with the necessity of meeting fixed charges on the "funded make-believe," the need for more capital in business is insatiable or indefinitely extensible. In effect, the less goods are produced, the more capital is needed. This is the practice of trading on the equity of material goods, and the equity continually grows thinner. The result is a curtailment of production, or an avoidance of the material gain to be achieved by a more efficient use of the industrial arts. In the absence of capitalistic sabotage this greatly inflated credit situation would collapse, involving a cancellation of at least half the money values carried on the books of the business community.

But the community still holds the superstition that the modern captain of industry is primarily a master technician. This belief is evidence that the community still has an instinct of workmanship, despite the fact that business principles have put it in abeyance as far as regards any practical effect. The mature captain of industry is in the position of a toad "who has found his appointed place along some frequented run where many flies and spiders pass and repass on their way to complete that destiny to which it has pleased an all-seeing and merciful Providence to call them." He is not the creative driver of industry, but the prehensile businessman, the captain of solvency occupied with the make-believe of money values. The captain of solvency is the type for the kept classes, the keeper and dispenser of their keep, just as was the war lord of the barbarian raids. These spokesmen of the kept classes are for the community merely a bill of expense, but by virtue of the perversion of the instinct of workmanship by business principles, the large absentee owners are held in esteem and respect. Their work differs only insubstantially from the early Portuguese and Spanish enterprise in pillage and devastation. Modern finance has proved to be a game of luck and skill, with the lack of scruples characteristic of such games which prescribe a formally even chance for all players. Under the canons of business and the developing technology, the self-made captain of solvency has made himself by seizing the gains which were created by the community's joint product and to which, by his own activity, he has contributed only a negative value. This stage of business maturity, which might be called the stage of vested interests, has been progressively reached in the controlling key industries.

Again Veblen discusses the farmer, with his illusion of independent status, as a typical example of the middle-class and working population. The farmers' community spirit in material concerns "has been notably scant and precarious, in spite of the fact that they have long been exposed to material circumstances of a wide-sweeping uniformity, such as should have engendered a spirit of community interest and made for collective enterprise, and such as could have made any effectual collective enterprise greatly remunerative to all concerned." But the farmer has cherished the illusion of obtaining something for nothing in the face of the great massive, impersonal interests which, under the prevailing law and order, are united in an unbreakable frame. In his principles of self-help the farmer is similar to the modern captain of finance. Subtraction through salesmanship is the aim of pioneer cupidity. Since this aim is not related to workmanlike, tangible performance, and since it is no longer concerned with specie, but with some form of credit instrument which conveys title to a run of free income, it can have no "saturation" point, "even in fancy, inasmuch as credit is also indefinitely extensible and stands in no quantitative relation to tangible fact." The driving force is not "an imperative bent of workmanship and human service," but an "indefinitely extensible cupidity."

Veblen uses the country town as another indication of the operation of modern capital. Its name may be Spoon River or Gopher Prairie, Emporia, Centralia, or Columbia. Its retail trade is a characteristic development of business as usual, and its occupation with speculative real estate and with living off the farmer is of the same nature as the activity of captains of finance in security deals which are useless to the general material welfare. "Real estate is an enterprise in 'futures,' designed to get something for nothing from the unwary." Even the location of the country town is determined "by collusion between 'interested parties' with a view to speculation in real estate," and it continues throughout its life history "to be managed as a real-estate 'proposition.' Its municipal affairs, its civic pride, its community interest, converge upon its real-estate values, which are invariably of a speculative character, and which all its loyal citizens are intent on 'booming' and 'boosting'—that is to say, lifting still farther off the level of actual ground-values as measured by the uses to which the ground is turned." The banker is the characteristic type, and he is "under the necessity—'inner necessity,' as the Hegelians would say—of getting all he can and securing himself against all risk, at the cost of any whom it may concern, by such charges and stipulations as will insure his net gain in any event."

The inhabitants of the country town constitute a monopoly against the specific farming region subject to the town, and are at the same time involved in cross-purposes among themselves, just as the investment syndicates constitute a monopoly over certain corporations, while at the same time the members of the syndicate engage in strategic manœuvres among themselves. But the country town has also a relation to big business which is comparable to that of the industrial corporations to their effective rulers, the investment bankers. "In a way the country towns have in an appreciable degree fallen into the position of toll-gate keepers for the distribution of goods and collection of customs for the large absentee owners of the business."

The inhabitants of the country town are under the necessity of contributing plentifully to church funds and similar collections, because of the incentives of fear and shame and prestige. To the believers in country-town virtues it is self-evident that a derangement of "the bizarre web of their incredible conceits" and grotesque religious verities and animistic beliefs, "none of which will bear the light of alien scrutiny . . . would bring the affairs of the human race to a disastrous collapse." In the South the peculiar institution of slavery has had much the same effect as the country town has had in the North.

Veblen's discussion of "The New Gold" begins with an account of the debauchery and manslaughter of the Indian population and the destruction of the fur-bearing animals through the application of business principles. The "New Gold" of the West is like the production of gold by capitalisation. The entire traffic is pure waste. Ninety percent of those who come out alive have nothing to show for their dissipation of time and goods. The game of dealing with speculative mining shares is, like other games of chance and skill, a closed circuit of profit and loss, in which the buyer of the securities gets nothing, for a price, and thus the traffic is characterised by a detachment from material fact. By what amounts to a tropismatic reaction the inflation of prices, or the inflated values of assets, in other words, the increase of capital, caused by the new gold is uncritically held to be good for the community. Money values are the underlying business realities, and in order to maintain and increase them sabotage is resorted to. When the case becomes desperate, however, and the unreality of the make-believe of money values cannot be overlooked, there comes a breakdown, a slaughter of the innocents called liquidation. The present international complication of insolvent credits provides the material for such an episode.

It is well known "that the scale of prices went out of touch with the material realities of production and consumption some years ago and has so continued since then; that the present scale of money-values in tangible property and in securities is quite unsound; that the outstanding volume of credit obligations has turned into a fantastic tissue of footless make-believe; and that the only way out of a desperate situation is to go to work." The country needs goods, and the resources are available, but the premise of unshrinkable money values binds the hands of the people who alone have power to act, and the result is ever-increasing hardship and indebtedness. Vested interests, corporation finance, do not admit deflation of assets in the ordinary course of business. European corporations have written off such valueless assets, but America is the land of unshrinkable absentee ownership, and the effect of guaranteed earnings, as in the railroads, for example, will doubtless be the charging of more than the traffic can bear. So great is the magic of the price system and the frame of mind which creates enlarged opportunities for corporation finance.

The American plan of corporation finance, characterised by seizure and conversion, devastation and monopoly, is shown clearly in what has befallen "The Timber Lands and the Oil Fields." Manpower is also discussed as a natural resource, subject to the same business principles that have guided activities in the oil industry, where the enterprising "knights of trover and conversion . . . go about their business in all haste and without afterthought." Under the prevailing conditions of law and custom the competition which results in waste and exhaustion of resources is sound business enterprise, "just as the Big Business and monopoly control" of large absentee owners "in which it invariably heads up is also sound business."

Once again Veblen devotes the second part of his book to a less obscure presentation of the material of the first part. "The federal constitution was framed by the elder statesmen of the eighteenth century; whereas the new industrial order of things is created by the technicians of the twentieth century." The spirit of the horse-trading farmer and the collusive retailers of the country towns is that of big business. The organisation of new ways and means in industrial processes and manpower is "subject to irresponsible control at the hands of a superannuated general staff of businessmen"—superannuated "in point of aims and methods, bias and preconceptions," not in physical senility. Their responsibility does not run in terms that fit the latterday technology. "Neither the tenuous things of the human spirit nor the gross material needs of human life can come in contact" with the impersonal routine of big business and the investment bankers in such a way as "to deflect its course from the line of least resistance, which is the line of greatest present gain within the law." This routine results in a vigilant sabotage of production, whether seen in its effect on labour policy or on the production of goods.

But America need not experience "a period of acute liquidation, so long as the effectual bankruptcy of all civilised Europe does not pass from *de facto* to *de jure;* provided always that the Federal Reserve continues to administer the American credit situation with a firm hand, and provided also that the nation's Business Administration does not live up to its election promises in the way of businesslike legislation. It may yet be within the power of the American banking community and the Federal Reserve to postpone the formal bankruptcy of Europe indefinitely, if European statecraft can be brought to substitute common sense for politics in any sensible degree." Veblen's discussion of European investments seems to apply equally to the operations he usually describes as foreign investments, that is, the great security operations of the corporate financiers, foreign to the industrial mechanism and increasingly removed from the industrial base, from the purchasing power of the community. In the traffic of the masters of credit and solvency, with the key industries under their control, "neither the industrial manpower nor the underlying population come into the case except as the counters in the computation of what the traffic will bear."

By their control of credit, the investment bankers control the strategic key industries, which in turn control the continuation industries of manufacturing proper, which in turn control agriculture, which supplies the manpower and means of subsistence. The manufacturing corporations compete among themselves, to the greater gain of the investment banker and to the cost of the underlying community. The farmer is caught in a system of absentee ownership, which reaches out in all-pervading network of credit, corporate capitalisation, and big business, managed on the principle of the greatest amount of gain in terms of price. A community which lives close to the soil, however, like Russia, can surpass the most advanced technological nations which are controlled by absentee ownership and finance.

The modern technology increasingly throws responsibility into the hands of technicians, who by virtue of their activity become more and more intolerant and constructively sceptical of the prevailing conventional truth lying beyond the borders of tangible fact. But neither the industrial system nor the brotherhood of technicians, in whose habits of thought this industrial system is contained, has yet reached an absolute and unmitigated state of mechanisation and brute logic. The logical outcome of such a state would be the abrogation of absentee ownership. Under the modern dispensation and division of labour, the captain of finance is still the discretionary figure, even though he has become an absentee, an outsider, so far as concerns any creative work. Sovereign jurisdiction is in the hands of laymen working at cross-purposes. They are governed not by the calculus of production but by that of net gain, in terms of price, the claim of absentee ownership. Their life of business expediency is irrelevant, incompetent, and impertinent, and not germane to creative industry. In the technician's computation, pecuniary personal gain is an alien factor, since it is a calculus not of material fact or of the general material welfare, but of money value alone.

In the light of the interlocking nature of modern industry and its continual advance, "the safe and sane plan of common sense now dictates that industrial operations must be conducted by competent technicians." This should be especially true of "the oversight and control of the industrial system at large as a going concern; of the balance, articulation, and mutual support among the several lines of production and distribution that go to make up the system." "The technological system is an organisation of intelligence, a structure of intangibles and imponderables in the nature of habits of thought." The mechanistic logic of physics and chemistry runs counter "to the miraculous convictions of religion and the magical 'forced movements' of nationalism," as embodied in absentee ownership. Under the modern scheme of the arts, the owners can be dispensed with. But the technicians, like other men, are citizens of the world and the pervading animistic bias that runs in terms of the magical symbols of money has acted to commercialise the engineer. As a result America faces a fatal decline in its technological powers.

The managers of the continuation industries, manufacturing concerns, have only "a vicarious or delegated power," since "their initiative and discretion are bounded by the measures which may be taken independently by the management of the key industries." The inordinate productivity of industry, and the continual increase of and demand for capitalisation, have resulted in a closed market; that is, the market for goods of any sort, and particularly for securities, is limited by the constant purchasing power available at any given time, rather than by the productive capacity of the community. This limitation is inherent in the nature of the price system, which is a credit price system for the achieving of free income by means of large absentee ownership. The management of industry by large investment interests for profit is essentially in the nature of inveterate ceremonial observance.

The financial concerns are competitive sellers in a closed market, and their competitive strategy is in the last analysis directed towards a lowering of production costs, that is, the wages of manpower. Workmen still have the prejudice that human work should be of some objective human use, but the bias of salesmanship is towards getting something for nothing. Should the workmen lose their prejudice and engage in salesmanship, the present great industrial adventure would come to a close, "presumably after a more or less protracted period of disorder and decay." The failure to reach this perfection in the wage relation is due perhaps to an apparently native workmanlike bent, in the nature of an ancient habit, which "will not tolerate an unreserved shift from workmanship to salesmanship." In a footnote Veblen somewhat qualifies this assertion. In any given case, he said, "a native bent of this kind" can be altogether neutralised by long, severe, adverse habituation. An appreciable number of individuals are virtually exempt from this bent, because of the dominating influence of other propensities.

The working population may already believe in the efficacy of salesmanship with their heads, but they do not yet know it with their hearts. Wherever such action is taken by workingmen or farmers, it is centred against specific personalities and for the presumed benefit of some specific organisation, or vested interest. The standard labour unions seek to get better pay, but in the nature of the case their efforts amount to nothing more than a process of catching up, since the better pay is in terms of price, and the general level of prices continues to rise under current conditions of credit, capitalisation, and salesmanship. As consumers they lose what they gain in higher wages. The same applies to the farmer. They do not yet realise that they are confronting a state of affairs based on the immemorial right of ownership. The underlying, working population is only a creative factor in the system, not an executive factor. In the strategy of business enterprise at large it has a passive role—as "manpower to be employed at discretion in the pursuit of earnings on capitalised industry, according to the law of balanced return," or as "a body of ultimate consumers to be supplied at discretion in the pursuit of commercial gains, according to what the traffic will bear." The underlying population, however, is learning in practical consequences to use sabotage effectively, and, as in the contests between pecuniary strategists, "with each recurring wrangle the preamble of vituperation and sanctimony becomes more abridged and the argument shifts more quickly and more overtly to its final terms—the big stick of coercive inaction, passive resistance, unemployment, sabotage."

Ultimate responsibility rests upon the managers of key industries, and on such men as millers and packers, whose work is in the same category as the key industries, from the standpoint of effective control. Because of the closed market it is necessary that they spend great and continually increasing amounts on salesmanship. Corporations are forced to keep up appearances with their competitors by increasing their sales expenditures. This rising cost of salesmanship becomes an overhead charge on the business, and it constantly increases, since the costs of salesmanship are subtracted from the available purchasing power of the community, thereby necessitating further sabotage and further increase of selling costs.

The fear of shame, of losing prestige, is the guiding incentive in purchasing advertised articles. The publicity agents of the sovereign remedies sound like the dealers in "that universal solvent of business exigencies, the creation of new credit obligations." Salesmanship is a capitalisation of credulity. "It is a trading on that range of human infirmities which blossom in devout observances and bear fruit in the psychopathic wards." But the devices of salesmanship, like those of corporation finance, are useful to their possessors, as a means for securing a "competitive share in the usufruct of the underlying population, its services, workmanship, and material output."

Veblen's discussion of salesmanship reaches a climax in a seven-page note on "The Propaganda of the Faith." The secular adventures in salesmanship and publicity, he declared, are "raw recruits, late and slender capitalisations out of the ample fund of human credulity," in comparison with the Propaganda of the Faith, which is "the largest, most magnificent, most unabashed, and most lucrative enterprise in sales-publicity." Nothing else has reached its "pitch of unabated assurance which has enabled the publicity-agents of the Faith to debar human reason from scrutinising their pronouncements. . . . Saul has slain his thousands . . . but David has slain his tens of thousands." It is a traffic in "divinely beneficial intangibles" based on the same "ubiquitously human ground of unreasoning fear, aspiration, and credulity," on which the intangible assets of modern corporations are based. The *summum bonum*, "a balanced ration of divine glory and human use," has its secular counterpart in the law of balanced return of privation. The audacity and achievement of the publicity agents of the Faith indicate "the limits eventually to be attained by commercial advertising in the way of capitalisable earning-capacity."

The salesmen of the faith have achieved the perfect ideal of modern salesmanship: to promise everything and deliver nothing. "All that has been delivered hitherto has—perhaps all for the better—been in the nature of further publicity, often with a use of more pointedly menacing language; but it has always been more language, with a moratorium on the liquidation of the promises to pay, and a penalty on any expressed doubt of the solvency of the concern." The salesmen play on an increasing fear and credulity, and the goods they promise to deliver fall under the categories of Hell-fire and the Kingdom of Heaven, "to which the most heavily capitalised of these publicity concerns of the supernatural adds a broad margin of Purgatory." Delivery of the goods is not desired by the ultimate consumers, any more than they desire the collapse of industrial civilisation which is threatened by the captains of finance if their charges are not met or if they are eliminated from the economic organisation. The result is a tremendous waste of resources and manpower, with nothing delivered except "a further continued volume of the same magisterial publicity that has procured a livelihood for its numerous personnel and floated its magnificent overhead charges in the past."

The tremendous waste includes not only the "establishments formally chartered to do business exclusively in the retail distribution of sacred sales publicity," but also the "equipment and personnel engaged in the fabrication, sorting, storage, ripening, and mobilisation of the output," the "very considerable number of schools for the training of certified publicity-agents in Divinity and for generating a suitable bias of credulity in the incoming generation," and organisations and periodicals devoted to pushing the work both at home and abroad. "The manpower employed in this work of the Propaganda is also more considerable than that engaged in any other calling except Arms, and possibly Husbandry. . . . All told—if it were possible—it will be evident that the aggregate of human talent currently consumed in this fabrication of vendible imponderables in the nth dimension, will foot up to a truly massive total, even after making a reasonable allowance of, say, some thirty-three and one-third percent, for average mental deficiency in the personnel which devotes itself to this manner of livelihood."

Veblen's discussion of "The Larger Use of Credit" might be considered the most important chapter in the book, since it presents the base of the entire argument, credit being the instrument of absentee ownership. The argument, said Veblen, leans to a peculiar degree on the chapters on "Credit and Capitalisation" in *The Theory of Business Enterprise,* and on Mitchell's *Business Cycles.* "In the business enterprise of this new era" the pivotal factor "is the larger use of credit." The volume of credit increasingly exceeds the material objects and operations upon which it conceivably rests. Today the control of the key industries by the massive credit institutions, acting in effect in collusion, prevents an unadvised breakdown of the inflated credit price. Therefore, if the price level suffers a material decline, it will be contemplated with equanimity by the massive credit interests, since such a break could be brought on only by deliberate action of the chief parties interested. In a footnote, however, there is a suggestion that by such a statement Veblen merely intends to emphasise the responsibility of the credit interests for privation and devastation.

If these concerns had let the inflated situation of the war period reach a climax, a drastic liquidation would have resulted, with effective cuts in capitalisation and price so that industry could easily have made up the waste of the war. If the industrial production had been allowed to run free, the increase in tangible wealth would have equalled by now "all the book-values of those inflated assets which their financial guardians have been safeguarding with unemployment and commercial paper through these years of privation and unrest." To deal with corporation finance by drift of circumstance rather than by design means a more stable order of things in business, but a more precarious order of things in industry, upon which business ultimately rests and to which it must eventually render an accounting.

Out of the exigencies of the nineties, created by the investment bankers themselves, and out of the maturing of ownership under the impact of the new technology, comes the investment banker as the most important institution of the community. "He is the source or the channel, as the case may be, of capitalisation and of corporation credit at large--a source if he represents a banking-house of the first magnitude, a channel if his place in the economy of Nature is that of a subordinate." The investment banker "initiates movement or pressure in the conduct of business, or he transmits initiative and pressure." In effect, he is the master of the fiscal affairs of business. By virtue of their collusion the investment bankers constitute the "One Big Union of the Interests," the "General Staff of the business community." The responsibility for the material welfare of the community rests on them, since it is upon their good will and wisdom that production depends. In Morgan's time "the great pioneering creator of mergers and holding companies came to stand as the chief of investment bankers and the dean of the congregation of corporation finance." Subsequently the investment bankers have increasingly obtained control of the industrial system, and their energies have been taken up with a standardised routine of investing funds and allocating credits for their own greater gain. The bonus, which was the entering wedge for control, was a pure credit transaction. It amounted to a redistribution of the old values under cover of a make-believe creation of new assets. In effect, recapitalisations were primarily of this sort, and amounted to the creation of new capitalised wealth by new extensions of credit. The great gains of investment banking are derived from such transactions of pure credit. These intangible assets, capitalisations of usufruct, are an absentee's claim to a share in the country's income, and constitute a valid claim to get something for nothing.

The general body of owners and workmen lose more than the pecuniary magnate gains, since the operations involve considerable costs. Their intangible assets, in the nature of magical items, can be used as collateral to make further gains at the cost of the underlying community, and ordinary cupidity will of course force them to continue this process. It is a cumulative process, masked by the continual inflation of prices as new credit is continually pumped into the system. Investment banks are closely allied with some one industrial interest, as well as with commercial banks. This double use of assets is the essence of modern capitalisation and the source of the great gains in financial strategy. It is in reference to this that Veblen calls the investment bankers "captains of duplication."

It is the nature of the work of modern banking that it should lend itself to syndicates, that is, to collusive operations. Teamwork is necessary to put over security issues and engage in financial deals. There are only a few large massive credit concerns, and their resources and their control of commercial banking and the key industries enable them to create credit almost at will. The lesser and outlying members of the craft must wait faithfully on the motions of these masters of solvency, on pain of being left out on the next occasion for gain.

The investment bankers, severally and collectively, constitute the absentee government of current business and industry. Their absentee ownership, like all absentee ownership, is in effect a claim to free income. Such an income is achieved by withholding needed credit extension from enterprises which are doubtful, from the standpoint of gain to the investment banker. Thus "the power and sanction commanded by these custodians are of a permissive sort. That is to say, their strategy and administration are necessarily of a negative, quiescent, sedative character, something in the way of a provisional veto power, a contingent check on untoward undertakings and excursions"; in effect a species of fiscal sabotage. Concomitant with the increasing scope of free capitalisation and credits is the increasing use of the injunction on the underlying population. Both in effect serve the ends of the larger absentee ownership. "Both combine judiciary with executive powers, and the powers of both are of an inhibitory sort, essentially powers of retardation and inertia, powers which take effect by way of penalising activities that are not otherwise obnoxious to law and morals." The activities and demands of the working interests, in their attempts to become *de facto* a business interest, are a threat to capitalisation and therefore a menace to business prosperity.

The fabric of credit and capitalisation "is essentially a fabric of concerted make-believe, resting on the routine credulity of the business community at large." Consequently it is always in a state of unstable equilibrium. The manipulation of credit and capitalisation is a confidence game, and, since the industrial interests are rivals for a fixed total amount of purchasing power, the peace between them, as well as that between them and the community, is in the nature of a negotiated peace, which is likely to break down at any time. The illusion of material prosperity is kept up, however, by a never-ceasing process of flotation of securities, which results in an inflation of security values and in turn provides for further issues and manipulations, all of which are met at the cost of the community. "In the long run the cumulative expansion of credit, re-inforced with a resolute businesslike restriction of output all along the line, has proved to be the determining factor in that parallelogram of economic forces the resultant of which has been a sustained upward trend of general prices and a cumulative capitalisation of intangibles." The farmers and workmen who constitute the underlying population are in effect "a species of natural resources," which are for the benefit of absentee ownership and which the absentee owners hold in usufruct, as if they were "in the nature of inert materials exposed to the drift of circumstances over which they have no control, somewhat after the analogy of bacteria employed in fermentation." With the increasing cost of labour trouble, of sabotage of wages, as the price of capitalisation in-creases, the costs of production also increase, and the imposition of further privation becomes necessary.

In the war against industrial manpower the big interests act in concert, as in the campaign for an open shop. In effect the modern corporation is a method of collusion for the benefit of the allied and associated powers at the cost of whom it may concern. It is a conspiracy of owners, and violates the traditional principle of self-help, but it is the only way business can function under the modern large-scale industrial organisa-tion. Against these large corporate units the old-fashioned craft union, as distinct from the industrial union, can hardly be effective. Law and order, the weapons of industrial warfare, are on the side of capitalised overhead charges as against the industrial manpower. The *status quo ante*, as represented by capitalised overhead charges, must be preserved, and the constituted authorities, being practical, businesslike men, en-deavour to preserve a system that will not work.

Under the improvements in technology and business, the net effect of this general working at cross-purposes is a chronic margin of de-ficiency, whereby the goods and services making up the livelihood of the community fall short of current needs by a progressively wider margin. But such a discrepancy will doubtless continue to be covered by the creation and capitalisation of new credits, with new fixed charges.

In fact the cut in material supply, coupled with rising costs and rising prices, will entail an urgent and progressive need of new capital to serve as working capital. Such a view of things is not held by the certified economists and substantial citizens. By received preconceptions they hold that "credit is deferred payment, capital is assembled 'production goods,' business is the helper of productive industry, salesmanship is the facility of the 'middleman,' money is 'the great wheel of circulation' employed in a 'refined system of barter,' and absentee ownership is a rhetorical solecism." But "it is conceivable that the civilised peoples might yet save themselves alive out of this impasse, in spite of their addiction to business, if it were not for their national integrity," which comes down to the same thing, the belief in the make-believe of capitalised overhead charges. Still "there is always the chance, more or less imminent, that in time, after due trial and error, on duly prolonged and intensified irritation, some sizable element of the underlying population, not intrinsically committed to absentee ownership, will forsake or forget their moral principles of business-as-usual, and will thereupon endeavour to take this businesslike arrangement to pieces and put the works together again on some other plan." Absentee ownership is not necessarily wrong in principle, but its concrete working out in the modern system of credit has created a precarious state of affairs.

"The net aggregate amount of these differential gains which so accrue to these special Interests at the cost of such ill will and distress to the common run will ordinarily foot up to no more than a vanishing percentage of their net aggregate cost to the underlying populations that are employed in the traffic. In the material respect these institutional holdovers work out in a formidable aggregate loss of life and livelihood; while in the spiritual respect their staple output is a tissue of dissension, distrust, dishonesty, servility, and bombast. The net product is mutual and collective defeat and grief." In the calculable future it is not to be expected that popular sentiment will effectively run counter to "that strategy of businesslike curtailment of output, debilitation of industry, and capitalisation of overhead charges" involved in the established system of ownership and bargaining. This chronic derangement, involving "a progressively widening margin of deficiency in the aggregate material output and a progressive shrinkage of the available means of life," with progressive capitalisation and overhead charges until a collapse is reached, recalls Veblen's declaration in *The Theory of Business Enterprise* that depression is normal and that business prosperity is achieved by an extraneous factor in the nature of waste.

Thus Veblen's formulation of the inherent contradiction of modern capitalism is that credit must be continually expanded in order to keep the industrial system going in the face of property rights and industrial efficiency. This expansion necessitates sabotage, labour troubles, and increased labour costs, which in turn necessitate further credit expansion, trading on a thinner equity of tangible assets, until the assets disappear.

The best summary of the book is a description of the third term of Veblen's course, "Economic Factors in Civilisation," called "The Industrial Revolution," which was scheduled for 1923 at the New School. This description declared: "The past 150 years may fairly be called a period of Industrial Revolution. Sweeping changes have taken effect in the ways and means of industry and have greatly altered the material conditions of life, and have thereby altered civilised men's habits of life in detail. These changes in the habitual ways and means of living have been and continue to be large, swift, and profound, beyond example; while the resulting changes due to follow in the habits of thought which govern civilised men's conduct and convictions have been and continue to be slight and slow, by comparison. So that it is now an open question whether the civilised peoples will be able to bring their principles of conduct up to date and with passable consonance with the new material conditions of life."

Veblen took the manuscript to Huebsch, and one of Huebsch's men, working on *The Freeman*, has said: "Veblen seemed more mouselike than ever. Huebsch told me that Veblen had stolen into his office like an interloper who wished to ask for a dime, but sat fidgeting in a chair for about an hour while Huebsch made conversation, and had finally with a great effort of will dumped an untidy parcel of manuscript on the desk, stating that it was something he had written but probably not of the least interest to the publisher or anyone else."

The reviews were relatively mild. The only strenuous objections came from the radicals, who had not yet learned to pierce Veblen's rhetoric. The reviewer in *The Liberator* said: "*Absentee Ownership* borders on Marxian analysis and interpretation. Yet Veblen insists on steering clear from the scientific line of socialism in his conclusions," declaring that "the standard formalities of 'Socialism' and 'Anti-socialism' are obsolete in face of the new alignment of economic forces."

Before the book was sent to Huebsch for publication, Veblen took a chance on the stock market. Dr. Boughton had been told by a friend in an oil company that the company's stock was bound for a sizable rise, and she asked Veblen if he wished to purchase some. He was interested in setting aside some money for his old age, and decided to buy the stock, although fully aware of the inconsistency of his action. Shortly afterwards the company figured in the oil scandals as the concern whose purchase price, when it was bought by a larger concern, was changed within twenty-four hours by an amount which was claimed to represent the funds needed to pay off the Republican party debt. But Veblen made money on his venture. One of his brothers declared humorously that his pecuniary success showed that he had finally become properly educated. The brother said that some of Veblen's work in *The Journal of Political Economy* and *The Theory of Business Enterprise* indicated his incomplete knowledge of business, "but he learned more later. When he really learned the science of business and finance, he went at it and made some money for himself." But, as so many had said before, the brother declared: "I do not think anyone ever really knew him."

Ellen Rolfe did not lose touch with Veblen. She knew when his second wife died in 1920. In a letter she said that "Mr. V. sends me his books," and she told a friend that she had been writing to him quite impersonally about her faith in theosophy. She attempted to convert him to theosophy, and he answered her kindly. She still felt that he would come back to her. Not long before her death she wrote that he remained in her memory as the quiet-mannered country boy of college years, neither crass nor blunt nor high-stepping, but of kindly although not sacrificial feelings. "Though the way grew very rough, it was my great good fortune to have married this one who has performed his mission so well." "It has pleased him in his super-activity to hold mankind up to the mirror to show them how their joints worked." In the final day of reckoning there could be "no better showman to point out the sheep from the goats to themselves." He was a natural mechanic, an inventor, anthropologist, linguist, nature lover, scientist, an ideal idler with the intelligence to gratify his curiosity in a leisurely way that never wore him out. He "roams the universe idly," with "never a moment of conscientious service." Even the idea of death does not affect him. He knows that might was born in him. No inner disquiet could ever take toll of the serenity of his outlook. Attention and praise were the due of his genius, for "the unusual loves to find acceptation." She did not entirely blame him for their difficulties. She termed herself "the romantic drudge, the first wife, who stems poverty, uncertainty, unfulfilment, 'temperament,' the sordid push upward, and asks for herself nothing, except perhaps that her heart be not too bitterly broken in the days when women begin to consider her prize worth attention."

Beginning in 1923 the same former Chicago student who had previously contributed $4500 to Veblen's salary now contributed $500 annually to Veblen's support. In the summer of 1924 Veblen was very uncertain of his direction. He wrote Lubin: "I don't know what I am likely to do next," and he wrote Mitchell that he was "still on the wind." He had some expectation of going to England in the winter of 1924 or the spring of 1925, to study British imperialism, for he had never ceased to be curious as to the explanation for England's hegemony over the rest of the world. England, he felt, was a predatory organism, just as were the United States and Germany, but the English seemed more efficient than others in their predatory activities. They seemed to know when they had reached the point of all the traffic can bear, whereas the Americans usually crossed the point. In England life seemed to run smoothly, without the overt brutality characteristic of the larger business operations in America and Germany. At a time when Americans felt that financial control had passed to the United States, Veblen had no doubts that the English financier would in the sequel be shown still to have control of the financial resources of the world. He seemed to feel that all his previous analysis was preliminary to such an investigation and that in a study of British imperialism he would merge the various currents of his thoughts. Alvin Johnson attempted to raise sufficient funds for Veblen, and at first the prospect seemed promising. Veblen even arranged for a passport, but finally it proved that funds were unavailable.

Veblen was quite pleased to learn that a doctoral dissertation had been written on his work at the University of Paris. The author was an American, William Jaffé, and before reading his book Veblen wrote him: "You seem to have been borrowing trouble, if I may comment." "It has also occurred to me, and I am taking the liberty to make the suggestion that if your dissertation were translated or rewritten in English you might find a certain (restricted) market and attention for it in this country. If such a thing should interest you, I would also suggest that you see Mr. Huebsch, my publisher."

Most of the professors at Jaffé's examination on his thesis seemed never to have heard of Veblen. One was annoyed at Veblen's contempt for luxury articles, maintaining that *articles de luxe* were evidences of a higher civilisation. One, however, William Oualid, showed acquaintance with Veblen's work, and wanted to know how Veblen came to have a point of view much more European than American. The most distinguished French economist in the orthodox tradition, particularly in finance, who had a high respect for Marx, seemed to feel that a study of Veblen was a waste of time. He said that he had read *The Theory of the Leisure Class* and found it worthless.

In Germany, Sombart had had a high admiration for Veblen since the appearance of *The Theory of Business Enterprise;* Max Weber thought much of *The Theory of the Leisure Class*. But such men were not considered economic theorists by the orthodox. The latter, represented by such men as Joseph Schumpeter, had much the same opinion of Veblen as had the American economists when *The Theory of the Leisure Class* first appeared. The most distinguished of their number said that he first saw Veblen at a meeting of the American Economic Association, and that Veblen, leaning against the wall near the threshold of a room, with a red scarf about him, looked like a common *poseur*. He added that he considered the distinction between making goods and making money only too obvious, and utterly useless in economic analysis. Marx, he felt, was a great thinker, but Veblen was little better than a charlatan.

In England, too, the conventional economists did not have a very high respect for Veblen. In *The Economic Journal*, the official publication of the Royal Economic Association, the only review of Veblen's works was that of *The Theory of the Leisure Class*, appearing in 1925, just after an English edition had been published of a number of his writings. The reviewer said: "There is naturally no suggestion in this tale of unrelieved gloom, of any service rendered by the leisure classes, nor any indication why the community should have continued so long to tolerate their existence. The whole treatment of the subject, and even more the style in which it is written, must make it most acceptable reading to the exponents of the class war." Jaffé's book on Veblen was reviewed at the same time and by the same reviewer, who commented "nor again, beyond a casual mention of the fact that Mr. Graham Wallas dislikes Veblen's irony, does [Mr. Jaffé] make any reference to the concentrated venom of Veblen's writings. But the average reader needs a walk in the sun to clear his head of sulphuric acid fumes between every two volumes." But Patrick Geddes stayed up all night to finish *The Theory of the Leisure Class*. In a note in *The Sociological Review* Victor Branford said that "in sum, the view of contemporary civilisation in the West, presented by Mr. Veblen's remarkable series of studies running through and beyond the two decades that have witnessed the world crisis of the War, comes nearer, perhaps to a sociological interpretation of current life and affairs than can be found elsewhere. But what a reflection on the body of professed sociologists that they should have left this supreme task of describing and interpreting the characteristic processes of contemporary civilisation in the West to a professor in Economics!"

Appreciation of Veblen was slowly growing in the academic halls of America. In 1924 Washington University gave him an honour that was not without a touch of irony. His name was carved on the wall of the building devoted to the School of Commerce and Finance, now called the School of Business and Public Administration. Veblen's name was surrounded not by those of Marx and Lassalle, but by those of such orthodox leaders as Hobson, Gossen, Jevons, Schmoller, List, Böhm-Bawerk, Smith, Taussig, Ricardo, Clark, Malthus, Mill, Marshall.

In that year Mitchell was president of the American Economic Association, and in his presidential address he said: "One topic . . . is fairly sure to receive much attention—the topic defined twenty-four years ago at the thirteenth annual meeting of the American Economic Association by Dr. Veblen," in his paper on "Industrial and Pecuniary Employments." "This is the relation between business and industry." [1] At the same session Veblen submitted a paper on "Economic Theory in the Calculable Future." This paper, like his first before the Association, was not delivered in person, ostensibly because of ill health. The meeting was held in Chicago, and Veblen felt that the trip would be too much of a hardship. He was not at all satisfied with his paper; it was less than eight pages in length, not enough space for Veblen's roundabout style to achieve its best effect.

Economic science, Veblen declared, has suffered an increasing bifurcation as a result of the operations of modern industry and absentee ownership on a large and ever-increasing scale. Economists must align themselves either with the state of the industrial arts or with the price system. The logic of business is alien to that of industry and incompatible with it. There is a great probability that the logic of business enterprise and of bellicose nationalism will overpower the evolutionary trend of economics and set back the industrial advance. Prevailing economics is of a monographic nature, based even more unreservedly than in the past on the traditional common-sense preconception of the price system. To the conventional economists, as well as to most other men, business considerations are understandable and of paramount importance, the technological half of the current economic world remaining to them obscure and, at the best, subsidiary. The final and conclusive terms, the objective beneficent end of the analysis, are increasingly the realities of business traffic and differential gain. The economist or businessman is not interested in the ulterior effect of the pursuit of differential gains, except by way of uttering an irrelevant *obiter dictum*, since these gains are the final terms of his own activity, and he takes it for granted that the pursuit of differential gains is good for the community.

Thus "economic science should, for its major incidence and with increasing singleness and clarity, be a science of business traffic, monographic, detailed, exacting, and imbued with a spirit of devotion to things as they are shaping themselves under the paramount exigencies of absentee ownership considered as a working system; and the personnel of the science, the body of economists in ordinary, in the degree in which they run to form under the training of the schools and the market, should be partisans of this system, and of a reasonably intolerant temper." There will, of course, be controversies, but such controversies "should in an increasing degree run in terms drawn from the current business traffic," from the controversies of captains of finance, concerned with the pecuniary advisability of disputed policies. No argument on economic matters can be respected today unless it is set forth as a "business proposition," in terms drawn from current corporation finance.

Technological matters are considered only in so far as they become instruments of differential gain against other businessmen and ultimately against the community. Technological enterprise perforce seeks a gain in productive efficiency at large, and from the technological standpoint the various industrial concerns work as a team. But from the standpoint of business strategy they are competitors in a strategy of mutual defeat. Monopoly, which is the basis of business gains, is pure waste from the standpoint of the technical half of the industrial world. National statecraft, patriotic inflation, armaments, function for the ends of big business. "And such economists and commissions of economic inquiry as are drawn into the service of the national establishment are drawn in for no other purpose and on no other qualifications than such as are presumed to serve the bankers and traders of the nation against the outsiders," the underlying population. Increasingly the faculties of economic science are taken up with the art of salesmanship and the expedients of sales publicity.

This conclusion is a long distance from that of "Why Is Economics Not an Evolutionary Science?" written a quarter of a century before, where Veblen had declared: "Under the stress of modern technological exigencies, men's everyday habits of thought are falling into the lines that in the sciences constitute the evolutionary method; and knowledge which proceeds on a higher, more archaic plane is becoming alien and meaningless to them. The social and political sciences must follow the drift for they are already caught in it."

Veblen's paper was discussed by Raymond Bye, professor of economics at the University of Pennsylvania, and by John Maurice Clark of Chicago University, the son of Veblen's old teacher. Clark said that "Veblen is far from being negligible with the large group of his disciples and the larger group of those who have been driven to rethink their premises and reorient their efforts by the challenge of his pitiless subversions of orthodoxy. . . . The wide effect of Veblen's doctrines is itself an evidence of some sort of manifest destiny." But Clark objected to Veblen's bifurcation of economic science. "A far truer statement would seem to be that the organising of human efforts involves two sets of functions, one technical, the other concerned with giving the technical efforts necessary direction and guidance." No one has ever shown "how social efficiency can be organised on a technical basis alone." The path of progress "calls for an evolution of our scheme of values, not for a 'technocracy' which ignores value." Clark also objected to Veblen's statement that "the nation has *no other function* than the pursuit of commercial rivalries, all of them affairs of international mutual defeat." [2] It could not, he said, stand a moment's candid examination if taken literally. According to Clark, Veblen himself presented the refutation to the objections against his statement that economists are becoming devoted to monographic work and to the service of business.

A move was under way to get the American Economic Association to recognise Veblen's position by an offer of the presidency. Some of the younger members had for some years been dissatisfied with the way in which they believed the association was being run by a small group of insiders with the result that the persons nominated for the presidency were not always the most eminent leaders in American economic thought. They were particularly nettled by the way in which Veblen was ignored for men whom they believed inferior to him. Therefore Paul Douglas had in 1923 started a movement for nominating candidates by petition as well as by the selections of the nominating committee. J.M. Clark was made head of a committee to investigate the question. The committee discussed also the possibility of an occasional election of an honorary president. In this office "the Association wishes to recognise scholarly service of high distinction without adding to it the burden of executive work." [3] This suggestion was also made by Douglas, and Veblen was the scholar to be so honoured. It was said that Laughlin might be given the distinction after Veblen if the proposal was approved. The committee could come to no decision at the 1924 meeting, and nothing came of either of the plans.

President Mitchell, however, appointed a nominating committee which was made up of Veblen's friends. Taussig was chairman, and the other members were Commons, Millis, and two younger men—James Harvey Rogers and Douglas. It looked as if Veblen was to be the next president. But in committee meetings Allyn Young's name was also put forward. He had been a colleague of Millis and Commons, and had just been made a colleague of Taussig at Harvard. It was said Veblen was really a sociologist not an economist, and the question was raised whether he would take the presidency seriously or would attend the coming meeting. Moreover, he was not a member of the association. On the other hand, it was contended that Young had been active in the association for many years, and that as secretary he had given much labour and time to its affairs. After a number of meetings of the nominating committee, the old generation won out. Early in the spring Douglas started a petition asking for the nomination of Veblen at the following meeting. This move met with some opposition from the older members of the association, but was supported by such men as Mitchell and A.B. Wolfe. Several hundred signatures were quickly acquired and presented to E.R.A. Seligman, who was chairman of the nominating committee. Seligman secured the consent of the nominating committee to Veblen's candidacy, and offered the nomination to Veblen, on condition that he become a member of the association and deliver an address. Veblen refused the offer, and after Seligman had left he said to a friend: "It gave me great pleasure to refuse him. They didn't offer it to me when I needed it." The whole matter was dropped. At the election one of Veblen's former students suggested that Veblen's bust, draped in an American flag, be placed on the presidential platform.

Doubtless it would have been a fine sentimental gesture if the association had elected Veblen despite his refusal, thereby showing that at least his own profession did not conform with his logic of institutions. But among the members there was no little division of opinion about Veblen. Many of the older members disapproved of him because of his marital experiences. They also resented the somewhat lofty tone that he assumed towards his contemporaries, and most of them disagreed with his economic theories. One of the members of the 1924 nominating committee said that he felt "a deep emotional opposition to Veblen which was as real as the admiration which many of us bore him."

Veblen turned back to the literature of his people, to "one of those things men do when they grow old." In 1925 he issued his translation of *The Laxdœla Saga*. It was now thirty-seven years since he had first undertaken the work. He told Huebsch that he would lose money in publishing it, but Huebsch was not concerned, since he had never made money on Veblen's books. At first Veblen thought of publishing the saga as a Christmas gift book, with illustrations by his friend Nordfeld, but nothing came of this plan.

Whatever the date of the translation may be, Veblen's introduction was certainly of a recent date. The discussion in the preface has about as much relation to the saga itself as Veblen's discussion of the preconceptions of economic science had to the specific economists and schools that he mentioned in those early essays. The different historical episodes and factors discussed in the preface, such as the blood-feud, the Propaganda of the Faith, the Viking Enterprise, the Icelandic Aristocratic Republic, had been used by Veblen before, but in this limited space they merge with one another, and appear merely as different ways of portraying the nature of modern capitalism. For an understanding of Veblen this is one of his best essays.

In Veblen's analysis the institution of the blood-feud can be taken as a symbol of the system of free contract and ownership, and the classic sagas as a symbol of classical economics and the traditional ideas of ownership. In all the "classic sagas which have come down from the saga period," the "paramount exigencies of the blood-feud . . . shape the outlines of the narrative and create the critical situations of the plot and give rise to the main outstanding incidents and episodes. . . . The blood-feud was then a matter of course and of common sense, about the merits of which no question was entertained—no more than the merits of national patriotism are questioned in our time." *The Laxdœla Saga* reflects the state of affairs "touching the Scandinavian and the English-speaking peoples at the point of their induction into their feudal and ecclesiastical status in early-christian times." The two pillars of the new institutional structure were Sin and Servility. "And both of these concepts are in principle alien to the spirit of the pagan past. The sagas of the classical period reflect that state of experience . . . which prepared the way for these new canons of right and honest living; canons according to which the common man has in the nature of things no claims which his God or his masters are bound to respect. They are at the same time the canons which have since then continued to rule the life of these Christian peoples in Church and State."

The discipline of the Viking Age induced in these people a frame of mind which would incline them to a conviction of sin and to an unquestioning subjection to mastery, in other words, to an acceptance of the Propaganda of the Faith. The concrete working out of the principle and logic of the blood-feud, "with its standardised routine of outlawry and its compounding of felonies," facilitated conversion to the fundamentals of the New Faith. The Viking Age of Big Business prepared the ground for the new feudal order of society. Viking enterprise "was an enterprise in piracy and slave-trade, which grew steadily more businesslike and more implacable as time went on. It was an enterprise in getting something for nothing by force and fraud at the cost of the party of the second part; much the same, in principle, as the national politics pursued by the statesmen of the present time." It became a settled right of common sense that the common man, the underlying population, "had no rights which the captains of the strong arm were to respect." "And like any other business enterprise that is of a competitive nature, this traffic in piracy was for ever driven by its quest of profits to 'trade on a thinner equity,' to draw more unsparingly on its resources of manpower and appliances, and so to cut into the margin of its reserves, to charge increasingly more than the traffic would bear. . . . Between increasing squalor and privation on the material side and an ever-increasing habituation to insecurity, fear, and servility on the spiritual side," the population was driven finally to believe that "this world is a vale of tears and that they all were miserable sinners prostrate and naked in the presence of an unreasoning and unsparing God and his bailiffs. . . . This standardised routine of larceny and homicide ran through its available resources and fell insensibly into decay. . . . The medieval church in Iceland stands out on the current of events as a corporation of bigoted adventurers for the capitalising of graft and blackmail and the profitable compounding of felonious crimes and vices." This oppression was implicit also in the growth and function of that "System of Boss Rule that made up the working constitution of the Icelandic Commonwealth" and eventually accomplished the "incredibly shameful" degradation of the people.

Some of Veblen's footnotes in the text are among the best examples, outside of his lectures, of his use of anthropological material to exemplify aspects of modern civilisation. Of one man who "grew to be a man of wealth and power, and a great chieftain," Veblen said in a footnote, "Such a 'chieftain' was a local ruler, by custom, prestige, patronage, and the strong arm, not by law. At this time (second quarter of the tenth century), as well as under the later-organised Republic, there was in point of law, no executive or police in Iceland. The nearest modern analogue of the Icelandic *hofdingi* and his powers, dignities, and duties, would be the political '*Boss*,' as he functions in American politics and in American municipal affairs. So that, in effect, the democracy of Iceland, both before and during the period of the Republic, was a comprehensive and elaborate system of 'Boss' rule; with no recourse to any ulterior authority, except to a judiciary which owed effectual allegiance to the Bosses of the system. . . . There is nothing in the way of an ostensible popular government interposed between the Bosses and their underlying population. There were parliamentary bodies, local and central, which were in effect, controlled by the Bosses. How nearly the American democracy may approach this type-form is apparently a question of the future."

"The *Hamingia*—good luck, destiny, *mana*—of any person was a congenital attribute. It was conceived to be transferable in some degree; so that its usufruct might inure to the benefit of a second party; and in any case its influence for good would extend to the lucky person's near friends and conduce to their success and profit. It was a magical force, of a spiritual nature, but greatly valued for the material benefits to which it conduced. . . . The friendship of any 'lucky person' was greatly valued—might almost be said to have been capitalised."

"Originally, in pagan times, the functions of the *Godi* were primarily of a shamanistic or quasi-priestly sort. To these there came to be added certain secular duties, connected with the local and seasonal folk-motes." In Christian times and under the Christian perspective the *Godord*— "the office or dignity of *Godi*—had become hereditary, but it was also otherwise transmissible, and, indeed, vendible. A godordsman would be a substantial citizen, and presumably a man of large means. The great political bosses of the twelfth and thirteenth centuries were commonly incumbents of one or more, sometimes fractional, godords, by inheritance, purchase, or proxy." The *Hersir* in Veblen's interpretation seems to have much the same function. The "*Hersir* was a 'Squire,' a country gentleman of wealth and family, who was by custom invested with a degree of authority in local concerns."

When the translation appeared, Veblen was asked the obvious question: "Is your particular style derived from imitating the ancient Icelandic, or have you written your own style into the translation? 'The man's head came off and he died soon after, as was to be expected'— any competent critic would set down as a Veblenism." Veblen's answer was, "I have translated the matter very literally."

L.M. Hollander, an authority on the saga literature, has said in *Scandinavian Studies and Notes* that Veblen's is one of the best translations of an Icelandic saga. But a few renditions are faulty, as a result of the author's leaning towards "raciness or smartness," as shown in such phrases as "a tough job," "with such a hell-bent ugly customer," "I will make no bones about bumping off one or both." The translation of *Hersir ríkir* as a "country gentleman of large means" gives an entirely false impression. A proverb which should have been translated as "don't depend on others" is given "the rather left-handed" form, "delegated business goes to the wolves." Hollander considered it unfortunate that Veblen should have viewed the saga as a sociological document, and declared that some of his generalisations were wide of the mark, especially that concerning the Christianisation of the North. "A little less sociology and far more expressed appreciation of the saga man's art, would have been in place," in the too lengthy preface.

For a few months in 1925 Veblen visited Lubin, who was connected with the Robert Brookings Graduate School, and faithfully attended every session of Lubin's class on classical economics. He was asked to deliver a series of lectures at the school, and the stipend was rather large, but he refused the offer. In 1926 Douglas started a movement for a *Festschrift* for Veblen, to be subsidised by the American Economic

Association, but it was difficult to secure financial support and the plan did not materialise. When Veblen heard of the proposal, he objected to it, and declared: "I am not dead yet."

Then occurred the British General Strike. Veblen once more felt as he had when President Wilson left for Europe. He said that it was the second opportunity for an upturn that had presented itself during his lifetime, and when it failed he declared that British labour, as always in the past, preferred to save the British Empire. The British Labourites, he said, had no plan of action; he had given them a suggestion but they never took it. Their dismal failure helped to complete the breakdown of Veblen's faith in the possibility of a new order by relatively peaceful means. He reread Carpenter's poem *Towards Democracy*, which in his Chicago days he had found so stimulating, but now it seemed to him merely trivial.

Ellen Rolfe died in May 1926. Although she was still a theosophist, she had arranged in her will that her body be given to a research group in the interests of science. Examination showed her physical development to have been greatly retarded, scarcely even to have passed beyond early adolescence. With her death the twilight began for Veblen. He was even now a legendary figure, and he himself said that he had already reached the crest of his popularity.

Veblen's days in the East drew to a close. He did not like to return to his property in California, which was near Stanford, for it was, he said, like going into cold storage. But that was the only choice he could make. He expected to stay in California only until something happened, but he had no definite plans. Accompanied by his stepdaughter Becky he went back to the West, a defeated man, and this time there was to be no return.

CHAPTER XXIV

ON the way to California Veblen stopped for a while with his sister in Minneapolis. He seemed as active as ever and busied himself fixing the locks of her house and making repairs. He went down for a while to San Diego, where his brother Andrew lived. On February 22, 1927, while still in San Diego, he wrote Lubin: "It is already some weeks since we got a card announcing the presence of Miss Alice; and the delay in acknowledging it has not been due to lack of sentiment on my part but only to my own dullness due to a persistent and debilitating cold. . . . There is not much to be said for this place (which is damp and chilly) and less to be said for myself (who am still unfit for anything) and Becky and I will probably be leaving for the east—probably for the Island—again in a few weeks." When he came north to Palo Alto, neither of his absentee properties was available for a home. The cabin was in disrepair and the house near Stanford, which was in a poor section, was occupied by a woman tenant who refused to move or pay the rent. A third shanty had been built on the property by Ellen Rolfe, but when Veblen presented himself there he was confronted by a simple and hearty old man who in plain words claimed title in the name of the tenant of the other shanty. She had told him, he said, that he could live there as long as he liked. Veblen, according to Hans Storm, Camp's brother-in-law, sat down on the doorstep and laughed silently, his shoulders shaking. "There was too much in that laugh to make it exactly pleasant to see: the irony of Thorstein Veblen having to defend the institution of absentee ownership before the unenlightened, the bitterness of a man turned out of his own house, and, also, the inherent weakness of a contemplative person confronted by a hale and hearty extrovert."

After getting possession Veblen lived for about a year in the town shack. Its yard was a tangle of shrubs and weeds. "The house," said Storm, "was bare and barnlike, inside and out; dusty, and so devoid of ordinary comfort that one felt as if someone from a very alien culture were camping in it—someone to whom our chairs and beds and tables are but useless curiosities. In mistaken concern various persons brought him rugs and cushions, but he really did not like these things; the chair he built for himself was a high-backed settle of bare wood." But there was no ascetic gesture in Veblen's taste for simplicity. "I simply have a tough skin," he said. "You would not wear a coat like this, it is too scratchy, but you see, I don't mind it." The clothes he wore at home were so coarse they would almost stand alone. "The heaviest of work-shoes, purchased from Sears, Roebuck, served him for everyday wear in the house." He bought much from the mail order houses, because he liked the rugged utility of their goods.

He was always an efficient workman. Once when Camp was chopping wood, Veblen was distressed to see his waste of motion, and showed him how to use the axe efficiently. When Camp quickly mastered the art, Veblen was highly gratified.

In having the mountain cabin repaired he was very particular that redwood blocks be used for the foundation instead of pine, since redwood would better resist decay. For the cabin he built himself an outdoor chair which was a familiar piece of furniture on old New England farms, with their rail fences, and he said that such a chair was not possible in the typical Middle Western farms, with their barbed-wire fences. Not a leaf or a weed or an insect was disturbed. Wood rats had free access even to the larder, and a skunk would brush itself against his leg, as a cat would. Veblen would stand or sit very quietly for long periods. He was never sentimental concerning "Nature," never even articulate. He seemed to consider the human relatively unimportant among living things.

He was still very fond of children, but after a neighbour's two children had lived with him and Becky for a few months, he agreed with their mother, rather too enthusiastically, that children need a world of their own apart from adults.

Mrs. Gregory, his old friend and student during his first years at Chicago, did not know that Veblen was in the West, but she opened her door one afternoon to find him standing nonchalantly before her. They talked, as always, of everything except himself. He said that it had taken him nearly two hours to walk the few blocks from Camp's house, because he had had to rest so often, but he told it humorously and gave no satisfactory answer to questions about the state of his health.

Veblen had a profound contempt for all forms of mysticism, considering it meaningless nonsense. "If there is a difference between religion and magic," he said, "I have never been able to find it out." On one occasion Storm picked up a copy of Merezhkovsky's *Birth of the Gods* at Veblen's house. He read the preface, which ends with the statement, "the living world is the abstract space in which the body of Christ is being formed," and asked Veblen, as a scholar, what the preface was about. Veblen replied: "It is about four pages and a half." He did not have a very high opinion of Spengler. One of Ellen Rolfe's former protégés told Veblen that a German of profound vocabulary, a mystic, who was then holding women's clubs and such organisations spellbound, had told her that his was the greatest intellect of the present age. Veblen nodded judiciously. "He should know. Only a mind as great as that *could* know." He expressed a good-natured ridicule for the anthropologist B. Malinowski, because "he claims to be reporting only facts, whereas actually on every line he builds up his own charming theories." Veblen read much of the recent literature. He chuckled with continual delight while reading Norman Douglas's *South Wind,* and he considered Aldous Huxley "a bright boy."

Veblen was still addicted to practical jokes. According to a story of Ardzrooni's, Veblen, in one of his walks, found a hornet's nest and shortly thereafter met a farmer with an empty sack. He asked the farmer if he could borrow the sack for a short while, returned to the nest, put the hornets into it, returned the sack to the farmer, and said "thank you." The farmer, says Ardzrooni, is still looking for Veblen. Something of the same strain is revealed in another story. An unscrupulous neighbour, who thought that Veblen was at the mountain cabin, was stealing from Veblen's property some drain pipes, lumber, and other materials purchased for a new garage. All the while Veblen sat smiling quietly, in the shadow of a tall bunch of cane growing in front of the house. The thief never knew that Veblen knew; neither did Veblen know that another neighbour was witnessing the entire spectacle.

In 1927 J.M. Clark, in discussing recent developments in economics, said that Veblen has, "more than any other man, altered the course of American economic thought until the orthodoxy of yesterday is today the thing everyone is trying to overthrow, replace, or modernise. . . . He may be taken as the largest personal impulse behind the modern critical movements." [1] But some of Veblen's ablest students were not very anxious that it be known that Veblen was their intellectual father, though they would admit their debt in private. The country seemed destined for a perpetual prosperity, and thus the millennium, and many of his former friends were saying that Veblen was outmoded. The older generation formally conceded him a high place in economics, but their concession was more a conventional observance than an underlying belief.

In a discussion in *The Quarterly Journal of Economics* of Mitchell's first volume of *Business Cycles,* Schumpeter put Schmoller and Veblen in the same class and said that "unless acquainted with the embers of recent controversial flames, no reader would think of the names of Veblen or Schmoller in reading it." Both men, in their equipment, had "glaring defects . . . natural and acquired." Schmoller exerted "an influence which is in part responsible for what everyone—especially every German —admits to be an unsatisfactory state of economic science in Germany.

. . . Had [Veblen] been able to have his way, had his teaching not met a phalanx of competent theorists, we should perhaps have to make a somewhat similar statement as to America."

Six months before his death in 1929, Veblen said in substance to his neighbour, Mrs. R.H. Fisher: "Naturally there will be other developments right along, but just now communism offers the best course that I can see." The youth movement in China was the last revolutionary flash which deeply interested him, and he was greatly distressed over its failure.

In conversation Veblen was seldom serious about his own writings. When he was asked whether he was the author of *The Theory of the Leisure Class*, he answered: "If I am, it has been a long time ago and I promise never to do it again." Ardzrooni told Veblen that he thought *The Theory of Business Enterprise* should be revised in order to include a discussion of the Federal Reserve system. Veblen agreed and suggested they both go to Washington Island to do the work, but they did not go and the book was not revised.

In 1927, just before his seventieth birthday, Veblen wrote an article entitled "An Experiment in Eugenics," but it was not Veblen at his best. The material is not new, and it lacks the snap of his previous work. His other work, whatever its appearance of irrelevance, pivoted around his fundamental distinction between modern property rights and the institutional requirements of the community, but this essay so lacks direction that much of it seems awkward and pointless. The underlying theme and the superstructure do not march together as they formerly did, but get in each other's way, so that the article seems to end nowhere.

The Scandinavian countries, said Veblen, would make an excellent test for the eugenics theory. They have been the source of great emigrations since antiquity and prehistoric days. According to the eugenics theory, the strong and able, the aggressive, in general the superior, would be the emigrants and the inferior and the generally unfit would be left to breed succeeding generations of emigrants. Thus a comparison of the present Scandinavian peoples with the general European population might show the value of the eugenics argument.

In the middle of the essay Veblen makes a digression to discuss why emigration from the Scandinavian countries was interrupted between the eleventh and eighteenth centuries and began again in the nineteenth. There was no surplus population available during this interval, in which the "feudalistic state and the medieval church were definitively installed in the Scandinavian countries." But a surplus population became available when these barbarian institutions lost their grip. "The Black Death also came during this interval and ran with exceptional severity" over the area. In *Absentee Ownership* Veblen had said that the two factors of the community's material efficiency and advance are the technological arts and population, with the latter conditioned by the former. Now the factors required are the absence of a kept class and the natural fecundity of the people, with the latter conditioned by the former.

In order to have a selective emigration of the superior there must be a habitual surplus margin of population, which presumes a habitual margin of livelihood in excess of current need. This in turn will presume the effective absence "of an idle or non-productive class of ultimate consumers," that is "kept classes." Under the pagan scheme the priesthood and other kinds of ecclesiastical personnel, gentry, nobility, royalty, were not exempt from industrial employment; that is, they did not draw their living from the industry of the working population. "Workmanship was then still an honourable distinction to which all classes and conditions of men aspired," and thus the country's productive work afforded a habitual margin of livelihood. Natural fecundity resulted in a surplus population for emigration. But with the coming of the feudalistic state and the medieval church, the ecclesiastical and similar kept classes multiplied and dominated the community "in a teamwork of misrule, extortion, and waste." The means of livelihood fell, and there was a consequent cessation of the habitual production of a surplus population. The substitution of Lutheran ecclesiasticism in place of Roman Catholicism made no substantial difference. The Lutheran church also operated on the "same old plan of charging all that the traffic would bear." The domestic establishments of the married priesthood served the same purpose as monasticism, the purpose of "tracelessly consuming any available margin of livelihood." In the nineteenth century, however, the grip of feudalistic state and church upon the underlying population was broken to some extent.

Norway can be taken as a good illustration, negatively, of the effect of kept classes on population. Norway is too poor in resources to support a landed gentry or a similar proprietary class. Thus the natural fecundity of the people was not restricted and a surplus population could develop.

Illegitimate births are altogether in contravention of the established law and order of Holy Church. Although the people of the Scandinavian countries are sufficiently law-abiding, devoutly and abjectly Lutheran, in some parishes, according to one authority, illegitimate births have risen as high as 30 or even 35 percent of the total birth-rate. "All this in spite of the obstinate endeavours of the clergy to discourage this illicit traffic." In a footnote, Veblen elaborated this statement in a style comparable to his discussion of the Propaganda of the Faith in *Absentee Ownership*. "As Adam Smith might have expressed it, illegitimate births 'do not afford a revenue.' By reason of this disability they have come in for a negative 'prestige value,' as not having the countenance of Holy Church. Inasmuch as they are celebrated with no circumstances of publicity, they do not lend themselves to the routine of sacramental excise from which the clerics of Holy Church derive a substantial portion of their livelihood. On these, and perhaps on other grounds, illegitimate births have had the fortune to become sinful, not to say shameful. So that there comes to be about this whole traffic a certain air of reluctant fortuity and irresponsibility, such as will call to mind the 'forced movements' of lower animals. In a manner of speaking, such births may be rated as an undesigned triumph of the hormones over the proprieties; or, theologically speaking, as a triumph of the ancient injunction to 'be fruitful, and multiply, and replenish the earth,' as against those later-devised Divine Ordinances that have been found advisable in view of the Holy Fisc."

The article was rejected for publication. When asked why he wrote nothing more, Veblen said: "I am seventy years old, and I have decided not to break the Sabbath. It is such a nice Sabbath." He was well aware of the fact that it was being asked everywhere if Shaw, whose seventieth birthday was being celebrated the same year with considerable blowing of trumpets, "had anything more to say." Veblen knew that he had finished writing, but the knowledge did not make his position any more tolerable.

At seventy he was eager for discussion, and he was lonely. The irony of his position, said Storm, was that, "while he lacked the companionship he wanted, he was given a surfeit of adulation, which he did not at all appreciate. 'Could you tell me,' wrote a young disciple, 'in what house in Chicago it was that you did your early writings, and if possible in which very room?'" Such persons would come to see him, "sometimes from considerable distances, not because they had anything to say to him, but because they wanted to sit at the feet of the Master. People with ponderous works which would never be published, and with theories of the universe which had, alas, been stated many, many years ago, but totally without a sense of humour, paid him a reverence no god should merit. The meetings with them were stupid or distressing. Veblen was kind to them. He was without the defences of a public person." When former students visited him he was extremely pleased, and would regret their leaving. He had a number of loyal Stanford friends. His nephew Oswald Veblen would visit him, and he asked a former student of his own at Stanford to see Veblen now and then and report on his condition. But these men had other duties, while Veblen had nothing to do.

As the end drew on, Veblen felt extremely lonely and neglected. He thought that everyone had forgotten him, and complained that he was not getting the proper care and attention. He even drew up a new will, but he neglected to sign it. Finally he would not see even old and true friends. Davenport, teaching summer school at Stanford, left his card twice at Veblen's Stanford home, but Veblen never got in touch with him. Davenport was angry, but when he was leaving town Ardzrooni met him at the station and persuaded him to return once more.

Although business prosperity was increasing, Veblen's material fortunes were on the decline. The raisin industry collapsed and Veblen's money invested there was lost. His oil stocks were worthless. He had lent the son of a former housekeeper a large sum of money in Stanford and, as a settlement, he took over the man's ranch, but regretted it because the rent he received barely paid the taxes. His income from royalties was around $500 to $600 a year, and his former Chicago student and colleague still contributed $500 a year. Altogether this one individual contributed $8000 to Veblen's support from 1919 to 1929, according to the records of the New School for Social Research, through which the transactions were handled. Others gave varying sums from time to time while Veblen was in California. His attitude concerning money furnished a good illustration of a friend's statement that Veblen never appreciated the necessity of being understood. When he was told that a former student was going to raise some additional money as a gift for him, he remarked that it was not a bad idea. Veblen continually worried over his finances, even when it was not strictly necessary, and up to the very day of his death he was trying futilely to get his money out of the raisin industry.

Another factor contributing to Veblen's uneasy state of mind was his great desire to return East to the centre of things. A former student came to visit him in April 1928, and with her Veblen joked and laughed in quite the old way. He said that the only thing that bothered him was exhaustion, that he could do nothing without being greatly fatigued, and the doctor did not know why. He wanted to return to Washington Island, and Becky said that he had a "nostalgia" for the place. He said he was only "waiting for the clock to strike," which it would do equally well in any place. Funds were supplied him for his trip, but he did not go.

In 1929 Mitchell was asked by a publisher to prepare a volume of lengthy extracts from Veblen's work, and a suitable introductory essay. Although he was extremely busy, Mitchell considered the task a moral obligation, and he sent the introductory essay to Veblen in June 1929. Veblen replied: "I have no fault to find and no changes to make. Indeed, I should trust you farther than myself, any day, to make the right selections to reprint. . . . And, as a certain Icelandic adage says, 'It is not for me to shake my fist at my good luck.'"

During that summer he planned to return to the East, but a relative dissuaded him because of his apparent ill health. Mrs. Fisher has said that one day, while he was sitting alone with her on the ridge, Veblen declared that "he heard members of his family, long since dead, speak to him in Norwegian, as exactly and clearly as I was speaking to him then." He died on August 3, 1929. The records gave heart disease as the cause.

Veblen died on a Saturday, but announcement was not made until Monday. His stepdaughter was under a strain, and immediately after his death Ardzrooni was telegraphed for, but he could not leave at once. Both Ardzrooni and Davenport, who was in Palo Alto at the time, were at a loss as to Veblen's wishes in the matter of burial. They decided to have him cremated and scatter the ashes over the Pacific Ocean. Pallbearers included Camp, Davenport, Stuart, and another former Stanford student, Frederick Anderson of the Romance language department of Stanford. Later Ardzrooni found a piece of writing among Veblen's papers which indicated that the funeral arrangements accorded with Veblen's wishes. The note was unsigned, written in pencil probably within a week of his death: "It is also my wish, in case of death, to be cremated, if it can conveniently be done, as expeditiously and inexpensively as may be, without ritual or ceremony of any kind; that my ashes be thrown loose into the sea, or into some sizable stream running to the sea; that no tombstone, slab, epitaph, effigy, tablet, inscription, or monument of any name or nature, be set up in my memory or name in any place or at any time; that no obituary, memorial, portrait, or biography of me, nor any letters written to or by me be printed or published, or in any way reproduced, copied or circulated."

In the will dated November 1924, Veblen left Becky $10,000 and the residue to both stepdaughters. He gave a quittance in full to Orson Veblen for any sum which he owed Thorstein except any remainder of a loan of $2,500 covered by a promissory note and secured by a mortgage. However, the estate consisted for a while of what he might have called negative assets. Down to 1932 the royalties that came in were needed to pay off debts.

Veblen's associates and students were deeply stirred by his death. John Bates Clark wrote: "It is a grief to me that Veblen is with us no more," and the obituary note in *The American Economic Review* was written by J.M. Clark. Everywhere it was said that Veblen's ideas, although radical at their inception, were now coin of the realm, and even his obscurity was accounted for upon this ground. Dr. Anna Youngman, associate editor of that avowed organ of the business and financial community, *The Journal of Commerce*, wrote on the editorial page that Veblen's "own published work unfortunately suffered greatly from the misinterpretation of critics who mistook his irony for sober expressions of opinion and read into his dispassionate analyses of economic society a bias that was conspicuously absent from his spoken utterances." In an

article in *The New Republic*, Mitchell said that it had been his own
great fortune to have studied with Veblen when Veblen began writing
his important work. In *The Economic Journal*, Mitchell reminded his
readers that the only review which *The Economic Journal* had made of
Veblen's work was a notice in the issue for September 1925 of *The Theory
of the Leisure Class*, "a volume published twenty-six years earlier, and
just then reprinted for the ninth time. . . . Veblen demands much of
his readers, and not everyone who sips will have the stamina to drink."
In receiving an LL.D. degree that year from the University of Chicago,
his alma mater, Mitchell declared that when Chicago lost Veblen and
Dewey it lost the finest of its men. "There was the disturbing genius of
Thorstein Veblen—that visitor from another world, who dissected the
current commonplaces which the student had unconsciously acquired, as
if the most familiar of his daily thoughts were curious products wrought
in him by outside forces. No other such emancipator of the mind from
the subtle tyranny of circumstance has been known in social science, and
no other such enlarger of the realm of inquiry." [2]

The Nation said: "It must always be a matter of regret that the movement vigorously pushed by [Veblen's] friends a few years ago to have him
elected president of the American Economic Association . . . should
have been blocked by the regulars in that organisation. If Veblen today
looks down from some Olympian height, it is doubtless to smile at the
grip of the vested interests on the minds of some of those who devote
themselves to the impartial study of the working of those interests." John
Hobson, writing in *The Journal of Sociology*, said that Veblen "has never
received any adequate recognition of his great and original contributions
to sociology and economics in his own country." In *Wallace's Farmer*
Henry A. Wallace declared that Veblen had tried to have the Food Administration do its avowed job, but "as might be expected, he didn't get
along so very well in the Food Administration and soon retired." Wallace
added: "He was one of the first men in the United States to demonstrate
that there was such a thing as a business cycle and many of the men who
are now working with the business cycle received their original impetus
either directly or indirectly from Veblen." "His books will live on for
centuries," and in a hundred years people reading them may realise that
he was one of the few men "who knew what was going on." But "not one
farmer in a thousand ever heard of him."

A significant obituary note was written in the Jewish socialist newspaper,
The Forward, by Veblen's former colleague at the New School, Horace
M. Kallen. "The newspapers have it that Thorstein Veblen was seventy-
two years old when he died. That is probably true. But he might have
been twenty-seven or one hundred and twenty-seven for all the difference

that years seemed to make in his physical appearance and the posture of his mind. There was something unchanging and eternal about him, frail and suffering invalid though he was. His significance to the development of political economy and sociology is still to be evaluated. Very great as his influence has been both on his own contemporaries and the later generations of economists and social thinkers, the bulk of it still lies in the future. I have a shrewd suspicion that Veblenism may be to the intellectuals of the future what Marxism has been to the humanitarians of the past." Nevertheless, without Veblen such men as Dewey, said Kallen, would not have attained their great heights. "And as for the professional economists of the present generation and the fundamental aspirations of current economics, they owe to Veblen more than to any single mind of his own time."

Stephen Leacock said: "I boast in my classes that I knew Veblen," and D.R. Scott, professor of accounting at the University of Missouri, declared in the preface of his *Cultural Significance of Accounts:* "To the late Prof. Veblen, I am indebted for the viewpoint expressed in the following discussion." Mitchell reiterated in class that Veblen was still to be fully appreciated, that his influence lay in the future.

Shortly after Veblen's death a recession occurred and the greatest depression in the world's history began. At this time Veblen was remembered almost entirely for *The Theory of the Leisure Class.* Up to February 1930, the total sales of his ten books, excluding *The Laxdæla Saga,* were approximately 40,000, and over half of this was represented by *The Theory of the Leisure Class.* He was still viewed primarily as a satirist.

In the issue of *The New Republic* for October 22, 1930, Michael Gold, communist and man of letters, reviewed Thornton Wilder's work in an essay entitled "Wilder: Prophet of the Genteel Christ." Veblen, said Gold, foretold the development of the American wealthy as the greatest of all leisure classes, in 1899, "in an epoch-making book that every American critic ought to study like a Bible. In *The Theory of the Leisure Class,* he painted the hopeless course of most American culture for the next three decades. The grim, ironic prophet has been justified. Thornton Wilder is the perfect flower of the new prosperity. He has all the virtues Veblen said this leisure class would demand; the air of good breeding, the decorum, priestliness, glossy high finish as against intrinsic qualities, conspicuous inutility, caste feeling, love of the archaic, etc." Subsequently in an editorial called "The Economic Interpretation of Wilder" the editors said that "perhaps no other literary article published in *The New Republic* has ever aroused so much controversy. . . . We have received, and are still receiving, dozens of letters about it," mostly in protest. The critics of Gold and his economic interpretation seem not to have heard of Veblen, but they accepted Gold's statement of what Veblen was supposed to have said and attacked both of them. One critic, Carl Thurston, made a flank attack, however, in a manner not unlike Veblen's own procedure: "Michael Gold . . . advises American critics to study *The Theory of the Leisure Class* as a Bible. Why doesn't he do so himself? If he had ever properly digested Mr. Veblen's remarks on 'conspicuous waste,' he could never have attacked Mr. Wilder so savagely for being a poet instead of a preacher of revolution. The class without leisure has its own forms of conspicuous waste, and the habit of spitting on tulips to show the world that it prefers onions, is one of them. For Mr. Gold, it is transfigured, by its origins, into a religious rite." On December 17 *The New Republic* presented "The Final Round" and said that the controversy was hereby "called on account of darkness."

In August 1931, Lewis Mumford devoted an article to Veblen in *The New Republic*, presenting him as an authority on art. Veblen's discussion, in *The Theory of the Leisure Class*, of the canons of beauty, with particular reference to architecture, was held to be unequalled. Mumford called attention to the neglect of Veblen in the social sciences, saying that about a year previously he had examined economic and sociological journals to see whether anyone had added to the rather perfunctory appreciations that appeared soon after Veblen's death, but could not find a word about him. "A sympathetic economist explained that Veblen's economics had been displaced by the detailed analysis of the so-called statistical school, and his theories were out of the current because they did not account for the actual prosperity that had come about under unrestricted mass production after 1921." Francis Tyson of the University of Pittsburgh replied that Mumford should have gone over the files of *The New Republic*, and read in the September 4, 1929, issue, a discussion of Veblen's strange genius and great contributions "by the oustanding exponent of statistical economics, Professor Wesley C. Mitchell!"

A significant incident in the growing appreciation of Veblen was the conversion of John Cummings, who, when he wrote his review of *The Theory of the Leisure Class* in 1899, could not believe that Veblen's new art in economic writing and thinking would ever be generally accepted or would ever become popular with the man on the street. A letter by Cummings written in 1931 not only indicates that economists and the laity had caught up with the position that Howells had taken when the book was published, but it also shows how great were the differences between that position and the common-sense philosophy which prevailed in the nineties. "It was hard for me to accept him or his philosophy. It went against my grain. I was eager to find it lop-sided and unreal. . . .

My review gives good evidence that I did not at the time fairly appreciate the contribution Veblen was making to our economic and social philosophy. I have often wondered how I could have been so blind. In the years since we have all seen the accumulating evidence of the widespread influence of Veblen's analysis of social and economic behaviour, as set forth in his *Theory of the Leisure Class.* . . . I know that I should write a very different review . . . today.

"I was a product of the gay nineties. My economic thinking was in conventional terms of academic training and of the classical economists and it was difficult off-hand for me to think at all in any other terms. With Veblen one really had to learn the alphabet all over again. It is difficult for me today to appreciate how strange his new alphabet was at that time. . . . Veblen was cubistic and for the time incomprehensible." Looking back to that time Cummings doubted "if Veblen took my review of his book very seriously. . . . In my academic conventionalism I was just another interesting specimen for observation and analysis—and probably kindly commiseration. I might see the light some day. Whether I did or not was a matter of indifference to him. He had the poise and self-confidence that go with all sound scholarship. He knew he was eternally right, and if others did not know it, that was no affair of his. They would probably find out in time. . . .

"And they have found out. Today if you have friends in to dinner . . . they will probably express their appreciation in terms of *The Theory of the Leisure Class,* whether or not they know that they are doing so, and say something about the conspicuous consumption in these hard times of unemployment." In his review Cummings had declared that Veblen's propositions were those of a master of sophistical dialectics and indicated a bias. Now he said "there was . . . no personal equation whatever in his thinking. . . . His scientific work was purely objective, which is all the more extraordinary because of its purely theoretical and philosophical character. . . . His sweeping generalisations and deductive analyses were fundamentally inductions from observed facts of everyday experience."

As the depression lengthened and grew worse, and as the government was being forced to resort to such measures as the Reconstruction Finance Corporation, in aid of finance and large business, the profounder meaning of Veblen's work was given an opportunity to express itself. One of the most significant indications of this was an article by the ever-young John Dewey in the April 27, 1932, issue of *The New Republic,* entitled "The Collapse of a Romance." The article was aimed at the romantic spirit of business and received economics, as distinguished from a matter-of-fact appreciation of the irrational, uncertain foundation upon which business rests. Business is gambling, and its postulates are insecurity and uncertainty, which it thrives on and increasingly creates, in order that more business may be done. Thus the prevailing breakdown is abnormal only because normal insecurity has got out of hand to the extent that it cannot be concealed from general recognition, and the essentially romantic nature of business becomes apparent to those who have open eyes.

Although business is intrinsically a gamble in uncertainties to secure profit, although it is essentially a confidence game, the manufacture and transportation of goods are "technological operations," based on physical materials and energies. "The locomotive runs on coal and steam, not on psychical acts of 'confidence.'" These technological operations are not business, whose differentiating mark is profits, but business uses them as instruments in a game in which the trumps are held by capital. Because of the wide reach of the game the insecurity of the masses eventually spells insecurity for the holder of the trumps. Business deliberately increases the uncertainty of life. Money is supposed to be a medium of exchange, and as such it would add to the security of existence, but it is in fact "a medium for *controlling* exchange." Hence the concentrated possession of money is a means of intensifying insecurity, for to control exchange means to stop it, "to tax it, to deflect it. To create a risk and then make a profit by assuming it, is a good rule—for those who control money." But the romance of business, which violates logic and reason, is not yet exhausted, for the romantic notion prevails of introducing planning into business. "What could be more romantic than the idea of retaining business, which is the process of placing wagers on uncertainties for the sake of profit, and at the same time introducing stability and security into it?"

Stuart Chase, who had always praised Veblen, began his review of Ida Tarbell's life of Owen Young, in *The Saturday Review of Literature* in June 1932, with the statement: "Thorstein Veblen, the greatest economist this country has produced, died in obscurity a few years ago. Day by day as the depression deepens, the soundness of his analysis, the awful import of his prophecy, becomes more apparent. It is a pity that he should not have been spared to witness, a faint, sardonic smile upon his lips, the brood of black ravens which have come to roost." Chase declared that he had "never forgotten" the distinction between business and industry from which Veblen deduced the business cycle and a general shortage of purchasing power, and he wondered what Veblen would have made of Young, the lawyer executive of General Electric.

The shift in the type of literary spokesman for Veblen is significant. The conservatism of Howells had given way to the Jeffersonian liberalism of Hackett, and was now giving way to a liberalism of the left, signified by John Chamberlain in his popular and epoch-marking *Farewell to Reform*. In this book Chamberlain declared that Veblen died "at the crest of a period of 'progress,' and at a time when men were 'deducing' from the spectacle of a 'New Era' and the antics of the stock market, an eternal plateau of prosperity. Few there were to do him reverence at his death. But now he shines like a star of the first magnitude." As the state of affairs continued to get worse, it was not uncommon to hear it said that Veblen would now have had the greatest laboratory experiment of his experience to observe.

In the fall of 1932 Veblen's name flashed into front-page news. In August the newspapers of New York carried an account of a solution for the depression given them supposedly by Howard Scott. The *New York Herald Tribune*, under the headline, "10-Year Survey Points to End of 'Price System,' " told of the work of a group known as "Technocracy," who had been conducting an "energy survey" of North America at Columbia University, under the direction of Howard Scott, consultant engineer, and under the auspices of the university's department of industrial engineering and the Architects' Emergency Committee of New York. The article said that Steinmetz and Veblen had been members of the group, and it named a list of members which included, of the old group, Bassett Jones and Ackerman. For ten years they had been at work, quietly and without publicity, tracing the industrial and social development of the United States over a period of a hundred years, and had concluded that the log-cabin era of business was out of date and that the obviously obsolescent price system must be superseded by a new order of technology. The social system was being forced into a revision by the impact of modern technology upon the price system. Technological efficiency had so greatly increased that unemployment must also increase steadily. At the same time the debt structure against the material equipment had reached a fantastic figure, resulting in a breakdown of the economic structure. Bonds had been floated that would not mature for hundreds of years, and interest was still being paid on debts contracted for equipment long out of existence. Such manœuvres as those of the Reconstruction Finance Corporation were futile. Inflation through pumping additional credit into the system might seem a palliative, but in the nature of the case it could only aggravate the situation eventually. Such measures as a five-day week and low-cost housing would have the same effect. The group predicted 20,000,000 unemployed within two years. Scott was quoted as saying: "We now regard it as our social duty to do our best to disseminate this information in answer to the growing demands of a public which has realised that none of its leaders of the past is equipped with knowledge adequate to cope with the present dilemma." He spoke of expanding the group immediately to include leaders from all the sciences, technical and humanistic, and he declared that price should be replaced by "energy determinants" as a measuring rod.

Immediately afterwards every corner of the land was discussing technocracy, although the expected study had not appeared. Press and radio gave it wide publicity. Schools of business and teachers' colleges began preaching about technocracy. Scott was eagerly sought to address businessmen, and his meetings were sponsored by leading captains of industry. His portrait appeared in *Business Week*, and *The Nation*, on the basis of the newspaper story, declared that "Technocracy's report is the first step toward a genuine revolutionary philosophy for America."

Although Veblen was mentioned only as a member of the old group, along with Steinmetz, he soon took the centre of the stage. For obvious reasons the newspaper story immediately suggested *The Engineers and the Price System*, and newspapers began speaking of this book as the basis for the philosophy of the movement. Press and magazine articles began to declare that "Thorstein Veblen is the theoretical founder of Technocracy." The publishers readvertised the book and it became a best seller, with an average sale of 150 copies a week. English instructors who had never read Mencken because he was supposed to be radical, now heard of Veblen. Wall Street gentlemen asked bookstore dealers to secure for them all of Veblen's works. One magazine account said that "Howard Scott is not the only person that the Technocracy furore has lifted from obscurity to fame. An old man named Thorstein Veblen who died in 1929, and whose works were read previously only by the intelligentsia, would be astonished if he were to learn that his name is on everyone's lips today."

In fact, Veblen began to receive too much attention. The technocrats in some cases declared that they had nothing to do with Veblen, and in other cases that Veblen had received his ideas from Scott. Thus Harold Rugg of Teachers College of Columbia University, who was one of the group, after calling Veblen one of the most distinguished American students of the social sciences, declared in his *The Great Technology* that the articles making up *The Engineers and the Price System* were influenced by Scott. The pamphlet on technocracy, published by the technocrats, even contained a special two-page note on the matter of priority. "There has been much discussion," it said, "concerning the origin of the body of ideas for which the term Technocracy now stands. Speculation concerning this point has focused attention upon the work of Thorstein Veblen as the source of inspiration, with particular reference to *The Engineers and the Price System*, as the animating force. Such conclusions are quite contrary to the facts." Veblen's book was written after contact with Scott, and moreover Veblen "indulges in extrapolations that are at wide variance with the work accomplished by Technocracy." Although Scott's published statements are of a later date than those of Veblen there is no question as to "the complete independence of the two men and their theories. . . . You cannot state Scott's theory in terms of Veblenian formulations, nor can you express Veblen's economic theory in terms of Scott's theory of energy determinants." It was admitted, however, that the discussions of the two men on price and credit were practically the same. Veblen had come to his conclusions by hacking his way through the preconceptions of economic science, while Scott found his direction by way of physical science. But in establishing their own independence the technocrats could not avoid Veblen's rhetoric. "The body of ideas for which Technocracy acts as spokesman, is seemingly foreshadowed in the recent drift of modern common sense, as it has gradually taken form under the impact of physical science and technology. Veblen was caught in that drift and he gave it both acceleration and direction. Scott likewise was caught in it; but being free of the preconceptions of economic science, he was able to turn his knowledge of physical science, to bear directly upon the problem of the physical operations of a social mechanism that had already passed under the dominating control of science and technology."

There were good reasons for differentiating the two movements, for, as the fame of Veblen increased, the difficulties of the technocrats rose with it. It would have been better for them not to have mentioned Veblen's name. His subversive doctrines were pointed out, particularly the memorandum on a Soviet of Technicians, and Allen Raymond, a reporter on the *New York Herald Tribune*, caused no little trouble by a series of articles and a book on the matter. "Shortly after the World War," he said, "a group of persons led by Thorstein Veblen, economist and revolutionary, sometimes called the 'bad boy' of economics, began to meet in New York City. In those times it was considered that Veblen, a man of international reputation, was the leader of this group." Scott, Ackerman, and Jones were under the influence of Veblen. Ackerman had told the reporter to read *The Engineers and the Price System* to understand technocracy, and after reading it the reporter declared that it was "a savagely ironic attack on the management of industry by representatives of the owners, followed by the perfectly serious proposal that the engineers who constitute the 'general staff' of modern technological industry, form a Soviet, educate the public by gradually developed research and publicity" to understand those defects in the capitalist order which Veblen considered an abomination. At the proper time the engineers would lead the forces of labour in seizing control of the industrial processes and abolishing property rights in the pursuit of profit. That is, the conclusions of the book are that the country would benefit by the overthrow of capitalism and by the establishment of control in the hands of a Soviet of Technicians. The personnel of the group today, declared the reporter, is essentially as it was when Veblen wrote the book, and the energy tables which are being prepared are doubtless those called for by Veblen as preparatory work for the revolutionary overturn. As long as Scott is the prophet and leader of Technocracy, all of its conclusions as well as its data are open to suspicion.[3]

It began to be generally asked whether Scott's group was preparing seriously for their Revolution of the Engineers and whether it dared to follow Veblen's lead. Even *The Nation* took this question seriously and proposed that technocracy submit its plans and claims to a committee it had chosen of scientists and economists. In January 1933, in an open letter to Scott, *The Nation* declared, however, that "Technocracy has performed a genuine service by focusing public interest on the two central problems of capitalist society—machines and money. Unless the present system can give the people jobs and the means to buy the essentials of life, it is headed for drastic change. Your survey, more than any other economic research in recent American history, has captured the attention of the country. It has dramatised the problems involved in the displacement of men by machines and the inadequacy of the present system of currency and credit for balancing production and distribution." Learned societies and organisations set up investigating bodies. As yet the technocrats had not presented their detailed survey, data and plans.

George Soule, in *The New Republic,* asked whether the movement was "Good Medicine or a Bed Time Story," and concluded it was the latter. He told the story of what had taken place since the breakup of the group in 1921. "Its centre is Howard Scott, who combines vehemence, ingenuity, and assurance. He began to . . . collect adherents back in 1921, when as at present there was much talk of the imminent breakdown of capitalism." His group then was called the Technical Alliance, and "was supposed to be collecting information from the strategic places in every industry against the day, when, as Thorstein Veblen predicted, the rule of the businessman would welter in the general confusion and the engineer would be called upon to run things in alliance with labour. But the day did not come, most of the adherents turned their attention to other pursuits. . . . With the flowering of the present depression, part of the old group coagulated, attracted new members, found a refuge in the Engineering Department of Columbia University. . . . In the meantime, Scott had begun to use the name. Then came the publicity in newspapers and magazines, and the growth of a popular following." Harold Ward, a member of the group, in attempting to reply to Soule, presented the tenets of the movement in the customary vague fashion and added, "all of which, to the shoulder-shrugging erudite, will seem but an echo of Thorstein Veblen, whose little volume on *Engineers and the Price System* (as clearly stated recently by Frederick L. Ackerman . . .) was written *as a result* of many long discussions with Scott twelve years ago." His statement brought an immediate response from one who signed himself a "Veblenite," declaring that "hanging in the air like that, the statement carries with it the imputation that Veblen couldn't have written the book without Scott's aid and stimulus. But the distinctions between industry and business that give *The Engineers and the Price System* its basic value are all in Veblen's *The Theory of Business Enterprise*, published in 1904, and are, indeed, implicit in *The Theory of the Leisure Class* (1899). Veblen's amazing insight deserves better at the hands of Mr. Ward. If Technocracy proves to be a bubble, there is danger of Veblen being pricked with it—which would be a real misfortune."

Before much of 1933 had passed, technocracy proved indeed to be a bubble, as anyone acquainted with the first movement might have predicted. Its popularity indicated not only the power of publicity, but also the depressed state of the public mind. Veblen was not pricked with it, however. As the result of an essentially accidental connexion, his name reached and held a higher position than it had ever held at any time during his lifetime.

Henry Wallace, about to become Secretary of Agriculture, said that Veblen "more than any other economist in his day saw the inevitability of many of the things that are now happening. . . . He planted many seeds which will inevitably have a profound effect on the future of our nation." Even Bukharin, leading theoretician of Soviet Russia, paid his respects to Veblen, even though he disagreed with Veblen's programme. In his report on "The World Crisis, U.S.S.R., and Technology," read before the Fifth All-Union Congress of Engineers and Technicians in 1932, and published in *Pravda*, Bukharin discussed two solutions for the crisis offered by the "bourgeois ideologists." There is no reference in the report to technocracy. The first solution is the one suggested by a number of Italian, German, French, English, and American engineers and economists. Thomas Nixon Carver is mentioned as the American representative of the group, and is disposed of. The second solution is that suggested by Veblen. "The literature of the Veblenian school must be regarded as an interesting phenomenon. Contrary to the views of other engineers and economists, Veblen holds that the capitalists are parasites, and that the real leaders of industry are the engineers. He puts forth an original concept as a guide for the future, i.e., the idea of engineerocracy, the rule of the engineers. . . . But even this concept could not bear any criticism notwithstanding the fact that it stands apart from the usually suggested remedies. For is it possible in reality that the capitalist should call upon the chief-engineer and tell him: 'I'll go to the Sahara Desert for an airing in accordance with the medicine prescribed by Krzhizhanovsky [a leading Soviet engineer and chairman of the State Planning Commission]'? He would not go there voluntarily even for the sake of pleasing the engineer. He must be overthrown. But even an American engineer (if he dared to make such an attempt) could not overthrow capitalism without the leadership of the working class. Hence, the first prerequisite: a united front between the engineers and the working class. [The engineer] may attempt to betray the worker, but when the latter reaches the stage of development when he is capable of overthrowing the capitalistic system, not even the most expert technician will be able to deceive him. Therefore, the way out lies not in engineerocracy but in the dictatorship of the proletariat."

In the January 1933 issue of *The World Tomorrow*, McAlister Coleman, writing under the title "Veblen Comes Back," said that Veblen's books were *verboten* in socialist libraries because Veblen had pointed out over twenty-five years before that the Social Democratic party in Germany was a party not of revolution but of reform, and was destined to become innocuous. The subsequent course of events in the party, said Coleman, has justified Veblen's prediction. In reference to the fact that a biography of Veblen was being written, he said in conclusion that "there could be no more appropriate time than this for the telling of the life story of a man who wrote so penetrating a biography of the entire capitalist system and incidentally did so much to write its eventual obituary."

With the declaring of the national bank holiday in March 1933, Veblen's prediction in *The Engineers and the Price System* and in *Absentee Ownership* also seemed to be justified. *Imperial Germany* seemed to have foretold the fortune of Germany and other European nations in every important detail: the breakdown of the Social Democratic party in Germany, the sweep of Hitlerism, the collapse of the treaty and of the covenant of the League of Nations, European debt defaults *de jure*. Japan seemed to be fitting itself to Veblen's analysis, and business enterprise throughout the western world was being faced with Veblen's two alternatives in the form of fascism and communism. His statement that the solution for the drift to the industrial republic was a process of increasing habituation to warlike enterprise was being borne out in an ever-increasing race in armaments, converting the entire world into an armed camp on a scale far greater than before the World War.

In the United States, with the establishment of the N.R.A. and similar controlling bodies, Veblen's alternatives—a feudalistic regime or a radical new deal—seemed to be battling for primacy. The Senate investigation into modern corporation finance revealed what Veblen, as early as "Some Neglected Points in the Theory of Socialism," had declared to be the logical concomitants of modern business. What had been considered then the personal idiocyncrasies of Veblen were now accepted as the impersonal inevitabilities of modern emulative enterprise. Jerome Frank, the general counsel for the A.A.A., wanted to start a Veblen club in Washington. Virgil Jordan, president of the National Industrial Conference Board, has said that Veblen's "influence upon the present economic, political, and social situation and upon current governmental policies has probably been greater than that of any other American thinker. No one can fully understand what is happening today in this country without knowing something about Veblen and his thought."

The influence of the rhetoric of *Absentee Ownership* was vividly illustrated at the 1933 Conference for Progressive Political Action, which included representatives of farm organisations, unemployed leagues, trade unions, radical and progressive parties, technocratic clubs, teacher and student organisations. According to an account in *The New Republic*, headed "A New Radical Party," Thomas R. Amlie, Norwegian-American of Wisconsin, former member of Congress, and product of the La Follette School of practical politics, solidified and electrified the delegates by an analysis of the economic debacle which was "Marxian without being obscure or doctrinaire." His central point was a proposed twenty-second amendment to the American Constitution, providing that "the absentee ownership of any industrially useful article by any person or persons not habitually employed in the industrial use thereof, is hereby disallowed within the United States." All laws in conflict are "hereby declared inoperative." Congress is to set up machinery for "the administration of said property in which absentee ownership has been cancelled for the common welfare of the people of the United States." The amendment, said Amlie, would not disturb any person's possession of his home, personal effects, or farm if worked by himself. "It would leave to be scientifically administered the natural resources and productive machinery of the nation for the benefit of all the people, by gearing productive capacity to consumptive capacity, and would result in a universal standard of living such as is now only enjoyed by the rich."

As 1933 closed, Ernest Sutherland Bates, in a biographical sketch in *Scribner's*, could say of Veblen, "a lone wolf, with all the pack against him, he had one powerful ally, Time," which has finally justified him. "Could he now observe his posthumous renown it is safe to say that he would regard it with his wonted irony." All his contemporaries are forgotten, and "out of an entire generation of political and economic thinkers, he alone produced a body of thought that lives on."

In 1934 there was a veritable deluge of popular books in which Veblen was given a prominent place. Mumford, in his *Technics and Civilisation*, acknowledged his debt to Veblen, along with Geddes and Branford, and James Rorty dedicated to Veblen his book on advertising. Critics of Stuart Chase's *The Economy of Abundance* asked what it contained outside of Veblen. More than one reviewer of Matthew Josephson's *Robber Barons* declared that its foundations were in Veblen.

Veblenism was heard even within the sacred precincts of the United States Senate. When Rexford Guy Tugwell was being quizzed by a senatorial committee as to his fitness to become Under Secretary of Agriculture, he was asked to explain the meaning of the phrase "anthropomorphic sequence in human existence," which had appeared in one of his articles. The inquisitors suspected that it had something to do with destroying the established law and order, and with Tugwell's declaration that the "anthropomorphic interpretation of events" was very plain, they understood no more than they had before. They would have been more enlightened, although, perhaps, no less disturbed, if they had gone to the fountain head of the idea in Veblen's discussion in *The Theory of the Leisure Class* of the devout observances that make up modern capitalism.

John Chamberlain, in his daily review column in *The New York Times*, made frequent reference to Veblen and used him as a baseline for criticism. In 1934 Laughlin died, and according to an account in *The Journal of Political Economy*, his outstanding intellectual achievement was that he had brought Veblen to Chicago. Members of the law school faculty of Yale University organised a movement to raise funds for a portrait of one of Yale's most distinguished alumni. Those who saw only irony in this belated honour overlooked the fact that Veblen's quizzical expression was no less imperturbable in a portrait hanging in one of Yale's Gothic structures than it had been when Veblen as a student walked unnoticed through Yale's complacent quadrangles.

Between February 1, 1930, and September 1, 1934, approximately 5000 copies of Veblen's books were sold. *The Engineers and the Price System* accounts for over half of this number, and *The Place of Science in Modern Civilisation* was second. *The Theory of the Leisure Class* came third, with fewer than 500 copies, but it is this that seems destined to remain Veblen's most popular book. In September, 1934, it was issued in a cheap edition by Modern Library, with an introduction by Stuart Chase.

In the same month appeared a collection entitled *Essays in our Chang-*

ing Order, which contained almost all of Veblen's important papers not hitherto collected. The variety is greater than in *The Place of Science,* but as in that volume every essay and editorial it contains, with the single exception of "Kant's Critique of Judgment," is built around Veblen's fundamental contrast. His basic thesis is the same, whether his subject be " 'The Overproduction Fallacy,' " or "The Economic Theory of Woman's Dress," whether it be "Between Bolshevism and War" or "Economic Theory in the Calculable Future." Veblen's essays, like his books, are different means of expressing the same argument, rather than different fields of inquiry. Change and development there were in Veblen's ideas, but his guide lines remained always those of a sophisticated, sceptical, Norwegian agrarian thrown into contact with the impersonal calculus of the credit economy as it took form in modern corporation finance.

Another cycle in Veblen's life history is now in the making, and the question as to the exact nature of his influence remains still to be answered. Edgar Lee Masters' statement that Veblen "certainly set up an ironic shout and shot the system with fireworks" might well be accepted by many of Veblen's followers, but the nature of the shout is so alien and so involuted, its overtones are so misleading, that men of widely conflicting views claim equally the authority of Veblen. Has his thinking actually become so assimilated in prevailing common sense that, as one scholar has said, "there would be no point in republishing *The Theory of the Leisure Class,*" or is he so far ahead of his time that the best of the economists, as another scholar has declared, are only beginning to catch up with him? Is the vital and profound meaning of *The Theory of the Leisure Class* taking precedence of its satirical appearance? The answers rest with the future.

BIBLIOGRAPHY OF THORSTEIN VEBLEN

1882. "J. S. Mill's Theory of the Taxation of Land," Johns Hopkins University, *University Circulars*, Feb., p. 176.

1884. "Kant's Critique of Judgment," [1] *Journal of Speculative Philosophy*, July, pp. 260–274.

1891. "Some Neglected Points in the Theory of Socialism," [2] *Annals of the American Academy of Political and Social Science*, Nov., pp. 345–362.

1892. "Böhm-Bawerk's Definition of Capital and the Source of Wages," [1] *Quarterly Journal of Economics*, Jan., pp. 247–252.

"'The Overproduction Fallacy,'" [1] *Quarterly Journal of Economics*, July, pp. 484–492.

"The Price of Wheat Since 1867," *Journal of Political Economy*, Dec., pp. 68–103 and appendix pp. 156–161.

1893. Review of Thomas Kirkup's *A History of Socialism*, in *Journal of Political Economy*, March, pp. 300–302.

Review of Otto Warschauer's *Geschichte des Socialismus und Communismus im 19. Jahrhundert*, in *Journal of Political Economy*, March, p. 302.

"The Food Supply and the Price of Wheat," *Journal of Political Economy*, June, pp. 365–379.

Review of B.H. Baden-Powell's *The Land-Systems of British India*, in *Journal of Political Economy*, Dec., pp. 112–115.

1894. Review of Karl Kautsky's *Der Parlamentarismus und die Volksgesetzgebung und die Socialdemokratie*, in *Journal of Political Economy*, March, pp. 312–314.

Review of William E. Bear's *A Study of Small Holdings*, in *Journal of Political Economy*, March, pp. 325–326.

"The Army of the Commonweal," [1] *Journal of Political Economy*, June, pp. 456–461.

Review of Joseph Stammhammer's *Bibliographie des Socialismus und Communismus*, in *Journal of Political Economy*, June, pp. 474–475.

Review of Russell M. Garnier's *History of the English Landed Interest* (*Modern Period*), in *Journal of Political Economy*, June, pp. 475–477.

Review of Émile Levasseur's "L'Agriculture aux États-Unis," in *Journal of Political Economy*, Aug., pp. 592–596.

"The Economic Theory of Woman's Dress," [1] *Popular Science Monthly*, Nov., pp. 198–205.

1895. Review of Robert Flint's *Socialism*, in *Journal of Political Economy*, March, pp. 247–252.

The Science of Finance, translation of Gustav Cohn's *System der Finanzwissenschaft*.

1896. Review of Karl Marx's *Misère de la Philosophie*, in *Journal of Political Economy*, Dec., pp. 97–98.

[1] Republished in *Essays in Our Changing Order*.
[2] Republished in *Place of Science in Modern Civilisation and Other Essays*.

Review of Enrico Ferri's *Socialisme et Science Positive*, in *Journal of Political Economy*, Dec., pp. 98–103.

1897. Review of Richard Calwer's *Einführung in den Socialismus*, in *Journal of Political Economy*, March, pp. 270–272.

Review of G. de Molinari's *La Viriculture—Ralentissement de la Population—Dégénérescence—Causes et Remèdes*, in *Journal of Political Economy*, March, pp. 273–275.

Review of Antonio Labriola's *Essais sur la conception matérialiste de l'histoire*, in *Journal of Political Economy*, June, pp. 390–391.

Review of Werner Sombart's *Sozialismus und soziale Bewegung im 19. Jahrhundert*, in *Journal of Political Economy*, June, pp. 391–392.

Review of N. Ch. Bunge's *Esquisses de littérature politico-économique*, in *Journal of Political Economy*, Dec., pp. 126–128.

Review of Max Lorenz's *Die Marxistische Socialdemokratie*, in *Journal of Political Economy*, Dec., pp. 136–137.

1898. Review of Gustav Schmoller's *Über einige Grundfragen der Socialpolitik und der Volkswirtschaftslehre*, in *Journal of Political Economy*, June, pp. 416–419.

Review of William H. Mallock's *Aristocracy and Evolution: A Study of the Rights, the Origin and the Social Functions of the Wealthier Classes*, in *Journal of Political Economy*, June, pp. 430–435.

"Why Is Economics Not an Evolutionary Science?" [2] *Quarterly Journal of Economics*, July, pp. 373–397.

"The Instinct of Workmanship and the Irksomeness of Labour," [1] *American Journal of Sociology*, Sept., pp. 187–201.

Review of Turgot, *Reflections on the Formation and the Distribution of Riches*, in *Journal of Political Economy*, Sept., pp. 575–576.

"The Beginnings of Ownership," [1] *American Journal of Sociology*, Nov., pp. 352–365.

"The Barbarian Status of Women," [1] *American Journal of Sociology*, Jan., pp. 503–514.

1899. *The Theory of the Leisure Class: an Economic Study of the Evolution of Institutions*; title changed in 1912 to *The Theory of the Leisure Class: an Economic Study of Institutions*.

"The Preconceptions of Economic Science," [2] *Quarterly Journal of Economics*, Jan., pp. 121–150; July, pp. 396–426; Jan., 1900, pp. 240–269.

Review of Simon Patten's *Development of English Thought*, in *Annals of the American Academy of Political and Social Science*, July, pp. 125–131.

"Mr. Cummings's Strictures on *The Theory of the Leisure Class*," [1] *Journal of Political Economy*, Dec., pp. 106–117.

1900. Review of Sir William Crooks' *The Wheat Problem, Revised, with an Answer to Various Critics*, in *Journal of Political Economy*, March, pp. 284–286.

Review of Arnold Fischer's *Die Entstehung des socialen Problems*, in *Journal of Political Economy*, March, pp. 286–287.

Review of Paul Lafargue's *Pamphlets socialistes: Le droit à la paresse; La*

[1] Republished in *Essays in Our Changing Order.*
[2] Republished in *Place of Science in Modern Civilisation and Other Essays.*

religion du capital; L'appetit vendu; Pie IX au paradis, in *Journal of Political Economy,* March, pp. 287–288.

Review of G. Tarde's *Social Laws; An Outline of Sociology,* in *Journal of Political Economy,* Sept., pp. 562–563.

Review of Basil A. Bauroff's *The Impending Crisis; Conditions Resulting from the Concentration of Wealth in the United States,* in *Journal of Political Economy,* Dec., pp. 159–160.

"Industrial and Pecuniary Employments," [2] *Publications of the American Economic Association,* Series 3, 1901, pp. 190–235.

1901. *Science and the Workingmen,* a translation of *Die Wissenschaft und die Arbeiter* by Ferdinand Lassalle, republished by German Publication Society in *The German Classics,* 1914, vol. 10.

"Gustav Schmoller's Economics," [2] *Quarterly Journal of Economics,* Nov., pp. 69–93.

1902. "Arts and Crafts," [1] *Journal of Political Economy,* Dec., pp. 108–111.

Review of Jules Gernaert's and Vte. de Herbais de Thun's *Associations industrielles et commerciales: Fédérations—Ententes partielles—Syndicats —Cartels—Comptoirs—Affiliations—Trusts,* in *Journal of Political Economy,* Dec., pp. 130–131.

Review of G. Tarde's *Psychologie économique,* in *Journal of Political Economy,* Dec., pp. 146–148.

1903. "The Use of Loan Credit in Modern Business," *Decennial Publications of the University of Chicago,* Series I, No. 4, pp. 31–50, republished without substantial change in *The Theory of Business Enterprise.*

Review of Werner Sombart's *Der moderne Kapitalismus,* in *Journal of Political Economy,* March, pp. 300–305.

Review of T.H. Aschehoug's *Værdi—og Prillærens Historie,* in *Journal of Political Economy,* March, p. 306.

Review of Maurice Lair's *L'Impérialisme allemand,* in *Journal of Political Economy,* March, p. 306.

Review of J.A. Hobson's *Imperialism: a Study,* in *Journal of Political Economy,* March, pp. 311–319.

Review of Brooks Adams's *The New Empire,* in *Journal of Political Economy,* March, pp. 314–315.

Review of Theodore E. Burton's *Financial Crises and Periods of Industrial and Commercial Depression,* in *Journal of Political Economy,* March, pp. 324–326.

Review of Lester F. Ward's *Pure Sociology: a Treatise Concerning the Origin and Spontaneous Development of Society,* in *Journal of Political Economy,* Sept., pp. 655–656.

Review of Ludwig Pohle's *Bevölkerungsbewegung, Kapitalbildung und periodische Wirtschaftskrisen,* in *Journal of Political Economy,* Sept., pp. 656–657.

Review of S. Tschierschky's *Kartell und Trust: Vergleichende Untersuchungen über dem Wesen und Bedeutung,* in *Journal of Political Economy,* Sept., pp. 657–658.

---

[1] Republished in *Essays in Our Changing Order.*
[2] Republished in *Place of Science in Modern Civilisation and Other Essays.*

1904. "An Early Experiment in Trusts," [2] *Journal of Political Economy*, March, pp. 270–279.

The Theory of Business Enterprise.

Review of Adam Smith's *An Inquiry into the Nature and Causes of the Wealth of Nations*, in *Journal of Political Economy*, Dec., p. 136.

Review of Francis W. Hirst's *Adam Smith*, in *Journal of Political Economy*, Dec., pp. 136–137.

Review of Jacob Streider's *Zur Genesis des modernen Kapitalismus*, in *Journal of Political Economy*, Dec., pp. 120–122.

1905. Review of Robert Francis Harper's *The Code of Hammurabi, King of Babylon about 2250 B.C.*, in *Journal of Political Economy*, March, pp. 319–320.

"Credit and Prices," [1] *Journal of Political Economy*, June, pp. 460–472.

1906. "The Place of Science in Modern Civilisation," [2] *American Journal of Sociology*, March, pp. 585–609.

"Professor Clark's Economics," [2] *Quarterly Journal of Economics*, Feb., pp. 147–195.

"Socialist Economics of Karl Marx and His Followers," [2] *Quarterly Journal of Economics*, Aug., pp. 578–595; Feb. 1907, pp. 299–322.

1907. Review of Sidney A. Reeve's *The Cost of Competition, An Effort at the Understanding of Familiar Facts*, in *Yale Review*, May, pp. 92–95.

"Fisher's Capital and Income," [1] *Political Science Quarterly*, March, pp. 112–128.

1908. "The Evolution of the Scientific Point of View," [2] *University of California Chronicle*, May, pp. 396–416.

"On the Nature of Capital," [2] *Quarterly Journal of Economics*, Aug., pp. 517–542; Nov., pp. 104–136.

1909. "Fisher's Rate of Interest," [1] *Political Science Quarterly*, June, pp. 296–303.

Review of Albert Schatz's *L'individualisme économique et sociale: ses origines—son évolution—ses formes contemporaires*, in *Journal of Political Economy*, June, pp. 378–379.

"The Limitations of Marginal Utility," [2] *Journal of Political Economy*, Nov., pp. 620–636.

1910. "Christian Morals and the Competitive System," [1] *International Journal of Ethics*, Jan., pp. 168–185.

"As to a Proposed Inquiry into Baltic and Cretan Antiquities," memorandum submitted to Carnegie Institution of Washington, published in *American Journal of Sociology*, Sept. 1933, pp. 237–241.

"The Mutation Theory, the Blond Race, and the Aryan Culture," paper submitted to Carnegie Institution of Washington and later elaborated into the two papers following:

1913. "The Mutation Theory and the Blond Race," [2] *Journal of Race Development*, April, pp. 491–507.

"The Blond Race and the Aryan Culture," [2] *University of Missouri Bulletin, Science Series*, Vol. 2, No. 3, April, pp. 39–57.

1914. *The Instinct of Workmanship and the State of the Industrial Arts.*

---

[1] Republished in *Essays in Our Changing Order.*
[2] Republished in *Place of Science in Modern Civilisation and Other Essays.*

1915. "The Opportunity of Japan,"[1] *Journal of Race Development*, July, pp. 23–38; Review of Werner Sombart's *Der Bourgeois: zur Geistesgeschichte des modernen Wirtschaftsmenschen* in *Journal of Political Economy*, Oct. pp. 846–848.

Imperial Germany and the Industrial Revolution.

1916. Review of Maurice Millioud's *The Ruling Caste and Frenzied Trade in Germany*, in *Journal of Political Economy*, Dec., pp. 1019–1020.

1917. "Another German Apologist," review of *England, Its Political Organisation and Development and the War Against Germany*, by Eduard Meyer in *Dial*, April 19, pp. 344–345.

An Inquiry into the Nature of Peace and the Terms of its Perpetuation.

"The Japanese Lose Hopes for Germany,"[1] letter to *New Republic*, June 30, pp. 246–247.

"Suggestions Touching the Working Program of an Inquiry into the Prospective Terms of Peace,"[1] memorandum submitted to the House Inquiry, through Walter Lippmann, Dec., published in *Political Science Quarterly*, June 1932, pp. 186–189.

"An Outline of a Policy for the Control of the 'Economic Penetration' of Backward Countries and of Foreign Investments,"[1] memorandum for House Inquiry published in *Political Science Quarterly*, June 1932, pp. 189–203.

1918. "On the General Principles of a Policy of Reconstruction," *Journal of the National Institute of Social Sciences*, April, pp. 37–46; republished in part as

"A Policy of Reconstruction,"[1] *New Republic*, April 13, pp. 318–320.

Report ad interim to Raymond Pearl on trip through prairie states in behalf of statistical division of Food Administration published in *American Economic Review*, Sept. 1933, pp. 478–479.

"Passing of National Frontiers,"[1] *Dial*, April 25, pp. 387–390.

"Using the I.W.W. to Harvest Grain,"[1] memorandum for Statistical Division of Food Administration, published in *Journal of Political Economy*, Dec. 1932, pp. 796–807.

"A Schedule of Prices for the Staple Foodstuffs,"[1] memorandum for Statistical Division of Food Administration, published in *Southwestern Social Science Quarterly*, March, 1933, pp. 372–377.

"Menial Servants during the Period of the War,"[1] *Public*, May 11, pp. 595–599.

"The War and Higher Learning,"[1] *Dial*, July 18, pp. 45–49.

The Higher Learning in America, A Memorandum on the Conduct of Universities by Business Men.

"Farm Labour and the Country Towns," memorandum for the Statistical Division of the Food Administration and published in an elaborated form as:

"Farm Labour for the Period of the War,"[1] *Public*, July 13, pp. 882–885; July 20, pp. 918–922; July 27, pp. 947–952; Aug. 3, pp. 981–985.

"The Modern Point of View and the New Order," *Dial*, Oct. 19, pp. 289–293; Nov. 2, pp. 349–354; Nov. 16, pp. 409–414; Nov. 30, pp. 482–488; Dec. 14, pp. 543–549; Dec. 28, pp. 605–611; Jan. 11, 1919; pp. 19–24; Jan. 25, pp. 75–82. Republished as:

---

[1] Republished in *Essays in Our Changing Order.*

1919. *The Vested Interests and the State of the Industrial Arts;* title changed in 1920 to *The Vested Interests and the Common Man.*

"Bolshevism Is a Menace—to Whom?" [1] *Dial*, Feb. 22, pp. 174–179.

"The Intellectual Pre-eminence of Jews in Modern Europe," [1] *Political Science Quarterly*, March, pp. 33–42.

"On the Nature and Uses of Sabotage," [3] *Dial*, April 5, pp. 341–346.

"Bolshevism Is a Menace to the Vested Interests," editorial, *Dial*, April 5, pp. 360–361.

"Sabotage," editorial, *Dial*, April 5, p. 363.

"Congressional Sabotage," editorial, *Dial*, April 5, p. 363.

"Immanuel Kant on Perpetual Peace," [1] editorial, *Dial*, May 3, p. 469.

"Peace," [1] *Dial*, May 17, pp. 485–487.

"The Captains of Finance and the Engineers," [3] *Dial*, June 14, pp. 599–606.

"*Panem et Circenses*," [1] editorial, *Dial*, June 14, p. 609.

"The Industrial System and the Captains of Industry," [3] *Dial*, May 31, pp. 552–557.

" 'Open Covenants Openly Arrived At' [1] and the Elder Statesmen," editorial, *Dial*, July 12, pp. 25–26.

"A World Safe for the Vested Interests," [1] editorial, *Dial*, July 12, p. 26.

"The Red Terror—At Last It Has Come to America," editorial, *Dial*, Sept. 6, p. 205.

"The Red Terror and the Vested Interests," editorial, *Dial*, Sept. 6, p. 206.

"Bolshevism and the Vested Interests in America," [3] *Dial*, Oct. 4, pp. 296–301; Oct. 18, 339–346; Nov. 1, 323–380.

"The Twilight Peace of the Armistice," [1] editorial, *Dial*, Nov. 15, p. 443.

The Place of Science in Modern Civilisation and Other Essays.

1920. Review of Keynes's *Economic Consequences of the Peace*,[1] in *Political Science Quarterly*, Sept., pp. 467–472.

"Wire Barrage," memorandum printed in second edition of *Essays in Our Changing Order* (1964).

1921. *The Engineers and the Price System.*
"Between Bolshevism and War," [1] *Freeman*, May 25, pp. 248–251.

1922. "Dementia Præcox," [1] *Freeman*, June 21, pp. 344–347.

1923. "The Captain of Industry," [4] *Freeman*, April 18, pp. 127–132.
"The Timber Lands and Oil Fields," [4] *Freeman*, May 23, pp. 248–250; May 30, pp. 272–274.

"The Independent Farmer," [4] *Freeman*, June 13, pp. 321–324.

"The Country Town," [4] *Freeman*, July 11, pp. 417–420; July 18, pp. 440–443.

Absentee Ownership and Business Enterprise in Recent Times; the Case of America.

1925. "Economic Theory in the Calculable Future," [1] *American Economic Review*, March, Supplement, pp. 48–55.

The Laxdæla Saga, translated from the Icelandic with an Introduction.

1927. "An Experiment in Eugenics," published for the first time in *Essays in Our Changing Order.*

[1] Republished in *Essays in Our Changing Order.*
[3] Republished in *The Engineers and the Price System.*
[4] Republished in *Absentee Ownership and Business Enterprise in Recent Times; The Case of America.*

REFERENCES

NOTE: The following students of Veblen have allowed me the use of their notes taken in Veblen's courses: Spurgeon Bell, Abraham Berglund, William R. Camp, Virginia J. Cowan, Burton L. French, Harry C. Green, Julia Guyer, A.F. Larson, Isador Lubin, J.D. Magee, Archibald B. Maynard, J.B. Sears, Margery Stallcup Smith, Charles Henry Swift, John G. Thompson, Myron Watkins, Fred Yoder. The Ward correspondence, with the exception of Ward's letter to the Library of Congress, has been supplied me by Dr. Bernhard J. Stern who is engaged in a study of the life of Ward. Since a good deal of the material is of a confidential nature, names have not been cited in a number of cases. When the published source of a statement is clear from the text, no footnote reference is given. Generally footnotes are given for quotations otherwise unidentified, and statements open to controversy.

CHAPTER I

1. Laurence M. Larson, "The Norwegian Pioneer in the Field of American Scholarship," Publications of the Norwegian-American Historical Association, *Studies and Records*, Vol. 2, p. 64 (Northfield, 1927); "Norwegian Immigrant Songs," translated and edited by Martin B. Ruud, Publications of the Norwegian-American Historical Association, *Studies and Records*, Vol. 2, pp. 2–3 (Northfield, 1927).

2. Knut Gjerset, *History of the Norwegian People*, Vol. 2, p. 45 (New York, 1927); L.M. Larson, *op. cit.*, p. 64.

3. Andrew A. Veblen, *Veblen Genealogy*, p. 101 (San Diego, 1925).

4. *America in the Forties: The Letters of Ole Munch Raeder*, translated and edited by Gunnar J. Malmin, Norwegian-American Historical Association, *Travel and Description Series*, Vol. 3, p. 77 (Northfield, 1929).

5. Publications of State Historical Society of Wisconsin, *Collections*, Vol. 26, *The Movement for Statehood, 1845–1846*, edited by Milo W. Quaife, p. 95 (Madison, 1918).

6. From address of Rev. Adolph Bredesen, cited in O.N. Nelson, "Historical Review of the Scandinavians in Wisconsin in O.N. Nelson, *History of the Scandinavians and Successful Scandinavians in the United States*, Vol. 2, p. 115 (Minneapolis, 1897).

7. Theodore L. Nydahl, "Social and Economic Aspects of Pioneering as Illustrated in Goodhue County, Minnesota," Norwegian-American Historical Association, *Studies and Records*, Vol. 5, p. 53 (Northfield, 1930).

8. Thorstein Veblen, *The Theory of the Leisure Class*, p. 179 (New York, 1899).

9. O.N. Nelson, "History of the Scandinavian Immigration" in O.N. Nelson, *op. cit.*, Vol. 1, pp. 71–72.

10. Thorstein Veblen, *Imperial Germany and the Industrial Revolution*, p. 318 (New York, 1915).

11. Karen Larsen, "A Contribution to the Study of the Adjustment of a Pioneer Pastor to American Conditions: Laur. Larsen, 1857–1880," Norwegian-American Historical Association, *Studies and Records*, Vol. 4, p. 13 (Northfield, 1929); Laurence M. Larson, *op. cit.*, p. 64; Andreas Ueland, *Recollections of an Immigrant*, p. 20 (New York, 1929); "Norwegian Emigrant Songs," *op. cit.*, p. 4.

12. O.E. Rølvaag, *Giants in the Earth*, p. 285 (New York and London, 1929).

13. Mersene E. Sloan, "Memories of the Eighties at Carleton," *Carleton College News Bulletin*, May 1922, p. 5.

14. "A Swedish Visitor of the Early Seventies," translated by Roy W. Swansen, *Minnesota History*, Dec. 1927, p. 399.

15. Carleton C. Qualey, "Pioneer Norwegian Settlement in Minnesota," *Minnesota History*, Sept. 1931, p. 271; Theodore L. Nydahl, *op. cit.*, p. 59; O.M. Norlie, "Religious Aim and Character," *Luther College Through Sixty Years, 1861–1921*, pp. 40, 44 (Minneapolis, 1922); Karen Larsen, *op. cit.*, p. 13.

CHAPTER II

1. William W. Folwell, *A History of Minnesota*, Vol. 3, pp. 104–108 (St. Paul, 1926).

2. William C. Edgar, *The Story of a Grain of Wheat*, p. 156 (New York, 1903).

3. Folwell, *op. cit.*, Appendix 10.

4. Folwell, *op. cit.*, Appendix 9.

5. Folwell, *op. cit.*, p. 46.

6. John D. Hicks, "The Political Career of Ignatius Donnelly," *Mississippi Valley Historical Review*, June–Sept. 1921, pp. 88, 92, 94, 97; Rasmus S. Saby, *Railroad Legislation in Minnesota, 1849–1875*, p. 122 (St. Paul, 1912).

7. Rev. President J.M. Sturtevant, "The Claims of the Higher Seminaries of Learning on the Liberality of the Wealthy," *New Englander*, Jan. 1862, Vol. 29, p. 96.

8. *Catalogue, 1879–1880*, p. 25; Rev. M.McG. Dana, "Western Colleges; Their Claims and Necessities," *New Englander*, Nov. 1880, p. 91.

9. *Catalogue, 1879–1880*, p. 25.

10. Rev. M.McG. Dana, *The History of the Origin and Growth of Carleton College*, pp. 29–30 (St. Paul, 1879).

11. Rev. Delavan L. Leonard, *The History of Carleton College*, pp. 330, 331 (Chicago, New York, 1904); Mersene E. Sloan, *op. cit.*, p. 4.

12. Franz F. Exner, "William Wallace Payne," *The Carleton Circle*, Feb. 1928, p. 53.

13. *Catalogue, 1878–1879*, p. 24.

14. *Catalogue, 1879–1880*, p. 30.

15. Sturtevant, *op. cit.*, p. 87.

16. *An Inquiry into the Human Mind, on the Principles of Common Sense*, p. 108; *Essays on the Intellectual Powers of Man*, p. 434, Hamilton's Edition of Reid's Works, Vol. 1 (Edinburgh, 1880), 8th ed.

17. "Philosophy of the Unconditioned," 1828; republished in *Discussions on Philosophy and Literature*, pp. 22, 43 (New York, 1857).

18. Laurens P. Hickok, *Rational Psychology*, p. 13 (New York, 1861); *Empirical Psychology*, pp. 68, 69 (New York, 1857, 2nd ed.), and revision with Julius H. Seelye, p. 43 (Boston, 1882).

19. *Mental Philosophy*, pp. 483, 484, 491, 492, 496, 497 (New York, 1875); *Moral Philosophy*, pp. 143, 145, 153 (New York, 1880 ed.).

20. Laurens P. Hickok, *A System of Moral Science*, p. 243 (New York, 1858, 3rd ed.); John Bascom, *Ethics*, p. 274 (New York, 1879).

21. *Manual of Political Ethics*, Vol. 1, pp. 115–116 (Philadelphia, 1874, 2nd ed.).

22. John Bascom, "Natural Theology of the Social Sciences," *Bibliotheca Sacra*, Vol. 25, No. 2, Jan. 1868, p. 12.

23. Noah Porter, *The Human Intellect*, p. 595 (4th ed., 1875, New York); James McCosh, *Energy: Efficient and Final Cause*, pp. 7, 47 (New York, 1883).

24. *Manual of Political Ethics, op. cit.*, p. 111.

25. J.N. Cardozo, *Reminiscences of Charleston*, pp. 9–10 (Charleston 1866).

26. *The Elements of Political Economy* by Francis Wayland, recast by Aaron L. Chapin, preface, pp. 4, 16, 170, 171, 175, 199, 231, 239, 300, 306, 315, 353, 387, 391 (New York, 1878); Francis Bowen, *American Political Economy*, pp. 15, 21, 104, 108, 110 (New York, 1870); "The Utility and Limitations of the Science of Political Economy," 1838, republished in *Gleanings from a Literary Life*, p. 124 (New York, 1880); J. Laurence Laughlin, "Seyd on Bimetallism," *The Literary World*, March 13, 1880, p. 90; Sturtevant, *Economics*, pp. 280, 282, 292, 294 (New York, 1881 ed.); Amasa Walker, *The Science of Wealth*, 1866, p. vi and condensed ed., (1872) p. vii; John McVickar, *Introductory Lecture to a Course in Political Economy*, p. 34 (London, 1830); "Inaugural Address of Francis Lieber" in *The Addresses of the Newly Appointed Professors of Columbia College*, p. 80 (New York, 1858); John Bascom, *Political Economy*, pp. 10, 81 (Andover, 1859); "The Natural Theology of the Social Sciences," *Bibliotheca Sacra*, Jan. 1868, pp. 13, 16, April 1868, p. 281, Oct. 1868, pp. 652, 656–659, 685; Simon Newcomb, "The Let-Alone Principle," *North American Review*, Jan. 1870, pp. 2, 8; Arthur Latham Perry, *Elements of Political Economy*, p. 120 (New York, 1866); E.D. Wilson, *First Principles of Political Economy with Reference to Statesmanship and the Progress of Civilisation*, pp. 29–30 (Philadelphia, 1879).

27. Lyman Atwater, "The True Progress of Society," *Princeton Review*, Jan. 1852, pp. 21, 33–34.

28. "Kant and His Philosophy," 1839; republished in *Critical Essays*, p. 65 (Boston, 1842).

29. John Stuart Mill, *Autobiography*, pp. 273–274 (New York 1873 ed.).

30. Francis Bowen, *Gleanings from a Literary Life, op. cit.*, preface.

31. Eliza M. Garman *Letters, Lectures and Addresses of Charles Edward Garman*, pp. 5–6 (Boston and New York, 1909).

32. "The Philosophy of Wealth," *New Englander*, Jan. 1877, pp. 170–172, 174; "Unrecognised Forces in Political Economy," *New Englander*, Oct. 1877, pp. 713, 719, 722, 723; "The Labour Problem and the Schools," *The Citizen*,

Minneapolis and St. Paul, Sept. 13, 1877; "Business Ethics, Past and Present," *New Englander*, Mar. 1879, p. 161; "The Nature and Progress of True Socialism," *New Englander*, July 1879, pp. 572, 579, 581; "Spiritual Economics," *New Englander*, May 1880, p. 318; "The Philosophy of Value," *New Englander*, July 1881, pp. 464, 467.

33. M.McG. Dana, "Western Colleges," *op. cit.*, p. 90.

34. Karen M. Larsen, *op. cit.*, p. 14.

35. Rudolf von Tobel, "Ellen Rolfe Veblen," *Carleton Circle*, Dec. 1926, p. 64.

36. *Rice County Journal*, July 1, 1880.

37. Arthur C. Paulson, Bjørnson and the Norwegian-Americans, 1880–1881," Publications of the Norwegian-American Historical Association; *Studies and Records*, Vol. 5, pp. 97–98 (Northfield, 1930).

38. Henry Demarest Lloyd, "Lords of Industry," 1881, republished in *Lords of Industry*, pp. 34, 46 (New York and London, 1910).

CHAPTER III

1. President Gilman, "Inaugural Address" in Johns Hopkins University, *Inauguration of President Gilman*, p. 21 (Baltimore, 1876); Johns Hopkins University, *First Annual Report*, p. 18.

2. J. Mark Baldwin, *Between Two Wars, 1861–1921*, p. 118 (Boston, 1926).

3. R.M. Wenley, *The Life and Work of George Sylvester Morris*, p. 147 (New York, 1917).

4. G. Stanley Hall, *Life and Confessions of a Psychologist*, pp. 242, 244, 245 (New York and London, 1923); Johns Hopkins University, *Seventh Annual Report*, pp. 61, 65.

5. Noah Porter, *Human Intellect, op. cit.*, p. 60.

6. R.M. Wenley, *Kant and His Philosophical Revolution*, p. 271 (Edinburgh, 1910).

7. J.P. Mahaffy, "Kant and His Fortunes in England," *Princeton Review*, Vol. 82, July 1878, p. 205.

8. Noah Porter, "The Kantian Centennial," 1881; republished in *Science and Sentiment*, p. 446 (New York, 1882).

9. Henry James, *The Letters of William James*, Vol. 1, p. 208 (Boston, 1920).

10. George S. Morris, *Kant's Critique of Pure Reason*, p. 10 (Chicago, 1880).

11. Abstract in Johns Hopkins University, *University Circulars*, Feb. 1882, p. 176.

12. "The Fixation of Belief," 1877, and "How to Make Our Ideas Clear," 1878, republished in *Chance, Love and Logic*, pp. 12, 21, 43 (London and New York, 1923); Ellery M. Davis, "Charles Peirce at Johns Hopkins," *Mid-West Quarterly*, Vol. 2, Oct. 1914, p. 56.

13. "The Christian College," *Fifteen Years in the Chapel of Yale College*, p. 382 (New York, 1888).

14. *Noah Porter, A Memorial by Friends*, pp. 191–192 (New York, 1893).

15. *Yale College in 1884, Some Statements Respecting the Late Progress and Present Condition of the Various Departments of the University, for the Information*

of Its Graduates, Friends, and Benefactors, by the Executive Committee of the Society of the Alumni, June 1884, p. 9.

16. "Spencer's Theory of Sociology," 1880; republished in *Science and Sentiment, op. cit.,* pp. 378–379.

17. *Annual Report of the President,* 1865, p. 6. John Spencer Clark, *The Life and Letters of John Fiske,* Vol. 2, p. 260 (Boston and New York, 1917); Edward L. Youmans, *Herbert Spencer on the Americans,* pp. 36, 38, 39, 45, 50 (New York, 1883).

18. "Reply to a Socialist," 1904; republished in the *Challenge of Facts and Other Essays,* p. 61 (New Haven, 1914).

19. "Non-Competitive Economics," *New Englander,* Nov. 1882, p. 846.

20. *War and Other Essays,* p. xvi (New Haven, 1919).

21. "Professor Sumner's 'Social Classes,'" 1884; republished in *Glimpses of the Cosmos,* Vol. 3, pp. 303–304 (New York and London, 1913).

22. "The Forgotten Man," 1883, published in *The Forgotten Man and Other Essays,* pp. 488–489 (New Haven, 1918); *Protection and Revenue, in 1877;* A Lecture delivered before the New York Free Trade Club, April 18, 1878, pp. 1–5.

23. E.G. Bourne, *The History of the Surplus Revenue of 1837,* p. 1 (New York, 1885); *Yale University Catalogue, 1883–1884,* p. 63, and *Yale University Catalogue, 1884–1885,* p. 109; *Yale Pot Pourri, 1883–1884,* p. 65; *Yale Banner,* 1884, p. 54.

24. *Letters of William James, op. cit.,* Vol. 1, p. 232.

25. "Spencer's Data of Ethics," *Princeton Review,* Dec. 1879, p. 636.

26. *The Elements of Moral Science,* pp. 125, 151 (New York, 1885).

27. *Ibid.,* pp. 136–137.

28. Kant's *Critique of Practical Reason and Other Works on the Theory of Ethics* (Abbot translation), p. 33.

29. *Kant's Ethics,* p. 71 (Chicago, 1886).

30. Norman K. Smith, *Commentary to Kant's Critique of Pure Reason,* p. 578 (London, 1918); James Ward, "Immanuel Kant," in *Essays in Philosophy,* pp. 347–348 (Cambridge, 1927).

31. The words of Harold Höffding, in *A History of Modern Philosophy,* Vol. 2, pp. 385–386 (London, 1900), based on Kant's *Prolegomena to any Future Metaphysics* (see Carus translation, p. 7).

32. René Willek, *Immanuel Kant in England, 1793–1838,* p. 27 (Princeton, 1931); N.K. Smith, *op. cit.,* p. 333; Kant's *Prolegomena to any Future Metaphysics,* p. 151; Friedrich Lange, *History of Materialism,* Vol. 2, p. 155 (Boston, 1882).

33. James McCosh, *Criteria of Diverse Kinds of Truth as Opposed to Agnosticism,* p. 2 (New York, 1882); *First and Fundamental Truths,* p. 29 (New York, 1889); *A Criticism of the Critical Philosophy* (New York, 1884); Porter, *Human Intellect, op. cit.,* p. 629.

34. H. Vaihinger, *The Philosophy of "As If,"* pp. xxx, xlvi (London, 1924).

35. "Final Purpose in Nature," *New Englander,* Sept. 1879, pp. 679, 698.

36. *Outlines of Metaphysics,* translated and edited by George T. Ladd, p. 1 (Boston, 1884).

37. "The New Psychology," *Andover Review; A Religious and Theological Monthly*, March 1885, pp. 247–248.

38. "Workingmen's Grievances," *North American Review*, Vol. 138, May 1884, p. 508.

39. "Workingmen's Grievances," *North American Review*, Vol. 138, May 1884, p. 519; "The Silver Danger," *Atlantic Monthly*, Vol. 53, May 1884, p. 681, "The Refunding Bill of 1881," *Atlantic Monthly*, Vol. 49, p. 205.

CHAPTER IV

1. *Scandinavia*, March 1886, p. 58.

2. *Scandinavia*, Feb. 1886, p. 33.

3. From the play "Wives Submit Yourselves unto Your Husbands," by Kristofer Janson, *Scandinavia*, Feb. 1885, p. 50.

4. John D. Hicks, "The Origin and Early History of the Farmers' Alliance in Minnesota," *Mississippi Valley Historical Review*, Vol. 9, Dec. 1922, pp. 202, 206, 207, 208, 209.

5. Henrietta M. Larson, *The Wheat Market and the Farmer in Minnesota, 1858–1900*, p. 162 (New York, 1926).

6. Stuart Daggett, *Chapters on the History of the Southern Pacific* (New York, 1922); Charles E. Russell, *Stories of the Great Railroads*, Chapters V–X (New York, 1908).

7. Nathaniel W. Stephenson, *Nelson W. Aldrich*, pp. 62, 103 (New York, 1930); James A. Barnes, *John G. Carlisle*, p. 102 (New York, 1931).

8. *A Plain Man's Talk on the Labour Question*, pp. 66–67, 90 (New York, 1886).

9. "The South-Western Strike of 1886," *Quarterly Journal of Economics*, Jan. 1887, p. 219.

10. Newcomb, *op. cit.*, pp. 142–143, 191.

11. "Henry Carter Adams," *Journal of Political Economy*, Vol. 30, April 1922, p. 205.

12. Henry George, Jr., *Life of Henry George*, pp. 473, 494–495 (New York, 1900).

13. Barnes, *op. cit.*, p. 102.

14. Graham Taylor, *Pioneering on Social Frontiers*, p. 136 (Chicago, 1930).

15. *Science*, Vol. 8, Oct. 29, 1886, pp. 38.

16. *The Study of Political Economy; Hints to Students and Teachers*, pp. 46–47 (New York, 1885); *The Elements of Political Economy with Some Applications to Questions of the Day*, preface and p. 265 (New York, 1887).

17. *Protectionism; The —Ism Which Teaches That Waste Makes Wealth*, p. 5 (New York, 1887); "State Interference," 1887, republished in *War and Other Essays*, p. 222 (New Haven, 1911).

18. "Political Economy in America," *North American Review*, Feb. 1887, p. 118; *Science*, Vol. 8, July 9, 1886, p. 34.

19. *The Laxdæla Saga*, Translation by Thorstein Veblen, Introduction (New York, 1925); *The Collected Works of William Morris*, Vol. 7, p. xx (New York, 1911).

20. John W. McKail, *The Life of William Morris*, Vol. 2, pp. 243–244 (London, 1901).

21. "What 'Nationalism' Means," *Contemporary Review*, Vol. 5, July 1890, p. 18.

22. Paul R. Fossum, *The Agrarian Movement in North Dakota*, p. 37 (Baltimore, 1925).

23. Caro Lloyd, *Henry Demarest Lloyd, 1847–1903*, Vol. 1, pp. 141, 128–129 (New York, 1912).

24. Agnes W. Dennis, "New Forces Astir," in Ernest L. Bogart and Charles M. Thompson, *The Industrial State, 1870–1893*, p. 176 (Springfield, 1920).

25. Fred E. Haynes, *Third Party Movements Since the Civil War with Special Reference to Iowa*, pp. 230–231, 236, 239 (Iowa City, 1916).

26. John D. Hicks, *The Populist Revolt*, p. 160 (Minneapolis, 1931).

27. Theodora Bosanquet, *Harriet Martineau*, p. 63 (London, 1927).

28. "Sketch of William Graham Sumner," *Popular Science Monthly*, Vol. 35, June 1889, p. 262.

29. *Principles of Political Economy*, Book IV, Chap. 7; "On the Definition of Political Economy, and on the Method of Investigation Proper to It," *Early Essays by John Stuart Mill*, pp. 132–133 (Bohn Standard Library ed., London, 1897).

30. Thomas Edward Cliffe Leslie, "The History of German Political Economy," 1875; republished in *Essays in Political Economy*, p. 93 (London, 1888).

31. *An Introduction to Political Economy*, p. 322 (New York, 1889).

32. Sir Henry Maine, *Popular Government*, pp. 50, 52 (London, 1885; Spencer, "The Man Versus the State," p. 69 (London, 1884); *Principles of Sociology*, Paragraph 616.

33. David G. Ritchie, *Darwinism and Politics*, pp. 4–5 (London, 1889).

34. Leonard Huxley, *The Life and Letters of Thomas Henry Huxley*, Vol. 2, p. 284 (New York, 1902).

35. Arthur Latham Perry, *Williamstown and William's College*, p. 665 (1899).

CHAPTER V

1. Jessica T. Austen, *Moses Coit Tyler, 1835–1900*, p. 263 (New York, 1911); G. Stanley Hall, editor, *Methods of Teaching History*, second ed., p. 135 (Boston, 1902).

2. John D. Hicks, "The Political Career of Ignatius Donnelly," *op. cit.*, pp. 120–121; Haynes, *op. cit.*, p. 258.

3. "The West and the Railroads," *North American Review*, Vol. 152, April 1891, pp. 446–447.

4. Haynes, *op. cit.*, pp. 263, 266, 436, 514.

5. W.W. Folwell, *op. cit.*, pp. 249–250.

6. Davis R. Dewey, *National Problems, 1885–1897*, pp. 248–250 (New York and London, 1907); J. Laurence Laughlin, "The Study of Political Economy in the United States," *Journal of Political Economy*, Vol. 1, Dec. 1892, p. 3.

CHAPTER VI

1. Henry B. Fuller, "The Growth of Education, Art and Letters," in Ernest L. Bogart and John M. Mathews, *The Modern Commonwealth*, pp. 30–31 (Springfield, 1920).

2. "The University of Chicago," *The Nation*, Sept. 22, 1892, p. 217.

3. Henry James, *The Letters of William James*, Vol. 1, p. 334 (Boston, 1920).

4. Thomas W. Goodspeed, *A History of the University of Chicago, Founded by John D. Rockefeller*, pp. 202, 377 (Chicago, 1916); Thomas W. Goodspeed, *William Rainey Harper*, p. 125 (Chicago, 1928); G. Stanley Hall, *Life and Confessions of a Psychologist*, pp. 296–297 (New York and London, 1923).

5. T. W. Goodspeed, *William Rainey Harper*, *op. cit.*, p. 99.

6. George L. Collie, "A Distinguished Son of Wisconsin: Thomas C. Chamberlain," *Wisconsin Magazine of History*, Vol. 15, June 1932, p. 427.

7. *The Annual Register, 1892–1893*, p. 210; "The Study of Political Economy in the United States," *op. cit.*, p. 6.

8. Charles S. Peirce, "Evolutionary Love," 1893; republished in *Chance, Love and Logic, op. cit.*, pp. 272–275.

9. George Romanes, *Darwin and After Darwin*, 2nd ed., Vol. 1, pp. 4–5 (London, 1893, 2nd ed.).

10. John D. Hicks, *The Populist Movement, op. cit.*, p. 463.

11. Robert M. Lovett, "Memories of William Vaughn Moody," *Atlantic Monthly*, March 1931, p. 387; Hamlin Garland, *Roadside Meetings*, p. 262 (New York, 1930); William Tufts, "What I Believe," *Contemporary American Philosophy*, edited by George P. Adams and Wm. P. Montague Vol. 2, p. 339 (London and New York, 1930); Jane Addams, *Twenty Years at Hull House*, p. 178 (New York, 1910).

12. Jane Addams, *op. cit.*, p. 178.

13. Henry B. Fuller, "The Development of Arts and Letters," in Ernest L. Bogart and Charles M. Thompson, *op. cit.*, p. 212.

14. Caro Lloyd, *op. cit.*, Vol. 1, p. 163.

15. Graham Taylor, *op. cit.*, pp. 112–115.

16. Agnes W. Dennis, *op. cit.*, p. 187.

17. James A. Barnes. *op. cit.*, p. 331.

18. Carlos C. Closson, Jr., "The Unemployed in American Cities," *Quarterly Journal of Economics*, Jan. 1894, p. 192.

19. *American Federation of Labor; History, Encyclopædia, Reference Book*, 1919, p. 27 (Washington, 1919).

20. Frederick Whyte, *The Life of W.T. Stead*, Vol. 2, pp. 45–46 (New York and London, 1925).

21. William T. Stead, *If Christ Came to Chicago*, p. 17 (Chicago, 1894).

22. *The Cyclopædic Review of Current History*, edited by Alfred S. Johnson, 1893, p. 636.

23. George Adam Smith, *The Life of Henry Drummond*, p. 480 (New York, 1901).

24. *Quarterly Calendar of the University of Chicago Founded by John D. Rockefeller*, Nov. 1893, pp. 3, 7.

25. "University Settlements," *Quarterly Journal of Economics*, Vol. 6, April 1892, p. 279.

CHAPTER VII

1. F.E. Haynes, *op. cit.*, pp. 340–341; John D. Hicks, *The Populist Revolt, op. cit.*, p. 32; William T. Stead, "Coxeyism and Its Commonwealers," *Review of Reviews*, June 15, 1894, p. 569; Henry Vincent, *The Story of the Commonweal*, p. 194 (Chicago, 1894).

2. Jane Addams, *op. cit.*, p. 214; *Report of the Chicago Strike of June–July 1894, by the United States Strike Commission*, pp. 29, 34–35, 36, 41 (Washington, 1894); Henry James, *Richard Olney and His Public Service*, pp. 42, 52 (Boston and New York, 1923); Waldo Browne, *Altgeld of Illinois*, p. 121 (New York, 1924); Robert McElroy, *Grover Cleveland, the Man and the Statesman*, p. 162 (New York and London, 1923); Brand Whitlock, *Forty Years of It*, p. 91 (New York and London, 1914); *Henry Demarest Lloyd, op. cit.*, Vol. 1, p. 147.

3. Samuel Gompers, *Seventy Years of Life and Labor*, Vol. 1, p. 413 (New York, 1925).

4. Horace White, *The Life of Lyman Trumbull*, p. 426 (Boston and New York, 1913).

5. *Report of the Chicago Strike, op. cit.*, pp. 37–38; Jane Addams, *op. cit.*, p. 218.

6. *Public Opinion*, Aug. 30, 1894, p. 516.

7. *The Quarterly Calendar*, Aug. 1894, p. 21.

8. *Public Opinion*, Aug. 16, 1894, and Aug. 23, 1894.

9. *Report of the Chicago Strike, op. cit.*, pp. 27–28, 34, 51–53.

10. "Revolutionary Statesmanship," *Harpers Weekly*, Nov. 24, 1894, p. 1107.

11. *Publications of the American Economic Association*, Vol. 10, No. 3, Supplement, p. 53, Vol. 9, pp. 483–484, 491, 492, 501, 505.

12. "The Chicago Strike," *Publications of the American Economic Association*, Vol. 9, pp. 511–512; Vol. 10, Supplement, pp. 62–64.

13. *Publications of the American Economic Association*, Vol. 10, Supplement, p. 117.

14. *Psychological Review*, May 1894, p. 405.

15. *Introduction to Comparative Psychology*, p. 314 (London, 1894).

16. *Ibid.*, p. 53.

17. Jacques Loeb, *Comparative Physiology of the Brain and Comparative Psychology*, p. 12 (New York, 1900).

18. Charles R. Henderson, "Sociology and Theology," *American Journal of Sociology*, Nov. 1895, p. 381.

19. W.B. Selbie, *The Life of Andrew Martin Fairbairn*, p. 338 (London, New York, Toronto, 1914).

20. Boas, "The Social Organization and the Secret Societies of the Kwakiutl Indians," Report of the United States National Museum, 1895, pp. 341, 342, 343, 344, 353, 354, 364; Boas, "First General Report on the Indians of British Columbia" in *Report of the Fifty-Ninth Meeting of the British Association for the Advancement*

of Science, 1889, p. 834; Horatio Hale, "Remarks on the Ethnology of British Columbia: Introductory to the Second General Report of Dr. Franz Boas on the Indians of That Province," *Report of the Sixtieth Meeting of the British Association for the Advancement of Science*, 1890, pp. 556–557.

21. *Eminent Authors of the Nineteenth Century*, translated by Rasmus Anderson, pp. 141–142 (1886).

22. Wesley C. Mitchell, "Thorstein Veblen: 1857–1929," *New Republic*, Sept. 4, 1929, p. 66.

CHAPTER VIII

1. Waldo Browne, *op. cit.*, pp. 40, 231–232, 233, 243; Brand Whitlock, *op. cit.*, p. 100; Ralph E. Heilman, "Chicago Traction," *American Economic Association Quarterly*.

2. *Quarterly Calendar*, May 1895, p. 7.

3. *Quarterly Calendar*, Aug. 1895, p. 15.

4. *New York Evening Post*, Oct. 5, 1895.

5. *American Journal of Sociology*, Sept. 1895, p. 210.

6. *Public Opinion*, Oct. 17, 1895, p. 489.

7. *Public Opinion*, Nov. 7, 1895, p. 582; *Henry Demarest Lloyd*, Vol. I, p. 211, footnote.

8. *Elgin* [Illinois] *News*, Nov. 8, 1895.

9. *Quarterly Calendar*, Nov. 1895, p. 17.

10. *Public Opinion*, Dec. 26, 1895, p. 849.

11. Cary McWilliams, *Ambrose Bierce; A Biography*, p. 239 (New York, 1929).

12. Barnes, *op. cit.*, p. 451.

13. Charles R. Henderson, "Business Men and Social Theorists," *American Journal of Sociology*, Jan. 1896, p. 388.

14. "Scope and Method of Folk Psychology," *American Journal of Sociology*, Jan. 1896, pp. 439, 442–443.

15. *Annual Register, 1894–1895*, pp. 73–74.

16. "Social Selection," *Journal of Political Economy*, June 1896, pp. 449, 457, 458.

17. Charles Zueblin, "A Sketch of Socialistic Thought in England," *Journal of Political Economy*, March 1897, p. 653.

18. George H. Mead, "The Definition of the Psychical," The University of Chicago Founded by John D. Rockefeller, *Decennial Publications*, First Series, Vol. 3, p. 98 (Chicago, 1903).

19. *Schopenhauer's System in Its Ethical Significance*, pp. 19, 136, 181, 288, 310–311 (Edinburgh, 1896).

20. "Hedonistic Interpretation of Subjective Value," *Journal of Political Economy*, Dec. 1895, p. 70; "Subjective and Exchange Value," June 1896, pp. 363, 376, 383, 384.

21. E.L. Bogart and J.M. Mathews, *op. cit.*, p. 172.

22. Thomas W. Goodspeed, *A History of the University of Chicago; the First Quarter Century, op. cit.*, p. 397.

23. *University Record*, July 3, 1896, pp. 222–223; July 17, 1896, pp. 253–254; July 24, 1896, pp. 269–270.

24. *University Record*, Aug. 7, 1896, pp. 305, 306.

25. *Ibid.*, pp. 300, 301, 302, 303.

26. Frederick C. Howe, *The Confessions of a Reformer*, p. 147 (New York, 1925).

27. Edward Stanwood, *A History of the Presidency*, p. 545 (Boston, 1898).

28. *Harpers Weekly*, July 18, 1896.

29. John D. Hicks, *The Populist Revolt*, *op. cit.*, p. 372.

30. Waldo Browne, *op. cit.*, p. 299.

31. H.H. Kohlsaat, *From McKinley to Harding*, p. 52 (New York and London, 1923).

32. F.J. Stimpson, "The Ethical Side of the Free Silver Campaign," *International Journal of Ethics*, July 1897, p. 403.

33. Browne, *op. cit.*, p. 287.

34. *Idem.*

35. Kohlsaat, *op. cit.*, p. 52.

36. Edward Stanwood, *op. cit.*, p. 527; Harry Thurston Peck, *Twenty Years of the Republic 1885–1905*, p. 211 (New York, 1913); Paxton Hibben, *The Peerless Leader; William Jennings Bryan*, p. 201 (New York, 1927).

37. "The Election of 1896," *Live Questions*, p. 691 (Chicago, 1899).

38. Hibben, *op. cit.*, p. 201.

39. "Trusts in Case of Bryan's Election," *Review of Reviews*, Oct. 1900, p. 444.

40. Kohlsaat, *op. cit.*, p. 53.

41. Peck, *op. cit.*, p. 516.

42. Howe, *op. cit.*, p. 149.

43. *Harpers Weekly*, Nov. 21, 1896, p. 1138.

44. Graham Taylor, *op. cit.*, p. 66.

45. John H. Gray, "The Street Railway Situation in Chicago," *Quarterly Journal of Economics*, Oct. 1897, pp. 88–89.

46. Henry Demarest Lloyd, *op. cit.*, Vol. 2, p. 282.

47. Samuel Moffet, "Charles Tyson Yerkes," *Cosmopolitan*, Aug. 1902, pp. 413–414; *Henry Demarest Lloyd*, *op. cit.*, Vol. 2, p. 283.

48. W.A. Todd, *Nation*, Nov. 18, 1897, p. 392.

49. T.W. Goodspeed, *A History of the University of Chicago*, *op. cit.*, pp. 310–311.

50. "Municipal Ownership," *Independent*, May 6, 1897, p. 571; "Some Practical Aspects of Socialism," *Proceedings of the Fifth Annual Convention of the Wisconsin Bankers Association*, 1897.

51. *Live Questions*, *op. cit.*, p. 862.

52. "Professor Patten's Theory of Social Forces," *International Journal of Ethics*, April 1897, pp. 350, 352, 353, and also "Reply," by Caldwell in July issue, pp. 496–497; "Professor Titchener's View of the Self," *Psychological Review*, July 1898, pp. 402, 408.

53. *Psychological Review*, Nov. 1897, p. 663.

54. *Journal of Political Economy*, Dec. 1897, p. 92.

CHAPTER IX

1. Werner Sombart, *Socialism and the Social Movement in the Nineteenth Century*, p. 124 (Atterbury translation, New York, 1898).

2. Charles Zueblin, "A Sketch of Socialistic Thought in England," *op. cit.*, p. 661.

3. William Archer, "American Jottings," *New York Times*, May 18, 1899.

4. Lincoln Steffens, "Chicago: Half-Free," 1903; republished in *The Shame of the Cities*, p. 254 (London, 1904).

5. Hibben, *op. cit.*, p. 215; *Life in Letters of William Dean Howells*, edited by Mildred Howells, Vol. 2, p. 90 (New York, 1928); Sumner, "The Conquest of the United States by Spain," 1898; republished in *War and Other Essays*, *op. cit.*, p. 334; Lovett, *op. cit.*, p. 390.

6. Henry James, *Charles W. Eliot, President of Harvard University, 1869–1929*, Vol. 2, p. 224 (Boston and New York, 1930); *University Record*, Oct. 21, 1898, pp. 180–184; John P. Altgeld, "Omaha Speech—the Situation," *Live Questions*, *op. cit.*, pp. 874–875.

7. Report of the United States Industrial Commission, Vol. 1, Part 2, pp. 104–118 (Washington, 1900).

8. "Social and Ethical Interpretation of Mental Development," *American Journal of Sociology*, Sept. 1899, pp. 184–188.

9. "Postulates of Psychology," *Philosophical Review*, Sept. 1898, pp. 451–452.

10. "The Postulates of a Structural Psychology," *Psychological Review*, March 1899, p. 186.

11. "Pragmatism," *Mind*, Oct. 1900, pp. 451, 456.

12. *University Records*, Dec. 8, 1899, p. 220.

13. Edward W. Bemis, "Academic Freedom," *The Independent*, Aug. 17, 1899, pp. 2197, 2198.

14. Publications of the American Economic Association, *Papers and Proceedings of the Twelfth Annual Meeting, 1899*, pp. 113, 120 (New York, 1900).

CHAPTER XIII

1. Publications of the American Economic Association, *Papers and Proceedings of the Thirteenth Annual Meeting, 1900*, pp. 69, 70 (New York, 1901).

2. *International Socialist Review*, May 1901, pp. 739–740.

3. *University Record*, Dec. 7, 1901, p. 277.

4. Alexander Dana Noyes, *Forty Years of American Finance* (New York and London, 1909); *Hearings before the Committee on Investigation of United States Steel Corporation*, Vol. 8, Appendix: Part 1 (Washington, 1911), pp. 300–301, 304, 331, 334; E. C. Kirkland, *A History of American Life*, p. 477 (New York, 1932).

5. "The Society of the Future," *Independent*, July 18, 1901, p. 1651.

6. Jane Addams, *op. cit.*, p. 404.

7. *Addresses and Presidential Messages of Theodore Roosevelt, 1902–1904*, with

an introduction by Henry Cabot Lodge, pp. 291–294 (New York and London, 1904).

8. *Henry Demarest Lloyd,* Vol. 2, *op. cit.,* pp. 190, 198, 207, 230, 235; Theodore Roosevelt, *An Autobiography,* pp. 468, 469, 474 (New York, 1913); Haynes, *op. cit.,* pp. 400–401; Elsie Glück, *John Mitchell, Miner; Labor's Bargain with the Gilded Age,* pp. 114, 117, 130 (New York, 1929); Caroll D. Wright, *The Battles of Labor,* pp. 153–154 (Philadelphia, 1906).

9. "Feudalism or Commonwealth," *Independent,* May 29, 1902, pp. 1276, 1277, 1279.

10. *Glimpses of the Cosmos, op. cit.,* Vol. 6, p. 144; Letters to Mrs. J.O. Unger dated Dec. 13, 1903, and letter to Ross dated Dec. 13, 1903, cited in Bernhard J. Stern, "Giddings, Ward and Small: An Interchange of Letters," *Social Forces,* March 1932, p. 316.

11. "Credit," University of Chicago, *Decennial Publications,* First Series, Vol. 5, pp. 9, 10, 11, 12, 26 (Chicago, 1903).

CHAPTER XV

1. Parker H. Sercombe, *Correct Thinking; A Herald of the New Learning,* (Chicago).

2. Letter to Mrs. J.O. Unger, April 1, 1905.

3. Charmian London, *The Book of Jack London,* Vol. 2, p. 21 (New York, 1921).

4. Frank W. Taussig, "Economics," in *The Development of Harvard University Since the Inauguration of President Eliot, 1869–1929,* edited by Samuel Eliot Morison, p. 188 (Cambridge, 1930).

CHAPTER XVI

1. Wesley C. Mitchell, "Thorstein Veblen: 1857–1929," *Economic Journal,* Dec. 1929, p. 649.

2. *Fourth Annual Report of the President of the University,* 1907, p. 34.

3. "Class Conflict in America," *American Journal of Sociology,* May 1908, p. 780.

4. "Capital and Interest," *Political Science Quarterly,* Sept. 1909, pp. 513, 516.

CHAPTER XVII

1. *Hearings before the Committee on Investigation of United States Steel Corporation, op. cit.,* pp. viii, xx, xxi, xxii, xxiii, xxiv, 19, 21, 251.

2. *Ibid.,* "House Report," pp. 58, 59, 69, 126, 128, 129, 130, 147, 209, 211, 212.

3. George Ward Stocking, *The Oil Industry and the Competitive System: A Study in Waste,* p. 54 (Boston and New York, 1925).

4. *The Industrial History of the United States*, p. 474 (New York, 1930).

5. "The Mechanistic Conception of Life," 1912; republished in *The Mechanistic Conception of Life: Biological Essays*, p. 31 (Chicago, 1912).

6. *The Instinct of Workmanship, and the State of the Industrial Arts*, pp. 315–316 (New York, 1914).

7. *Biennial Report of the Board of Curators, 1912*, p. 151; *1916*, p. 317.

CHAPTER XIX

1. "The Socialist Attitude on the War," *The Class Struggle*, July–August 1917, pp. 10, 13, 18.

2. Charles Seymour, *The Intimate Papers of Colonel House*, Vol. 3, p. 171 (Boston and New York, 1928).

3. William Hard, "Mr. Burleson, Section 481½ B," *New Republic*, May 17, 1919, pp. 77, 78.

4. Based on "Report of Committee on Academic Freedom in Wartime," *Bulletin of the American Association of University Professors*, Feb.–March 1918, pp. 29–47.

5. *Amherst College Catalogue, 1917–1918*, p. 94.

CHAPTER XXI

1. "Thorstein Veblen," *New Republic*, Aug. 5, 1931, p. 315.

2. "The New Psychology and the Social Order," *Dial*, Nov. 1, 1919, p. 367.

3. *Dial*, July 12, 1919, p. 27; July 26, 1919, p. 43; *New Republic*, Nov. 19, 1919.

4. *Revolutionary Radicalism: Its History, Purpose and Tactics with an Exposition and Discussion of the Steps Being Taken and Required to Curb It, Being the Report of the Joint Legislative Committee Investigating Seditious Activities, Filed April 24, 1920, in the Senate of the State of New York*; Part I, *Revolutionary and Subversive Movements Abroad and at Home*, Vol. 1, pp. 1093, 1094; Vol. 2, p. 1414 (Albany, 1920).

CHAPTER XXII

1. "Statement of Clark Controversy for Free Speech," *Clark College Monthly*, March 1922, pp. 200, 203, 205, 210, 215; "Report of the Committee of Inquiry Concerning Clark University," *Bulletin of the American Association of University Professors*, Oct. 1924, pp. 68, 69, 70.

CHAPTER XXIII

1. "Quantitative Analysis in Economic Theory," *American Economic Review*, March 1925, p. 7.

2. *American Economic Review*, March 1925, Supplement, pp. 56–57.

3. *Ibid.*, p. 147.

CHAPTER XXIV

1. "Recent Developments in Economics," in *Recent Developments in the Social Sciences*, edited by E.C. Hayes, p. 250 (Philadelphia, 1927).

2. "Research in the Social Sciences," in *The New Social Science*, edited by L.D. White, (Chicago, 1930).

3. J.K. Atkins, "Thorstein Veblen—Father of Technocracy," *Technocracy Review*, Feb. 1933, pp. 16, 19; Howard Scott *et al.*, *Introduction to Technocracy*, pp. 59–61 (New York, 1933); Allen Raymond, *What Is Technocracy?*, pp. 6, 12, 120, 130–131, 134 (New York and London, 1933).

APPENDICES

THE following appendices contain information which has come to light since the original publication of this book. The first includes five unpublished letters from Veblen, to J. Franklin Jameson, the eminent historian. Written when they were both graduate students, they have importance for the light they cast on a period of Veblen's life of which very little is known. I should like to note that the late Elizabeth Donnan while preparing (with L. F. Stock) *A Historian's World: Selections from the Correspondence of James Franklin Jameson* (The American Philosophical Society, Philadelphia, 1956) called my attention in 1954 to these letters.[1] In addition to the unpublished letters there is reprinted in this appendix two later revealing references to Veblen, from Jameson's letters in *A Historian's World*.

As the editors of that volume write, "Proud of his New England birth and scornful of anything 'westernish', he [Jameson] was yet able to recognize the unusual powers of Thorstein Veblen, a fellow student [at Johns Hopkins]. . . . The acquaintance which began at that time was never dropped though communication between the two was infrequent." Jameson himself in an unpublished letter in 1910 to Robert S. Woodward, President of the Carnegie Institution of Washington, asserted that Veblen: "is an extraordinary man, indeed in many respects his attainments may fairly be called marvelous. I have known of him chiefly as a most ingenious student of economic phenomena. . . ."

The second appendix contains the address (with minor revisions) which I prepared for the session of the American Economic Association meetings in 1957, commemorating the centenary of Veblen's birth. The version here is taken from the symposium, *Thorstein Veblen: A Critical Reappraisal* (1958).[2]

---

[1] Jameson's papers were originally in the Carnegie Institution of Washington where he had served as director of the Department of Historical Research. After publication of *A Historian's World*, they were transferred to the Library of Congress.

[2] Permission to reprint given by the publisher, Cornell University Press, is gratefully acknowledged.

I

THE VEBLEN - JAMESON CORRESPONDENCE

285 York St., New Haven, Conn.
April 2, 1882

My dear Mr. Jameson:

I had expected to write you sooner than this but procrastination to-gether with lack of anything to write about has made me put it off.

I came to New Haven without any adventure and found things here pleasanter than I had expected. The College here is to my mind an improvement on J.H.U. I like the school and the teachers very well, although I miss Prof. Morris. But I console myself with that I should have missed him if I had stayed at Baltimore also.

I am taking Political Economy under Prof. Sumner, two classes in Philosophy under Pres. Porter, and am very well pleased with both, particularly with Prof. Sumner.

I met Mr. Norton when I came here and he has been as kind and made himself as useful to me as he could, more so than I could have asked.[1]

I have heard from out West lately, and I understand that Mr. Williston, who filled Prof. Clark's place at Carleton College this year, is not to stay there longer than to the end of the year. I shall probably hear again, if the report is well founded, and if so shall be glad to send you word. Prof. Williston does not seem to take well with the boys there.[2]

Sincerely yours
T. B. Veblen

285 York St., New Haven, Conn.
June 2, 1882

Dear Mr. Jameson:

I ought to have written you sooner, especially as I had promised to write to you again about a certain matter as soon as I should know more definitely what to say, but as I found out that you already knew all that I would be able to tell I wrote nothing more about it.

Recitations in P.E. have closed for the year here, but I have yet some work under the President which will go on till commencement.

---

[1] Edwin C. Norton (1856-1943) was an Amherst classmate of Jameson; he later became dean of Pomona College.

[2] Jameson had written the president of Carleton College in February 1882, for a position. The opening paragraph in the following letter refers to the same matter.

At the J. H. U. the work has closed some time ago, I hear — Do you come up for a Ph. D. this Summer? If so I should be very glad to hear how you find the examinations.

I am beginning to like New Haven better lately than I did when I first came. The weather was extremely hard until these last days, and the town has looked muddy and shabby; but now, that Spring is coming, it does very well, indeed it is a very handsome looking town.

The Base Ball game between Yale and Harvard took place the other day — Yale was beaten, as you may have heard — and Jumbo was here yesterday. It has been some surprise to me to see how kindly the puritan of today takes to Baseball and circuses. I noticed a Prof. from the Theological Seminary at the Baseball game. Athletics and c. is decidedly the most characteristic virtue of Yale, and perhaps of New Haven, and I am afraid it covers a multitude of sins.

Where do you expect to spend the Summer?

Sincerely yours
T. B. Veblen

285 York St., New Haven, Conn.
October 9, 1882

Dear Mr. Jameson:

Your kind letter of August 18th reached me only last week. I failed to get it while at home this Summer and so it was forwarded here after I came back to school. I am sorry to have missed getting the letter last Summer for if I had I might have had an opportunity to meet you here this Fall, as it says you were coming through here in the early part of Sept. I had seen from a J. H. U. circular that the degree had been given you, as well as the position as Associate, and beg to tender my best wishes for a successful and happy school year. I am glad to hear Gould got the fellowship.[1] I was afraid it would be awarded otherwise.

I staid at home through most of the holidays, but did no reading at all, and now I am back at Yale and going on with the work about the same as last year.

How do you find the work this year? Do you like the change? Do you hear any of Dr. Ely's lectures? If so perhaps you could tell me what he is doing.

Sincerely yours
T. B. Veblen

---

[1] Elgin Ralston Lovell Gould (1860-1915), was a graduate student at Johns Hopkins between 1881 and 1886, his studies being interrupted by frequent illness. He achieved considerable prominence as a statistician, and as a collaborator of Seth Low in reforms in New York City.

140 Howe St., New Haven
February 12, 1883

My Dear Mr. Jameson:

It is already quite a while since I got your letter but somehow, like a bad housekeeper that I am, I have not answered. I suppose you folks in Baltimore are just now resting after the first semester's work and getting ready for what comes next. As for us, our year is divided differently and we are in the middle of the second term, and as busy as we can be. I have eleven hours a week this term, mostly in Philosophy. Just now, Hegel is all the rage, that is with me, and, by consequence, with Pres. Porter. Hegel is "tough"; very much so in fact, but I like him more the more I see of him. The president does not agree with Hegel, but so far I have not let myself be disturbed by that. I have not written disquisitions on vexed points of political Economy this year, neither have I been encouraged to do so. You may perhaps not know that I got up a certain essay last year, while at the J. H. U., which Dr. Ely advised me to send to a periodical to have printed. Well, I sent it and, as might have been expected, the "periodical" died of it. That discouraged me a little, though it increased my admiration of the Dr., who, as I understand, had a grudge against the "periodical".

How did you find the Swedish that you were taking up when I came away?[1] Is Mr. Swift, who was Fellow in Philosophy last year, in Baltimore now?[2]

The weather here is bad and has been bad; I believe, the most disagreeable winter I have ever seen.

Yours very truly,
T. B. Veblen

285 York St., N. Haven
May 16, 1883

Dear Mr. Jameson:

If I am not mistaken your year's work at J. H. U. closes now before long, that is recitations close as I understand about the end of this month, and I suppose you are happy to find a vacation at the end of it. As for us, we go on till near the end of June, and I don't know but I shall stay here or in this neighborhood through the summer holidays and go on with my reading about the same as during term times.

---

[1] Veblen while at Johns Hopkins had helped Jameson to locate source material for his projected doctoral dissertation on the early Swedish settlements on the Delaware.

[2] Morrison Isaac Swift (1856-1946) spent most of his life in social reform movements.

If you have watched the course of events closely at J. H. U. you may have noticed my name as an applicant for a fellowship there in Philosophy. When I left the place I had hardly expected ever to go back, and the notion of applying for a fellowship would never have entered my head but for the suggestion of Pres. Porter. Some two or three weeks ago the President spoke of it, and though I had then and have now no hope of getting the position I was induced, by his repeatedly speaking about it and advising it, to send in an application about the beginning of the month. The application can of course do no harm—that is my recurring consolation — and at the same time it was an easy way to please the President. So, if chance, which I understand has very little to do with these matters, should give me the place I should again find my place among the hopeful young men of J. H. U. I am still of opinion that on the whole Yale is preferable to J. H. U. so far as Political Economy goes, but as you know in the event of getting a fellowship there would be other circumstances to be taken into consideration.

Prof. Sumner's two years' course of lectures on U. S. political and financial history will be completed at the close of this year. He is now at Hayes' election. I have liked the lectures very much and think they have grown more interesting the farther they have gone on.

I was very sorry to hear from your letter, that Mr. Gould has been failing this year, and shall hope to hear of his coming out of it all right.

Forepaugh's circus and the anniversary exercises of the Theological Seminary, together with the national anniversary of Norway, come tomorrow, so that you see I am on the eve of a great holiday.

Sincerely yours
T. B. Veblen

Jameson to Lord Bryce, October 31, 1917

". . . . Your foot-note on page 18 [of Lord Bryce's presidential address before the British Academy] about forms of the Norwegian language, brings to mind what I was told thirty years ago, by a young Minnesota Norwegian who was one of my companions at the Johns Hopkins University. He said that nearly all the people of his township in Minnesota had come from one valley in Norway, and that late comers from that valley told him, on visiting the village, that they were preserving old dialectic forms which in the valley itself had become extinct by reason of the constant influence of the Danish newspapers from Copenhagen and Christiana [now Oslo] — the same fossilizing of colonial dialect that is so familiar in the case of Canadian French, South African Dutch, and in a way, the English of Ireland and America. . . ."

Jameson to President Woodward, November 20, 1918

"Some time ago Professor Thorstein Veblen told me that he was preparing to publish a book on the higher education in the United States which he had written before the war. I urged him to take account in it of the new situation in which the United States would be put at the end of the war in respect to the sustainment of learned and scientific researches and laid before him much the same thoughts in that regard that I have at times expressed to you. . . . Lately I received from him for criticism, some pages of text which he resolved to include in his book on account of my representations. He has, with his usual cleverness, expressed the thing much better than I could and therefore I send his pages to you herewith. . . . The remedy or devices which he suggests for meeting the situation is d. .nctly . . . his own. . . . But whatever method may be best for achieving profitable results I feel no doubt of the main doctrine of Mr. Veblen's memorandum, nor of the cogency and intelligence with which he has stated it."

The editors then stated: "The work to which Jameson referred was Veblen's *The Higher Learning in America*, N. Y., B. W. Huebsch, 1918, of which pages 48-58 were those prompted by Jameson's suggestions. The section begins: 'The progress and the further promise of the war hold in prospect new and untried responsibilities, as well as an unexampled opportunity. . . . The fortunes of war promise to leave the American men of learning in a strategic position, in the position of a strategic reserve, of a force to be held in readiness, equipped, and organized to meet the emergency that so arises, and to retrieve so much as may be of those assets of scholarly equipment and personnel that make the substantial code of Western civilization' (52). His proposal is for a great central university where teachers and students of all nationalities may meet as guests of the American people."

II

THE SOURCE AND IMPACT OF VEBLEN'S THOUGHT

THE celebration of the one-hundredth anniversary of Veblen's birth by such organizations as the American Economic Association and Cornell University may be taken as recognition of his impact on the growth of economic thought. That his work continues to be a source of considerable controversy is indicative of its vitality. Some men effectively catch the drift of development and have a vision of things to come. Such men become active forces in that very development, and their names become landmarks and turning points. Time alone is the final judge of a candidate's right to inclusion in this select list. For Veblen time has rendered its verdict.

As John Maurice Clark has said, he was "one of the great formative influences in the transformation of our economic thought in the past half-century."

Veblen's story is complicated by his historical setting, his personality, and his style of writing. Perhaps as the biographer of Veblen, I have an advantage, slight though it may be, in the task of clarifying the picture of the man and his role. It is almost a quarter of a century since I sent *Thorstein Veblen and His America* into the world. Since then, additional information on his career and background has become available, and many things have happened in the world of affairs and the world of economic science. These developments should provide the opportunity for a more mature understanding of this enigmatic figure. It is, therefore, in the light of what I like to think of as a richer experience, but which may well be excessive boldness, that I attempt an assessment of the source and impact of Veblen.

In Veblen we have at least two men. There is the economist, and there is the artist, a most unusual combination. Generally the two do not mix. In the history of Anglo-American economics, which actually forms one mighty stream, the only other case that comes to mind is that of David Hume.

Let me take up Veblen the artist first. Veblen is a person interested in writing and communication. Of his style the prominent novelist, Hans Storm, wrote that it was

faintly suggestive of the great geographers in its impressive unornateness and stolidity in front of new discoveries, but refined and yet again refined and pared until it lay hard against the bare rock and resisted by virtue of the hardness of the rock itself. . . . [Veblen] brought into economic writing the rules of good poetics . . . in which every word is understood not only in its immediately purposeful meaning, but with all its nimba of picturesqueness, background, and suggestion.

As a writer too, he is full of whimsy and humor. He loves to tease, to exaggerate, to present fantastic and poetic images, to utilize symbolism and allegory, and to mobilize folklore. He will even use archaic words and phrases to fit the mood of an archaic economic and social order. As he unfolds various aspects of western civilization, he is a throwback to the saga-tellers of his Norwegian forebears and the writers of epic poems with their tales of intermingled tragedy and comedy. The anthropologist and archeologist in him, fed by his northern pride and heritage, provided him with an almost inexhaustible arsenal of examples, illustrations, and "models."

As he spins tales, so he spins webs that entrap the reader into the recognition of the seriousness of phenomena that he may have taken for granted. Veblen merely picked his Don Quixotes from the realm of economics. Behind the humor and the dead pan there is often a stark tale that is reminiscent of the privileged court jester. Veblen's shafts respect no class or group. There are no exceptions, not even himself. With his artistic temperament went the peccadillos that are conventionally associated with it.

Having been reared in one culture and having matured in another, Veblen had a heightened instinct of curiosity. That curiosity received, in the course of his academic training in the seventies and the eighties, the benefit of the discipline and inspiration that seminal minds and provocative teachers give to promising youth, thereby enabling them to go beyond and transform the established positions, to lift them to a higher plane, as it were. For Veblen was indeed fortunate.

At sturdy Carleton College he studied under the profound philosophic economist, John Bates Clark, who on the one hand was developing his comprehensive marginalist economics beginning with his own version of marginal utility and on the other hand was formulating his creed of Christian Socialism. Clark soon saw the promise of Veblen and encouraged him to go on to graduate work at Johns Hopkins with philosophy as his major and economics as his minor.

His stay at Johns Hopkins was brief but rewarding. He had the advantage of studying logic with Charles S. Peirce, the founder of pragmatism. He was impressed with the lectures of George S. Morris, the teacher of John Dewey and one of the advance guard of the trained Hegelians from the German universities. There was on the social science staff at Johns Hopkins his contemporary, Richard T. Ely, the *enfant terrible* of economics, who was already impressed with Veblen. Veblen established lifelong friendships with fellow students, for example, that future noted American historian, J. Franklin Jameson.

Veblen then went on to Yale, where he had the benefit of the William Graham Sumner of the *Folkways* and the gruff philosopher, Noah Porter, who was making a last stand on behalf of the traditional common-sense philosophy, as it was called, against the onrush of Spencerian evolution and the Kantian and Hegelian idealist systems.

Thus at the very beginning of his career Veblen stood in the thick of the battle of conflicting philosophic systems. But fortunately for us, on his return to academic halls at Cornell in 1891 he left philosophy for economics, although he never lost his original interest.

As an economist his relation to his times is doubly significant, for he played a dual role. He was a theorist, and a catalyst of reform. He came upon the scene between two ages of social and intellectual ferment. As in the realm of affairs, so in the realm of knowledge, there are great tides. Periods of reform and reconstruction rise to great crests; then come troughs marked by consolidation of gains, conservatism, and sometimes reaction. The last great crest of the seventies and eighties was marked by the triumph of the doctrine of evolution in science and a world-wide movement of political and social reform. In economics it was epitomized by the wave of interest in the German historical school. In its native land this movement had sought to broaden economic analysis beyond the narrow foundation of the older classical school of economics, and to that end it had attempted to develop such powerful instruments of research as statistics and history, including comparative economic development. It also sought to give greater scope to the ethical nature of man than the dominant vulgarizers of the classical economics would permit.

In the realm of policy it sought to meet the wave of discontent, and the threat of socialism, by a variety of reformist devices. These included the appeal to the churches to take an active part in solving such critical social questions as the relation between employers and employees, the appeal to government for easing the restrictions on trade unions, and the support of national social security legislation such as workmen's compensation, old age, and sickness insurance. It included also a concern with the problems of conserving natural resources and regulating "natural monopolies." On the one side the movement seemed to provide the beginning of a richer synthesis for expanding knowledge, and on the other side a basis for policies that would check the damage of excessive individualism without embracing the socialism of Karl Marx.

To the younger generation of reforming American economists, encouraged by such eminent elders as General Francis A. Walker and Carroll D. Wright, this German historical movement, flanked as it was by a similar movement in Great Britain, seemed to offer the promise of adaptation to the needs of the developing American economy. As such it provided a basis for the "new economics." This included the revised classical tradition, which embraced the doctrine of marginal utility. In accordance with their Anglo-American heritage, the exponents thought that economic reform could be achieved largely by voluntary organizations and by state and local units more than by the national authority. "Planning" was city planning, and "regulation" was largely that of railroads and other "natural monopolies" by state commissions.

After the turn of the century came stabilization, security, and consolidation, a frowning on innovation and the depreciation of further reforms. The turning away from "social inventions" had its counterpart in the lack of enthusiasm for any kind of innovation in economic analysis. Thus, for example, the original leader of the movement of mathematical economics, Simon Newcomb, voiced doubts of the usefulness of further work in this area, and he expressed the hope that economists would turn their energies to educating the public in the simpler "abstractions," as he called them, of the Ricardian economics of an earlier age. Economics had only just begun to have autonomy as an important area in its own right rather than as a limited, narrow topic in the course in moral philosophy. In such heated political struggles as that over "free silver" there was not a little feeling that moderation in matters of policy was essential to protect the infant profession. Narrow practical and intellectual ends became dominant, or so it seemed.

Of the older generation of leaders of the movement for reconstruction, some went into administrative work, others specialized in less controversial subjects such as public finance, and still others devoted themselves to the more abstract problems of the rationale of a static state. But even these protected themselves against the charge of lack of immediate, practical reference by claiming that their analysis tested the validity of the existing economic system's right to survival. Social innovation was considered outside the realm of science.

But because liberal reform found hard sledding, there appeared to be a greater need for a basic revaluation and reorientation. For this the special qualities and abilities of Veblen seemed particularly valuable. He was well equipped to survive intellectually in an age where basic thinking appeared to be at a discount. He just escaped being an immigrant. In effect he was an "outsider" and therefore not easily engulfed in the passing mood. He had a special feeling for languages and old-world, particularly northern, sagas and cultures. His extraordinary linguistic equipment opened to him developments and literature in a variety of areas and lands. His cosmopolitan scholar's pervasive sense of history, along with his knowledge of anthropology, psychology, and the biological sciences, gave him perspective. Having received his doctorate in philosophy, he had special equipment for theoretical discussion on the relation of economics to other fields of knowledge. He had the comprehensive reach of the student of culture, the precision so essential for systematic thinking, and that rugged consistency, courage, and independence that refuse to bend to the expediencies of changing winds and fashions.

These qualities distinguished him at the outset. With his strong sense for the fundamental, he fixed attention on central economic institutions of his time, and indeed of our own time — for example, the corporation and the technological process. Veblen implicitly recognized that the corporation is a mighty instrument for organizing production and promoting efficiency. But he regarded it as something much more than a mere embodiment of external mechanical forces. Rather it was a complex human organism that lent itself to manipulation by passions and spirits that ran counter to the objective of its function in the economy. More fundamental still it gave play to the intrigues and rivalry of inner groups whose habit of thinking in terms of money as an abstract aim overlay their functions in the institution. This habit at times ran counter also to the needs of the community, when it bred a reduction of output and employment to maintain solvency or increase profits. As the corporate form gains increasing sway over the economic life of the community, the consequences, if left uncontrolled, become all the more serious.

Veblen's view of technology, like his view of the corporation, was intimately related to his conception of human nature. Man to Veblen was a natural force acting upon all other forces of nature. Man was distinguishable by his special characteristics of imagination, playfulness, economic effort, and tasteful production. To a large extent science and the machine are embodiments of these attributes. But there is an aspect of machine technology which leads to purely reflexive and habitual activity, and sometimes machine technology has been abused to produce ugly things. This explains Veblen's simultaneous emphasis on and admiration of technology as well as his occasional concern over its effects. The techniques and institutions that man creates have a way of turning around, creating a life all their own threatening to become his masters and gods. Veblen saw constantly re-enacted in history a dramatic saga between man's material interests and the institutions he creates to give them expression.

Veblen's views of technology, human nature and corporations, and money and economy do not add up to a closed structure of thought in the typical nineteenth-century sense. Such systems begin with an over-

whelming major premise and ineluctably drive, fall the chips where they
may, toward a grand, simplified, logical conclusion, as the stationary state
of a David Ricardo, the positive religion of an August Comte, the classless
society of a Karl Marx, and the idealized order of free contract of a
Herbert Spencer, where even a policeman would not be needed. Veblen
is less doctrinaire and less dogmatic. Where the authors of the great closed
systems seek to dominate and organize, Veblen suggests, tempts, pleads,
and even hypnotizes. In his method he is more evolutionary, more sensitive
to psychological forces, more aware of the relations between the social
sciences, and more cognizant of surprising changes in the configuration
of forces. He combines forces and elements often thought of as disparate
or irrelevant to each other. This is the reason why he occasionally surprised and even shocked his reader or fellow economist. His approach
makes him at home with the spirit of the twentieth century and projected his influence forward.

Although bereft of the attractions of the great system-makers and the
magic of the great programmatic reformers, his influence has been wide,
pervasive, and enduring. Vital and original minds were drawn toward
him from the beginning.

There were first of all his own students. Here as elsewhere I can only
refer to a few. Veblen moved Herbert J. Davenport to cleanse of apologetics the main tradition of economics with his critical volume, *Value and
Distribution*, and then his general treatise, *The Economics of Enterprise*,
which still stands as a classic of modern price analysis. There was Robert
F. Hoxie, perhaps the finest analytical mind the United States produced
in the field of labor, who developed a functional analysis of types of
unions with special emphasis on what he called business unionism. There
was Ezekiel H. Downey, a pioneer in the first great step of social security
legislation, namely, workmen's compensation laws. In his classic defense
of such legislation, *History of Work Accident Indemnity in Iowa*, he
explained that, since the human organism was imperfectly adapted to a
mechanical environment, work injuries are attributable to inherent hazards
of industry and should be met by industry.

There was Wesley C. Mitchell, who found in Veblen's work not only
inspiration for pioneering studies on business cycles and the money
economy but also specific helpful theories, such as in his business cycle
theory the important relationships in Veblen's emphasis on the capitali-
zation process. As Mitchell wrote in a private letter in 1910, while working on his monumental *Business Cycles:* "The theory propounded [on the
breeding of crises] is fairly close to Veblen's on the most important point
— a decline in prospective net earnings leads to a shrinkage of business

credit and thus brings on a liquidation of outstanding accounts." Further-more, in Veblen's emphasis on "behavior" and men's actions, rather than on their introspective rationalizations, lay much of the stimulus that re-enforced Mitchell's bent for systematic quantitative analysis and drove him on to making such work a permanent basic feature of economic theory.

There was Walter W. Stewart, who in modern central banking made effective use of Veblen's distinction between industry and business. In his diagnosis of Britain's loss of competitive position in the 1930's, he ascribed the larger and more permanent part of the difficulties to the lag in technological advance and accumulated industrial shortcomings rather than to the current financial maladjustments. In this country Stewart, like Mitchell, was influenced by Veblen to use quantitative data, both financial and industrial, to test from time to time the performance and adequacy of our banking institutions. Finally, let me just mention DR Scott, author of *The Cultural Significance of Accounts*, as further evidence of the stimulus and influence of Veblen on his students.

Let us now turn to his influence on his contemporaries. Perhaps the best external evidence of the wide recognition of Veblen among the most distinguished economists of the day was the petition in 1925, with nearly 225 signatures requesting the nominating committee of the American Economic Association to select Veblen as president. Among the signers were eleven future presidents of the association, Morris A. Copeland, Paul H. Douglas, Edwin F. Gay, E. A. Goldenweiser, Alvin H. Hansen, Frank H. Knight, Frederick C. Mills, E. G. Nourse, Sumner H. Slichter, Jacob Viner, and A. B. Wolfe.

The constant references in economic studies to *The Theory of Business Enterprise* at any event belie the misgivings that Veblen originally had about publishing the book, misgivings chiefly, he said, "that it would pass unnoticed by the gild of economists to which it is addressed."

More revealing of his influence was the seepage of his ideas into a wide variety of original enterprises in economics. There was his impact on Carleton Parker, who pioneered in focusing the attention of economists and management on the need in the study of industrial relations to under-stand the psychological forces involved. There was Veblen's impact on John R. Commons' work, especially *Legal Foundations of Capitalism* and *Institutional Economics*, not only through Commons' use of Veblen's distinction between business and industry, but more specifically through Commons' development of such concepts as the "going concern" and "intangible property" as distinct from "tangible property." As an admirer of both, A. B. Wolfe stated: "Commons arrived at substantially the same, though greatly amplified conclusions as to the role played by intangible assets." Veblen was stimulating also to the son, John Maurice Clark, of his old Carleton teacher, as the younger man sought to work out a positive position vis-à-vis Veblen's and Davenport's criticisms of John Bates Clark, which centered on social productivity versus private acquisition. Veblen had an influence on such business-cycle theorists as Alvin H. Hansen which dates back to the days when Hansen was working on his doctoral dissertation, *Cycles of Prosperity and Depression in the United States, Great Britain and Germany*, and runs through his later productions in Keynesian economics.

In the field of consumption patterns, of course, Veblen's attraction has been enormous, especially evident in such stimulating studies as those of Hazel Kyrk, Theresa S. McMahon, and Jessica B. Pexiotto.

Veblen's "pecuniary emulation" and "conspicuous consumption," especially when given a less colorful name, such as the "demonstration effect" – the increase in consumption expenditures through contact with superior goods – helped to bring about a revision of the conventional demand theory, including a special aspect of this theory, the "consumption function," as analyzed, for example, by James S. Duesenberry, in *Income, Saving and the Theory of Consumer Behavior*. Falling into the same category and given increasing attention especially by those interested in geometric presentation was the case that has acquired his name, the "Veblen case." This has been well described by Sidney Weintraub in *Price Theory* as consisting of goods that "appeal to the snob as a vehicle for 'conspicuous consumption' . . . only when the price goes sufficiently high to prevent these items from being widely bought."

In the areas of the regulation of corporations and security markets Veblen's works have had a practical effect. Witness the popularity of *The Modern Corporation and Private Property*, by A. A. Berle, Jr., and Gardiner C. Means, and of a number of other provocative works dealing with the "managerial revolution" and the corporation, and with the "organizational man" as exemplifying a way of life. Incidentally, Justice Louis D. Brandeis cited Veblen in a famous minority opinion against the encroachment of the great corporations (*Lee* v. *Liggett Co.*).

In economic history there immediately comes to mind Harold A. Innis, the one Canadian economist who has been president of the American Economic Association. He noted as early as 1929 that Veblen was the "first to attempt a general stock taking of general tendencies in a dynamic society saddled with machine industry just as Adam Smith was the first to present a general stock taking before machine industry came in." Veblen's story in 1915 of how aristocratic, imperial Germany exploited the developments of the machine technology turned out to be so prophetic of the rise and fall of Nazi Germany that a new edition of *Imperial Germany and the Industrial Revolution* was called for. Currently economic historians have suggested its applicability to the Soviet Union.

In recent years *An Inquiry into the Nature of Peace and the Terms of Its Perpetuation*, along with *Imperial Germany*, has come to the fore as among the few books of the World War I era that have endured. Here Veblen's technique has its fullest scope. He takes up in its widest background and with a grand perspective of economic and international relations the greatest of all problems and makes his contribution toward a reconstruction of the world on a more peaceful basis.

Of his predictions and prophecies, which have so often been accurate, I shall refer to only one. This is a prediction that has not been generally noticed. In the closing page of *The Theory of Business Enterprise*, he observed that the "*full* dominion of business enterprise was necessarily a transitory dominion" (italics mine). That dominion is now less complete than ever.

Veblen's early vogue began in the realm of literature through the reception accorded his one really popular book, *The Theory of the Leisure Class*. Although originally, as Veblen put it, "opinion seems to be divided as to whether I am a knave or a fool," the book had the good fortune to be enthusiastically reviewed as a work of genius by the dean of American letters, William Dean Howells and the famous Irish journalist, novelist, and translator of Plotinus, Stephen McKenna. McKenna wrote in *The Criterion* that it was

... a book, too, which is immensely educative; no one could take it up and even dip into it, casually here and there without feeling a distinct freshening of interest in the deeper signification of the most commonplace principles, habits, venerations, and dislikes of everyday existence. At every step one is flung back from the present as by a catapult, into the most distant past. One gets a new sense of the depth of the ways of men; a keener perception of the oneness of mankind through all the variations of all the centuries ...

In portraying the effects of pecuniary standards on culture, Veblen dissected men's most cherished values in their current form and showed that they were curiously wrought-out products of a historical process stamped with the dollar sign. The full weight of this was caught by his readers only in later years, especially in times of depression and war. Today the book is also increasingly appreciated for the guidance it offers in raising the economic level of underdeveloped countries and above all in strengthening the national defense. Again on December 2, 1957, the New York *Times* editorial page reminded the country that Veblen long ago called attention to the "problems which arise because of men's slowness to adjust their cultural attitudes to the rapid changes imposed by scientific and technological advance."

Ever since Professor J. H. Tufts called attention in 1904 in *The Psychological Bulletin* to the penetrating psychological analysis in *The Theory of the Leisure Class* and *The Theory of Business Enterprise*, social psychologists have obtained leads from Veblen's works.

Certainly no economist of his day or ours has commanded the respect of so many leaders in so many other disciplines: in literature and the fine arts, philosophy, psychology, sociology, political science, anthropology, history, and even the biological and physical sciences.

Veblen is a "philosophical radical," in a twentieth-century American setting. Unlike his British counterparts he was free from Benthamite psychology, was not a system-builder, and was without a positive political program. Yet his indirect influence upon men active in public affairs was very considerable particularly following the great depression, when many of our economic institutions became subject to criticism and revision. Veblen had made it abundantly clear that "prosperity" of business enterprises was not necessarily co-incidental with the welfare of the community at large. During this period some of Veblen's ideas, available for decades, fell at last on fertile soil and took root. His regret might have been that so many of them in application led to a further aggrandizement of the state. So while it may be impossible to point to a single piece of legislation that he would have proposed, there can be no doubt that men who had never read his books came unknowingly under the influence of his thought. No one can say exactly when or how Veblen's ideas, once widely regarded as radical and violently rejected by most of one generation, gradually became a part of our accepted common stock of ideas. We do know, however, that historically such slow and pervasive infiltration is characteristic of an intellectual forerunner.

The cultural role of Veblen is that of all creative artists as described by the sociologist, Charles H. Cooley: "The 'significance' of an artist means I suppose, his contribution to a culture of which his work is a part, so that to understand it you must understand *him*."

This was Veblen. Here is a man who was often inchoate, obscure, tangential, unintelligible, and one-sided. He made his generous share of mistakes. Ultimately his value lies in his role as an emancipator of the human mind. He tears down the walls of the institutions, prejudices, and fond illusions that imprison the human spirit. He sharpened the use of reason and presented it as a tool to those who would penetrate to the secrets of society. He transcended the function of the economist, but he also fulfilled it. He marked an epoch in the cumulative growth of the science and the development of western culture.

INDEX

Abbott, Lyman, 136
Absentee ownership, 418-419, 436, 447, 458-459, 489, 516; stability of, 378-379, 413-414, 441-444, 461-462
Absentee Ownership and Business Enterprise in Recent Times; The Case of America, 456, 466-485, 501, 515
Academic freedom, 61, 109-110, 122-123, 153, 190, 210-211, 253, 254, 255, 311, 383, 403, 405-406, 425-426, 463-464
Ackerman, Frederick, 454, 462, 510, 512, 514
Action at a distance; in business, 290, 444, 470-471; in industry, 290; in science, 290
Action, philosophy of, 41, 76, 114-115, 129-131, 139-141, 151, 152, 153, 163, 209-210
Activity experience, philosophy of, 50, 140
Adams, Henry Carter, 61
Adams, Herbert Baxter, 39, 61, 77, 91
Addams, Jane, 107
Advertising, 177-178, 210, 288; in church, 479-480
Æsthetics, 22, 126; pecuniary basis of, 102-103, 177, 204, 327
Agrarianism, 14-16, 29, 58-59, 72, 80, 88, 100, 105, 106, 123, 135-136, 202, 204, 233, 264, 383, 384, 386-390, 391, 419, 473, 478, 483, 505; in Norway, 2-3; in socialism, 223, 268-269, 367-368
Agricultural crisis, 14, 104
Agriculture aux États-Unis, L', review of, 104
Aldrich, Nelson, 59-60
Aliens, 5, 6, 7, 8, 10, 11, 17, 29, 33, 41, 42, 57-58, 304, 319; intellectual, 323, 424-426
Alison, Archibald, 22
Allen, William, 256
Allen, William V., 135
Alsberg, Carl C., 460
Altgeld, John P., 99, 108, 122, 139, 150; criticisms of, 109, 135-136
American Economic Association, 61, 373, 451-452, 488, 489-492, 495-496; criticisms of, 64-65, 505
American Federation of Labor, 99, 100, 108, 198, 384, 387, 419, 429, 431, 442, 443, 445, 478, 483
American Historical Association, 61
American Legion, 465, 470
American Railway Union, 107-108, 137
American Social Science Association, 61
Amherst College, 394-395
Amlie, Thomas R., 516
Ammon, Friederich, 126, 143
Anarchists, 61, 88, 99, 103, 106, 136, 137-138, 206, 232, 243, 244
Anderson, Frederick, 504
Anderson, Maxwell, 422
Anderson, Rasmus, 36, 67
Angell, James Rowland, review of Patten's *Development of English Thought,* 151
Animism, 126, 474, 517; attitude of modern

science on, 52-53, 156, 163-164, 186, 189-190, 290; attitude of modern technology on, 159-160, 163-164, 182, 184-185, 189-190, 231, 290-291, 345, 369; in barbarian culture, 169; in corporate ownership, 169-170, 226, 343, 363; in economics, 114, 155, 160, 328; in gambling, 185-186; in higher learning, 189-190; in ownership marriage, 172; in pecuniary occupations, 184-185; in system of status, 158-159; of the captain of industry, 184; of the criminal, 184; of leisure class women, 187-188
Anthropology, 125, 277, 280, 300, 333-337; in common-sense philosophy, 20; in conventional economics, 27-28, 97-98, 127, 128-129, 132-133, 168-169; in materialistic interpretation, 101-102; on ownership, 115-116, 168-172
Anthropo-sociology, 126-127
Arbitration, 206, 207; compulsory, 110; criticisms of, 109, 111
Archæological Institute of America, 295, 299, 300
Archæologists, criticisms of, 276
Archer, William, 149
Ardzrooni, Leon, 312, 353, 411, 447, 449, 450, 453-454, 455, 456, 459, 460, 462, 499, 500, 503, 504; "The Philosophy of the Restriction of Output," 457
Aristocracy and Evolution: A Study of the Rights, the Origin and the Social Functions of the Wealthier Classes, review of, 148-149
"Armistice, The Twilight Peace of the," 436
Arnott, Virginia, 272, 273
Art, 327; in industry, 204-205, 233; representative, 319-320
Artists, 252, 259
Aryan race, conception of ownership of, 97, 240; culture of, 296-297; language of, 297
Aryanisation, 297
Ashley, William, 112
Assets, intangible, 201, 222, 228, 246, 278, 281, 283, 284, 287-288, 414, 415, 420, 481, 482, 483; tangible, 288, 301, 420
Associational-hedonistic psychology, 20, 46-48, 65, 125, 128, 129-130, 141, 292-293; in ownership, 149, 157, 265, 281-283, 284-285; criticisms of, 47, 49-50, 76, 114-115, 131-132, 139-140, 141, 151-152, 155-158, 203, 276-277
Associations industrielles et commerciales, review of, 213
Atkinson, Edward, 112
Atwater, Lyman, 26
Atwood, Wallace W., 463-464

Bacon, Francis, 203
Baden-Powell, *The Land-Systems of British India,* 97-98
Baer, George, 207

557